a typographic
a typographic
a typographic
WORKBOOK

a typographic
a typographic
a typographic

A PRIMER TO HISTORY, TECHNIQUES AND ARTISTRY

Kate Clair

a typographic
WORKBOOK

John Wiley & Sons, Inc

New York · Chichester · Brisbane · Singapore · Toronto

Copyright
Data

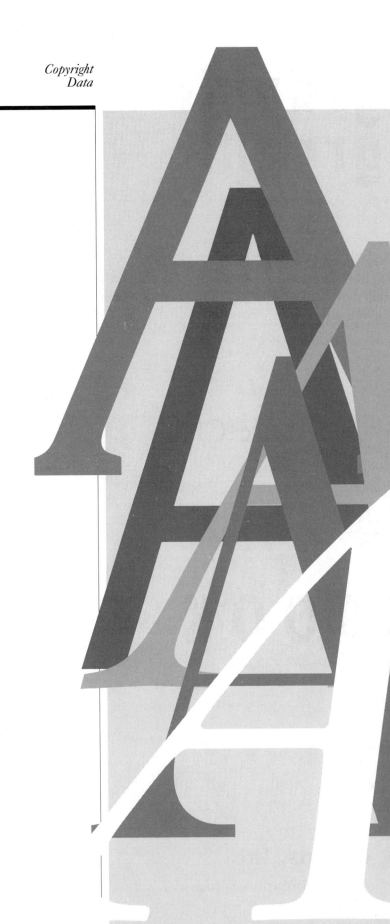

Designations used by companies to distinguish their products
are often claimed as trademarks. In all instances where those
designations appear in this book, and John Wiley & Sons, Inc. is
aware of a trademark claim, the product names are followed by
™ or ® symbol. Readers, however, should contact the appropriate companies for more complete information regarding trademarks and registration.

Copyright © 1999 by John Wiley & Sons, Inc.
All rights reserved.

Published simultaneously in Canada.

No part of this publication may be reproduced, stored in a
retrieval system or transmitted in any form or by any means,
electronic, mechanical, photocopying, recording, scanning or
otherwise, except as permitted under Sections 107 or 108 of the
1976 United States Copyright Act, without either the prior written permission of the Publisher, or authorization through payment of the appropriate per-copy fee to the Copyright Clearance
Center, 222 Rosewood Drive, Danvers, MA 01923, (978) 750-
8400, fax (978) 750-4744. Requests to the Publisher for permission should be addressed to the Permissions Department, John
Wiley & Sons, Inc., 605 Third Avenue, New York, NY 10158-
0012, (212) 850-6011, fax (212) 850-6008,
E-mail: PERMREQ@WILEY.COM.

This publication is designed to provide accurate and authoritative information in regard to the subject matter covered. It is
sold with the understanding that the publisher is not engaged in
rendering professional services. If professional advice or other
expert asssistance is required, the services of a competent
professional person should be sought.

This book is printed on acid-free paper.

Library of Congress Cataloging-in-Publication Data:

Clair, Kate
    A Typographic Workbook: A Primer to History,
    Techniques, and Artistry

ISBN 0-471-29237-0

10 9 8 7 6 5 4 3

This page is set in
ITC Fenice Light 8.5/12

Introduction

Introduction

Typography really is the paint that a designer uses on the canvas. As a painter, the better you refine your knowledge of paint, brushes and canvas, the better equipped you will be to use your tools. The more you know about how pigments, binders and mediums were developed, and how they interact, the richer an understanding and appreciation you'll have for your medium. The more you refine your acuity and sensitivity to brushes, and their uses, the better your choice of appropriate brushes will be. The more you practice painting, and master basic strokes and theories of color, the faster your skills will grow and your eye will become refined, able to distinguish great painting from mediocre painting. Ultimately, the more you know about the tradition of painters that you are becoming a part of, the more you will be able see the continuity and exploration which preceded you and recognize your place in that spectrum of time.

And so it is with typography. The more that you know about the tradition of creating, setting and designing with type, the more you will come to understand your place within the continuum of designers and typographers. As you study the parts of letters, you begin to appreciate the subtle distinctions of fonts, and to consciously understand the associations a specific font evokes. As you learn the considerations of spacing letters together, you become able to make assessments of type in your visual environment. As you begin to distinguish one font from another, you feel a kinship with the person who made the decision to use a sans serif face for the headline. You comprehend typography more fully by knowing the traditions of casting lead type, methods of designing a typeface on a computer, and subtleties of spacing text type. You will evaluate and discriminate the quality of type in your visual environment, critiquing and learning as you embrace it with greater understanding and respect.

Hopefully, my book will inspire you to "paint" with type, and provide a rich understanding of the medium, the history and the technology that you must master for your chosen field. I hope it will be a book that you will refer to often throughout your time as a student, and will appreciate more as time goes on, and you enter the professional field as a designer, illustrator, advertiser, web designer, typographer, etc.

This workbook integrates the historical information about the development of the alphabet with the technical information about typography. The history presented here is merely an overview, not an attempt at a complete history. But it gives a sense of the evolution of some of the fonts that you will be studying. And it also provides a frame of reference for the technological typographic advancements throughout history.

The text type settings change throughout the book. This is to give you the experience of reading a variety of text settings. The point size and the tracking of the settings are consistent, for comparative purposes. The point sizes of the fonts may not appear to be the same size from one page to the next, but they are.

This page is set in
Fenice Light 8.5/12.

Introduction

The intent is that you will not only be learning about type, but that you will respond to the different fonts in text settings as you read through this book. Ultimately, you should try to appreciate not only the aesthetics of the fonts you are reading, but the emotive associations you experience subconsciously to each font, as the text type changes throughout the book. You may also want to discern which fonts are the most comfortable to read, and establish the reasons behind their reading ease.

There are self quizzes at the end of each chapter to assist you in gauging your progress and comprehension. The questions also help you to review the important points of the chapter. There are topical projects listed throughout this workbook for you to apply the information after reading it. These exercises are designed to reinforce new ideas by reviewing the new terms and concepts.

Why is it important to study the field of typography? How did writing systems develop historically? Why is it important to understand the development and history of type? Why should students of design care about the many implications inherent in preserving thought, culture, history, philosophy, mathematics and medicine with written symbols? Where would society be today, without the fields of lettering and typography?

The answers to these questions (undoubtedly clarified in the pages of this tome) enrich young designers, not only about their own culture, but about the tradition of design they are entering into—which requires organizing the written word on the page.

It is intriguing to compare one's place in society with that of ancient scribes and medieval monks. Typography students should consider themselves part of a continuum of visual people—working with, communicating with images and type on the page. Although the writing surfaces and tools for writing have changed throughout the millennium, although the typefaces and the means of production are constantly evolving, still the functions and objectives of the type-oriented craftsperson have principally remained the same.

I hope this book will serve to inspire young designers who are joining the ranks of the creative souls who preceded them. May you embrace the field of typography and its history, with profound appreciation and an ever-inquisitive attitude…and learn each day.

This page is set in
ITC Fenice Light 8.5/12.

Dedication/
Acknowledgements

DEDICATION

This book is dedicated to Dick Coco, my greatest friend and eternal soulmate, who patiently put up with our life's disruption while this work was undertaken.

ACKNOWLEDGEMENTS

A sincere thanks goes to Lisa DeLay and Dan Kilgore, who helped me maintain my sanity while they carefully numbered each figure and digital file in this book. They were a lot of fun to work with, even when the studio did resemble an insane asylum (their contributions to this atmosphere certainly lifted our moods). I'd like to thank Allison Jeffery for her fine work on the illustrations of well known typographers for this text.

The Research Committee at Kutztown University contributed by granting one class release time to assist in the final rewrite of the manuscript. From the Grants Office at Kutztown University, Sandra Hammann and Elaine Hamm must be thanked for their patience in helping me fill out numerous forms for student assistants to be paid. The librarians from Kutztown University's Rohrbach Library were very supportive and efficient. They helped with last minute details of maps for reference, publisher information, book suggestions and copyright information; they include Sandra Allen, Joanne Bucks, Rick Dyson, Bruce Gottschall, Cathy Hartwick and Anita Sprankle.

From the Communication Design Department at KU, Laurel Bonhage, Kevin McCloskey, Elaine Cunfer, Dennis Johnson, John Landis, Martin Lemelman, David Bullock, Karen Kresge, Miles DeCoster, Brenda Innocenti, Nunzio Alagia, Don Breter and Tom Quirk, I'd like to thank all of my co-workers who put up with me when I was severely underslept while completing this book. I would especially like to thank Lucy Williams, the greatest department secretary, for all of her help. To David Bullock, my department chair, for proofing a few chapters, a sincere thanks. To my colleague Laurel Bonhage, who helped with the first draft of this text when it was just a graduate-school research project, I'd like to thank her for her energy in embarking on this project. I must thank Margaret Cummins, Leigh Frantz and Jim Harper at Wiley for their assistance in the last minute details and scheduling of this book. I would also like to thank Tenth Avenue Editions and Clive Giboire for their help with preparing this book for printing.

I'd like to thank Joseph and RoseMary Clair, who dutifully always acted interested in this project. To many supportive colleagues, too numerous to list, I would like to thank them for refraining from asking about the progress on the book when it wasn't a choice topic of discussion.

To the students and alumni of Kutztown University's Communication Design Department, who graciously allowed me to use their school work in this text, without anything but the glory of their work being published, being listed in the index and a copy of the final text as payment, a sincere debt of thanks. To the person, they all agreed to let me reproduce their work, even when they *knew* that I would no longer be grading them. I am indebted to them all for their cooperation and generosity.

To my design professors at Tyler School of Art, Stephanie Knopf and Paul Sheriff, to whom I owe my appreciation for the field of typography, a long overdue thank you. And certainly I must sincerely thank Joe Scorsone, who has been a mentor, role model, and friend, and who awakened me to the beauty and subtlety lurking in the field of type.

I'd lastly like to thank Dick Coco for being an endless source of tremendous understanding, compassion and support throughout the many trying phases of the completion of this text. His unfailing faith in me is a truly selfless gift. His sense of humor came in handy, too! His managing of all of the day-to-day details of our lives for two solid years cleared my mind to finish this book. I only hope that I can someday repay this caring. I regret that this book took so much time from our lives together.

This page is set in
Fenice Light 8.5/12.

Table of Contents

Table of
Contents

Table of
Contents

This page is set in
ITC Fenice Light 8.5/12.

Table of
Contents

Chapter 8
Measuring Type/Leading/
Kerning/Ligatures 128-145

Chapter 9
Five Historic Families of Type 146-153

Chapter 10
Optical Adjustments to Typefaces 154-163

Chapter 11
Typeface/Font/Family of Type 164-169

Chapter 12
Readability & Legibility 170-176

Chapter 13
Matching Type with Message 177-182

Table of
Contents

Table of
Contents

Ancient Writing Systems

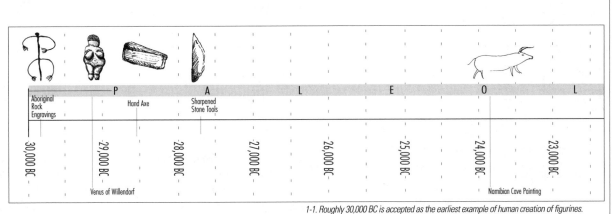

1-1. Roughly 30,000 BC is accepted as the earliest example of human creation of figurines.

INTRODUCTION

"Ancient" is generally defined in the western culture as "before the fall of the Western Roman Empire, 476 AD." We study the precursors of our alphabet, through Ancient Greece in this chapter. Ancient Rome is covered with the Middle Ages. Many students are unfamiliar with ancient history, and few consider the writing systems of this era. Ancient Egyptian (African), Greek and Roman societies were quite highly developed, with magnificent architecture, legal courts, codes of law, epic plays, elaborate religious myths, indoor plumbing, comfortable homes with servants (often captives from military conquests), and reasonably good nutrition. Some historians argue that these developments would hardly have been possible without the tool of written communication. Consider the development for yourself. Remember that in BC time, as you move forward in time, the year numbers get smaller, and then you start counting up in AD; so that 500 BC is 400 years earlier than 100 BC. This chapter begins with considerations of society at 30,000 BC.

PRE-WRITING SOCIETIES

Trying to imagine human existence before there was either oral or written communication is difficult. Without *oral* communication the level of subtle communication in humans' lives is not clear; people lived by practices similar to the instinct of animals. Tribes of humans knew to head south when the weather was cold; they knew to gather food; they knew to seek shelter from rain and cold; they knew to follow their instincts to procreate.

Once verbal communication was developed, people were able to interact with other humans, to organize activities, to assist each other in a coordinated fashion, to structure their lives so that they lived more comfortably and predictably. By about 30,000 BC, there is evidence of creative works or votive forms

> Oral languages must always precede written languages–the written words are merely the symbolic representation of the spoken words.

This page is set in
ITC Fenice Light 8.5/12.

1

*Ancient
Writing Systems*

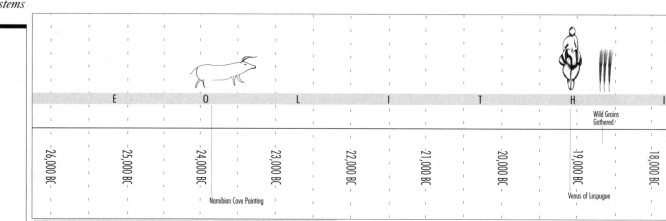

| E | | O | | L | | I | | T | | H | | I |

Wild Grains Gathered

-26,000 BC · -25,000 BC · -24,000 BC · -23,000 BC · -22,000 BC · -21,000 BC · -20,000 BC · -19,000 BC · -18,000 BC

Namibian Cave Painting

Venus of Lespugue

1-2. This timeline highlights some of the innovations of early nomadic and agrarian people.

Mnemonics, or

memory devices, were

used by tribal elders

to recall

vast amounts of

information such as

myths, histories,

cures and legends.

These memory aids

were passed down

from one generation

to the next.

such as the Venus of Willendorf (see timeline above). About 10,000 years ago (8000 BC or so), humans began to cultivate the soil, and gradually shifted their nomadic lifestyle to a more settled one with the development of an agrarian-based society.

THE DEVELOPMENT OF ORAL COMMUNICATION

As oral communication developed beyond simple human interaction necessary for existence, humans could express thoughts, feelings, etc., verbally. It is interesting to wonder whether these sentiments were present in our species *before* humans developed the capacity to express them in words; or if the expressions of thoughts, hopes and fantasies were possible *because* humans developed the means of expressing subtle differences through the use of refined, specific speech.

With the development of oral communication, and as humans found temperate areas to settle year 'round, near sources of fresh water, different societal structures developed. Hospitable climate and agricultural knowledge may be the strongest contributing factors to the development of human civilization. Around 8000 BC, with the adjustment from gathering food to growing it, life changed. Because there was not a constant battle with the elements or endless foraging for food, people had time to devote to other activities, and humans were able to refine their living conditions.

Humans were able to sustain increased population growth more readily by simply growing more food. A favorable climate allowed them first and foremost to plan on the sequence of seasons and grow food accordingly, rather than spending daily hours rummaging through forests for food. Some anthropologists believe that the domestication of animals was a strong factor in developing human society. Nomadic people were able to transport their food with them by driving the animals ahead of the tribe; then the animals could be slaughtered as needed for sustenance.

The change from nomadic to settled, agriculturally-based life also allowed for more substantial homes. With their basic needs for food and shelter attended to, humans began to turn their attention to refining tools, organizing the tribe, perfecting the healing arts, recording genealogies, defending against predators, pondering the stars and appeasing the spirits.

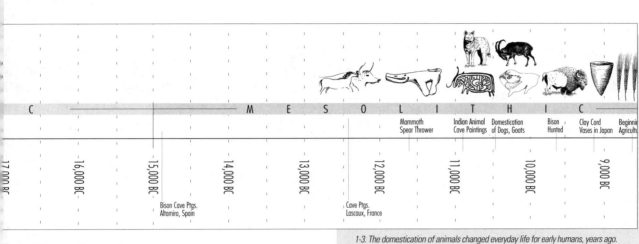

						Mammoth Spear Thrower	Indian Animal Cave Paintings	Domestication of Dogs, Goats	Bison Hunted	Clay Cord Vases in Japan	Beginning Agriculture
17,000 BC	16,000 BC	15,000 BC	14,000 BC	13,000 BC	12,000 BC	11,000 BC	10,000 BC	9,000 BC			
		Bison Cave Ptgs. Altamira, Spain			Cave Ptgs. Lascaux, France						

C ——————— M E S O L I T H I C ———— C

1-3. The domestication of animals changed everyday life for early humans, years ago.

VERBAL-BASED SOCIETIES

In a settled community, before the invention of the written word, a hierarchy of society evolved. When information was handed down by word of mouth, the people with the most power were those who had been entrusted with the "memory" of the tribe; those who were chosen by the tribe's elders to commit to memory the myths, legends and genealogies of the tribe.

Mnemonics, the use of memory tricks and devices to recall great amounts of information, were well developed by these elders. They had great power and personal status within the community and were often relieved of the menial tasks of fulfilling the basic day-to-day needs of the tribe. This prestigious position also required great accuracy in the recall of information.

HANDING DOWN KNOWLEDGE VERBALLY

These elders often had exclusive choice of their replacement, deciding to whom they would bestow all the knowledge of the tribe. The training to remember all of the important information of the tribe took many years of memorization and recall. Frequently the next generation of elders were trained in memory and storytelling from the time they were very young children.

The respect for elders in the community was unquestioned. Some indigenous peoples today associate the various stages of aging (often based on their hair color) with status in the tribe. In fact, in some Native American languages, the word for "gray-haired" means "knowledgeable" and the term for "white-haired" means "close to the knowledge of the gods." Because of their language structure, there are no words to express these concepts separately. In a Native American tribe, aging and its inherent wisdom is revered; their words display this respect because aging and knowledge are inextricably woven into one concept, literally one word. Language can affect our perception of reality.

Many sacred spiritual rituals were also handed down verbally in great secrecy and memorized by successive generations. Carrying out these sacred rituals was an honor, so those who were informed were willing to undergo arduous training in memory in order to master them. In a verbal-based culture, there is a premium on one's mnemonic ability; to remember and to have stored mental knowledge or experience gives one a strong po-

> Oral traditions are limited in terms of precise accuracy due to the personal editing that is undertaken in each successive generation of storytellers or elders.

This page is set in
ITC Garamond Light 8.5/12.

1 **Ancient Writing Systems**

1-4. This timeline shows that there seems to be a creative explosion across cultures in building, worship, writing and creating around 4,000 BC.

WRITING SUBSTRATES & TOOLS

It is important to note that the changes in the appearance of a lettering style, in the shapes of letters, is often influenced by the tool or instrument (reed, brush, pen, chisel, etc.); the substrate or material used to write on (stone, clay, bark, metal, papyrus, parchment, etc.), the availability of the substrate; and the artistic as well as economic climate of the times. The tools and materials will influence the fluidity, shape and weight of the characters. The aesthetic sensibility and artistic development of a people will direct the appearance of the letters or symbols. Some scripts, like written Hindu, are very curvilinear; Hebrew has a flowing appearance; and our Roman-based alphabet is quite vertical. The appearance of a writing style is based on all of these factors: tools, substrates, and aesthetics.

Sidebar is set in Futura Book Italic 8.5/17

This page is set in
ITC Garamond Light 8.5/12.

sition in the tribe. Healing rituals, incantations and herbal remedies were likewise only the knowledge of the initiated, privileged few, and were often handed down within families.

LIMITATIONS OF ORAL TRANSMISSION OF KNOWLEDGE

It is important to realize that no one from one generation could speak directly to those of later generations without intermediaries before the invention of writing. All communication was contemporaneous and temporal when it was solely oral. We assume that there were no precise words or phrases that had lasting influence over the centuries, unless they were handed down and reiterated by one generation to the next. For ideas to have lasting influence, they had to be restated by each generation and ran the risk of personal editing, inaccuracies, embellishments, memory lapses, or disagreement and therefore omission of details.

IMAGE-MAKING VS. INTENDED COMMUNICATION

It is important when studying the development of our own writing system to realize that simple expression of visual ideas cannot be considered an alphabet. For instance, the cave paintings in Lascaux, France (very early images created by humans approximately 12,000 BC, or 14,000 years ago), do communicate the form of the animals, but they don't qualify as pictographic (alphabet) communication because they are not a codified system of standardized symbols. The pictorial signs must become simplified and must be used consistently to represent the same idea in order for a series of pictographs to be considered as writing rather than image making.

MAKING THE TRANSITION FROM SPEAKING TO WRITING

Today, there are many spoken languages throughout the world which have no written form. Although people speak

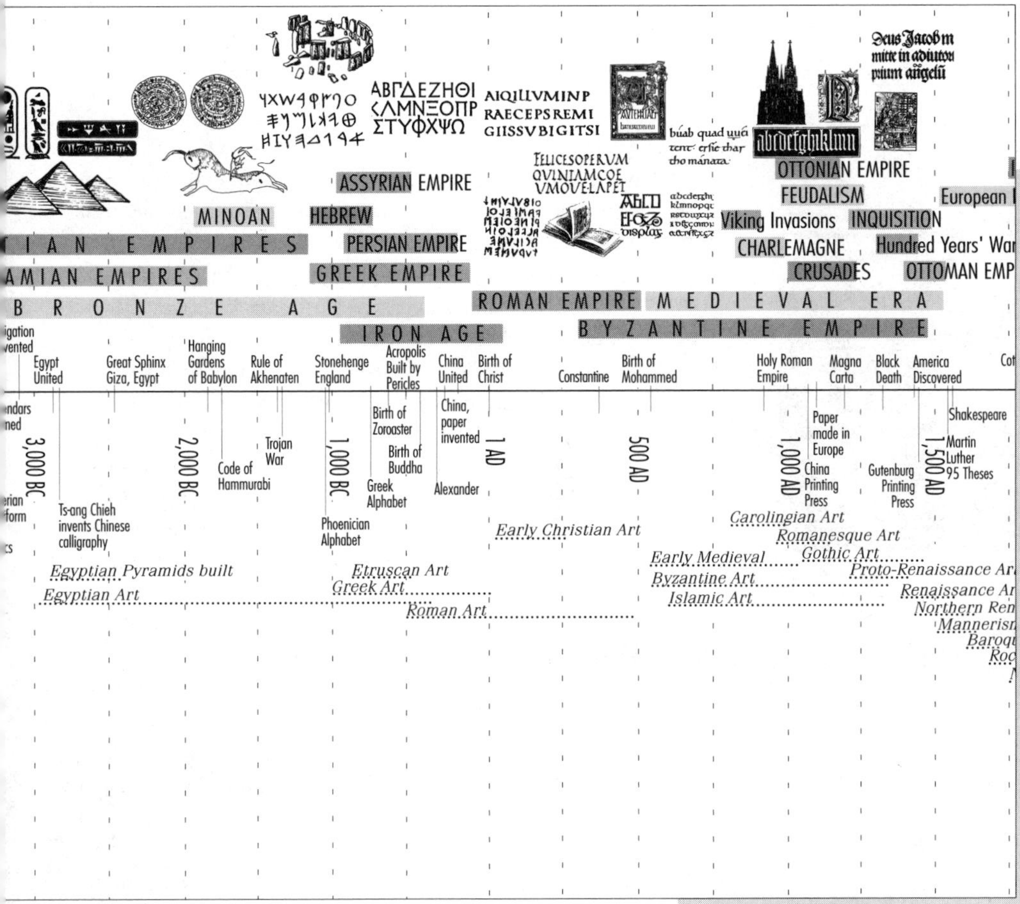

*Ancient
Writing Systems* 1

1-5. This timeline shows the changes in writing systems over the centuries.

[Timeline labels:]

ASSYRIAN EMPIRE
MINOAN HEBREW OTTONIAN EMPIRE
...IAN EMPIRES PERSIAN EMPIRE FEUDALISM European
...MIAN EMPIRES GREEK EMPIRE Viking Invasions INQUISITION
CHARLEMAGNE Hundred Years' War
CRUSADES OTTOMAN EMP...
B R O N Z E   A G E   ROMAN EMPIRE M E D I E V A L   E R A
I R O N   A G E   B Y Z A N T I N E   E M P I R E

[Timeline events:]
...igation invented Egypt United | Great Sphinx Giza, Egypt | Hanging Gardens of Babylon | Rule of Akhenaten | Stonehenge England | Acropolis Built by Pericles | China United | Birth of Christ | Constantine | Birth of Mohammed | Holy Roman Empire | Magna Carta | Black Death | America Discovered | Cot...

3,000 BC | 2,000 BC | 1,000 BC | 1 AD | 500 AD | 1,000 AD | 1,500 AD

Birth of Zoroaster
China, paper invented
Code of Hammurabi | Trojan War | Birth of Buddha
Greek Alphabet | Alexander
Paper made in Europe
China Printing Press | Gutenburg Printing Press
Shakespeare
Martin Luther 95 Theses

...ndars ...ned
...erian ...form
Ts-ang Chieh invents Chinese calligraphy
Phoenician Alphabet
Early Christian Art
Carolingian Art
Romanesque Art
Egyptian Pyramids built | Etruscan Art | Early Medieval Gothic Art | Proto-Renaissance Ar...
Egyptian Art | Greek Art .... | Byzantine Art | Renaissance Ar...
Roman Art .... | Islamic Art .... | Northern Ren...
Mannerism
Baroq...
Roc...

the language, there is no corresponding alphabet. In order to write these languages, it may seem logical to use an existing alphabet (Roman, Cyrillic, Arabic, etc.) to transliterate them (or sound them out). The limitation of transliterating is that each existing alphabet has the likelihood of bringing with it the association of the socio-religious values of the culture it grew out of originally–Arabic would likely bring overtones of the tenets of Islam; the Greek or Roman alphabet would bring ideals of Christianity, democracy, and a capitalist ethic; and Cyrillic may likely bring along Russian ideals and values. We must remember that the forms of the alphabets are currently associated throughout the world with the culture that initiated them. Ultimately it makes the most sense to allow an alphabet to develop out of the culture of a people rather than to impress onto the pre-writing society the alphabet of another people. If we don't allow the language to develop its own written form, we are stripping those people of the right to develop their own unique writing system that reflects their society's aesthetic.

PICTOGRAPHS AS THE BASIS FOR WRITTEN COMMUNICATION

Repetition of agreed simple shapes is the essence of writing. In order to communicate, the simplified drawings must be recognized and interpreted by numerous people. Pictographs are the assumed beginning of most alphabets, yet each culture represents their pictographs differently,

Although visual art communicates, it is necessary to have a designated set of consistent pictographs or symbols which can be read or deciphered in order to have a written language.

This page is set in ITC Garamond Light 8.5/12.

1   *Ancient*
       Writing Systems

1-6. Cylinder seals were rolled into wet clay to show ownership, to show contents in shipping, or to commemorate events or for ceremonial purposes. The wet clay could be used to wrap over the top of a vessel to assure that the contents were not tampered with. These were created in Mesopotamia about 1500 BC.

> Our concept of history would be much shorter and far less detailed if it all had to be memorized.

and these pictographs are simplified differently based on each culture's tools, raw materials, leisure time, mechanical advancements, and aesthetic sensibility.

In the development of a pictographic system, the symbols reflect the ideas and perceptions of the *verbal* language they represent. The verbal concept must precede the pictograph. So that a culture of Eskimos which has twenty different *spoken* words to represent specific types of snow (as opposed to our snow, sleet, ice, hail, and slush) *needs* twenty different *pictographs* for the varieties of snow that they perceive based on their verbal language. The verbal language reflects the necessity for distinguishing subtleties of various forms of freezing water. Yet because they communicate simply, pictographs have only limited use to a society.

WRITING AND RECORDING HISTORY

The study of written communication is the study of the evolution of history. Before writing there was no *recorded* history; it was all verbal. Without lettering and type, there would be a more condensed version of history, one that a human could commit completely to memory. History would be subject more to personal interpretation and editing; we would not know some of the details we *do* know about the lives of ordinary people in earlier cultures. Also, because lettering and type are closely tied to technological advancements in the manufacturing of tools, writing substrates (whether clay, stone, or parchment) reflect the raw materials and mechanical abilities of a particular people or society.

EARLY WRITING SOCIETIES

It is interesting to note that writing systems were developing within about a thousand years of each other in Sumeria (Middle East), Egypt (Africa) and China. All three cultures date the refinement of their pictograph-based writing system to between 3000 BC and 2000 BC. (Cuneiform dates to around 3000 BC, hieroglyphics dates to around 2800 BC, the precursors of the Kanji Chinese alphabet date to around 1800 BC, and Sanskrit in India dates to about 1500 BC.) Clearly the introduction of writing allowed these cultures to more rapidly develop a highly organized society, and record codes of law, history, literature, philosophy, medicine, mathematics, and religion.

PICTOGRAPH-BASED WRITING SYSTEMS

Early picture writing (when a simplified drawing of an image represented the object it looked like) is assumed to be the first step in developing most written languages. These pictographs may have been introduced for any number of reasons. Some historians assume that writing began with small tags of clay inscribed with pictographs that were attached by string to jugs; the pictographs represented the

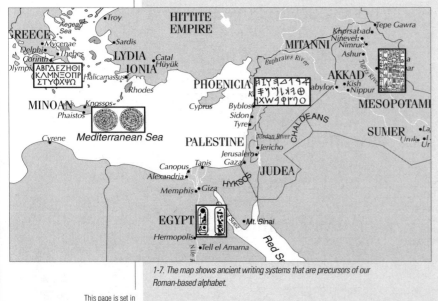

1-7. The map shows ancient writing systems that are precursors of our Roman-based alphabet.

This page is set in
ITC Garamond Light 8.5/12.

contents of the vessel during shipping. Others think that writing was used at first to record gifts to the temples that people were required to donate as tribute each year. Another theory posits that writing evolved as a means to show ownership; a small distinctive mark or series of marks on an object designated to whom it belonged, or who crafted it. Some assume that pictographs developed out of drawing, as a sort of shorthand representation of a memorable event.

Whatever the origins, writing allowed the recording of events, the transcription of history, the codification of legal practices, the development of mathematic theory, the creation of literary epics, the recording of healing herbs and the expansion of mercantile practices. In short, without writing, it is difficult to predict how society would have developed, or to know how it did develop.

Exactly how and why writing developed is not clear. It *is* clear that distinct but possibly related alphabets developed in different ancient cultures, in various places, within a thousand years of each other, around 3000 BC. For a short while, some cultures had rather elaborate writing systems while people in other lands were using simple pictographs.

Simplified drawing of objects, *pictographs* are appropriate for nouns, but not for communicating complex ideas, feelings, concepts, and actions. Modern examples of pictographs indicate gender-separate toilets, places to stay overnight, and eating areas. Pictographs are vital when there is a need to communicate in the absence of a common language or script. Historically pictographs functioned as a writing system for a society for a while, but as the use of written communication broadened, so too must the images or symbols which represented that communication.

THE TRANSITION FROM PICTOGRAPHS TO IDEOGRAPHS

Over time, pictograph-based languages developed into a system to represent ideas and concepts other than nouns. Pictographs were combined to signify *ideas*, rather than simply representing objects. When pictographs must be *interpreted* with knowledge rather than simply *recognized* and identified to be read, they are considered ideographs. An *ideograph* (also *ideogram*) is the combination of two or more pictographs to represent a concept—the pictograph of woman combined with the pictograph of child may represent the idea "pregnant" even though it does not show a pregnant woman.

Ideographs are also defined as pictographs that come to mean something other than their original intent. For example, the pictograph of the "hand" changes to an ideograph when it is combined with other symbols to mean "to give," "to greet," "to offer": things *associated* with the hand rather than the hand itself. Ideographs mark the true beginning of a language that must be decoded by outsiders.

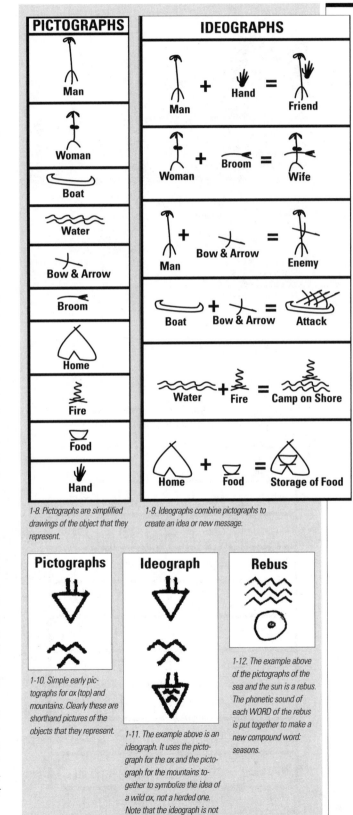

1-8. Pictographs are simplified drawings of the object that they represent.

1-9. Ideographs combine pictographs to create an idea or new message.

Pictographs

1-10. Simple early pictographs for ox (top) and mountains. Clearly these are shorthand pictures of the objects that they represent.

Ideograph

1-11. The example above is an ideograph. It uses the pictograph for the ox and the pictograph for the mountains together to symbolize the idea of a wild ox, not a herded one. Note that the ideograph is not trying to show a wild ox, running free in the mountains.

Rebus

1-12. The example above of the pictographs of the sea and the sun is a rebus. The phonetic sound of each WORD of the rebus is put together to make a new compound word: seasons.

This page is set in ITC Garamond Light 8.5/12.

1 *Ancient*
Writing Systems

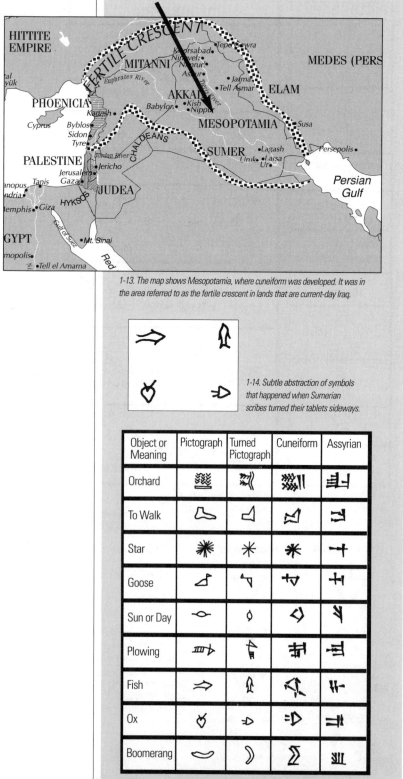

1-13. The map shows Mesopotamia, where cuneiform was developed. It was in the area referred to as the fertile crescent in lands that are current-day Iraq.

1-14. Subtle abstraction of symbols that happened when Sumerian scribes turned their tablets sideways.

Object or Meaning	Pictograph	Turned Pictograph	Cuneiform	Assyrian
Orchard				
To Walk				
Star				
Goose				
Sun or Day				
Plowing				
Fish				
Ox				
Boomerang				

1-15. This chart reveals the transition from pictographs in clay, then turning the characters sideways, the introduction of the wedge-shaped stylus, and the gradual abstraction from the object depicted.

This page is set in Bodoni 8.5/12.

Ideographs cannot be looked at and understood; there is an element of abstraction to ideographs. They represent the idea presented, but they are not a simplified drawing of the concept. Ideographs need an interpreter or translator. Since an ideograph is the integration of pictographic symbols to represent conceptual ideas, note that a culture could not have ideographs if it did not already have a working vocabulary of pictographs. Also, every culture has different combinations of the somewhat universal pictographs to represent concepts based on the foundation of their specific verbal language, their spiritual beliefs and their social structure.

SUMERIAN CUNEIFORM

The Sumerian culture grew out of the southern fertile land, "the fertile crescent" between the Tigris and Euphrates Rivers in Mesopotamia. Most of the surrounding land is limited in its ability to sustain agriculture. (This is the area occupied by current day Iraq; it was referred to as Mesopotamia by the Greeks, meaning "land between two rivers.") The land has low-lying hills surrounding it to the north that act as a natural barrier preventing attack from outside aggressive forces. The regular supply of fresh water from the two rivers enabled the culture to grow its own food, to settle, to develop a system of government, and eventually to create a form of writing.

Abundant local clay from riverbeds served as the logical material for record keeping. The Sumerians turned their clay-like riverbed soil into their writing surface; it was formed into tablets and written on when wet, then laid in the sun to dry.

It is important to realize that the appearance of written communication is affected by the writing surface and the tools used to write the original forms, as well as by the pictorial sensibility of the people. The Sumerians used clay tablets to write on with a pointed stylus dragged through the clay. By about 3200 BC, pictographs were used to write simple records. Cuneiform is generally hypothesized to be the oldest writing system, based on the dating of artifacts. By 3100 BC, a codified system of pictographic symbols had been developed that scribes understood.

CUNEIFORM TABLETS ARE TURNED SIDEWAYS

Over the next two hundred years, by about 3000 BC, scribes gradually turned their tablets sideways for efficiency, now writing was from right to left rather than from top to bottom. This change was probably made so that the scribes would not mar their work while the clay was still soft. When they incised the clay tablet in vertical columns starting on the right, any right-handed scribe ran the risk of smudging the characters if his hand dragged over them as he composed the next vertical column. By changing the tablet's orientation, scribes made writing faster (they didn't have to be so careful) and made pictographs less literal since they were all turned sideways. The sideways pictographs related less visually to the item they referenced. This adjustment and the abstraction of the symbol from the item referenced was the first break from the pictographic roots of the Sumerian writing system.

INTRODUCTION OF THE TRIANGULAR-TIPPED STYLUS

The Sumerian written language was modified over the centuries. By about 2500 BC the scribes' writing speed was greatly increased when they replaced the pointed stylus with a triangularly tipped one. Characters now were composed of a series of wedge-shaped strokes pushed into clay rather than a pointed tool dragged through the clay. The use of these wedge-shaped forms further abstracted the symbols which composed the language called *cuneiform*.

THE TRANSITION FROM IDEOGRAPHS TO REBUSES AND PHONOGRAMS

Gradually these symbols were put together and used in *rebus-like* manner. Rebuses are pictographs of short words, put together to sound out longer words, so that the symbols for bee+tray=betray, or moon+light=moonlight, or basket+ball=basketball. Rebuses allowed the creation complex words from simple pictographs.

Another innovation with pictographs was the development of *phonograms*. Phonograms use the first phonetic sound of grouped pictographs to sound out the word, so that *gun+ostrich=go*, or *crane+aunt+leg=crawl*. Phonograms had to be read to be understood.

The Sumerians were eventually overrun by the militant, horse-charioted Assyrians, from north of Mesopotamia, who were quick to try to adopt cuneiform as a practical writing system. Even after the Assyrians simplified cuneiform (so that they could learn it more easily) there were still 560 different characters in use. Cuneiform is not an exclusively ancient writing system since it continued in use until about 100 AD.

MINOAN WRITING

Some historians hypothesize that the ancient inhabitants of the island of Crete (known as Minoans after their ruler, King Minos) may have been the earliest to invent writing, but the remains of the writing of the Minoans are limited, and the evidence for this is inconclusive. The Minoan culture is believed to have been wiped out by a tidal wave caused by a volcanic eruption on a neighboring island.

The Minoan symbols have not yet been deciphered. Of the examples of the Minoan alphabet, a few found in the city of Phaistos are on clay disks, with the symbols spiralling into the center. Some historians have theorized that these are "story" disks; others believe that they may have been made

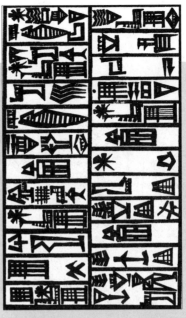

1-16. Old Akkadian pictographs from ancient Babylonia from the time of King Sarganisaralim. These pictographs pre-date the wedge-shaped cuneiform writing.

1-17. Above is an ancient, sun-dried clay tablet that was inscribed with the wedge-shaped cuneiform while the clay was wet.

1-18. An example of cuneiform writing with the wedge-shaped characters placed in long boxes that appear to be cartouches borrowed from Egypt.

Ancient Writing Systems **1**

1-19. An example of cuneiform writing with the wedge-shaped characters written in vertical rows.

This page is set in Bodoni 8.5/12.

1
Ancient
Writing Systems

1-20. The drawings of the phaistos disks above show simple pictographs that have not yet been deciphered. The symbols are arranged in a continuous swirl towards the center.

1-21. The map shows Knossos, on the island of Crete, where the Minoan civilization was located in the ancient world.

1-22. Above are two cartouches for the pharaohs of Egypt. On the left is the cartouche of Rameses II, King of Egypt from 1324-1258 BC. On the right is the cartouche of Cleopatra II, Queen of Egypt from 69–30 BC.

1-23. Above are the hieroglyphs used in ancient Africa for the seasons. Notice the simplicity yet the beauty of their design. At the left is Akhet–Winter, the four months of sowing. In the middle is Pert–Spring, the four months of growing. On the right is Shemu–Summer, the four months of inundation.

This page is set in Myriad Tilt 8.5/12.

from stamps pressed into the soft clay. The Minoan script has not yet been translated. Some historians believe that the Minoan alphabet may provide a link between the ancient hieroglyphics and ancient Phoenician, but this is debated.

EGYPTIAN HIEROGLYPHICS

Egyptian hieroglyphics began in Africa largely as pictographs around 2800 BC. Early examples of pictorial hieroglyphics around 2600 BC in the tombs of pharaohs are magnificent. They show detail and are often carved in stone relief with color added. This level of visual detail required an intensive human effort and was not maintained for everyday written records. As limited writing was gradually introduced for business records, the writing of hieroglyphic symbols was simplified to clear linear outlines. Details were omitted in favor of the speed of writing.

Hieroglyphics generally ran in vertical columns on the page. These columns of characters were read from top to bottom usually, but not always starting with the rightmost column. These vertical columns of pictographs were separated by thin rules between the columns. In hieroglyphics, all of the people and animals faced in the same direction. To read hieroglyphics, you must read "into" or "towards" the front of the people or animals. Design format in hieroglyphics required one or two colored horizontal rules across the top and bottom of the columns.

CARTOUCHES SIGNIFIED SACRED NAMES

The names of pharaohs (who were believed to be direct descendants from the gods) were enclosed within the ankh symbol for infinity, an oval with a line. Placing their name within the ankh represented their immortality. The names were written as phonograms. (A phonogram combines the first uttered sound of the symbols to sound out the proper name; for instance, the image of a lion would represent the sound of the letter "L.") Many scholars believe that phonograms lead to the development of a phonetic alphabet in which one symbol represents one sound in the spoken language. However, ancient Egyptians never made this transition. Hieroglyphics were in use from 2600 BC to 400 AD, for approximately 3000 years, but they never really evolved into a fully *phonetic* alphabet, in which one abstract symbol represented each phonetic sound in the spoken language.

In hieroglyphics, the phonogram system was not standardized; scribes did not have a set selection of symbols agreed upon to represent the various sounds. The same phonetic sound could be represented by a variety of symbols, depending upon the scribe's location or schooling; over 300 different symbols had to be known in order to "read" hieroglyphics. The Egyptians never simplified their system to the 24 consonant sounds needed to represent the utterances of their spoken language. This may be due to the fact that many words in their language had consonant duplicates; without the vowels, it *was* impossible to tell the words apart.

HIEROGLYPHICS: THE REBUS

The hieroglyphic pictographs were eventually put together in a rebus-like manner. The transition to rebuses marks the beginning of a phonetic relationship between the verbal uttered word for an object and the symbols that represent the sound of the word; it begins the detachment from the physical object of the pictograph. Rebuses have to be deciphered; unlike pictographs, they can't be figured out.

It is a short step from rebuses, to phonograms, to a truly phonetic or acrophonic alphabet. In *acrophony*, the vowel sounds were often omitted when words were sounded out. Only the consonants in the language were represented, and the vowels were figured out by the word's context. Hebrew, which is believed to originally date back to about 2000 BC, is an example of an alphabet that uses acrophony. In Hebrew, there are no calligraphic symbols for the vowel sounds, but they are sometimes represented as dots to clarify the meaning of the word.

PAPYRUS: THE ECONOMICAL WRITING SURFACE

The introduction of papyrus as a writing substance and a reed brush to write with around 2400 BC changed the form of the Egyptian pictographs. The use of a brush allowed the pictographs to take on a fluid, sinuous, graceful appearance. Corners were rounded off to hasten writing, and hieroglyphics were often constructed from one continuous flowing brush stroke.

Just as the writing implement affected the appearance of the written symbols, so did the *substrate* (writing surface) affect the appearance of the writing system. It is important to realize that humans were innovative with the natural resources at their disposal. Economics dictated that an abundant raw material be used to write on. The Egyptians capitalized on a weed in the Nile River called cyperus papyrus that grew between three to ten feet tall, and could grow five inches thick in the stem. Papyrus was used from at least 2400 BC to 500 AD as the primary writing surface throughout the ancient western world. It was cheaply made, lightweight, and transportable, and could provide a smooth writing surface.

THE COSTLY MANUFACTURING OF SCROLLS

Due to the time involved in the manufacturing of scrolls, the cost of materials and the limited number of scribes, the price of a scroll was prohibitive for most ancient Egyptians. Some merchants must have known some words in order to carry out their business. Yet when the copying of scrolls was so painstakingly slow, scrolls were a symbol of great wealth. They were sought after as status symbols as well as collections of information (sort of like having a high-powered web-browser today).

HIERATIC SCRIPT: WRITTEN WITH FLUIDITY

Due to the use of papyrus and reed brushes, the pictorial hieroglyphics were simplified by 1500 BC, into a calligraphic style known as *hieratic script* which means literally "priestly writing". Hieratic script developed with a reed "pen" (a dried reed cut at an angle and dipped in ink to write) and gradually resulted in characters that were more abstracted from their pictorial roots. This hieratic script was used exclusively for religious literature at first, but gradually was adapted for commerce and daily business use as well as for the rituals..

DEMOTIC SCRIPT

Around 500 BC this hieratic script eventually evolved into *demotic script* (means "of the people") which was used more widely. This writing style was even further simplified and abstracted from the pictorial hieroglyphics. Although ordinary people could use this script, the average person did not have wide access to scholarly information nor training as a scribe.

1-25. Hieroglyphics were generally stacked vertically as shown above, with all of the symbols facing one direction. They are "read" towards the front of the symbols.

1-24. An example of hieroglyphics written on papyrus with a reed brush. The fluidity of the brushstrokes changed and softened the drawing of the hieroglyphics.

1-26. This example of Egyptian hieroglyphics shows the organization into vertical columns with dividing rules between each column. The columns were read by reading into the direction that the symbols faced.

This page is set in Myriad Tilt 8.5/12.

1 *Ancient*
   Writing Systems

Object or Meaning	Pictograph	Hieroglyph	Script Hand	Hieratic	Demotic
3 Animal Skins tied Together					
A Vessel for Fluids					
A Harpoon					
A Corded Bundle of Papyrus					
A Whip					

1-27. The chart shows the transition from pictograph-based hieroglyphics to the brush-based Hieratic and eventually the abstract Demotic script.

PAPYRUS PRODUCTION

Papyrus is a paper-like substance made from the papyrus plant that grew wild along the banks of the Nile River. To make papyrus, this bamboo-like plant was soaked in water for a few weeks, the outer tough hide was stripped off, and the inner, soft, pulp-like striated fibers were beaten until they were flat These still retained their long, thin shape. Each flat, thin strip was lined up next to the other neatly. Another layer of flat strips was placed on top at 90° to the first layer. These were then layered with cloth to absorb the moisture, and a great weight was placed upon the layers of papyrus. They were allowed to dry for a few days, and then the papyrus was ready to write on. Usually individual pieces of papyrus were joined to make scrolls. Each sheet of papyrus was about 9 in. high and 15 in. long. These lengths were then joined together to make scrolls 20 to 30 ft. long.

Sidebar is set in Gill Sans Light Italic 8.5/15

DEAD SEA SCROLLS AT BURIAL

Scrolls at this time were too expensive for the average person. The Egyptian tradition of burying the deceased with the Dead Sea Scrolls (a series of religious writings, with the name of the deceased inserted, enabling a fruitful afterlife) has revealed that there was a wide variation in the scribes' skill levels. Scribes were paid to complete these scrolls by the family of the deceased. Some of the burial scrolls are not complete; the writing stops about half way through the scroll! In others there are obvious copying errors and misspellings throughout. Because the average person could not read, this was not jeopardizing the scribe's position or future contracts.

READING & WRITING PRIVILEGES

Throughout time, the dissemination of knowledge and the ability to read and write have often been reserved for the chosen few, the elite, the scholars and rulers, or the priests who controlled religious rituals and the early forms of taxation. The importance of memory in pre-writing societies is comparable to the importance of literacy in writing societies. Those who could read were looked to for advice in all types of disputes and emergencies; their knowledge and judgment were unchallenged. Scribes— those who could write—were believed in some cultures to have power over human life; if an Egyptian scribe wrote your name in the Book of the Dead, your time was up in this world! Doubtless, the scribes did little to dissuade this myth. Scribes were trained in Egypt from the time they were about five years old.

Today we have abolished this controlled system of learning writing and reading skills. (But a parallel to that practice today can be seen today in the knowledge of computer programming). In ancient times, hand-copied scrolls were expensive to produce (not many people were taught to write); any scrolls were cherished, valued and cared for from one generation to the next.

Frequently the luxury of knowledge is linked to the religious culture of a society because these religious enclaves have handed down the learning gained over the years to their initiates. The copying and selling of texts throughout the centuries has enabled religious enclaves to raise funds for support.

Much of our knowledge of ancient western cultures comes to us second-hand, from the parchment copies made from papyrus scrolls by monks during the Middle Ages. (The original texts on papyrus have not survived the moist Mediterranean climate; but Medieval copies on animal skins have survived.) We can only assume that monks copied these ancient texts faithfully, without editing them.

The democratization of reading was impossible for many centuries since the supply of hand-copied books could not meet the demand, and teachers only had a handful of pupils. Public lending libraries are only a very recent step in the process of attaining information. Those trained to read at a temple at a young age had to rely on the beneficence of the wealthy, and they were often employed to teach the offspring of nobles so that the scholar would have access to the coveted libraries. Rulers built up libraries of scrolls from their own land (the history and stories of their people), as well as writings, beliefs and ideas from other lands. Early scribes were commissioned by rulers to copy texts and these were traded.

PARCHMENT AS A WRITING SURFACE

One of Egypt's pharaohs was in a library-building competition with another ruler; he placed an embargo on papyrus, so none could be shipped abroad. This led to the development of an alternative writing substance. The search ended with the refinement of parchment as a writing surface. Parchment is a writing substrate made from the skins of calves, sheep and goats–originally developed as an alternative to papyrus. Vellum is the highest quality of parchment made from newborn calf skin. Parchment, unlike papyrus, could be written on both sides without the ink seeping through. And, unlike papyrus, parchment could be folded without cracking at the fold.

Some scholars believe that parchment allowed for the development of books (written on both sides of the page) rather than scrolls (writing only on one side). Yet, parchment, because it was made from animal skin, was also vastly more expensive to manufacture than papyrus. It was a better, smoother surface, but far more costly, and time-consuming to produce. Because books made with parchment were so expensive, they were sought after and collected by rulers as a sign of great wealth and power.

ANCIENT WRITING SYSTEMS

Other writing systems were well developed in the ancient world. China, India, Crete, Egypt, Sumeria and the Hittites had writing systems as early as 2000 BC. It is important to realize that these different writing systems coexisted in time (although they were exclusive to each culture), and the written forms were eventually translated, just like their oral languages.

It is difficult to determine which writing systems preceded the others. Scholars disagree on whether cuneiform influenced the development of the Phoenician alphabet that led to our Roman-based alphabet or whether the Phoenician alphabet is indebted to Egyptian hieroglyphics. Some scholars argue that our phonetic alphabet may be derived from the undeciphered pictographs of the Ancient Minoan civilization on the island of Crete, while others credit the Sinaitic script developed by Semitic workers in Egyptian turquoise mines as the first acrophonic adaptation of hieroglyphics. This last theory may be a reasonable assumption since the ancient *spoken* Phoenician was closely related to the ancient Hebrew spoken by the Semites of the day.

THE ANCIENT PHOENICIAN ALPHABET

However it developed, the majority of scholars do agree that by the year 1500 BC, over three thousand

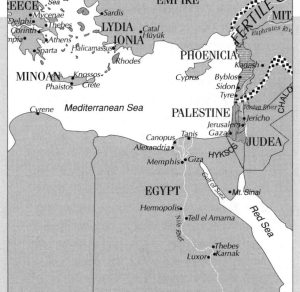

1-28. The map shows Egypt, where hieroglyphics originated.

PARCHMENT PRODUCTION

Parchment is a substance for writing that is made from the skin of goats and calves. First, the fur would be rubbed off the surface, then the skin would be stretched over a frame and left to be bleached in the sun. The surface of the skin would be smoothed with stones and liquid washes. Parchment was a substance, unlike papyrus, that could be written on both sides without the ink seeping through. Some scholars believe that parchment allowed for the development of books (written on both sides of the page) rather than scrolls (writing only on one side). Yet, parchment was also vastly more expensive to manufacture than papyrus. It was a better, smoother surface, but far more costly and time-consuming to produce. Perhaps this encouraged people to try to utilize both sides of the surface. Because the production of books made with parchment were so expensive, they were sought after and collected by rulers as a sign of great wealth and power.

Sidebar is set in Gill Sans Light Italic 8.5/ 21.5

This page is set in
Gill Sans Light 8.5/12.

1 *Ancient Writing Systems*

Some scholars posit that the ancient Semitic Phoenicians are responsible for devising a "true" alphabet which relied on a single abstract symbol to represent a particular sound. Whether it was adapted as a simplification of cuneiform or hieroglyphics is still debated. There were Semitic slaves in Egyptian turquoise mines in the Sinai desert who designed an adaptation of hieroglyphics to transcribe their oral language (ancient Hebrew). Examples of this ancient Semitic writing system exist today but have not yet been fully decoded. In this alphabet–known as the Sinaitic script–it is believed that each symbol represented the sound the word began with. Although printed reproductions of this script, which was usually inscribed in stone or clay, are difficult to find, they may represent the missing link in understanding how our own alphabet evolved from the various known scripts in the ancient world.

Sidebar is set in Futura Book Italic 8.5/13.5

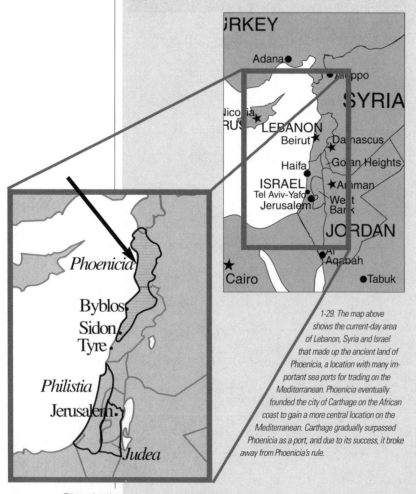

1-29. The map above shows the current-day area of Lebanon, Syria and Israel that made up the ancient land of Phoenicia, a location with many important sea ports for trading on the Mediterranean. Phoenicia eventually founded the city of Carthage on the African coast to gain a more central location on the Mediterranean. Carthage gradually surpassed Phoenicia as a port, and due to its success, it broke away from Phoenicia's rule.

This page is set in Futura Book 8.5/12.

years ago, ancient Phoenicia had developed an alphabet of twenty-two symbols that was phonetically-based and widely in use throughout their land. It is to this alphabet that we directly trace our own, and we have space here to only consider the formation of our Roman-based alphabet.

In the area of the ancient world known as Phoenicia (lands that are now parts of Lebanon, Syria and Israel), an alphabet grew up that is a precedent of the one you are reading. The Phoenicians were a seafaring and merchant people located at the crossroads of international trade in the ancient world. Phoenicia was considered the gateway to the Middle Eastern lands and all the goods and foods that it produced. Ancient people from land in current-day Europe traded with the Phoenicians to acquire the rare spices, jewels, brocades, silks, weavings, etc., from the eastern countries that came to the Phoenician docks via overland caravans. The culture of the Phoenicians was influenced by the many other countries that surrounded the Mediterranean Sea, as well as by the Arab and Persian traders. It was truly a cosmopolitan center of the ancient world, with sea travelers and traders from many different lands. The Phoenicians were in contact with the Egyptians, the Sumerians, the Greeks, the Minoans, the Etruscans (in what is now Italy) and dozens of other cultures. Because of this myriad of influences, it is difficult for scholars to track the roots of the Phoenician alphabet.

PHONETICS: HOW THE PHOENICIAN ALPHABET WAS DIFFERENT FROM OTHER ANCIENT WRITING

The important innovation that the Phoenician alphabet offered was breaking down oral speech into a series of sounds, and then attributing a symbol to represent each spoken sound. They freed written communication from its pictographic origins. No longer did the symbol have to "look" like the item it represented. This simplified the number of symbols necessary to know in order to read. With fewer symbols, both writing and reading were simpler to learn. The limited characters of the Phoenician alphabet allowed reading to become more widely available. Also, the Phoenician sound-based alphabet could be used to transcribe other oral languages besides their own, making early translation possible. This was particularly helpful for a city with people traveling from different lands, speaking different languages. Their alphabet provided a common written communication among various peoples.

The Phoenician alphabet was likely used in trading. The Sumerians' custom of using seals pressed into soft clay to identify the owner of a parcel may have been adopted by the Phoenicians (who used letters rather than symbolic pictographs to represent the owner's name or vessel's contents).

Thus, their alphabet could have spread gradually to other cultures. It seems logical that the use of Phoenician lettering would replace these older pictorial seals for identification.

THE ALPHABET IS EXPORTED FROM PHOENICIA TO GREECE

By about 800 BC, the Phoenician alphabet spread to ancient Greece, meaning that merchants in Greece began using the alphabet they learned and applying it to their own language. To write the Phoenician alphabet, the Greeks used an ivory or metal stylus, inscribed into a wax tablet to practice as student scribes or for temporary notes and letters.

It is important to note that the Greeks borrowed a fully developed alphabet from another culture (without conquering them) and simply adapted it for their own needs. Throughout history, some cultures have been known as innovators of ideas while others are known for adopting and improving the original idea or technological advancement. The Greeks simply lifted the entire twenty-two symbols of the Phoenician alphabet, changed five consonant characters to represent the vowels (which were omitted in writing by the Phoenicians), and added characters for the sounds in the Greek language that had no counterpart in Phoenician.

It may be that the Greeks had a tendency for "borrowing" ideas in this manner, or that the Phoenician alphabet lent itself to the task of writing Greek because it simplified the sounding out of any language. The Greek alphabet was made to read from left to right rather than from right to left as Phoenician had (although for a short while, it was written back and forth down the page, called *boustrephedon*).

GREECE AT ITS ZENITH

After the Greeks had the alphabet for only three hundred years, their culture was at its zenith. 500 BC is considered the Golden Age of Greece, when the arts and learning were at their peak. Whether we can attribute this development to the introduction of the written alphabet is difficult to say, but the written language does allow for the codifying of laws; the recording of elaborate epics, plays, and myths; as well as the documenting philosophical ideas and medical cures. All of these accomplishments would have been significantly more difficult without writing and more cumbersome with an extended pictograph-based writing system, rather than the phonetic-based alphabet.

Around 300 BC, Greece was becoming a powerful force in the west. From the northern city-state of Pella, Alexander the Great (356–323 BC) of Macedon overthrew the Persian empire of Darius. With the expansion of the Greek empire under Alexander, Greek culture was

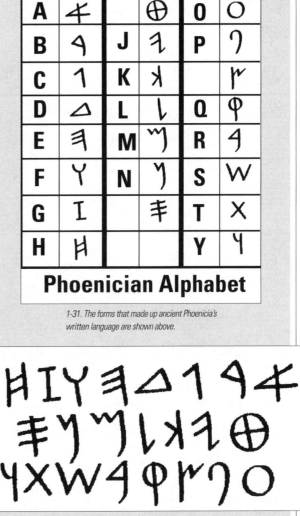

1-30. *Ancient Phoenician inscribed on a piece of the interior of a bowl.*

A	⟨			0	O
B	⟨	J	⟨	P	⟨
C	⟨	K	⟨	⟨	⟨
D	△	L	⟨	Q	φ
E	⟨	M	⟨	R	⟨
F	Y	N	⟨	S	W
G	I		⟨	T	X
H	⟨			Y	⟨

Phoenician Alphabet

1-31. *The forms that made up ancient Phoenicia's written language are shown above.*

1-32. *Phoenician alphabet (c. 1000 BC) reads from right to left on the page.*

This page is set in
Futura Book 8.5/12.

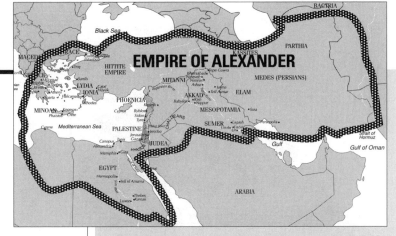

1-33. The map shows the extent of the empire of Greece's Alexander the Great in 324 BC.

Phoenician	Greek

1-34. Above is a comparison of some ancient Phoenician characters on the left, with early ancient Greek on the right.

spread throughout most of the ancient world. The spread of Hellenistic culture was significant: the Greek phonetic alphabet (precursor of our own alphabet) spread as far as Egypt, Mesopotamia and India. Greek language and writing spread throughout the ancient world, and the Greek alphabet became the basis of the Cyrillic, Etruscan and Latin alphabets.

Scrolls were used to transmit information at this time, and they were usually about 35 feet in length, 9 or 10 inches in height, and rolled up to about 4 or 6 inches in diameter. When Alexander died, his generals parceled out the lands that had been his empire, creating smaller kingdoms that were no longer powerful or unified. Yet the effects of common writing and language of the prior empire were established. As we will see in the next chapter, the ancient Roman Empire adopted much of Greek culture and exported their language, alphabet and customs to many of their conquered territories.

THE KEY TO ANCIENT EGYPTIAN HIEROGLYPHICS

As the ancient world became more dependent upon writing, translating from one language to the next became a necessary skill in the various cultures. Nineteenth-century archeologists had artifacts with undeciphered hieroglyphics on them for centuries before they had any idea of what the hieroglyphics meant. Because the transition away from hieroglyphics as the preferable format for writing was gradual, and the demotic script predominated over time, eventually no living person was able to comprehend the meaning behind the ancient Egyptian pictographs. Most of the writing in hieroglyphics was difficult to decipher because the subject matter frequently related to their ancient religion, and the names of the gods were no longer recognized—even by Egyptians. Their script had changed so much that they could not trace it back to the pictographic origins of their alphabet.

The Rosetta stone held the key to understanding the ancient hieroglyphics. This elaborately inscribed stone was created about 200 BC. It displays one message inscribed in three different alphabets: ancient Greek, hieroglyphics and Demotic script. It was not until this stone was unearthed by Napoleon's men in 1799 (when they invaded Egypt) that the translation of hieroglyphics was possible. By using the ancient Greek inscription as a "map," the archeologist Jean François Champollion was able to decipher the order and sounds represented by the hieroglyphic pictographs in 1822. The key was to recognize that the cartouches were sounding out proper names. Champollion also posed theories (later proved

---

WRITING COMPARED TO PLOWING

For a short while, Greek writing read from right to left on the first line and then from left to right on the following line and so forth, wrapping back and forth across the page in snake-like fashion. This structure on the page was called "boustrephedon" and comes from the Greek words meaning "as the ox plows the field." They wrote these new letters on the page the same as they plowed their fields, and the letters were reversed on the line reading from right to left. This shows how early reading and writing were closely related to the Greeks' everyday common activities.

Although you may think that eventually it becomes easier to read backwards, with some practice, it is still difficult to read text when you have to discern and flip the letters.

correct) about the structure of the Demotic script language on the tablet. These discoveries led to deciphering other hieroglyphic paintings and inscriptions.

ANCIENT CHINA: PAPERMAKING AND PRINTING

To give you more of a global as opposed to a western perspective, in 105 AD the Chinese had invented papermaking, which was eventually to become the writing/communication material of choice. Ts'ai Lun in China is credited with the development of papermaking. He used an assortment of vegetable fibers, such as mulberry bark, bamboo, silk, cotton rags, linen and hemp. These fibers were mixed with water and beaten until they broke down into a pulp. Then using a wooden frame with a screen on it, he lowered the screen into the watery, pulp mixture. By gently shaking the screen while raising it out of the watery mixture, an even coating of the fibers was caught against the screen. The thin mat of fibers was then flattened, weighted, pressed and when dried was a sheet of paper.

Also, by 270 AD, the Chinese were printing from woodblocks that were inked, sometimes in different colors, and multiple blocks were printed onto the same piece of paper. The raised surface of a block of wood that had been cut away was rolled with a water-based thin ink that soaked into the raised wood. A piece of rice paper was then applied to the wood and rubbed so that the ink was absorbed into the paper. The Chinese were printing on paper rather than engraving in stone or clay long before the western world made the transition. While the Greeks were still writing on

Chinese calligraphy was invented around 2000 BC (about 4,500 years ago) according to legend by Ts-ang Chieh, who was inspired to invent writing by studying the claw marks of birds and the footprints of animals. Chinese calligraphy is highly stylized abstract designs called logograms—graphic characters or signs that represent an entire word—in English, "% or & or = or + or @ or #" are examples of logograms. Some historians believe that, like Egyptian hieroglyphics, Chinese calligraphy was at one point a picture-based language. As a writing system, Chinese calligraphy is very complex and challenging to master; knowing all 44,000 characters is an indication of great learning. Elementary-school children must be able to distinguish between 5,000 and 10,000 characters to read. This is very different from our western twenty-six-character, phonetic-based alphabet.

Sidebar is set in Bodoni Italic 8.5/ 19

1-35. The Parthenon, built in ancient Greece, under Pericles.

1-36. Above is the ancient Greek alphabet at about 500 BC.

1-37. The Rosetta Stone showing the same inscription translated into three different written alphabets. It was carved in 200 BC. Champollion used cartouches to decipher the hieroglyphic inscriptions.

This page is set in Cheltenham Book 8.5/12.

1 Ancient Writing Systems

1-38. This table shows a comparison of various ancient alphabets.

papyrus scrolls or codices, the Chinese were developing printing from carved wood blocks. The Chinese even carved the textual pages of books out of wood blocks and printed from them by 300 AD. The mass production of Eastern books predates Europeans by fully 1200 years!

PROJECT: CREATING PICTOGRAPHS, IDEOGRAPHS, A SIMPLE ALPHABET

Using the examples at the right for inspiration, write/design ten simple pictographs below. They can be for objects in the world around you. Remember to keep them clear and simple.

Now try to use five of them in combination as ideographs, to represent an idea or concept. You can add new pictographs as needed.

Now try to create five rebuses below. Rebuses are when you combine pictographs of short words to sound out complex words.

Also, trace out your name using the ancient Phoenician and the Greek alphabets. Remember that the Phoenician reads from right to left. Lastly, try to create your very own symbols for an alphabet—see chart. They can be doodles, scribbles, etc.

OBJECTIVES
- To reinforce information on ancient alphabets from the text.
- To apply the alphabets in a hands-on project.
- To experience how symbols read visually and as sound elements.
- To consider spacing and density considerations of ancient scribes.
- To appreciate the abstraction/arbitrary nature of the symbols of any phonetic alphabet.

PICTOGRAPHS

IDEOGRAPHS

REBUSES

NAME IN ANCIENT PHOENICIAN

NAME IN ANCIENT GREEK

NEW SYMBOLS FOR AN ALPHABET

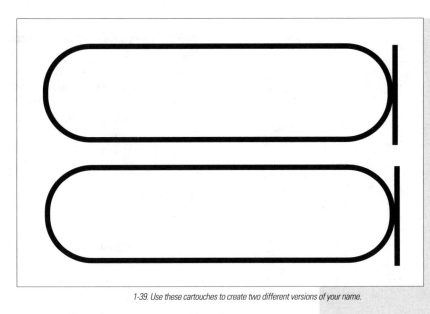

1-39. Use these cartouches to create two different versions of your name.

PROJECT: CUSTOM-DESIGN YOUR OWN CARTOUCHE

Using the hieroglyphics listed in the table at the side, create two cartouches in the ovals above that use phonographs to sound out your first name. Arrange the hieroglyphics so that they are both aesthetic in appearance, and so that their order can be determined. Use some of the alternate hieroglyphs in the second design. Pay attention to line quality and weight of the strokes, as well as the relative sizes of the symbols and even placement.

Position the hieroglyphs so that they all face in the same direction. Reading towards these "into the face of the creatures" is the direction your cartouche will be read.

OBJECTIVES

- To reinforce information on the use and implementation of hieroglyphics.
- To apply the knowledge of hieroglyphics in a hands-on application.
- To experience how hieroglyphics read visually and consider design decisions in placing them together in a cartouche.
- To consider the spacing and density decisions made by ancient scribes.
- To appreciate the skill required to draw ancient hieroglyphics.
- To gain hands-on experience fitting a series of hieroglyphics comfortably and clearly into a cartouche.
- To understand the facing of hieroglyphics for correct reading.
- To reinforce the awareness that cartouches were used for proper names.

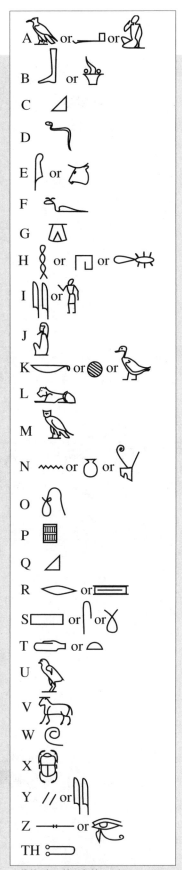

Ancient Writing Systems 1

1-40. Use these hieroglyphics as phonograms to draw your name in the cartouches above.

This page is set in ITC Fenice Light 8.5/12.

1 *Ancient*
   Writing Systems

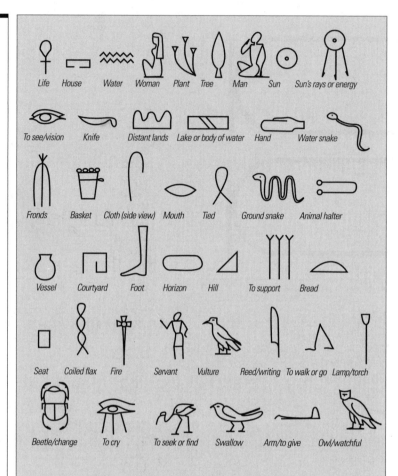

1-41. From the hieroglyphics above, construct a few simple sentences.

PROJECT: COMPOSING SIMPLE SENTENCES IN HIEROGLYPHICS

Using the hieroglyphics listed in the table on the left, create two simple sentences in the area below. You can stack the hieroglyphics in columns, but they will read in vertical columns from right to left. Remember to face the symbols in the direction that they are meant to be read.

OBJECTIVES

- To reinforce knowledge of the meaning of a few simple hieroglyphs.

- To apply the knowledge of hieroglyphics to a hands-on application.

- To experience how hieroglyphics read visually and consider design decisions in placing them together in a phrase.

- To consider the limitations of pictographic communication experienced by ancient scribes.

- To appreciate the multiple interpretations possible with pictographs as opposed to alphabetic communication.

- To gain hands-on experience fitting a series of hieroglyphics into a vertically stacked column.

- To understand the accuracy required in the drawing of hieroglyphics.

- To experience the challenges of consistent size, spacing and line quality in the drawing of hieroglyphics.

Ancient Writing Systems-Review

1. What was a personal attribute that was important before the development of writing? _____

_____

2. What was a possible use of writing when it was first developed? _____

_____

3. What did the first written communication represent? _____

4. Hieroglyphics were developed about (year) _____ in (country) _____

5. What is a pictograph? _____

_____

6. What is an ideograph? _____

_____

7. Describe a rebus. _____

_____

8. Describe a phonogram. _____

_____

9. How were phonograms used in hieroglyphics? _____

10. How was papyrus made? _____

_____

11. Why are cuneiform and the hieroglyphics so different in appearance? _____

_____

12. Why was the Phoenician alphabet widely adopted in the ancient world? _____

_____

This page is set in ITC Fenice
Light 8.5/12.

Ancient
Writing Systems

13-16. Identify these writing systems, and name the culture associated with them.

1-41.

13. _____

1-42.

14. _____

1-43.

15. _____

1-44.

16. _____

17. Why did the Sumerians choose to inscribe into clay tablets? _____

_____

18. When and where was cuneiform developed? _____

19. What are some advantages of a written language? _____

_____

20. Name three places where early writing systems were initiated. _____

_____

21. In your own words, compare a pictograph-based language with a phonetical-based language. _____

_____

_____

_____

_____

_____

22. How would you trace the origins of our alphabet? _____

_____

_____

_____

23. What is the connection between cultural concepts and our language/words? _____

_____

_____

_____

24. What do the forms of an alphabet tell us about the culture of the people? _____

_____

_____

_____

_____

Roman Empire–Middle Ages Lettering

2   *Roman Empire–Middle Ages Lettering*

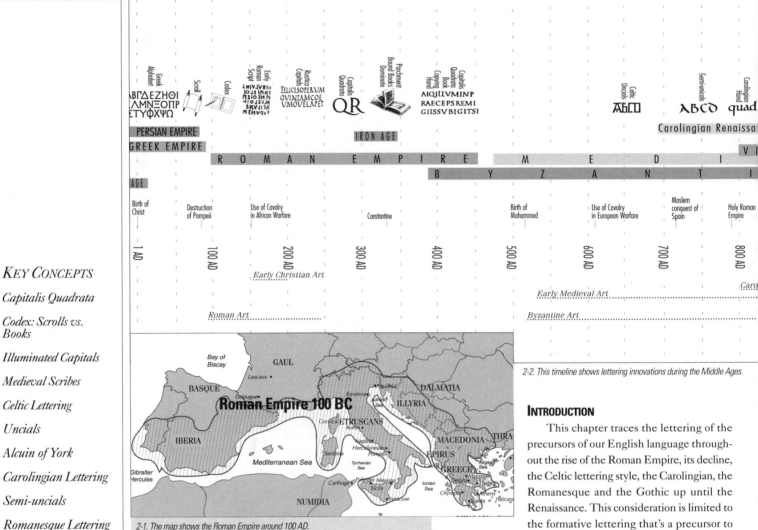

2-2. This timeline shows lettering innovations during the Middle Ages.

2-1. The map shows the Roman Empire around 100 AD.

KEY CONCEPTS

Capitalis Quadrata

Codex: Scrolls vs. Books

Illuminated Capitals

Medieval Scribes

Celtic Lettering

Uncials

Alcuin of York

Carolingian Lettering

Semi-uncials

Romanesque Lettering

Gothic Lettering

Lombardic Initials

Rotunda Lettering

Littera Antiqua

Papermaking

Rag Paper

Vellum

Woodblock Printing

INTRODUCTION

This chapter traces the lettering of the precursors of our English language throughout the rise of the Roman Empire, its decline, the Celtic lettering style, the Carolingian, the Romanesque and the Gothic up until the Renaissance. This consideration is limited to the formative lettering that's a precursor to our alphabet, to act as the bridge to the letters that you are reading.

THE IMPACT OF THE ROMAN EMPIRE ON LETTERING

During approximately forty years (from 185 BC to 145 BC) the growing Roman Empire waged horrendous battle against the Greeks in a series of intermittent onslaughts. The Romans were trying to extend their empire by conquering neighboring lands. The Romans finally succeeded in their effort to overrun Greece in 146 BC.

The Roman alphabet (the earliest form of our own alphabet) was derived from the Greek alphabet via the ancient Etruscans who settled just above Rome. The early Etruscan script reveals the debt owed to the Greek alphabet. The Roman alphabet consisted of 21 letters. During Roman military encroachment and empire expansion, this alphabet was

2-3. Etruscan Script, 600 BC. This example reveals the indebtedness of the Roman alphabet to the Greek.

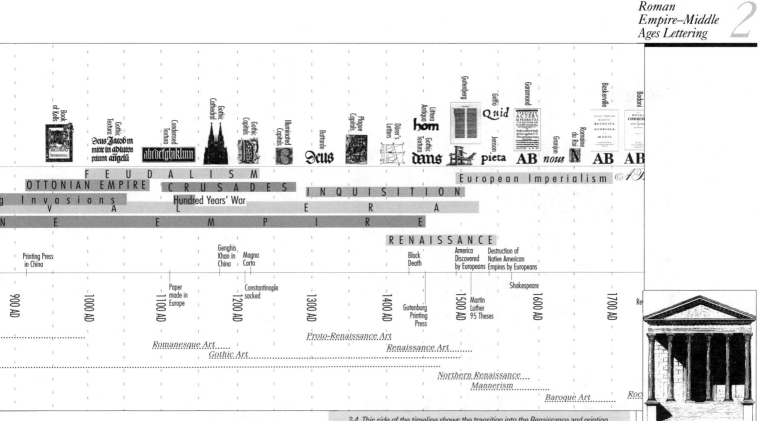

2-4. This side of the timeline shows the transition into the Renaissance and printing.

spread from England in the north, to Spain in the west, to Egypt in the south, and to the Persian Gulf in the east by the year 100 AD when the Roman Empire was at its largest. Roman pride in conquest of these foreign lands was memorialized in commemorative inscriptions of capital letters emblazoned on large arches.

ROMAN TRIUMPHAL ARCHES

Not only did the Romans conquer a people and force most of their able-bodied men and women into slavery, but they also physically memorialized their conquest in huge architectural projects known as triumphal arches built across main thoroughfares of the major cities they conquered; sort of a daily reminder to the people of the land that they were indeed subjugated by the Romans. The Romans built many of the first roads and bridges connecting the cities of their empire to move troops and chariots. Classic Roman capitals were used in these inscriptions praising the Romans. The capitals, spelling out exaltations to the Romans, were carved in stone and were often painted in a red clay color.

A preeminent example of the beauty of structure and weight of the Roman capitals is the inscription at the base of Trajan's column in Rome carved in 114 AD. This inscription is regarded to be the finest example of quality chisel-cut lettering and shows the introduction of serifs. *Serifs* are horizontal extensions at the end of a stroke of a letter.

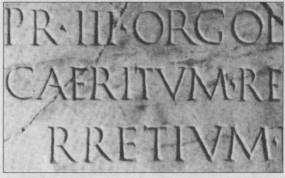

2-5. Engraved Capitalis Quadrata from Trajan's Column shows the beauty, balance and precision that the Roman alphabet had attained by around 114 AD. These letters are well proportioned and refined in terms of weights of the strokes.

2-6. Roman alphabet about 400 BC. Letters were painted on stone before they were chiseled.

2-7. Roman temple architecture was adopted from the Greeks.

2-8. Roman bridges, part of their road network, were frequently constructed of arches to span rivers.

This page is set in Caslon 540 8.5/12.

2-9. Handsomely engraved Capitalis Quadratus. These letters were engraved in stone, and then were usually painted with a red-ochre paint to help them stand out.

ABCDEFGHIJK LMNOPQRST UVWXYZ

2-10. Square Roman capitals, about 300 BC. These are squatter and thicker than the earlier engraved versions of Capitalis Quadrata and are created with a flat-tipped pen held at 90°.

2-11. Rustica was a condensed face that took up less space, and so became quite popular because parchment was expensive. This is from 500 BC, and is written with a pen angle of about 60° to write it.

About 100 BC, the Roman Empire was at its strongest with all of current-day Europe and parts of Africa beyond Egypt under its domination. It maintained this strength as a unified political and cultural unit. This extensive empire had a single language (Latin), one writing style and a consistent government.

ROMAN LETTERING

Just as the Greeks had borrowed the alphabet from the Phoenicians, the Romans borrowed from the Greeks. The Romans adapted the Greek alphabet for their own language and also adopted much of Greek civilization, culture, art, philosophy and legal system for their empire.

The Roman lettering was finely crafted and refined as their empire grew in strength. For years it was believed that the serifs were necessitated by the stone-cutting technique to create clean, precise "stops" for the strokes of the letters with the chisel. But, recent studies suggest that the serifs may have been created by the reed letterer who laid out the text in wash on the stone as a guide for the stone mason. The stone mason followed the reed brush's tendency to create thick and thin strokes in the letterforms and the serifs as well. After being incised in the stone, the letters were filled with red paint to look like writing on papyrus, but most of the inscriptions that remain today have lost their former coloring.

CAPITALIS QUADRATA TO RUSTICA

Capitalis Quadrata is the written counterpart of the classic capitals. Written with a reed pen, their thick and thin strokes have an organic unity of curves and straight lines that form square-shaped elegant capitals. These capitals were transformed into Rustica capitals, a condensed variation of the Capitalis Quadrata. The Rustica capitals were popular during this time (there are even examples of ancient graffiti in these letterforms) from about 100 BC to 100 AD. Rustic capitals were an extremely condensed version of the Roman capitals and were less rigidly constructed. They evolved to save space—parchment and papyrus were expensive and this lettering style allowed scribes to get 1 1/2 the information in the same space, and eventually included linking letters when possible to increase speed.

CONSTANTINE ENDS CHRISTIAN PERSECUTION

By 325 AD, Christianity was the recognized religion of the land. The Roman Empire adopted Christianity, and the formerly pagan people no longer tortured Christians. Around 330 AD (while the Chinese were printing on paper in multiple colors), Constantine united the East and West portions of the Roman empire and expanded it into current-day Russia. He set up many small bands of military personnel in the conquered lands to assure that he would receive tribute or taxes from the conquered people. He also moved the capitol of the empire from Rome to Constantinople (named for him).

THE ROMAN EMPIRE IS DIVIDED

In about 395 AD, the Empire was segmented into the East and West dominions, ending the religious cohesiveness of the Empire. That same year, the Roman Empire was overrun by outsiders called the Visigoths and Barbarians from the north. At first the Romans were only losing control of their outlying areas, but gradually the invaders overthrew the city of Rome itself. Shortly afterward, about 476 AD, the Eastern empire was overrun by Germanic barbarians who ransacked and looted cities, leading to their eventual breakdown.

THE SCROLL VS. CODEX CONTROVERSY

The earliest codex or left/right paged book was two wax-coated boards tied together and written on with the pointed end of a stylus. The other flat end of the stylus was used for erasing. This wax-coated board was used for temporary communication, for notes and correspondence. The wax booklet was also used by students and scribes in training and used for writing and studying. In a parchment codex, both sides of the parchment could be used for writing; this in turn meant that codices required less writing material and could be produced for less expense. They took up less room in storage, could be stored more easily and were less cumbersome when searching for a specific area of text than the lengthy scrolls.

Because papyrus's vertical strands on the back side make it a poor two-sided writing surface, scrolls were written on only one side. Papyrus was too fragile to be folded into pages; it would eventually crack and tear in two. *Parchment* (animal skin) could be folded in two, stitched together, and made into a codex. Gradually codices became recognized as a Christian preference distinguished from the older, pagan scrolls. Early Christian scholars compared different accounts of the same event from the different Gospels; codices were easier to search through than scrolls. From about 1 AD until about 400 AD, scrolls and codices were used side by side, but the practicality of the codex as a preferred format eventually dominated.

THE DEVELOPMENT OF BOOKS

With the production of parchment as a writing surface around 100 AD, the development of books as we know them began. The form of a book, or *codex*, with a left, *verso*

TOOLS & LETTERS

Ancient Roman writing, formed with flat-tipped reed pens, affects many of our current typefaces in their thick and thin weight variations. The angle of the pen, as well as the direction of movement, produced lines of differing widths. This thickening of the lines, especially when curved, is called stress. The appearance of our own writing styles and typefaces are based on the tools used to create the letters thousands of years

Sidebar is set in Futura Book Italic 8.5/17

2-12. The scroll was gradually replaced in popularity by the book format with pages that we know. Parchment may be responsible for the development of the book because it could be written on both front and back, unlike papyrus, which was too thin and translucent and cracked when folded.

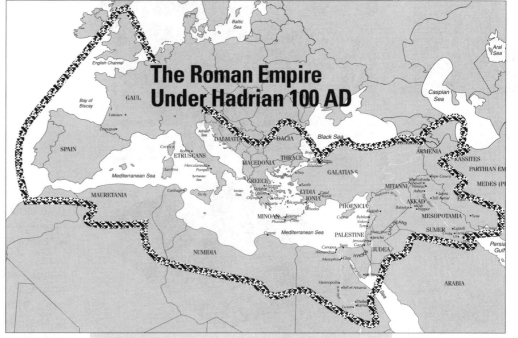

The Roman Empire Under Hadrian 100 AD

2-13. The map shows the Roman Empire around 100 AD, under the Emperor Hadrian.

2 Roman Empire–Middle Ages Lettering

2-14. Above is the ancient Roman everyday script hand used for business notations, records, loan documents and accounting.

Europe in 500 AD

2-15. This map shows Europe around 500 AD, after the disintegration of the Roman Empire.

2-16. Stone fortresses were built during the Middle Ages to protect the inhabitants from bands of looters.

2-17. Monastic orders copied texts to preserve knowledge. Monks lived a repetitive life of study and were revered by locals. For many born to low status, joining an order gave them an opportunity for respect and education, as well as a life of less arduous labor.

This page is set in Palatino Roman 8.5/12.

2-18. Expensive volumes often had elaborate leather covers, inlaid with jewels and closed with a handsomely crafted clasp.

and right, *recto* page began to be developed at this time. (Oddly enough, the terms recto and verso come from the description of the sides of the sheet of parchment; recto is the right or good side, the inside of the skin; verso is the back side, not as smooth, the fur side.) Although scrolls and codices were used interchangeably until around 400 AD, the codex form gained popularity from 100 AD.

THE EVERYDAY ROMAN SCRIPT HAND

About this time, 400 AD, there also developed an everyday script Roman hand used for recording business transactions, bookkeeping and correspondence. In order to save time, space and writing materials, this script became quite popular and marks the beginning of the lowercase letters known today. It was thought to be easier to read because of the flowing nature of the letters. The shapes of these letters were dramatically changed from the shapes of the original Roman capitals. Long sweeping flourishes created ascenders and descenders.

Local chanceries or government scribes developed their own variation of the rapid Roman everyday cursive, introducing ligatures, ascenders and descenders. With the Roman adoption of Christianity, there was a great demand for more Bibles and for the scholarly interpretations of the Bible. The ligatures, ascenders and descenders would eventually find their way into the religious texts.

THE CRUMBLING OF AN EMPIRE

Rome was sacked by succeeding waves of invaders starting in 410 AD with the Visigoths, then the Franks, the Vandals, and then the Burgundians. These invaders never overthrew the senators (or landed class outside of Rome), but after ransacking the city, they went on to settle in lands to the north and east of Rome; the Huns and Slavs in the west prevented them from settling the western territories. As a trading city and as the headquarters of the Empire, many nobles were living in Rome, and it was logical that bands of looters would head for a wealthy center. Rome was again sacked and ravaged in 533 AD when Justinian attempted to regain control of the city. The city seemed to be a less safe place to live; people moved to the estates of landed nobles and traded their liberty for protection by the lord. The men were vassals and had to guarantee defensive military service in case of attack.

LETTERING AS A DECLARATION OF FAITH

The ornamentation of early papyrus scrolls had been limited mainly to the carving of the *sticks* to which the scroll was attached rather than to the lettering of the *words* themselves. With the increase of Bibles in codex format, the importance placed on the beauty of the sacred word became competitive and imaginative. The monks creating these sacred texts were committed to penning a beautiful Bible to exalt their God. Also, the reference to God as the Light led to the use of gold leafing to "illuminate" the words. Initial caps of each section became highly stylized over time and included images of characters in the story (histrionic capitals); Bible covers were imbedded with jewels.

THE MIDDLE AGES: ISOLATION AND RELIGIOSITY

After the fall of the Roman Empire in 476 AD, the centers of civilization had been looted, beginning what is called the thousand years of the Middle Ages, or the Dark Ages. Feudalism, an economic system where serfs work for the lord in exchange for protection, gradually took hold throughout the lands. There were no longer cities as centers of culture because they had been destroyed by the warring marauders in the previous decades and were perceived as open targets for such attacks in the minds of commoners. Over the next few centuries various bands of barbarians would scour over Europe, ransacking and pillaging.

The Roman Christian Church became the primary uniting factor throughout Europe and the power of the clergy was unquestioned. The Christian notion of an all-powerful God, father figure, was prominent in all facets of daily life yet conversely there was great belief in evil spirits by average people, carried over from the days of pagan beliefs. The task of copying texts was completed primarily by monks in monasteries. The era of the continuous expansion of the Roman Empire had come to a close.

FEUDAL COMMUNITIES

Each feudal lord set up a small self-sufficient community, so there was no need for interacting with other peoples and only limited need for trading. These medieval communities were usually surrounded by a protective wall or set up on a high land mass for protection; all of the nobles and serfs lived within the wall.

Secluded monasteries were established for religious orders in the countryside. In these geographically isolated sites of learning, the copying of the ancient Roman and Greek manuscripts was carried out. The monks raised their own animals and crops for food; they lived a peaceful life of quietude and study. Manuscripts could be sold by the monastery for funds or used in trade for goods. Cultural achievements from this era were hampered because there was no forum for the interaction of ideas, philosophies or influences, and only limited travel.

This period did stabilize the people because they settled into the feudal society and no longer looked to conquer other lands and build an empire. In the monasteries, many of the ancient texts were copied, and the Medieval copies are the only remaining versions today because the originals, likely on papyrus, could not withstand

2-19. Regional variations on the uncial hand.

2-20. Regional variations on the uncial hand.

2-21. Monastic orders were generally responsible for the preservation of ancient texts through copying them onto parchment during the Middle Ages.

2-22. Elaborate books with jeweled covers were prized possessions among the nobles and wealthy.

2-23. Some of the Celtic initials were executed by less skilled artists, but maintain a delicacy of form and detail.

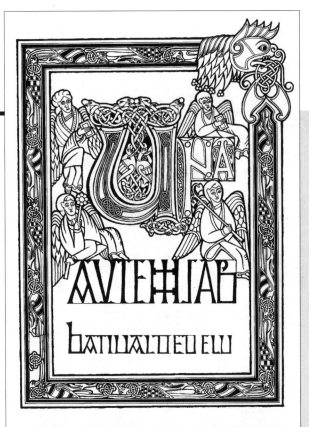

2-24. The front page to the Gospel of Luke, Book of Kells, about 700 AD. The text begins: "Now upon the first day of the week, very early in the morning," from Luke, 24:1. This Bible from Kells marks the highlight of the Irish lettering and illumination style.

abcdefghij klmnopqr stuvwxyz

2-25. Uncials named for the inch-wide guidelines they were written on. This was a wide face that eventually developed a smaller or miniscule version–half uncials. Half uncials later became our current lowercase letters.

This page is set in Palatino Roman 8.5/12.

2-26. These examples of Celtic knotwork "B's" show the variation and imaginative forms that decorated the capital letters of the Bible.

the dampness of Mediterranean weather. With the separation and isolation of the peoples of Europe, divergent regional styles of lettering developed in these copies of ancient texts.

THE DEVELOPMENT OF DIVERGENT COPYING HANDS IN EUROPE

Regional dialects became pronounced, and as they mixed with the languages of conquering peoples, different languages evolved throughout Europe (which were mainly based on the ancient Roman language Latin from the days of the Roman Empire; these are referred to as the romance languages). Because there was no center for learning, the variations in the lettering styles became more pronounced as the years passed, so that scholars are able to tell where Medieval manuscripts were produced by examining the lettering and illumination style.

THE CHRISTIANIZING OF IRELAND AND CELTIC LETTERING

Just before the sacking of Rome in 476 AD, around 430 AD the missionary St. Patrick set out with Bible manuscripts to convert Ireland. Perhaps because it was geographically removed from the mainland of Europe and was not as subjected to the frequent invasions from nomadic tribes of warriors, Celtic manuscripts and lettering design flourished without many outside influences. The work shows extraordinary variations of letterforms and geometric ornamentation. Celtic decoration and letter innovation mark new directions in lettering and illumination styles. Pages introducing each of the Gospels are completely utilized to illustrate one word or phrase magnificently. Complex interlacings of precise Celtic scroll work interspersed with animals and supernatural creatures are carefully executed with geometric accuracy paid to the minute details. Bright, intense colors are set side by side to intensify the thick texture of twisted ornamentation highlighted in gold leafing. The rounded uncials appear with upper- and lowercase clearly defined, and the Celts introduced word spacing, which improved readability.

At this time, the concept of illuminating meant to illustrate or make clear the stories of the Bible, as well as to brighten the page with the reflective gold accents. The scribes believed that they must use the beauty of the illustration to help the illiterate understand the meaning of the text. Only the most precious materials (gold, silver and jewels) were used in the creation of a Bible, the most precious text. The concept of God as light in the Bible also directed the choice to use reflective gold leafing on the sacred pages. During this period, the average person could not read, and relied on the pictorial carvings and paintings in churches to recall the scenes from the Bible and the stories and lessons that accompanied them.

The Transition to Celtic Round Uncials

Beginning primarily in the Celtic lands, a new rounder form of the Roman alphabet was created called *uncials* which were written on four guide lines that were one inch (in Latin, uncial) apart. These uncials are the precursor of our upper- and lowercase letters. Many scholars believe that lowercase uncials grew out of a desire to apply the small letters to the manuscripts of the Bible for the practical purpose of saving parchment, and to develop beautiful letterforms for the sacred text that were also quick to write. Celtic uncials were distinguished by their roundness, their diminished serifs, and their new subtle ascenders and descenders. In the interest of saving time, scribes rounded off corners. Uncials appear to be lowercase letters today, but sentences were sometimes begun with the same uncial characters that were used in the rest of the sentence.

From the time of the development of the Phoenician alphabet until the introduction of uncials, all Roman letters had previously been uppercase (even though scripts had been used for everyday writing). With the introduction of semi- or half uncials, the foundation for lowercase or miniscule letters was established. *Semi-uncials*, or smaller scale letters, began to appear around 600 AD, and they saved space. With the eventual extension of some of the ascenders and descenders begun in uncial lettering, it is easy to comprehend how our lowercase evolved. These characters eventually developed regional and national stylistic traits. The concept of reading to oneself may have influenced the use of the small letters because books were made smaller, for meditation or reflection, and these letters saved space. In addition, the words were easier to read with clearer distinctions of the small letters with their slight ascenders and descenders, rather than all capital lettering.

A Unifying Force in Lettering: Charlemagne's Empire

During the Early Middle Ages (from 500 to 750 AD) the lands that had been part of the Roman Empire were disintegrating into independent feudal communities. The Latin language evolved into regional dialects. Yet there were still attempts by strong military leaders to conquer and consolidate large territories into a kingdom. In 768 AD the Gauls' leader Charlemagne (whose empire eventually extended through much of current Europe) was known as a military king, as well as a ruler who favored learning and the arts.

On Christmas day in the year 800 AD, Pope Leo III crowned Charlemagne the emperor of the Holy Roman

2-27. These Celtic capitals are based on a rigid box formula; they are angular and geometric, almost abstract in their simplicity.

2-30. This handsomely designed Celtic "T" uses restraint of ornamentation for a classic sensibility.

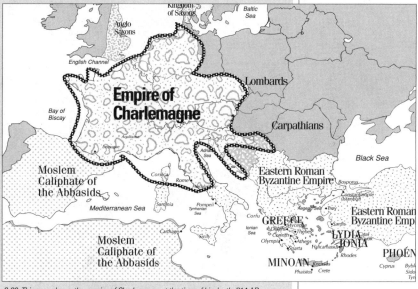

2-28. The two initial capitals on the left incorporate animal forms into the knotwork. The "S" on the left appears to show a dragon making up the letter, and the "U" also is made partly of some creature. The "S" on the right relies on very geometric, intricate knotwork.

2-29. This map shows the empire of Charlemagne at the time of his death, 814 AD.

This page is set in Palatino Roman 8.5/12.

2 Roman Empire–Middle Ages Lettering

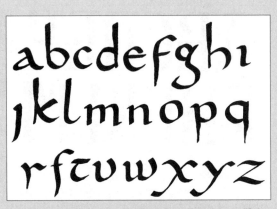

2-31. Carolingian manuscript hand about 800 AD. This writing style was codified for the monks during Charlemagne's reign.

2-32. Although this monk is shown copying alone, they usually worked in class-room-like scriptoriums, in monasteries, copying each text. Sometimes the text was read aloud to the copiers who wrote as they heard.

2-33. Monasteries copied and bound books as means of raising funds.

This page is set in ITC Serif Gothic Light 8.5/12.

Empire, a move that may have been calculated to gain military support against invaders trying to overthrow Rome. Under Charlemagne's reign, in 786 AD, a standardized copying (or lettering) style was decreed throughout the empire. Charlemagne appointed an English monk scholar, Alcuin of York, to oversee the copying of many ancient manuscripts.

Alcuin, who many assume was a Celtic-trained monk, assembled a crowd of letterers in 789 AD at Charlemagne's court at Aachen. He chose a hand that was similar to Celtic uncials as the imperial lettering style. Alcuin is credited with the introduction of the Carolingian (meaning during the reign of Charlemagne) style of lettering that was dictated as the standard copying script at this time throughout the empire of Charlemagne.

THE CAROLINGIAN LETTERING STYLE & THE MINISCULE

Like Celtic uncials, the Carolingian hand is a style of writing in which the characters are round and full. There is a twisting of the pen throughout the downward stroke of the ascenders, giving a slightly tapered appearance to the letters. With this standardized hand, the lowercase letters of the Roman alphabet became uniform. The use of larger uncials to introduce a sentence was in practice at this time around 800 AD. Punctuation was not standardized and adopted until after printing was invented, the end of the 1400s.

By 1000 AD, the Carolingian hand was widely used with many variations throughout the empire. Carolingian lettering was widely used by monks copying ancient texts. This style of writing was what later Italian Renaissance printers would copy when they developed printing fonts, mistakenly thinking that they were copying an ancient hand from Roman times.

With the breakdown of Charlemagne's empire (his empire was eventually divided between his three sons) and the barbarian raids, little lettering was accomplished. When copying was done, local tastes prevailed and the standardized hand of an empire became a relic of the past.

THE MEDITERRANEAN EXPANSION OF MOSLEMS

The Moslem Arabs were expanding across Persia, Arabia and around the southern banks of the Mediterranean at an unprecedented rate between 620 AD and 730 AD. They did offer a political stability and laws to the conquered lands; however, locals were given the choice of conversion or death. The Moslems ruled Arabia, Palestine, parts of ancient Persia, and Egypt by 650 AD. Next they expanded across north Africa, and in 711 AD, they crossed from Morocco to Spain at the Straits of Gibraltar. They overtook Spain and were not halted until 732 AD, when they were overpowered at the Pyrenees mountains separating France and Spain. Because of their conquests, the Arabs controlled all shipping on the Mediterranean. They overpowered Sicily in 827 AD, and attacked and invaded Rome in 846 AD, looting St. Peter's Cathedral, which was not at that time enclosed within the city walls.

Around this same period, the Vikings began to raid Europe by land and sea. They intermittently attacked Europe from about 830 AD to 851 AD. They ransacked the Lindisfarne monastery in Scotland in 793 AD and then went on to invade Ireland in 835 AD, France in 843 AD and England in 851 AD. These raiders had no appreciation for the culture they were destroying; they stole all the precious metal work they could find and melted it down. Monasteries were a prime target for these bands because the orders were known to have elaborate gifts donated to them from wealthy patrons and kings.

With the disintegration of Charlemagne's empire, compounded by the Viking raids that began around 800 AD, the uniform Carolingian lettering tradition petered out. Most coastal communities were too preoccupied with their protection to be concerned about lofty books and lettering.

THE ROMANESQUE HAND INVITES INNOVATION

The Romanesque lettering style was formulating from from around 800 AD to 1000 AD. It is recognized by the extensive manipulation of the forms of the letters featuring innovative additions to the strokes of the letters. Inspired by earlier Celtic and Rustica lettering, the Romanesque integrates insets, overlaps, and fused letters in manuscripts and engravings. There are a geometric experimentation and a truncation of crossbars that are inventive. Lettering is freed from the prior austere organization to be more creative and intuitive. Often multiple forms of the same letter are used in a single manuscript as if to telegraph the creativity of the scribe. Here the goal appears to be syncopated rhythm on the page and a broad spectrum of alternate letterforms to choose from.

Romanesque era lettering differs depending on location and is so varied that the influences are difficult to trace. Gradually, the Romanesque hand was transformed into the more consistent Textura style of lettering. This consistency may have occurred under Otto's empire around 960 AD. The Gothic hand is more prevalent in the Germanic areas and was used there late into the 1800s and early 1900s.

THE DEVELOPMENT OF THE GOTHIC TEXTURA HAND

In the area that is now Germany, the Romanesque style developed a typically Gothic character over time, becoming condensed, angular and incorporating heavy vertical strokes with almost all curves disappearing. These "black letters" were made with great precision and were evenly spaced to such an extent that the texture on the page resembled a woven fabric; for this reason it is referred to as *Textura*.

There were no spaces used between words at this point, and the copy extended from the left to the right margin in

2-38. This medal shows the use of Romanesque lettering around the figure. Rarely are two of the same letters drawn the same in such a piece.

2-34. This chart shows some of the Romanesque alternate characters and the tendency for insetting of characters to save space.

Romanesque Variations

A						N				
B						O				
C						P				
D						Q				
E						R				
F						S				
G						T				
H						U				
I						V				
J						W				
K						X				
L						Y				
M						Z				

2-35. This practice of the Gothic hand shows the use of a grid to determine the proportions of the letters, and to maintain consistent vertical strokes.

2-36. This Romanesque lettering engraving shows the creative variety of the forms of the letters.

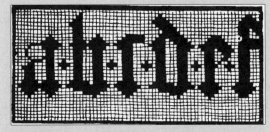

2-37. This practice of the Gothic hand shows the use of a grid to determine the proportions of the letters, and to maintain consistent vertical strokes.

2-39. In the Gothic era, the ornamentation of capitals was handsome, yet restrained.

This page is set in ITC Serif Gothic Light 8.5/12.

2-41. Round capitals, known as Lombardic, were often selected to balance the verticality of Gothic manuscripts.

2-42. This example shows the condensed verticality of the Gothic Textura; letters were packed so closely together that they are difficult to differentiate. The dot over the "i" started to be used at this point, to distinguish it from an "n" or an "m" or part of a "u."

2-40. Secular scribes lettered books, diplomas, legal documents, loans and mortgages.

2-43. The initial caps above feature intricate, probably Celtic-inspired scroll work. The caps are so ornamented and interlaced with plant forms that they lose readability Above is a "C," an "M" and a "T." The knotwork is not as intricate and angular as in Irish examples.

2-44. Gothic Textura about 1400 AD. Note the condensed, vertical rhythm of the letters on the page.

2-45. This map shows the empire of Otto the Great, around 973 AD.

This page is set in ITC Serif Gothic Light 8.5/12.

two columns on the page without exception. The length of the ascenders and descenders was shortened and the space between lines of text was reduced so that less parchment was used. Gothic was a difficult hand to read; the dot over the "i" was implemented to distinguish it from a stroke of an "n," "m," or a "u." Because this style of lettering was used predominantly for religious texts, it became unavoidably linked with associations of the church, and still resonates with religious overtones for us, hundreds of years later.

Some typographers compare its strong vertical, angular style to the spires of the Gothic architecture at the time. It has a very severe appearance on the page, and its relentless verticality and angularity make it seem harsh visually.

THE RISE OF THE SECULAR SCRIBE

By around 800 AD, the time of the widespread adoption of the Carolingian hand in Charlemagne's empire, a class of scribes was developing who weren't monks, but who were employed to copy secular texts. These commercial writers were employed by publishers who pressured them to write with greater speed. This may have affected the different forms the Carolingian hand took in different parts of Europe. The copiers also drew up contracts, loan documents, legal agreements and deeds. These copyists were busy copying texts for the educated elite of the day since books were not affordable for the average person. Bibles, if a wealthy family had one, were handed down from one generation to the next, and cherished.

THE OTTONIAN EMPIRE

The centuries of 800 and 900 are marked with little consistency in the reigning powers in Europe. In 936 AD, Otto I came to power in the area of Germany, and the period of his rule is known as the Ottonian Period. The Pope in Rome played an important role from time to time but was not consistently a powerful force. The lack of centralized political stability reinforced the separateness that had developed in the early years of the Middle Ages.

Isolationism in small feudal communities was akin to survival at this time. This era was marked by great devotion to religion. Natural phenomena were explained as curses or blessings from an almighty power. Pilgrimages to faraway lands were a commonplace homage of faith, a means of purifying oneself of sins, proving one's devotion, or gaining additional grace. This was also the era of honor, purity and chivalry. People did not question their clerics. Most lived by strong convictions of ethical religious and moral codes of behavior.

PILGRIMAGES AND THE "HOLY" WARS

From about 1096 AD to about 1291 AD, the Crusades were waged from central Europe against the lands in the Middle East. Turkish, Syrian and Arabian lands were at-

2-46. The map shows the routes of the Crusades during the Middle Ages.

tacked, and the Holy Land of Jerusalem was frequently under siege in an attempt to try to regain control of this land of significance. The land around Jerusalem is considered sacred by three different religions: for Christians it is the place of the birth and death of Christ, for Jews it is the site of Solomon's Temple, and for Moslems it is the site of Mohammed's ascension to heaven.

The Christian Crusades were made in the name of the almighty power and were considered justifiable by the warriors who were trying to regain Jerusalem for the Christians. Ostensibly the wars began as a means to secure the pilgrimage routes to holy lands (Jerusalem and other sites of religious shrines to saints) from looters. Bands of marauders would wait along the pilgrimage route and hold up those planning to visit the sacred places. These "holy" wars were often sanctioned and blessed by the Pope at the time, if not funded by his coffers. A look at the map of Europe at the time shows that the militant Moslems were spreading their religious beliefs in the lands all around the Roman pontiff; this fact makes his urgency to secure routes for the pilgrims more understandable.

THE INNOVATION OF RAG PAPER

One of the innovations that made books cheaper in the Middle Ages was the faster production of paper from rags. When paper could be made from rags and plant fibers rather than from sheep and calf skin, the cost of books was reduced. The cheaper paper production became, the more that could be produced. In about 1100 AD, papermaking was introduced in Sicily, and by the close of the 1200s a small paper mill was well established in Fabriano, Italy, and one was established in France fifty years later.

Paper mills were established on rivers because they would use the power of the running water to turn great water wheels, and they would use the river water in the fabrication of the paper. Watermarks eventually identified and distinguished the papermakers, and cheap rag paper be-

2-47. Coats of arms were introduced in the Middle Ages to identify knights in battle or jousts. They were emblazoned on metal shields and identified the family.

2-48. The code of chivalry among knights gave men a place of regard in society. However, their warfare was brutal and dangerous; many were wounded or died in battle.

2-49. The transition from making books from animals skin to making them with rag paper reduced the cost of creating a text. The rags were soaked in vats of water until their fibers broke down, and they became mush. A screen in a frame was lowered into this mush and jostled until a thin film was evenly spread over the screen as it was pulled out of the vat. This film was dried between blankets, and the water was pressed out; when dried, the film was a piece of rag paper.

This page is set in Rockwell Light 8.5/12.

2 *Roman Empire–Middle Ages Lettering*

2-50. This book plate shows how knighthood also looked to scholarship and learning as part of its code of chivalry.

2-51. This example of northern Gothic lettering shows the delicacy that the letters could have when carefully crafted; notice the full capitals which offer a visual break from the verticality of the Textura.

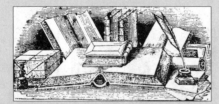

2-52. Lombardic initials were often integrated with Textura creating an interesting contrast.

2-53. With the growth of universities, the demand for books increased, leading to the expansion of the number of secular scribes who copied books.

2-54. These medieval book plates illustrate the plague wrenching or cajoling people from this earth and its cares. These may have been created to act as a warning to others, or in thanks of a life inexplicably spared by the plague.

came plentiful in Europe. Parchment or vellum was still used for important texts, but the availability and affordability of rag paper made the cost of books decrease. Also, the growing middle class of guild members was literate and was interested in owning books, once they could afford them.

THE LATE GOTHIC PERIOD

The 1200s to the 1400s is considered the Gothic period. The Gothic aesthetic in art and architecture was at its zenith throughout Europe. In architecture, the spires of cathedrals soared ever higher in their attempt to reach out to heaven, supported by flying buttresses. Tall, vertical churches with vast areas of stained glass were popular. The stained glass depicted Biblical stories for the illiterate, and the more they depicted, the easier the teaching and preaching was for the clerics. Monasticism was at its peak in Europe during the Gothic period, with many different orders founded and co-existing in monasteries. Churches were often built in towns along the pilgrimage routes to provide a place for pilgrims to stop, rest overnight and to worship.

The feudal society that began during the Middle Ages was transitioning into the settlement of cities. No longer were bands of looters considered as great a threat. This era was marked by the powers of the lords being curtailed by reasonable laws. Increased agriculture led to international trade. Trade centers were established on the sites of prior cities. Money began to replace land as the measure of wealth.

THE FOUNDING OF UNIVERSITIES AND THE RISE OF GUILDS

Universities were founded in cities, and a broader spectrum of society was being educated than ever before. Trade and commerce were growing, and cities were being organized. Craftsmen had multiplied, and many were now settling in the cities and were organizing into guilds and training young apprentices.

Because of the universities, the need for books increased dramatically. Book production was commonplace, with some guilds specializing in the lettering, others in the ornamentation and others in binding. Toward the end of this period, there was a transition away from the religious orders' monopoly on education and book production; the universities were secular, and the texts they reviewed were often the classical Greek and Roman texts–not the clerical Latin translations.

The study of ancient texts led professors to adopt a philosophical movement called *Humanism*. Humanism was a school of thought that placed humans at the center of the universe, without divine intervention (a heretical concept). It was based on reevaluating the ancient texts firsthand, and it adopted many of the philosophical beliefs of the ancient Greek and Roman cultures.

THE BLACK PLAGUE

During this era, about the time of the resettlement of cities, the Bubonic Plague hit Europe. It is frequently called the Black Death, and it decimated the population of Europe. In the forty years between 1347 AD and 1377 AD, more than *40 percent* of the population died—that is, more than 25 million people. A selective natural quirk rendered some people immune to the plague, or spared those who were not exposed. Sanitary conditions at the time were appalling and the spread of germs was rampant. Living conditions of filth were the norm for the lower classes. The plague was brought from the East in the fleas that lived on rats that came on board docked ships. When these ships returned to the Mediterranean and sold their cargo, the rats went on land and the fleas spread the plague to the mainland. It is called *Black Death* because corpses turned black from the plague; the illness was lethal in about four days after a flea bite.

Those who survived the plague felt a need to procreate and to celebrate. Society in many cities was turned upside down by the death of so many people. Looting wasn't even necessary with almost half of the people dead. Many survivors were able to walk into the homes of the wealthy who were killed by the plague and take them over. It is possible that some of the religious monuments that were built during this period were a symbol of thanks from the people who survived the plague. There are many book plates, illustrations and initial capitals that represent the plague as a skeleton coming to whisk the unexpecting people from life.

THE EARLY FORAYS INTO PRINTING

By the 1400s wood block printing was common in Europe. Usually illustrations from the Bible, folktales or playing cards were cut from blocks of wood and printed. But printing was not considered a viable means for reproducing the text of books. If all the letters on every page had to be carved by hand into wood, it was doubtful that it would be an efficient process. Some books that were primarily illustrative were cut from wood blocks, printed on rag paper and bound, but these were a rare exception.

ROTUNDA COMPARED TO GOTHIC LETTERING

In the early 1400s, two dominant lettering styles were beginning to emerge in Europe: the Gothic Black Letter or Textura, and the Rotunda letters. Both would serve as examples in movable type experimentation. The Rotunda or Humanistic hand or Littera Antiqua was a more open, rounded form than the condensed, angular black letter, and was popular in France and Italy. The darker, narrow, condensed Gothic hand was preferred into the 1900s in German areas.

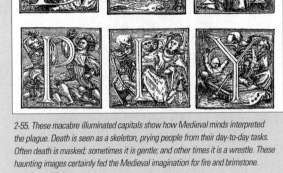

2-55. These macabre illuminated capitals show how Medieval minds interpreted the plague. Death is seen as a skeleton, prying people from their day-to-day tasks. Often death is masked; sometimes it is gentle; and other times it is a wrestle. These haunting images certainly fed the Medieval imagination for fire and brimstone.

2-56. Round, full Lombardic initial caps were often used with Textura, as seen in this early printed example. This also shows how tightly Textura was written.

2-57. An example of a simple early woodcut illustration that was printed and distributed; it looks rudimentary and rough in its craftsmanship.

2-58. This example of Rotunda lettering shows its adaptation from the Gothic; it is wider and less ornate. It almost seems like a fusion of Gothic and Carolingian.

This page is set in Rockwell Light 8.5/12.

2-59. This cathedral was likely built around 1200 AD. It is typical of Gothic architecture's attempt to reach the heavens through towering vertical spires.

2-60. Gothic lettering can have grace and elegance when carefully executed.

BOOK SECURITY AND COMPUTER SECURITY

Eight hundred years ago, no middle-class people had books in their houses; books were an expensive luxury item and few people could read. Even in early university libraries, the books were huge, oversized, heavy manuscripts. Scholars were not allowed to take them out (even if they could carry them). The manuscripts were chained to the stacks. You could come in and open them, and read them on the desks in front of the stacks, but that was as far as you could go. This is very similar to our current attitude towards computers. But, as time goes on, and computers get smaller, cheaper and more portable (as books have become), we will all carry computers with us rather than books! Some predictors of the future suggest that we will eventually think of computers that way we now think of paper notepads—won't that be something!

Sidebar is set in Gill Sans Italic 8.5/24.

The inspiration for the Humanistic hand was from the older, Carolingian form of writing. In fact scholars who read ancient Roman manuscripts that had been copied during the Carolingian period thought that they were reading the original texts, and assumed that the writing style in the manuscripts was from ancient Rome, hence the name Littera Antiqua which means "ancient letters."

Developed during the proto-Renaissance, Littera Antiqua was based on the Carolingian script that was only 600 years old. Square Roman capitals were combined with the curving, round lowercase letters. The Littera Antiqua style also served to differentiate secular, Humanistic or ancient texts from Gothic lettered religious texts in the geographic areas that adopted it. Littera Antiqua was the formal style of lettering that was used for secular manuscripts.

AN OVERVIEW OF THE LETTERING OF THE MIDDLE AGES

During the Middle Ages, lettering had undergone two different periods of standardization. The period began with a variety of styles showing some Celtic influence. There was the introduction of a consistent hand under Charlemagne, followed by the variations of Romanesque. Then there seems to have been a Gothic consistency, which may have been standardized under Otto; and finally there was the branching into Rotunda, Textura, Batarde, and Humanistic styles of lettering, all coexisting in time, with scribes who probably knew all of these styles of writing.

SETTING THE STAGE FOR THE RENAISSANCE

As the cities began to grow in importance just before the Renaissance (which literally means a "rebirth" of learning) around 1450 AD, there was occasional political strife and turmoil between the emerging cities. Art was primarily created under the patronage provided by wealthy lords. The Medici family in Florence was known for sponsoring great works of art and architecture from Renaissance artists. The Popes also were patrons of artists, commissioning sculpture, architecture and frescoes to decorate religious buildings.

When Islamic Turks closed the overland routes to India and the Far East, nations seeking spices and silks were forced to sponsor explorers to find alternate routes. This led to Columbus's journey to America in 1492 AD (proving the world to be round), and Vasco da Gama's successful attempt in 1497 AD to reach India by sailing around Africa. Humans were beginning to be the center of the universe and understand the world and explain its forces in other than supernatural terms. Humanism would flourish during the Renaissance in Europe.

PROJECT: CREATE AN ILLUSTRATED INITIAL

Select a text that you would like to illustrate. Keep it short—three to seven lines in length. Using the lowercase letters provided at the right as a model, carefully letter the words you have selected, leaving room for the addition of a decorative, illustrated capital. Remember that the capitals illustrate what's going on in the story, so you may want to choose your text accordingly. You can mimic any of the style of initial capitals that are shown throughout the chapter, or do research at the library for further reference or create your own, unique style of illuminating the capital. There are tremendous liberties taken with the form and readability of the letters that are illuminated. They can be twisted, gnarled and contorted; they do not have to look like traditional capitals placed in text. They can be contained to a box, or more free-form and organic, or just a part of the illuminated capital can extend from the box. Feel free to experiment, and have this text reflect your own style, sense of design, and humor. Think about which part of the text to illustrate carefully.

Begin by doing fifteen thumbnails of your illuminated capital. Rough in the type, or photocopy it down so that you can see how it will work with the capital.

Next do two half-sized roughs, and finally, complete the final text and illuminated cap on some high quality, acid-free paper. Create a piece of art that you would want to frame and hang on your wall and reflect upon. Remember that throughout history, great artists were also accomplished letterers.

OBJECTIVES

- To experience the time and effort that it takes to execute hand-lettering with skill.
- To appreciate the planning that an illuminated capital requires to be read as a letter and as an image.
- To recreate the sense of hand-crafted letters.
- To plan the spacing and aesthetic arrangement of type on a page.
- To experience the detailed hand work required for exceptional illuminated capitals.
- To comprehend the time that is required for precise lettering and illuminating.
- To adopt a sense of the tradition of the hand-letterer/artist that calligraphers continue today.
- To make considerations of paper texture, colors of inks, their reflectivity and appropriateness with subject.
- To encourage further research of illuminated capitals and their nuances and quirks.

2-61. This font, Wilhelm Klingspor Gotisch Regular, is based on the lettering Batarde.

This page is set in ITC Fenice Light 8.5/12.

2-62. The capitals in the font Wilhelm Gotisch Regular are not as condensed, nor as Gothic in appearance as the lowercase featured on the previous page.

Roman Empire-Middle Ages Lettering-Review

1. How was Roman lettering spread throughout the empire? _____

_____

2. How did the predominant governing structure of the Middle Ages affect the appearance of the lettering styles? _____

_____

3. Why is the Celtic lettering style so distinct from the hands of the rest of Europe during the Middle Ages? _____

_____

4. Describe how Celtic lettering differed in appearance from continental styles. _____

_____

5. What did "illumination" mean as it pertained to Medieval manuscripts? _____

_____

6. How were ancient texts preserved during the Middle Ages? _____

7. What book was the most common one to be copied in the Middle Ages? _____

8. Why was the Carolingian hand developed? _____

_____

9. What are "uncials," and where did the term come from? _____

10. What typographic innovation developed from uncials? _____

11. What was the prevalent language during the Middle Ages, and why? _____

_____

12. How did this language affect the subsequent development of regional dialects? _____

_____

13. Who was Alcuin of York? _____

_____

This page is set in
ITC Fenice Light.5/12.

2 *Roman Empire–Middle Ages Lettering*

14. What is the term Textura used to describe, and why? _____

_____

15. What innovation in the Middle Ages made the production of books cheaper? _____

_____

16. How does the Gothic style of lettering differ from Carolingian? _____

_____

17. What is the significance of the monasteries and their copying of texts (what texts did they copy, and why are we thankful today)?

_____

_____

_____

18. Why was writing known only by a few classes of people in the Middle Ages? _____

_____

19. How were illuminated caps related to the text? _____

_____

20. Why were books treated with such security measures during the Middle Ages? _____

_____

21. Describe the Gothic aesthetic and how it influenced typography. _____

_____

22. What happened at the end of the Middle Ages that caused a greater demand for cheaper books? _____

_____

23. How were the Romance languages formed during the Middle Ages? _____

_____

24. Why were the Crusades undertaken? _____

25. What was the predominant religion during the Middle Ages, and why? _____

_____

26. Who owned books during the Middle Ages, and why? _____

Renaissance Typography/Printing

INTRODUCTION

In this chapter, we will discuss the invention of printing during the Renaissance, and all the mechanics that went into refining printing and early innovations in printing. Just before the Renaissance, cities grew in importance again. Universities were founded in cities, and students flowed into these learning centers. Guilds were organized for the craftsmen, and they instituted a system of apprenticeship. There was increased trade, travel, and learning. There was peace and prosperity. Columbus sailed to America in 1492. Resurgence of interest in ancient Roman and Greek thought led to the philosophical movement known as Humanism.

The innovation of printing with movable, reusable type, developed during the Renaissance, has been considered an epoch-making event in the course of human development. Today we live in the era of the epoch-making development of the personal computer, which can be clearly paralleled to the impact of printing with movable, reusable type.

In referring to centuries, the name of the century, the thirteenth century, is one number ahead of the years of that century, 1201–1299, because the first century, 1–99 had no hundreds in it. So the fifteenth century covers the years 1400–1499.

THE RENAISSANCE

Often described as the "rebirth of learning," the Renaissance is generally agreed to have lasted from around 1400 until around 1600. This rebirth meant an exaggerated fascination with all things of ancient Greek and Roman origin. The writing, music, theatre, philosophy, medicine and law of the ancient cultures was deified. This was in sharp contrast to the predominantly Christian-based learning of the Middle Ages; some considered this reevaluation of "pagan" culture heretical. Even ancient religion was inspected and compared to Christianity in Europe during the Renaissance; these ruminations were finding their way into print, as book production was getting cheaper. The refinement of the

3-1. Gothic textura about 1400. Note the condensed, vertical rhythm of the letters on the page. This was a popular, formal book-copying hand in the Germanic area.

3-2. Humanistic book-copying hand about 1450, called Littera Antiqua because it was based on the Carolingian lettering in Carolingian copies of ancient texts, which Renaissance scholars thought was the original ancient hand they were written in. This rounder, fuller book hand was favored in Italy and France.

3-3. Carolingian book-copying hand, codified under Charlemagne; mistakenly thought to be the ancient writing style by Renaissance era scholars who thought that Carolingian copies of ancient texts were the originals, and were enamored with this "ancient" lettering.

KEY CONCEPTS

Littera Antiqua

Gutenberg

Precision Mold

Tacky Ink, Chase

Movable, Reusable Type

Gutenberg's 42 Line Bible

Kerning, Mortising Ligatures

Nicolas Jenson

Aldus Manutius

Francesco Griffo

William Caxton

Claude Garamond

Robert Granjon

Copperplate Printing

This page is set in ITC Stone Serif 8.5/12.

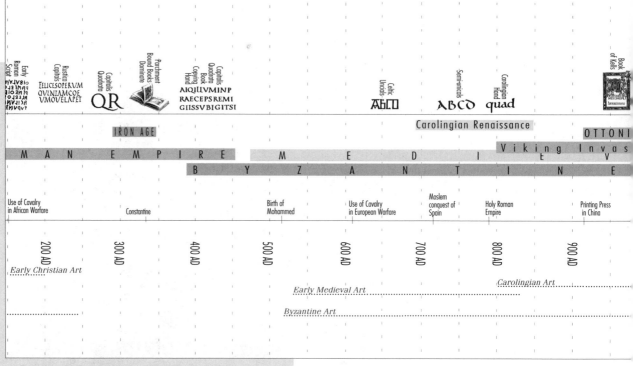

3-5. Johann Gutenberg, widely considered the father of print-ing in the western world. He devoted most of his life to the pursuit of refining printing, only to die a pauper.

3-6. This is a woodcut of an early platen pressure press, similar to the one used by Gutenberg to print his 42 Line Bible over five years from about 1450 to 1456, in Mainz, Germany.

This page is set in ITC
Stone Serif 8.5/12.

printing press, the innovation of movable reusable type, and the manufacture of cheaper paper allowed the production of books to increase during the Renaissance, and the cost of the previously hand-copied manuscripts had plummeted. With more printed books came greater literacy, broader availability of books and wider dissemination of learning.

THE BEGINNING OF PRINTING

The invention of the printing press and movable, reusable type radically changed the course of human history, and many have compared it to the information explosion in our own era created with the dawn of personal computers. From the time when oral tradition dominated human interaction through the development of writing systems, never had there been such a quantum leap in the mode of communicating as there was when Gutenberg refined printing. Mass reproduction of texts enabled more wealthy landowners, merchant and guild classes to own books. No longer were books exclusively in the price range of nobility.

Just as the proliferation of books changed the structure of communication and work throughout Europe, so, too, will computers change the way we interact with others, transmit information to them and work to earn a living. Computers will become as commonplace and as compact as books have become . . . they will be taken for granted in every household, and we will use them to assist us in more and more of our daily lives. In order to appreciate the changes that computers will make in society during our lifetime, it is helpful to understand the roots of our current typographic communication system, and

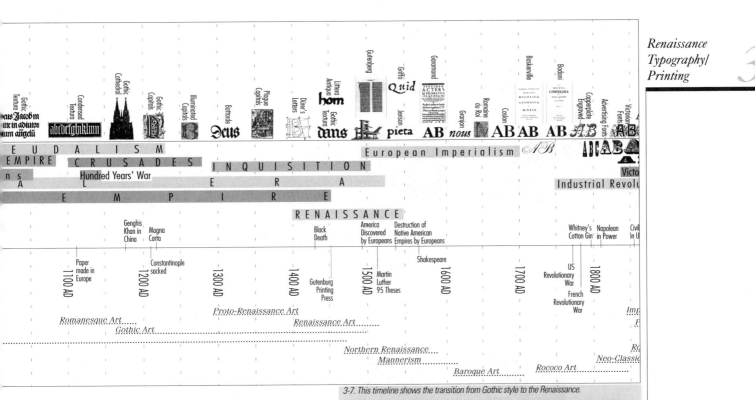

3-7. This timeline shows the transition from Gothic style to the Renaissance.

try to translate some of the printed book's impact on historic society to help project the changes computers will wreak on our current society.

GUTENBERG AND MOVABLE, REUSABLE TYPE

Johann Gutenberg is credited with the development of movable, reusable type. Certainly, Gutenberg's commitment to refining the printing process, to solving a series of problems and challenges is legendary. Some historians argue that Laurens Coster of Holland developed the art of printing slightly before, or right around the same time as, Gutenberg; others argue that Coster merely sold some of Gutenberg's trial forays into printing. Others propose that we know too little of the actual details of Gutenberg's life to credit him with the invention of printing. This controversy is unresolved and remains a contentious issue among historians.

GUTENBERG: THE METAL CRAFTSMAN

This version of the invention of printing story is one that is generally accepted in the field. We do know that Gutenberg was always borrowing money from people. Gutenberg was a craftsman who was accomplished in working with metals and casting. As early as 1438 AD, he was working to figure out how to print the text of books (illustrations at this time were printed from wood blocks). He joined forces with Johann Fust, a goldsmith, who agreed to underwrite the cost of Gutenberg's printing experimentations, provided Gutenberg repay him.

Gutenberg's press was adapted from a press that was used for the pressing of grapes to make wine. He de-

3-8. In this poster and invitation by KU student Hunter Brown, an early form of the platen pressure press, adapted from a wine press, can be viewed.

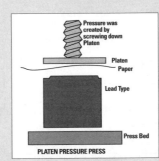

3-9. This diagram shows the printing process refined by Gutenberg that relied on pressure to transfer the image from the lead locked up in the chase onto the paper.

This page is set in ITC Stone Serif 8.5/12.

3
*Renaissance
Typography/
Printing*

3-10. Fust and Schoeffer (the rascals) used the symbol above as the printer's mark in the back of each Bible, in the colophon. A colophon replaced the scribe's date and signature at the end of a text; printers put their mark and the date instead. Today colophons are used to identify the press, the paper, the inks used, and any unusual press tricks; few printed pieces have colophons.

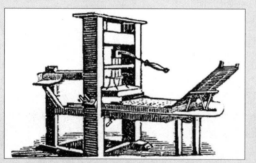

3-11. This press is similar to the one perfected by Gutenberg. He worked out a process for registering a page correctly and for getting a clean image.

THE USE OF COLOPHONS

Colophons came into use when the copier of a book came to the end of the piece, and dated and signed the last page of the work. Sometimes the scribes would add a short phrase about themselves, their location or the reason why they undertook the writing of that particular text. This tradition was carried over by early printers, who included a printer's mark in the colophon as a means of identifying and authenticating the work. Today, colophons are printed in only limited-edition books. They include information about the press, the paper, the printer, the designer, the illustrator and the inks, as well as the length of the run. Most are usually numbered as well.

Sidebar text is set in Stone Serif Italic 8.5/18

This page is set in Stempel Schneidler Roman 8.5/12.

veloped a method to cast type in single pieces that varied in width but were precisely the same height (using the precision mold); he devised a chase to hold the type on the press, experimented with and finally mixed suitable inks that would stick to the cast lead type. He also perfected techniques for registering a page to make a good impression, and a method to keep extra ink off the edges of the page. In short, Gutenberg made printing a viable reproduction process.

MOVABLE, REUSABLE TYPE

Gutenberg's brilliance was in realizing that it was feasible to have individual, reusable characters rather than cutting or casting an entire page as one solid piece. These accomplishments, however, were not without their trials and tribulations; much of his life and work ends as a tragedy. Many of Gutenberg's explorations into the technology of printing required funding. A great deal of money from Johann Fust helped finance his experimental workshop; and when Gutenberg finally refined the printing process, Fust sued him for the money owed, foreclosed on Gutenberg in November of 1455, locked him out of his print shop, and prevented him from selling the books that were a few months away from completion. These were books that Gutenberg had labored over for *five years* with his staff! Thus, Fust became the owner of the press and the techniques that Gutenberg had labored to perfect! Peter Schoeffer, Gutenberg's assistant, became a partner with Fust and managed the press. Together they finished printing the around 180 Bibles that Gutenberg had initiated, and they made a fortune. Fust and Schoeffer signed and completed the Bibles the following August. Oddly enough, these Bibles have been referred to as *Gutenberg's* 42 Line Bibles . . . at least Gutenberg got the *credit* he rightly deserved! Schoeffer eventually married Fust's daughter and conveniently became his son-in-law and business partner.

THE PRINTING CHALLENGES

A few of Gutenberg's greatest challenges were in the casting of type. He had to develop a method to cast type so that each piece would be precisely the same depth for inking, the same height so that the letters would line up along a base line, yet also find some means to cast letters that were different widths—like an "m" and an "i," for example. Gutenberg finally perfected such a system, with the development of the ingeniously simple precision mold.

First a punch was cut of the letter from hardened iron. The letter had to be accurately cut on the punch as a raised surface in reverse and had to be precisely the same size as the other letters. The letters of Gutenberg's Bible were cut to closely resemble the best Gothic manuscript lettering of the time. Frequently metalsmiths were employed as punch cutters at the beginning of the printing revolution because they were accustomed to working in fine detail in metal. The punch had to be driven into the brass matrix at a precise depth; this created the negative mold from which the final character would be cast in a lead alloy.

THE ADJUSTABLE PRECISION MOLD

Gutenberg developed a precision mold which was used to cast a solid piece of lead type about one inch high. It was composed of two "L"-shaped pieces of metal that could be opened and closed to accommodate letters of varying widths, while still maintaining the exact height and depth. Into the top of this precision mold, a negative impression of a letter in brass was placed. This piece was known as a *brass matrix*.

A mixture of molten tin, antimony and lead was poured into the precision mold assembled with the matrix. The mold was then clamped shut and swung around by the rope handle to assure that the molten metal flowed into all the small pieces of the letter, and to prevent any air bubbles in the molten metal—which would render it worthless. (The air bubbles would cause the shape of the letter to be imperfect or cause the platform of the character to malform when pressure was applied on press.)

The precision mold was then opened, and the cast letter was removed. It would still need to be smoothed and have burrs removed, but it was the perfect height and depth for printing. One letter was complete!! This was quite a bit of work to get one letter for printing, but the character could be used over and over again and have multiple copies printed once it was set as a page, and it was ultimately faster to cast many letters than to copy a page by hand. Gutenberg's workers cast over 15,000 lead characters for the setting of his 42 Line Bible.

THE GOAL: TO IMITATE A HAND-COPIED BOOK

It is difficult for us now to realize that Gutenberg's ultimate goal was to create a manuscript that looked as though it had been hand-lettered by a scribe. In order to achieve this, he patterned the letterforms he cast to look like the writing of the scribes of the time. It is also important to note that there was *no other* form of writing or lettering at this time other than that of the scribes. He had no other logical choice than to copy the existing lettering standard in the field.

To further fool the prospective customer, Gutenberg cast almost 270 different pairs of kerned or ligatured pairs of characters. These joined letters more closely resembled the handwriting of the scribes. To approximate handwriting, ligatures or connected letters were cut as one punch. The

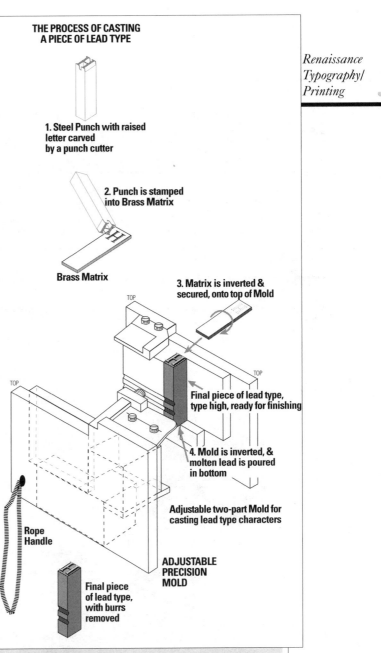

**THE PROCESS OF CASTING
A PIECE OF LEAD TYPE**

1. Steel Punch with raised letter carved by a punch cutter

2. Punch is stamped into Brass Matrix

Brass Matrix

3. Matrix is inverted & secured, onto top of Mold

TOP

TOP

TOP

Final piece of lead type, type high, ready for finishing

4. Mold is inverted, & molten lead is poured in bottom

Adjustable two-part Mold for casting lead type characters

ADJUSTABLE PRECISION MOLD

Rope Handle

Final piece of lead type, with burrs removed

3-12. The drawing above, based roughly on Gutenberg's Precision Mold, shows the process for casting a piece of lead type, from the cutting of the punch for each letter, (both upper- and lowercase), to making the matrix, to placing the matrix in the mould and then casting the final piece of lead type.

Ligature: when two characters were cast on the same lead base

3-13. Gutenberg cut 270 different pairs of ligatured letters to have his Bibles more closely resemble the hand-copying of the scribes.

Kern: when a part of a letter overhangs the base and rests on platform of the next letter

3-14. Gutenberg also shaved the lead on some characters to kern certain letters more tightly.

This page is set in Stempel Schneidler Roman 8.5/12.

3 *Renaissance*
Typography/
Printing

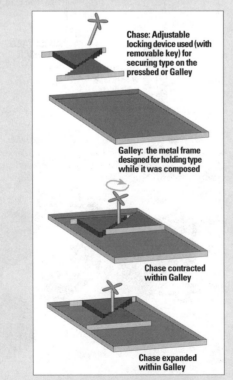

3-15. This example shows an excerpt of a page from Gutenberg's Bible, reproduced at approximately 100%. The circles reveal ligatured characters cast as one piece of type.

3-16. Early printed initial caps, like the two on the left, mimicked the scribes; they were heavy and Gothic in character. With the refinement of copperplate engraving in the 1600s, more delicate detail could be achieved in the initial capitals.

Chase: Adjustable locking device used (with removable key) for securing type on the pressbed or Galley

Galley: the metal frame designed for holding type while it was composed

Chase contracted within Galley

Chase expanded within Galley

3-17. Above are simplified drawings of the chase and the galley first designed by Gutenberg. The chase could also be used to lock up type in the pressbed.

This page is set in Stempel Schneidler Roman 8.5/12.

nature of cast type requires side spacing as a part of every character. For those letters that appeared too far apart, *mortising,* or the cutting away of a part of the body of the type, allowed the kerning of two separate lead letters. *Kerning* was when a part of the base was filed away, and part of one character rested on the platform of the next letter. Today kerning refers to the adjustment of letter spacing within words, usually tightening up the space to make the word appear easier to read.

HAND-ILLUMINATED VS. PRINTED INITIAL CAPITALS

At first, only the text was printed and space was left for the large decorated initials to be drawn in by hand. This further simulated the hand-copied books of the era. But, as printing began its widespread growth at the end of the 1400s, punch cutters gradually began designing these ornate initial capitals as well. They were frequently printed in a different color or colors than the body text. Through the decades, punch cutters developed type fonts that were different from the manuscript lettering of their day.

THE FIRST PRINTING INK

Gutenberg developed an ink with enough tackiness that it would stick to the metal letters. Unlike Oriental ink that was thin and soaked into the wood and then into the paper giving a blurred edge to the characters and images, Gutenberg's inks had to stick to the nonporous surface of the metal letters yet still be transferred to paper under pressure. It couldn't be too runny or it would not stick solely to the raised portion of the letters, and would make a mess. He likely borrowed some of his ideas for the ink from oil paints, which were introduced around 1430. The final mixture was made from boiled linseed oil that had lead and copper mixed with it for a rich blackness.

THE GALLEY FOR COMPOSING A PAGE

One of Gutenberg's other inventions was the galley that held the type in place when the top of the press was forced down over the composed page and the ink transferred to the page. The pressure required to transfer the tacky ink to the paper necessitated that the type was locked up in a galley that clamped tightly around the composed text so that it could not shift or move. The galley used the bed of the press to maintain its tension in place.

Gutenberg also developed a method for registering the type on the page accurately. A paper mask was placed over the perimeter of the press bed to prevent any ink from getting on the margin of the page. The chase is another invention; it was used to compose and proof type when setting up a page, before the letters were slid onto the press bed.

CREATING GUTENBERG'S 42 LINE BIBLE

Using the scribe's writing as a model, Gutenberg's 42 Line Bible was printed somewhere between 1450 and 1456 in Mainz, Germany. Gutenberg was not able to see his first finished sample come off the press because he had been thrown out of the business by Johann Fust, his creditor, a few months earlier. One page of Gutenberg's Bible contained 4,000 to 5,000 pieces of type, but 2 or 3 times that number of characters were required so that one page could be composed while the other was on the press. The Bible is called 42 Line because each page is composed as two columns each 42 lines deep. A stock of 15,000 to 20,000 characters was required for the type alone plus spaces between the words, which were made in the same way, but were flat and shorter and did not print. A proof could be pulled and errors corrected for all copies of a book—unlike scribes' mistakes, which remained, differently in each book.

The intent behind all this experimentation was to create a book that looked as though it had been copied by hand. Completed around 1455, the Gutenberg Bible was a two-volume piece, measuring roughly 12" wide by 16" tall, with a total of 1,282 pages in both. It is assumed that the edition was of approximately 180 copies, most were on rag paper and about one quarter were printed on vellum. They took roughly five years to complete—and that was considered amazingly fast! Only 48 copies of this Bible are known to exist today.

Many of the first books printed were sold at the price a scribe would have been paid to copy them, and the printed books cost less to produce. People could not tell the difference at first. When they could be distinguished, printed books were at first considered inferior to their counterparts that were hand-lettered.

Some of the guilds of letterers had printed books outlawed in their towns because they were afraid that they would be put out of work. Over time, however, many scribes began laying out the books that the press composers followed; they created a prototype in hand-lettering that would be followed and reproduced on the press; hence, they did not lose work.

EARLY TYPEFACES

The earliest cast typeset faces were actually modifications of scribes' hand-lettered alphabets. Gradually books departed from the manuscript model, and typefaces were cut that used Littera Antiqua as a model hand. Some typefaces were designed specif-

3-18. Gutenberg's 42 Line Bible, printed about 1450-1455, is the earliest example of a full-length, textual printed book in the western world. This book is called the 42 Line Bible because most of its pages were printed with 42 lines per column. In early printed manuscripts, the illuminated capitals were usually drawn in by hand. These printed books often were difficult to distinguish from their hand-copied counterparts.

3-20. This is Gutenberg's Bible text type reproduced at 100%. Imagine setting over 1200 pages in lead type this size, by hand, and then printing roughly 200 versions of each page!

3-19. With a platen press, 200 lbs. per square inch of pressure have to be applied to get the impression of the ink onto the page. It required a great deal of physical labor to print. These presses were also used to adhere the leather to cover boards of books.

3-21. The platen press requires the use of pressure to get the imprint of the ink onto the page.

This page is set in Windsor 8.5/12.

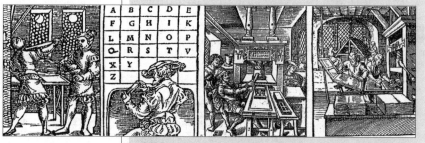

3-22. Printing shops sprang up across Europe in a flurry. There were almost two hundred print shops across Europe during the early 1500s. The woodcuts above show composers on the left, the press being operated in the middle, and the inking of type on the right.

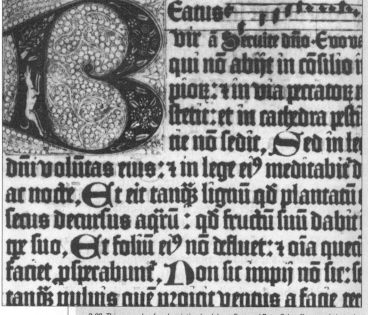

3-23. This example of early printing by Johann Fust and Peter Schoeffer reveals how the printers were trying to recreate the only books they knew, those that were hand-lettered. The text as well as the initial cap were printed. Frequently early printed initial caps were printed in two colors, and gold was added by hand. Registering the two colors required careful planning and alignment.

3-24. Above is an example of the Humanistic cursive hand that was popular as an everyday hand during the Renaissance.

This page is set in
Windsor 8.5/12.

ically for printed books—making the type smaller and more legible (due to the form of the letters) and books more affordable (because the letters were smaller than hand-written, books required less material). Many of the first typefaces cut for books were actually modifications of an historic form of lettering (such as Carolingian or Uncial) that was reexamined. This was the beginning of typographic design; typography became an art to study and pursue separate from the art of lettering.

ASSEMBLY-LINE PRODUCTION OF BOOKS

Many historians consider Gutenberg's workshop to be one of the earliest examples of assembly-line production. Unlike earlier craftsmen, each person in Gutenberg's shop was working on a part of the process, either in the composing, the printing, the binding, or the lettering, or on the covers. Each individual worked on a specialized component of the book or a part of the assembling process, rather than making an entire book from start to finish. In fact, the printing of books is an example of early mass production.

The news of printing spread quite quickly. In the area of Germany where Gutenberg started, other printers sprang up. Gutenberg himself is believed to have set up a separate press and to have continued printing in Mainz after Fust took over his enterprise. He was at one point somewhat destitute, and was taken on as a craftsman for the Archbishop of Mainz in 1465. Gutenberg died three years later in 1468.

THE SPREAD OF PRINTING: JENSON IN ITALY

When printing spread to Italy, the patrons showed a distaste for the Gothic Textura lettering. They preferred a Roman style letter, like Littera Antiqua, one that was more open and round like the Rotunda lettering. By 1458, Nicholas Jenson, a French engraver who was the master of the mint at Tours making dies for coins, was dispatched to Mainz by King Charles VII to bring back information on the new art of printing. Jenson later settled in Italy (never returning to France due to the unstable monarchy) and developed the first pure Roman typeface. In this type, there was little contrast between thick stem and thin hairline strokes; serifs were blunt and heavily bracketed. The stress in the letterforms was oblique. The baselines of all the characters of type aligned more accurately in Jenson's type than in any other printed font of the era. The caps are shorter in height than the ascenders, so that they did not stand out too much on the page. The lowercase "e" had a distinctive slanted cross stroke. The black face influence was left behind. Versions of Jenson's Old Style typeface remain as Cloister Oldstyle. This typographic style became known as Old Style type. Cloister, Garamond and Goudy are examples of Old Style faces. Old Style type has a soft organic feel to it; the serifs seem to grow out of the stem. The serifs are often rounded gently at the ends and are cup-shaped, with generous bracketing.

THE FIRST PUBLISHER

About the time that Columbus was discovering America, Aldus Manutius, an Italian scholar and tutor, saw cheaply priced printed books as a means of making ancient manuscripts available for students, and as a means of making a profit. At the age of 40, Aldus, along with a financial backer and a printer, began printing reference books which changed the concept and purpose of all books. He wanted to publish smaller texts, rather than huge heavy books. He was not creating a book to be placed on a lectern and read aloud from; he created a personal book, to be placed in a pocket and read to oneself (known today as the pocket-sized book). Through Manutius's efforts, Venice became a printing center that exported many small affordable books.

Manutius is credited with creating the first modern book—in terms of typographic design—as well. In 1495 using a calligraphic Roman face of Francesco Griffo's design, the book's typographic layout was open and airy in design, without heavy borders on the pages. This was probably done as a cost-saving measure; without borders, the press setup time was less, meaning that books could be produced more quickly, for less money. Roman type (similar to Littera Antiqua) was to become the standard in printing, surpassing the importance of black letter (Textura). One possible explanation for this is that the Roman face was easier to read silently, especially if the type was small. This legibility at a small size reduced the cost of books and made them more widely available to the general public. Manutius was a fastidious editor and proofreader, and his books were seen as a standard for accuracy in spelling and syntax from the ancient manuscripts.

He continually experimented to produce books more cheaply, which meant that he could make more profit. The Roman face he is responsible for funding by Francesco Griffo incorporated different weights of the hairline and stem strokes and delicate serifs. The typeface was more uniform in the shape, size, weight and scale of the characters than Jenson's face had been, as well as smaller, which meant fewer pages needed for the texts. Manutius was first and foremost a businessman who was interested in the bottom line. He tried to create good quality content in the most affordable production of the books he published.

THE INTRODUCTION OF THE ALDINE ITALIC WITH GRIFFO

In 1506, influenced by the Papal Chancery cursive handwriting used at the time for papal documents, Manutius developed the first italic type with Francesco Griffo. It was originally intended as a book face for the lowercase only and relied on Roman (vertical) capitals. Because the characters were much narrower than Roman, Manutius set entire books in the italic version. With it, he could get more words on a page, use less paper in the production of books, and could sell books more cheaply. (The term italic may likely have originated because it was associated with the unique fonts used in Manutius's books—italic, meaning from Italy.)

3-25 Nicolas Jenson, a French engraver, is credited with the development of the first pure Roman typeface; one that veered from the predominant Blackletter fonts.

enim id scrutádum nobis módo est. Post H
pietate successit: fœlice hac hæreditate a par
coniunctus quum geminos genuisset castit
dicitur abstinuisse. Ab isto natus é Iacob q
prouétum Israel etiam appellatus est duob
uirtutis usú. Iacob eim athletá & exercétem
quam appellatióne primú habuit: quú prac
pro pietate labores ferebat. Quum auté iam
speculationis fruebat bonis: túc Israelem i

3-26. Above is Nicolas Jenson's Roman typeface. It was so popular in France and Italy that it replaced the black letter which was preferred by the German peoples long after Roman was favored in Italy.

3-27. Aldus Manutius, an early publisher of pocket-sized books. His texts were known for the accuracy of proofreading and editing.

3-29. This illustration shows the convenience of paperback books in reading.

Dique ad q̃sto sincero & sancto Imperio, finito
gno parlare, humilmente fecime seruo cernuo, & c
exiguo auso di subito parendo. Sopra quelle deliti
tro, posime adsedere, Cum la mia lanacea toga, anc

3-28. Above is an example of the font Francesco Griffo cut for Aldus Manutius's books.

This page is set in Windsor 8.5/12.

3
Renaissance
Typography
Printing

3-30. Above is an engraving of a Renaissance Era scholar, shown with a small book for study.

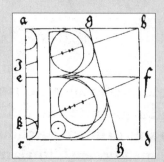

3-31. Above is an example of one of Manutius's pocket-sized books that utilize Griffo's italic for the lowercase. Note that the uppercase letters are in Roman at the beginning of each line. Because the italic was thinner, it was used for the entire book's text.

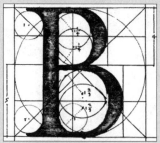

3-32. This is Giovanni Battista Palatino's "B" showing its construction. Palatino was a letterer who published writing guides to teach people how to write.

3-33. This is Dürer's version of the geometry to construct the capital letter "B." Artists saw letters and lettering as a legitimate avenue for their expertise in proportions.

This page is set in ITC New Baskerville Roman 8.5/12.

Manutius's fame is due to his undying attempts to make books cheaper, offer accurate translations and generally make them more available to scholars. After the introduction of the first italic face, a quarter century passed before sloping italic capitals appeared in type. Griffo also cut the typeface Bembo, which is named after Cardinal Bembo, who was the first to utilize this typeface. It has been redesigned and still is widely in use in books today.

THE LETTER AS ART

In the 1500s, during the Renaissance in Europe, interest in books, their design and specifically the design of letters became a subject of study. During this era, painters and sculptors saw the patronage of the wealthy as commonplace, and they all worked for clients in order to earn a living. Artists often were fine letterers as well, considering the art of lettering as important as the art of drawing, and as important as writing poetry. It is not surprising that artists turned their skill to the designs of many items, including letterforms, during the Renaissance.

Some of the most renowned artists of this era felt that the proportions of the perfect letter were just as predictable as the proportions of the human body. In his *Divina Proportionne* of 1509, Leonardo daVinci analyzed the construction of letterforms with geometric elements. DaVinci also compared the proportions of letters to the proportions of the human body. In 1525 Albrecht Dürer wrote an essay entitled *On the Just Shaping of Letters* as part of a treatise on applied geometry. Dürer constructed letters by inscribing them in a square of specific size, building the character from the elements of the square and the arcs of circles. Complete instructions and alternate designs for each letter were given in the text. Dürer, known for his impressive woodcut illustrations, made an important contribution to the craft of lettering and type design with this essay.

It is important to realize that artists of this period often created woodcuts for printing and did not see fine art, graphic art and typography as the separate fields we perceive them as today. Knowing the proportions of the human figure was just as important as knowing the correct proportions of letters. Type was seen as another artistic expression or avenue, one that could be analyzed, studied, and mastered like human anatomy, not simply as words on the page. Perhaps this is because these artists were in touch with hand lettering as an art, and they strove to be Renaissance men.

PRINTING IN ENGLAND: WILLIAM CAXTON

In England the first printed book was created in 1476 by William Caxton, an Englishman who had studied the art of printing in Bruges, Flanders. The first book printed in the English language was set in a flourishing and angular Gothic face (popular in France at the time) called *Batarde*. Some calligraphers consider Batarde to be a fusion of the Rotunda style and the Gothic Textura hand; others consider it a unique lettering hand.

Caxton worked for a few years in Bruges and then set up shop in England around 1478. The printing of books in English standardized spelling and punctuation in the English language. It also set the trend for the use of Gothic typefaces in English printing that lasted much longer than in France and Italy. The royalty eventually limited printing to the cities of London, Oxford and Cambridge, and all manuscripts had to be submitted to a censor for a license to be printed!

THE RELIGIOUS REFORMATION AND WITCH-HUNTING

In 1517 Martin Luther nailed his ninety-five theses to the door of the Wittenberg church in Germany, calling for reforms in Catholicism. When he refused to recant his ideas, he was excommunicated and began a new religion that became known as the Lutheran religion. Other Reformists broke from the Church in France and Switzerland, and Henry VII began the Church of England in 1534 when he wanted to divorce his wife. The Reformation caused tremendous upheaval in Europe; the different religions were eventually the cause of wars. There was no longer a unifying spiritual force throughout the various countries.

A Counter-Reformation movement began with the Council of Trent in 1545, calling for changes within the Church. These changes caused some extreme reactions, such as the witch-hunting Inquisition and book-burning in Spain and the disbanding of longstanding monasteries in England. In the face of religious persecution, many religious people, like the Puritans, moved to more hospitable areas or set off to settle a new land, free from religious persecution.

THE PINNACLE OF THE RENAISSANCE

The 1500s mark the time that the Renaissance in Europe was in full bloom. Some scholars would refer to each other by ancient Greek or Roman names, and they would write in the ancient tongues. Ancient Greek and Roman society was considered the ultimate achievement in sophisticated culture, and the aesthetics, books and theatre of the past were revered and copied. This is the century when the Mona Lisa and the Sistine Ceiling were painted. Oil paints allowed artists to achieve much more detail in their work, and scientific analysis of perspective gave artists a better understanding of how to represent three-dimensional objects on the two-dimensional plane of the canvas.

Broader literacy meant people of all classes were interested in books. As the lower classes yearned for reading material, the large-format manuscripts lost their appeal in

3-34. William Caxton printed the first book in English in 1477. This publication standardized punctuation and spelling.

3-35. This is the font used in William Caxton's text printed in English in 1477. Caxton was influenced by the German preference for black letter type, over the lighter Roman faces like Jenson's. This font is more curvilinear than the Gothic black letter.

3-36. William Caxton's printing mark, used to to identify his books in the colophon at the end.

3-37. This is an example of the lettering known as Batarde; it has some of the flourishes and curves of Rotunda, and the verticals of and is condensed like Textura.

3-38. This early printed example of a page in English it about the English Usurer. Notice that the "U's" are replaced with "V's," because the "U" and the "V" were seen as the same character at this point.

This page is set in ITC New Baskerville Roman 8.5/12.

3-39. Intricate initial capitals were used to enhance the appearance of Renaissance books. This elaborate letter is a capital "I."

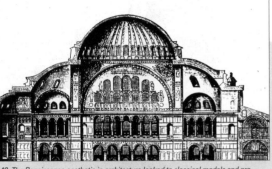

3-40. The Renaissance aesthetic in architecture looked to classical models and proportions to design buildings and create interior spaces.

3-41. The map above shows the country/provincial areas of Europe during the Renaissance.

3-42. This Book of Hours was printed in 1531 by Geoffrey Tory. The delicate woodcut illustration was possible in the workable boxwood. There is a sense of classic proportions and elegance to this page, with the focal point of the dark bird within the lighter linear elements.

favor of smaller, lightweight, cheaper books. Calligraphers were, however, still employed to draft important legal documents for businesses and state decrees. The importance of handwriting as a symbol of one's station in life also began at this point. It was assumed that only those of the highest upbringing had the time to master fine handwriting.

Writing masters were employed to teach people refined handwriting skills. Some writing masters even published books displaying their skills. No longer was writing learned only by a few scribes; now it could be learned by the public at large. Yet printers in the 1500s faced the problem of state and religious censorship of their work. Ideas expressed in the classic Greek and Roman texts were often at odds with the clergy or royalty. Yet the Humanist philosophy (which placed man rather than God at the center of the universe) was able to gain acceptance throughout Europe despite the attempts to prevent its spread through censorship.

CLASSICAL AESTHETICS APPLIED TO BOOK DESIGN

The appearance of the Renaissance printed material reflected the artistic sensibility of the era. Gone were the dark heavy borders filling every inch of available space that were popular in the hand-lettered texts. If borders were utilized, the images were represented as outline or contour drawings. Press work was refined, and a high quality of accuracy, consistency and cleanliness was achieved by the finest printers of this time. Illustrations were usually executed as copperplate etchings, which necessitated that they be printed separately from the text because a separate press was required.

FRANCE OFFERS A NEW LOOK IN TYPE: GARAMOND

Claude Garamond grew up in France in the printing business from the time of his youth. His greatest accomplishment was to free typefaces from their reliance on calligraphic forms. He did not look to the calligraphers of the day for his inspiration. Just as previous lettering was affected by the substrate and the implement it was written with, Garamond designed a typeface that was sensitive to the metal it was designed with. Garamond's Roman typefaces were introduced in Paris in 1530.

Garamond was not a printer, but he set up a business that exclusively cast letters to be sold directly to printing shops. Garamond was the first full-time punch cutter and typefounder in history. His work begins the separation of the type foundry from the same workshop as the printer. Up until this point, the overseer of the type production was usually the overseer of the printing as well.

Garamond cut a face that is considered one of the best in all typographic history; it was so widely accepted that it was used almost exclusively for 200 years throughout much of Europe. Based on the Aldus Roman face, it added nobility, simplicity and a careful blending of the parts into readable, classic letters. His type had a snugness of fit that allowed tighter word spacing which was more readable and created a more even tone on the page. In Garamond's typeface, the lowercase letters are as beautiful as the large capitals. They were the first lowercase letters that were used in the titles of books; previously titles had been only in capitals. Since there are more lowercase letters in any page, it was sensible for Garamond to focus on the form of them since the lowercase often determines the legibility of the face. Garamond's successful typeface was considered an Old Style face.

These new letters gained rapid acceptance in France and were responsible for France's complete switch away from the black letter style. Garamond's Roman faces would monopolize the printing industry in France and Italy well into the 1700s. Today's Garamond faces are redrawn, and although adapted, they are based on the same forms and nuances.

PRINTING INNOVATIONS: THE INCUNABULA

It could be argued that the greatest contributions to printing and typography were made within the first century after the invention of printing. The period of the first fifty years after the introduction of printing is referred to as the Incunabula, which means "swaddling clothes" or "cradle" in Latin. (In many countries infants are "swaddled" or wrapped very tightly just after birth to recreate the feeling experienced in the womb.) Most of the books printed early in this period were of religious nature, but by the end of the century many were secular. The contributions of the first century after the introduction of printing included: the Old Style family of types, small capitals, italics, printer's marks, type registration on the page, two-color printing, colophons (to credit the printer) and the movable type itself. Contributors included: Gutenberg, Coster, Jenson, Aldus, and Garamond.

To give you a sense of the enthusiasm of printing, in 1450, Europe's monasteries and libraries housed fifty thousand volumes, but, by 1500 it is estimated that *nine million* books were produced. There were over thirty-five thousand different editions printed in the first fifty years after printing was invented! The boom of printing gradually grew to include short lived broadsides printed on one side, posters, and leaflets.

By 1500, printing establishments had been set up in 140 cities on the continent. Some historians argue that without printing, the political revolutions of the next centuries (American and French) would not have been possible. Printing enabled ideas to be spread over great distances and did not require forums of people to be assembled. Besides establishing ideas regarding the rights of humans, printing also unified and standardized the languages throughout Eu-

3-43. Claude Garamond, 1480-1561, cut the punches for a few early Old Style fonts. Variations of his design are still used today.

reftituit. Fuit hic (vt Annales ferunt) Othonis eius qui ab infigni pietate magnitudinéque ar nente illo pernobili claffico excitus, ad facrú in Syriam contendit, communicatis fcilicet c atque opibus cú Guliermo Montifferrati regu à proceritate corporis, Longa fpatha vocabat

3-44. Above is an example of Claude Garamond's original font, an Old Style font with heavy bracketing and cupped serifs.

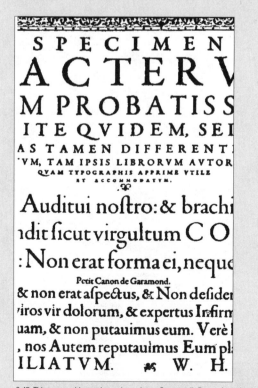

3-45. This typographic specimen sheet shows Garamond's Roman face, that he cut about 1592. It was extremely popular in France and Italy.

This page is set in
Frutiger Light 8.5/12.

3 *Renaissance*
    Typography/
    Printing

3-46. Elaborate initials
show the influence of
Baroque art.

3-47. These initial caps
were likely engraved in copper due to the fine details.

3-48. This "E" and "I" are so
ornate that they are difficult
to discern.

3-49. Granjon worked with Garamond as an apprentice and later
cut ten italic faces that were well balanced. He also cut the first
typeface that was influenced by the hand lettering that was
popular at the time.

Simon Vostre & tant d'autres, do
Christian nous résume ici les tr
merveille dans cette œuvre nouvelle
    Encouragée par plusieurs mon
primerie n'avait, jusqu'au comm
XVIᵉ siècle, inspiré en France au

3-50. Above, a Granjon Italic is featured. The weight of the strokes is quite delicate,
and the capitals are slanted along with the lowercase letters, unlike earlier italics,
which simply used the Roman capitals with the italic lowercase.

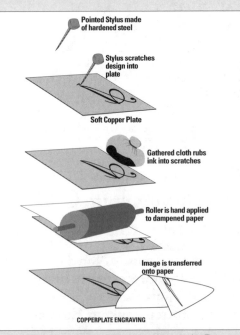

3-51. The diagram above shows the process of copperplate engraving. There was a
limit to the run that could be pulled from a copper plate because the impression in
the copper would wear down over time, due to the softness of the metal.

rope at this time. Printing also lead to the democratization of information, as books were produced more cheaply, upper and lower classes were reading the same information. This explosion of information has been compared to the mass information that has been disseminated since the popularization of television after the 1950s, and could be compared to the explosion of information available on the web today.

PREVALENCE OF ITALIC FACES

In the mid 1500s Robert Granjon, a young man who worked with Garamond, cut ten italic faces that were considered outstanding. One was designed as a companion to the Roman Garamond. There were characteristics to these faces which made them different from the Roman faces: "m" and "n" have small hooks at the end of their final stroke, rather than a serif; the "k" often has a loop rather than an upper diagonal stroke; and the "f" has a longer and more graceful descender. These changes in the italic reveal the handwriting origin of the faces, but they were clearly "printing" typefaces that were designed for printing, not simply an imitation of handwriting.

Yet, in 1577, Granjon did cut the first typeface to simulate handwriting rather than hand lettering. As noted throughout many developments of alphabets, the script that was written for everyday use differs dramatically from the careful hand lettering used in texts. His most famous face was Civilité, which was based on the popular handwriting of the day. Granjon's Civilité marks the first time that typography was influenced by the cursive handwriting of the day. It was really a cursive face, characterized by linked lowercase letters. This development led to the printing of scripts, a whole class of specialized typefaces.

COPPERPLATE ENGRAVING

Another form of printing had been used from about the time that Gutenberg developed movable type. *Copperplate engraving* is a process in which the image is engraved or scratched into the surface of a soft copper plate using a hardened-steel engraving stylus that is pointed like a needle. Also known as *gravure* or *intaglio*, this process required incising into a thin plate of copper. The images created with this process were much more refined than those created with wood blocks. Fine hairline-thick lines could be cross-hatched to create shading and the illusion of depth. Once the image was engraved into the copper plate, the ink was then applied heavily over the entire surface, and the excess ink was rubbed off the surface of the plate. The ink remained only in the crevices. The paper was then dampened and put under pressure against the plate to pick up the image and the type. The limitations of this process were that the plate, because it was made of soft copper, would not hold up for many impressions. But the quality of the detail of the illustration was much better with engraving than with woodcuts. This method could also be used for printing more than one color.

HANDWRITING AS A SYMBOL OF BEING WELL BRED

Refined handwriting had become popular in the Renaissance as a sign of status. When a fancy script face was cut in copperplate, it was an instant success. Elaborate handwriting was a sign of being very well bred, so there were many handwriting masters at this time. Flourishes and curlicues with thick and thin strokes and the linking of letters were very popular. Everyday handwriting scripts were always different from the faces that were lettered in books.

Granjon's Civilité was quite popular, and it was one of the only script faces that was cast in lead. In the 1600s copperplate engraving was used to recreate the popular scrollwork of the writing masters. Because it could reproduce the fine lines of the scripts, it was the natural choice for reproducing faces that were becoming popular in handwriting at this time. The difference between lead type and copperplate engraving is that the lead type can be reused, whereas the copperplate is inscribed with a single message; a couple hundred are printed, and then the plate is repaired and stored or ground down to be used again. Civilité was not very legible and its popularity faded quickly. Copperplate engraving gradually replaced woodcuts as the illustration medium of choice in books because such fine detail and shading could be created.

EARLY PRINTED BOOKS

Although there was press refinement and Roman-based fonts that were developed shortly after the invention of printing with movable type, many books were printed that still used the heavy Gothic text and dark woodcuts, particularly in Germany and northern areas of Europe. There was also a proliferation of religious texts, warning people to be just in their daily lives. Many of the innovators in book design, such as Manutius, were overshadowed by the preponderance of cruder, Gothic-styled book design. Eventually the more open page designs gained favor, but it was a slow and gradual process.

3-52. This elegant script was only able to be printed by copperplate because the fine curves could not be cast in lead; and they could not withstand the pressure of the press.

3-53. This writing sample from 1592 shows how elaborate handmade documents had become, with filigreed pen work and scrolls showing great mastery of pen techniques.

3-54. Above is an example of a Gothic-styled page. The text is very densely packed on the page and the illustration is a dark, heavy woodcut. This page describes hell and damnation.

3-55. In this Gothic page, entitled The Parliament of Devils, the illustration of satanic creatures dominates the page, and is intended to scare the reader into living a good life.

3-56. Both reading and fine handwriting were considered the hallmarks of an educated person.

3-57. This is an example of elaborate Gothic capitals that became popular in the 1500s. Initials such as this were often used to promote lettering-teacher's skills.

3-58. Swirling curves create this elaborate "B," likely done in copperplate engraving.

3-59. This "J" is Gothic and Baroque in style; it is detailed with extensive filigree.

This page is set in Fenice Light 8.5/12.

3 *Renaissance Typography/ Printing*

3-60. The T-shirt design above utilizes Nicolas Jenson's font, as well as an engraving of him.

3-61. This T-shirt commemorates Claude Garamond with a layered design.

3-62. This T-shirt is dedicated to William Caxton and the font he designed.

PROJECT: TYPOGRAPHER COMMEMORATIVE T-SHIRTS

Select a well-known figure from the history of typography, and design a two-color T-shirt inspired by the type and design sensibility of this person. You can use the face of the person or not as you see fit. It can be as simple or as complex a design as you desire. It can incorporate the sleeves, the back, etc. It can be serious, silly or irreverent. It can be true to the era of the designer, or it can be anachronistic on purpose. It can work to challenge viewers, or it can inform them. The T-shirt can be a purely aesthetic design, or it can have a verbal message. Use your newly gained knowledge of typography and any examples you can find at the library.

Go to the library, and do further research on the person of your choice. Try to design a T-shirt that other designers would appreciate; it can even be funny. This is your opportunity to create a T-shirt that you would want to wear. The design can be simple and minimalistic, or it can be complex and layered; suit your own tastes. The final size will be determined by the design; some may be large, others may be small. What is most important is that you design with a sense of the historic era that you are trying to learn more about. Angled text may not be appropriate for a T-shirt on Bodoni; but on the other hand, it could be a very innovative solution to this problem. There are no limits to this project, except the two-color limit; but the two colors can be any colors.

Begin doing research, then random-associate about the information you have gathered. Next, do fifteen thumbnail sketches to get your ideas down; be sure to plan them on the T-shirt. Finally refine two as color studies, at half size, and then complete the final version, either by heat-activated T-shirt transfer, or by silk screen.

OBJECTIVES

- To research a type designer in depth.
- To use a typographer's style as visual reference.
- To consider type on the three-dimensional plane of clothing.
- To design for a specific audience.
- To utilize type as the primary visual medium.
- To inspire designers to know about the tradition of their craft.

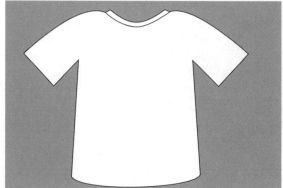

3-63. Use this template to design your own T-shirt.

Renaissance Typography/Printing-Review

1. What is the Renaissance, and what important typographic innovation took place during it? _____

_____

2. What happened at the beginning of the Renaissance that changed the lives of everyday people? _____

_____

3. What was the first printing press adapted from? _____

_____

4. Who developed printing, when and where? _____

_____

5-8. Name at least four of his other inventions—besides printing (and describe). _____

_____

_____

_____

_____

_____

9. What "font" were the earliest books printed in, and why? _____

_____

10. What is the first printed book called, and why? _____

_____

11. How many pieces of type were cast in the first printing workshop? _____

_____

12. Why is printing considered one of the first applications of mass production? _____

_____

13. Who was Aldus Manutius, and what did he contribute to the history of type? _____

_____

3 Renaissance
Typography/
Printing

14. What did Francesco Griffo contribute to the history of type? _____

_____

15. Who was Garamond, and how did he change the roles in the production of books? _____

_____

16. What was significant about Garamond's font? _____

_____

17. What was Robert Granjon known for? _____

_____

18. Why were his typefaces considered different from others that preceded his? _____

_____

19. What is Textura, and why is it called Gothic? _____

_____

20. What are ligatures? _____

_____

21. What is mortising? _____

_____

22. What is kerning, and how was it used in early printing? _____

_____

23-24. Name two practices that were used to make early printed books look like hand-copied ones.

_____

_____

_____

25. How was the scale of books affected during the Renaissance, and how was this related to literacy? _____

_____

26. Name two Renaissance artists who wrote about the correct proportioning of letters. _____

_____

27. Who printed the first book in English? _____

28. How did this book affect the written language? _____

_____

29. Why was handwriting so important in the Renaissance and during the early years of printing? _____

_____

30. Why is the story of the first printer somewhat of a tragedy? _____

_____

31. What is a colophon? _____

Colonial & Industrialized Typography

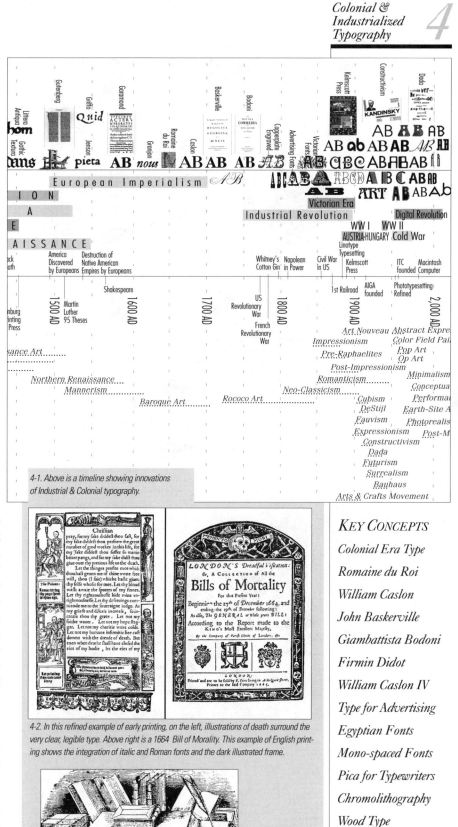

4-1. Above is a timeline showing innovations of Industrial & Colonial typography.

INTRODUCTION

This chapter traces the advancement of typefaces and styles throughout the colonial and Industrial Revolution eras. During this time, type production became much faster with the introduction of mechanization into the printing process. Printers are credited during this time with proliferating concepts of freedom and liberty which encouraged the revolutions and the establishment of some of the national governments that we now know. In type design we witness a transition from clean, practical, readable text faces, to ornate faces popular in the Victorian era, when type was used for early advertising as the Industrial Revolution surged forward, creating markets for mass-produced goods.

COLONIAL ERA TYPOGRAPHY

Printers flourished in the 1600s and 1700s, although there was not a great deal of innovation in the equipment of the industry. America began to be colonized (for some as a refuge from the witch hunts) with the 1607 settlement at Jamestown, Virginia. The pilgrims landed in Plymouth, Massachusetts, and the Dutch settled New Amsterdam (New York) in 1623. Absolute monarchs who believed in the Divine Right of Kings reigned throughout Europe. William Shakespeare lived and produced plays during this period, dying in 1616, seven years before his entire works were published in 1623. Bach and Vivaldi lived at the end of this century, and wrote their great symphonies. Operas began to be staged in this age when Baroque music and art was in style. Baroque art was based on the expression of emotion and feeling in vibrant colors. Some historians see the Baroque style connected to the Counter-Reformation of the Roman Catholic Church, which emphasized spirituality and emotional aspects of the Catholic religion. Baroque artists turned to classical themes, and others set Christian heroes in ancient settings.

Novels, journals, and political pamphlets were widely available to the emerging European middle class, and there was an unquenchable thirst for the printed word. Novels had tremendous impact on the moral and cultural norms of

4-2. In this refined example of early printing, on the left, illustrations of death surround the very clear, legible type. Above right is a 1664 Bill of Morality. This example of English printing shows the integration of italic and Roman fonts and the dark illustrated frame.

4-3. Books were a main import to the colonies from Europe; there was a constant demand for reading material.

This page is set in Flare Gothic Light 8.5/12.

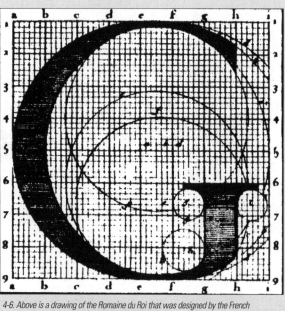

4-6. Above is a drawing of the Romaine du Roi that was designed by the French Academy of Sciences to be a mathematically and geometrically perfect font.

4-4. The handwriting craze as a symbol of status continued into colonial days. Above is a device for holding the pen at the correct angle and preventing blotches and smudges with your hand.

4-5. The split-nib quill pen was the instrument of choice for writing masters.

parts. Les Hérétiques domptez,
orite Royale reftablie, rendoie1
nt. Mais il manquoit au Roy t

4-7. Above is an example of the final Romaine du Roi font, printed. It is not likely that all of the details of the enlarged drawings were maintained when the punches were cut because the scale was so different, and the punches were cut by hand.

4-8. Official writers were used to draw up legal documents and loans in colonial times; some were employed as secretaries to wealthy landowners.

4-9. This decorative initial displays some of the French preference for ornate, three-dimensional leaves contrasted with flat areas of patterns.

4-10. This capital captures the excessive decoration of the Rococo era of type.

This page is set in
Flare Gothic Light 8.5/12.

the time. Posters and broadsides, as well as newspapers (the first was printed in Strasbourg in 1609), were found in most cities throughout Europe. In Amsterdam, books were printed in condensed type to fit into vest pockets. The first Bible was printed in English by Robert Baker in 1612.

The first press was established in the American colonies in 1640. By 1775, despite the tax on paper and advertising, there were fifty printers in the thirteen colonies. These presses spread the word of the Revolution throughout the new world; without printing, the American Revolution might not have been possible. Books were still a frequently imported item from England to the colonies at this time.

THE MATHEMATICALLY PERFECT FONT

In 1692, in an effort to approach the design of typefaces scientifically, King Louis XIV in France ordered the French Academy of Sciences to develop its own geometric formula for typography. Headed by a committee of scholars and mathematicians, they worked out a detailed theory of design based on a grid of 2,304 little squares. In 1702, Phillippe Grandjean, Royal punch cutter, cut a face called the Romaine du Roi (Roman of the King) in keeping with the designs of the Academy. The "G" shown on the left is an example of the geometric formula approach of the Academy. This face exaggerated the difference in weight between the stem and the hairline stroke, reduced bracketing, and created thin, horizontal, squared-off serifs. This face was to be used exclusively by the Royal printing office of France at the time; any other use was a crime. This typeface marks the first time that a mathematical, precise analysis was used to design the letters, as opposed to a calligraphic or artistic approach.

ROCOCO ERA TYPOGRAPHY

The 1700s is known as the Rococo period of design. The flowery, ornamented style of fashion and design reflected a monarchy who lived lavish lives of indulgence—a lifestyle that would soon be overthrown in favor of a government ruled by the people (1789-1793 French Revolution). The royalty continued to enjoy a life of extravagance and frivolity unaware of the danger that was brewing in the hearts of those condemned to a life of miserable, hunger-stricken poverty.

The flamboyance of the style of the Rococo era was expressed as fine lines and curving flourishes. Copperplate engraving was better suited to this style than the rigidity of letterpress printing. The handwriting craze of earlier years was reinforced, with masters creating elaborate cards exhibiting their talents to lure in students. These elaborate flourishes and scroll works were sought after as a sign of refinement. The upper classes were completely out of touch with the harsh reality of the living conditions of the poorer classes in France and other European countries.

STANDARDIZATION OF TYPE MEASUREMENT

During this era of excess, in 1737 Pierre Fournier le Jeune, a French printer and type designer, standardized the measurement system of typefaces. He published his first *Table of Proportions* which named the different sizes of type. His later works introduced the idea of a family of type, and the use of compatible type that could be mixed in one printed piece for consistency. Fournier's final work codified the point system for measuring type that is still in use today. This system was later refined by Françoise Ambroise Didot. It is sometimes referred to as the Didot system, and Fournier's is referred to as the Pica system of type measurement. The Pica system of type measurement was widely used in England and America.

COLONIZATION/MECHANIZATION AND TYPOGRAPHY

Colonization was essential for the raw materials that were needed in the European countries as a source for tax revenue for the kingdom, and the colonies provided a ready market for the goods manufactured in Europe. While the French aristocracy was contributing money to support the move toward the independence of colonial America, their own lower classes were dissatisfied and heading toward a revolution. Ironically, some historians are convinced that the success of the American Revolution in the colonies inspired the French lower classes to fight for their freedom a decade later, in 1789.

Mechanization was beginning in this century, and the end of the century was marked by a steam engine being placed in a cotton-spinning factory in Nottinghamshire in 1785, and Eli Whitney's invention of the cotton gin in 1793. That same year Louis XVI and Marie Antoinette were executed by guillotine in France, beginning the Reign of Terror in France in which any noble person could be sentenced to guillotine death by the verdict of the lower classes as a crowd. In 1799 Napoleon Bonaparte, a young general, seized dictatorial power in France. The burgeoning of the Industrial Revolution was a few decades away.

SEPARATING THE "I, J, U," AND "W" IN ENGLISH

In the 1700s printing flourished in England due to the freedom of the press that was enacted in 1694. About the end of the 1700s, the mixup over "I, J, U, V," and "W" in the English language was resolved: the "J, U," and "W" were given separate sounds and full place in the alphabet, which then became the version we are all familiar with, our present 26 letters.

4-11. Ben Franklin was a prolific and important colonial printer.

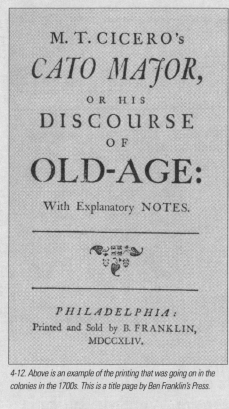

4-12. Above is an example of the printing that was going on in the colonies in the 1700s. This is a title page by Ben Franklin's Press.

4-13. Books in the colonies were always in demand, but most were imported from Europe, rather than being produced in the colonies.

This page is set in
Clarendon 8.5/12.

4 *Colonial &*
Industrialized
Typography

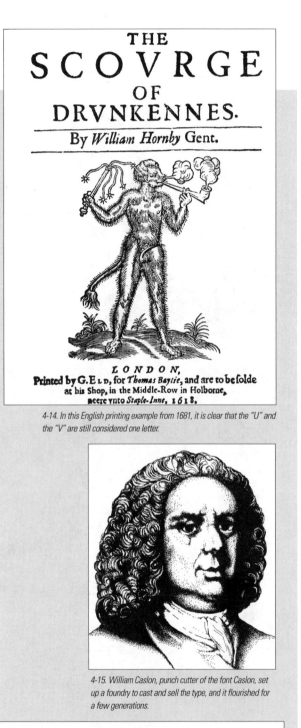

4-14. In this English printing example from 1681, it is clear that the "U" and the "V" are still considered one letter.

4-15. William Caslon, punch cutter of the font Caslon, set up a foundry to cast and sell the type, and it flourished for a few generations.

ENGLISH ROMAN.

Quousque tandem abutêre, Catilina, patientia nostra? quamdiu nos etiam furor iste tuus eludet? quem ad finem sese effrenata jactabit audacia? nihilne te nocturnum præsidium palatii, nihil urbis vigiliæ, nihil timor populi, nihil consensus bonorum omnium, nihil hic munitissimus

ABCDEFGHIJKLMNOPQRSTVUW

4-16. Caslon's Old Face was known for the clarity of the lowercase letters, as well as the accurate alignment of the baselines, which was believed to allow for easier reading.

While England was growing as a center for printing, a new pointed split-quill pen used in England's enlarging commerce led to "round" handwriting, based on thick and thin hairline strokes. This new pen and handwriting style ushered in a renewed interest in fine handwriting. Professional scribes were still employed to write up official legal documents, loan agreements and state decrees.

TYPE TASTES IN ENGLAND

Around 1730, William Caslon, a goldsmith, designed a type (roman and italic) named Old Face. This typestyle was an instant success in England. It was balanced in the proportioning of the letters. Caslon's design relied on some ancient inspiration as well. The characters had a slightly heavier weight to the thick strokes, which increased their legibility. This heaviness was directly opposed to the light type Romaine du Roi in France. Caslon's type created exceptionally legible words when set as a page of text because no flourishes would distract the reader. Caslon's type became the standard of the era, especially for books printed in English. Both the Declaration of Independence and the Constitution (when they were printed) were first printed in Caslon. Caslon italic and swash capitals are often used to convey an American antique feeling. The font relied on an organic style to the letters but with more of a refinement to the weights of the strokes than Garamond. Caslon's heavily bracketed font Old Face is considered an Old Style font.

WRITING MASTER TO TYPE DESIGNER

During the 1700s John Baskerville began his career as a professional writing master. He was also an accomplished stone cutter. After making money as a manufacturer of japanned ware (objects that were layered with lacquer and then had decorations carved into their surfaces) for a few decades, he returned to letters and particularly printing. Like Gutenberg, Baskerville perfected many elements of the printing process. He designed type, cast it carefully, refined the "packing" of the press, introduced a new smoother surface to paper, improved the design of the printing press, and refined the mixing of ink so that he achieved a rich, almost purple black.

At 41, he decided to try his hand at printing and, dissatisfied with the existing typefaces, Baskerville set out to design a face that would meet his expectations. Considered a Transitional Style type (between the Old Style and the Modern faces), Baskerville's font marks the beginning of the influence of the mechanization of printing into the field of type design.

The new typeface (in Roman and italic) was introduced in England by Baskerville with his publication of Virgil in 1757. Gone are the craftsman-like qualities of the Old Style type, to be replaced by more precise faces. No longer was the typeface based on a pure pen stroke; especially in the serifs, there was a departure from earlier typefaces. The result was a relatively heavy face with extreme thins and straight serifs. These new letters had a near perfection unlike the earlier cruder faces. The new font was somewhat straighter and more vertical in the stress of the strokes and used a mechanical line with flatter serifs. The height of the lowercase was considered small compared to the capitals, and the lowercase was extremely wide. The serifs showed less bracketing and were more pointed at the ends as opposed to the earlier more rounded forms. This engineered face probably has the most in common with the Romaine du Roi, which was designed by mathematicians. Baskerville was very secretive about how he accomplished some of his refinements of printing his font.

Baskerville has recently been recognized as history's first *type designer* as opposed to one who is also the punch cutter. John Handy was Baskerville's punch cutter. Baskerville may be one of the earliest type designers to work out his forms first on paper and to later refine them rather than directly cutting the punches in metal. Baskerville considered every part of the printing process in the design of his type. For the first time, the refinement of the paper and the printing technology were considered during the drawing of a typeface.

Baskerville knew at the outset that he did not want a heavy impression of the letters pushed into the paper. He made his own extremely black printing ink by boiling linseed oil, aging it with black resin, and burning the lamp black himself...this was a committed perfectionist! In search for a smoother printing surface, he invented the first woven paper, rejecting the traditional laid texture paper, and he hot-pressed his paper while it was damp to assure added smoothness. He revised the press and packed the blanket behind the sheet to be printed with a harder material than was used before.

All of this work was met with great disdain from the general public; few people liked the new

4-17. John Baskerville did not live to see the success of his font and his printing innovations. Baskerville, a Transitional font, is well known for its thin, delicately bracketed serifs.

have received, that I still preserve my former
the commonwealth: and wish me joy in the othe
marriage. With respect to the first, if to mean
interest of my country and to approve that mean
ry friend of its liberties, may be considered as
my authority; the account you have heard is ce

4-18. This is an example of Baskerville's font that was crisper and lighter on the page than any of its precedents.

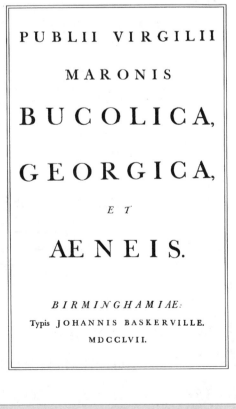

PUBLII VIRGILII

MARONIS

BUCOLICA,

GEORGICA,

ET

AENEIS.

BIRMINGHAMIAE:

Typis JOHANNIS BASKERVILLE.

MDCCLVII.

4-19. In the layout of his books, Baskerville used a clean, sparse layout of the title pages, allowing the type to dominate in the design.

4-20. Modes of transportation to speed up travel were investigated. The first hot-air balloon was sent up in 1783 in France by Etienne and Joseph Montgolfer.

4-21. Industrialization forged forward. The first steam-powered locomotive engine was created in 1829 by George Stephenson.

This page is set in
Clarendon Light 8.5/12.

4 *Colonial &*
Industrialized
Typography

4-22. With industrialization, the world was changing dramatically. Henri Giffard of France flew the first dirigible in 1852 at 6 mph.

4-23. Giambattista Bodoni, the originator of the Modern style font, Bodoni, worked in Italy.

✳ ╡ PAPALE ╞ ✳

Quousq; tandem abutêre, Catilina,

SALUZZO

4-24. Bodoni was known for a sparse type layout on the books he oversaw the printing of in Parma.

Quousque tandem abutêre, Catilina, patientiâ nostrâ ? *audacia? nihilne te noctur-*

4-25. Above is an example of Bodoni's Modern font.

look of Baskerville's type and books. They thought that the paper was too smooth, the ink too black, and were afraid that the reflection caused by the paper would hurt their eyes—imagine what they would think of monitors today! Baskerville was admired in France and the colonies for his type design, his ink, and his simple, clean layouts. He was known for using generous amounts of white space in his layouts, which were devoid of ornaments; they relied exclusively on the type for the design format. Unfortunately, this undaunted innovator died before truly knowing whether or not his work in printing and commitment to excellence were ever accepted by the general public.

TYPOGRAPHY IN ITALY

Giambattista Bodoni, working in Parma, Italy (around the same time that Baskerville was working in England), introduced the first truly Modern Style typeface in 1788 under the influence of Baskerville. Bodoni may have seen the work of Firmin Didot in France who was likely influenced by the Romaine du Roi. Bodoni's type had extreme weight variations between the thick and thin strokes. The round letters were narrow rather than full, and the serifs were thin lines that were not attached to the stem (no bracketing). The serifs ended in sharp right angles.

The Modern style faces of Bodoni and Didot were also possibly influenced by the engraver's tool, which is a thin, pointed stylus used for working on metal plates. The refinement of this tool may have allowed for the creation of more precise letterforms. This type has a classical feel to it because of the geometric precision of the characters. Modern typefaces had come as far as they could from the hand-lettered Old Style faces, which had little contrast between thick and thin lines, and had heavily bracketed serifs and a slanted stress. The new faces were very mechanical and sharply defined, with contrasting thick and thin stroke weights with extra thin, flat serifs and the vertical stress to the letters of Didot and Bodoni.

Considered a Modern Style face, Bodoni's face has extreme differences in the weights of the thick stem and the fine hairline strokes; no bracketing of the serifs; and strong vertical stress to the letters. The lowercase letters that have a small x-height in proportion to the cap height, letters that are narrower rather than fuller, and ascenders that are the same height as the capital letters.

These geometrically based faces mark the move toward the appearance of mechanization; no longer is there an organic quality to the characters. Bodoni designed his type by repeating some basic shapes.

THE DAWN OF INDUSTRIALIZATION

The close of the 1700s was marked by political revolutions in America and France and the transition from an agrarian and hand-crafted economy to a mechanized and mass-produced one. It seemed in some industries that the transition happened overnight, and families were forced to sell their farmland and move to cities when their farming livelihood was threatened. The change had dramatic effects on the society, the art, the writing and the economy of the time. The change to the Industrial Age was littered with many unemployed, many overworked, and a few wealthy factory owners. It will be interesting in our own era to compare the industrial transition to the technological transition our societies are now experiencing.

The 1800s ushered in the Industrial Age with a frenzy. Every possible application of steam power to allow faster production of goods was applied. English slums grew at a staggering rate as workers who had previously earned a subsistence living on meager farms moved to the cities, and the squalid conditions were exacerbated by this overcrowding. A middle class emerged from this revolution, and the overall standard of living of all classes was raised during this period due to the mass reproduction of goods.

Wealth was no longer measured in land owned. During the Industrial Age, wealth was measured in capital, that is the amount of money one had invested in machinery or factories to produce goods. The growing urban population created a demand for the goods produced and also comprised the workforce that enabled the production. With the increased production of goods, there was also an increase in the need for printed materials to advertise the goods. Mass production, or breaking down the manufacturing process into component parts, became the standard in factories. In the early part of the century, the efficiency of steam-powered engines was applied to the field of printing.

THE GROWTH OF NATIONAL IDENTITIES

This was also the era of Napoleon's rise to power, and his attempts to militarily take over all of Europe. He was defeated by Wellington at Waterloo in 1815. In 1860 Italy was united as one nation, and Germany was unified under Bismark in 1870. Most European countries had colonized distant lands in an effort to gain cheap raw materials and in the interest of "Christianizing" the natives. Railroads and steamships cut down travel time, and the telephone and telegraph were introduced in this century. Employment was sometimes shaky in this new industrial economy. Workers were sometimes replaced by machinery that was faster, or they were let go when production was too high and had to be slowed.

FOURDRINIER'S WOOD PULP PAPER MACHINE

In about 1803 Henry Fourdrinier in England engineered a continuous-roll, paper-making machine which revolutionized the manufacturing

4-26. Firmin Didot, working in France about the same time as Bodoni, designed the Modern font Diderot.

AVIS

AUX SOUSCRIPTEURS

DE

LA GERUSALEMME

LIBERATA

IMPRIMÉE PAR DIDOT L'AÎNÉ

SOUS LA PROTECTION ET PAR LES ORDRES

DE MONSIEUR.

LES ARTISTES choisis par MONSIEUR pour exécuter son édition de LA GERUSALEMME LIBERATA demandent avec confiance aux souscripteurs de cet ouvrage un délai de quelques mois pour en mettre au jour la première livraison. Il est rarement arrivé qu'un ouvrage où sont entrés les ornements de la gravure ait pu être donné au temps préfix pour lequel il avoit été promis : cet art entraîne beaucoup de difficultés qui causent des retards forcés ; et certainement on peut regarder comme un empêchement insurmontable les jours courts et obscurs d'un hiver long et rigoureux. D'ailleurs la quantité d'ouvrages de gravure proposés actuellement par

4-27. Didot's type layouts were as sparse and understated as his typographic design. Notice the simple placement of elements and harmonious balance of the page.

Plus beau, plus fortuné, toujours cher à la paix,
Ton règne ami des lois doit briller d'âge en âge;
Tous nos droits affermis signalent tes bienfaits.
Le ciel t'a confié les destins de la France:

4-28. Above is an example of Didot's Modern font.

This page is set in Hardwood 8.5/12.

4 Colonial & Industrialized Typography

4-29 Copperplate engraving allowed for the detailed shadowing on this raised letter.

4-30. This engraving shows the use of a cylinder press used in the printing process.

4-31. Letter writing was a popular past time of the wealthy Victorians. Fine handwriting was a sign of leisure and fine education.

This page is set in Hardwood 8.5/12.

4-32. This font, called Crayon, uses a linear pattern to create a gray tone.

4-33. This font, known as Karnac, uses curlicues to give a decorative sensibility that was popular in the advertising of Victorian and industrial products.

4-34. Called Heather Lightface, this font features swirls and unusual finials to add elegance and uniqueness to the overall face.

4-35. This font, Arboret, is a fanciful Victorian font. Such fonts were tremendously popular during the Industrial Revolution. The garlands and details refer to abstracted elements from nature, something too rarely enjoyed by the new urban factory workers.

4-36. William Caslon IV's sans serif font was unpopular at first and nicknamed grotesque because of the lack of the familiar serifs.

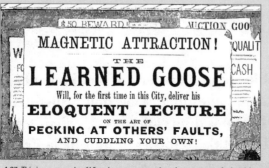

4-37. This is an example of Victorian era posters, the primary means of advertising events and products. Often these typographic posters were placed on top of each other.

of paper. Previously paper had been made one sheet at a time, by hand out of old rags. This was slow and expensive, and the final product was not uniform. This old type of paper had to be printed damp in order for it to be soft enough to be pushed against the metal type. By 1840, a process was developed to make paper out of wood (rather than rags) in one long, continuous sheet. Now paper was cheap and plentiful, and consistent enough in weight that it could easily be put through a press. (Today there is experimentation making paper from bamboo, considered an expendable weed.)

MECHANIZATION OF PRINTING

In printing, mechanical innovations were speeding up the field; in 1814, two steam presses which printed 1,100 sheets an hour were built by Friedrich Koenig for *The Times* of London. Before that, on a hand-operated press, 250 sheets per hour was considered fast. The steam press increased the rate of production of a newspaper by over 400%. This was the beginning of making inking rollers and curved plates. Presses were soon running out thousands of pages per hour. By 1851 the Hoe rotary press ran 20,000 sheets per hour, and by 1960 the rate was 70,000 or more complete newspapers per hour which are 96-pages long and 8 columns wide. This explosion in the quantity of reading material made it more affordable to the general public, greatly reduced illiteracy and satiated the public's growing appetite for the printed word.

INTRODUCTION OF SANS SERIF FONTS

Although the serifs on type had been added by the ancient Romans (the original form of the Greek and Phoenician letters was sans serif), all printed type had been serif up until the 1800s. The introduction of William Caslon IV's sans serif type in 1816 was referred to as "grotesque" in Europe and "Gothic" in America because it had a barbaric look due to its strangeness. But, by 1832, the novelty had worn off, and Stephenson Blake produced a broad range of sans serif faces that were popular in the U.S.

A NEW ERA IN TYPOGRAPHY: ADVERTISING

The year 1820 could be considered the boundary between type functioning primarily for the dissemination of information (with tasteful "book faces" predominating) and the use of type in "display faces." Also, at this point, the Industrial Revolution's impact on the printing industry was felt, and it became a more mechanized as opposed to a handiwork field. Around 1820, the world, and America in particular, was expanding economically and industrially at a rate no one had ever known before. Society was changing dramatically; immigrants to America were rapidly absorbed into the workforce and exploited as a cheap labor force.

To serve the needs of this growing industrial power, advertising was demanding more unusual "display faces" for use on the posters, stationary, catalogues, time tables, trade cards, labels and other necessities of a manufacturing and marketing economy. Because of the increase in printed matter, posters had to scream out their messages in a crowded visual environment. The classic typefaces designed for reading books were not suited for shouting about a merchant's wares. Soon variations of fancy fonts became the norm in advertising, and large typefaces (2″ and 3″ tall) cut from wood were required for the increased size of headlines. (Wood was used for display type because it was cheaper and lighter in weight than lead at large sizes.) Sans serif types were often incorporated into posters because they were thick and heavy and added blackness to the page, calling attention to the message.

New type forms were developed for advertising, with thick black strokes and heavy slab serifs. These fonts acquired the name "Egyptian" because of England's preoccupation with the archaeological discoveries going on at the time along the Nile. These faces had stems and slab serifs of nearly equal weight, making them especially visible in advertising broadsides.

This is one of the first times that the needs of advertising had an impact on the world of type design. Formerly changes in typefaces were due to the limitations or freedoms allowed by the tools and materials at hand, printing considerations, or aesthetic judgments of the type designers; now advertising's needs were determining the appearance of typography. The P.T. Barnum style of type, with swelled, stretched, three-dimensional letters incised, flowered and shaded to catch the attention of the buying public soon became the norm. Typical characteristics of Egyptian typefaces are a visual evenness of weight; little or no bracketing between stem and serif; thick, square, slab serifs; short ascenders and descenders; and a tall x-height of the lowercase letters.

THE PRACTICAL WRITING MACHINE

Around this same time, the typewriter was being refined as a mechanical instrument. It would eventually become the writing machine of choice for secretaries in business, replacing the writing of neat records by hand and composing of business correspondence by hand, which was what most of the male secretaries did in those days. A primitive typewriter was patented in 1714, but it was not until 1829 that William Austin Burt patented a practical writing machine in the U.S. The earliest models produced only capital letters and primarily embossed the letters; they were primarily considered a tool for the blind.

The typefaces for the refined machines resembled Bodoni, but the thin serifs did not allow the operator to make good quality multiple copies. The mechanics of the typewriter also created an identical space for an "i" as for a "W." Typefaces in which all the characters are allotted equal space regardless of their own width are known as *monospace*. The monospacing of the letters on the page did not allow for a fluid motion of reading and produced an uneven staccato rhythm in words. To counteract this, the serifs of thin letters were extended to fill the space allotted to each character. This new lettering designed specifically for the typewriter became known as Pica. The marketing of the typewriter has frequently been compared to the proliferation of personal computers that became popular in the 1980s.

4-38. The Industrial Revolution relied on posters for all types of advertising. They were the mass media of the era.

4-39. With the prepackaging of foods, labels and product identities became important for consumers in the marketplace.

4-40. This font, Coffee Can, was quite popular on circus and all advertising posters, and still resonates with circus associations today.

4-41. Tall, vertical fonts were cut out of wood; originally used on promotional posters, these have exaggerated serifs that add a darkness to the page.

4-42. The typewriter allowed people to create finished looking documents more easily.

4-43. Early mechanical typewriters were found in every office, with male secretaries.

4-44. Above is a version of Pica, a monospaced font designed for typewriters; notice the extension of serifs on the narrower characters.

This page is set in
Times Roman 8.5/12.

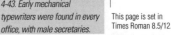

4 Colonial &
Industrialized
Typography

4-45. Detailed packaging was popular during the Victorian era. Products that were not essential had to create a reason to be desired in the minds of consumers.

4-46 Many elixirs (cure-alls) were marketed during the Victorian era. These herbal remedies relied on alcohol as an ingredient.

4-47. On many early labels, type appears to be fitted together like a jigsaw puzzle, filling every nook and cranny.

4-48. On this example of Victorian packaging, the type is very clear and legible, even though numerous banners make up the areas that type is placed in.

4-49. In this engraving of composers at work, it is interesting that there is a Victorian era woman setting type alongside the man.

Typewriters allowed individuals for the first time in history to create finished, printed-looking documents in the privacy of their own homes or offices. Oddly enough, the first secretaries were exclusively male (few women worked at this time in history), and there were highly publicized typing competitions to see who could type the fastest–sort of an Olympics of the business office!

Typing caught on very quickly, and began the decline of the scribe for the writing of legal and court documents. In a few decades, typewriters were in many offices. It was only with the invention of the electric typewriter in 1935 that *variable* spacing became an option and type designers were free to invent new letterforms for the typewriter. As the typewriters could accommodate subtler adjustments of spacing and replaceable heads allowed the changing of typefaces, the desire to create faces for it was stimulated. This was an example of technology determining the form that typefaces took, rather than the materials or the marketplace determining the appearance of fonts as they had in prior times.

STONE/CHROMOLITHOGRAPHY PRINTING

Although invented around 1796 by Aloys Senefelder, the lithographic process was implemented at the beginning of the 1900s as a commercial printing tool. This printing style was based on the principle that water and grease do not mix. The image was drawn with a grease marker onto the stone. The stone was then coated with a mixture of water and gum arabic. This did not adhere to the grease image, but did adhere to the rest of the stone. When the oil-based ink was applied to the surface of the stone, it adhered only to the image area, which could then be printed.

Because the artist or designer drew directly onto the stone, this method of printing allowed a great deal of freedom and spontaneity in type design, as well as wider use of multiple colors. The tradition of decorative initial capitals that goes back to the days of Medieval manuscripts was revived in chromo-lithographic printing, as was hand lettering in general. Lithography was used for many of the theatrical posters of this era, which were lavish and colorful to attract viewers. Type could gracefully curve and sweep across labels and posters with ease thanks to stone lithography. Whimsical initial capitals were popular with the lithographic process, and there were often quite a few stones used in the production of one piece. As many as ten or twelve different ink colors were used in a single piece!

THE USE OF WOOD TYPE

As the size of type increased for visual impact on posters, the weight and cost of the lead type became expensive, and was difficult to cast at these larger sizes. In 1827 an American named Darius Wells produced large hand-cut wooden type, and later a router that could cut the wood type more quickly and accurately. Wood type made the production of large scale type less costly, and it was lighter to handle on the press. Wood type meant that there was no limit to the size of the type that could be printed, and larger was better. Frequently posters were printed in condensed and extended typefaces so that all the lines were of an even length. Posters were very popular at this time for advertising; they were the mass media of the era. Town ordinances eventually limited the numbers, the size and the places for posting them.

THE VICTORIAN INFLUENCE ON TYPE DESIGN

The last half of the 1800s is referred to as the Victorian era, after Queen Victoria who ascended the British throne at eighteen years old in 1837. She ruled the United Kingdom until 1901. This era was marked with strong moral and religious beliefs, optimism, and attention to social conventions and manners. There was a naive sweetness and romance to this era, which likely reflects the sentiment of the youthful queen. This time was known for its more tender attitude toward youth, and marked the wide publication of picture books for children. There was a love for detail and intricacy of design that can be seen in everything from architecture, to furniture, to clothing, to graphic design styles. Some of the Victorian taste for decoration can be nauseating when overdone, or a magnificent display of craftsmanship when carefully applied. This taste for unnecessary decoration was eventually rebelled against by the subsequent artistic movements whose followers were seeking more contemporary, functionality-driven design.

When the Victorian aesthetic was applied to type design, the result was not always promising. The love for minute detail with flowers, leaves, and ribbons frequently led to typefaces that were filigreed and embellished, and some that were difficult to read. Designed primarily for use on posters, many of the faces were successful in catching the viewer's eye. There were some innovations in the forms of letters that were quite beautiful, and faces that harkened back to lettering detailing of the Middle Ages.

Many Victorian faces feature curlicues, natural leafy decoration, or ornamentation similar to that found in the architecture of the era. Some historians believe that type designers of this era form a bridge to the typographers in the Arts and Crafts Movement, because both groups of craftsmen value the Medieval workmanship and a certain level of decorative ornamentation.

Most of the faces from this Victorian era are used only in limited applications today. They are considered specialty or novelty faces, well suited for initial capitals or headlines; their poor readability often prohibits their use for extended body copy.

The faces that are considered the "workhorse" faces are those that have stood the test of time and are still visually appealing and easy to read. These standardized faces are more challenging to design. But the Victorian specialty fonts can be used very effectively in logo design, poster design, and headlines when the visual association with the Victorian era is the goal. Because they are not seen often, they stand out as unique and call attention to themselves, which can be very effective in design.

4-50. With the advent of wood type, extremely tall, condensed fonts such as this one, Tombola, were designed that could fit entire phrases on one line, and stand out in the visual-poster environment.

4-51. Also cut from wood were the very wide fonts such as this one, Lambada, with thick slab serifs, called Egyptian fonts. These fonts enabled poster designers to use one word to take up an entire line of a poster.

Colonial & Industrialized Typography 4

4-55. This historic drawing shows a woman operating a platen style, sheet-fed letterpress.

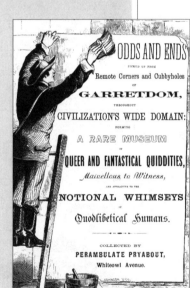

4-52. On this poster, notice the variety of fonts that are used to draw the eyes of the passersby. Fonts of varying widths were used to make all of the lines justified.

4-53. The posting of oversized advertisements to catch the public's attention was a common occupation.

4-54. These wonderfully ornate initial caps are intricately designed with Victorian patterning.

This page is set in Times Roman 8.5/12.

4 *Colonial &*
Industrialized
Typography

4-56. The detailed shaded, filigreed character above would not have been possible without the refined control of copperplate engraving because this fine detail was too small to cast in lead.

4-57. Eventually, cameras became more compact, like the one above, and they were cheaper and more widely available.

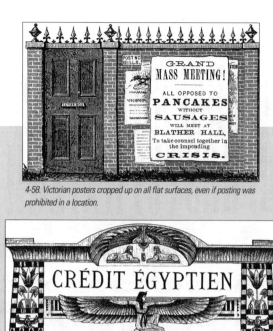

4-58. Victorian posters cropped up on all flat surfaces, even if posting was prohibited in a location.

4-59. This example of a Victorian logo shows the fascination with the excavations that were taking place along the Nile River in Africa during this era.

4-60. As late as 1841, this Pennsylvania Dutch calendar uses Textura for the cover.

4-61. This calendar cover from 1873 shows the use of Gothic Textura as preferred for Germanic areas late into the 1870s

4-62. Photography was popular and democratized family portraits; subjects had to stay still for a few minutes with the model above.

4-63. The first mass-marketed Kodak camera was developed in 1888. It was a box-type camera like the one above and sold for $25 and could be used for 100 pictures.

4-64. Negatives were originally developed with a wet developing process which was later simplified with dry plates.

THE USE OF THE CAMERA IN DOCUMENTING THE CIVIL WAR

The last half of the nineteenth century also marks the Civil War from 1861 to 1865 in the U.S., and the Reconstruction era in the south. Although ostensibly the reason for the war was opposition to race-based slavery, it was also caused by the industrial economic base of the north conflicting with the plantation economic system of the south. In short, the factories were in need of cheap labor. The Civil War was the first war to be documented on still film, and firsthand accounts of the battles were carried in newspapers. One million American men were lost in the war, the largest U.S. war casualties of any other armed conflict. Some credit this war with the advent of photojournalism and the craving for immediate documentation of news. The distribution of dailies, or newspapers, was broadened by the desire for updated news of the war front, and numerous presses cropped up to meet the demand.

The industrialization of the printing process enabled books and newspapers to be produced faster, which ultimately lowered the price. During the Industrial Revolution in the U.S., immigrants were absorbed into low-paying factory jobs that required little training. In the near future, the 20th century would bring two world wars, the invention of electricity, and the mass ownership of the automobile, the Great Depression, women's suffrage, the Civil Rights Movement and the Vietnam War.

4-65. This title page from 1900 shows the use of classical elements.

4-66. This title page from 1899 uses a sparse layout with Greek-inspired ornaments and clean type.

PROJECT: DESIGN A VICTORIAN POLITICAL TYPE POSTER

Your project is to design a Victorian styled typographic political poster. Select a political person who is very well known and whose name is broadly recognized. This person can be from history or from current-day events. You will need at least one image for reference of this person. Write a list of at least forty words to describe this person. The words can even be phrases or accomplishments that the person is known for. They can be personal words or terms that relate to the person's professional accomplishments in Congress, or abroad. You are free to choose a current or former president, first lady, any member of Congress, a well-known governor, or an international leader of another country from current-day politics or from history.

Your goal is to create a Victorian-styled advertising poster for the person. There must be at least ten terms or phrases to describe this person. Choose the terms for their honest evaluation of the politician, or poke fun at him/her. Do a simple caricature of the person to use somewhere in the poster. Integrate the caricature of the person with the type in a creative manner. The objective of this project is to get you to think about the appropriateness of fonts for the person, as well as for words, and to pay attention to spacing fonts, considering kerning and ligatures.

Set up the terms on the computer; others can be photocopied together from fonts that you find in books in the library. You can give your poster a very Victorian feel or it can feel more contemporary. You will be working in black, white and gray only. The final size will be 9" x 17" in a vertical format. You will likely have to set up a simple mechanical, and then photocopy your original 11" x 17" paper. Feel free to use any rules, ornaments or dingbats that you find, or create your own. However, you may want these flourishes to resonate with the sense of the person and their era.

Try not to stretch and squish fonts on the computer. Your poster should have some small and some tall lines, as you can see in the poster samples in this chapter. After research at the library, begin by doing a series of fifteen thumbnail sketches. Next, decide on the words, and trace them in a variety of fonts. Finally photocopy the tracings, and paste them together to make two half-sized roughs. Select one, and create it full-sized.

OBJECTIVES

- To encourage careful attention to the kerning nuances of different typefaces.
- To look at various letter combinations and the spacing challenges they propose.
- To examine the same letter combinations in different typefaces.
- To analyze appropriate fonts for interpretive value.
- To encourage the use exclusively of type to convey an idea.
- To introduce type as a visual communication medium.
- To think of type as an interpretive, expressive medium.

4-67. This poster, by KU student Rhonda Schmig, captures the essence of the type sensibility of Teddy Roosevelt's era. The integration of the tall and short areas of type work well to create an overall unity. Even the ruled dividers are carefully selected in keeping with the historic period.

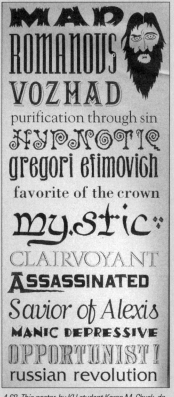

4-68. This poster, by KU student Karen M. Chuck, describes Rasputin using the Victorian poster style.

This page is set in ITC Fenice Light 8.5/12.

Colonial & Industrialized Typography-Review

1. What is the Romaine du Roi, and who designed it? _____

_____

2. How do copperplate engraving and letterpress printing differ? _____

_____

3. How does the printing technology affect the appearance of typefaces? _____

_____

4. Who was William Caslon? _____

_____

5. What was significant about the font he designed? _____

6. Who was John Baskerville? _____

7-8. Name two of John Baskerville's accomplishments (other than type design). _____

_____

9. What was significant about the font that he designed? _____

10. Who is Bodoni, and what is significant about the font that he designed? _____

_____

11. What typographic changes came about as a result of the Industrial Revolution? _____

_____

12. What are Egyptian fonts, and why did they gain popularity in the early 19th century? _____

_____

13. What are sans serif fonts? _____

14. How were they accepted when they were first introduced? _____

15. How did the development of the typewriter affect typographic design? _____

_____

16. How did the Industrial Revolution affect the production of books? _____

_____

17. How would you describe Victorian fonts? _____

18. What are the measurement systems for fonts? _____

_____

19. How did the refinement of offset lithography affect the appearance of typography? _____

_____

20. How did the Industrial Revolution affect the visual environment of the people living at the time? _____

_____

21. What are some of the changes that were resolved in the writing of the English language by the end of the 1700s? _____

_____

22. Why was refined handwriting considered so important by the aristocracy during the 1600s? _____

_____

23. After books were printed, what were scribes employed for? _____

_____

24. Why is type on early typewriters compared to computers? _____

_____

25. How was the first sans serif type accepted? What was it called? _____

_____

26. Why did Darius Wells create a machine to cut type out of wood? _____

Parts of a Character

This page is set in
Bookman Light 8.5/12

Roman

5-1. **Roman face**—*denotes the upright, vertical position of a letter,
as opposed to a slanted, italic form; type fonts based on the design
of ancient Roman capitals.*

Uppercase

5-2. **Uppercase**—*capital letters, historically placed in the upper of the two
drawers used in hand composition of lead type; also called majuscule.*

Lowercase

5-3. **Lowercase**—*small letterforms, originating from the semi-uncial lettering style;
includes ascenders and descenders. The name comes from the placement of the letterpress case of small letters in the lower of the two wooden type cases used by
hand compositors; the small letters were placed so that they were within hands'
reach, also called lc, or miniscule.*

INTRODUCTION

In this chapter, we review the names of specific
parts of letters. Knowing the names of the parts of
characters is essential for a designer who will communicate with typesetters, other designers and
clients in the future. When you need to explain why
you've chosen a particular font for a headline or for
body copy, it can be very helpful to use the correct
terminology to describe the parts of the letters that
resonate with certain associations. Also, in the
process of learning the names of the different parts
of a character, you will begin to notice the subtle differences in how a particular area is structured or
transitions from one shape to the next. This, in
turn, leads to a fuller appreciation of fonts in general, and it improves your ability to discern one
font from another, by noting and appreciating these
distinguishing details.

Learning the details of type is also the initiation
of a designer—the opportunity to learn a new lexi-
con and to become familiar with the jargon of the field.
If words indeed make our reality, then knowing the
vocabulary of typography is necessary for designers
who are using type as the paint on their canvas.

BENEFITS OF KNOWING TYPE DETAILS

Knowing the details of type allows you to speak
with confidence about a font selection and justify
your decision articulately. You will eventually develop
your own typographic sense, deciding which fonts
you prefer, the font that you feel is effective, and the
fonts that you find emotive. Long before you get to
this point, you will have to begin to look at type more
critically, understanding why a designer chose a
particular font, and analyzing how well you think it
has been used or how you would change it. In order
to recognize fonts more readily, you must come to
know the parts of a character very well so that you

*Parts of a
Character*

5

can compare the nuances of one face to another. Minute details in serifs can determine the difference between a font appearing elegant, engineered, or casual. You will likely attribute personalities to fonts that you become familiar with. You may even find yourself sketching out your own font at some point in the future!

ROMAN AND ITALIC

These two styles of fonts are easily distinguished: italic is always slanted, or sheered, to the right. Many typophiles argue that you can tell the true quality of a font by examining the italic and its relationship to the Roman face. The italic should retain a sense of the Roman and its style, but it should also be distinctly different from the Roman, incorporating the hooked finials, the descender on the "f"-curved terminals and some loops in characters. Maintaining the essence of the font, yet creating an italic that harmonizes with the Roman is not an easy task.

UPPERCASE AND LOWERCASE ASCENDERS AND DESCENDERS

Upper- and lowercase letters are distinguished by the presence of ascenders and descenders. The capitals are all the same height. The ascender line and the cap height line may be the same in some fonts; sometimes the caps are a bit shorter than the ascenders.

Ascenders are the parts of the strokes of a font that extend above the waist line or x-height line of the font. *Descenders* are the parts of strokes of letters that extend below the base line of a font. Ascenders and descenders are found only in the lowercase letters of an alphabet. They help readers to recognize words more easily due to the distinct shapes created when they are combined into words.

HAIRLINE STROKE AND STEM STROKE

The *hairline stroke* of a character is the thinner of the strokes. The *stem stroke* is the thicker or main stroke of a letter. The design of the transition from the hairline to the stem stroke often gives a font much of its unique appearance.

SERIFS, BRACKETING, AND SANS SERIF TERMINALS

Serifs are the "feet" that you see on the bottom of the letters that you are reading. They are extensions from the strokes of letters. Serifs are thought to be retained from the days when type was cut into stone with a chisel, but this is debated. Serifs come in many

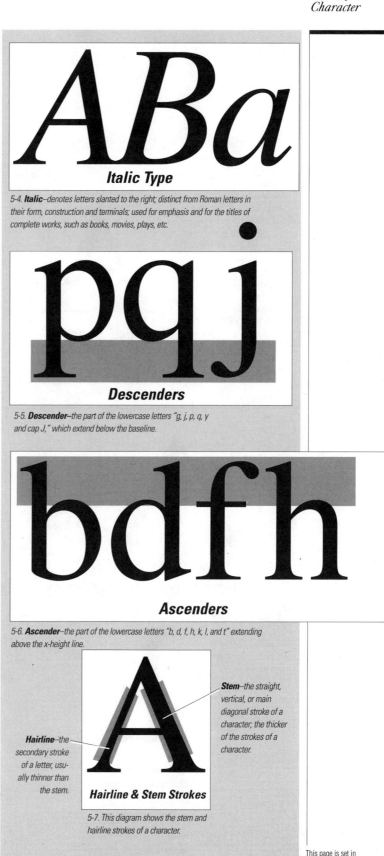

Italic Type

5-4. **Italic**—denotes letters slanted to the right; distinct from Roman letters in their form, construction and terminals; used for emphasis and for the titles of complete works, such as books, movies, plays, etc.

Descenders

5-5. **Descender**—the part of the lowercase letters "g, j, p, q, y and cap J," which extend below the baseline.

Ascenders

5-6. **Ascender**—the part of the lowercase letters "b, d, f, h, k, l, and t" extending above the x-height line.

Stem—the straight, vertical, or main diagonal stroke of a character; the thicker of the strokes of a character.

Hairline—the secondary stroke of a letter, usually thinner than the stem.

Hairline & Stem Strokes

5-7. This diagram shows the stem and hairline strokes of a character.

This page is set in Bookman Light 8.5/12.

5 *Parts of a*
   Character

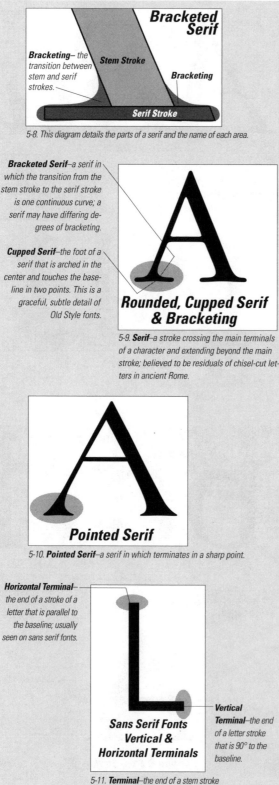

Bracketed Serif

Bracketing– the transition between stem and serif strokes.

Stem Stroke

Bracketing

Serif Stroke

5-8. This diagram details the parts of a serif and the name of each area.

Bracketed Serif–a serif in which the transition from the stem stroke to the serif stroke is one continuous curve; a serif may have differing degrees of bracketing.

Cupped Serif–the foot of a serif that is arched in the center and touches the base-line in two points. This is a graceful, subtle detail of Old Style fonts.

Rounded, Cupped Serif & Bracketing

5-9. **Serif**–a stroke crossing the main terminals of a character and extending beyond the main stroke; believed to be residuals of chisel-cut letters in ancient Rome.

Pointed Serif

5-10. **Pointed Serif**–a serif in which terminates in a sharp point.

Horizontal Terminal– the end of a stroke of a letter that is parallel to the baseline; usually seen on sans serif fonts.

Vertical Terminal–the end of a letter stroke that is 90° to the baseline.

Sans Serif Fonts Vertical & Horizontal Terminals

5-11. **Terminal**–the end of a stem stroke of a character; different types: sheared, straight, acute, horizontal, ball, convex, concave, rounded, flared, hooked, tapered, and pointed.

This page is set in Bookman Light 8.5/12.

different sizes and shapes; they can be rounded, pointed, tapered, slab, or ruled. The base of a serif can be flat, or it can be arched or "cupped."

Sans serif fonts do not have serifs; their strokes end in square or rounded or or splayed or angled terminals. Sans means "without" in French, so they are "without" serifs. The ends of sans serif strokes are called *terminals.*

Bracketing is the design of the area that attaches the serif to the stroke of the letter. A serif can be bracketed or not. Bracketing is not essential. There can be heavy bracketing on a serif or very little bracketing. Only serif fonts have bracketing; sans serif fonts do not since they do not have serifs. Bracketing is also a means of discerning one font from another. Once you start to recognize fonts, you can often use bracketing to check which font you are looking at.

BODY HEIGHT, X-HEIGHT, WAIST LINE, MEAN LINE

The *body* of a character is the part of a letters that falls between the baseline and the *waist line,* or *x-height line.* The x-height line is considered the height of the lowercase letters. The "x" is used to measure the body of a font because it touches both the base-line and the waist line in two flat terminals. The x-height is important to know when it comes to evaluating the readability of a font. The x-height line is also referred to as the *mean line* of the font.

STRESS OR BIAS OF A FONT

The *stress,* or *bias,* of a font is the angle determined by the direction of the thicker stem strokes of a Roman character. The angle or obliqued stress was historically caused by the flat tipped pen held at a consistent angle. The thickest area of the stroke is referred to as the maximum stress of the letter. The maximum stress of a character is often not directly parallel in serif typefaces, due to the angle of the stress.

Most sans serif fonts also have a stress, but it is sometimes less pronounced than in serif fonts, which have a more clearly defined stem and hairline stroke.

BOWLS, CROTCHES AND COUNTERS IN A FONT

The *bowl* of a letter is the round stroke that encloses space. The bowl is the term used for the stroke, and the *counter* is the term used for the space that is enclosed. If the bowl stroke touches a stem stroke, it creates a closed counter, as for example, in "a b, d, g, o, p, or q." If, however, the bowl does not touch a stem stroke, it creates an open counter, as in "a c, e, f, h, j, m, n, s, or u."

Even angled strokes can create counters, as in a "v, w, x, y, or z." Counters can be open or closed depending on the letter. The *crotch* is the term for the interior space created by the juncture of two angled strokes of a character, as in the "K, M, N, V, W, X, Y, and Z." An *acute crotch* is an angle of less than 90°, an *obtuse crotch* is when the strokes of a character meet at an angle greater than 90°.

APEXES AND VERTEXES

The *apex* of a letter is the area where two upward-pointing angled strokes come together. The apex of a character usually extends slightly past the cap line to make it optically appear the same height as other letters. There are different types of apexes, for example, pointed, rounded, sheared, hallowed, and flat.

The *vertex* of a letter is the inverse of the apex; it is the juncture of two downward slanting strokes. The vertex also has a number of variations, such as the flat, sheared, pointed or rounded versions. Remember the vertex is the term for the outside of the stroke juncture, and the crotch is the term for the interior of the juncture.

ARMS AND LEGS IN TYPE

Arms and legs are the names of parts of letters that extend out from the main stroke of the letter and are free on the terminal end. The strokes that extend out either straight or are angled upward are called the *arms* of the character. The strokes that extend downward from the stem of the letter are called *legs*. You will notice that these terms are given to extensions that are similar to our own appendages.

X–Height line, Waist line or Mean line—*this line defines the height of the body of the lowercase letters. The lowercase x is used to determine this line because it meets the waist line at two flat areas.*

Baseline—*this is the line on which the bases of all the letters align.*

Body height—*the distance from the base line to the x-height line.*

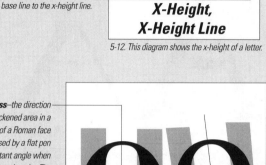

X-Height, X-Height Line

5-12. This diagram shows the x-height of a letter.

Vertical Stress—*the direction of the thickened area in a curved stroke of a Roman face initially caused by a flat pen held at a constant angle when making a curved stroke. The thickest point is the "maximum stress."*

Biased Stress—*the direction of the thick strokes and curves in a typeface is called either biased, oblique or slanted. The biased stress of italic faces is usually at a greater angle than Roman faces.*

Vertical & Biased Stress

5-13. The stress of a character is the direction of the thick strokes.

Open Counter—*the partially enclosed space within a character that is open on one end; for example, the white space in a "c, h, m, n, u, v, w, or y."*

Crotch—*the interior space formed by the joint of two strokes of a character, as in a "K, L, M, N, V, W, X, Y, or Z;" an acute crotch is less than 90°, obtuse crotch is more than 90°.*

Closed Counter Space—*the enclosed area formed within a bowl of a letter; for example, in an "a, b, d, g, o, p, or q."*

Open & Closed Counters

5-14. This diagram compares open and closed counters.

Closed Bowl—*the curved stroke that makes a fully enclosed space within a character; the curved stroke meets the stem; for example in an "a, b, B, d, D, g, p, P, R, or q."*

Open Bowl—*the curved stroke that makes a partially enclosed space within a character; the curve does not meet with the stem completely.*

Closed & Open Bowls

5-15. The examples above compare open and closed bowls.

This page is set in Bookman Light 8.5/12.

5 *Parts of a
Character*

Flat Apex   **Pointed Apex**   **Extended Apex**   **Hallowed Apex**   **Rounded Apex**

A A A A A

Apex–Flat, Pointed, Extended, Hallowed, Rounded

5-16. **Apex**–*upper point of letters with an ascending pointed form–this point usually extends past the cap line; examples of different types: rounded, pointed, hallowed, flat, extended.*

Vertex

5-17. **Vertex**–*the downward pointing, free-ending juncture of two angled stems; the point touches just below the baseline. Examples of different types of vertices: rounded, pointed, hallow flat, extended, found on the letters "w" and "v."*

Arm–*the horizontal or diagonal upward-sloping stroke that attaches to the stem and is free on one end.*

EYKR

Arms and Legs of Letters

5-18. *This diagram shows the arms and legs of type characters.*

Leg–*the downward-angled stroke that is attached to the stem on one end and is free on the other terminal end.*

EARS AND SPURS IN TYPE

An *ear* in type is the small terminal stroke (sometimes rounded or tear-dropped) projecting from the top of lowercase Roman "g, r, f, and a." The ears are different from one font to the next, and they can be used to distinguish fonts.

A *spur* is a small stroke that connects the curved stroke to the vertical stroke in the uppercase "G." The spur usually has a small extension on it, which varies from font to font. Some fonts, particularly sans serif fonts, have little or no spur on the "G."

THE CROSS BAR AND THE CROSS STROKE

The *cross bar* in type is the horizontal stroke that connects two other strokes in a character. Both ends of the cross bar meet and are joined by a stem or hairline stroke.

The *cross stroke* is a horizontal stroke that intersects across one of the main strokes of the character, but is free on one or both ends. Usually cross bars and cross strokes are the same width as the hairline stroke of the font. Cross bars and cross strokes can be curved, angled, or stepped, depending on the font.

LOOPS, LINKS AND TAILS

A *loop* is the lower bowl or descender on the lowercase "g." The *link* is the stroke that connects the loop to the upper bowl in the lowercase "g."

The *tail* is the swashed stroke that differentiates an "O" from a "Q." The tail can be simple and functional, or magnificent and decorative.

Loops, links and tails are often good places to inspect a font for the idiosyncratic tendencies of a type designer. Frequently these parts of letters show a great sense of the personality of the type.

SPINES, EYES AND SHOULDERS IN TYPE

The *spine* is the name given to the sinewy, double curving stroke in the letter "s." The spine is often the thickest part of the letter "s." This term is easy to remember because the back of the "s" is shaped the same as the human spine.

The *eye* in type is the specific term given to the counter of the lowercase "e." The eye is very important to type designers because it is often the first area to plug up on press if the type is very small.

Shoulders are the name of the transition from the vertical to the curved stroke in letters. Shoulders are found in "f, h, j, m, n, and u." The design of the shoulders in a font is very subtle and the weight has to be refined perfectly to create an undistracting area. The shape of these transitions determines whether a font appears round, oval or squared off.

Ears

5-19. **Ear**–the small terminal stroke (sometimes rounded or tear-dropped) projecting from the top of lowercase Roman "g, r, f, and a."

Spur

5-20. **Spur**–the nodule descending from the vertical stroke of an uppercase "G"; it connects the straight to the curved stroke but is separate from both.

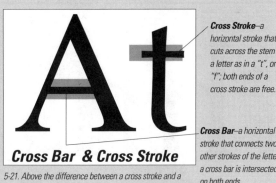

Cross Bar & Cross Stroke

Cross Stroke–a horizontal stroke that cuts across the stem of a letter as in a "t", or "f"; both ends of a cross stroke are free.

Cross Bar–a horizontal stroke that connects two other strokes of the letter; a cross bar is intersected on both ends.

5-21. Above the difference between a cross stroke and a cross bar is shown.

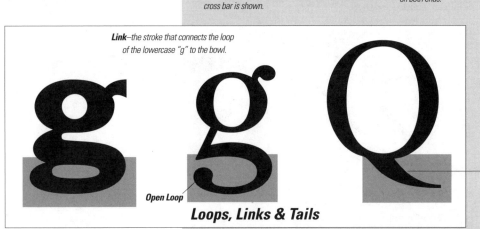

Link–the stroke that connects the loop of the lowercase "g" to the bowl.

Open Loop

Loops, Links & Tails

Tail–a downward sloping short stroke or arc of a character starting from the stem and ending free, as on an uppercase "Q." Sometimes, the legs of uppercase "R" and "K" are referred to as tails.

5-22. **Loop**–the lower portion of the Roman lowercase "g" distinguished from the bowl as a flourish rather than a necessary part of the letter.

This page is set in Bookman Light 8.5/12.

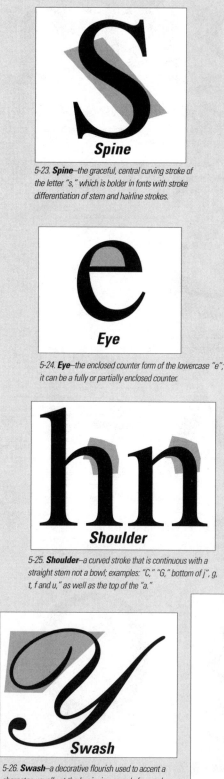

5-23. **Spine**–*the graceful, central curving stroke of the letter "s," which is bolder in fonts with stroke differentiation of stem and hairline strokes.*

5-24. **Eye**–*the enclosed counter form of the lowercase "e"; it can be a fully or partially enclosed counter.*

5-25. **Shoulder**–*a curved stroke that is continuous with a straight stem not a bowl; examples: "C," "G," bottom of j", g, t, f and u," as well as the top of the "a."*

5-26. **Swash**–*a decorative flourish used to accent a character, usually at the beginning or end of a word. Swashes can be curled, twisted, or graceful extensions added to letters to call attention to it.*

5-27. **Flags**–*the small swash-like strokes used on calligraphic fonts to add flourish to the vertical strokes.*

SWASHES AND FLAGS

A *swash* is a decorative flourish used to accent a character, usually at the beginning or end of a word. Swashes can be curled, twisted, or graceful extensions, added to letters to call attention to the letter and to provide a sense of elegance to the type. Swashes are often alternate characters in a script font.

A *flag* is the small swash-like strokes used on calligraphic fonts to add flourish to the vertical strokes. Flags are most often seen on black letter type fonts.

BEAKS AND BARBS

A *beak* is a half serif at the ends of an "E, F, L, or T." Beaks sometimes extend in two directions from the arm. Beaks are half serifs that are at the end of only straight strokes in letters.

A *barb* is a half serif found at the end of a curved stroke, such as a "C, G, or S." Barbs sometimes extend in both directions from the curved stroke.

TERMINALS

A *terminal* is the end of a stroke in a font. There are endless possibilities to the design of terminals. There can be flat, hallowed, rounded, sheared, teardrop, or angled terminals. The terminal determines much of the appearance of a sans serif font. The design of terminals is as specific to a sans serif font as the design of the serif is to a serifed font. In serif fonts, the ear of the "a" and the "c" are often ball or teardrop terminals.

POINT SIZE IN TYPE

The *point size in type* is the measure of the font. It comes from the days of lead type, when the slug that letters were cast on had to include space for the ascenders, the body and the descenders of all the letters. So, point size is measured from the ascender line to the descender line. Although the days of lead type are past, the point size is measured this same way, even on computers. Point size includes ascenders, the body and the descenders of a font. This may not seem logical at first, but it makes sense if you understand that lead type had to be cast in such a way that the baselines of all of the characters would line up.

KNOWING TYPE TERMINOLOGY

Knowing the names of the parts of type can help you if you are trying to find the right font for a job, or if you are looking for a specific design of a font from a supplier. Knowing these terms will allow you to talk about the details of the type accurately . . . whether with colleagues or with clients.

Parts of a
Character

Beaks

5-28. **Beak**—a half serif at the end of the horizontal arms of the "E, F, L, T or Z."

Barbs

5-29 **Barb**—a half serif at the end of the curved strokes of a "C, G or S."

Acute Terminal Teardrop Terminal Ball Terminal Sheared Terminal Vertical Terminal

Horizontal Terminal

Terminals: Acute, Teardrop, Ball, Sheared, Vertical, Horizontal

5-30. **Terminal**—the end of a stroke of a character; different types: sheared, straight, acute, horizontal, ball, convex, concave, flared, hooked, tapered and pointed terminals.

Ascender Line or Cap Line—the line that the caps and ascenders touch. (Sometimes these two lines are the same; sometimes, as in Old Style fonts, the caps are smaller than the ascenders.)

Baseline—the line along which the bases of the letters align.

Descender Line—the line which the descenders of a font touch.

POINT SIZE

Point Size

5-31. **Point Size**—is measured from the ascender line to the descender line. It includes the body of the letter as well as the ascenders and descenders.

This page is set in Bookman Light 8.5/12.

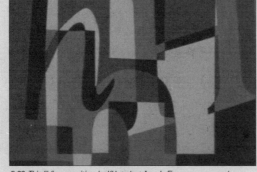

5-32. This composition of "L's," by KU student Todd Ritzman, accentuates the verticality of the structure of the letter "L."

5-33. This "h" composition, by KU student Angela Fies, uses grays and transparencies to create an almost Cubist sensibility to the overall piece.

5-35. This composition overlaps lowercase "g's" in a variety of gray tones.

5-34. This composition, based on "i," by KU student Eugene Yoder, uses transparencies and crisp, distinct areas of gray and black with angles to explore this project.

5-36. In this composition of "M's," the white space balances the positive dark areas.

PROJECT: DESIGN WITH ONE CHARACTER

The project is to design a creative layout using one character. It can be abstract or very organized. Choose one letter of the alphabet. Using both the capital and lowercase version of that letter, select one serif and one sans serif font. Enlarge the letters, and create an abstract pattern. You can blow up the letters on tracing paper, and use another piece of tracing paper to determine the layout by tracing the letters over one another. You can also enlarge them on the copy machine for the layout, but make sure that you have accurate drawings of the letters to work from.

Using either the italic or the Roman versions (and either upper- or lowercase letters), create your design using one letter. You have four versions of the letter in the serif face to work with, (Roman uppercase, Roman lowercase, italic uppercase, italic lowercase) and four versions of the letter in sans serif to incorporate into your design.

For example: if your letter is "F," use both lowercase or uppercase F from the serif and the sans serif, in italic and Roman. Create a design from at least five different F's.

You are limited to black, white and gray in your design. The final size will be 11″ x 17″, (either vertical or horizontal) and will be executed in cut paper. On an overlay, mark the names of the parts of the letters from the terms in this chapter.

Begin by doing 15 thumbnails of the design at a small size, drawn to scale. You need not use the entire letter in the design some of it can bleed off the paper. In fact, you may want to use only a small portion of the letter, but you cannot cut up or cut off the letter unless it is cut off by the edge of the sheet. You can overlap parts of letters, work with the shapes created from this overlapping, etc. You can apply transparency to overlapping parts of letters. The design can be random or highly stylized and organized. This should be an exciting, creative layout when you are done. The design should utilize the three colors effectively.

OBJECTIVES:

- To appreciate the detailed nuances of different typefaces.
- To view letters as forms, and experiment with combinations.
- To draw letters at the size type designers work.
- To utilize type as a visual element and an abstract design.
- To develop a design sensibility with abstract shapes.
- To design within a limited color palette.
- To experiment with random vs. planned design solutions.
- To balance the use of color/tone in the overall design.
- To examine the stroke variations in fonts when enlarged.

Parts of a Character-Review

1. What does Roman mean in relation to typography? _____

2. What does italic mean in relation to fonts? _____

3. What is uppercase in a font? _____

4. What is a descender? _____

_____

5. What is an ascender? _____

_____

6. What is the hairline stroke of a font? _____

_____

7. What is the stem stroke of a font? _____

_____

8. What is a serif? _____

_____

9. Name two different types of serifs. _____

10. What is bracketing? _____

_____

11. What is the x-height of a font, and from which lines is it measured? _____

_____

12. What is the bias or stress of a font? _____

13. What is a bowl in a character? _____

14. What is a counter in a letter? _____

_____

15. What are examples of letters that have crotches? _____

16. What is an apex? _____

17. Draw and label three different types of apexes.

18. What is a vertex? _____

19. What are an arm and a leg of type? _____

20. What is an ear in type? _____

21. What is a spur on a character? _____

22. What is a cross bar in type?   _____

23. What is a cross stroke in type?_____

24. What is a loop on a character? _____

25. What is a tail on a character? _____

26. What is the link of a character? _____

27. What is a spine of type? _____

28. What is an eye in type? _____

29. What is a shoulder in type? _____

30. What is a swash on a letter? _____

31. What are flags on a font? _____

32. What are beaks in relation to fonts? _____

33. Which characters have barbs? _____

34. What is a terminal in type? _____

35. Draw and label three different types of terminals.

36. How is the point size of a font measured, and from which line to which line? _____

37. Why is the point size of a font measured in this way? _____

20th Century Typography

INTRODUCTION

This chapter discusses type design, technological advancements and typographic innovations in the 20th century. By the end of the 1800s (nineteenth century), commercialism and the Industrial Revolution had crept into almost every aspect of American and European life. Some historians theorize that there is a great excitement and experimentation at the turn of a century, and certainly this was true of society at this time. Bauhaus and the Dada movements are not far in the future. The theory of evolution was published by Charles Darwin in his 1859 *Origin of Species*. By simply presenting the hypothesis that humans could have been descended from apes, he shocked Victorian society. There has been much controversy ever since. In psychology, Sigmund Freud was developing theories of the ego, super ego and id.

The steam locomotive had allowed both edges of the American continent to be joined, and the telegraph was a means of long distance, immediate communication. The Impressionists in France were changing the way we viewed art and reality. The world was changing at an unprecedented pace. This new era seemed to be marked by a relentless increase in speed, as if the world was on a drug. Products had to be made faster, travel had to be faster, information had to move faster . . . sort of similar to our own age. It can be dizzying to live in a society based on change and increasing speed.

THE ARTS & CRAFTS MOVEMENT

In contrast to the mass production of banal products, lacking in design, a group of artists formed the Art Workers' Guild in 1884 to create functional creations that were also aesthetic. This movement praised the work of individual craftsmen, and the artists were convinced that with the ever faster production of mass goods, aesthetic values, or design was compromised, and resulted in products that were ugly

6-1. William Morris, founder of the Kelmscott Press and an influential member of the Arts & Crafts Movement.

type, in black and red.
be printed, at Twenty
of which 8 are for sale
these have already been
published by William N

6-2. William Morris's Golden type, which he designed and used in his Kelmscott publications. These lavish, oversized books were quite expensive.

6-3. Above is the nameplate used to identify books produced by the Kelmscott Press. This press symbolized the return to an appreciation of the handcrafts.

This page is set in
Optima 8.5/12.

6-4. *A page from a Kelmscott Press'* The Canterbury Tales, 1896. *These books harkened back to the Middle Ages, when books were handcrafted on irregular paper. Morris was reacting to the industrialization and lack of aesthetics and craftsmanship of the era.*

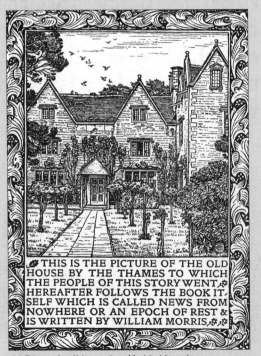

6-5. *This page from Kelmscott shows Morris's elaborate home, where the Kelmscott Press and workshop was situated.*

and of poor quality. In the light of these many industrial and mechanized products, William Morris and others yearned for a return to the values of individual craftsmanship as opposed to industrial production. In 1861 he founded Morris & Company to create hand-crafted home furnishings for the mass consumer. The attempt to stem the increasing ugliness of the industrial blight brought about a retro-Movement now referred to as the Arts & Crafts Movement.

The Arts & Crafts Movement was not as successful in the mass-marketing as intended; because the goods produced from the craft resurgence at Kelmscott and other centers were handmade, they were only affordable to wealthy citizens of the era. But the devotees of this school were trying to produce home furnishings (wallpaper, fabrics, furniture, books, architectural fittings) of high quality and good design. Although elitist, their efforts began a series of attacks on mass-produced goods that ultimately raised the quality of the factory products.

KELMSCOTT PRESS

Morris established the Kelmscott Press in 1889 and turned to the printed books of the 1400s for inspiration. He studied the arts of printing, papermaking, bookbinding and type design for three years before producing his first book. His books were large, oversized tomes, and Morris designed a Roman typeface for them, after the style of Nicholas Jenson, called *Golden*. These heavier, blacker faces were surrounded on the title page by dark, ornate woodcut borders and ornamental initials, and were inspired by Medieval manuscripts. Morris's fastidiousness for craftsmanship extended to the quality of his paper, which was a linen rag (not wood pulp) made with an irregular surface akin to the older paper, and was exclusively produced for all his printing.

Through his efforts, printing was reaffirmed as an art form, as opposed to a mechanical process devoid of human input. The use of beautiful and lavish decoration in his book design was considered essential to the emotional experience of the book. Morris cut three typefaces; one was named Golden, one was Chaucer, and the other Troy. Although these faces did not become the style of the day, Morris's work did account for the proliferation of private presses and limited-edition books throughout Europe and America. Morris's example was a fine indication of the craftsmanship required for outstanding printing. He applied this same care and perfectionism to his furniture design, wall hangings, fabrics and wallpaper. He clearly made objects for everyday use that were works of art. Ironically enough, he may be one of the earliest industrial designers known, applying his artistic talent to products for the home. He also championed the notion that well-designed type affects the reader's perception and comprehension.

NEON TYPE/CAMERAS FOR THE WEALTHY

Also at the end of the century, in 1889, neon tube lighting was developed; the look of our nighttime cities has never been the same since. By bending the tubes into script or sans serif type, messages flickered from restaurant and tavern windows. The only limitation was the skill of the glass blowers to shape the tubes. This scientific discovery dramatically changed the average person's interaction with typography in the environment. Glowing neon signs stood out against the black night. We take this interaction with typography for granted today.

In this same year, 1889, the first camera was produced by Kodak, and mass-marketed to Americans, allowing them for the first time to take their own portraits and photos. Photography had been invented about forty years before this and documented the Civil War in detail, but Kodak made photography and cameras available on a large scale to the wealthy and upper classes by developing the film at its plant.

SPEEDING UP THE COMPOSING OF PAGES

Printing at this point had changed dramatically since Gutenberg's day, but the setting of type had made only one true leap. Originally cast in molten lead, known as *Hot Type* because of the heat required in the melting of the lead; each letter was laid in a *galley* or *composing guide*, one character at a time. This meant a great deal of hand work for the composing of daily newspapers. In the late 1800s the New York newspapers offered a *half million dollar* award to anyone who could improve on this process and cut the time for composing a page of type by 25%. *Three thousand* patents were issued to inventors who were working on a mechanized typesetting machine and competing for the award!

Otto Mergenthaler designed the first linotype machine in 1886. By utilizing a typewriter keyboard linked to *matrices* (or *molds*) of letters, the linotype machine would set an entire line of type at a time, as one piece or *slug* of molten metal, rather than setting each character individually. The operator would sit at a typewriter keyboard and type in the newspaper articles. The lines were assembled into columns of type automatically by the machine, and fit very closely together. This hot-type method of typesetting a line at a time allowed a faster pace for composing type as compared to the hand method, and was put to practical use in 1886. It was not until 1960 that a further breakthrough was implemented in the production of type.

The linotype machine could compose *ten times* faster than hand composition. This productivity allowed newspapers to drop their price and enabled them to print more copies. Because of the reduced time in the composing room, the newspapers could be on press sooner, and more copies could be printed in the same amount of time, meaning more profits.

6-6. Above is a platen-style, sheet-fed letterpress press, used for small printing jobs.

6-7. This is the Model 5 Linotype, a standard keyboard typesetting machine.

6-8. The composing of pages for daily newspapers was a labor-intensive undertaking when each letter had to be set by hand and then resorted and set the following day.

6-9. Hand-composing lead type was painstakingly slow and tedious.

20th Century
Typography

6

This page is set in
Optima 8.5/12.

6 20th Century Typography

6-10. The Wright Brothers flew the first plane from Kitty Hawk, North Carolina in 1904.

6-11. Guglielmo Marconi made the first crossatlantic radio transmission in 1901.

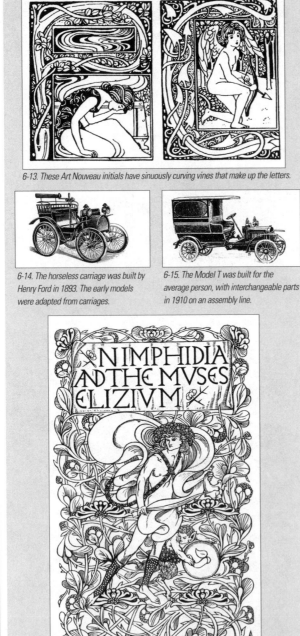

6-12. These Art Nouveau initial capitals are integrated with human figures accentuating their curves and softness.

6-13. These Art Nouveau initials have sinuously curving vines that make up the letters.

6-14. The horseless carriage was built by Henry Ford in 1893. The early models were adapted from carriages.

6-15. The Model T was built for the average person, with interchangeable parts in 1910 on an assembly line.

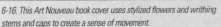

6-16. This Art Nouveau book cover uses stylized flowers and writhing stems and caps to create a sense of movement.

This page is set in Weiss 8.5/12.

CHANGES AND INNOVATIONS

The first two decades of the 1900s had significant innovations in science and technology. Electricity was introduced for lighting of streets and homes, replacing gas lights as a cheaper alternative. In 1901 the first radio transmission was completed from Britain to America by Guglielmo Marconi; the Wright brothers completed their first engine-powered flight in 1903; and Henry Ford produced the first fifteen Model T's in 1908. Originally referred to as the "iron wagon," the auto replaced the horse as the primary means of travel in a matter of decades. Russian Ballet was introduced to European audiences in 1909. Surrealism and Cubism developed out of a society that was changing at breakneck speed. In Cubism, painters attempted to represent all views of a subject at one time, and Surrealism was inspired by the dream state and the unconscious mind that was introduced by Freud around 1915.

THE WAR TO END ALL WARS

All of these attitudes of innovation and improvement were changed with the outbreak of World War I on August 1, 1914. The Austro-Hungarian Empire was attempting to take over neighboring countries. WW I had more casualties than the total of every war since added together. The trench warfare was horrific, with the dead and wounded crowding out the living. Worldwide, ten million men's lives were lost in this war by the time Germany surrendered on November 11, 1918. Roughly one quarter of the men of that generation perished in this war. The Bolshevik Revolution also took place shortly after the turn of the century, with some five million lives lost in Russia. In 1917 the Bolsheviks overthrew the power of the Czar Nicholas II, and started a Communist society under Lenin. Stalin later annihilated millions of farmers and property owners to institute state ownership. Unbridled disregard for traditions marked the beginning of the 1900s in all fields. WW I reigned in some of the artistic experimentations because it had devastating repercussions throughout Europe. The anti-art Dada movement was artists' response to WWI's senselessness and the suffering it caused.

ART NOUVEAU

The influence of the aesthetic of the Victorian era and the Arts & Crafts Movement flowed together creating an art movement called Art Nouveau, based on graceful, sinuous, curving lines and statuesque young women. This style was widely applied to posters produced in this era by stone lithography, and there was a renewed interest and attention given to hand lettering in these pieces. Alphonse Mucha's posters display an elegance and superb integration of type and illustration. Because the artist drew directly on the stone, the illustrator was often the letterer. These dual roles imbued these posters with a very cohesive sensibility to the overall design, with type and illustration beautifully integrated. Otto Eckmann and Henri van de Velde stand out in this era as type designers who tried to capture the sense of Art Nouveau with cast lead typography. Van de Velde designed organic initials in lead that captured the writhing of the era.

When he was producing books, William Morris's Kelmscott Press was widely admired by printers throughout Europe and America who were familiar with it. In Germany, Morris's influence upgraded the quality of book design, inspired finer printing craftsmanship, and led to new typeface designs and experimentation.

RUDOLF KOCH'S NEULAND: A GERMANIC CRAFTED FONT

Rudolf Koch was inspired by Morris's books. Known as a deeply reverent Christian man with a distinctly Medieval preference in type, Koch was a teacher of calligraphy at the Arts and Crafts School in Offenbach. There, he tried to develop personal variations of some of the Medieval faces. After serving in WW I, he continued designing typefaces for the Klingspor type foundry. This is when he designed the heavy face Neuland, a typeface that has been popular in book cover design and has the feeling of a woodcut letter because of its simple, rustic, angled curves. Koch also designed the sans serif face Kabel, which is very frequently used in children's product applications. It is a beautiful face that reads well, with a carefree playfulness to the letters. The angled terminals make the characters appear to dance and skip along the baseline rather than march rigidly as the squared-off terminals appeared.

FREDERIC GOUDY & INSPIRED PRIVATE PRESSES IN THE U.S.

In America, the type designer and printer Frederic Goudy was directly inspired by Morris's Kelmscott Press, as were many other American printers of this era. The emphasis on excellent quality paper and impeccable press work raised the overall standards in the printing industry. Goudy even ran his own Village Press until it was ruined in a huge fire. Goudy is credited as the first full-time type designer in history. He cut a total of 122 faces combining beauty and function. For inspiration, he looked back to the Renaissance for the Humanist inspiration of many of his typefaces. He cut the face Goudy Old Style, a face that reveals its relationship to the calligraphic pen. He wrote books on lettering and edited journals that dealt specifically with book design and layout.

EDWARD JOHNSTON & ERIC GILL: CLASSIC LETTERERS

The overwhelming array of whimsical Victorian type a few decades earlier may have precipitated a desire for simpler, more streamlined typefaces. Some type designers looked to the Roman classics for inspiration, while others looked to the earlier original sans serif face introduced in 1816. Edward Johnston, a central figure in the English revival of fine calligraphy and the study of letters, devoted much of his life to teaching the art of lettering. In some accounts Johnston is considered the primary mover in England's resurgence in hand-crafted lettering. In his enthusiastic classes he trained a generation of fine calligraphers in

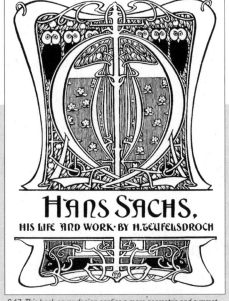

6-17. This book-cover design applies a more geometric and symmetric approach to the Art Nouveau interlacing.

6-18. This is Epoque, an Art Nouveau font modeled after designs of Henri van de Velde.

6-20. Rudolf Koch designed Neuland, Kabel, and Klingspor. He lived from 1876 to 1934 and worked in Germany.

6-19. Rudolf Koch's Neuland has a woodcut feel to the rough-hewn letters.

ABCDEFGHIJ
abcdefghij
KLMNOPQR
klmnopqr
STUVWXYZ
stuvwxyz
1234567890

6-21. Rudolf Koch's Kabel is a clean and informal sans serif font.

6-22. Above is the nameplate from Frederic Goudy's press. Goudy defied all odds of success when he rebuilt his foundry twice after it burned to the ground.

This page is set in Weiss 8.5/12.

6 20th Century
Typography

6-23. Frederic Goudy designed
over sixty fonts. He lived from
1865-1947 and worked in America.

6-24. This is Goudy Old Style Italic.
It has some elegant hooked terminals.

6-25. This is Goudy Old
Style and bold.

6-26. Eric Gill began as a
carver of letters in stone for
headstones. He designed Gill
Sans, and lived in England
from 1882 to 1947.

6-27. This is Gill Sans Italic
and Bold Italic.

6-28. This is Gill Sans in light and bold; it has a lot of
personality for a sans serif font.

many different lettering, calligraphic and script faces, and
raised the quality of the craft through his disciplined
dedication and inspired teaching.

Johnston is also credited with the creation of the first
modern sans serif typeface in 1916 for the London Underground
subways. This face marks a departure from earlier sans serif faces
in the forms of many of the letters. There is a tremendous
amount of innovation and exploration in the forms of the individual characters. This typeface served as an inspiration for future
type designers. Some historians feel that Eric Gill's (one of
Johnston's students) Gill Sans face is deeply indebted to
Johnston's Railway Type. Johnston also wrote books on lettering to further the interest in the field.

Eric Gill, a student of Edward Johnston, began his career
as a letterer and stone cutter. He started designing typefaces
and his first one Perpetua, was a traditional serif face inspired
by classical models. He made a break with classic faces in 1928
when he designed a handsome sans serif Gill Sans. This typeface
is a sans serif font that has beautiful calligraphic details to
some of the letters. It is distinctive on the page and yet very
legible. The subtle nuances and sensitivity to the weights of the
characters make it an excellent typeface. When it was introduced
in England, Gill Sans received rave reviews. It has stylistic
characteristics similar to Johnston's Railway Type. Gill also
designed the typefaces Joanna, Perpetua and Bunyan.

OFFSET LITHOGRAPHY

In 1905, rotary offset lithography was introduced by Ira
Rubel. Like stone lithography, offset was based on the principle that oil and water don't mix. In this new version, however,
the stone was replaced with a thin aluminum alloy plate that
wrapped around a cylinder. The image from this plate was offset
onto the surface of a rubber roller and then printed onto the
paper. These improvements revolutionized the industry:
press preparation time was reduced and presses could run
faster with the plates on cylinders as opposed to flat surfaces.
Although offset lithography is the most common form of
printing today, it took fifty years before it dominated the
industry, and surpassed letterpress printing.

THE ROARING 20S

The 1920s, known as the Roaring Twenties, were a time of
celebration and freedom, giving women the right to vote.
The world was at peace, but there was also a devastating
depression in Europe, with Germany being the hardest
hit. The German mark was so devalued that it took baskets
of money to buy a single loaf of bread, and some of the
worthless currency was literally burned and used to fuel
furnaces when winter set in.

The style of design in the decade between the World
Wars is varied, and many different influences in the art world

have repercussions in design. Art Deco, Futurist, Constructivist, Art Nouveau, Suprematist, Impressionist, Expressionist, Cubist, De Stijl, Surrealist, Jungenstil, Dadaist, Social Realist and Bauhaus ideas were coexisting in the art/design circles throughout Europe. It is difficult to try to create a linear timeline of these styles because so many of them coexisted and overlapped in time; they were often simultaneously the vogue of different cities.

DADA'S REJECTION OF THE TYPOGRAPHIC MESSAGE

Dada rejected the organization of type on the page. Type was to be used as an expressive medium and arranged by chance, not to be read. The Dadaists created layouts by random and intuitive placement of type and abstract elements. They rejected the rigid horizontal and vertical format that had strait-jacketed printing of the past, and introduced a new typographic sense. They composed on the bed of the press. Using an assortment of letters in various sizes found at hand, they incorporated printing rules, boxes and bars as part of their composition or in ways that represented letters. They created chaos on paper and felt that it justifiably represented the sense of the era. Dada art was confusing, perhaps offensive, sometimes poetry, and it was unaccepted. All structure and organization in typography was obliterated after WW I. The male population had been cut by 25% in the war generation. There was a philosophical nihilism and angst among warfare survivors, not to mention the psychological scars from the brutal warfare conditions. The Dadaists liberated printing tremendously and expressed incredible energy and exploration in their work.

ART DECO'S INFLUENCE ON TYPE

Art Deco is characterized by technical geometric linear designs usually incorporating bilateral symmetry. Elaborate frames are frequently used in Art Deco designs. Dark areas of tone or color, geometric shapes and thin parallel lines are incorporated into Art Deco typefaces and design. A. M. Cassandre is a type designer and graphic designer of this era who is known for his design of the typeface Peignot. His work was influenced by the Cubists, as well as the Art Deco aesthetic. He struggled to simplify his design work, and create clean forms. His typefaces explore contrasts of line weight in black and white, as well as introduce innovative forms for many of the characters. His typefaces are not looking backwards to older styles, but forging ahead with new variations.

THE BAUHAUS AESTHETIC: KANDINSKY AND BAYER

The German design school founded after WW I was called the *Bauhaus*. The Bauhaus' mantras were that "form follows function," and "less is more." Although they

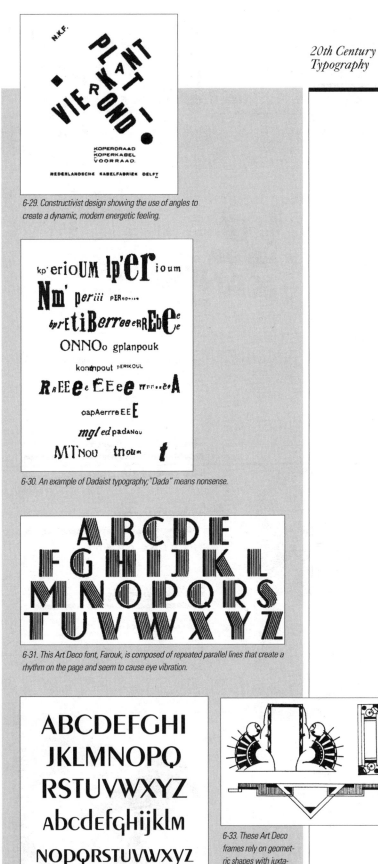

6-29. Constructivist design showing the use of angles to create a dynamic, modern energetic feeling.

6-30. An example of Dadaist typography; "Dada" means nonsense.

6-31. This Art Deco font, Farouk, is composed of repeated parallel lines that create a rhythm on the page and seem to cause eye vibration.

6-32. This font is Peignot designed by A. M. Cassandre. It resonates with an Art Deco design sensibility due to the dark and light contrast.

6-33. These Art Deco frames rely on geometric shapes with juxtaposed dark areas to create visual syncopation.

This page is set in Stone Sans 8.5/12.

6-34. *Above is Herbert Bayer's Universal font, which attempted to eliminate the need for capitals.*

6-35. *Constructivist poster by Herbert Bayer utilizes angled bars for organization and clarity.*

6-36. *Constructivist cover by El Lissitzky for* The Isms of Art, *1924. This cover uses a pattern of type and dark bars to organize the space and the type, creating a modern aesthetic.*

6-37. *This poster by El Lissitzky, entitled* Beat the White with the Red Wedge, *from 1919 is a quintessential Constructivist design with angular shapes and off-balanced weight.*

existed for only fourteen years, the philosophy of the Bauhaus has had strong repercussions on twentieth-century design. They believed that clean, spartan design, devoid of decoration, giving way to the "truth" of the materials, was the goal of good design. The Bauhaus philosophy was that aesthetically beautiful, well-designed objects could be achieved through industrial manufacturing (this can be seen as a direct challenge to the handcrafted, unique object, quality materials philosophy of the Arts and Crafts Movement).

Walter Gropius is responsible for founding the Bauhaus in 1919. He worked along with Laslo Moholy-Nagy, Wassily Kandinsky, Paul Klee, Lionel Feininger and Josef Albers. Because this modern art was seen as contrary to traditional German ideals, the teachers eventually had to move the school and were later forced by the Nazis to close it completely in 1933. But the philosophy of the Bauhaus lived on long after the school was shut down; many of the teachers emigrated to the U.S. where they influenced a generation of artists, designers and architects.

In an effort to ever simplify the sans serif types, Herbert Bayer, a student of the Bauhaus school in Germany, took the sans serif ideal to its logical extreme in 1925. His "universal type" attempted to serve all typographic needs by reducing the letters to the simplest, most basic forms; he discarded capitals, claiming them unnecessary. This type innovation was successful, but this typeface was not widely reproduced. Bayer is also known for his creative design work later in his career that applied the principles of the Bauhaus to corporate promotional materials.

RUSSIAN CONSTRUCTIVISM: EL LISSITZKY

With the rise of the philosophy of the Bauhaus and the philosophies of Bolshevism in the twenties, more and more "fine" artists were rejecting the traditional canvas as a medium, and taking up a study of design. In Russia, the ideas of the De Stijl movement, the Cubists, and the Futurists inspired new art movements called *Constructivism* and *Supremacism*. They renounced "art for art's sake" and applied their talents to posters, books, magazines, exhibitions and type design in an effort to create an art that was "for the people." It was the politically correct thing to do at the time. They were trying to create "modern" art for the new "modern" Communist society. Constructivist style is based on a radiating use of angled planes photomontage; simple; bold linear elements; and a strong use of the diagonal as the focal point of the design.

El Lissitzky was a Constructivist designer whose typographic layouts were innovative and influenced subsequent designers. In his work he tried to break from the restraints of verticals and horizontals in layouts, utilizing

This page is set in
Stone Sans 8.5/12.

instead the diagonal as a primary design element. Letters were made out of geometric bars and printing rules, and photomontage was usually employed. He frequently worked in a red, white and black color scheme. Lissitzky is responsible for lecturing widely on the ideals and philosophy of the Constructivists and spreading their prominence.

DE STIJL MOVEMENT IN THE NETHERLANDS

The De Stijl movement began in the Netherlands in 1917. The work of this group can be characterized in Mondrian's paintings. Their work is recognized by abstract geometric forms used to express universal principles of balance. Heavy black bars at right angles were used in type layouts to separate space and information. Like other art movements of this era, they attempted to reject the values of the former era, making a break with the representational paintings of the past and forging ahead in new directions. Théo van Doesburg applied these De Stijl theories to many creative ventures and in 1919 designed a typeface called "An Alphabet," which is exclusively based on a square. Curves and diagonals are omitted in favor of a clean, modern, geometric aesthetic. Although never a commercial success, this font still resonates with a contemporary feeling today.

MINIMAL TYPOGRAPHIC DESIGN: JAN TSCHICHOLD

A designer who was influenced by the Bauhaus and Constructivist ideals of minimal decoration was Jan Tschichold. In 1928 he codified the typographic principles of these movements in the pamphlet *The New Typography* for a wider audience of designers, printers and letterers. He advocated asymmetrical layouts, diagonals, and sans serif geometric typefaces structured in a grid layout. Decoration is deemed unnecessary, and clear communication should dictate all layout decisions. Color on the page was achieved by balancing light, bold, condensed and extended sans serif typefaces. White space was seen as an integral and essential element of any layout. He renounced these views later in his life (around 1940) and began to reassess the value of classical typefaces and layouts.

A GEOMETRIC TYPEFACE: PAUL RENNER'S FUTURA

Another early sans serif designer, Paul Renner, designed Futura in 1927. This font is based on the simplification of the letterforms to geometric shapes. Early exploratory versions of this face show that the designer was trying to be extremely innovative in the design of letters. Many alternate characters in the

6-38. This is An Alphabet, by Théo van Doesburg, in 1919 has omitted all curves and diagonals from the design of the characters.

6-39. De Stijl layout utilizing geometric principles and simplicity of balance.

6-40. Jan Tschichold's cover for an insert on typographic design from 1925 that revolutionized German typesetting and cemented the transition away from Textura as a text font.

6-41. Futura was designed by Paul Renner in 1927; it has a geometric basis to the letters and a clean contemporary sense. It's a well-designed font in all of the weights.

6-42. Paul Renner, designer of Futura, which was the first geometrically designed sans serif face and was quite successful.

This page is set in Stone Sans 8.5/12.

ABCDEFGH

abcdefghij

IJ**KLMNOP**

klmnopqr

QRSTUVW

XYZ

stu**vwxyz**

1234567890

6-43. This is Stanley Morison who
designed Times New Roman with Victor
Lardent. This font was used to redesign
of the nameplate of The Times of London.

6-44. Times New Roman, designed in 1932
by Stanley Morison and Victor Lardent for
efficiency on press and for optimal characters
per line for The Times newspaper of London.

ABCDE

FGHIJ

abcdefghij

KLMN

OPQR

klmnopqr

STUVWXYZ

stuvwxyz

1 2 3 4 5 6 7 8

9 0

6-45. Times New Roman Italic and Bold.

original design are very unusual, and would have added an irregular syncopation to the letters on the page because the bowls of the letters vary in their height. The geometry of this sans serif face was a departure from earlier faces. In the final design, the round characters were based on a perfect circle, and the angled characters were based on pointed triangles. It was eventually broadened to a family of type including thirteen variations of weight. This font has a beautiful economy of form and a strong sense of balance and functionality. It is still used often today.

THE EFFECTS OF THE GREAT DEPRESSION AND CRASH OF '29

With the Wall Street Crash of 1929, the decade of the Great Depression began. International trade had essentially been stopped by the passage of the Hawley-Smoot tariff, which placed high taxes on any imported goods. Banks closed and businesses failed. Food supply was scarce because it cost midwestern farmers more to ship their crops and livestock to market than they would get in return for them. Soup lines in cities became a common sight.

The Fascist dictator Adolf Hitler would come to power in Germany by 1934, Benito Mussolini in Italy, Francisco Franco in Spain, and Joseph Stalin in the Soviet Union. Demoralized people looked to extremist leaders to vanquish the difficult conditions of their daily lives. Unfortunately, they traded freedom for a *promise* of stability and a rosier future; they *thought* it couldn't get much worse. There were parallel ripples in the U.S.

When Franklin D. Roosevelt was elected to the White House in 1932 by a clear majority, the policies of the New Deal were instituted, thanks to Presidential manipulation of the Supreme Court. Roosevelt began the largest public-spending policies the country had ever known, a move which some historians and economists believe to have deepened and extended the Depression.

Movies had been silent up until this point, but "talkies" were introduced in 1927; they were a major hit and a relief from the day-to-day reality of the Depression. Even during the Depression, the average family owned an automobile, and larger supermarkets began to replace the small-town grocer. Commercial airlines, ocean liners, and high-speed trains were making the world seem smaller.

TYPE FOR DAILY NEWSPAPERS

Daily newspapers were sought for news on the crash or the job circumstances. Linotype eventually developed typefaces which were specifically designed for the newspapers. These faces had to withstand wear on high speed machines, avoid filling in the eye of the "e," and allow the greatest number of letters to the inch while providing good legibility. Not since the days of Baskerville had the printing technology had such an impact on the design of typefaces. These were very practical considerations which were better addressed at the outset of designing the type to ensure a more workable typeface.

In London, Stanley Morison (who was a typographic advisor to the British Monotype Corporation) was selected to redesign a typeface for use in *The Times* newspaper. The font, designed with Victor Lardent, was named Times New Roman and was used for the first time in the October 1932 issue. Its legibility was immediately recognized. Morison used shorter ascenders and descenders, heavy stroke weights and slightly condensed characters to create a readable typeface that fit more characters per line. Modern aesthetics were being embraced by established publications, leading to broader acceptance of this new approach to typographic design.

THE U.S. ENTERS WW II

In 1941, when Japan attacked Pearl Harbor, the U.S. entered the second World War. The country was just getting over the effects of the Depression and was flung into the middle of a worldwide conflict. Harry S. Truman ended the conflict by dropping the atomic bomb on Hiroshima and Nagasaki on August 6, 1945. Although this was a devastating decision, the end of the war years, the war rations, the war recycling and the Victory gardens was embraced by the country.

The 50s represented the beginning of the Cold War and the buildup of military weapon arsenals by the major industrial powers and the USSR. This decade was also the beginning of the technology revolution where space travel was the guidepost of a country's military power. Women had entered the work force during the war years, and Americans were more educated and mobile thanks to the WW II GI, bill, which guaranteed free college tuition to war veterans.

America was involved in the Korean War from 1950 to 1953. It ended while Eisenhower was president. Television was common in American homes, Abstract Expressionists were being reviewed by New York art critics, polyester fabrics were in, tape recorders (reel to reel) were newly invented, plastics became popular, and frozen food was introduced. In 1957, the Soviets launched Sputnik, and the race to the moon began with the aid of growing, albeit limited, computer technology of the space program at NASA.

ADRIAN FRUTIGER'S UNIVERS NUMBERED FAMILY

Adrian Frutiger, a Swiss-born designer developed an entire family of sans serif faces from 1954 to '57 named Univers. It encompassed a variety of weights, italics, condensed and extended fonts. Frutiger optically adjusted parts of the typefaces so that there would be an even texture to the resulting type. A designer now had twenty-one variations of the Univers font to choose from or to incorporate into the same piece. He devised a numeric system for referring to the

6-46. This is Univers 39 and 59, by Adrian Frutiger. The design of the Univers family took from 1954 to 1957.

6-47. This is Univers 47, 48 and 57.

6-48. This is Adrian Frutiger, designer of the entire Univers family, ITC Frutiger, and other fonts. The design of the twenty-one weights and styles of Univers was a three year undertaking.

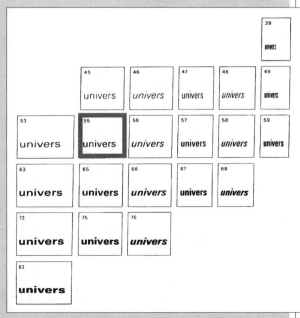

6-49. This layout of Univers places all of the weights and italics in relation to each other in an attempt to visually explain the logic of Frutiger's numbering system.

6-50. This is Helvetica Light and Bold, designed in the 1950s by Max Meidinger and Eduoard Hoffman.

6-51. This is Helvetica Compressed.

6-52. This is Hermann Zapf, designer of Zapf Chancery, Palatino, Optima, Melior and other fine fonts.

6-53. This is Palatino, designed by Hermann Zapf in 1950.

6-54. This is Optima in designed by Zapf in 1958.

weight, width, and italic form of type. 55 was the norm or standard version of Univers, and the higher the tens digit number, the bolder the face; for example 75 is bolder than 55, and 35 is lighter. The styles with ones digits lower than 5 were extended faces and those with higher than 5 were condensed. If the second number was an even one, the font was italic. If it was an odd number, the font was Roman. This font was a mammoth undertaking, and was three years in the making. It marks the first conception and planning of a full font family designed by one individual to assure consistency. It was a daunting task!

THE SWISS DESIGN STYLE: MEIDINGER'S HELVETICA VS. FRUTIGER'S UNIVERS

In the 1950s a new sense of typographic design was emerging in Germany and Switzerland known as the *Swiss style*. Based on an underlying grid structure of layout, asymmetrical arrangement of objects, and the use of different weights of a sans serif type, this design formula offered many possibilities when handled creatively. The goal of the originators was to override the style of individual designers in favor of communicating the message as clearly as possible. Some of the philosophy of the Swiss school harkens back to Bauhaus aesthetics. New sans serif typefaces were designed to express the Swiss school philosophies. The work of the Swiss designer Josef Müller-Brockmann is an example of the Swiss school.

Another well-used sans serif face was created at this time. Max Meidinger created Helvetica for the Haas Type Foundry in Switzerland in the mid-50s. Using a larger x-height than Univers for better legibility, Helvetica was an immediate success. A variety of designers created the various weights and condensed versions of this face, so that there tends to be less unity in the family as a whole than there is in the Univers family. But Helvetica embraces graceful curves in its design, making it less geometric in structure than Univers which appears squared off. However, if any typeface has been overused, it is Helvetica, which is synonymous with generic because it has flooded the visual environment. It graces everything from computer screens, to generic food packaging, to highway signs.

A CLASSIC TYPE DESIGNER: HERMANN ZAPF

A German type designer who spanned four decades of type production began his climb to fame in the 50s. Hermann Zapf was an accomplished calligrapher who turned his hand to type design. One early face was Palatino in 1950, which reveals his familiarity with calligraphy. Melior was next in 1952, a broad, elegant, square face. Looking back for inspiration to sans serif inscriptions of the 1400s in Florence, he developed the sans serif face Optima in 1958. Using the slightly thickened or splayed ends of the strokes of the letters to replace serifs, these letters are simple and graceful. Optima is a highly legible, Humanistic sans serif typeface.

It does not look cold and mechanical. Zapf was able to work from inspiration of the past but to imbue the faces with a clear legibility and modern sensibility. He also wrote *Manuale Typographicum,* which is a book devoted to typefaces, with quotes on typography, completely designed by Zapf.

FENICE: NOVARESE'S ELEGANT FONT

Aldo Novarese and Alessandro Butti, working in Italy, designed new sans serif faces that were in vogue at this time: Microgamma and Eurostile. These two share some common features: they are square, spartan typefaces that look highly engineered and mechanical. Microgamma is exclusively an uppercase face, Eurostile is both upper- and lowercase. These faces also have a very tight character fit and look very compact on the page, which may have been influenced by the tighter spacing of phototypesetting.

Aldo Novarese also went on to design other fonts, including ITC Novarese, ITC Fenice, and ITC Mixage. All of these are clean, simply elegant fonts with attention to the balance of the letters and weights. Novarese's fonts are recognized because they read exceptionally well.

FREEMAN CRAW: A DESIGNER OF STABLE TYPEFACES

Freeman Craw is an American type designer of this era who designed three faces that were quite popular: Craw Clarendon, Craw Modern, and Ad Lib. All are very balanced, stable and industrial looking faces. They have large x-height in proportion to the cap height (especially Craw Modern), and the characters are a bit extended. The beauty of these faces is the sensitivity to the thick and thin contrast of the strokes which is carefully refined. Craw Clarendon has a very clean, industrial appearance.

PHOTOTYPESETTING: COLD TYPE

There had been many attempts to merge the technology of typesetting with the technology of photography, but none were successful. Although experimentation began in the 1920s to convert a *linotype machine* (lead lines of type) to a *phototypesetter* (photographically produced type), it was not until the 1950s that the technology of phototypesetting was widely available. Phototypesetting machines worked by using a negative of the character instead of a matrix. The negative was placed between an enlarging lens and photosensitive paper. Using a computer interface, a character was sized to the correct point size, then a light exposed the negative and the photosensitive paper received the light and developed the single character. With one negative of a font, phototypesetters could set type from 4-to-36 point type. The font negatives were designed as precise discs or ribbons that rotated at high speed to expose the characters after they were punched in and coded for size, etc., by an operator. The photosensitive paper was then loaded into a light-tight cassette and developed in a series of rollers and fluid baths.

20th Century Typography

6

6-55. This is ITC Fenice in a variety of weights, designed by Aldo Novarese.

6-56. This is Eurostile, designed by Novarese.

6-57. This font, Craw Clarendon, was designed by Freeman Craw. It's very clear and open.

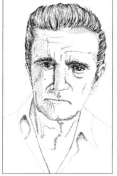

6-58. This is Aldo Novarese, designer of ITC Fenice, Eurostile, ITC Novarese and other fonts.

6-59. This font, Orbit Inline, embodies the sensibilities of the 60s with the high platform shoes relating to the weight at the bottom of the characters.

6-60. This font, Moore Computer, was designed for optical readability by computers. The characters are distinguished from one another through the use of solid areas that are strategically placed; there are no curves or angles.

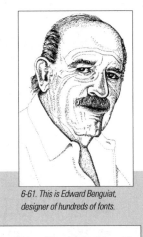

6
20th Century
Typography

6-61. This is Edward Benguiat,
designer of hundreds of fonts.

ABCDEFGHIJ
abcdefghij
KLMNOPQR
klmnopqr
STUVWXYZ
stuvwxyz
1234567890

6-62. This is ITC Bookman
designed by Benguiat.

ABCDEFGHIJ
abcdefghij
KLMNOPQR
klmnopqr
STUVWXYZ
stuvwxyz
123456789

6-63. This is ITC Souvenir,
designed by Benguiat.

ABCDEFGHIJ
abcdefghij
KLMNOPQR
klmnopqr
STUVWXYZ
stuvwxyz
1234567890

6-64. This is ITC Korinna
designed by Benguiat.

ABCDEFGHIJ
abcdefghij
KLMNOPQR
klmnopqr
STUVWXYZ
stuvwxyz
1234567890

6-65. This is ITC Panache designed
by Benguiat.

ABCDEFGHIJ
abcdefghij
KLMNOPQR
klmnopqr
STUVWXYZ
stuvwxyz

6-66. This is ITC Benguiat designed by Benguiat.

Phototypeset type is referred to as *Cold Type*, as opposed to the older lead type, which is referred to as *Hot Type* because of the heat necessary to cast the lead lines of type. Character spacing could be sensitively controlled even within small-sized body text in phototypesetting. Letters could be superimposed; lines could be overlapped. More important, it allowed the designing and production of new typefaces because the burdensome cost of casting them in metal was removed. Type was sharper and blacker; it could be enlarged up to 500% without affecting its integrity. Photocomposition was also more economical because it eliminated steps in the production process. In short, it allowed designers to explore whole new and exciting possibilities with type.

PHOTOTYPESETTING AND TYPE DESIGN

Phototypesetting had serious repercussions on the appearance of type and the choices that designers made. No longer were designers limited in the size they could enlarge type to, or in the tightness of letterspacing that they could achieve. Phototypesetting meant that type could be curved, extended, condensed, angled, printed in textures, and overlapped easily because the lead did not have to be cut away between the physical characters in order to set a very tight headline. Spacing of letters for improved readability became a far more precise art when phototypesetting was used. It also led to the proliferation of typefaces, because it was no longer labor intensive to cut punches for the font in all different sizes. New fonts could be introduced more quickly.

By the early 1960s phototypesetting machines had been invented that eliminated vertical and horizontal spacing limitations and worked at dizzying speeds. Photo display lettering could be expanded, condensed, compressed, extended, curved, obliqued or otherwise made to conform to a desired space. There were no longer rules limiting the use of type. One character could fill an entire page for effect, and it often did. Because it was an option, type was crammed together with unprecedented compactness, sometimes pushing the limits of legibility.

INTERNATIONAL TYPEFACE CORPORATION

The notion of designing type for legibility and ease of reading is the guiding principle behind the International Typeface Corporation, or ITC as it is known. This establishment was founded in 1970 by Aaron Burns, Herb Lubalin, and Ed Rondthaler. ITC redesigns older, classic typefaces, improving them for legibility, balance and phototypesetting. This usually means increasing the proportion of the x-height to the height of the capitals and opening up the counter forms, so that they are tall and clear. In an ITC face, the entire family is designed to have a consistent feel. ITC buys the rights to new faces that have been developed, commissions designs from existing type designers, and reviews classic faces for possible redrawing. They license a tremendous number of faces per year. Their commitment is to designing superior, beautiful digital faces with high legibility. If you want an ITC face, you have to specify it and purchase it from your type supplier. ITC faces are also precisely the same whether you buy them in America, Europe, or any other foreign country. They are licensed, and you can count on their consistency.

EDWARD BENGUIAT: A PROLIFIC TYPE DESIGNER

Edward Benguiat is an American corporate designer who has designed over five hundred successful typefaces. The font Benguiat is a serif face which incorporated interesting angles and curves into the letters. The serifs are sharp and pointed, and the bracketing is very heavy. The overall effect of the face is a slightly harsh feeling from the thorn-shaped serifs. He also designed ITC Benguiat Gothic, ITC Tiffany, ITC Souvenir, ITC Bookman, ITC Panache and ITC Korinna. Benguiat Gothic is a sans serif face that ends with rounded terminals and utilizes curves in the construction of the characters; they break new directions in the use of curved rather than horizontal cross bars. Benguiat's fonts are unique, showing a great deal of experimentation in the forms of the characters. His inspiration of letterform variation seems to be freshly conceived and is refreshing.

THE 1960S AND THE INFLUENCE ON TYPE DESIGN

The decade of the 60s began as a period of post WW II economic strength and expansion for American industry. The gross national product had never been higher, and American factories were supplying goods for the recovering European countries. The U.S. was the dominant manufacturing force in the world. The baby boomer generation was coming of age, and took society by storm as beatniks, hippies, and the flower children toward the end of the decade. Some of the generation was anti-establishment and politically active in demonstrations. The Civil Rights Movement and the Women's Liberation Movement preoccupied some of the college-aged population. John F. Kennedy succeeded Eisenhower in the White House, and the Washingtonian era of Camelot began. America was prosperous, comfortable, and middle-class consumers.

Type design in the 60s borrowed much from the taste of Op Art or Psychedelic Art. Neon colors were new and were often used with virtually unreadable results (of course, the image did burn into your retina, producing a closed-eye, after-image). Hand lettering was employed on posters to make the letters swirl and curve into each other with dizzying effects. The overall impact of the posters was likely inspired by the then-popular psychedelic drugs. This phase is sometimes compared to the Art Nouveau style

6-67. *This rock concert poster for the Steve Miller Band is almost unreadable. The type has to be figured out. It seems to writhe around the figure, oblivious to readability concerns.*

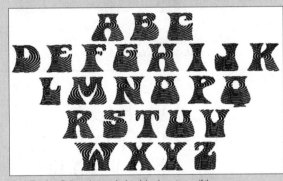

6-68. *This font, Bullseye has manipulated the characters as if they were on stretchable putty. The ripple design adds an Op Art effect to the letters.*

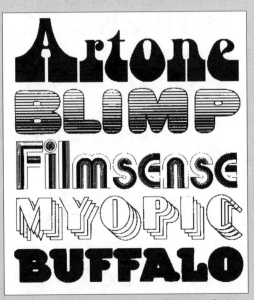

6-69. *The fonts above were designed by Seymour Chwast; they reflect his illustration sense, especially Artone which is so fluid and graceful.*

This page is set in Industrial 736 8.5/12.

6 *20th Century*
     Typography

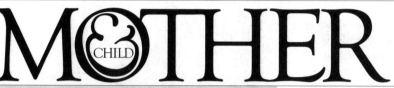

6-70. This is Herb Lubalin, a man
gifted with the creative genius to
truly paint with type.

6-71. This proposed logo for a magazine that never materialized is probably Herb
Lubalin's most famous piece of typographic design. The ampersand creates a womb
for the word child, inside the "O" of Mother. Lubalin was famous for his inventiveness with integrating letters and his ingenious typographic vision.

of organic lettering taken to the extreme.
Legibility was no longer at issue–
observers were *challenged* to figure out
the message of a rock poster.

SEYMOUR CHWAST'S WHIMSICAL TYPEFACES

Seymour Chwast (who is primarily an illustrator) designed
five display typefaces that embody the aesthetic of this era
called *Artone, Blimp, Filmsense, Myopic,* and *Buffalo*. Artone literally applies the platform shoe and bell bottom fashion sense
to the font, creating an extremely high slab serif with a great
deal of bracketing. Blimp is a round, pumped-up sans serif
that uses a linear pattern for gradation. Filmsense is a sans serif
face with rounded characters that uses black, gray and white
tones to define the letters. Myopic relies on the repetition of
the form of the letter as though it is stacked, for its uniqueness, and Buffalo is a modified bold sans serif face. These
display faces captured the style and design sensibility of the
era; because of this they look dated today. Their affiliation with
the 60s cannot be denied or separated. They will always
resonate with that association and designers can utilize them
when it is appropriate and desirable to recall this era.

6-72. This is Lubalin's design for the nameplate of the first issue of Avant Garde
magazine, which he art-directed. This served as the inspiration for the font of the
same name. The letters all overlap and tuck into one another.

ABCDEFG
abcdefghi
HIJ**KLMN**
OPQRST
jklmnopq
UVWXYZ
rstuvwxyz
1234567

6-73. This is Serif Gothic by Herb
Lubalin.

ABCDEFGHIJ
abcdefghij
KLMNOPQR
klmnopqr
STUVWXYZ
stuvwxyz
1234567890

6-74. This is Avant Garde by Lubalin.

HERB LUBALIN'S FLAIR FOR INNOVATIVE TYPOGRAPHY

One type designer who did take advantage of the design
possibilities of phototypesetting was Herb Lubalin. He used
type to express ideas, emotions and surprises more than any
other designer in history; this man is known for his intuitive
sense of designing, in fact illustrating exclusively with type.
Although a prolific designer, he also designed a few typefaces.
The font Avant Garde developed from the lettering design
for a masthead Lubalin designed for a magazine (of the same
name) which he art-directed. Unable to find characters that
had the qualities he was looking for, he simply created his own
for the masthead. This font is known for its extensive selection of alternate characters and unusual ligatures that Lubalin
designed due to his own preference for tight letterspacing.

Serif Gothic is an elegant face he designed that is based
on curves. It has small, delicate spur serifs on the ends of the
terminals. Lubalin Graph is a slab serif face version of Avant
Garde. Lubalin retained the proportions of the Avant Garde
letters, created custom ligatures and added the square
Egyptian slab serifs. As a founding member of the International Typeface Corporation, he designed their publication
U&lc (Upper and lowercase) for many years.

THE RADICAL 70S AND TYPE DESIGN

With the end of the 60s, the beginning of the 70s were
a very different picture. Drugs were funneled into the U.S.
for recreation, and the effects of psychedelic drugs were
frequently reported. Marijuana was smoked, and the sexual

This page is set in
Janson 8.5/12.

6-75. This is Lubalin Graph, designed by Herb Lubalin.

revolution began with the introduction of birth control pills and free love. The miniskirt was in, and long hair for males was a groovy protest of the establishment. Platform shoes, bell bottoms, hip huggers, fake eyelashes, the smiley face and rock music were all hip. America was embroiled in Vietnam and anti-war demonstrations. The peace sign became the symbol for the war protest movement and draft dodgers. Television brought the harshness of the war into American living rooms, and the nation waffled in its support of the troops.

John F. Kennedy and Martin Luther King, Jr. had been assassinated and most of the Black Panthers (a radical pro-Black Power group) had disbanded. Black was beautiful, but still was segregated in some areas of the south. Women had earned some rights, but *Roe* v. *Wade* was still a few years away, and girls still died from complications of illicit abortions. Richard Nixon brought the troops home from Vietnam and signed the last balanced budget America ever knew. Secretary of State Henry Kissinger made strides toward Middle Eastern peace, Nixon visited China, and nuclear détente was signed with the Soviet Union, marking the beginning of the thawing of the Cold War era. The scandalous Watergate hearings ended with Nixon's epoch-making resignation from the office of the President.

The 70s was the decade that Japan launched its subtle war on U.S. consumers by flooding our markets with inexpensive cameras, calculators, televisions, and cars. This eventually forced American companies to reorganize in the 80s to compete for their share of the U.S. markets. The Abstract Expressionists were replaced by Op and Pop artists in New York. Happenings and Performance Art began to gain ground at this time. Conceptual, Environmental, and Minimal artists followed in the 70s.

MINIMALISM & CONCEPTUAL ART'S IMPACT ON TYPE

The aesthetics of Minimalist art were applied to graphic design, and there was a resurgence of interest in the Swiss style of design and layout in the 70s. The 70s was the

6-76. This is Matrix, designed by Zuzana Licko in 1986.

6-77. This is Modula by Zuzana Licko in 1985.

6-78. This is Lunatix by Zuzana Licko in 1988.

6-79. This is Beowulf, a font designed by Erik van Blokland and Just van Rossum in 1990.

6-80. This is Tegentonen designed by Max Kisman, in 1990.

This page is set in Bembo 8.5/12.

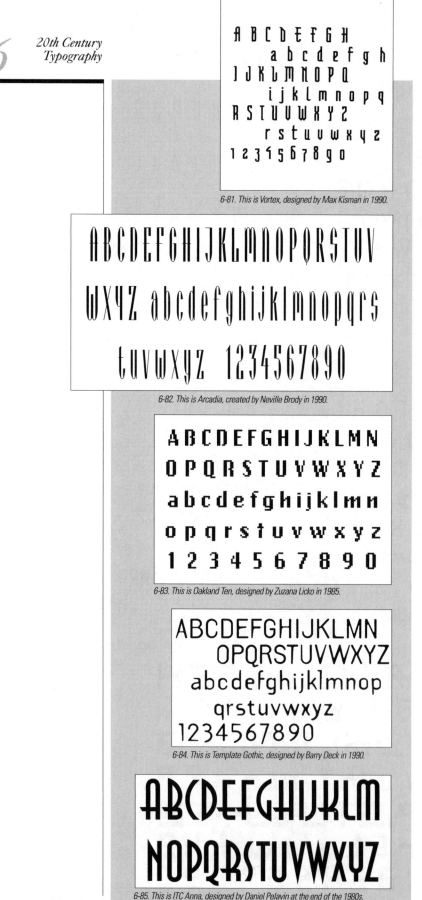

6-81. This is Vortex, designed by Max Kisman in 1990.

6-82. This is Arcadia, created by Neville Brody in 1990.

6-83. This is Oakland Ten, designed by Zuzana Licko in 1985.

6-84. This is Template Gothic, designed by Barry Deck in 1990.

6-85. This is ITC Anna, designed by Daniel Pelavin at the end of the 1980s.
This is a display font only; there is no lowercase to this font.

decade of disco music, leisure suits, gas lines, oil embargoes, Iran hostage-taking, and a sweatered President Carter reminding Americans to set thermostats at 65° F. Import cars went farther on a tank of gas, and foreign car manufacturers expanded their American market share. The country was in an economic recession and people turned to jogging, yoga, transcendental meditation, encounter groups and analysts rather than drugs for the answers. Baby boomers were middle-aged and settling down with families; the radical protest era faded as they grayed.

THE RISE OF CORPORATE TYPE AND DESIGN GUIDELINES

Corporate design became structured at the end of the 70s with strict program guides determining the grid and type choices that designers could use in corporate communication. Corporations strived for consistent visual programs and images. The 80s was the decade of the Savings and Loan Crisis, unbridled government spending by Congress, the rise of the environmental movement as the "cause celebre" of the new generation, and Reagan was in office. Early rock music and tie-died shirts made comebacks; punks, skinheads, skateboards and rap music were awesome. Compact disc players, home camcorders, silk ties, Walkmen, fiber optics, lasers and genetic engineering were new in this decade. AIDS changed the sexual scene late in the 80s in America–caution meant life or death. Drugs were not cool, but weightlifting and aerobics were.

Americans reduced smoking and starting eating healthfully (somewhat). Personal computers were gradually making their way into most American homes, just as television had in the 50s. Southern cities were experiencing a tremendous growth as population moved to the Sunbelt. Silicon Valley was christened.

POST-MODERNISM/MEMPHIS INFLUENCE ON TYPE DESIGN

At the end of the 80s, Post-Modernism and Memphis style industrial design were in vogue. Post-Modernism was based on a integrated, eclectic approach to design, and Memphis was expressed best in the high contrast in furniture designs of unique geometric forms and vibrant colorful patterns and colors. Some typefaces were designed with these sensibilities. Typestyles were more influenced by the retro movement among some of America's prominent designers. Rather than create fresh ideas, these people were looking to movements of the past for inspiration and reusing and reissuing these ideas with the era's messages. Dada type design of random mixing, Constructivist designs, wood block illustrations, and photomontage techniques were all revisited as the current design vogue. Letterers were paid to hand-letter wood or lead type that was no longer available, and the old was seen as new.

Daniel Pelavin looked to the Art Deco era of the 20s to create ITC Anna that was released at the end of the decade. This font is a condensed, sans serif face with some rounded characters and square terminals. It is clearly reminiscent of the Roaring 20s, and some of the characters are related to hand lettering done during that decade.

COMPUTERS AND DIGITAL TYPE DESIGN

The introduction of computers affected type design. In the past, fonts were designed at very large sizes, by hand. Each letter was painstakingly drawn and redrawn as it was refined. The drawings of characters were then placed together to check for the fit of characters and the harmony of the font. Letters were often refined at 14" high or more, so that the details of each letter could be examined. Of particular importance were the transition areas of the letters, where the strokes change from the hairline to the stem weight stroke. The stress of each letter can also be carefully studied at enlarged size. The compatibility of shapes and curves are easily finessed when the characters can be seen extremely large.

Neville Brody, a typographer from London, designed condensed, square and angular fonts that resonated with the Russian Constructivists' influence. In Industria Inline and Arcadia, Brody's characters are more than a strict recreation of the style of a bygone era. His characters do show different and contemporary variations of counter forms, as well as unorthodox shapes to some of the letters, which give the faces an unusual and appealing quirkiness. They feel industrial and computerized at once, yet they are not spartan. His geometric fonts are contemporary because of their minimalism and their efforts to be different and innovative from the historic typefaces he is referencing.

Max Kisman has also designed number of innovative fonts for digital use. He has created Vortex, Traveller, Jacques Slim, and Tegentonen. His fonts have an offbeat angularity to the characters. Some are very condensed and formal; others are more casual. Zuzana Licko, working with Emigré designed Matrix, Modula, Lunatix and Elektrix.

6-86. This is Traveller Regular, designed by Max Kisman in 1991.

6-87. This is Prototype, designed by Jonathan Barnbrook in 1990.

6-88. This is Industria Inline, designed in 1990 by Neville Brody.

6-89. This is Jacques Slim, Regular, and Fat, designed by Max Kisman in 1990.

This page is set in Bembo 8.5/12.

6-90. This is Keedy Sans Bold, designed by Jeffery Keedy in 1989.

6-91. This is Arbitrary Sans Serif Bold, designed by Barry Deck.

6-92. This is Hard Times Regular, designed by Jeffery Keedy in 1990.

She even started designing fonts back in the ImageWriter days, creating bitmapped versions for the QuickDraw printers. Jeffery Keedy has made some wonderful contributions with Keedy Sans and Hard Times, which is a fusion font. On some terminals there are serifs; on others there are none. The digital fusion fonts offer an interesting area for typeface development, and only time will tell if these forays in type design will have interest for generations to come, and perhaps create their own branch of font styles. They have endless possibilities.

Today, type design is an unusual fusion of technical skills, classic geometry, and artistic balance—not to mention functionality. In the final font design, attention must be paid to each character, as well as to the harmonious unity of the overall font. The *negative spaces*, or *counters*, of the letters must be critiqued, as well as the strokes. The font must reproduce well at a variety of sizes, with the printing technology of the day. With digital technology many standard, traditional rules of the weight and strokes in type design were broken. Digital fonts can be created as a fusion, manipulation or combination of other fonts.

There is much more to designing a font than merely the design of 26 upper- and lowercase letters. There are also the numerals, the monetary symbols, the accented characters, the punctuation symbols, the small caps, the fractions and the mathematical symbols. In addition, the spacing of the characters has to be exquisite and finessed to provide the best readability. Even with the tools of technology, the design sense of the typographer is still essential.

PROJECT: 20TH CENTURY TYPOGRAPHER SERIES EXHIBITION POSTER

Your project is to design a poster for an exhibit of the work of a 20th century type designer. Select a typographer whose work you admire from this chapter, and research him/her further at the library. Then, using his/her typeface(s) design a two-color poster for an exhibit of his/her typographic work. You can use the face of the person or not as you see fit. The focus of the poster and the focus of the exhibit are typographic. They can be as simple or as complex a design as you desire.

Consider incorporating working drawings of the font if you find them in other reference books. It can be a purely aesthetic design, or it can have a verbal message. The final poster will be sold for framing, so plan size accordingly.

Begin your design process by doing fifteen thumbnail sketches, and then on the computer try to combine a series of them to create ten more ideas. Experiment with color in your designs. Once you've worked through this process, you are ready to design the final poster, full size. Be sure to indicate the time, date and place of the exhibit, as well as the name it is given. Also, you may want to advertise a lecture by the person whose work is being exhibited.

OBJECTIVES

- To research a 20th century type designer in depth.
- To use only one typographer's fonts as visual reference.
- To design for a specific event.
- To limit the designer to two colors, plus their screen combinations.
- To utilize type as the primary visual medium and utilize space on the page creatively.
- To encourage designers to know more about the tradition and contemporary practitioners of their craft.

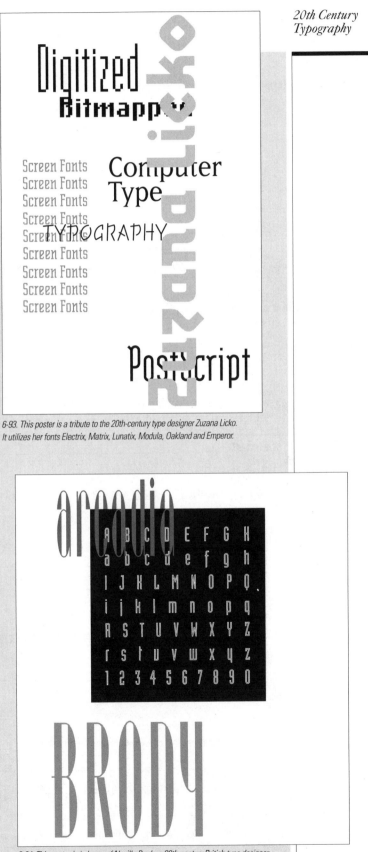

6-93. This poster is a tribute to the 20th-century type designer Zuzana Licko. It utilizes her fonts Electrix, Matrix, Lunatix, Modula, Oakland and Emperor.

6-94. This poster is in honor of Neville Brody, a 20th-century British type designer. It utilizes his fonts Industria Inline and Arcadia.

This page is set in Fenice Light 8.5/12.

20th Century Typography-Review

6 *20th Century*
Typography

1. What was the Arts & Crafts Movement? _____

_____

2. Who was William Morris? _____

_____

3. Name three of his innovations (other than typefaces). _____

_____

4. What is the difference between *Hot Type* and *Cold Type*? _____

_____

5. What is the linotype machine and what is significant about it? _____

_____

6. What is a slug? _____

_____

7-8. Who was Frederic Goudy and what were two of his contributions to typography? ___

_____

_____

9. Who was Eric Gill? _____

_____

10. Describe the Dada movement's approach to typography. _____

_____

11. What was the Bauhaus? _____

_____

12. Describe the Bauhaus' contributions to typography. _____

_____

13. What was Herbert Bayer's contribution to typography? _____

_____

14. Describe Constructivist type layout. _____

_____

15. Describe Paul Renner's contribution to typography. _____

_____

16. Who was Hermann Zapf, and what were his contributions to typography? _____
_____

17. What was Adrian Frutiger's contribution to typography? _____
_____

18. What are some of the special considerations of a typeface design for a newspaper? _____
_____

19. How was Helvetica designed? _____
_____

20. What are some of the fonts designed by Herb Lubalin? _____
_____

21. What are some characteristics of 1960s type design? _____
_____

22. What is the ITC? _____
_____

23. What is phototypesetting? _____
_____

24. How did phototypesetting affect the appearance of typography? _____
_____

25. What are some of the contributions of Ed Benguiat? _____
_____

26. Who is Daniel Pelavin? _____
_____

27. Who is Neville Brody? _____
_____

28. How has the creation of fonts changed with the advent of computers? _____
_____

This page is set in
Fenice Light 8.5/12.

Changes in Printing Technology

7 *Changes in Printing Technology*

7-1. The earliest presses were pressure presses. This is an example of a pressure press; the paper was placed between the type and the platen. The platen was cranked down onto the lead type, and the ink was transferred from the type onto the paper.

7-2. Printing was a multi-step process. It has been considered the first application of assembly-line production since the production was broken down into a series of tasks that were performed by different workers.

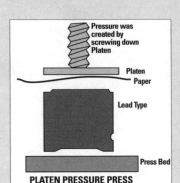

7-3. Originally, presses required a great deal of physical pressure to print a page of type. The pieces of lead type were locked into a frame to prevent them from shifting or moving.

This page is set in Serifa Roman 8.5/12.

INTRODUCTION

In this chapter, we will review the basics of printing technology from Gutenberg's time to current computerized presses. Printing has changed tremendously from the days of pressure-based "wine presses" to today's disk-to-plate technology. Production time is a fraction of earlier processes and costs have been reduced. However, with greater technology comes greater complexity. This chapter traces printing from the days of lead type, through photocomposition, to dot matrix, then to laser output and finally to offset lithography.

PLATEN LETTERPRESS

The earliest printing press was a modified grape press for making wine. Letterpress printing is a variation of the original platen press. The platen press required the use of a flat, horizontal press bed. On the press bed, all type or images to be printed had to be precisely *type high* or .918" tall. This was essential for even distribution of ink and a uniform impression on the page. Anything taller could tear through the paper; anything shorter would not get inked and would not print.

The bed of the press had a frame around it that was shorter than type high so that it would not print. The type (either lead or wood) had to be arranged on the press bed, and then *furniture* or blocks of wood and metal, were placed from the edge of the type on the press bed to the edge of the press. They locked the type in place in all directions to prevent it from shifting when the platen was screwed down with force onto the type. A great deal of pressure was needed to impress the ink onto the paper; this is where "presses" got their name.

Proofing sheets were run to assure that the type appeared in the desired place on the page, and to correct any typesetting errors. Each letter or line was placed on the galley or composing plate one at a time in letterpress. It takes a great deal of time to set up the press for this printing process.

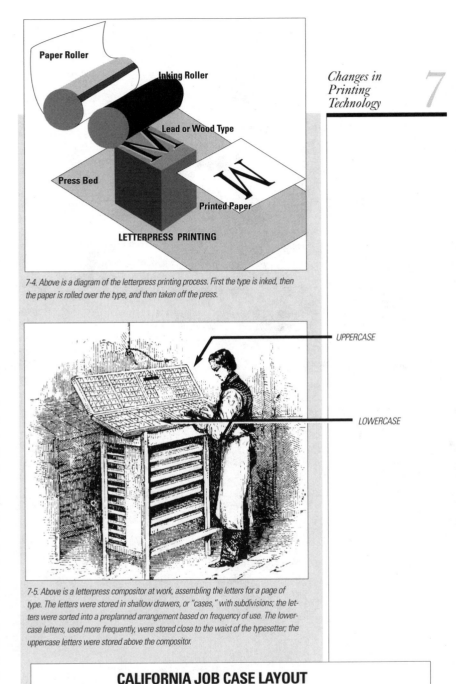

ROTARY LETTERPRESS

In rotary letterpress printing, an inking roller passed over the type on the press bed, followed by a paper roller that rolled the paper over the inked type and picked up the impression of the type. The pressure was supplied by the physical weight of the metal roller. The paper had to be hand-fed onto the paper roller in early models. The paper was released at the end of the press and the type was re-inked by the inking roller on the way back. The inking roller then picked up a fresh supply of ink from the ink feeder and the process repeated.

Letterpress printing was at first constrained by horizontal and vertical structure in the layout of the type on the page. This was easily broken when Dada artists began experimenting with composing directly on the press bed, printing from unconventional objects and locking up the type so that it wasn't square.

Letterpress is an art to be mastered. It required the packing material (paper or wool blankets), behind the roller that carried the paper. The packing behind the paper could affect the quality of the impression. The ink had to be mixed to just the right viscosity so that it would stick to the type, yet come off cleanly on the paper, without any smudges or runs. Older ink that sat on the shelf sometimes got thick and had to be mixed with oil to get it to the right consistency. Heat and humidity would also affect the runniness of the ink and the paper's ink absorbency. Trial and error was necessary to get the second color to print exactly where it was supposed to print, and this was time-consuming and costly.

But the letterpress is a very tactile, artsy, romantic printing press. Some printers can judge the correct tack of the ink by the sound that the inking roller makes as it picks up ink from the ink feeder. You can smell the ink, hear the press running and watch your piece come off—sometimes you have to reload the paper, and turn the crank of the rollers by hand. Letterpress printing is printmaking that is slow and methodical, by an individual press producing work at a speed that humans can comprehend and watch. Many artists' books are created by artists who have purchased these old presses and now personally operate them. They can be adapted for use with woodcuts, linoleum cuts and found objects that are trimmed or mounted to type high.

SETTING LETTERPRESS TYPE

Type for a letterpress machine was originally set each character at a time. This is where the name upper- and lowercase came from to describe the capitals and small letters. The type was sorted according to its

7-4. Above is a diagram of the letterpress printing process. First the type is inked, then the paper is rolled over the type, and then taken off the press.

7-5. Above is a letterpress compositor at work, assembling the letters for a page of type. The letters were stored in shallow drawers, or "cases," with subdivisions; the letters were sorted into a preplanned arrangement based on frequency of use. The lowercase letters, used more frequently, were stored close to the waist of the typesetter; the uppercase letters were stored above the compositor.

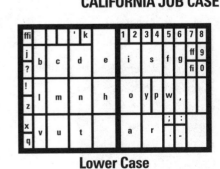

CALIFORNIA JOB CASE LAYOUT

Lower Case

Upper Case

Letters were arranged according to frequency of use, and were alotted space that related to how many characters were on an average page. The lowercase was laid out to save motion when setting type for a page. The J and U are at the bottom of the upper case because they were introduced into common use long after the lay of the case had been determined.

7-6. Above is the layout of the type cases used for letterpress composing. These shallow drawers are called California Job Cases.

This page is set in Serifa Roman 8.5/12.

7-7. *Above is an operator loading paper into a rotary mechanized letterpress.*

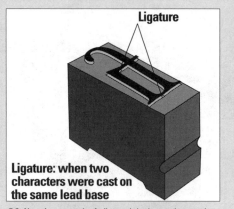

Ligature

Ligature: when two characters were cast on the same lead base

7-8. *Above is an example of a ligature in lead type, when two characters are joined at the serifs or cross bars, and are cast as one character on a single slug of lead.*

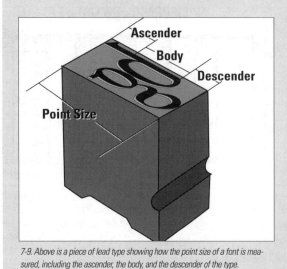

Ascender

Body

Descender

Point Size

7-9. *Above is a piece of lead type showing how the point size of a font is measured, including the ascender, the body, and the descender of the type.*

This page is set in Serifa Roman 8.5/12.

point size and placed in very wide, long drawers that had very little depth to them. The type was arranged in a pre-determined fashion in these drawers based on which characters were used the most frequently. These shallow drawers held the sorted type and were called *California job cases.* The type was also sorted according to whether it was small letters or capitals. The capitals were kept in the upper drawer or "case," and the small letters (which were used more frequently in composition) were kept in the "lower case," where they were more readily accessible. Although this hand sorting of type is rarely done any more since the introduction of the linotype machine, the phrases "uppercase" and "lowercase" have stuck from that era and are used today to describe capital and small letters.

Another term that carries over from this era is the term *leading* to describe the space between lines of type. In the letterpress era, spacing between lines was created by placing thin strips of lead that were less than type high between the rows of letters. The spacing could be opened up by adding additional strips of lead or by using wider strips of lead. These strips of lead were called *leading*, and they came in one point increments. There were one point, two point, three point, four point, etc., leading strips that determined the thickness of the spacing between the printed lines. It is difficult today to imagine that the space was determined by the width of a physical piece of lead, but it is easier to imagine if you can see some old lead type.

Today we refer to interline spacing as leading, and measure it from the baseline of one line to the baseline of the next line. The baseline is used because it is a constant line in type design. The point size of the type is placed as the numerator of a fraction and the leading is placed as the denominator—for example, 10/12.

The measurements of fonts, from ascenders to descenders, harkens back to the lead type. Each mold had to be made exactly the same length on the type surface. This area had to accommodate space for ascenders and descenders, regardless of whether the character had them. This was so that the type could line up in rows on the press. All of the matrices had to be designed with the baseline of the characters at a consistent place so that the fonts' bases lined up precisely when printed.

THE LETTERPRESS CHARACTER—A PIECE OF LEAD TYPE

There is a whole dictionary of terminology for the parts of a piece of lead type. It was important to have terms to describe these parts so that the hand compositors could discuss a broken or disfigured piece of type accurately. To begin with, the height from the bed of the press to the flat surface of the raised character that will print must be precisely .918" high, or type high, so that it prints very clearly.

The base of the lead character that sits on the press bed is notched down the center. The notched area is called the *groove*. The two edges that sit on the press bed are called *feet*. The vertical height of the lead character is called the *body* or *shank*. One side of the body (that corresponds to the base of the character) has a curved depression running horizontally near the base of the lead character. This was used to align the characters, and the strips of lead placed between lines of type for spacing had a protrusion that fit precisely into this depression called the *nick*. The thickness of the lead used would determine the appearance of the white space between the lines of type.

The very top surface of the letter that is printed is called the *face*. When you look down on the face of the lead character, the surface from which the character is built up is called the *platform*; at the edges, it's called the *shoulder*; this area does not print. The section of the letter that is raised up off the platform is called the *beard* or *neck*, and it is usually a diagonal structure to reinforce the face of the character. Remember that the character is reversed before it is printed, so that the impression on the page will be "right-reading."

Although letterpress technology has been superseded, it is interesting for designers to know the terminology that is part of the heritage of the field. It will allow you to get "design" jokes in the future at conferences with some of the esoteric knowledge you have gained about typography. It also enables you to understand how some of these names or terms may be applied to new parts of type in the future. Hopefully it enhances your appreciation for the medium of type as an artistic tool for communication. As technology changed, some of the lead type terms have remained. When the linotype machine was adopted, some of this terminology was applied to the solid (fused) lines of lead type, and some of it became unnecessary.

MERGENTHALER'S LINOTYPE MACHINE

The introduction of Mergenthaler's linotype machine in the printing industry had overnight repercussions. Entire composing rooms of twenty peo-

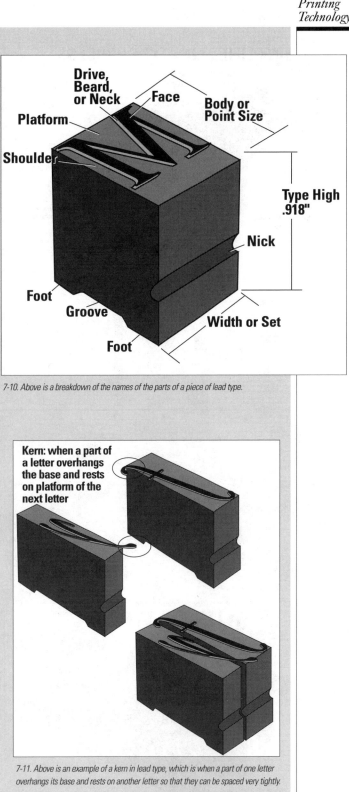

7-10. Above is a breakdown of the names of the parts of a piece of lead type.

7-11. Above is an example of a kern in lead type, which is when a part of one letter overhangs its base and rests on another letter so that they can be spaced very tightly.

This page is set in
Americana 8.5/12.

7
*Changes in
Printing
Technology*

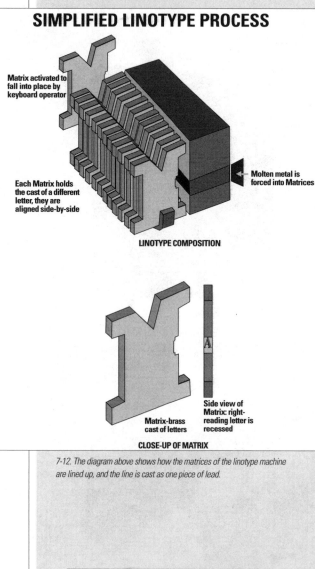

SIMPLIFIED LINOTYPE PROCESS

Matrix activated to fall into place by keyboard operator

Each Matrix holds the cast of a different letter, they are aligned side-by-side

Molten metal is forced into Matrices

LINOTYPE COMPOSITION

Matrix-brass cast of letters

Side view of Matrix: right-reading letter is recessed

CLOSE-UP OF MATRIX

7-12. The diagram above shows how the matrices of the linotype machine are lined up, and the line is cast as one piece of lead.

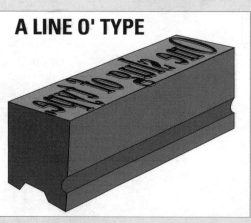

A LINE O' TYPE

7-13. Above is a diagram of a line of type, cast as one piece from a linotype machine.

This page is set in
Americana 8.5/12.

ple had been needed to hand-assemble a newspaper each day. With the linotype machine, this same composing could be done in half the time by three keyboard operators. This one machine forced many people to be retrained or find other work.

The linotype machine works by having the *matrices* or *molds*, of each character linked to its corresponding key on a typewriter keyboard. As the operator types, the matrices come down a tube and are lined up next to each other, and spaces, capitals and punctuation have their corresponding matrices. Once the operator gets the signal that the end of the column width has been reached, they have to insert a hyphen, or backspace and eject the partial word at the end. Once the line is determined, a button is pressed, and the molten lead is poured into the matrices. This creates a line of type cast as one piece, hence the name of the device.

The molten lead line is cooled quickly, shaken out of the matrices, and fed down a chute, where it lands next to the previous line. The top and bottom edge of linotype is not smooth, but notched so that the lines sort of clamp together. The matrices of the letters are returned to their places via chains and pulleys, and the process begins again for the next line.

If the operator makes a typing mistake, the line could be discontinued, or cast and then removed from the column of type. After a mistake, composers would run their finger down the keyboard, creating the nonsense phrase ETAOIN SHRDLU to call attention to the line so that it would be pulled during proofing. Occasionally, this line was missed, and it printed.

The spacing on the linotype machine was difficult. Kerning could be accomplished, and justifying was possible, but they required keystroking during the process of inputting the text. The transition from linotype, or hot type, to phototypesetting, or cold type was gradual. Some designers were highly in favor of lead type and argued that photo-set type wasn't as clear or as crisp as lead type, while others simply liked the subtle impression of letterpress type on the paper. Phototypesetting would never have advanced as quickly as it did if offset lithography was not becoming a viable printing option.

OFFSET LITHOGRAPHY

Automated offset lithographic printing was refined in the 1930s. The main breakthrough is that offset no longer used heavy lead type. Instead it is a process in which the image from the photographically exposed plate is "offset" onto a rubber roller, which then transfers the image to the sheet. This allowed anything to be printed which could be photographed. Offset also applies the theory that oil and water do not mix, as lithography does. The innovation of the roller allowed faster printing.

In offset printing, the mechanical boards prepared by the designer are shot and a negative film is made of the layout. Images or halftones in the design are stripped into place and the negative is exposed to develop an aluminum alloy printing plate. This thin, flexible plate is then wrapped around the plate cylinder on the press. The plate picks up ink from one roller, offsets the image onto a rubber roller, and the paper then picks up the image from this rubber roller. The paper *never* touches the plate; in fact, the paper would wear down the surface of the aluminum alloy printing plate very quickly because the paper has a hard surface. The soft, rubber offset cylinder doesn't harm the printing plate. The printing plate is made of an aluminum alloy that is not very durable if the printing were done directly to paper, but the plate prints onto the soft, rubber offset roller. Unlike letterpress printing, it is not necessary to compose the page letter by letter, or line by line. When type could be produced photographically, the lead and the heating were entirely removed from the production of type process.

COLD TYPE REPLACES HOT TYPE

When hot type was being replaced by *cold type*, or *phototypesetting*, few designers trusted the new photo type. Designers would have type set from a linotype machine, and then a few proof copies were pulled in black ink and sent to the designer. The designer then pasted this type onto the mechanical board that would be shot and printed by offset lithography. It seems as though this process was a bit backward when we look at it today, but there was a time when this was standard procedure. Before phototypesetting was widely available, or commercially feasible, this was the only alternative. Likewise, at this point, if you wanted headlines kerned for better readability, it was necessary to cut the letters apart, cut out the space between characters and then paste the letters together back into words. Spacing between lines could also be changed in this hand-cutting method. Design was very labor intensive at this point. The process wasn't foolproof, but the alternative with lead type and letterpress was to physically shave or sand down the edges of metal or wood characters so that they would fit more closely in the headline.

PHOTOTYPESETTING

In 1949, René Hogonnet and Louis Marius Moyroud piloted a phototypesetting machine at the American Newspapers Publishers Association conference that set type from photographic masters or negatives. This prototype of photocomposition, called the Photon, was in production in 1954.

7-14. Designers used to work with t-squares, triangles and rubber cement to layout "galleys" received from phototypesetters. Once everything was measured, glued down, and instructions were written for the printer, the boards were shot as negatives and then burned into plates which were hung on the press and printed.

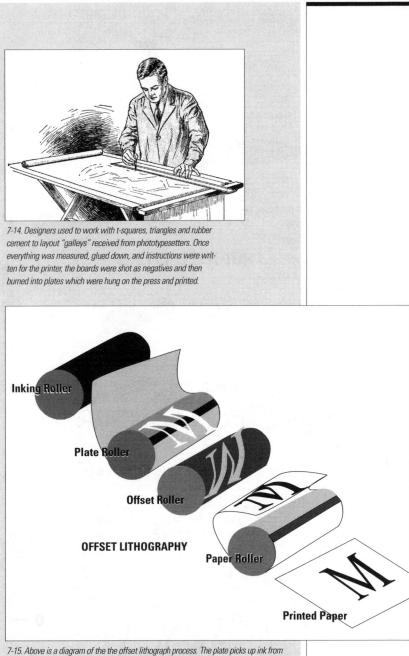

OFFSET LITHOGRAPHY

Inking Roller

Plate Roller

Offset Roller

Paper Roller

Printed Paper

7-15. Above is a diagram of the the offset lithograph process. The plate picks up ink from the inking roller, and then transfers the image onto the rubber offset roller. Then the image is "offset" from the offset roller onto the paper on the paper roller.

This page is set in
City Medium 8.5/12.

7 *Changes in*
Printing
Technology

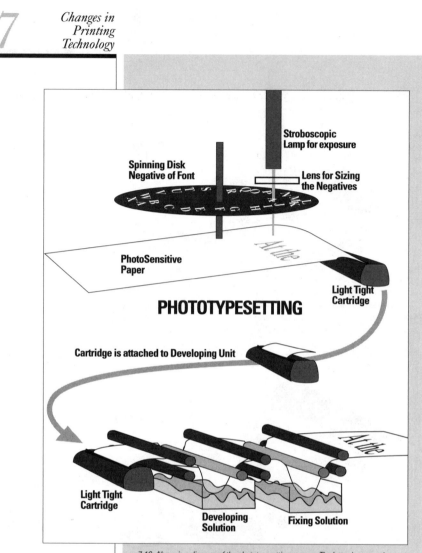

7-16. Above is a diagram of the phototypesetting process. The letter is exposed onto photosensitive paper by a beam shot through a negative. The paper is then scrolled into a light tight cartridge. The cartridge is connected to the developing unit, where it passes through a series of chemical baths to develop it.

7-17. Examples of the possibilities of photocomposited type are shown above. These would have been impossible in lead type.

This page is set in
City Medium 8.5/12.

Phototypesetting meant that the work-intensive design process could be streamlined. Now, designers roughed in the headline by hand, in the typeface they wanted, at the size they wanted, with the letterspacing and line spacing they wanted, and sent this rough layout to the typesetter with type speccing marks on it. The typesetter sat at a computer terminal and input the text, coding it for font, size, spacing, etc. Then the signals were sent to a machine that spun a disk of the negative of the font. A stroboscopic lamp was used to shoot light through the master of the font; a lens adjusted the size of the letters. The light exposed the images of the letters onto *light-sensitive* or *photographic* paper. This paper was fed into a light-sealed cartridge. The cartridge was removed and attached to another unit that fed the paper through the developing fluids and baths so that the type was developed on the paper; these long columns of phototypesetting were called *galleys*, and were assembled by hand, with triangle and T-square, into mechanicals that were shot photographically.

If the chemicals were weak, the type would come out gray on the paper, and the job had to be rerun with fresh chemicals. If the spacing of the headline was not accurate to the layout, the typesetter might try to rerun it or ask the designer to cut it together where needed. Typesetting had come a long way at this point. These phototypesetting machines were considered quite fast, outputting up to 50 lines of text per minute, creating type faster than it could be typed in at the keyboard of the phototypesetting machine.

Phototypesetting allowed new design possibilities. Type could be blown up to any size! Designers were not limited by the stock fonts of the *printing* firm they worked with. Type could be *overlapped*—something that was not possible in linotype on letterpress. Soon type could be forced to conform to a circle, create angles, be skewed, stretched or twisted. The possibilities were endless. Type could be crammed together in headlines—and it was. Tight letterspacing became the vogue in the 70's—the tighter the better. Some phototypesetters could also print the type with textures, lines or dots rather than merely in solid black.

DIGITAL PHOTOTYPESETTING

In 1972, phototypesetting was combined with computerized printing technology for the first time. Rather than use a physical negative as the master of the font, the font was created as a digitally represented master. Each character was encoded as digital or computerized information. The earliest versions of digital typesetters used an electron beam to transfer the digitized font into a visual font onto a *cathode ray tube* (CRT). The CRT then transferred this visual font onto photosensitive paper, creating output exactly the same as earlier phototypesetting equipment. This typesetting technology allowed 3,000 lines to be set every minute since the physically spinning disk film negative of the font was eliminated from the process. The CRT has been surpassed by the laser beam as the instrument for transmitting the image of the digitized information onto the photosensitive paper.

DOT-MATRIX PRINTERS AND FONTS

Computer printers began with very simple type and the dot-matrix printer. Yet because the letters from a dot-matrix printer were slightly broken, it was considered difficult to read. Nonetheless, many businesses were willing to forgo this difficulty in order to maximize the convenience of the computer in the early days. Similar to monospaced fonts that were first created for the typewriter (which eventually evolved to variably spaced and alternate fonts with the electric typewriter), the early dot-matrix fonts were monospaced. This means that the lowercase "i," a very thin character, was allotted the same width as the uppercase "W," a very wide character. This leads to extremely awkward spacing, poor readability, and an aesthetic so bad that many potential users preferred to stay with the better quality output from sophisticated electric typewriters. Typewriters weren't as convenient as computers, but in the long run they put out a much-better-looking and easier-reading product.

Dot-matrix printers generally have the same resolution as the type you see on the screen; both are 72 *dots per inch* (dpi). This dpi ratio was chosen at first because type is measured in points, and there are 72 points in an inch. The theory was that the screen and the existing system should coincide. 72 dots or pixels per inch means that each side of a square inch has 72 pixels or dots in it. The printers are measured in dots per inch, the monitors are measured in pixels per inch. (Monitors can have more than 72 pixels per inch, such as 82 or 92 or more in current models. The more pixels per inch, the more accurately your screen fonts are displayed on the monitor.)

Apple Computer™, the maker of the ImageWriter™, attempted to find an alternative to the unappealing dot-matrix fonts. Rather than trying to make the computer printout look more like a typewriter printout, they tried to work *within* the limitations of the 72 dpi resolution, and designed visually pleasing fonts that would work well at all sizes. Apple was one of the first computer companies to realize that the solution laid in working *with* the limited technology of dot-matrix printers and designing fonts that worked well with it, rather than trying to fight it. They employed a type designer (Charles Bigelow) to create Chicago exclusively for the 72 dpi resolution of a Mac. This font worked well on the screen of 72 pixels per inch, and printed well on the dot-matrix Quick Draw™ printers at 72 dots per inch; it is used as the default font for the interface on all Macintosh™ computers. This was just the beginning of the process of computer printers affecting the appearance of fonts and type. No longer is it the scribe's hand, the writing implement or the substrate that is written on; but now it is the limits of the current technology that is changing and determining the face of our alphabet.

DOT-MATRIX OUTPUT

If you look closely at a dot-matrix output, you can actually see the separate tiny dots that make up each letter. Usually, in dot-matrix printers, each dot on the paper is made by a separate pin hitting the ribbon against the paper, (although this is not the only method). There are different numbers of pins in dot-matrix printer heads; they range from 35 pin wires (five across in seven vertical rows) to 24 vertical and horizontal rows of pin wires. The more pins there are in the model, the smaller they are, and the closer they are together, the better the final printed dot matrix-character. More pins ultimately produce a more accurate and faster character on the paper because rather than just printing a row of three or seven dots high at a time, they are able to print a row of 24 dots deep

7-18. Above is an example of dot-matrix printing. The letters were composed of little dots that had tiny spaces between them. It was hard on the eyes.

7-19. The example of Chicago above shows how it looked when it was output on first generation dot-matrix printers. It is built out of the 72 dot structure.

7-20. Above is Chicago redesigned for optimal readability and with smoother letters for use with laser printers.

This page is set in ITC Garamond Condensed 8.5/12.

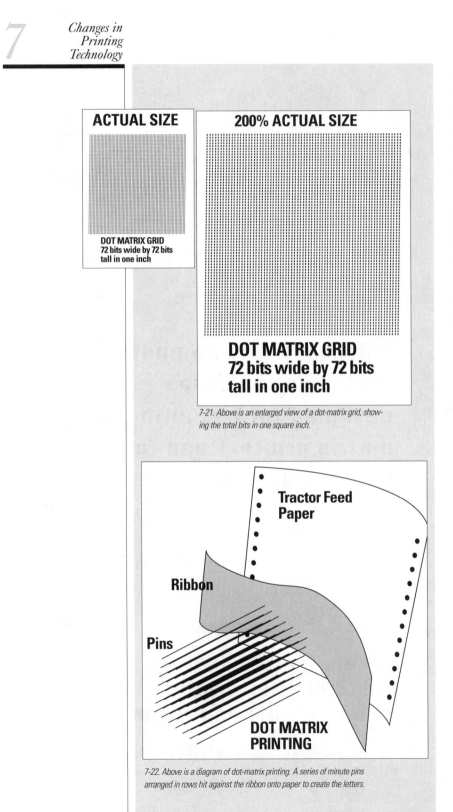

ACTUAL SIZE

DOT MATRIX GRID
**72 bits wide by 72 bits
tall in one inch**

200% ACTUAL SIZE

DOT MATRIX GRID
72 bits wide by 72 bits
tall in one inch

*7-21. Above is an enlarged view of a dot-matrix grid, show-
ing the total bits in one square inch.*

Tractor Feed
Paper

Ribbon

Pins

**DOT MATRIX
PRINTING**

*7-22. Above is a diagram of dot-matrix printing. A series of minute pins
arranged in rows hit against the ribbon onto paper to create the letters.*

at a time. Dot-matrix printers print a few thin lines of dots (determined by the number of pins high on the print head) across the page, skipping or printing the dot as the computer instructs the pins. The paper platen then moves up one fraction of an inch, and the printer head slides back across the page printing first from left to right, then right to left, down the page, activating lines of pins at a time as indicated by the printer instructions. In an ImageWriter printout, there are 72 dots high by 72 dots wide, per inch, or 5184 dots per square inch.

To improve the appearance of the dot-matrix output, Apple introduced a creative feature on their "Best" version of the printing mode on the ImageWriter. Each line was printed over twice, but the second hit was slightly offset from the first by a tiny fraction, to smooth out some of the curves and diagonals, reducing the appearance of the stepped effect. This took twice as long to print, but the separate dots were no longer visible, and the letters were darker and somewhat smoother. This double striking also gave the appearance of 144 dpi output. Some current dot-matrix printers can output type directly at resolutions higher than 72 dpi.

CHARACTER/ DAISY-WHEEL PRINTERS

Gradually the computer and printer manufacturers experimented with alternatives to dot-matrix type. One alternative was to incorporate some of the technology of the typewriter into the computer. The impact daisy-wheel or thimble-style printer was designed with type which looked like a typewriter font. These printers worked on the same principle as manual typewriters, so the shaped, raised character was pressed from a rotating *daisy-wheel* master against a ribbon onto the paper. The type produced by these printers was far superior to the dot matrix visually, but the impact version of printers were a step backwards from electronic typewriters. The impact printers made the same noise and had the same reverberation of the old manual typewriters. They could be annoying to be around when they were printing, you had to change daisy wheels in order to get an italic or bold, and they were slow because each character had to be smacked onto the paper in succession.

INK JET/BUBBLE JET PRINTERS

Ink jet printers form the characters out of little dots (similar to the dot-matrix version), but the liquid ink is shot out of minute jets that are in the replaceable cartridges. Similar to dot-matrix printers, a printer head slides back and forth, spraying ink as the paper is rolled forward. Unlike dot-matrix printers, ink jets are much quieter because there is no impact; the ink is sprayed by microscopic nozzles onto the page, so the tiny splotches of liquid ink appear to run together. This forms a more solid black than the individual dots in the dot-matrix version because the sprayed ink fills in the spaces between the dots.

With *bubble jet printers*, a bubble of ink is formed when the ink is heated by a heater plate within the nozzle of each cartridge. The bubble expands, which forces a drop of ink to be squeezed through the nozzle. As it contracts, it creates a vacuum, which sucks ink from the cartridge into the ink jet nozzle, and the process starts anew.

Color ink jet printers have four ink cartridges, one each for cyan, magenta, yellow and black; these are the same ink colors that are used on printing presses. Some ink jet printers are very flexible and will print on a variety of surfaces; others are more finicky about the paper. The difficulty is that drying times of the ink on the surfaces varies depending on the absorption of the paper; if drying times are long, ink can easily be smeared.

LASER PRINTERS

Laser printers were introduced in 1985. They gave a cleaner, smoother appearance to the type, so no longer was there a pixelated, step appearance to curves and angles as there had been with dot matrix. Laser image printers create the printout by drawing the image onto a metal drum with a fine beam of laser light. This drum is then electrostatically charged positive, attracting dry toner (a mixture of carbon, metal shavings and plastic dust) to the laser pattern on the metal drum. The paper passes over an electrostatic negatively charged wire which attracts the toner from the drum onto the paper. The image is then adhered to the paper by a fuser unit and heat process, which melts the plastic particles and affixes the carbon toner to the paper.

The printing resolution of LaserWriters™ is 300, 600, 800 and 1200 dots per inch. The original laser printers were 300 dots high by 300 dots wide, or 90,000 dots per square inch. The individual dots on a laser printout are not capable of being discerned by the human eye.

Laser printers now allow the creation of many different typestyles and sizes with a legibility of 300 dots per inch, which reduces the problem of the jagged diagonals. But, they are not at the high quality resolution of the 2400 dpi of phototypesetting machines, which creates a flawless character with perfectly smooth edges.

Most laser printers use the PostScript™ language developed by Adobe™ as the format in which the construction of the font is directed from the computer. Most fonts designed for laser output are drawn in the computer as outlines created from bezier curves with a few active anchor points. These outlines can be mathematically scaled up or down to print the outline in proportion at any given size. The outline tells the printer the shape and the size to create and it is filled in automatically to produce the black or gray characters on the page.

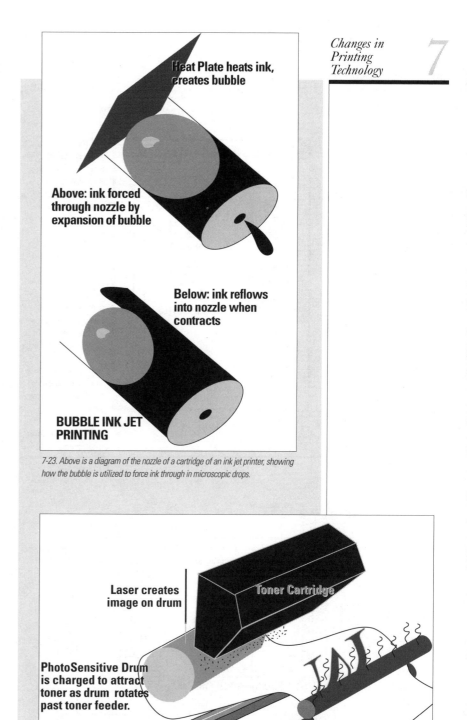

Changes in Printing Technology 7

Heat Plate heats ink, creates bubble

Above: ink forced through nozzle by expansion of bubble

Below: ink reflows into nozzle when contracts

BUBBLE INK JET PRINTING

7-23. Above is a diagram of the nozzle of a cartridge of an ink jet printer, showing how the bubble is utilized to force ink through in microscopic drops.

Laser creates image on drum

Toner Cartridge

PhotoSensitive Drum is charged to attract toner as drum rotates past toner feeder.

Electrically charged wire attracts toner from drum onto paper.

Heated Rollers fuse toner to the paper.

LASER PRINTERS

7-24. This illustration shows a simplified drawing of the inner workings of a laser printer.

This page is set in Melior 8.5/12.

7 *Changes in Printing Technology*

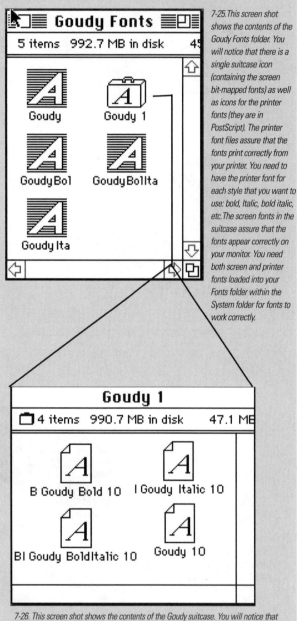

7-25.This screen shot shows the contents of the Goudy Fonts folder. You will notice that there is a single suitcase icon (containing the screen bit-mapped fonts) as well as icons for the printer fonts (they are in PostScript). The printer font files assure that the fonts print correctly from your printer. You need to have the printer font for each style that you want to use: bold, italic, bold italic, etc.The screen fonts in the suitcase assure that the fonts appear correctly on your monitor. You need both screen and printer fonts loaded into your Fonts folder within the System folder for fonts to work correctly.

7-26. This screen shot shows the contents of the Goudy suitcase. You will notice that the icons of the screen fonts look different from the icons of the printer fonts. The screen fonts are much simpler. If you keep all the variations of weight and style of one family in the same suitcase, it will simplify and reduce the size of your Font folder. Also, you need each style of the screen font in only one point size (here it's 10) if you are running ATM, Adobe Type Manager™, which scales the one size of screen font to any size needed, and prevents screen jaggies on your type.

This page is set in ITC Frutiger Light 8.5/12.

IMAGESETTER PRINTERS

Imagesetters™ are digital typesetting equipment for professional quality output. They produce photographic quality output, because they print out at up to 2400 dots per inch, and the characters are perfectly smooth. These machines (Linotronic™, Varityper™ and CompuGraphic™) can also print photos as halftones and print to film as well as paper, streamlining the printing process. If you output to film, the output is more expensive, but you save the cost of having the boards shot as negatives and halftones stripped in, to make the plates from.

The Linotronic 100 outputs type at 1270 dots per inch, or 1.6 million dots per square inch. The more advanced Linotronic 500™ has the capacity to print 1690 dots per inch or 2.85 million dots per square inch. The top of the line Linotronic 300™ outputs type at 2540 dots per inch resolution. This means that it has the capacity to print 6.45 million dots per square inch. The differences in the resolution of these high end machines cannot be detected with the human eye, they can just barely be seen under a magnifying glass. But it is good to know the resolution of the type you are buying; it can be important if you decide to photographically enlarge type from a typesetter.

HOME COMPUTERS/TELEVISION WEB BROWSERS

The proliferation of the personal computer and laser printers has raised the quality of the visual presentation of written correspondence in the business world. No longer is the typewriter considered the standard. The industry has dictated that laser output with a variety of fonts should be used. Like the invention of the typewriter itself, the laser printer has enabled individuals to create documents that were previously only possible through expensive complicated processes that were not practical for an everyday letter. Individuals with a personal computer can now create books that look as if they were printed. With modems and fax machines information can be transmitted in seconds, leading to an international information explosion that the human mind finds boggling. Online computer network services allow users to converse with users in other countries, download information from web sites, and research information at all times of night and day.

The computer is becoming a window to the rest of the world, and more and more Americans are plugging in. The future workplace will likely be the home. Some corporations are responding well to employees' requests for home work rather than commuting to an office. A whole new industry of network offices linked via computers to the actual physical office where a person is employed (but located in the suburbs to reduce traffic congestion) is becoming very popular.

SCREEN FONTS

Computerized typesetting for the Macintosh format consists of two different types of fonts. There are *screen fonts* and *printer fonts*. They are related and yet very different. Screen fonts allow a user to get an approximation of how the printed version of a font will appear on paper. It accurately shows the font at the correct height, displays italic or bold faces, and indicates line and page breaks as they will print on paper. They do not, however, show the font perfectly accurately, nor do they show how it will look when printed at higher than 300 dpi output.

PRINTER FONTS

Printer fonts are the PostScript™ language files that tell the printer how to create the vector version of the font for printing based on the font on the screen. They must be installed in the *fonts folder* of your *system folder* in order for fonts to print correctly. Each of the different weights and italic versions of the printer fonts must be present as a separate file.

INTERNATIONAL TYPEFACE CORPORATION

In the face of this global expansion of computers and fonts, there is some semblance of order within the font community. The International Typeface Corporation (ITC) was founded in an attempt to standardize fonts. Up until this point, many different type foundries had created their own versions of some of the classic fonts, so that a Caslon font from the American Type Founders' manufacturer was different in appearance, set width, character count, x-height, italics and ligatures than a Caslon font from the Stemple Foundry™, or from Monotype Corporation. Given any historic font, innumerable drawings and redrawings had been made from the original font. When ordering type, designers did not always know what to expect. Unless you meticulously comped type from the supplier you always used, some of the qualities might change, and a headline in the same font would look entirely different if you bought it from a different supplier than the specimen sheet from which you worked.

The International Typeface Corporation (ITC) attempted to make sense of a system that had grown out of control. It was an innovative answer to the copycat fonts. It licenses a face after redrawing all the characters for improved readability, and it uses ITC in front of the name of the face to guarantee that it is one of its own fonts for example, ITC New Baskerville. By redrawing the classic faces and improving their legibility, (usually by increasing the x-height to cap-height proportion), ITC has introduced a new standard into the field of typography. Its type is available from vendors all over the world, and it is reassuring to know that when you specify an ITC face, it will be exactly what you expect, regardless of where you are.

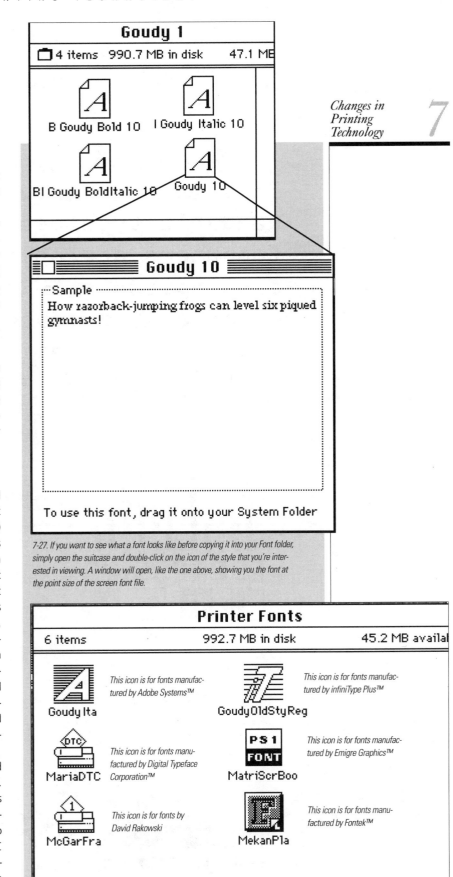

7-27. If you want to see what a font looks like before copying it into your Font folder, simply open the suitcase and double-click on the icon of the style that you're interested in viewing. A window will open, like the one above, showing you the font at the point size of the screen font file.

7-28. The various icons used for printer fonts is nothing more than a means of font manufacturers to distinguish themselves; it is almost like a logo to identify who licensed the font.

This is a computer-
readable typeface.
Computers are able to
distinguish a "3" from an
"8" or a "B" because of the
way they are designed.

7-29. This is a computer readable font called OCR-A (OCR stands for Optical Character Recognition). The characters are designed primarily for error-free computer reading.

7-30. This logo, by KU student Tara Cannon, was created using computer technology to assemble the type and symbols. Designers are able to save a great deal of time by creating final designs on the computer so that they can be scaled and colored easily.

ITC also publishes a quarterly newsletter called *U&lc* that uses type innovatively in its layouts and showcases some of ITC's new font releases. It is particularly helpful for designers to see how well a new text type will read before they decide to buy it for a job. The newsletter frequently displays paragraphs of body copy set in the entire family of a font, and this is particularly helpful when a designer is planning to use various weights of a new font for headlines and subheads. The *U&lc* newsletter can be a great tool to keep young designers learning about typography apprised of changes in the field.

COMPUTERS AND TYPOGRAPHY

In the early days of interfacing computers with type, it was not the designing of type that was an issue, but the automatic optical readability that was required so that a computer could clearly distinguish a printed "8" from a "3," or from a "B." There were many developments made in this field, and the first successful attempt produced a computer-readable typeface, but a font that had little aesthetic appeal. Gradually, computer manufacturers became more sensitized to this lack of aesthetics and undertook the task of designing a more attractive optically readable typeface. The newer optically readable type, begun around 1963, relied on a finer grid of 72 dots per inch which allowed the appearance of diagonal and curved parts to the typeface.

THE MACINTOSH MAKES COMPUTER DESIGN EASY

Apple Computer released its Macintosh computer in 1984; this computer was based on a visual interface—the user did not have to type in complex syntactical commands. Finally, computers were easy! Fonts had to be designed for the optimum readability on the black-and-white screen, as well as to reproduce well on the dot-matrix printers that were available. As noted earlier, type designs are often determined by the effects of the technology used to reproduce them. Not only did the screen resolution and the printer resolution have to be planned in concert, but they also had to resemble each other from the screen to the dot-matrix-"printed" page.

It should be noted that not only did Apple Computer implement the human-based (graphic user) interface (making the computer idiot-proof), but it was also the first company to make the decision to represent the page as white on the screen, rather than black. Apple's decision really enabled designers working on the screen to visualize what their printed work would eventually look like on the page.

7-31. The logo above was designed by KU student Brian Barto; the computer was important in the the precise kerning of the letters in this final version.

The screen attempted to accurately represent the fonts at the sizes and boldness on the page. (This has gotten better over time, but the WYSIWYG rule, meaning "What You See Is What You Get," has not been entirely perfected. There still is awkwardness of screen letter spacing and lack of consistency from screen to printer.) But, no longer was the type on the screen green or peach against a black background. The operator now could see how the final page would look.

These innovations in screen/printer consistency, as well as the user-friendly interface, enabled designers to dabble in computer-type design. The results opened a new era in type design. Many of the old hard-and-fast rules of good type design were bent, if not broken. The weights of the strokes of characters were stretched and explored and these new experimental fonts had merit.

TYPE SUPPLY HOUSES

Type corporations, such as ITC, Bitstream, Adobe Type Systems, and Monotype, had to start adjusting how they produced type and began to make computer-compatible fonts. They adapted their existing fonts for computers; the first font to be released by ITC for use on personal computer as well as for linotronic output (high resolution) was the Stone family designed by Sumner Stone and completed in 1987. This family had three variations, Stone Serif, Stone Sans Serif and Stone Informal, which has a modified serif. Each of the three versions came in three weights of italic and three weights of Roman, so that the family is made up a total of 18 fonts. It is a comprehensive system, and all the fonts share the same proportions, thereby giving greater compatibility. As with Frutiger's consistent design of the Univers system, Stone's conception of these compatible families of fonts assures a logical aesthetic consistency to the overall program.

GAUGING THE QUALITY OF COMPUTER FONTS

Often a digitized font can be judged by the attention paid to the design of the italic version of the face. With the advent of computerized type came the tendency of fonts to be designed with a slanted version of the Roman as the italic font, rather than designing different characters for the italics (which would incorporate the subtle adjustments to the letters that have always been the hallmark of italic fonts). This computerized *sheering* of the font to make a *pseudo-italic* led to the "uglying" down of fonts. The italic version of fonts often boast subtle nuances of design—softer teardrop terminals, hooked finials, loops replacing diagonal strokes, and elegant capitals inspired by scripts. Often the design of the italic font reveals the calligraphic skill and taste of a type designer. Fortunately, the italic versions of the Stone family are distinct designs that were planned as complements to the Roman faces.

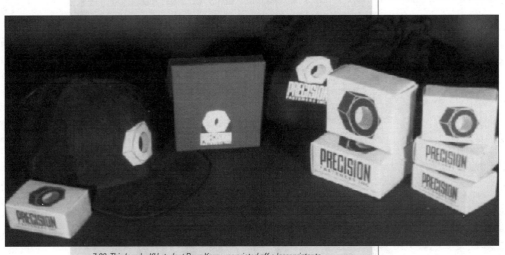

7-32. This logo by KU student Doug Kozo was printed off a laser printer to create labels and proposed applications of the logo on hats and T-shirts.

ABCDEFGH
abcdefgh
IJKLMNOPQ
ijklmnopq
RSTUVWXYZ
rstuvwxyz
1234567890

7-33. This composite font is Fudoni Bold Remix, created by Max Kisman. Kisman admits that this font is a computer fusion of parts of the traditional fonts Futura and Bodoni. The final result is an unpredictable and intense font that has an attitude.

7-34. This is Beowulf, created by Max Kisman in 1991. It appears to be composed of random parts of fonts that have been integrated with various characters from different sources.

COMPUTER-TYPE DESIGN

Today the use of computers in designing type is essential. The computer screen allows minute adjustments to curves by zooming in to a detail of a character. The bezier curve tool has replaced the french curves of yesteryear. It would be interesting to know how many type designers still draw the letters by hand and then scan them in, and how many work directly on the screen. More and more designers are relying on computers for immediate options and creations with typography. It has become a marvelously creative tool to make typographic ideas immediately accessible and viewable.

Font-manipulation programs allow users to try to design new fonts, to adjust existing fonts or to fuse two or more fonts. The type innovation of the next decades will be exciting to witness. In the historical context, it is interesting to note that just as there was a proliferation of typeface design at the turn of the last millennium, due to the Industrial Revolution so, too, at the turn of this millennium, has the Digital Revolution caused a sharp increase in the number of typefaces in production. Of course, frequently, when the numbers of typefaces proliferate, sometimes the quality standards stagnate. History teaches us that there will likely be a return to fine typography in reaction to the temporary reduction of quality and mass creation of novelty fonts. Good, solid, easily readable fonts transcend any of the changing trends and styles in typography.

PROJECT: CREATE A FEW CHARACTERS OF A FONT

This is a project to get you to appreciate the challenges of designing your own font. Your objective is to come up with four characters for a new font. Your font should be a novelty font, not a text font. It would be planned as a headline font. Select four characters that you would like to design and begin by evaluating existing fonts.

Either dive into an illustration program or begin by drawing out some of your ideas on paper. Photocopy and cut pieces of font together—use whatever means of creation that you feel the most comfortable with. Do whatever you want to create a new form for the letters, let your imagination wander and draw inspiration from all facets of your life. Consider getting some books from the library on historic and contemporary font design. Examine the fonts of other countries or certain lettering styles. It's important to realize that your font need not look like any other font that you've seen; it should try to break new ground.

Begin by trying to do medium-sized sketches of the letters, then enlarge and refine them by whatever means you choose to work. The final size of the letters is 8" tall. Mount the four final letters on board, and trim flush.

OBJECTIVES

- To research new fonts that have been designed.
- To use a variety of fonts as visual reference.
- To explore different means of creating a font.
- To try to expand the limits of headline fonts.
- To experience the process that type designers go through.
- To consider elements of letters that give them harmony.
- To encourage designers to know more about the process of designing a typeface.
- To begin to pay attention to your creative process.

7-35. This font, designed by KU student Michael Spina, is named Scathe and was created on the computer, not through hand drawings.

7-36. This font, designed by KU student Michael Spina, is named Collage and was created on the computer; some refinements were made through hand drawings.

This page is set in Fenice Light 8.5/12.

Changes in Printing Technology-Review

1. What is type high, and why is it important? _____

_____

2-3. What is the difference between letterpress and offset lithography? _____

_____

_____

4. Why is letterpress printing so time-and-labor intensive? _____

_____

5. Where do the terms upper- and lowercase come from? _____

_____

6. What is leading, and where did the term come from? _____

_____

7. What is the printing surface of lead type called? _____

_____

8. What is a kern in lead type? _____

_____

9. What is a ligature in lead type? _____

10. What is the shoulder in lead type? _____

11. What is the neck in a piece of lead type? _____

12. What is the linotype machine? _____

_____

13. What is phototypesetting? _____

_____

14. Describe the difference between hot type and cold type. _____

_____

15. In offset lithography, why is the image offset from the plate onto a rubber roller? _____

_____

16. What are some of the advances in type layout brought on by phototypesetting? _____

_____

17. How does digital typesetting differ from linotype? _____

_____

18. What is computerized typesetting? _____

_____

19. How can dot-matrix printers be compared to primitive typewriters? _____

_____

20. How does dot-matrix print relate to the screen of the computer? _____

_____

21. How are dot-matrix letters created on the page? _____

_____

22. What are character printers? _____

_____

23. How do ink jet printers differ from dot-matrix printers? _____

_____

24. Describe the process of a laser printer. _____

_____

25. How did imagesetters change the speed of producing design work? _____

_____

26. What is WYSIWYG? _____

_____

27. In a laser printer, how is the toner attached to the paper? _____

_____

28. What are the two parts of a computer font, and why do you need both pieces of software? _____

_____

_____

29. Why is it important to understand how the printer and the computer interact? _____

_____

_____

_____

_____

_____

_____

_____

This page is set in
Fenice Light 8.5/12.

Measuring Type/Leading/Kerning/Ligatures

8 *Measuring Type/ Leading/Kerning/ Ligatures*

KEY CONCEPTS

Points/Picas

Point Size of Type

Type High

Set Width of Type

Body Height

Spacing Letters

Kerning Pairs

Ligatures

Word Spacing

Headline Spacing

Caps vs. Lowercase

Reversed Type

Phrasing in Headlines

Bad Breaks

TNT: Tight Not Touching

Leading/Line Spacing

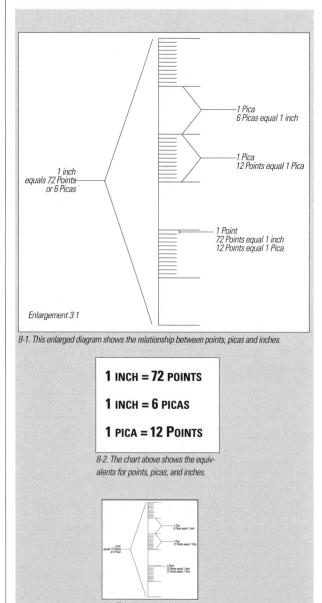

8-1. This enlarged diagram shows the relationship between points, picas and inches.

1 INCH = 72 POINTS

1 INCH = 6 PICAS

1 PICA = 12 POINTS

8-2. The chart above shows the equivalents for points, picas, and inches.

8-3. This illustration shows points, picas, and inches at actual size.

INTRODUCTION

In this chapter, first the measuring systems for type and leading are explained. Next the visual appearance of type size is covered. Then spacing is considered and is built upon. We start with the spacing of a few letters in a word, then move to spacing words and phrases in headlines (including leading), and finally to considerations specific to headline spacing.

Have you ever been tired while reading and you find yourself rereading the same line two, three, maybe four times, until you realize that you're starting to memorize it? Typographers might argue that you may *indeed* be tired, or you may be the victim of poorly spaced type that is tough to read. By paying attention to the details of spacing headlines, and the point size, leading and line length of text type, designers can create type that is more likely to be read because it *is easier* to read.

THE POINT/PICA SYSTEM OF MEASURING TYPE

To communicate with the typographer, the designer must be knowledgeable in the terminology of points, picas and leading. Measurements based on the standard U.S. ruler (inches, feet, etc.) have little relation to the language of letterforms. Type is measured in points: 72 points equal roughly one inch (.996264 of an inch) and 36 points are equal to roughly a half inch. (There are exactly 72 points to the inch when using digital technology.) See the examples at left for the relationship between points, picas and inches; example 8-1 is enlarged, and example 8-3 is at actual size.

The Parisian, Didot, was responsible for refining and standardizing the type measuring system still used today. Twelve points make a pica in the American and English systems of measurement. And, six picas equal one inch. In France, twelve points equal a a measure called the *cicero,* as opposed to a pica. In 1886 the US Type Founders Association adopted the point/pica system as the uniform measurement for type in the U.S.

Didot assigned a name to each type size, and each point size became known by this name. The point system has replaced Didot's name-based system and is universal today; the only two names that remain common are the agate and the pica. Even the agate measure, used to calculate column depth in newspaper columns, is becoming obsolete in favor of column depth measured in inches, centimeters and millimeters.

The point is a typographic measurement, and the pica is used for horizontal linear measurement of column width. Designers and typesetters use rulers that show points, picas and inches. Line length and column widths are usually measured in picas.

The point system is used for measuring the size of type, as well as the thickness of rules or lines. You can have a 1-, 2-, or 4-point rule. You can also have a .25 or a quarter point rule, which is quite thin. A hairline rule is the thinnest rule available (see figure 8-5).

MEASURING THE POINT SIZE OF TYPE

The point size of type is measured from the height of the ascenders down to the descenders. This includes the height of the *body* of a character plus ascenders and descenders. Although the height of a particular font is consistent, the width of characters changes with the letter. Letters are measured from the descender line up to the cap line or ascender line, whichever is higher. This is difficult to grasp at first, but it makes sense if you refer back to the metal type. The point measurement is taken from the outside edges of the slug or base (in lead type) on which the letter was cast or carved. (See figure 8-4 to right.)

As we observe a piece of lead or wooden type, it is clearly a rectangular block with the printing surface on top (the letter is reversed). In order for the baselines of all the characters to line up correctly, the letters *without* descenders have to be cast on a piece of lead that is the same height size as the letters *with* descenders. Below the characters that don't have descenders is a flat area of lead, called the *base* or *platform,* that is recessed so that it won't print. This extra space on a piece of lead type assures that the bases of the characters will align across the page accurately. A piece of lead type is a block that *had* to include the descender area when it was measured because all the characters allowed space on the slug for descenders, whether they had them or not. Likewise, letters without ascenders included space for the ascenders so that the type lined up evenly on top and bottom. Because of the roots in lead type, all characters are measured so that the point size includes the descender, the body and the ascender. So point size is always measured from ascender line to the descender line. (See example 8-6).

THE HISTORY OF LEADING

Leading, or *line spacing,* is the term for the space between lines of type. This term originated from the days of handset composition, when a compositor would literally place small thin strips of lead between the lines to give a little extra space between the lines of type. This extra space allows readers to maintain their place on a particular line and jump smoothly to the next line, without rereading the same or the preceding line. The leading was placed according to the instructions given to the compos-

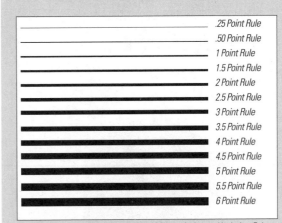

8-4. The point size of type is shown as the measure from the ascender or cap line (whichever is higher) to the descender line.

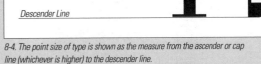

	.25 Point Rule
	.50 Point Rule
	1 Point Rule
	1.5 Point Rule
	2 Point Rule
	2.5 Point Rule
	3 Point Rule
	3.5 Point Rule
	4 Point Rule
	4.5 Point Rule
	5 Point Rule
	5.5 Point Rule
	6 Point Rule

8-5. The rules above show the graduated thickness of rules used in design. Rules can be set in increments of one tenth of a point.

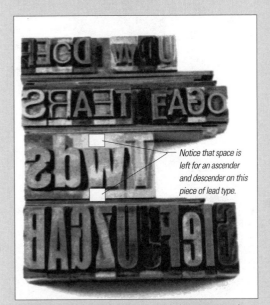

Notice that space is left for an ascender and descender on this piece of lead type.

8-6. These actual pieces of lead type show that the letters are reversed so that they will print correctly. Notice that all of the type pieces align at the top and bottom, and that space is left on every piece of lead type for ascenders and descenders.

8 Measuring Type/ Leading/Kerning/ Ligatures

Cap and Ascender Line

X-Height, Bodyline, Waist Line or Mean Line

Baseline

Descender Line

Measuring Point Size includ

8-7. Because of its historic roots in lead, the size of a font is measured to include the ascenders and the descenders.

8-8. Above are a few pieces of leading lying flat, and one standing on end as it would if placed between two lines of type.

Face: the flat surface of the character that prints

Base, Platform or Shoulder: the flat surface below the area that prints

Beard: the edge of the raised letter

Nick: indent used in aligning type

Set Width: the width of the character of type

Point Size: measured from the ascender to the descender

Groove: raised area between feet

Foot: the flat surface that sits on the press bed

8-9. The names of the parts of a piece of lead type are shown above. This information is for the interest of today's digital designers.

Type High: the measure from the press bed to the inking roller, .918".

8-10. These actual pieces of lead type show the consistency of type high, and how the width of individual characters varied. You can also see that the ascender and descender areas had to be included in the piece of lead type, whether the letter had them or not, so that all of the type would line up evenly.

This page is set in ITC Berkeley Oldstyle Book 8.5/12.

itor. 1-point leads were used to add 1 point of space between lines, and they were physically one 72nd of an inch thick. 2-point leads were used to add two points of leading etc. Today, leading is measured in typeset copy from the baseline of one line to the baseline of the next line.

EXPLAINING TYPE HIGH

Type high is .918". *Type high* is the measure from the base of the press bed to the inking rollers. Anything placed on the press bed that was type high would print. Anything less than type high would not print. That is why the base of a piece of lead type is recessed, and why strips of leading (used to space lines) are shorter than .918", because you wouldn't want the lead strips to print.

THE SET OR WIDTH OF A TYPEFACE

The *width*, known as the *set* of a piece of lead type, is dictated by the individual letter and the particular typeface. The set determines how many characters will fit on a line in the typeset copy. The set of a face determines how long a selection of body text will run when it is typeset. The more letters there are to the line, the shorter the final selection will run. The fewer letters there are to the line, the longer the same selection will run when it is set in that particular face. The same paragraph set in a condensed font will run shorter than if set in a regular or an extended font. This is because the overall number of letters in the paragraph is the same—but the condensed font fits more characters to each line, and thus will have fewer lines.

THE VISUAL APPEARANCE OF TYPE SIZES/BODY HEIGHT

When different fonts measure the same from descender line to ascender line, they are the same point size. Yet there are other considerations that determine the *appearance* of the size of the typeface. Some typefaces will appear to be larger than others because they have a larger *body height* to the lowercase letters. Body height is the measure from the baseline to the *x-height line*, or the line that runs horizontally across the tops of the lowercase letters, excluding ascenders. (See example 8-6 of measuring point size on page 129.) The *x-height line*, also known as the *waist line*, the *body line* or *mean line* is a term used because the lowercase "x" is the standard for the body-height measurement. The "x"

es Ascenders & Descenders

was chosen because it has two horizontal edges that touch the mean or waist line of the font, and two horizontal surfaces that touch the baseline (as opposed to rounded or pointed parts of a letter touching the waist line at just one delicate point).

Since there is variation in the height of the body of lowercase letters in proportion to the size of the uppercase letters, the fonts with a larger *body* height *appear larger* than those with small x-heights. It is important to realize that as the proportion of the body height of a font is enlarged, the area for ascenders and descenders is reduced. So faces with large x-heights also have shorter ascenders and descenders than their small x-height counterparts.

Given different typefaces in 60-point type (see example 8-12), the x-heights will all be different, thus giving the appearance that some fonts are larger than others, even though the fonts measure the same from descender line to ascender line. The x-height gives the illusion of the size of the font on the page in text, or in a headline, because there are far more lowercase letters on the page than there are uppercase letters. If the x-height is larger, then the font appears large. The font you are reading, ITC Berkeley, has a small x-height and the copy appears extremely small and delicate on the page, but American Typewriter, the text in a few pages, is the same point size but appears much larger due to its larger x-height.

TYPE-SPECIMEN BOOKS

Type-specimen books give a designer a sense of what different fonts look like at a variety of sizes. The fonts are set in the same copy in a variety of standard text point sizes, as well as a few characters at display size. Type-specimen books can be helpful for a designer to compare different weights of the same font, and to see whether reducing the text setting by 1 point, say from 10 to 9 point, will adversely affect readability. These specimen books also allow designers to compare the readability of different fonts at the same point size. 9-point Helvetica reads very differently than 9-point Stone Sans, which reads very differently than 9-point Goudy Oldstyle. (This book gives you a tool to compare text settings of different fonts, and to *experience* how well each one reads as you read through the text; you can also review the examples in Chapter 21.)

8-11. The lowercase "x" is used to measure the body of a font because it has two flat surfaces that meet both the waist line and the baseline, giving an accurate measure.

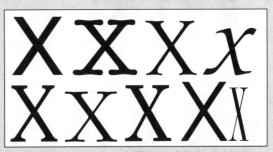

8-12. The "X's" above are all 60-point CAPITAL letters. Notice how their heights vary even though they are all the same point size. This is because the point size includes the descenders, and they vary in length.

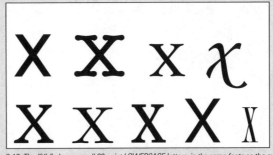

8-13. The "X's" above are all 60-point LOWERCASE letters, in the same fonts as the example above. The body heights vary even though they are all the same point size. This is because the point size includes ascenders and descenders, and they vary in length.

This page is set in ITC Berkeley Oldstyle Book 8.5/12.

8 Measuring Type/ Leading/Kerning/ Ligatures

8-14. This photo of actual lead type above shows a few strips of leads standing up, and one lying down. The leads were placed between lines of copy to space out the lines, hence the word "leading" for line spacing.

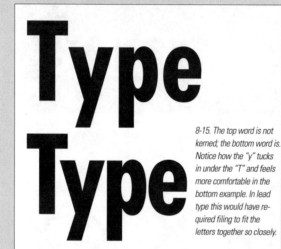

8-15. The top word is not kerned; the bottom word is. Notice how the "y" tucks in under the "T" and feels more comfortable in the bottom example. In lead type this would have required filing to fit the letters together so closely.

8-16. Although the point sizes of the type below are the same, they appear to be different sizes because of the difference in their x-heights.

Rather than wasting time deciding on a font in front of the computer screen, it is very helpful to utilize type-specimen books so that you can narrow down your text choices efficiently. Poring over type-specimen references will also make you more familiar with a variety of fonts. And since type is a primary element of design, this familiarity will help your design. The differences of fonts at reading sizes are at first barely discernible to the untrained eye. It takes designers a few years before they begin to feel familiar with typefaces, and can predict those that will read well at 8 points and those that are better set at 9 or 9.5 points. The greater your sensitivity to typography, the faster you will be able to work as a designer. Also, you will start to distinguish the personalities that fonts resonate and make your type selections accordingly.

Typically, type comes in sizes ranging from 4 points to 96 points. Type larger than 96 points originally would have been measured for typesetting in inches, but digital type usually ranges from 2 to 720 points. (Large type would have likely been created in wood rather than metal to reduce the weight of the type in setting up the press.) Type between 4-point and 6-point is used mostly for legal, technical or ingredient/nutritional copy; 7-point through 10-point sizes of type are more standard sizes for text. 11- through 22-point type is used for subheads and callouts. Display type is 28 points and larger; it is used for headlines and subheads. The space between the lines of type (the leading or line spacing) has as much effect on the readability of the type as does the point size and x-height of the text. (The apparent change in type size when the x-height changes is seen in the text of this book, since the point size, leading, line length and tracking are consistent throughout the chapters—only the fonts change.)

X-Height Line	
Baseline	*60-point Zapf Chancery*
X-Height Line	
Baseline	60-point Bodoni
X-Height Line	
Baseline	60-point Times Roman
X-Height Line	
Baseline	60-point Univers Condensed

LEADING OR LINE SPACING

Today, we take the measure of the width of the lead and add it to the point size of the type we are specifying. So if you want 10-point type set with 2 points of leading between lines, you must specify it as 10/12 (ten point type on twelve points of leading). The second numeral denotes leading, which is equal to the point size of the type plus the extra points of leading you want between lines.

Leading is measured from the baseline of one line to the baseline of the next line. This format is used because the baseline in text is consistent, whereas the body height and ascender height vary. When you measure from one baseline to the next, you include the height of the descenders, the leading, the ascenders and the body of the type–the same elements used in measuring the point size–plus the width of the leading. This is why the leading includes the height of the type itself, and is written as 9/11 rather than 9/2.

In some computer-layout programs, you have the option of having leading measured traditionally, from baseline to baseline, or as digital line spacing, which is measured from the center of one line to the center of the next. This means that the type sits more centered in the text box but otherwise makes little difference.

SPACING LETTERS WITHIN WORDS

Tightening the space in between letters in a word, as in a headline, is called *kerning*. This term seems to come from the German word for corner, which is kern. In the days of lead type, kerning two characters meant that the hand-setter had to remove both letters from the tray, file down the sides of each of their lead characters and then try to fit them together again, more closely. It may be that the process of filing down became known as kerning or *cornering*, the type. The term "kerning" has remained through the ages and is applied to the tightening of letters on the computer screen.

There are certain combinations of characters that should always be kerned. Generally, the tighter the spacing within words, the easier it is for the eye to recognize the shape of the word, which results in faster and easier reading on the part of the reader. The refinement of the spacing within words in a selection of body copy will affect the *density* of the type on the page, or how dark a tone of gray the text type creates on the page. You are striving to create an even, 50% tone of gray on the page with well-tracked body copy. If the text starts to get darker, the text type is probably too tightly tracked, or too bold. You also run the risk of white spaces at ends of paragraphs sticking out too dramatically if the type is dark.

In any event, kerning letters in a headline-sized font does improve readability. But it is important to realize that many fonts have built-in, automatic kerning tables that adjust type whenever two kerning characters are next to each other. A typical font can have from 200 to 500 sets of kerned characters built into the font, depending on the forms of the characters and the fastidiousness of the type designer and the font manufacturer.

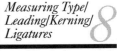

Leading is expressed in points, and is measured from the baseline of one line to the baseline of the next line.

LEADING

**DESCENDER AREA
LEADING AREA
ASCENDER AREA
X-HEIGHT AREA**

The darkened area is the measure of the leading between the two lines of type.

8-17. This example shows how leading is measured in typeset copy.

Unkerned Type

Kerned Type

8-18. In the above example, the effect of kerning on readability is exemplified.

All of these paragraphs are set in the same point-size text, 12 point, with -6 tracking and 15 points of leading. But notice how the appearance of the size of the type changes as the size of the x-height changes.

All of these paragraphs are set in the same point-size text, 12 point, with -6 tracking and 15 points of leading. But notice how the appearance of the size of the type changes as the size of the x-height changes.

All of these paragraphs are set in the same point-size text, 12 point, with -6 tracking and 15 points of leading. But notice how the appearance of the size of the type changes as the size of the x-height changes.

8-19. In the above example, the same paragraph is set in Bodoni, Centennial Light, and Optima. Compare how the x-height changes from one font to the next, and some appear much larger than others.

This page is set in ITC Berkeley Oldstyle Book 8.5/12.

8 Measuring Type/ Leading/Kerning/ Ligatures

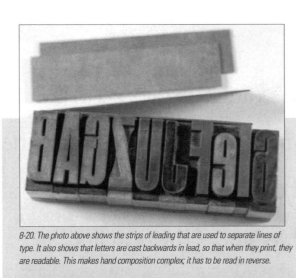

8-20. The photo above shows the strips of leading that are used to separate lines of type. It also shows that letters are cast backwards in lead, so that when they print, they are readable. This makes hand composition complex; it has to be read in reverse.

KERNING PAIRS

AC AT AV AW AY FA Fa Fe Fi Fo

Fu LT LV LW LY OA OV OW

OY PA L' L- P. P, P; P: P- P—

R- R— Ta Te Ti To Tr Tu

Tw Th Ty Wo Wi Wr We Wu

Wy W. Wa W, Wh W: W; W-

W— Ya Ye Yi Yo Yu Al An AG

AO AQ AU AV BA BE BL BP

BR BU BV BW BY CA EC EO

FC FG FO GE GO GR GU HO

IC IG IO JA JO OH OI OK OL

OM ON OP OR OT OU OX PE

This sidebar is set in Clearface Bold 16/25; -10 tracking

8-21. This list of kerning pairs shows capital and lowercase combinations that need special kerning that is built into the electronic spacing

KERNING TABLES

Kerning tables are the list of kerned-pair combinations of letters that are available in the font in upper- and lowercase. The same two characters that need to be kerned in uppercase will not necessarily need kerning in lowercase because the forms of the letters change. Type designers know that some characters scream to be kerned—for example, any letter set next to a cap "W, T, V, or Y." Likewise, the open space below the arm on the "T" or "F" makes you want to tuck the next character in closer to these caps. In other cases, you may even overlap the letters a bit for characters with an ascender, such as in the Wh combination, and create a ligature.

Refer to the table of kerning pairs in example 8-19 at the left. These tables exist to help the typesetter and designer, and you can see that most of the examples are kerned tighter than they would otherwise appear if set in normal, unkerned text.

When kerning characters in a word, if the bowls of two rounded characters touch, it is called *kissing*. Kissing can add areas of darkness that may be undesirable, depending on the font, the word, and the tightness of the rest of the phrase. The ultimate effect you are striving for in the spacing of letters in a word is an even appearance of tight but consistent letter spacing that improves readability but does not call attention to itself because it is too tight. With some serif fonts, you will be surprised at how much you can overlap the serifs on two vertical characters, such as an "l" and an "i," without the characters appearing to be too tightly kerned together. But these same vertical characters may need to be opened up a bit to prevent visual vibration, which is created when the two or more verticals are placed too closely together.

COMPUTERIZED KERNING

With the advent of computerized type, letters can be kerned within 1/1000th of an *"em" space* (width of a lowercase "m") in some programs. The refinement that is now available through desktop computers is more precise than was possible with traditional typesetting. The problem now is that the average computer user does not always know enough or see enough of the details of typography to utilize these refinements to improve the appearance of type on the page. Hence, although they are blessed with a machine with superior capacity to improve typography, inevitably the readability and spacing of type on the page have been reduced as novices are cranking out unrefined pages of type to be read.

In most layout programs, you can kern between two specific characters in addition to kerning across a selection of type. Tracking is when you evenly letter space out the characters in a word. Computers have made tracking a very refined typographic technique. The craft of typography is being watered down, and the standards are being lowered by the proliferation of poor quality typography set by untrained typists. As a designer, it's important to learn the kerning capacity and settings of the program you're using. Mastering kerning and tracking will result in more attractive and more readable type and headlines in your work.

LIGATURES

Often, when kerning type within a word you will create *ligatures*. When you join parts of letters, or overlap serifs, you are creating ligatures. Ligatures are two letters that are joined to improve the spacing in a word, and they harken back to the days of Medieval scribes. A standard ligature is the joined cross bar of two lowercase "ff's." In some fonts, you can get the kerned version by a key command on the keyboard; in others, the ligature version is automatically transferred in when the two "f's" are typed in succession. In some fonts, it depends on the application-wide settings for ligatures; in others, you need the expert version of the font, and in yet other fonts the ligature version shows up only in italic versions of ff. Gutenberg copied the ligatures of the scribes' handwriting when he cast lead type over five hundred years ago. It seems as though Gutenberg was more concerned with fooling prospective book buyers with this typographic detail than he was with maintaining an even letter spacing throughout the text (but, of course, we do not know this; perhaps he hated bad letter spacing!).

It is important to remember that spacing the letters in a word or headline affects the readability just as much as the font you've chosen, the word spaces, the line spacing, the line breaks, and the size of the font you've chosen. Poor letter spacing can distract the reader and reduce the impact of your message. Ligatures in headlines or logos cannot be fussed over too much. Likewise, the spacing of the product name in package design must be precisely spaced, or you'll forever regret your haste.

To check the spacing and ligatures in a word or headline, there are a few tricks that designers have been using for years. These are to look at the word upside down to see if the spacing looks even. Look at it backwards, from the back of the page, with light coming through to check for the evenness of spacing. Lastly, look at the word in the mirror to see if the spacing looks consistent when reversed. These options all require the designer to look at the white space between the letters, rather than the letters themselves, and to consider the letters as abstract shapes. As the letters become abstracted because you are seeing them backward or upside down, you will be more critical of distribution of the white spaces between the characters because you will have less of a tendency to read letters.

This is an example of a headline that needs kerning.

8-22. This headline is set at the default spacing without any kerning.

This is an example of a headline that's been kerned!

8-23. In this lower example, notice how the kerning helps the readability of the words by making them hold together more clearly.

Ligatures are connected letters within a word.

8-24. Ligatures help the readability of words in headlines. Beware of extra kerning in headlines when words have rounded or angled characters in them.

This page is set in American Typewriter Medium 8.5/12.

8 *Measuring Type/*
Leading/Kerning/
Ligatures

Rarely is it wrong to set headlines very tightly.

8-25. Headlines have their own spacing rules. In the example above, the word spaces are kerned at -35, while the headline is kerned at -14. The space between "to" and "set" is kerned at -40; the words that have angled characters at the end or beginning couldn't be kerned as tightly. The spacing around the "dli " in "headlines" had to be opened up a bit because the verticals felt too close together.

UPPERCASE
Upper- and Lowercase

8-26. The example above shows how upper- and lowercase letters reveal the shape of a word more clearly due to ascenders and descenders. All uppercase letters line up too perfectly; each letter has to be individually recognized to read the entire word.

Headlines in caps/lowercase are easier to read than those set in all caps BECAUSE THE ASCENDERS AND DESCENDERS HELP US TO READ WORDS BY THEIR SHAPES, RATHER THAN IDENTIFYING EVERY LETTER.

8-27. This example tries to reinforce the fact that lowercase letters read more easily than all uppercase, which take longer to read.

This page is set in American
Typewriter Medium 8.5/12.

WORD SPACING

The general rule of thumb for word spacing is to visualize the width of a lowercase "l" in the font when planning the spaces between words. This means that word spacing changes based on the width of the font and the point size of the words.

Spacing type effectively for the optimum readability may be the single most important sensibility that the designer must hone while studying his/her craft. Poorly spaced type can render even the best design awkward. Type must be spaced using the intuitive sense of the designer, there is no hard-and-fast rule. Each designer's sense of type spacing differs. Often a trial-and-error approach is best when spacing is concerned. Designers often talk in terms of tightening up letters or opening up letters in a headline just a hair—meaning just a hair's width of space. Type-spacing accuracy can get neurotic! But frequently, the last round of fine-tuning in a headline can make all the difference in the overall look and legibility. A few rounds of tweaking type is necessary to get it right, and this is something that only a trained eye in type can assess. You will develop your eye and aesthetic sense of spacing type over time by critiquing everything you read and see.

GENERAL RULES FOR HEADLINES

Headlines are probably the most important typographic element in an ad, brochure, magazine spread, poster or newspaper article. A headline should be just long enough to get the reader's attention and encourage further reading. If the headline doesn't get the reader involved, the rest of the copy will probably not be read.

Headlines are usually set in display-sized type which visually prioritizes them on the page. The rules governing headline type are not necessarily the same for body or text type.

In headlines, you can crowd, tip, fit in, under, tint, decorate, or do almost anything logical that does not detract too much from the readability. You can actually play typographic tricks with a headline if it seems appropriate for the message and represents the client appropriately. Today, with the use of computers, you can apply a great variety of effects to headline type. These include changing the dimension or point size of the different letters within the headline, italicizing the letters, making them bold, changing proportions, putting them in an arc or another shape, and twisting or distorting them in some way. There are options to fill them with textures, photos, illustrations, or layer them four and five levels deep. Clearly, these effects are gimmicky and should be used when appropriate and with restraint.

Headline type can be set in the same formats as body copy: flush left, flush right, justified or centered. Because of the short length of headlines, (usually between one to five lines), more variations than these four basic options exist. Free form, in which the headline position fits around the rest of the elements within the piece, is one option. Lining type on a common vertical from a visual is another possibility. It is important to note that, due to its size, all headline type must be carefully kerned because of the problematic relationship of certain letter combinations. Word spacing and line spacing must be considered carefully as well. Usually it is necessary to kern letters tightly and reduce word spacing and leading for the headline to read comfortably.

It is not uncommon for ascenders of lower lines and descenders of upper lines to share the same space in headlines that are tightly crammed together. The shapes a headline can take are extremely varied, but whatever the shape of the headline, the arrangement should accent the type's message. Some subjects are better expressed with traditional styles of type and arrangement, while others might call for a flamboyant or contemporary treatment.

HEADLINE LETTER SPACING AND WORD SPACING

Because the words in headlines are so large and so few, headlines have specific considerations in terms of letter spacing, word spacing, line spacing and phrasing; it is imperative that they are easy to read. Subtle spacing adjustments can improve readability tremendously. The general rule for word spacing in text is to allow the width of a lowercase "l" for the spaces between words. This is enough space to distinguish one word from the next, but not enough to cause white gaps in the design. However, in headline spacing, this rule is often broken. In headlines, this space can even be reduced further and words can be cheated together a bit depending on the letters involved. If you do tighten word spacing, you have to tighten the overall tracking of the headline as well. Kerning generally improves readability because the words visually hold together better.

The rule of thumb for word spacing is to visualize a lowercase l between words.

8-28. The example above illustrates the use of the lowercase "l" to determine word spacing.

Depending on the letter combinations in headlines, you can space them differently.

8-29. Notice that the "iff" in differently is spaced very tightly, as is the word "space" above. Often, after tracking a headline, you have to go in and open up the areas between the vertical characters, as in the "dli" above, so that they don't appear too tight and create a dark area in the headline that calls attention to itself.

The shape of the font can also affect the spacing of words and letters in a headline.

8-30. Some very wide serif fonts, like Bembo in the example above, cannot be kerned too tightly without looking spotty. The wide counters of the "o's" start to look crowded if they're kerned too tight. Also, the long terminal at the top of the lowercase "f" prevents a vertical stroke from being kerned too tightly after the "f" without looking awkward.

This page is set in American Typewriter Medium 8.5/12.

8 *Measuring Type/ Leading/Kerning/ Ligatures*

Regular Leading vs. Negative Leading & Kerning

8-31. The example at the top illustrates the default settings on a computer for tracking and leading compared with the version below, that is custom kerned and leaded. This explains how two operators of computers can turn out vastly different quality of type; like so much about typography, the details make a world of difference.

Word spaces in type are sometimes measured in fractions of "em" spaces. An "em" space, or "mutt" space, is the square of the point size of the type. This means that an "em" space in 8-point type is 8 points wide. Generally, this width is also represented by the lowercase letter "m," hence the name of the space. "En" spaces, or "nut" spaces, are also referred to in spacing type–they are equal to half the width of an "em" space, or half the width of the point size. These spaces are also used to indicate paragraph indents.

8-32. Although "em" spaces are rarely referred to in digital type, as a designer, it is still good to know the history and development of the term.

Word spacing in headlines is always different depending on the last character of the former word and the first character of the next word. Because each character is shaped slightly different, you must use your judgment when adjusting the word spacing in a headline. This can also be affected by the selection of fonts, and whether they are set in caps, or upper- and lowercase. If one word ends in a "l" and the next word begins with a "i," you may be able to tighten the word spacing more because of the white space caused by the vertical strokes of these characters. On the other hand, if the one word ends in a round character and the next word begins with a "d", you may *not* be able to tighten this word spacing as much as the previous example because the protruding bowls of the characters make them appear to stick out into their surrounding white space. Adjusting word spacing in a headline must be done on a case-by-case basis, with the goal being the appearance of even word spacing across the headline, and comfortably tight word groupings.

When spacing letters in a headline carefully, it can help to consciously over-tighten the letters together on the computer at first, then slowly open the tracking, then judge where the space between individual letters is too tight, and open these areas up. The next task is to match the screen spacing to the computer printout. Do not be fooled by the spacing of the screen fonts that appear on your monitor; they are always spaced differently than the printer fonts that come from your laser printer. Go by the printouts, even if the type on the screen looks horribly spaced. The principle of "WYSIWYG," which stands for "What You See Is What You Get," does not apply to computers; screen fonts only approximate the printer fonts. What you see on the printout is accurate. It is the printout that you should base the spacing refinements on; the screen font is merely a representation of the final piece.

NEGATIVE LEADING IN HEADLINES

When designing headlines, it is important to pay attention to the leading. Negative leading is often utilized in headlines to give a tight, unified fit to the lines. *Negative leading* is when you have 120-point type on 80 points of leading. In this case, the ascenders and descenders share the same space and have to be carefully integrated in the space to prevent overlapping (see 8-31). It often requires some refining of the type so that descenders from an upper line are not hitting into ascenders from a lower line. But, with some adjusting, negative leading can be very effective in headline design. This allows the type to be as large as possible in the costly advertising space. When using negative leading, designers sometimes omit the dot on the "i's" so that it does not interfere with the descenders from the line above. (To get a lowercase "i" without the dot, use shift-option B on the keyboard.)

PHRASING IN HEADLINES

Phrasing must be considered in the setting and spacing of headlines. *Phrasing* means paying attention to the meaning in the lines of type in a headline and how the lines break. More specifically, it means breaking the lines of type so that they make sense when read. Headlines that are broken into more than one line should be divided based on the copy's message. The line breaks should be determined by the sense of the words. Your goal should be to keep descriptive words or phrases together; you also want to try to keep negative or positive modifiers on the same line as the word they modify. Create logical phrases, such as adjective-and-noun combinations. Bad breaks in phrasing not only read poorly, but can also change the meaning of the headline tremendously.

The line breaks should be in logical places, and the font should be changed if necessary to accommodate this. It also helps to read a headline out loud, with pauses at the end of each line, to check if the breaks make sense. Also say the phrases out loud, in different combinations with a pause at each line break, to hear whether or not they make sense to your ear. The designer who fails to do this is doing an injustice to the message.

PLACING THE HEADLINE/READABILITY IN HEADLINES

The placement of the headline within a design is key to the eye's movement throughout the piece. Most ads, magazine spreads, etc., are designed to "begin" with the headline. Traditional headlines are placed across the top of the page. This position is a logical location, but there are no rules determining the placement of a headline. The designer has the skill and ability to place the headline anywhere on the page and to create an appropriate layout around it. The design of the headline and the layout are planned as one cohesive, integrated whole. As long as the headline upholds its primary function, which is to get attention and be read, then the placement is successful.

Studies show that there is no significant difference in the readability of 14- to 30-point type. The white space around the type, however, will increase legibility. A general rule might be to set the head slightly smaller and allow additional white space *around* the headline (but not necessarily *between* the lines).

The fact that lowercase letters are easier to read (due to the unique shapes formed by ascenders and descenders) than uppercase holds true not only in body copy but for headlines as well. Headlines set in all caps are more difficult to read, per-

This is an Example of a Headline Set with Negative Leading.

8-33. This example show that headlines generally feel more comfortable when set with negative leading (which is when the point size of leading is less than the point size of the type, as in 45/38 above).

This is an Example of a Headline Set Solid.

8-34. In this example, the point size of type is the same as the point size of the leading set at 45/45 or set solid.

YOLI RUNNING SHOES ARE SO GOOD, YOU'LL FORGET THE NAME.

*Headline
not broken
for sense.*

8-35. In the example above, the headline has not been phrased for sense. The breaks seem awkward.

YOLI RUNNING SHOES ARE SO GOOD, YOU'LL FORGET THE NAME.

8-36. In this example, notice how the phrases make sense and seem to read better. The example also uses negative leading to help readability.

Sans serif fonts create fewer ligatures in tightly kerned headlines.

8-37. Because there are no serifs in sans serif fonts, fewer characters touch when they are tightly kerned; the ear of the "g" touches the "h" above, and the "if" and "tu" run together; but in general, there is less interaction between letters in sans serif than in serif fonts in headlines.

This page is set in ITC
Clearface Regular 8.5/12.

WHEN USING (PARENTHESES), – "EN" OR —
"EM" DASHES, OR • BULLETS IN ALL-CAP
COPY, YOU HAVE TO BASELINE-SHIFT THEM
UP. The dashes – and • bullets are designed so
that they center on the lowercase x-height.
The (parentheses) are designed so that they
take into account lowercase descenders.

8-38. Above, some of the refinements of using bullets, dashes and parentheses in
all-caps body copy are explained. The dashes, bullets and parentheses in the copy
above have not been shifted up as recommended.

Reversed type, or white letters on a
black background, is more difficult to
read than its black-on-white counterpart. **The reason for this is that the
white type appears smaller in
comparison to the large area of
black.** Also, in printing, fine lines are often very fine *after the
ink seeps into the paper, leading to a
smaller appearance of the type as well.*

8-39. Depending on the weight of the strokes, reversed type can be difficult to read.

*Phrasing is when you attempt
to break the lines in a headline
so that line breaks
create natural pauses
that make sense.*

8-40. Notice how smoothly this example reads. Attention to phrasing can
really help a headline read faster.

*Bad phrasing not
only throws off the
meaning of a head-
line, but it makes it
more difficult to
read.*

8-41. This example seems slow and staccato to read.
It's difficult to understand at first.

haps 15% slower. The reader is forced to read all uppercase
headlines letter by letter, rather than in saccadic jumps as with
lowercase characters, where we recognize entire words. This,
however, doesn't mean that one should *never* use all uppercase characters in a headline; some work great this way! Since
there are generally few words in a headline, there is a certain
amount of latitude that the designer can take. You can also
try using caps and small caps.

REVERSED TYPE IN HEADLINES

Reversed type, or white letters on a black background, is
said to be approximately 15 to 40% more difficult to read than
its black on white counterpart. This is generally not an issue
with headlines because of the larger size of the type and the
shortness of the line length involved. However, be prepared for
reversed type to *shrink* optically. Because the type is the only
white element on a large field of black, the black overpowers
the eye and sort of closes in on the type, making the white type
appear smaller. It is wise to go up one or two point sizes when
a headline is to be reversed. Also take care to select a typestyle
that's not too light in the weight of the strokes because thin
strokes in characters will appear *very* thin when reversed out
of black, and they may close up when printed. Select a typestyle that's regular or bold in weight, and make careful decisions about line lengths, letter spacing and line spacing.

ALIGNMENT/OPTICAL ALIGNMENT IN HEADLINES

Refined alignment of characters is necessary when you
set a stacked headline flush left or flush right. It is tricky to
align characters vertically in a headline. When type is stacked,
frequently some characters, such as an "A" or an "O," have
to be cheated a bit to the left to give the appearance of correct optical alignment. This is a subtle but helpful hint to apply
to advertising layouts or book-cover design. Poor optical
alignment is most obvious when the typeface is large and
clearly seen.

The designer cannot rely on mechanical flush left settings;
the letters must be lined up optically for the best readability.
The capital letters "A, C, G, J, O, Q, S, T, V, W, X, and Y" represent special alignment challenges because they are either
rounded or angled characters, or characters that have unusual
shapes to them. If these characters are mechanically set flush,
they will seem out of line to the eye. Frequently, rounded or angled characters have to be cheated a bit past the flush left line
that defines the edge in order to appear in line. The upper
stroke of a capital "T" often has to be moved past the defining
edge quite a bit to make it appear in line with the other letters.

To align characters optically on the computer, it is often
necessary to put a *soft return* or *shift return* after the end of
each line. Then type a space at the beginning of each line. Lastly,
you highlight the space and change the tracking of the space

as necessary to optically align the characters. With a high amount of negative tracking, -30 or more, you can make a character shift to the left, which is often necessary when optically aligning lines in a headline (see example 8-41 for an optically flush-left headline).

PUNCTUATION IN HEADLINES

Optical alignment also applies to the concept of *hanging punctuation*. If you have a headline that has a quote at the beginning, it is a good idea to hang the punctuation and to vertically align the rest of the flush left lines of type by eye. Otherwise, the edge of the type is rough and irregular. Hanging punctuation is important in headlines for optimum readability. The quotes are still seen, but they are not a distraction.

Likewise, punctuation marks (hyphens, bullets, parentheses, quotation marks) have to be specially treated in headlines. They need to be set outside the flush-left or flush-right headline in order to read optically aligned. This is called hanging punctuation (in the margin) and will give the appearance of vertical alignment (See example 8-43 of hanging punctuation at left).

Often punctuation marks look better in the headline if they are set a few point sizes smaller than the point size of the headline. This is because the punctuation marks are designed to be clearly readable even when the font is at a text type size. These marks are proportionally rather large for the font. When they are set at the same point size as the rest of the headline, they often seem dominant in a headline. Reducing their size reduces their impact, allowing the words to be the emphasis.

When you reduce the point size of quotes or apostrophes, you often have to baseline-shift them up into place. This is because they are designed to align at the top of the point size; when you make the quotes a smaller point size, they shift into place for the top of the smaller-point-sized type.

Conversely, if you set a headline in all caps, be aware that you will have to shift up any bullets or dashes in the headline because they are designed to center on the x-height of the characters. Parentheses likewise have to be shifted up in all-cap copy because they are designed to take into account the descenders of the font and will appear to hang too low on all-cap headlines.

TIGHT, NOT TOUCHING

The general rule in spacing type, especially body copy, is the *tight-not-touching* or the *TNT,* approach. The tighter the characters can be brought together, generally the better the readability of the text type. But if this rule were applied to larger-point-sized type, it would likely appear not tight enough.

In very small text type (7 point and smaller), and in white type that is reversed out of a solid color, the TNT approach can be a good rule for spacing. If kerned too tightly, reversed or

These examples of headlines show the difference between optically flush left versus mechanically flush left, as well as hanging versus non-hanging punctuation.

8-42. This is an example of a headline that is set mechanically flush left. The left edge of the "T" is aligned with the left edges of the characters below it. Although this is correct mechanically, our eyes perceive these lines as better aligned in the example below.

8-43. In this example, although it looks flush left, the "T", "S" and "a" are adjusted further to the left to create visual alignment. Adjustments depend on the shapes of the characters in the particular font you are using.

8-44. Notice how the "T" in "This" is inset because the quote is set flush left.

8-45. In this example, the quotes hang to the left, and the "T" aligns optically flush left with the lines below. This is the correct format, with the punctuation hanging to the left.

This page is set in ITC Clearface Regular 8.5/12.

8 Measuring Type/ Leading/Kerning/ Ligatures

"Let's all go out together"
(full-sized punctuation)

8-46. In the headline above, the point of the punctuation has not been reduced, and the space around the apostrophe has not been kerned. The punctuation has not been hung and makes the headline appear off-balance.

"Let's all go out together"
(reduced punctuation & hanging punctuation)

8-47. Above, in the same headline, the point of the punctuation has been reduced, and the space around the apostrophe has been kerned. The punctuation has also been hung.

very small type can cause problems on press with characters running together. Some designers prefer to use the TNT rule for their body copy; others track their body copy from -2 to -6, depending on the font and the designer's typographic sensibility. You must determine the tracking settings that you judge to be the most comfortable to read for both text type and headlines, based on your own aesthetic sensibility and the intended audience. The text throughout this book is all globally tracked at -6. In general, this appeared to me to be comfortable for most of the fonts, but a few throughout the book appear to be tracked a bit too tightly, even to my eye, which generally prefers text a bit tight. You may want to take some time to flip through the pages, compare the settings of the text fonts, and see which ones feel comfortable, which read easily to your eyes, and which appear as though they are tracked too tightly. You may also want to compare which fonts appear small at 8.5 points and which appear quite legible.

The practice of evaluating all of the type that you see in your visual environment will lead to refining your typographic sense more quickly. A warning, however: you will no longer be able to go to the grocery store without subconsciously identifying the fonts that you see and the design decisions made in packaging–you'll even redesign your toothpaste tube in your head while brushing your teeth. If you see a font that you don't recognize, you'll have to find out its name. When you find yourself evaluating a new beer based on its label design rather than its taste, there's no turning back!

PROJECT: TYPOGRAPHIC SELF-PORTRAIT

Choose words from the list below that you feel describe yourself (or come up with your own words). Use as many as you like, with the minimum choice of five. Choose them so that they make sense in relation to each other. You will be working on an interpretive self-portrait limited exclusively to type. Use the font and the scale of the words to try to convey the message. Focus on the kerning of the different letters together, and the ligatures that you may want to create, as well as the interpretive quality of the words. You may choose to use antonyms or all synonyms, and put them in very different fonts or in fonts that either contradict or reinforce the meaning of the word, etc.

Awkward spacing will negatively affect readability. You must get the basics of spacing letters in a word mastered before you can begin to space words into headlines, titles, etc. The final design is limited to three different colors, black, white and gray. The final piece should be executed in cut paper. The words can be overlapping, transparent, interlacing, bleeding off the edge, etc. Make your layout choices so that they reinforce the idea you are trying to project for the viewer.

Try using different weights or italic versions of typefaces where you think it's appropriate, and any fonts that you want to use from your text or from other reference books in the library. You can photocopy faces up to the desired size. Consider incorporating punctuation marks into the words. Your final piece can be vertical or horizontal.

Complete 20 thumbnail sketches for this project. Make sure you have decided on the words you will work with, and do not deviate from them. Try different fonts for each word; try emphasizing different words. Consider the meaning behind the words and the fonts selected.

Masculine	Feminine	Unpredictable	Wild	Aggressive
Assertive	Handsome	Cute	Surly	Loud-mouthed
Zany	Tenacious	Outspoken	Subtle	Crazy
Offensive	Harsh	Different	Forceful	Nasty
Abusive	Confident	Passive	Submissive	Gentle
Quiet	Reserved	Shy	Social	Demonstrative
Baby	Honey	Sweetie	Underdog	Self-righteous
Buddy	Candid	Mouthy	Guy	Nerdy
Affectionate	Chatty	Talkative	Political	Distinguished
Interesting	Compelling	Intelligent	Talented	Determined
Gossip(y)	Clicky	Insistent	Intransigent	Relentless
Intense	Appetite	Hard-working	Committed	Sensitive
Slinky	Frail	Timid	Graceful	Slender
Flowing	Dainty	Equal	Silly	Self-conscious
Perfectionist	Accurate	Logical	Precise	Conscientious
Inarticulate	Ditzy	Brainless	Blonde	Bravado
Brawny	Upset	Childish	Dippy	Strong
Weak	Domineering	Powerful	Competent	Willful
Angry	Whiny	Friendly	Judgmental	Severe
Emotional	Articulate	Demanding	Nice	Open
Supportive	Tender	Brash	Uncompromising	

OBJECTIVES

- To appreciate the kerning nuances of different typefaces.
- To consider various letter combinations and the spacing challenges they propose.
- To examine letter combinations in different typefaces.
- To analyze appropriate fonts for interpretive value.
- To encourage the use of type exclusively to convey an idea.
- To introduce type as a visual-communication medium.
- To encourage thinking of type as an interpretive, expressive medium.

8-48. This typographic self-portrait by KU student Renee Alvarado uses numerous fonts and overlapping to create a complex, overall layered appearance in the final piece.

8-49. This typographic self-portrait by KU student Cat Schroeder uses well-chosen fonts appropriate for each word to convey the meaning behind each of the terms.

8-50. This typographic self-portrait overlaps descriptive words that are often contradictory about oneself.

This page is set in Univers 47 Light Condensed 8.5/12.

Measuring Type/Leading/Kerning/Ligatures-Review

1. What is type high in inches, and what does it mean? _____

_____

2. How did lead type affect the way that fonts are measured? _____

_____

3. How many points are in a pica? _____

4. How many picas are in an inch? _____

5. How many points are in an inch? _____

6. Why do fonts that are the same point size appear to be different sizes? _____

_____

7. How is the point size of a font measured? _____

8. Why is interline spacing called leading? _____

9. What is the set width of a font? _____

10. Why is upper- and lowercase easier to read than all uppercase? _____

_____

11. Why would you use a type specimen book? _____

12. Why is the body height of a font called the x-height? _____

13. What is considered optimum word spacing? _____

14. What does set solid mean when it comes to type? _____

15. Why is leading measured from baseline to baseline? _____

16. What is phrasing in headlines? _____

17. In headlines, what type of leading is normally used? _____

18. What is ligature? _____

19. What is kerning? _____

20. What is tracking? _____

21. What are kerning pairs? _____

22. What types of letters should you be alert to when kerning headlines? _____

23. What is a widow? _____

24. What is an orphan? _____

25. How does reversed type affect readability? _____

26. What are bullets, and what do you have to be aware of when using them? _____

_____

27. What are two tricks a designer can use when the copy is running too long for the space allotted? _____

_____

28. What should you do to punctuation in headlines to make it appear correct? _____

_____

29. When using parentheses in all-capital copy, what do you have to do? _____

30. What is hanging punctuation? _____

31. Why is there only one space after a period in body copy? _____

32. Which fonts can you kern more tightly, serif or sans serif? _____

33. What fonts should you avoid reversing, and why? _____

_____

Five Historic Families of Type

9 *Five Historic Families of Type*

KEY CONCEPTS

Old Style Serif

Transitional Serif

Modern Serif

Egyptian Serif

Sans Serif

Decorative Serif

Splayed Serif

OLD STYLE FONT CHARACTERISTICS

The following is a list of some of the attributes of Old Style fonts:

- *Little thick/thin contrast between stem and hairline weight.*

- *Heavily bracketed serifs.*

- *Oblique stress in the characters.*

- *Capital height is shorter than the height of the lowercase ascenders.*

- *Often cupped serifs.*

- *Terminals on some lowercase letters are shaped like teardrops.*

9-1. The list delineates the characteristics of Old Style fonts.

ITC GARAMOND BOLD

9-2. Above is ITC Garamond, an Old Style font.

INTRODUCTION

In this chapter we review the historic families of type. For ease of classification, most fonts are divided into one of the following categories: Old Style, Transitional, Modern, Egyptian, Sans Serif or Display fonts. These categories separate fonts on the basis of the structure of their serifs, terminals and the angle of the stress of the font. In general, the categories reflect the historic evolution of typefaces, but type from these different categories is mixed for contrast, and all coexist and are used in combinations today.

OLD STYLE FACES

Old Style fonts are organic in their feel on the page because of the generous bracketing on the serifs, which makes them appear to gently grow out of the stem strokes. The round, cup-based serifs have great similarity to the arch of the human foot, and the gentle curves of bracketing are reassuringly comfortable. The hairline strokes in Old Style faces have mass to them, and they reinforce the sense of stability and groundedness that resonates through these historic fonts.

Old Style typefaces are easy for the eye to discern because they tend to be heavy on the page. Because they were designed in the era when type punches were hand-cut and then cast by hand in lead, it was essential that there was sufficient mass to them for the human hand to manipulate during the cutting process. They also had to be strong enough to withstand the pressure of the adapted wine press without breaking or chipping. Their greatly bracketed serifs evolved as much from the practicality of the lead characters lasting longer as from the aesthetic preference for this style of font.

The calligraphic practice of allowing the height of the ascenders to pass beyond the height of the capital letters was carried over into Old Style faces. The x-height of the lowercase letters sometimes appears small by comparison to newer fonts, but this is only because we are more familiar with faces where the x-height of the characters has been enlarged to improve readability at small sizes.

There is a distinct grace in Old Style faces; their close relationship to handwriting is evidenced in the beautiful teardrop-shaped terminals on the lowercase "a's," "c's" and "r's." This subtle design element enhances the organic sense of the fonts; these terminals appear to bulge gently out of the stroke, like an emerging seed. The Old Style fonts can have a very classic or traditional feel when used carefully, or they can be used in contemporary applications when married with a font that contrasts with their historic style.

TRANSITIONAL STYLE FACES

As their name implies, Transitional fonts form the bridge between the organic design of the Old Style fonts and the mechanized structure of the Modern fonts. Transitional faces owe something to both camps. They still retain elegant although understated bracketing on the serifs, yet they are more precisely drawn than the Old Style fonts. The hairline stems have been gently thinned down, and the serifs end in tapered points rather than the bulbous "feet" of Old Style fonts. To improve readability, the width of the lowercase letters has been slightly extended, creating wider, fuller counter forms. The curves on this face are wide, round and heavy, almost giving the impression that they are extended.

Because of the refined hairline stroke, the stem strokes can appear too thick to be supported by the delicate hairlines. But the italic version of Transitional faces are unsurpassable. They combine elegance, balance, and penmanship details to create an outstanding italic that seems to dance along the baseline. There is so much energy and creativity in these characters that it is difficult to believe that they are over 200 years old. Baskerville Italic, for example, has graceful loops and creative thicknesses of line weight and curves that resemble the fine-penned flourishes of the era, as shown on the italic question mark (?). The designer of the font you're reading, John Baskerville, was a lettering teacher before he turned his interests to type design. The stress of the characters has modulated from the clearly angled stress of the Old Style fonts to a more upright bias in Transitional fonts, which owe less of their design to the marks of the scribes of the time.

MODERN STYLE FONTS

Modern fonts are the beginning of the mechanized appearance of type. No longer does the character's stress gently sit on the oblique; in Modern faces, the stress is a verti-

Transitional
ITC NEW BASKERVILLE

9-3. This is ITC New Baskerville, a Transitional font.

*TRANSITIONAL FONT CHARACTERISTICS
The following is a list of some of the attributes of Transitional Style fonts:*

- *Strong thick and thin contrast in weight of stem and hairline.*

- *Finely bracketed serifs.*

- *Almost vertical stress.*

- *Capitals are same height as lowercase ascenders.*

- *Lowercase letters are very short and wide, and almost appear extended.*

9-4. This list delineates characteristics of a Transitional style font.

Modern
BODONI

9-5. This is Bodoni, a Modern font.

This page is set in ITC New
Baskerville & Bodoni 8.5/12.

9

Five Historic Families of Type

MODERN FONT CHARACTERISTICS
The following is a list of some of the attributes of Modern Style fonts:

- *Extreme contrast of thick and thin in weight of stem and hairline.*

- *No bracketing of serifs.*

- *Strong vertical stress.*

- *Lowercase letters have small body height in proportion to cap height.*

- *Terminals on some letters are circular.*

9-6. Modern font characteristics.

cal, rigid, up-and-down format. The gradual emergence of the serifs from the stem strokes is replaced by precise 90° angles; there is no bracketing. The two strokes meet as if they were beams in a house. The former tapering ends of the serifs are replaced with sharp, square right angles. These are fonts that are built on precision with a sanitary, ascetic appearance to them. The calligraphic beauty of a character was sacrificed in order to maintain the consistency of the geometrically based font. Clean and crisp are words frequently used to describe Modern fonts. The characters are all slightly condensed, and the feeling from Transitional fonts of bowls that are too full is completely removed in Modern fonts.

The draftsmanship qualities of this font (Bodoni) make it appear architectural, and its mathematical properties render it timeless. It is a font that is designed more by logic than by guts or by hand or by eye, and it follows no trends of style or fashion. Its conservative appearance and upright structure imbue it with qualities of solidity over time, and rigorous attention to the details of the font. Interestingly, the italic face of Bodoni does have beautiful teardrop terminals and sweeping curved strokes that give a glimpse of the flair of the type designer. Structured and straightforward, this no-nonsense type can be used very tastefully, but it tends to break up at small point sizes (under 7 point) if the resolution of the hairline stroke isn't good, and reversing it out of a solid color at small sizes is not advisable because it will be difficult for the printer to reproduce the fine hairline strokes, which may fill in.

CLARENDON BOLD

Egyptian

9-7. This is Clarendon Bold, an Egyptian font.

EGYPTIAN STYLE FONTS

Egyptian fonts are a different breed altogether. They are similar to Modern fonts in their geometric precision and vertical stress in the characters, but the similarities end there. Egyptian fonts have the appearance of a *monoline font,* or a font that appears to be constructed of lines that are all approximately the same weight. This divergence from earlier fonts which had thick and thin strokes is a major step in type design. The innovation of the large, square serifs also call attention to themselves because of their dominant visual presence on the page. These fonts may or may not have bracketing, but they always are designed with thick, generous slab serifs.

The structure and presence of the serifs are as important as the forms of the letters themselves. The letters are based on simple geometric shapes in this font (Lubalin Graph). The round characters are perfect circles, and square characters are perfectly constructed at 90°. There is something about these fonts that is reminiscent of railroad ties and lumber; they almost seem as if they could have been cut out of wood. Often the x-height of the lowercase is tall because so much of the characters is taken up with the thickness of the serif, which gives the font great readability at small sizes. On the other hand, the staccato rhythm in the text created by the heavy serifs can act as small hurdles to interrupt smooth reading. These faces feel as though they are rugged enough to have children climb all over them. Their structure is sturdy, down to earth, and pragmatic.

SANS SERIF STYLE FONTS

Sans serif fonts come in many weights, shapes and styles. There are those that have modified serifs or splayed strokes, those that are based on geometric shapes, and those that harken back to the proportions of the Roman capitals. Sans serif fonts are such a broad group that many type suppliers have created their own subcategories by which they group sans serif fonts. This makes categorizing easier for a newcomer in the world of fonts.

Sans serif fonts appear at first to be serif fonts minus the feet, or what serif fonts look like when they put on their sweats at home and lounge around. That is, until you learn that there are very elegant sans serif fonts (Optima or Gill Sans, which you are reading, for instance) that hold a candle to any serif face in terms of style and grace. The assumption that all sans serif faces are designed to have unistroke appearance just because the overused one (Helvetica) is unistroke is a fallacy.

Many sans serif fonts vary the weight of the stroke to add interest and nuances of detail to the forms of the characters. They do not strive for a mechanistic appearance which denies the existence of the human hand. Some type designers have gone back to old and ancient inscriptions for their inspiration for new

EGYPTIAN FONT CHARACTERISTICS

The following is a list of some of the attributes of Egyptian style fonts:

- Little contrast of thick and thin in weight of stem and hairline.

- Large body height to lowercase letters.

- Thick, squarish or slab serifs.

- Little or no bracketing between stem and serif.

- Vertical stress.

9-8. Egyptian font characteristics.

Sans Serif

FRANKLIN GOTHIC CONDENSED BOLD

9-9. This is Franklin Gothic Condensed Bold, a Sans Serif font.

SANS SERIF FONT CHARACTERISTICS

The following is a list of some of the attributes of Sans Serif Style fonts:

- No serifs.

- Little stress, because weights of stem and hairline optically appear even.

- Large body height in proportion to capital height.

- Often squared-off terminals.

9-10. Sans Serif font characteristics.

This page is set in ITC Lubalin Graph Book & Gill Sans Regular 8.5/12.

9 *Five Historic*
Families of Type

Display Font Characteristics
The following is a list of some of the
types of Decorative and Display fonts:
- *Scripts*
- *Inline, outline, contour, shaded*
- *Ornate faces*
- *Historic faces*
- *Illuminated initials*
- *Rustic, textured faces*
- *Highly condensed faces*
- *Extremely extended faces*
- *"Western" faces*
- *"Circus" faces*

9-11. Display-font characteristics are varied, as listed above.

WILLOW

DISPLAY FONTS

9-12. This is Willow, which is reminiscent of the Arts and Crafts movement.

MONA LISA RECUT

Decorative

9-13. This is Mona Lisa Recut, which has a distinctive triangular dot over the "i".

IRIS

SPECIALTY FONTS

9-14. This very condensed font is Iris. It is only designed in capitals; there is no lowercase.

INSIGNIA ALTERNATE

Unusual Fonts

9-15. This is Insignia, a very wide font that has replaced all slanted strokes with angles.

EMBASSY

9-16. This is Embassy, a delicate script font that has a very traditional sense.

sans serif fonts. That something old can become new again in the hands of a designer is part of the magic of type design. Each artist who looks at a character is able to see something different in the font that triggers a new direction in type design.

It is advisable for a newcomer to fonts to beware of overused fonts that have lost their effectiveness in the world of communication because we are so often bombarded with them. It is helpful to seek out less recognized fonts that have fine readability as well as character in their type design, and to familiarize yourself with these lesser-known faces. Although it's a good idea at first to become familiar with a stable of tried-and-true fonts, it's important to vary your font use, to prevent getting into a type rut, where you use the same faces all of the time, regardless of whether or not they have just the *right* feel for the project.

DECORATIVE AND DISPLAY STYLE FACES

The Decorative and Display Faces cover a broad spectrum of type design and type history. They encompass elaborate Art Deco initial caps; engraved, majestic Arts and Crafts caps; silly, obscure, hard-to-read fonts like Baby Teeth; and novelty fonts like Frankfurter. These fonts are difficult to categorize because they include such a wide variety of typefaces.

One characteristic that Decorative Fonts share is that they have poor readability at text-face point sizes, from 8 to 11 points; they do not read well at small sizes. Display fonts were designed for optimal readability when used as one initial character of a paragraph, or as a few words in a headline, or simply as a single word in a logo.

New designers are often enamored with these unique type designs, but should be advised to utilize the novelty faces with caution. It is often true that less is more in type design, and a sparse use of a novelty font shows better sensitivity and restraint than setting the entire headline in the decorative font. Sometimes one word or one initial capital has more impact than an entire page of body copy.

This page is set in Gill Sans Regular & ITC Korinna 8.5/12.

PROJECT: CREATING A TYPE "FACE"

Choose one of the historic families of type to work with, and select one font from within that family. Using both the capitals or lowercase, numerals and punctuation, create a face from the characters. The face can be seen in profile, frontal or three-quarter view. It can be a very realistic face or more of a caricature. It should be recognizable as a face. You can angle or reverse characters, but you cannot cut them apart; they must retain their integrity. Letters can be blown up or reduced to different sizes within the same design. You can also use both the italic and Roman versions of the font you have selected.

Limit the colors of your design to black, white, and gray. The final size is 11″ x 17″, (either vertical or horizontal), executed in cut paper. Mount the final piece on white matte board, and trim flush.

Begin by doing 15 thumbnail sketches, roughly to scale. The easiest way to do these might be to trace the letters from the typefaces at the end of this book, or to photocopy them enlarged. You need not use the entire letter in the design; some of it can bleed off the paper. In fact, you may want to use only a small portion of the letter, but you cannot cut up or cut off the letter unless it is cut off by the edge of the sheet. You can overlap parts of letters and work with the shapes created from this overlapping; you can apply transparency to overlapping parts of letters. The design can be random or highly stylized or organized. This should be an exciting, creative layout when you are done, one that utilizes the colors effectively.

OBJECTIVES

- To encourage designers to look at the detailed nuances of typefaces from different families.
- To look carefully at the forms that make up letters in different families.
- To experiment and play with letters from different families.
- To utilize type as a visual element, an abstract design form.
- To observe the details of letters from different families more closely when enlarging and tracing them.

9-17. This face is composed from characters in the Optima font.

9-18. This face is made up of Janson Italic, and the man has a beard.

9-19. This face is composed of Times Roman characters, and it looks angry.

This page is set in ITC
Fenice Light 8.5/12.

Five Historic Families of Type-Review

9 *Five Historic Families of Type*

1. Name four characteristics of an Old Style font. _____

_____

_____

_____

2. Name four characteristics of a Transitional font. _____

_____

_____

_____

4. Name four characteristics of a Modern font. _____

_____

_____

_____

5. Name four characteristics of an Egyptian font. _____

_____

_____

_____

6. Name four characteristics of a Sans Serif font. _____

_____

_____

7. Name an Old Style font. _____

8. Name a Transitional font. _____

9. Name a Modern font. _____

10. Name an Egyptian font. _____

11. Name a Sans Serif font. _____

12. List four characteristics of Decorative & Display fonts. _____

_____

_____

_____

13. List four examples of different types of Decorative & Display fonts. _____

_____

_____

_____

14. How are Display fonts best used? _____

15. How did the technology of printing affect the development of these different styles of fonts? _____

_____

_____

_____

_____

_____

_____

_____

Optical Adjustments to Typefaces

10 *Optical Adjustments to Typefaces*

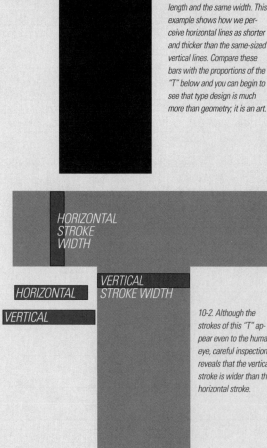

10-1. The black bars are the same length and the same width. This example shows how we perceive horizontal lines as shorter and thicker than the same-sized vertical lines. Compare these bars with the proportions of the "T" below and you can begin to see that type design is much more than geometry; it is an art.

HORIZONTAL STROKE WIDTH

VERTICAL STROKE WIDTH

HORIZONTAL

VERTICAL

10-2. Although the strokes of this "T" appear even to the human eye, careful inspection reveals that the vertical stroke is wider than the horizontal stroke.

INTRODUCTION

This chapter explores some of the decisions that type designers make when they design a typeface in order to make the font appear balanced and harmonious. We look at the differences between fonts that are designed as condensed and those that you might condense using the computer's capabilities. We also examine some height and width considerations specific to type design.

WHY HORIZONTAL LINES APPEAR THICKER

There are physical, human considerations that type designers have to take into account when they design a font. The human eye sees horizontal and vertical bars differently. Given the same weight rules, the vertically oriented one will always appear thinner to humans than the horizontally oriented rule. Some anthropologists theorize that humans perceive horizontal rules as thicker because during the evolution of humans, we had to constantly scan the horizon for potential predators, strengthening our horizontal spectrum. Some physiologists believe that it has to do with the structure of the rods in the eye (the rods that perceive horizontal widths are longer than those that perceive vertical width). For whatever reasons, this discrepancy in perceived thicknesses is a universal phenomenon among human beings.

DESIGNING A TYPEFACE

Type designers must take this information into consideration. Since horizontal strokes always appear thicker than verticals of the same weight (see example 10-2 at left), type designers must reduce the thickness of the horizontal parts of letters in a face they design to create an even weight appearance. This task is not as simple as it sounds because the horizontal strokes of most letters modulate gradually into the vertical strokes. The most difficult area of the letter to design is the transition from the horizontal to the vertical. It cannot appear too thick or be too sudden, or the human eye will detect the awkwardness.

If you look carefully at the selection of Helvetica at the left, you will notice that the horizontal parts of the letter "T" are slightly thinner than the vertical strokes. Yet, when we read the face, we feel that it is an even weight face, not a thick and thin face. The two bars below the "T" are in fact the same width and the same length. The change of orientation changes our perception of their relative length and width.

10-3. Notice in the example above that the angled and the circular characters are farther past the ascender and baseline than the square characters at the same point size. This is done so that the angled and circular characters appear as large as the square characters.

OPTICALLY CORRECT CIRCLES, TRIANGLES, SQUARES

These artistic subtleties of the weights of the strokes are often the finer points that make the difference between a successful and an unsuccessful font. Other visual considerations are the appearance of the comparable height of uppercase characters that are very differently shaped. The overall form of a "T" or an "L" is a square, but the overall form of an "O" or a "C" is a circle. Likewise, the overall form of a "W" or a "V" is triangular. These three basic shapes, the circle, the triangle and the square, are also perceived differently by the human eye. Four points of the square letters align along the baseline and the cap line. In the triangle and the circle, (which just barely touch the baseline and the cap line), they appear slightly smaller than the square. The square will always appear largest to the human eye.

Because of this, characters that are rounded or pointed are always designed to go slightly above the cap line, and slightly below the baseline. The reason for this is that if the bottom of a "V" sat directly with its lowest point on the baseline, it would appear to be placed too high since only a small portion of the letter actually hits the line. This can be contrasted with an "L," which has a long area of straight base to align along the baseline. If you look at the line of letters above, you will notice that the rounded characters and pointed characters are clearly larger than the characters that are based on a square.

Although this information may at first seem like esoteric details of type that you are interested in but unconcerned about (since you don't see yourself running out to design a font), it affects how you would align letters in a headline, or book jacket, or poster application. These details of typography may even affect how you would design a custom-logo type.

JOINED STROKES IN TYPE

There are more adjustments that type designers consider. When two lines come together and form a junction in a letterform (take "W" or "t," for example), the human eye perceives that area of juncture as heavier than the weights of each individual stroke. Perhaps because the strokes are so close, if these intersecting strokes were kept at their precise thickness, the area of the join would appear as a dark or uneven spot in the character. To prevent this, type designers slightly taper or thin strokes as they approach a juncture with another stroke, or adjust the amount that the strokes will overlap. There is a good deal of engineering and optics involved in the art of typeface design.

10-4. Notice how the horizontal strokes of this "O" are thinned to meet the thicker vertical strokes.

10-5. Notice how the strokes of this "V" gradually thin as they reach the vertex. The thinning of the strokes compensates for our eyes' tendency to add thickness or perceive thickness when two strokes come together.

This page is set in Goudy Oldstyle 8.5/12.

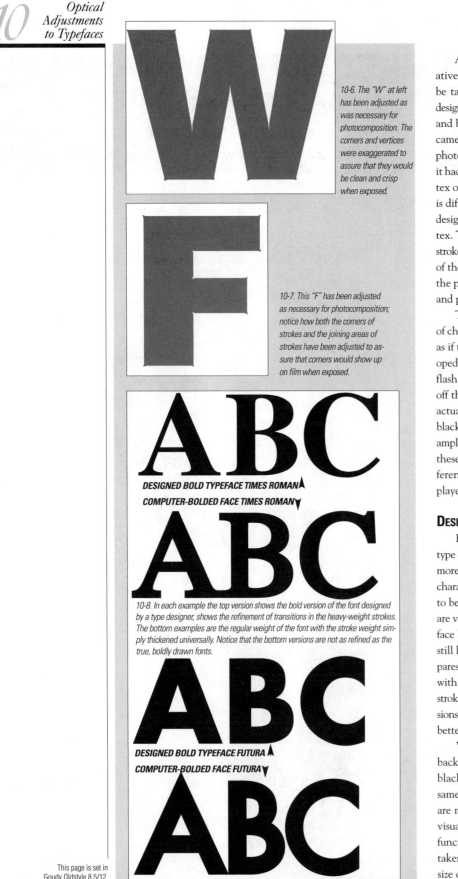

10-6. The "W" at left has been adjusted as was necessary for photocomposition. The corners and vertices were exaggerated to assure that they would be clean and crisp when exposed.

10-7. This "F" has been adjusted as necessary for photocomposition; notice how both the corners of strokes and the joining areas of strokes have been adjusted to assure that corners would show up on film when exposed.

DESIGNED BOLD TYPEFACE TIMES ROMAN
COMPUTER-BOLDED FACE TIMES ROMAN

10-8. In each example the top version shows the bold version of the font designed by a type designer, shows the refinement of transitions in the heavy-weight strokes. The bottom examples are the regular weight of the font with the stroke weight simply thickened universally. Notice that the bottom versions are not as refined as the true, boldly drawn fonts.

DESIGNED BOLD TYPEFACE FUTURA
COMPUTER-BOLDED FACE FUTURA

Also, when type was produced photographically, using a negative and a light source, other photographic tendencies had to be taken into account. Phototypesetting required that type designers adjust characters so that they did not become too heavy and black, and so that the edges did not appear rounded, but came to sharp points and square edges. The distortions of the photographic process required some changes to the type once it had been designed. Because there was a tendency for the vertex of a "W" to slightly fill in and become rounded off since it is difficult for the light to get into that tight, tiny angle, type designers had to unnaturally pinch the white space in the vertex. To do this, white space would be extended down into the strokes of the letters as a small white line, piercing into the blacks of the strokes (see example 10-6 at left). This exaggeration of the pointed area allowed the exposed type to look clear, sharp and pointed, as desired.

The opposite of this rule was applied to squared-off terminals of characters. In order for the corners of a sans serif "F" to look as if they are 90° corners when the font is exposed and developed, the negative had to be adjusted to ensure that the quick flash of light would pick up the corners crisply, and not round off the corners. To assure clean, sharp corners, type designers actually had to expand the corners, pinching out a small bit of black at the corners, extending the corners of the font (See example 10-7 at left). As more and more type is digitally produced, these optical adjustments are less necessary, but there are different considerations for the resolution of type as it is displayed on a computer monitor.

DESIGNING DIFFERENT WEIGHTS OF A FACE

Because of the subtle adjustments to each character, when type designers design different weights of the same face, there is more to do than simply thicken the weight of the line that the characters are drawn with. The subtleties of each character have to be reviewed at the heavier weight and adjusted so that they are visually comfortable. Frequently, the counter forms in boldface letters have to be opened up considerably so that they are still legible at small sizes. See example 10-8 at left, which compares the true bold font (at the top), designed by a type designer, with the faked bold version below, created by thickening the stroked outline on regular weighted characters. The true bold versions retain the thick and thin weights of the font better, and have better distinction between stem and hairline strokes.

When type is *reversed* (that is, printed in white on a black background), the human eye perceives the white letter on the black background as slightly thinner and smaller than the same character printed black on white. It may be that our eyes are more accustomed to black-on-white type, so we "read" it visually more accurately in terms of size, or it may be due to the functioning of our eye physiologically. This effect should be taken into account when deciding on the correct weight and size of type for a piece.

DESIGNING TYPE FOR USE AT DIFFERENT SIZES

Traditionally, type designers would refine three different versions of one font in each weight. This was done because of the wide variation in sizes: 4-point type has very different legibility concerns than 36-point headline type, or 100-point display type. In order for the font to appear the same at all these different sizes and maintain its personality and readability, it was necessary to design one version for body copy use at 4- to 14-point sizes. Another was designed for use from 16- to 36- point sizes, and a third was designed for uses larger than 36 points. Each of these three versions were refined separately. The small version for body copy for 7- to 12-point type often had a slightly larger x-height than was used at the larger sizes. This larger x-height improved readability and allowed more detail in the lowercase letters at these small sizes. The counter forms were also slightly enlarged to ensure that they would not close up at 6-point size. The eye on the lowercase "e" is the counter that is the *most* susceptible to closing up on press.

The next size, used primarily for heads in books, etc., was designed to read well at the medium size, from 12 to 36 points. The height of the lowercase was not so exaggerated, and the counters did not have to be enlarged. The display version of the font, or the one for applications over 36 points, is the version that we identify as the typeface. In this version, the subtleties of the bracketing on serifs and the weights of the strokes, the optical adjustments, and the transitions are refined so that the face will look correct if it is blown up five feet tall for a billboard. Every detail and proportion of the face is carefully worked out so that it is perfect at large sizes.

DESIGNING ITALIC FONTS

It is also important to realize that there is more to creating an italic version of a Roman face than simply slanting it. Some type critics judge the quality of a face by the italic version. They carefully inspect how much of the face is retained and how much is redrawn for the italic version before they judge whether the overall integrity of the font is maintained and translated into the italic face. Some characters change completely when they are created in the italic face, and most whole fonts are redrawn. Often, the italic version of a typeface usually has qualities reminiscent of hand-lettering. There is sometimes a longer extension put on the descender of the lowercase "f" as there is in calligraphy. The lower loop on the "g" is dramatically different from the Roman font. The lowercase "a" often changes its form from a bowl and an upper terminal to a single bowl form, and the lowercase "k" often incorporates a loop in place of the arm. The lowercase "s" occasionally changes to a script version, and the "t" gets a hooked terminal at the bottom. The bowl of the lowercase "p" sometimes extends past the stem stroke with a creative little swash. The lowercase "m, l, i, and n" frequently get hooked finials, and the lowercase "v, x, w, and y" can be gracefully redrawn with curves replacing the angles. Teardrop terminals are

Black-on-White Type 20 pts., 12 pts.

10-9. Compare the type above with the reversed version below. Notice that both are in a thick-stroked font, to improve readability when reversed.

White-on-Black Type 20 pts., 12 pts.

10-10. Reversed type generally looks smaller because it is surrounded by a large area of black, which seems to press in on the white letters, minimizing their size.

TRUE ROMAN TYPE- PALATINO

10-11. Compare the forms of the Roman letters above with the italic letters below. Notice that the italic version below is an entirely different design from the Roman, and it is not simply an "obliquing" or slanting of the Roman version.

TRUE ITALIC TYPE- PALATINO

10-12. You can see that the descender of the "f" changes, the "g" changes, the "k" gets a loop, and the "m" and "n" get hooked finials.

COMPUTER-OBLIQUED TYPE-PALATINO

10-13. This example shows an obliquing of the Roman, not a separate italic version. This slanting of the Roman is undesirable.

This page is set in
Goudy Oldstyle 8.5/12.

10 Optical
Adjustments
to Typefaces

OLD STYLE FIGURES

1234567890

10-14. Shown in the same point size, the numerals above are called Old Style figures, and feature ascenders and descenders. The numerals below are called Lining or Ranging figures, and they line up evenly on the baseline. The Old Style figures are more reminiscent of the handwriting of figures from ages past, before spread sheets and computers.

1234567890

LINING OR RANGING FIGURES

sometimes used on the lowercase "s" and "z" in place of serifs, as well as on some of the punctuation and symbols, such as the question mark "?," dollar sign "$," and the ampersand "&." Sometimes Old Style figures replace lining figures in the italic face.

LINING VS. OLD STYLE FIGURES

Lining or *Ranging figures* are those that are the same height as the capital letters and align along the baseline of the font. On the other hand, Old Style figures appear to bounce up and down in their placement, regardless of the baseline. In Old Style figures, the "0, 1, and 2" are small—the size of the x-height of the font. The "4, 5, 7, and 9" fall below the baseline, as if they had descenders. The "6" and "8" sit on the baseline, but their ascenders touch the cap line. Old Style figures can add character to an address or any use of numbers, and they are a pleasant change from everything lining up so solidly. Many fonts have them; you just have to buy the expert version of the font from the manufacturer. The expert version supplies the Old Style figures, caps and small caps, and fractions.

DESIGNING CONDENSED FONTS

Some fonts originate as condensed or extended faces and type designers never create a regular width font. Most fonts must change the structure of some of the characters in order to create the condensed version because the original structure would not work when simply computer-condensed. The refined adjustment of stroke transitions is not an option when a font is condensed on the computer. Fonts are encoded on the computer to be set at the width they were designed. Tinkering with the width settings of fonts on the computer not only reduces the quality of the appearance of the font, but creates an uneven distribution of weight that is distracting for the reader, and a bastardization of the font.

When a typeface is designed as a condensed typeface, it is designed so that the thickness of the stem weights of the letters is in proportion to the thickness of the hairline strokes. The horizontal and vertical strokes create a harmonious font. When a typeface is redesigned as condensed, the counters sometimes have to be slightly opened up to assure readability, and the horizontal strokes are reduced in length. When you try to condense a typeface on the computer, the face is merely squished together, throwing off all of the optical adjustments; in fact, it reverses all these adjustments. The horizontal strokes (which are designed to be thinner than the vertical strokes) are thickened when you condense a font on the computer. The line that is designed as the horizontal stroke gets crunched to-

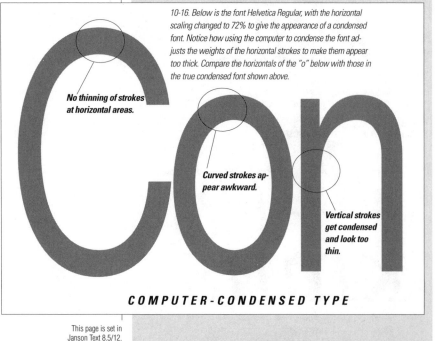

10-15. Below is a true Helvetica Condensed font. Note how well the transitions from thick to thin strokes are maintained and how the weights of the horizontal strokes seem comfortable and balanced.

Horizontal areas are gracefully thinned.

Junctures of curved and vertical strokes are refined.

Verticals are slightly thick.

TRUE CONDENSED TYPE

10-16. Below is the font Helvetica Regular, with the horizontal scaling changed to 72% to give the appearance of a condensed font. Notice how using the computer to condense the font adjusts the weights of the horizontal strokes to make them appear too thick. Compare the horizontals of the "o" below with those in the true condensed font shown above.

No thinning of strokes at horizontal areas.

Curved strokes appear awkward.

Vertical strokes get condensed and look too thin.

COMPUTER-CONDENSED TYPE

This page is set in
Janson Text 8.5/12.

gether, and the weight is increased. The vertical strokes are forced to become thinner, reversing the planned appearance of the font. The vertical strokes appear thinner because the outline condenses all parts of the letter, making the verticals very thin and the horizontals thick, and creating a very strange looking typeface.

When type designers create a condensed font, they do not reduce the thickness of the vertical strokes as the computer does. They design the vertical strokes at the same thickness as the original font, and adjust the length of the horizontal strokes, counter forms and the stroke transitions accordingly.

Adjusting the width of a face on the computer can also radically change the form of the bracketing on characters, as well as the lengths of the serifs themselves, thereby causing a change in the overall appearance of the font. It is important to realize that there is more to designing a condensed or extended font than simply pushing a few keys on the keyboard.

DESIGNING EXTENDED FONTS

The extended version of a font is one that is wider than the normal typeface. The characters are designed specifically for this new font. It means much more than simply stretching the letters horizontally. When you stretch a letter horizontally (as you can in some computer programs), you change the optical adjustments that are worked into the font. The thin areas of the letters (the horizontal strokes) get stretched thinner than they would otherwise be, and the weight of the vertical strokes is increased, so that they appear thicker than usual. This causes a very awkward and uneven appearance to the character. The horizontal strokes are too light, and there is no harmony to the letter; not to mention that the transitions from stem- to hairline-stroke weight are thrown off. When type designers draft an extended typeface by hand, they make the adjustments that maintain the integrity of the font, so that the horizontal strokes do not appear too thin, and the verticals do not appear too thick.

The reason that the horizontal strokes get thinner when you extend a font on the computer is that you are taking an area of a font that has been encoded as a line of a specific thickness that joins other parts of the character at certain curves, and stretching it. When you stretch this line, it is like stretching a rubber band; there is only so much mass determined for that line, and as it gets longer, it will get thinner because there are no alternatives.

Yet, as in all rules of design, these rules are meant to be broken. Some designers purposely change the widths of fonts on the computer to create the off-balanced feeling to the letters as part of the design. This can be effective as part of the overall design and the intended message. Furthermore,

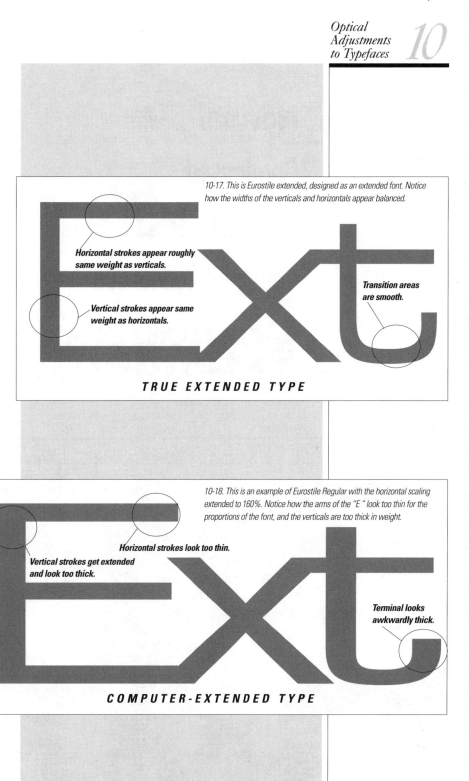

10-17. This is Eurostile extended, designed as an extended font. Notice how the widths of the verticals and horizontals appear balanced.

Horizontal strokes appear roughly same weight as verticals.

Transition areas are smooth.

Vertical strokes appear same weight as horizontals.

TRUE EXTENDED TYPE

10-18. This is an example of Eurostile Regular with the horizontal scaling extended to 160%. Notice how the arms of the "E" look too thin for the proportions of the font, and the verticals are too thick in weight.

Horizontal strokes look too thin.

Vertical strokes get extended and look too thick.

Terminal looks awkwardly thick.

COMPUTER-EXTENDED TYPE

This page is set in Janson Text 8.5/12.

10 *Optical*
Adjustments
to Typefaces

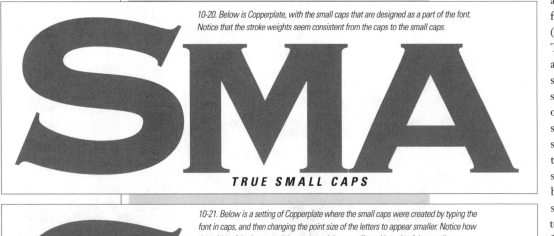

Normal
Condensed
Extended
Computer-Condensed
Computer Extended

10-19. The settings above show a comparison of fonts that are designed as condensed and extended versions of the original, compared with the computerized condensed and extended versions.

in contemporary type design, many of the traditional rules of weights and serifs are being eschewed in favor of creating alternative sensibilities to the faces *because* they break the rules. To part with the rules of traditional type design is perfectly okay, as long as you acknowledge the digression. Many artists argue that you can only successfully break from the traditions of the past after you have full knowledge and mastery of those traditions.

DESIGNING CAPS AND SMALL CAPS

Caps and small caps are an alternate typesetting option in place of caps and lowercase, and are often used in setting distinctive text type, standfirsts, or headlines. When you request type set in caps/small caps, all the lowercase characters will be set in caps that are approximately 75% of the height of the capital letter. These caps have been specifically designed for use with the full-size caps. In designing the small caps, the type designer has beefed up the weight of the hairline and stem strokes a bit on the small caps so that they appear as the same weight as the full caps. If you simply type in a selection on the computer and select the lowercase and set it in 10-point caps, and set the uppercase in 12-point caps (to sort of fake caps and small caps), the type will look uneven because the verticals of the small caps look too light and whimpy, which makes the darker full caps too prominent on the page (see examples 10-20 and 10-21 at right). The weight of a 10-point cap's strokes are much lighter than the 12-point cap's strokes. In the small caps, the type designer has adjusted for the appearance of difference in stroke weight. The strokes of the small caps that are designed for the font are a bit thicker than they should be at that point size, so the stroke weight of the small caps balances the stroke weight of the full-size caps. This allows the weight of the text to look even, and ultimately makes for easier reading. This is one of the more subtle points of type design, but an experienced designer should be aware of these adjustments.

10-20. Below is Copperplate, with the small caps that are designed as a part of the font. Notice that the stroke weights seem consistent from the caps to the small caps.

SMA
TRUE SMALL CAPS

10-21. Below is a setting of Copperplate where the small caps were created by typing the font in caps, and then changing the point size of the letters to appear smaller. Notice how the width of the letters and the stroke weights are affected by using false small caps.

SMA
COMPUTER-CREATED SMALL CAPS

This page is set in
Janson Text 8.5/12.

PROJECT: TYPOGRAPHIC CELEBRATION CARDS

Find two greeting cards that you like or come up with your own saying for one of the following holidays/events:

- Birthday	- New Year's	- Passover
- Divorce	- Marriage	- Easter
- New Child	- Vacation	- Chinese New Year
- St. Patrick's Day	- Kwanzah	- Groundhog's Day
- Halloween	- Thanksgiving	- Random Acts of Kindness Day
- Christmas	- Hanukkah	- Turning 50/Over the Hill

You can use any of the holidays from the list above, or any others that you come up with. The size of the final cards must be smaller than 8.5" x 11", but they can be any shape, and they can fold in any direction. The primary limitation is that they must be predominantly designed typographically. You can design your two cards to look similar in the use of color, texture and fonts, or they can be entirely different. You will also have to design an envelope for each card, so think in terms of the envelopes as part of the piece. You can consider type on the envelopes, or die-cuts, etc.

Consider all that you have learned as far as the weights and the design of specific fonts. In order to design with the type, you may need to break from the standard alignment of type on a baseline; this is perfectly acceptable.

Although you can use visuals, the type should be the primary element and the media that conveys the message. You need to think of the emotions that are being conveyed with the card and apply those emotions to the type. The type can be sad even though the message is happy, or vice versa.

On this project type can be set, drawn, scrawled, built three-dimensionally, engraved, collaged, or lettered. There is no limit to the means by which your type is produced. Let your creativity and imagination run wild.

Begin by completing a series of 20 thumbnail sketches, ten for each card. These sketches should add clarity to the intent of the cards, or serve to express the sensibility you felt from the topic. Type can work in concert with the message it is trying to convey, or undermine that message as a contradiction.

After your thumbnail sketches are resolved, progress to a full-sized pencil rough of each card. This rough layout should be tight enough for you to understand and make sense of when you try to set your type on the computer, cut it together by hand, or collage/create it. Remember to check your layout for readability and kerning where necessary.

Next you must begin assembly of the card, by whatever means is most appropriate. You may want to add hand-coloring to the images to separate them from the letters, or illustrate some of the letters or collage elements together. There are no rules for this project, except for the size limitation and the emphasis on type as your medium. Your cards do not necessarily have to be made of paper. Be creative, and have fun!

OBJECTIVES

- To understand type as an interpretive medium.
- To organize information using typeface distinction.
- To reinforce the hierarchy of typographic information.
- To review kerning and ligatures.
- To develop the ability to choose appropriate fonts for a project.
- To see type as an abstract design element.
- To question the relationship between type and message—how they reinforce one another, and how they can contradict one another.
- To communicate a simple message using exclusively type.

10-22. This card, designed by KU student Renee Alvarado, shows how type, its arrangement, and the use of other elements can create a festive typographic solution for a New Year's greeting card.

10-23. This Over-the-Hill card adjusts the type so that it visually creates the hill.

This page is set in Futura Light Condensed 8.5/12.

Optical Adjustments to Typefaces-Review

10 *Optical Adjustments to Typefaces*

1. Why are the horizontal strokes of a character thinner than the vertical strokes? _____

_____

2. What do type designers do where two angled strokes come together in a character? _____

_____

3. What do type designers do to rounded characters? _____

4. What do type designers do to two strokes that come together in a character at 90°? _____

5. What does the term "optically correct" mean as it applies to typographic design? _____

_____

6. What does a type designer do to design various weights of a font? _____

_____

7. What happens when you condense a font on the computer, rather than using a condensed font? _____

_____

8. What happens when you extend a font on the computer, rather than using an extended font? _____

_____

9. How can you detect a font that's been condensed on the computer by altering the horizontal scaling? _____

_____

10. What are four considerations of designing italic fonts? _____

_____

_____

_____

_____

11. How can you tell the difference between true small caps, and those that are reduced in size by the computer? _____

_____

12. Why is it important that designers know what the type designers are doing, and what their intent is? _____

_____

_____

_____

_____

_____

_____

_____

_____

This page is set in
Fenice Light 8.5/12.

Typeface/Font/Family of Type

11 *Typeface/Font/*
Family of Type

INTRODUCTION

This chapter defines and gives examples of a typeface, a font and a family of type. It explains the correct usage of these terms, what comprises each, and how they are interrelated. It also distinguishes the term typestyle from a font or typeface.

DISTINGUISHING A TYPEFACE FROM A FONT

There is a great deal of confusion between the meaning of typeface versus font. The word *typeface* is a term that is used very loosely, and often incorrectly. The term typeface refers simply to the upper- and lowercase letters and the design of the letters in a given design, by a given type designer. The term typeface does not imply a finished, complete font, ready for public use; it merely refers to the new "look" that a type designer has created for letters.

The term *font*, on the other hand, is correctly used to include the upper- and lowercase alphabet, all the sym-

TYPEFACE

ABCDEFGHIJKLMNOP
QRSTUVWXYZ
1234567890

11-1. Above is the complete Willow typeface; notice that there are no lowercase characters nor symbols. Typefaces are only composed of the letters and sometimes the numbers. A typeface is much smaller than a font.

11-2. Above is the complete set of characters in the Times Roman font; it includes mathematical symbols, monetary symbols, accented characters, trademark symbols and footnote symbols. A font is more extensive than a typeface.

bols, monetary symbols, numerals, punctuation, fractions, mathematical symbols, ligatures, dingbats, superior and inferior characters, small caps, and accented characters that are necessary for typesetting. There is much more to designing a font than merely the 26 letters of the alphabet in upper- and lowercase. A font has been refined; it includes the design of numerous symbols beyond simply the letters of the alphabet.

The word font includes much more than the term typeface. A font is a more complete, ready-to-use version of a typeface. The typeface refers to the basic design of the letters and the regular weight that the type is first designed in; it exists as one weight, and as either a Roman or italic version. A font is designed to have a stroke weight that optically appears consistent throughout all the characters. The stem weight and the hairline weight appear to be consistent from one letter or symbol to the next. Even the numerals are designed to correlate to the font visually to create a harmonious whole. The small caps have been designed so that their weights correspond to the stroke weights of the capital letters.

THE FAMILY OF TYPE

The *family of type* includes all the relatives of that one font, sort of a family reunion of all the fonts that look like each other. The Berkeley family listed in the chart above shows a standard series of weights and italics that make up a family of fonts. Usually, when a single font is selected for body copy, the corresponding weights of bold and italic are used to show emphasis in text, or for callouts and pull quotes.

A family of fonts includes all of the versions that are based on the original face—all of the different weights: extra light, light, book, demi, bold, extra bold, heavy and ultra, in both the Roman and italic versions. The family also includes the condensed versions

FAMILY OF TYPE

ITC Berkeley Oldstyle Book

ITC Berkeley Oldstyle Italic

ITC Berkeley Oldstyle Medium

ITC Berkeley Oldstyle Medium Italic

ITC Berkeley Oldstyle Bold

ITC Berkeley Oldstyle Bold Italic

ITC Berkeley Oldstyle Black

ITC Berkeley Oldstyle Black Italic

11-3. Above is the family of ITC Berkeley fonts, showing the variety of weights. Notice that the family includes all of the Roman and italic versions, as well as all of the various weights.

This page is set in Eurostile 8.5/12.

HELVETICA FAMILY

Helvetica Extra Light
Helvetica Light
Helvetica
Helvetica Medium
Helvetica Demi
Helvetica Bold
Helvetica Extra Bold
Helvetica Extra Light Italic
Helvetica Light Italic
Helvetica Italic
Helvetica Medium Italic
Helvetica Demi Italic
Helvetica Bold Italic
Helvetica Extra Bold Italic
Helvetica Extra Light Condensed Italic
Helvetica Light Compact Italic
Helvetica Condensed Italic
Helvetica Medium Condensed Italic
Helvetica Bold Condensed Italic
Helvetica Extra Bold Condensed Italic
Helvetica Demi Condensed Italic
Helvetica Extra Light Condensed
Helvetica Light Condensed
Helvetica Condensed
Helvetica Medium Condensed
Helvetica Demi Condensed
Helvetica Bold Condensed
Helvetica Extra Bold Condensed
Helvetica Condensed (all weights)
Helvetica Extra Condensed (all weights)
Helvetica Extra Bold Italic
Helvetica Compressed Italic (all weights)
Helvetica Extra Condensed Italic (all weights)
Helvetica Extra Light Extended Italic
Helvetica Light Extended Italic
Helvetica Extended Italic
Helvetica Medium Extended Italic
Helvetica Demi Extended Italic
Helvetica Bold Extended Italic
Helvetica Extra Bold Extended Italic
Helvetica Demi Extended Italic
Helvetica Extra Light Extended
Helvetica Light Extended
Helvetica Extended
Helvetica Medium Extended
Helvetica Demi Extended
Helvetica Bold Extended
Helvetica Extra Bold Extended
Helvetica Extra Bold

11-4. All the possible versions of Helvetica listed above are considered part of the same family.

of the face, in all the various weights: extra light, light, book, demi, bold, extra bold, heavy, and ultra, in both the Roman and italic versions. The family includes the extended fonts as well in all the weights: extra light, light, book, demi, bold, extra bold, heavy, and ultra, in both the Roman and italic versions. The family of a font also includes the outline and small-cap versions of the letters. In some typefaces, these options can create a rather large "extended" family of a font.

DESIGNING WITH TWO FAMILIES OF TYPE

It can be helpful to understand what comprises a family of type, particularly when you're working on an editorial project. A common rule of thumb for newsletters, newspapers and even magazines is to stick to two fonts, a serif and a sans serif for the overall design of the piece, but to utilize the entire family of each of these fonts. By limiting the selection to a single serif and a single sans serif family, there is a consistent typographic program and order through the use of those two fonts. The coordination of the family gives the designer a broad range of condensed, bold, and italic options, while the family unity lends harmony to the overall typographic design. There can be consistency, yet a wide variation and typographic contrast within a limited sphere . . . it is sort of like a symphony which offers listeners endless variation on a common musical theme that consists of the same notes, in the same order. As a designer, once you understand a family of type, you are free to utilize it to its fullest in a design format to create variation and contrast, in stroke weight, point size, form, structure, spacing and density between the two families you are using.

A TYPESTYLE VS. A TYPEFACE

The *typestyle* refers to whether the typeface is italic, bold, extended, or condensed. The typestyle is a descriptive term that modifies the original font. Typestyles are like variations on the theme of the original typeface. The typestyle will look different from the original face, but be related in the essential components of the design of the characters. A family of type is a collection of all of the related typestyles that are variations on a specific typeface.

SUPERSCRIPTS/SUBSCRIPTS/OLD STYLE & LINING FIGURES

Superscripts are exponents, such as in 10^4 and the upper numerals or numerators in fractions. *Subscripts* are used in chemical formulas, such as H_2O, to denote the number of molecules in a substance. Subscripts are also used in denominators such as the 2 in the fraction written stacked ($\frac{1}{2}$) or with a slash ($1/2$).

Numerals can be designed to align along the baseline and cap line (the format that we are accustomed to in texts), or they can be designed with ascenders and descenders, more reminiscent of handwritten numerals. Those that align at the cap and baseline are called *Lining* or *Ranging figures* or *numerals*; those that have ascenders and descenders are called *Old Style figures*.

THE UNIVERS FAMILY

The Swiss type designer Adrian Frutiger designed the font Univers, a somewhat square, well-balanced, sans serif font that is very clean with a functional practicality to the forms of the letters. In a valiant attempt to codify the family system, Frutiger developed a numerical system to determine the stroke width and the condensed or extendedness of the typeface within the family. He also designed the entire family as one massive undertaking, rather than adding variations at a later time, some of which are often designed by subordinates for most fonts and often lose the essence of the original typeface.

In the Univers numbering system, the Univers 55 version was considered the middle of the family, or the original design. As the stroke width got heavier, the tens digit increased, so that Univers 65 was a heavier weight than 55. Conversely, as the stroke weight got thinner, the tens digit number decreased, so that Univers 35 was lighter than 55. The ones digit referenced the condensed or extendedness of the font. The higher the ones digit, the more condensed the font is, with 5 being the original drawing; the lower the ones digit, the more extended the font. So Univers 59 is more condensed than 55, and 53 is more extended than 55. In addition, italic was indicated by an even number in the ones place, and Roman was indicated by the an odd number in the ones place. Univers 56 is the italic version of 55, Univers 38 is the italic version of 37. Although there was logic and order to this numbering system to the Univers family, it was never adopted as the standard for other families of type. Univers numbers are applied to Helvetica in some foundries. But the drawing of the variations of Helvetica are not as consistent as in the Univers system because they were completed by various type designers at different times and, therefore, lack the cohesiveness of Frutiger's comprehensive Univers system.

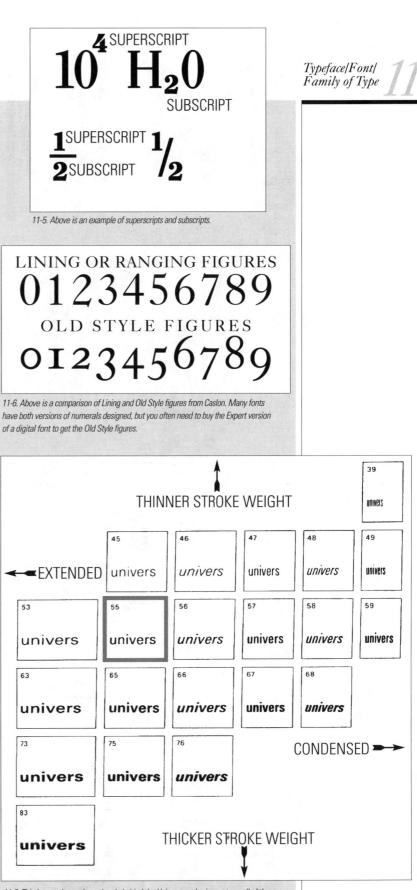

11-5. Above is an example of superscripts and subscripts.

11-6. Above is a comparison of Lining and Old Style figures from Caslon. Many fonts have both versions of numerals designed, but you often need to buy the Expert version of a digital font to get the Old Style figures.

11-7. This layout shows the rationale behind the Univers numbering system; all of the weights of the fonts in this family were designed by Adrian Frutiger. This gives Univers a tremendous sense of cohesiveness and unity.

11 Typeface/Font/
    Family of Type

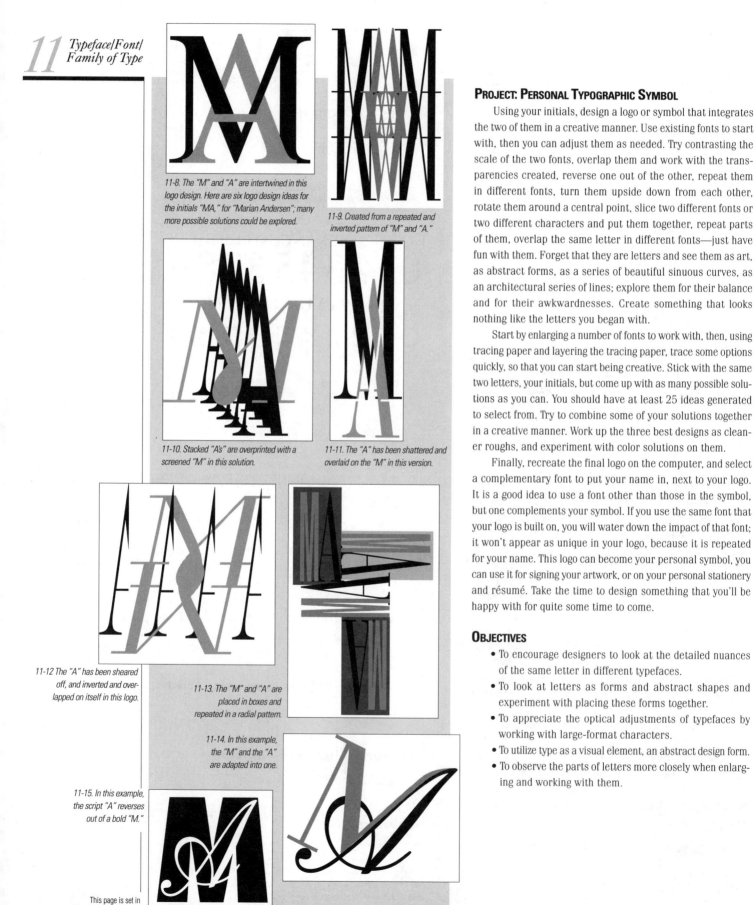

11-8. The "M" and "A" are intertwined in this logo design. Here are six logo design ideas for the initials "MA," for "Marian Andersen"; many more possible solutions could be explored.

11-9. Created from a repeated and inverted pattern of "M" and "A."

11-10. Stacked "A's" are overprinted with a screened "M" in this solution.

11-11. The "A" has been shattered and overlaid on the "M" in this version.

11-12 The "A" has been sheared off, and inverted and overlapped on itself in this logo.

11-13. The "M" and "A" are placed in boxes and repeated in a radial pattern.

11-14. In this example, the "M" and the "A" are adapted into one.

11-15. In this example, the script "A" reverses out of a bold "M."

This page is set in ITC Fenice Light 8.5/12.

PROJECT: PERSONAL TYPOGRAPHIC SYMBOL

Using your initials, design a logo or symbol that integrates the two of them in a creative manner. Use existing fonts to start with, then you can adjust them as needed. Try contrasting the scale of the two fonts, overlap them and work with the transparencies created, reverse one out of the other, repeat them in different fonts, turn them upside down from each other, rotate them around a central point, slice two different fonts or two different characters and put them together, repeat parts of them, overlap the same letter in different fonts—just have fun with them. Forget that they are letters and see them as art, as abstract forms, as a series of beautiful sinuous curves, as an architectural series of lines; explore them for their balance and for their awkwardnesses. Create something that looks nothing like the letters you began with.

Start by enlarging a number of fonts to work with, then, using tracing paper and layering the tracing paper, trace some options quickly, so that you can start being creative. Stick with the same two letters, your initials, but come up with as many possible solutions as you can. You should have at least 25 ideas generated to select from. Try to combine some of your solutions together in a creative manner. Work up the three best designs as cleaner roughs, and experiment with color solutions on them.

Finally, recreate the final logo on the computer, and select a complementary font to put your name in, next to your logo. It is a good idea to use a font other than those in the symbol, but one complements your symbol. If you use the same font that your logo is built on, you will water down the impact of that font; it won't appear as unique in your logo, because it is repeated for your name. This logo can become your personal symbol, you can use it for signing your artwork, or on your personal stationery and résumé. Take the time to design something that you'll be happy with for quite some time to come.

OBJECTIVES

- To encourage designers to look at the detailed nuances of the same letter in different typefaces.
- To look at letters as forms and abstract shapes and experiment with placing these forms together.
- To appreciate the optical adjustments of typefaces by working with large-format characters.
- To utilize type as a visual element, an abstract design form.
- To observe the parts of letters more closely when enlarging and working with them.

Typeface/Font/Family of Type-Review

1. Define a typeface. _____

2. Define a font. _____

_____

3. Define a typestyle. _____

_____

4. Define a family of type. _____

_____

5. List the characters that make up a font. _____

_____

6. List the elements of a family. _____

_____

7. What is the difference between Lining and Old Style figures? _____

_____

8. How does the Univers family differ from other type families? _____

9. Why do type designers have to design so much more than just the letters of the alphabet when designing a font? _____

_____

_____

_____

This page is set in
Fenice Light 8.5/12.

Readability & Legibility

12 Readability & Legibility

SHORT ASCENDERS & CONDENSED = POOR LEGIBILITY

hnm

*12-1. Condensed fonts often are less legible at small sizes because the letters are
difficult to distinguish; notice the similarity between the "h", "n", and "m" above.*

EXAGGERATED HOOKED TERMINALS, EXTREMELY CONDENSED & MINIMAL COUNTERS = POOR LEGIBILITY

*12-2. Sometimes subtleties or nuances of a font prevent clear legibility, as in the exagge-
rated finials in the font above that can connect and make characters unintelligible.*

*12-3. Depending on the style, script fonts can be extremely illegible when it comes to
the capital letters. It is virtually impossible to tell one letter from another above;
they are "T," "I," "S."*

INTRODUCTION

Readability and legibility are terms used to describe text
type and how it is set. Readability refers to the overall
appearance of how the type is spaced in the column—decisions which the designer makes about point size, leading,
tracking, and line length of a selection of copy. Legibility
refers to the decisions that the type designer made about
the forms of the letters of the alphabet, and the ability of
the reader to distinguish the letters
from each other. In order for text to
be optimally readable by the viewer,
both the legibility and readability considerations have to be addressed.

LEGIBILITY CONSIDERATIONS/
FONT DESIGN

Legibility is the ease with which
a reader can discern the type on the
page, based on the tone of the type
in relation to the background, and can
discern the letters from one another.
Letters must be identified to be read. Research has shown
that the eye travels across a line of type in saccadic jumps.
The eye sees a small grouping of
words for approximately one-quar-
ter of a second before jumping to a
second grouping and so on. It seems
that readers look most closely at the
top halves of the letters, rather than
at the bottom half. In order to be
legible, fonts can't have too small an
x-height, or it will be difficult to discern the letters. Likewise, if the ascenders and descenders are too short, it
becomes difficult to differentiate an
"n" from an "h," an "o" from a "p" or
a "q," or an "i" from an "l." In script
fonts, often the "I" and the "T" are dif-
ficult to distinguish; sometimes the "S" and the "J" are eas-

ily confused. The legibility of some display faces is so poor that they are never considered for body copy.

Some typefaces are more legible than others. Research has shown that serif faces read better generally than sans serif faces. Some *sans serif*, or *splayed* faces, like Optima, were designed with wider areas at the ends of the strokes for this reason, and they read better than other sans serif faces.

A selection of type must be set in a legible font before the details of readability can be analyzed. The size of type is very important to the legibility of the type. The most legible type sizes are 8, 9,10, and 11 point. Legibility relies further on the x-height of the face that you specify. If the style you select has a large x-height, then you should select 8-to 10-point type. Conversely, if the typeface you select has a small x-height, then you should use 10- or 11-point type. Smaller than 8-point type will not be an easy read because it doesn't allow for fast letter recognition. Thus, if smaller type is needed because of space requirements, try a condensed font, but select one with a large x-height proportion.

READABILITY & TEXT TYPE

The readability of type is affected by the font selection, the point size, spacing, tracking, line length and leading. Readability refers to the evenness of the tone of gray created on the page by a setting of text type. You want to create an even texture of gray with even line spacing that does not have dark and light areas to distract the reader's eye from the words.

Type set in all capital letters slows down the readability and uses approximately fifty percent more space. All-cap type is still generally acceptable in headlines, subheads, and picture captions, but for body copy caps and lowercase are more appropriate. The lowercase letters, with their more distinguishable letter shapes due to ascenders and descenders, assist in reading. The first initial cap at the beginning of each sentence is also a significant visual aid for the reader. Some body copy set in all caps can be completely illegible, so use caution when specifying all caps for body copy, or consider trying caps and small caps for a change. This will at least call the reader's attention to the beginning of a sentence.

Another typographic style that can slow down the reader is script or italic typefaces. While these faces are very appropriate in showing elegance and getting attention, caution must be used. Consider using script faces just for the initial cap to add an air of elegance to the body copy without sacrificing readability, or allow for plenty of leading to improve readability with italic fonts.

CONFUSION OF CHARACTERS = POOR LEGIBILITY

12-4. The letters "S," "J," and "I" above are difficult to distinguish; this font, Berthold Script Regular, has poor legibility.

Line length of type should be in proportion to the size of the type. If you use a long line length, use a large point size so that the type is easy to follow. Also, increase the leading so that the reader does not retrack on the same line repeatedly.

Simply opening up the leading will make the text significantly easier to read, and to flow from one line to the next. It often does not take a great deal of space to open the leading, but it makes your text easier to read and more accessible.

12-5. The example above shows how line length and leading must be considered of equal importance when designing type for optimal readability.

Take the same text, and set it two different ways, 10/11 and 9/12 or 9/12.5. You will be able to analyze the changes that size versus line spacing makes on the readability of the selection. This is set 10/11.

12-6. The example at the left shows that increased point size doesn't help readability nearly so much as increased leading, which makes tracking across the lines much easier and faster.

Take the same text, and set it two different ways, 10/11 and 9/12 or 9/12.5. You will be able to analyze the changes that size versus line spacing makes on the readability of the selection. This is set 9/12.5.

12-7. This selection is much easier to read due to increased leading, even though the point size of the type is smaller.

Type that is tracked too
loosely will be tiring to the
reader's eyes. The words
don't hold together and
they take too much time to
distinguish because the letter spacing is too wide.

12-8. Notice how long it took you to read the words above; the overly loose tracking slows you down.

Type that is tracked too tightly
will be tough on the reader's
eyes. The letters take too
much time to distinguish
because the letter spacing
is inadequate.

12-9. Notice how long it took you to read the words above; the overly tight tracking slows you down.

Rivers in body copy can be
very distracting to the eye.
Even though you may not
be consciously aware of
how tiring poor letterspacing may be on your eyes,
you will suffer eye fatigue
when reading poorly
spaced type full of rivers.

12-10. In justified copy, if the line length is too short, your type will have numerous rivers, making reading tedious.

LETTER SPACING AND ITS EFFECT ON READABILITY

Type designers spend as much time studying the spacing of the letters as they spend designing the letters themselves. Thus, one can assume that a well-designed typeface has a "natural" or "normal" letter space setting built into the design. This "normal" letter space is probably optimal for most body copy. When letters are set too loosely, the words do not form groups, and the spaces between the words are difficult to discern, causing the eye to slow down. If the letters of body copy are too tightly packed together, the letters can be hard to distinguish from one another, again causing the reader to slow down to read the copy. If text is tough to read, we are likely to pass over it. When a reader has to work to read the body copy, the designer has failed to get the client's or author's message across effectively. (Hopefully this textbook is a pleasure for the reader to read–typographically speaking.)

Attention to letter spacing is necessary because it helps the reader differentiate the separate words, increasing readability. Generally, letter spacing between two letters will need adjustments in display type, but not in body type. When a designer makes a change in letterspacing it subtly alters the balance of the spacing throughout the text. Letter spacing should be set so that words create clear groups without feeling crowded together.

When you change the letter spacing of text type on most typesetting equipment, the word spacing is likewise adjusted. When you specify very tight letter spacing, you also adjust the word spacing. The function of word spacing is to clearly separate the words from each other. It must also be uniform and consistent, and even in justified copy it should not be visually too irregular. (The copy that you are reading is justified text.)

LEADING, LINE LENGTH AND READABILITY

The third element that must be in harmony with letter spacing and word spacing is the leading, or line spacing. Leading can improve or confound readability. Research shows that increased leading improves legibility. Line spacing must never be less than your word spacing because if the linespacing is too tight, the reader's eye will tend to drop through the word spaces into the lines below. Heavy sans serif faces and bold faces sometimes require more leading and word spacing than their regular-weight counterparts. As a general rule of thumb, for text copy use from three to four points of leading beyond the point size of the type for good line spacing to maximize ease of reading. (The copy that you are reading has 3.5 extra points of leading between lines.)

READABILITY AND EYE-FOCUSING

The width of the column and the eye's ability to focus on an area also factors into readability of text. Studies indicate that the human eye can keep an area around four inches wide in sharp focus at one time without having to turn one's head. This means the eye can see or read a line 24 picas wide and find the beginning of the next line with only so much as a blink. We do blink about 25 times a minute, or every 2.4 seconds. When we do blink, we lose focus and have to refocus. A skilled reader, however, reads about 10 words or 60 characters in 2.4 seconds, blinking at the end of each 24-pica line width (or two) before starting the next line of text. (Now, don't stop reading here to count your blinks per line!)

There are many rules governing the optimal line length, but keeping body-text line measures between 13 picas and 26 picas is wise. Formulas for ideal line length include: make the measure in picas twice the type size in points, or make the measure of the column 1 1/2 to 2 1/2 alphabets long. The second takes into account the set width of the typeface. Generally you should use the shorter measure for fonts with smaller x-heights, fonts at smaller point sizes, or condensed fonts. Longer line lengths should be used with larger x-heights, larger point sizes, and wideset fonts. Light faces, bold faces, italics and monoweight sans serifs should be set on shorter line lengths for greater reading ease.

In multi-column layouts, you might not have the room for 20-pica-wide columns, but make sure that you don't go to less than 9 picas wide. Column widths less than 9 picas speed up eye movement when reading and is very tiring to the eyes. Readability is slowed down by line breaks and end- of-line hyphens. If space doesn't allow you anything more than a short column width, specify a tight-set face, or even a condensed face in a flush-left, ragged-right setting.

LEADING IN RELATION TO LINE LENGTH

Relating leading or line spacing to line length seems obvious here. The longer the line, the more leading you will need. The added leading will help the reader get across a long line of type without the eye jumping down mid-line to the next line. Long copy lines need to be well separated by extra leading so that the reader can distinguish the beginning of lines clearly. We've all had the experience of reading the same line of text a few times in a row because our eyes had difficulty in tracking from one line to the next. The longer the distance the eye has to travel to pick up the beginning of the subsequent line of text, the more important it is to have clear rows of white space (leading) between the lines of text.

HOW THE SETTING OF TEXT AFFECTS READABILITY

Studies indicate that flush-left, rag-right text is slightly easier to read than justified text. Almost all Medieval manuscripts were written in justified formats, creating neat, even pages. Justified columns create perfect rectangles or squares of copy with consistent margins, giving us a feeling of order and balance, as

Type set flush left is assumed to be more legible than type set centered or flush right. Decide for yourself if this true as you read through this selection of type.

12-11. The text above is set flush left; compare its readability to the examples below. Also, the same selection is reversed on the next page; evaluate how difficult it is to read reversed copy for yourself.

Type set flush right is assumed to be more difficult to read than type set centered or flush left. Decide for yourself if this true as you read through this selection of type.

12-12. The text above is set flush right; compare its readability to the other examples on this page. Also, the same selection is reversed on the next page; evaluate how difficult it is to read reversed copy for yourself.

Type set centered is assumed to be more difficult to read than type set flush left because there is no consistent left margin. Decide for yourself if this true as you read through this selection of type.

12-13. The text above is set centered; compare its readability to the other examples on this page. Also, the same selection is reversed on the next page; evaluate how difficult it is to read reversed copy for yourself.

This page is set in
Industrial 736 8.5/12.

Type set flush left is assumed to be more legible than type set centered or flush right. Decide for yourself if this true as you read through this selection of type. Also, does reversing the type out of black change the readability of the type?

12-14. Compare this flush-left setting with the version on the previous page.

Type set flush right is assumed to be more difficult to read than type set centered or flush left. Decide for yourself if this true as you read through this selection of type. Also, does reversing the type out of black change the readability of the type?

12-15. Compare this flush-right setting with the version on the previous page.

Type set centered is assumed to be more difficult to read than type set flush left because there is no consistent left margin. Decide for yourself if this true as you read through this selection of type. Also, does reversing the type out of black change the readability of the type?

12-16. Compare this centered setting with the version on the previous page.

This page is set in
Industrial 736 8.5/12.

the text on this page. Because of their right angles, these columns also blend well with photos, artwork and information graphics.

Non-uniform word spacing is the biggest drawback to justified copy, with frequent hyphenation at the end of lines the second drawback. Word spaces tend to be either stretched or squeezed to fit the line width; the consistent line length is achieved by enlarging or reducing the spaces between words. Some lines will have long gaps between the words, and some will have thin slivers, potentially ruining the overall even-gray appearance that the type should have on the page. Sometimes hyphenations are used, and they tend to slow down the reading a bit. It is particularly infuriating to find a hyphen in a place it simply doesn't belo-ng that was put there automatically so that the line would break correctly.

In justified copy you also have to be alert for *rivers*. In the type world, rivers are areas of white space that flow vertically through overly wide word spacing in justified copy. Rivers are distracting to readers and undesirable in your copy. If your layout needs to be conservative, quiet, or serious, you should specify a justified setting, but beware of rivers. Review copy carefully, and write to fit if possible.

Flush-left, ragged-right formats can be more interesting than justified ones because of the contrasting line lengths. Flush-left copy is easier to read because of its consistent word spacing and limited hyphenations. The contrasting line lengths may even help the eye track back to the next line correctly. If your layout calls for a more informal, contemporary style, you should select flush left, rag right.

Certain type alignments are less legible than others. Centered and flush-*right* copy arrangements are not considered "reading formats" because they do not have a fixed left margin as an indicator for a new line of type. Centered formats are classical and formal in balance and are frequently used for title pages, engraved wedding invitations, headlines, etc., where the amount of copy is strictly limited. Centered settings give the feeling of gravity and can be very elegant and poetic, especially with sufficient line spacing. Flush-right, ragged-left settings are the most unusual formats of the group. Although the read can be difficult, if used sparingly to create attention, these text settings can be effective and distinctive.

COLUMNS OF TYPE AND READABILITY

When a page has more than one column of type, the space between the columns, the *column margins* or *alleys*, need to be considered in terms of readability. Justified columns of type, 11 picas to 20 picas wide should have about 1 1/2 picas between them, if you want the text to be read easily. If the copy is set flush left, a little less space is needed in the alleys because the ragged right edge of the text joins the vertical alley. A vertical rule down the alley can help to separate the columns and won't be too distracting if it isn't too dark or thick. Alley widths are not as critical as letter spacing, word spacing and line spacing are for readable text. Alleys are primarily a part of the design of the page and can vary greatly. It is important to realize the overall impact the layout of the page can have on the reader. A page designed with narrow column margins looks heavy and appears serious. A page designed with wider columns, broader alleys and generous leading looks lighter and more inviting to read.

PROJECT: EXHIBIT POSTER & INVITATION

Your project is to design a poster and an invitation for an exhibit, using the copyright-free fonts and images. The size of the poster is 11″ x 17″; it can be designed vertically or horizontally. The size or scale of the invitation is up to you. The poster and the invitation should look related in the use of color, the use of type and the use of imagery. From the copyright-free books of historic images, choose visuals that relate to a theme or topic. Using historic typefaces, or fonts from the computers (or a combination), select fonts that you think will work with the subject matter that you choose. Make copies of the images and the fonts from the historic books. They will be used to advertise a museum show or exhibit. Here are some exhibit topics to choose from:

- Technology and Transportation
- Toys of Bygone Eras
- 19th-Century Musical Instruments
- Household Antiques
- Flowers and Herb Prints
- A History of Sports
- Creatures from Mythology
- Historical Automobiles
- Shoes from the 19th Century
- American Indian Crafts
- Quilts over the Centuries
- Insect Design
- Occupations of the Past
- The History of Hats
- A Kaleidoscope of Marine Life
- Hot-Air-Balloon Designs
- Handbags from the 1800s
- Furniture of the 1800s
- Architectural Details...A Historical Survey
- Walking Through History...Shoes from the Past
- Reptiles of Various Countries

These are just a few titles; you can pick one or create your own. You can also use other visuals from other sources; you may want to do an illustration of your own, or a collage, etc.

You should write all of the copy for this project: the name of the exhibit, one to two paragraphs of body copy, the name of the museum, the address, and the date and time of the show. You may want to get the logo of a museum to use. Answer the questions who, what, where, when, why, and how in your copy, and put the time and date on the poster and the invitation.

Set the body copy for the poster and invitation on the computer. Use as many images as needed from references. Think in terms of typographic hierarchy when working on this piece. Try photocopying the images onto different colored papers or try adding color by hand-coloring them.

Begin by doing 15 thumbnails, of the poster, and 15 thumbnails of the invitation and then two half sizes of each. Mount the final poster on thin board and trim flush on all sides; then make a distinctive envelope for the invitation.

OBJECTIVES

- To reinforce the use of type for readability in design.
- To teach students to utilize historic sources for reference images and fonts.
- To reinforce the three-stage process of design from thumbnails, to roughs, to finish.
- To apply the concept of companion pieces and visual/typographic links to establish the relationship between poster and invitation.

12-17. This poster and invitation, by KU student Brett Barto, use historic illustrations of insects and contemporary type treatment for a show entitled The Architecture of Insects.

12-18. This poster series, by KU student Dana A. Ronitz, uses dominant images integrated with large type, which was selected for its sensibility with the subject matter.

12-19. In this companion poster by Dana A. Ronitz, notice how the consistent use of type and placement carries the theme.

12-20. This invitation, by KU student Nathan Frohm, uses dominant type and a checkerboard arrangement of images balanced with a vertical font for the exhibit.

12-21. This poster, by KU student Mielinda K. Hands, uses strong type solutions to promote the exhibit.

This page is set in Fenice Light 8.5/12.

Readability & Legibility-Review

1. What are rivers, and when do you have to be aware of them? _____

_____

2. What determines the readability of a font? _____

_____

3. What determines the legibility of a font? _____

_____

4. How does line length affect readability? _____

5. What is the overall goal that you're striving for in body copy? _____

6. How do line length and point size of body copy relate to each other? _____

_____

7. In terms of the alignment of the setting of body copy, which is best for optimal readability? _____

_____

8. How can tracking affect readability? _____

9. How can leading affect the readability of a font? _____

10. How does frequency of blinking affect reading and body-copy decisions? _____

11. Why should a designer pay attention to readability and legibility studies? _____

_____

12. What causes reader fatigue? Why is this important to designers? _____

_____

Matching Type with Message

Traditional

INTRODUCTION

In this chapter, we will consider the process of choosing the right font for your message and audience. Mastering the selection of fonts is a sign of increased typographic sensibility. With the number of fonts expanding, selecting one can be daunting.

Today there are literally thousands of typefaces available to the designer—not to mention the computer programs to alter existing fonts. It's reminiscent of the proliferation of fonts during the height of the Industrial Revolution before the turn of the twentieth century. We're now in the digital revolution experiencing the same geometric expansion in font design. Just as legibility concerns of fonts were sacrificed during the Victorian era, in favor of type that had fanciful ornamentation, so too are today's fonts often compromising readability and traditional rules of type design in favor of techno and retro styles. As a designer, you need to become familiar with numerous fonts and experiment with them to learn to use them appropriately.

13-1. When the font selection and the meaning behind the words are in concert, the message is enhanced and understood more quickly and more readily. The use of a script font for the word "Traditional" reinforces visually the concept behind the word. There is no ambiguity, no levels of meaning.

Traditional

13-2. When the font and the message are opposed, it can perk the curiosity of the reader to see what's going on, or it can send a mixed message, which can be poorly received. Mixing the verbal and visual message can be effective in topics for alternative clients, or when the mixed or cryptic message is the intent.

CONSIDERATIONS WHEN CHOOSING A FONT

When specifying a font for a particular job, it is unlikely that there is only one appropriate typestyle. Well-designed typefaces are flexible and can be used in a variety of situations. It's important to define exactly what you want or need your type to do before you go looking through type-reference books to find just

what you're looking for. To define your font need, you must base your selection on the specific audience you need to reach and the message that must be conveyed. Obviously, if you design a

13-3. Popular fonts are those that embody a sensibility or style that is currently in favor. These fonts are less concerned with the traditional "rules" of type design and distribution of weights than with their visual freshness in the arena of type design. Time will tell whether the trendy or traditional fonts will prevail.

This page is set in
ITC Panache 8.5/12.

Bodoni
Optima
New Century Schoolbook
Modula
Embassy

13-4. The fonts above have radically different associations for the viewer. As you look at them, try to come up with appropriate applications for each font.

INDUSTRIAL 736

Classic

13-5. Classic fonts, such as Industrial 736 above, are noted for the clarity and legibility of the letters. They have a certain balance and harmony of design. They are never trendy, and they are never out of vogue. Good type transcends the whim of style. Classic fonts are always a safe choice for conservative clients.

HELVETICA REGULAR

Generic

13-6. Some fonts, such as Helvetica shown above, have so flooded our visual environment that we no longer see it as a unique font with a personality. It becomes an anonymous font that denotes nothing specific to the reader.

brochure for an insurance agency you will specify one type treatment, while a different font selection would be appropriate for the cover and interior of a rap CD.

Children and senior citizens need special considerations when it comes to type selection. Type for an elderly audience must not have glare or coating on the page, must be large enough to be clearly readable, and must be dark enough on the page to be easily read by those with limited sight.

Children need large letters that are clearly distinguishable from one another—for example, the capital "I" should look clearly different from the lowercase "l"—since children are just decoding the letters and learning to recognize them by their differences. Because of these needs, children's primers are usually set in very large serif fonts that make the differences between the letters very clear. These primers may also accustom the reader's eye to serif fonts earlier, which may lead to the preference of serif fonts in readability tests. These and other considerations explain the need to identify your audience before specifying type.

TYPE PERSONALITIES

Typefaces have different personalities. Type settings and leading arrangements generate different feelings. It is important for the experienced designer to recognize and use typefaces appropriately, relating the selection of the font to other design choices and decisions. Designers must make intelligent selections of type that answer the specific problem and represent the content of the subject matter.

We know that the oldest, most staid typefaces are the historic serif faces; the newer, more avant garde are the sans serif digitized faces that break from traditional "rules" of how the weights of the strokes relate to one another. How does this information relate to your client...your message...and your audience?

Many well-designed typefaces communicate a visual meaning. The font Bodoni radiates a feeling of elegance, clarity and tradition. Optima is clean and classic with an informal flair. New Century Schoolbook is a pragmatic, nuts-and-bolts, easy-reading face. Modula gives a stylishly radical impression, and Embassy is classy, sensual and beautiful (see example 13-4 at left). That doesn't mean these fonts are restrictive because these generalities can be overcome in a number of ways. One way might be to contrast them with another face; another is to use them at an unusual size or with an unexpected texture, such as Embassy script filled in with leopard skin, leather, or gold lamé for a tacky sensibility.

Designers make type selections based on their own knowledge, their intuitive judgment of the fonts, and their aesthetic sensibility as it relates to the message and the intended mood of the piece. The message of the words in the piece and the mood of the message are represented through the font. The designer must ask the client if the appearance of the piece should be serious, funny, educational, bizarre, contemporary, whimsical, frightening, happy or melancholy. Times Roman doesn't say bizarre, Kabel is not serious, and Eurostile isn't funny, or could it be (see example 13-7)?

GETTING TO KNOW A FEW FONTS WELL

Often it makes sense for young designers to master the effective use of the "classic" historic fonts before embarking on more experimental type design. There is quite a bit to be learned from serious considerations of standard serif fonts set in comfortable reading sizes, at a reasonable leading and line length. Refinements of tracking, flush settings, caps/small caps, headline spacing, subheads, hierarchy, bullets, tabs, initial capitals, etc., should be explored and appreciated before all of the "rules" of good, readable typography are challenged.

By limiting your use of fonts to four families of serif and four families of sans serif fonts that you experiment with broadly, and by mixing and matching the serif and sans serifs, the various weights and italics, you can develop a stable of well-known, tried-and-true fonts that will come through for you in a pinch. A general rule of thumb is to use a family of serif and a family of sans serif fonts in your design for balance.

Pick four serif fonts that belong to different historical families, some Old Style, some Transitional and some Modern. Select them because of readability and because you like the way the letters are formed. Start experimenting with how they look at a variety of sizes, leadings, trackings, and in different cases (upper–lower; caps–small caps).

Once you know a few fonts very well, it is easier to start appreciating the nuances of other fonts and how the subtleties of bracketing, stroke weight, beaks, counters, bowls, stress, etc., affect the appearance of a font. The more sensitized to type you are as a designer, the better your font selections will be and the more appropriate your overall design will be.

Once you can distinguish why Univers would be more appropriate to a specific job because it is a very square sans serif font, as opposed to say a rounder sans serif font like Avant Garde, you are making choices to carefully match the font with the message that you are trying to convey to the reader; this is a good sign.

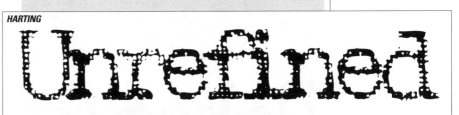

13-7. These three fonts are distinctly different in their style and in the resonance and connotative associations that designers have when viewing them.

13-8. Harting, shown above, gives a very rough, textured feeling. Finding just the right font does take some searching. The more familiar you are with fonts, the easier and faster your search will be, and the more rewarding your outcome.

13-9. Fonts do have personality. Some would clearly be more comfortable having their nails manicured, while others are more at ease in jeans. This font, Caslon 540 Italic, prefers to be dressed elegantly.

13-10. Lucida, shown above, is a no-nonsense, down-to-earth font. It appears strong and pragmatic and would definitely prefer comfort over style.

13-11. Hand-rendered fonts like Kid Type-Crayon above rarely retain the freshness and spontaneity of the original design. They can be used well for one word of a headline. If they repeat characters too often, the regularity of the characters undermines the intended uniqueness.

This page is set in
Sabon Roman 8.5/12.

13 *Matching Type with Message*

TRIPLE CONDENSED GOTHIC

STRUCTURED

13-12. The denotative analysis of this font is that it is based on vertical strokes and perpendicular lines, and curves are reserved for necessity. The intense verticality of the font makes us associate skyscrapers, vertical blinds, or tall, thin fashion models with it.

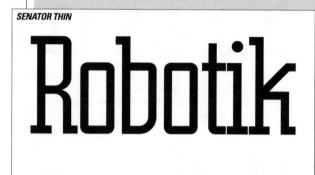

SENATOR THIN

Robotik

13-13. The denotative analysis of this font, Senator Thin, is that it is based on angular strokes and perpendicular lines. There is a slab serif, and the font appears to be a mono-weight stroke. The connotative analysis tells us that it seems mechanical, futuristic and alien to humans.

TIFFANY

Delicate

13-14. This font, Tiffany, seems to be very fragile and breakable because of the extreme thinness of the hairline strokes compared to the weight of the stem strokes. This is not a font that you'd want to carry on the subway during rush hour.

ARCADIA

Refreshing

13-15. The denotative analysis of this font, Arcadia, reveals that it is based on simple geometric shapes, such as the oval and square, and has a tall x-height and very condensed characters. This is a sans serif font with thick-thin-stroke contrast. The connotative analysis tells us that it seems bold, refreshing, unpredictable, legible and different.

This page is set in
Sabon Roman 8.5/12.

TYPE DENOTATION & CONNOTATION

The *denotation* of a specific font is an analytical description of its serifs and bracketing, how terminals are formed, and the direction and relative weight of strokes. This is a formal analysis of the structure and the physical details of the design of the font based on observation of the letters.

The *connotative evaluation* of the font is all of the associations that we as human beings, living in America in the 21st century, bring to our interaction with the font: what it reminds us of, the feelings or thoughts that we have when looking at it, where we think that we may have seen it before, what kinds of music it might conjure up in our minds, even the fashion we think of when seeing the font. These are the connotative associations that we have with fonts.

Remember that denotation is like a definition of the facts about the font. The connotation is what we feel about and associate with the font. To utilize type well as a designer, you have to be able to exploit the connotative associations of a font, yet be able to articulate the decision(s) that you made by defining the denotative attributes of the font when discussing your work with clients or colleagues.

THE RESONANCE OF A FONT

The *resonance* of a font relies heavily on the connotative associations that we have with the font. Most of the examples of large type in this chapter rely on the resonance that the font has. For instance, you can look at a font and immediately determine if it has historic, romantic, or business overtones. You can evaluate from your stored visual library whether it appears to be type from the 50s, from the computer, or from an exotic, faraway land. We judge the resonance of type everyday, simply by looking through magazines and associating the sense of the font with the product promoted. The font, the color and the layout tell us whether the product is serious, hygienic, romantic or indulgent. As a designer, you need to be aware of these resonant cues, and use them effectively to get your message across. Or, you could also satirically counter the resonance of a font as part of your message.

PROJECT: DESIGNING A TYPOGRAPHIC BOOK COVER

This project requires that you design the front, spine and back book cover. You should try to utilize type interpretively for this project. The focus of the cover should be type rather than an image, although a visual can be worked into the type. Because you may be used to thinking of book covers in terms of illustrations, this may take some thinking about, as well as some research. Choose a book that you've *read*–preferably one that you've read recently. It is even better if it is a book that really made you think or one that touched you deeply. Think about the essence of the book, or the plot in its most simplistic terms. This concept is what you will try to express in type.

You can substitute an image for one of the letters. You can have a character interacting with a letter of the type: sitting or leaning against a letter, or, yes, doing the lambada with a letter. You can adjust a letter to make it stretch out and wrap around other letters. You can adjust a part of a letter or place an image in a counter.

Plan the front cover of the book to be 6″ x 9″; you should include a review, or information about the author on the back cover. You probably should get the real book to work from, and to base your copy on. The spine should be 1″wide. It usually has the name of the author, the title, and the publisher on it.

Think about the resonance of the type and the color that you are planning to use. If your book is historic, you may want to find a font that is historic and scan it in for use. Think about whether the font should be elegant, simplistic, childlike, retro, new age, funky, uptight, relaxed, etc.

In terms of color, we read a lot into color selections as readers and purchasers of books. Often, as designers we overlook its impact. Should you be using Victorian colors, neon colors, subdued colors, masculine colors, medical colors, vibrant colors, jarring colors, haunting colors, or vibrating colors?

OBJECTIVES

- To review the selection of appropriate type for the title.
- To consider denotative and connotative associations of fonts.
- To review spacing considerations of fonts in a title.
- To utilize color so that it reinforces the content of the book.
- To begin to think of type as an illustrative, emotive element.
- To understand type as an interpretive medium.
- To organize information using typeface distinction.
- To refine the use of the hierarchy of typographic information.
- To reinforce a sense of kerning and ligatures.
- To choose an appropriate text font for a project.
- To see type as an abstract design element.

13-16. This book cover, by KU student Heidi Loudenslager Russell, places the type for the cover tightly together and adds color to the counter forms, creating an abstract pattern.

13-17. This book cover, by KU student Mary Munz, uses a basic grid structure to organize the type, and simple colors layered on top of a collage of historic photographs and stock data.

13-18. This book cover, by KU student Brian Benner, uses a label approach to the title, which is designed in fonts with arrow-like projections on them, resonant of the Southwestern design style. The borders also reflect the sensibility of Southwestern design.

Matching Type with Message-Review

13   *Matching Type*
       with Message

1. How is the parallel between the Digital Revolution and the Industrial Revolution manifested in type design? _____

_____

2. How is the message affected by the font that transmits it? _____

_____

3. How can a designer use connotation effectively? _____

_____

4. What is the resonance of a font, and why should a designer understand resonance? _____

_____

5. What happens when a designer tries to contradict the resonance of a font? _____

6. What are some considerations of the audience that a designer has to consider when selecting a font?_____

_____

7. What's the advantage of a new designer working with a limited palette of fonts? _____

_____

8. Describe how denotation and connotation interact with the message and the audience to help a designer select the most

appropriate fonts._____

_____

_____

_____

Type Specification & Proofreading

INTRODUCTION

In this chapter we will review the process of type specification, copy fitting and proofreader's marks. *Type specification,* or *speccing,* is the means by which a designer communicates with a typesetter. It is a very complicated process that seems as though it should be easier. You will be frustrated at all the steps to be remembered at first. It seems as though there must be a simpler way to explain the process, but it is one of those "I've Got It" processes. You don't really catch on until everything sort of clicks at once, and it all makes sense. Then you understand why you have to go through all those long, drawn-out steps, and they don't seem like gibberish anymore. Be prepared for frustration and confusion, and maybe it will come more easily to you.

Although most designers feel that in the age of computers, they really don't need to know how to spec type for a typesetter, it is still a good skill to have in case you are working somewhere, and you need to use type speccing to figure out how many characters will fit in the allotted space; and, like all knowledge, knowing a bit more won't hurt you.

In short, speccing type is the magic designers do (or did) when they take a client's typed manuscript and transform it into a beautiful layout with appropriate typefaces, readable body copy and clear headline emphasis. It is an exciting process to decide how you want your type set, and the first few times you get back your photocomposition output as galleys, you're amazed, the type looks so luscious and dark. Today, most pages are output as negatives rather than paper. It is always a good idea to have someone else look over your speccing. Typesetters will give you exactly what you ask for, even if they think it doesn't make sense. A good, conscientious typesetter may call to verify what you want, but don't expect this or count on it.

Smoking is Cool!

1 You start by spending lots of money,

2 You cough every morning,

3 You wind up on an oxygen tank!

14-1. Before the speccing of the type, this is what the manuscript looks like; it is simply typed copy, no creativity added.

14-2. After the speccing of the type, the same type has hierarchy, it visually appeals to an age group and it has an aesthetic sensibility.

This page is set in Lucida Regular 8.5/12.

Type
Specification &
Proofreading

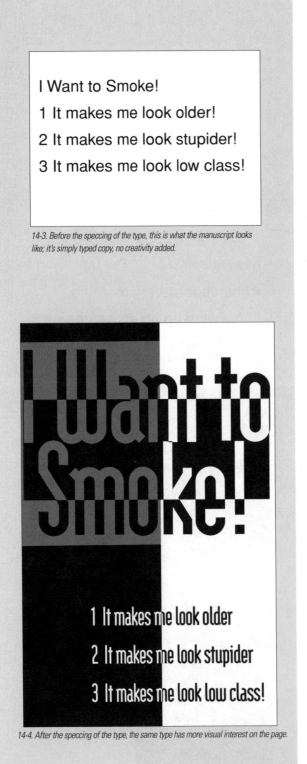

I Want to Smoke!

1 It makes me look older!

2 It makes me look stupider!

3 It makes me look low class!

14-3. Before the speccing of the type, this is what the manuscript looks like; it's simply typed copy, no creativity added.

1 It makes me look older

2 It makes me look stupider

3 It makes me look low class!

14-4. After the speccing of the type, the same type has more visual interest on the page.

Type speccing is a very humbling task; it brings us all back in touch with our own humanity. You must remember to write down *everything* that you want...if you forget the word "italic" for example, your type will not be set the way you envisioned it. Envisioning type the way you want it may be the single most difficult task a designer must do. Type speccing is tedious, precise, and either right or wrong. Take great pains to write all your instructions as clearly and as legibly as possible. No one wants to have to try to decipher bad type-speccing marks that are written carelessly. This is a sure way to have mistakes made in the final typesetting.

If you work with a typesetter, you should always treat your typesetter with respect and appreciation. There will be times when you will need a favor of a job rushed through or need to have a client's changes set overnight; a good rapport will go a long way in getting your favors taken care of. Always remember that they are just trying to do their jobs the same as you are. The better you treat them, the better they'll treat you.

WRITING UP THE TYPE SPECIFICATIONS

You must give all the instructions on your type clearly and succinctly. At first you may want to write your type specs out on a separate piece of paper, and only after you have proofread them, will you transfer them to the margin of the typed manuscript in red ink. Type speccing is a complicated process, and one numeral copied wrong or one word left out will waste a lot of time, money, and energy.

HOW TO SPEC TYPE

Below is a list of all the information you must consider giving the typesetter if you spec type. Read it through first, then follow it carefully.

You must indicate the following information:

1. The name of the typeface.

2. Whether the face is Roman or italic.

3. The weight of the face–whether it is light, medium, bold, etc.

4. The size of the typeface in points, represented as a numeral—for example, 12 followed by a slash / then followed by a numeral representing the point size of the leading, for example, 15; this would be written as 12/15, and means that you

would receive 12-point type (measured from ascender line to descender line) with space between the lines (leading—measuring from baseline to baseline) of 15 points. If you do not want any extra space between the lines, this is called *set solid*, and you must spell this out, or write it as 12/12.

5. Next, and this is important, you must indicate the width of the column measure in picas, which are used to measure horizontal column widths. So the width of your column is represented as a numeral, for example, 13 (picas), and a small, square box representing picas following it, or the word "picas."

6. Next, if you have paragraph indents, consider what would you like them to measure. The indents are usually indicated in "em" spaces. An *"em" space* is the square of the height of the typeface, and is usually equal to the width of a lowercase "m" in the font. Specifying a 1-em indent is standard for paragraph indents, but you may also want a larger indent and you can specify it by the number of em spaces you request for the indent.

7. Now you will have to write down whether you want your type flush left, flush right, or justified, or if you want the lines centered line for line. If you want the type flush left and rag right, this is written as F/L, R/R. If you want the type flush right and rag left, this is written as F/R, R/L. If you want both edges to align evenly, you must write out the word "justified." If you want the lines centered line for line, you must put in the line breaks (see symbols on pages 189–190), and then write out "centered line for line."

8. Also you must write whether you want the text all uppercase, upper- and lowercase as shown, caps and small caps, or all lowercase. U/lc stands for upper/lowercase, all U/C stands for all uppercase, and all l/c stands for all lowercase. Note: if you write U/lc, the typesetter will set the text in upper- and lowercase as it is typed on the manuscript unless otherwise specified. There will be times that you will need to make changes to the format of the manuscript, and these proofing marks should always be marked neatly in *red* so that they're clear for the typesetter.

9. If you want to introduce the text with a special treatment of the initial capital, it is usually best to put a box around the character and write out the

To specify type correctly, you really have to pay full attention to what you are doing. You need to follow the steps carefully, and to practice the process a number of times. It does require some simple math skills, as well as careful counting. If the type runs longer than the area allotted for it, you have to do some fancy footwork. You can make the point size of the type smaller or close up the leading. You can also select a condensed font in place of a regular one. The condensed font will allow the same information to be printed in less space. Sometimes you can make the column width of the type wider, which will reduce the overall number of lines of type. You can also tighten the tracking on the selection of copy that you are trying to fit into the space. Type speccing has largely been replaced by simply pouring the type into the layout on the computer. This practice allows designers to immediately make the adjustments necessary to fit the type on the page. Generally, this is a good practice, but it now means that designers have to know more about typesetting practice, such as the titles of full-length works are usually set in italics rather than underlined in body copy. In addition, am and pm are most correctly set in small caps. Lastly, designers must master both tabs and the formatting of tables, which can be involved.

14-5. This is an example of a typewritten manuscript to use for practice type speccing.

Copyfitting allows a designer to figure out if the text for a piece will in fact fit into the layout that's been designed. You must first estimate the number of characters in your given body copy. Then, you must estimate how many characters in the font that you want, in the size that you want, will fit into your layout.

It may help to think of this process as trying to figure the area of each selection of type. You must figure length times width in order to get the total number of characters. You must use a Character Per Pica (CCP) chart in order to spec type for copy fitting most accurately. After you have done this process a number of times, the steps become more second nature to you. Copy fitting does help to plan a piece very accurately, or it can be used to give an editor the number of characters that will fit in an area. Although it is tedious and a number of steps are involved, if you master the concept of copy fitting—that you're fitting type in a specified point size and font into an area—it will very likely come in handy some day and save you time when time is of the essence.

instructions for the initial capital—for example: Set cap in 48 pt. Helvetica, base-align with the fourth line of text, and set F/L with left margin, or base align with 1st line of text, and hang in left margin. There are many options facing a designer, and as your sensitivity to typography becomes more sophisticated, you will find that you want to try a number of different variations and combinations and your type speccing may become more complex. The best rule of thumb is: When in doubt about your speccing, spell out more than you think is necessary so that it is clear for the typesetter. Your typeset copy is usually output as negatives from which printers make proofs, then expose the printing plates; some printers go directly from disk to plates.

COPY FITTING

Copy fitting is the tricky process of figuring out how you will take the copy that has been supplied by the client and get it to fit into your beautiful layout without being forced to use 6-point type. When you copy-fit, you actually estimate the number of characters in the manuscript and then estimate the number of characters that would fit into your layout based on the font, the type size and the leading you've indicated in greeked copy. Usually, you find that the client has supplied more copy than you've planned for. Sometimes, the client has doubled the amount of copy that you designed in the layout. This is when you get out the "type shoehorn," and try to cram the copy in. You can adjust the layout, use a slightly smaller or more condensed font, or add pages to the design, or break down and ask the client if there's any way the copy could be edited to lose a few lines.

Designers have to know how to copy-fit so that they won't be paying for endless rounds of typesetting to fit text into areas that it's impossible for it to fit into. You will waste a lot of time and energy if you don't resolve to learning it right the first time. Like type speccing, it will take you a while to catch on to, and at first there seems as though there are a lot of extra steps. But there is no way around all the calculations you have to do to fit copy from one source into another.

In fitting copy, you take a typewritten, double-spaced manuscript and determine how much of the typewritten version will fit into each of the copy blocks that you have on your layout. Once you have determined that the copy will fit in a particular column width, in a specific point size and leading, you are ready to write up all the specs for the typesetter.

14-6. This is an example of a typewritten manuscript to use for practice type speccing.

THE GUIDE TO COPY FITTING

The following is a step-by-step list of the process of copy-fitting type.

1. Count the number of characters in an average line of the typewritten manuscript (this includes counting the spaces and the punctuation).

2. Count the number of lines in the typed manuscript.

3. Multiply the number of characters per line by the number of lines. This will give you an approximation of the total number of characters in the typed manuscript.

4. Now, look up the typeface you want to use in your body copy on the *character per pica (CPP) tables.*

5. Once you've found the font (remember to check for italic or bold if you want it), look up the point size that you would like the type in (9 point is very standard size for body copy). Now, go down vertically along the point size until you come to the name of the font that you have chosen. This figure tells you the number of characters of that particular font, in the size that you have chosen, that will fit in each pica. Write this number down.

6. Once you have the number of characters per pica, you must multiply that number by the pica width of your column indicated on your layout (13 picas is a common column width). When you have multiplied these two figures together you will know the number of characters per body copy line that you will get when the text is typeset in the face you chose at the size you selected.

7. Now, you must divide the total number of characters in your typewritten manuscript by the number of characters per body copy line. This will tell you how many lines of body copy you will have when it is typeset in the face you looked up at the size you selected.

8. Next, you must decide on the leading you want for your body copy. (Standard leading is 1 to 3 points more of leading than the type point size, so that you would have 9/10, 9/11, 9/12, 9/13.) Once you have chosen the leading you would like, find that leading on the leading gauge on your ruler, and measure with the leading gauge, the depth of the number of lines of body copy that you determined that you would have back in step 7.

14-7. In this logo, by KU student Lisa M. DeLay, to promote business within a county, the dollar symbol is used to show the recycling of money within the community, and the subordinate fonts are clean and simple.

14-8. This logo, by KU student Lisa M. DeLay, for an online promotional service for artists and designers uses type simply but creatively.

14-9. This logo, by KU student Jeanne Macijowsky, for an upscale shoe company integrates a capital "M" and a high-heeled shoe for the symbol. The selection of type shows familiarity with visualizing fonts, something that you have to do when you spec type.

14-10. This team, logo by KU student Joseph R. Whelski was proposed for the Las Vegas Blackjacks baseball team.

This page is set in Trump Medieval Roman 8.5/12.

Copy fitting is most help-ful when you are under a tight deadline and have to write copy to fit the layout. There may only be a day or two to put together the last two spreads of a monthly magazine. To save time, the designer can figure from the layout how much copy is needed, and then ask the writer to write to those speci-fications. This kind of organi-zation will save everyone frus-tration when there is already a short production time. It will also prevent unnecessary rounds of editing changes or layout revisions because the type will fit the layout. It's also rewarding to have knowledge of how many characters are needed as a writer, so that unneces-sary research isn't undertaken.

9. If the leading that you measured fits neatly into your layout, you are all set. If the leaded lines appear shorter than you had wanted, you may want to increase the leading a few points, then measure the new lead-ing to make sure that it will fit.

10. If the typed manuscript runs too long for the space that you have allotted for it, you have a few choices:

a. Make the point size of the body copy smaller.

b. Use a condensed version of the typeface that you had chosen.

c. Add a 1/2 or a full pica to your column width.

d. Extend the length of your copy block.

e. Reduce the leading that you planned by 1 or 2 points.

f. Add another copy block to the design.

g. Ask the client to cut 10 to 12 lines from the manuscript.

i. Ask the typesetter what the cpp (character per pica) figure will be if you tighten the tracking.

j. See how much it would cost to add another 1 to 4 pages to the piece for more room.

k. Do all the above if the type is running very long for the space in the layout.

A shorthand summary of the above steps is shown below for those who will work with it more readily as a visual/ mathematical process:

characters per line of manuscript x # of lines in manuscript = total characters in manuscript

characters per pica x column width in picas = number of characters in a line of typeset body copy

$$\frac{\text{total characters in manuscript}}{\text{number of characters in a line of body copy}} = \text{number of lines of typeset body copy}$$

This page is set in Trump
Medieval Roman 8.5/12.

PROOFREADER'S MARKS

As mentioned above, there will be times that you will have to make small adjustments to typed manuscript that has been supplied. Rather than retype parts that must be changed, you can mark them with *proofreader's marks* on the manuscript neatly in red, and the typesetter will know what you want and make the indicated changes.

The Mark and Its Definition	How the Mark Is Written in Text	How the Correction Appears
℘ means to delete the word or character or punctuation it touches; it is also a good idea to circle the item to be deleted with a circle.	Deletee character	Delete character
¶ means to start a new paragraph	This prior sentence is unrelated. The next sentence will start a new thought.¶Now is a good time for a break.	This prior sentence is unrelated. The next sentence will start a new thought. Now is a good time for a break.
⌒ means to run into the word or copy above	Connect to the previous line.	Connect to the previous line.
∧ means to insert a letter, word or punctuation mark; this is often represented in a circle, and if it is long, it is often written clearly in the margin beside the carat mark. Put the insert mark accurately and clearly in the text.	Include a leter omitted.	Include a letter omitted.
‾‾‾ means to set the word, character or title underlined in italics	Try italics for emphasis in text.	Try *italics* for emphasis in text.
∼∼∼ means to set the word or phrase underlined in bold	Use bold for words or phrases defined.	Use **bold** for words or phrases defined.
≡≡≡ means to set the word or phrase in all uppercase	Use all caps for subheads in text.	Use ALL CAPS for subheads in text.
/ when written through an uppercase character means to make it lowercase	LOWERcase can be effective in headlines.	Lowercase can be effective in headlines.
⌐ means to start a new line; indicates a line break.	Separate different thoughts onto a different line. They don't need to start a new paragraph. Used to get rid of hyphens.	Separate different thoughts onto a different line. They don't need to start a new paragraph. Used to get rid of hyphens.
stet means that the typesetter should not make the changes indicated, and should leave the passage as it was originally	*stet* This one means to disregard the proofing marks.	This one means to disregard the proofing marks.
# means space; when written as open up #, typesetters will understand your intent.	This is used when bad typists omit spaces.It can be between words or after periods.	This is used when bad typists omit spaces. It can be between words or after periods.
⌒ means to close up space	This is often used when basket ball is typed as two different words.	This is often used when basketball is typed as two different words.
∪ means to transpose letters or words as indicated	This is used when tow words or letters are reversed.	This is used when two words or letters are reversed.

This page is set in Univers
Light Condensed 8.5/12.

14 *Type*
Specification &
Proofreading

The Mark and Its Definition	How the Mark is Written in Text	How the Correction Appears

The Mark and Its Definition

‖ means to align vertically

⌿ through a letter means to correct the letter and to replace it with one indicated in the margin

═ means to set copy in small caps

I/M means to insert one em or mutt dash here

I/N means to insert one en or one nut dash here

❝/❞ means to insert quotes

❜ means to insert apostrophe

(/) means to insert parentheses

⌃ means to insert comma

⌃ means to insert semi-colon

⊙ means to insert period

⌃ means to insert hyphen

spl means to spell out

wf means wrong font

⌐ means to move text to the right; you should indicate distance in "em" spaces or picas.

no ¶ means to remove paragraph indent

⌐ means to move text to the left; you should indicate distance in em spaces or picas.

⌐⌐ means center copy

⌒ means to close up and delete space

How the Mark is Written in Text

‖ These lines should line
‖ up, but they don't.

w There is the dog?

Caps and small caps read well.

Use mutt dashes for a change in direction when there is no continuity. I/M

Use an "en" dash to replace "to" as in Feb. 2 3. I/N

He asked, When is the party? ❝/❞

That's not mine; its Harry's. ❜

Go to the store Macy's and research their shoes. (/)

Go left at the light and follow the road to the inn. ⌃

I don't know her she's never been in my class. ⌃

Don't think Just follow your heart. ⊙

This is a long awaited moment in history. ⌃

spl of the workers went on strike.

Pay attention to the fonts that you use. *wf*

• This can be useful in the runovers on bulleted items, to get the text to line up. ⌐

no ¶ This is when you want to remove the indent.

⌐ This can be helpful for text that is a long quote from a text that you want to indent.

⌐⌐ Move to the center of the column

This can be helpful. When two spaces are typed after all periods. It tells the designer to close up unnecessary space. ⌒

How the Correction Appears

These lines should line
up, but they don't.

                    Where is the dog?

Cᴀᴘs ᴀɴᴅ sᴍᴀʟʟ ᴄᴀᴘs ʀᴇᴀᴅ ᴡᴇʟʟ.

Use mutt dashes for a change in direction—when there's no continuity.

Use an "en" dash to replace "to" as in Feb. 2–3.

He asked, "When is the party?"

That's not mine; it's Harry's.

Go to the store (Macy's) and research their shoes.

Go left at the light, and follow the road to the inn.

I don't know her; she's never been in my class.

Don't think. Just follow your heart.

This is a long-awaited moment in history.

Ten of the workers went on strike.

Pay attention to the fonts that you use.

• This can be useful in the runovers on
  bulleted items, to get the text to line up.

This is when you want to remove the indent.

   This can be helpful for text that is a long
   quote from a text that you want to indent.

        Move to the center of the column.

This can be helpful. When two spaces are typed after all periods. It tells the designer to close up unnecessary space.

PROJECT: TYPE-SPECIMEN POSTER

For this project, you must choose a typeface and design a poster promoting the use of that typeface. Write one or two paragraphs of body copy that describe the font, and its denotative and connotative associations; this will be the body copy on the final piece.

The purpose of a type-specimen poster has three parts: to show the different qualities of a face, to show the entire alphabet, and usually to display the type in different sizes so that a designer can visualize the text face. Sometimes the different weights of a face are shown. Any body copy on the poster is shown in the font at text size.

The format is 11" x 17". You can design a horizontal or a vertical poster. The one requirement is that you show every letter of the alphabet, in upper- and lowercase. Design your piece to be as involved or as simple as you would like. You may want the focus of the design to be one or two characters blown up very large, or a more complex design with many different characters at different sizes. Letters can overlap, bleed off the page, or be printed in different colors. You may want to choose a few words that you feel describe the font to work into your design.

Begin by working up 20 thumbnail sketches of the design, then bring two to half-sized rough sketches. You can incorporate imagery as needed, but type should still be the primary element.

OBJECTIVES

- To encourage thinking about the connotation of a font.
- To encourage working with exclusively typographic layouts.
- To focus on the emphasis/priority on the page.
- To review the process of change and redo that's intrinsic to design.
- To reinforce the process of design from thumbnails to half sizes.
- To analyze different settings of typefaces closely.
- To organize information using typeface distinction.
- To reinforce a sense of kerning and ligatures.
- To encourage refinement of the hierarchy of type on a page.
- To reinforce copy fitting and speccing body copy.
- To develop choosing the appropriate copy type for a project.

14-13. This poster, designed by KU student Elaine Gustus, reinforces the curvilinear nature of the font Friz Quadrata. This piece was executed in rich tones in colored pencil.

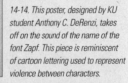

14-14. This poster, designed by KU student Anthony C. DeRenzi, takes off on the sound of the name of the font Zapf. This piece is reminiscent of cartoon lettering used to represent violence between characters.

14-15. This poster, designed by KU student Rachael Waters, emphasizes the width of the font Copperplate. The background uses newspaper to conjure up a bookish environment.

14-11. This poster, designed by KU student Carolyn Keer, accentuates Times Roman's association with newspapers.

14-12. The poster above, designed by KU student Stephanie E. Sheppard, uses Americana to create an American flag design.

This page is set in Univers Light Condensed 8.5/12.

Type Specification & Proofreading-Review

1. What does the 9 in 9/11 stand for? _____

2. What does the 12 in 9.5/12 stand for? _____

3. What is the CPP for Palatino Roman at 9-point type? _____

4. What is the CPP for ITC Fenice Light at 8-point type? _____

5. For Bodoni at 10-point type, how many characters fit on one line of an 11-pica column width? _____

6. For Times Roman at 9-point type, how many characters fit on one line of a 13-pica column width? _____

7. If you can fit 26.5 characters on a line, how many total characters will fit on 32 lines? _____

8. If you can fit 22 characters on a line, how many total characters do you have in 34 lines? _____

9. If you have 22 lines of copy with 60 characters per line, how many overall characters do you have? _____

10. If you have 65 lines of copy with 61 characters per line, how many overall characters do you have? _____

11. Will 670 characters set in Garamond Light at 9/11 fit in a 13-pica column width that's 22 picas deep? _____

12. How many lines will the above example run? _____

13. Will 708 characters set in Baskerville 9/11 x 12 picas fit in a column depth of 11 inches? _____

14. How many lines will the above example run? _____

15. Will 632 characters set in Janson 10/15 x 20 picas fit in a column depth of 6 inches? _____

16. How many lines will the above example run? _____

17. Will 546 characters set in Korinna 9.5/12 x 14 picas fit in a column depth of 7 inches? _____

18. How many lines will the above example run? _____

Typographic Hierarchy

INTRODUCTION

In this chapter we will review typographic hierarchy and how designers use it to make some type more prominent than the rest. *Typographic hierarchy* is a term that defines the order of importance that elements on a page are given, based on their placement, size and tonal boldness. Type hierarchy determines what the reader's attention is drawn to first, depending on how the page is laid out and which information the designer has given the most emphasis. The term *hierarchy* implies the large-to-small relationships in type elements, such as the main head, subheads, secondary subheads, callouts, captions, text type, listed items, sidebars, and running headers and footers.

It may be helpful for you to think of the hierarchy as the "voice" of the type: how loudly it yells on the page, how it speaks up every now and then, or how it talks in an even tone, or even whispers. The voice of the type or the personality of a message can be revealed more accurately through the use of different fonts. The following descriptions are of different typographic treatments that can be used on a page, and how they can be implemented for hierarchy, clarity and creative design.

RUNNING HEADERS & FOOTERS

Running headers and footers seem a logical place to begin a discussion of hierarchy because if they are needed in a text, they will be on every page and will work into the margin of the pages. Margin elements are usually quiet on the page in terms of size and color. Knowing that you need to include a header or footer may make you try to include a larger margin for them in your page layout. Headers and footers are usually not the most prominent elements on a page; in fact, they are usually quite quiet and reserved. They can include the name of the book or the name of the chapter. They can be set in small caps, in italic, or in a light sans serif face, or letter-spaced out above a hairline rule. They sometimes incorporate the *folio,* or page number, or the publication date into their design although this is not necessary.

Headers are typographic titles placed at the top of the page, and *footers* are type elements placed at the bottom of the page. These type elements are called *running headers* if

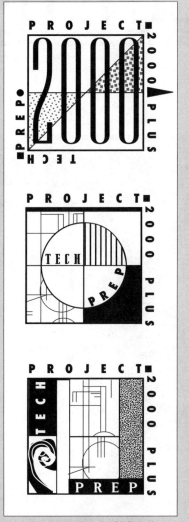

15-1. In these logos, by KU student Erin Earley, the type is used creatively in a variety of sizes to give priority to the information.

KEY CONCEPTS

Running Headers

Running Footers

Tabular Material

Runovers

Callouts

Dingbats & Flourishes

Pull Quotes

Sidebars

Author Bylines

Captions

Datelines

Folios

Initial Capitals

Headlines

Subheads

This page is set in
Kabel Book 8.5/12.

15 *Typographic*
Hierarchy

15-2. This logo by, KU student Beth Brader, uses hierarchy of type to contrast the
large, light LADY with the smaller type that's reversed out of the bar at the bottom.

15-3. Hierarchy in type often gives the designer license to give priority to different words in a headline. In this poster, by KU student Holly N. Tienken, the word
Shapes in the headline dominates the rest of the phrase.

This page is set in
Kabel Book 8.5/12.

they are placed at the top of every page of the piece, even if
the information changes from chapter heads to the book's
title on alternate pages. They are called *footers* if they're
placed at the bottom of the page, and *running footers* if
they're placed at the bottom of every page consistently. It is
important to realize that these elements are usually some of
the "quietest" elements in hierarchy on the page.

TEXT TYPE

Text type is the body copy of the piece. It is how the
bulk of the text is typeset. You should try to look at specimen
sheets from typesetters or the examples of text type at the
back of this book before deciding on a text type font, size
and leading. These specimen sheets show examples of standard text sizes of a font (such as 9-, 10-, and 11-point-size
type), and sometimes show them with different leading.
Often you are shown the type with one additional point of
leading, 9/10, 10/11, 11/12. This may be tighter than you want
the lines leaded. If this is the case, run copy out of the computer with different leadings to give yourself an idea of how
the leading will affect the type.

The text copy should not scream, but it should be legible,
and sometimes it must reflect the reading capacity of its audience. Type for senior citizens' magazines might be set a bit larger to make it more legible for those with limited or impaired
sight. Likewise, type set for children's books should also be set
oversized because children are just learning to decode letters.

The point size, leading and column-width ratio can determine how many characters will fit on a line in the typeset version. If there are too few characters on a short line length,
there will be many bad breaks and repetitive hyphens. It may
be better to go with fewer columns and a longer line length
so that more words can fit per line. One rule of thumb is that
the column width should be able to fit 1-1/2 to 2 full lowercase alphabets in the point size you have chosen. With justified copy, it is even more important that you allow yourself a
long line length, so that there will be fewer places where the
word spacing will have to be extended and you'll reduce the
risk of your copy being overrun with rivers.

But body copy fonts do not have to be boring. You can
choose a very fine face, leading, and point size that complement each other to create type that is both legible, readable
and beautiful. (Most typophiles would argue that indeed the
most beautiful body copy is also the most legible.)

It is important to realize that you must make an informed
decision about selecting the font for your body copy. It can
be the most important decision you make about the piece
because often variations of the body copy are used for the
callouts within the text, the subheads, and even the pull
quotes. If you are not happy with the font you've chosen for
the body copy, you may not care for its appearance in other
applications within the piece.

ENHANCING BODY COPY WITH INITIAL CAPITALS

Body copy that is well designed can also be enhanced on the page and draw readers into it through the use of large initial caps that either stand up from the text, are inset into the copy, hang in the margin, or overprint the copy in a screen. The body copy does dictate the character of the overall piece, as well as the "tone" that the piece is speaking in, so don't make your decision lightly.

Sometimes the first few lines of body copy are set larger than the rest of the copy or in small caps which is called a *standfirst*, to draw the reader into the copy. All of these tactics for drawing readers in can determine how many people read the full article or information. Without careful design decisions, the same information might go unread. Start to follow your own eyes on a page or a spread of a magazine. Try to be aware of what you read first, how your eye bounces around on the page, and how much of an article you read, and why, based on the typographic design.

LIMITING THE FONTS IN A PUBLICATION

The general rule for design is that you should work with only two fonts in a publication—a serif family and a sans serif family, and no more, unless absolutely necessary. The family means that you can use the bold, light, medium, italic, and small-caps versions of each font. When designing a page, it is a good rule of thumb to start out by limiting yourself to a *maximum* of four different families of type. I say four because you may want to incorporate a script face, a serif face, a sans serif face, and maybe a display font for initial caps. You will be free to use all the variations of these families, all the various weights in Roman and italic, but you don't want to overdo it with type variations on the page. It is better to limit yourself at the outset so that you can maintain some unity of design from page to page. Some skilled designers insist that you can layout an entire book with just one serif family and one sans serif family. Although this is true, it may be interesting to have a few more fonts at your disposal for design purposes.

A rule of thumb, though, is that you should not mix two different serif faces on the same page, especially two that are quite similar in structure, like Goudy and Garamond (both Old Style faces). Because they are so close in appearance, the differences will be lost on the reader, and it may look like your typesetter made a mistake and set the wrong font for parts of the page. You would be far better off going to another weight of the one serif font, contrasting the serif font with a sans serif face, or putting the information in italics to call attention to it, rather than selecting Goudy to contrast with Garamond.

Once you have determined the two, or three, fonts you will use, and which you will use for the body copy, there are still many more decisions to make. You want to find out how the body copy reads with different tracking options, and at a variety of point sizes and leading. You can run out variations of small

15-4. This logo creates hierarchy in the type by contrasting the size of the different elements. Designed by KU student Daniel Victor, the use of the spiraling DNA for the angled stroke of the "N" is creative and ultimately simple, almost obvious.

When you have type in a box as a sidebar or as a pull quote, it is important to remember to utilize the inset text feature Modifying that will give your text some room to breathe around the edges.

15-5. Text set in boxes needs some space between the edge of the box and the text itself. This box is set with 8 points of text inset.

Garamond contrasts better **with Helvetica Condensed, rather than with** Goudy (this font), for which it can be easily mistaken. This is Garamond, it looks very similar to Goudy.

15-6. The fonts in a piece are usually limited to one serif and one sans serif font for consistency. This example shows how difficult it is to distinguish two similar serif fonts which is why they should not be used together in the same piece.

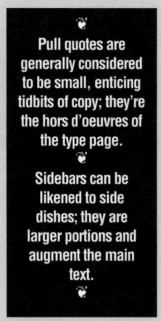

15-7. Pull quotes and sidebars break up the visual monotony of a full page of text.

15-8. This logo by KU student Danielle Doyle has three levels of hierarchy to the type. The "O" is a compass as well as a letter and acts as a symbol for this store. Next in hierarchy is the rest of the OUTLANDISH word, followed by OUTFITTERS.

THE HIERARCHY OF TYPE DETERMINES WHICH TYPE GETS READ FIRST—WHICH CALLS THE READER'S ATTENTION MOST PROMINENTLY. AS A DESIGNER, IT IS IMPORTANT TO UNDERSTAND AND UTILIZE TYPOGRAPHIC HIERARCHY TO ADD **EMPHASIS TO THE INFORMATION ON THE PAGE.**

15-9. Often boxes with a dark background will call more attention to themselves than white boxes on a text-filled page.

paragraphs on the computer and compare a variety of settings. Pay attention to the character spacing as well as the word spacing. You should familiarize yourself with all the weights and italic versions of these fonts, small caps if they are available, and any dingbats that you may want to use with them.

DINGBATS AND DECORATIVE FLOURISHES

Dingbats are beautiful, small graphic elements. They are basically little black images (they can be screened) that have been designed with the font to add at the end of paragraphs or sections, around pull quotes or under headlines. (There are specialty fonts exclusively composed of dingbats that can enhance your layout and be used as graphic elements.) They can be decorative or whimsical and add character to your body copy. Dingbats can be used in body copy as paragraph breaks, in place of returns. They can also be set at any point size you want because they are designed like a font. Dingbats include diamonds and bullets for listing items, as well as boxes, leaves, paragraph symbols, stars, arrows, pointing hands, and snowflakes, all of which can be arranged into patterns or borders as well. You may want to incorporate them into your layout when appropriate.

TABULAR MATERIAL & RUNOVERS

Tabular material refers to elements within the text that are listed, either in a table or with bullets. Often the bulleted elements are indented from the left margin 1 or 2 picas and set off with a bullet, diamond, or other dingbat. *Runovers* are the lines of copy that run under the bullet; they are usually aligned with the first letter of the text next to the bullet.

- OCCASIONALLY- they include a name followed by a dash; when you want the name to stand out from the description that follows, it's a good idea to set it in bold or italic.
- RUNOVERS- are the part of the bulleted text that wraps under onto the next line. It is considered best to have runovers flush with the first letter of the first line of text. This is accomplished by using the key combination of the back slash and the command key just before the first letter after the bullet. This will make all wrapped lines align under it.
- AVOID UNDERLINES- Even when used for emphasis, it is generally considered poor typography to underline words in typeset copy. (Even names of books, magazines, plays, etc., are set in italics in typeset copy.)
- ITALICS- will appear most comfortable in text copy if you select the space before and after the italicized word, and make these spaces italic as well as the word.

There are some refined decisions you have to make about tabular material: will the second lines run over back to the original left hand margin, will they stay flush with the indented text, will they line up flush with the bullet or diamond, or will the runover lines be indented themselves? Some of these decisions will be reduced if you are working with a small column width, where it would be impossible to incorporate two indents into the tabular material. Sometimes you may want all the tabular type set off in a different format or font from the text type. This should be done carefully, so that the gray texture of the body copy is not made choppy by the inclusion of heavy type for these bulleted items.

TABLES AND FORMS, LINES AND LEADING

Sometimes you will find that you need to set up a table or a form as a part of a document. This can be tricky because you want all the information to fit on one page while you maintain some of the font and leading format that the rest of the piece has. It is a good idea to use ruled lines that are as fine as possible in tables. This reduces their visual impact on the page, allowing readers to focus on the information in the table rather than on the structured lines of the table. This also gives you room for text in title blocks and allows you more space to fill in numbers. Also, you can then use heavier rules for emphasis either under a headline or to show a break in the table. It could be a good idea to print the rules of a table in the second color so that they're not too prominent.

For forms, you must set up the information in a logical fashion and allow enough room for someone to fill them in comfortably by hand. Try to use 18 or 20 points of leading between lines that have to be filled in by hand. If you go much smaller than this, you will have people cramming in the information very sloppily. The form you design should add clarity and structure to the information; it is often necessary to lay out forms roughly by hand as a visual aid and to clarify placement and order. On forms, as on tables, you can use the different typestyles creatively to set up a hierarchy. Perhaps all the text on the form is set in a light sans serif font, but the dividers of the form are set in a bold weight of the sans serif font one or two points larger. You would be amazed at how much bigger 12-point bold sans serif type looks when contrasted with 9-or 10-point serif text type.

CALLOUTS

Information within the text that is called out in boldface, etc., is referred to as a *callout*. Information that is separated from the article and inset into the text in a larger size is referred to as a *pull quote*.

- **CALLOUTS**- are short heads that follow bullets or dashes. They give you the option to set the callout in caps, small caps, italic, bold, bold italic, a sans serif font for contrast, or a bold sans serif so that they really stand out.

Callouts can be placed within the text, and you have to determine a consistent format to call attention to them. Either boldfacing the font or using italics makes sense; it's considered poor typography to underline callouts within text. Sometimes bold, *small* capitals can be effective. Depending on the font, how dark it is when bolded, and the level of hierarchy you want, you will determine the typographic treatment suited for callouts.

Name _____

Address _____

Phone _____

15-10. *For forms with lines that need to be written in, try to use 18- to 20-point leading to leave sufficient space for people to fill in between lines with ease. The form above uses 18 points of leading between the lines.*

Name	Information	Response
Name	Information	Response
Name	Information	Response
Name	Information	Response
Name	Information	Response
Name	Information	Response
Name	Information	Response

15-11. *In this table, the rules are .25 points and 2 points; the 2-point rules are screened at 30% black so that they don't overpower the text.*

Name	Information	Response
Name	Information	Response
Name	Information	Response
Name	Information	Response
Name	Information	Response
Name	Information	Response
Name	Information	Response

15-12. *In this table, the dark, thick rules overwhelm the information within the table.*

This page is set in ITC Officina Sans 8.5/12.

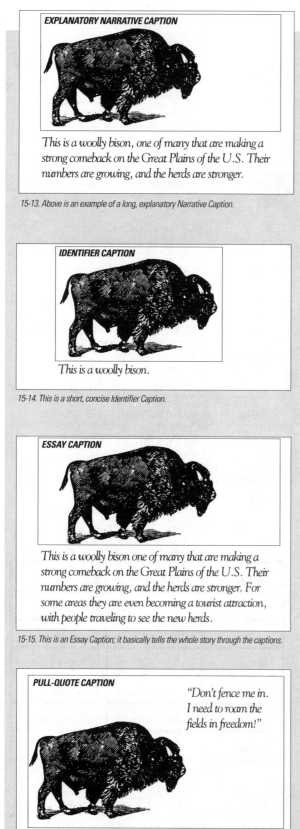

EXPLANATORY NARRATIVE CAPTION

*This is a woolly bison, one of many that are making a
strong comeback on the Great Plains of the U.S. Their
numbers are growing, and the herds are stronger.*

15-13. Above is an example of a long, explanatory Narrative Caption.

IDENTIFIER CAPTION

This is a woolly bison.

15-14. This is a short, concise Identifier Caption.

ESSAY CAPTION

*This is a woolly bison one of many that are making a
strong comeback on the Great Plains of the U.S. Their
numbers are growing, and the herds are stronger. For
some areas they are even becoming a tourist attraction,
with people traveling to see the new herds.*

15-15. This is an Essay Caption; it basically tells the whole story through the captions.

PULL-QUOTE CAPTION

*"Don't fence me in.
I need to roam the
fields in freedom!"*

15-16. This is a Pull-Quote Caption, which tries to personalize the photo.

This page is set in ITC Officina
Sans Book 8.5/12.

CAPTIONS

Captions are considered by some magazine editors to be
the most important type on the page because they can tell
the story with images and a few words. Captions are sentences placed near the photos or illustrations in a piece;
they're used to explain what is going on or to identify who is
in the image. Captions are often set in a different font from
the text type, so that there is no room for confusion between
the two. Sometimes captions are set one or two points larger
or smaller than the text type of an article.

Editorially, there are four different types of captions that are
treated distinctly typographically. These are:

- NARRATIVE CAPTIONS are frequently long and explain what is going
  on in the photo and relate it to the content of the text.
- IDENTIFIER CAPTIONS are short in length and identify only the figures and action in the image, without any extraneous words.
- ESSAY CAPTIONS are long captions which should be treated as
  body copy since they tell the story along with the photos.
- PULL-QUOTE CAPTIONS are statements attributed to one of the figures in the photo, to personalize it.

Captions are often set with a different line length than
the line length of the text. Sometimes captions are set on
very short line lengths in a small condensed font, but there is
no hard-and-fast rule of thumb, and just the opposite is
equally a good format. Photo essays in journalism rely on
long, easy-to-read captions to carry the story, and together
with the photos they transmit the information that is reinforced by the visual content of the photo-dominant spread.

AUTHOR BYLINES

Author bylines are the credit lines that are given to the
authors who write the text. They follow no strict format typographically, except that they are either placed at the top of
the text to introduce the article, or placed at the end, where
they are often followed by a very small bio of the writer.
Usually the format and placement for bylines is consistent
throughout a publication. These lines are usually set in a font
and style that distinguish them from the text. If the text is
F/L, the bylines are frequently set F/R. bylines can be set
larger or smaller than the text type, in caps and small caps,
and in a different font or in italics if desired. Often there is a
descriptive line under newspaper bylines, such as "Corres-
pondent for News Today"—this is used *for non-staff* writers of
the publication.

PHOTO/ILLUSTRATION CREDITS

Photo/illustration credits vary widely depending on the
publication. Some editors are diehards about having photo
credits run down the lower right-hand edge of every photo.
Others are committed to ganging all the image credits at the
front or end of an article or publication. Still others place the
image credits literally in the gutter of the publication where

you have to crank open the binding to find out who did the illustration. And some relegate photo credits to the same treatment as the author bylines at the end of articles. Visual credits need to be taken seriously; they're often printed in 3- or 4-point type, and are frequently seen in all caps, which are easier to read at minute sizes. Visual credits need to be legible if someone wants to check the credit, but generally they should seem invisible on the page.

Subsidiary type, such as the dateline in newspapers and magazines, the bylines, the subheads, the credit lines, etc., often reveal the typographic sophistication of the designer. Small type, judiciously placed so that is readable, not distracting, and so that it adds another level of rhythm to the work, can enhance the overall page. Conversely, large, horsey, subsidiary type that unnecessarily and inappropriately calls attention to itself on the page can be distracting to the reader, and is a red flag that the designer does not know how to handle type well. Also, do not let small numbers (3, 4, 5) of the point size of type worry you. If it's readable and legible, it's probably not too small.

INITIAL CAPITALS

Initial caps are larger or decorative capital letters that introduce a section of text type in an attempt to call attention to the text type. There are different names for different types of initial caps.

STAND-UP CAPS (or raised caps)–are caps that are larger than the text type, yet whose bases align with the first or second line of the text type. This causes the taller letter to stand up past the text type. It is sometimes necessary to add an extra line of space before the stand-up cap, so that there is some extra white space around the cap.

INSET CAPS OR DROP CAPS–are caps that are larger than the text type but are inset into the text type, so that they base-align with either the third, fourth, or fifth line of text type, and align flush left with the margin of the text type.

The cap line of drop caps usually aligns with the top of the first line of body copy. Insetting caps sometimes requires *mortising* the lines of text type around the form of the capital letter, so that there is not an awkward shape of white space next to a cap "T," "A," or "W." Mortising means that you back up the text along the edge of the cap. It looks most harmonious if the text conforms to the angled edge of the character that is inset. (Mortising is a term from the days of lead type, when the base of the large initial lead cap would have to be filed away or "mortised" so that the text type could fit in closer to it on an angle) (see examples 15-19 and 15-20).

15-17. The two credit lines above are very small, but still legible. The ones on the left are 3.5 points; on the right, 4-point type. Putting the credits in all caps makes

Bison Times • February 2020
This is 9-point Gill Sans, caps and lowercase, with the name and date is separated by a bullet.

BISON TIMES • FEBRUARY 2020 • PAGE TWENTY-ONE
This is 7.5-point Baskerville Italic, in caps and small caps; with spelled-out page number.

BISON TIMES • 198 • FEBRUARY 2020
This is 8-point Weiss, in caps and small caps; the page number is included.

Bison Times • A Quarterly Newsletter • February 2020
This is 8.5-point Janson Italic, in upper- and lowercase.

15-18. Above are examples of different settings for a dateline. The page number can be included, as well as a descriptive line about the publication.

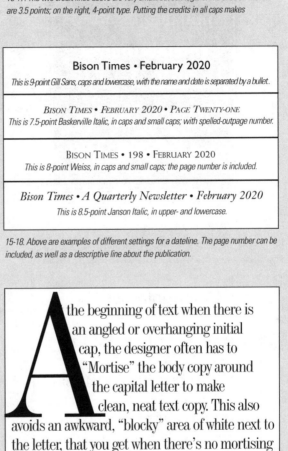

t the beginning of text when there is an angled or overhanging initial cap, the designer often has to "Mortise" the body copy around the capital letter to make clean, neat text copy. This also avoids an awkward, "blocky" area of white next to the letter, that you get when there's no mortising done by either a lazy or uninformed designer.

15-19. Above is an example of text that is mortised around the angled capital "A."

t the beginning of text when there is an angled or overhanging initial cap, the designer often has to "Mortise" the body copy around the capital letter to make clean, neat text copy. This is what no mortising looks like next to an initial capital; it's harder to read the first word.

15-20. Above is an example of text that is not mortised around the angled capital.

This page is set in ITC Officina Sans Book 8.5/12.

15 Typographic
     Hierarchy

When you design pull quotes, they should contrast with the tone of the text type on the page.

15-21. Above is an example of a reversed pull-quote set in Matrix Bold, 18-point type on 24 points of leading. This pull quote offers a dark contrast on the page.

Pull quotes can be reversed or set off in a white box for contrast on the page. The type should be easy to read.

15-22. This sample pull quote is set 18/30 in Industrial 736. The overall type is light and offers an airy break from text type on the page.

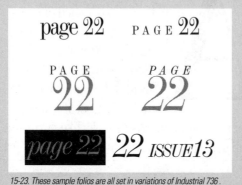

15-23. These sample folios are all set in variations of Industrial 736 .

HANGING CAPS–are initial caps that are larger than the text type and hang either somewhat or completely into the left margin next to the text. Partially hanging caps usually inset into the text as well as hang into the margin a bit. Completely hanging caps are those that hang entirely in the margin next to a selection of flush-left text.

FOLIOS/PAGE NUMBERS

Folios are the page numbers on the pages of a piece. They can be set large and screened back, set very small and bold, set small and light, or spelled out or handwritten. They offer the designer a place to express some creativity and try something new. They are usually placed on all of the pages consistently and treated the same on each page. Occasionally they are used as a place to incorporate a client's logo, or the name or date of the piece. They can be placed at the top of the page, the bottom of the page, or in the middle; they can even run vertically along an edge of the page; there is no predetermined rule. Page numbers are frequently incorporated into running headers or footers. Sometimes, they are part of the dateline of the piece, or are followed by the chapter title or the book title.

PULL QUOTES

PULL QUOTES ARE SMALL QUOTES FROM THE TEXT THAT ARE ENLARGED AND SEPARATED FROM THE TEXT TO GET THE READER INTERESTED IN READING FURTHER, OR TO PROVIDE AN OVERVIEW OF THE ARTICLE. THESE QUOTES CAN BE INSET INTO THE TEXT TYPE, HUNG PARTIALLY INTO THE COLUMN OF TYPE AND THE MARGIN. THEY CAN BE PLACED IN WHITE SPACE OR OFFSET IN A TINTED BOX. THEY ARE OFTEN SET IN A FONT THAT IS DIFFERENT FROM THE TEXT FONT, AND CAN BE PLACED IN BOXES, ACCENTED WITH PIECES OF AN IMAGE, SET TO CREATE A SHAPE, SCREENED BACK, OR ACCENTED WITH RULES OR DINGBATS. THERE ARE NO CORRECT WAYS TO DESIGN PULL QUOTES, EXCEPT THAT USUALLY NO MORE THAN TWO ARE USED ON ONE PAGE TO BREAK UP THE DESIGN, AND THEY SHOULD STAND OUT EASILY IN TERMS OF THE CHANGE IN THE FONT SIZE AND FONT STYLE FROM THE TEXT ON THE PAGE. IT IS SOMETIMES A GOOD DECISION TO CHOOSE A FONT THAT CONTRASTS WITH THE TEXT TYPE, AND A LEADING THAT ADDS A NEW RHYTHM TO THE PAGE VISUALLY.

SIDEBARS

SIDEBARS CONSIST OF SECONDARY INFORMATION RELATED TO THE TOPIC OF THE TEXT THAT THE EDITOR WANTS YOU TO READ SEPARATELY FROM THE ARTICLE. SIDEBARS SOMETIMES INCLUDE IN-DEPTH INFORMATION OR AN EXPLANATION OF AN ISSUE, OR THEY INTRODUCE A PARTICULAR PERSON'S POINT OF VIEW ON AN ISSUE. THEY

ARE OFTEN SET OFF FROM THE TEXT IN A DIFFERENT COL-
ORED SCREENED BOX, AND FREQUENTLY A DIFFERENT
FONT IS USED TO VISUALLY SEPARATE SIDEBARS FROM THE
REST OF THE ARTICLE. SIDEBARS OFTEN INCLUDE THEIR
OWN HEADLINES THAT SHOULD BE TREATED TYPOGRAPHI-
CALLY DIFFERENTLY FROM THE REST OF THE HEADS AND
SUBHEADS IN THE ARTICLE. IN SHORT, IT IS GOOD TO
THINK IN TERMS OF SIDEBARS AS SHORT STORIES IN THEIR
OWN RIGHT.

JUST BECAUSE THEY ARE CALLED SIDEBARS DOES NOT
MEAN THAT THEY COULDN'T GO AT THE BOTTOM OF ONE OR
TWO PAGES, OR BE PLACED IN THE MIDDLE OF A PAGE, ETC. THE
TEXT OF A SIDEBAR SHOULD BE A DIFFERENT FONT, DIFFERENT
SIZE, AND DIFFERENT LEADING FROM THE TEXT TYPE IF YOU
WANT IT TO STAND OUT DRAMATICALLY FROM THE ARTICLE. THE
CHANGE SHOULD BE MORE SUBTLE IF YOU WANT THE SIDEBAR
TO MELD IN WITH THE TEXT. GRAPHS AND CHARTS ARE OFTEN
RELEGATED TO THEIR OWN SEPARATE AREA OR SIDEBAR
WHERE THEY ARE EXPLAINED OR DISCUSSED IN RELATION TO
THE TEXT. THE SIZE OF SIDEBARS SHOULD BE FLEXIBLE TO
ACCOMMODATE VARIED LENGTHS.

HEADLINES & SUBHEADS

THE TWO LARGEST TYPE ELEMENTS ON THE PAGE ARE
THE HEADS AND SUBHEADS. THE *HEADS* ARE THE TITLES
GIVEN TO THE MAIN DIVIDERS OF SECTIONS IN THE TEXT.
THE *SUBHEADS* ARE THE TITLES OF THE SECONDARY
AREAS OF DIVISION IN THE TEXT. THE *HEADLINES* REFER
TO MORE INFORMATION AND ARE USUALLY SET LARGER OR
BOLDER THAN THE SUBHEADS, ALTHOUGH THIS IS NOT
ALWAYS NECESSARILY TRUE. HEADS SHOULD BE SET AT
SIZES THAT ARE EASY TO READ AND STAND OUT ON THE
PAGE. FOR SOME APPLICATIONS, THEY SHOULD SCREAM;
FOR OTHERS THEY SHOULD BE RESTRAINED.

SUBHEADS ARE OF SECONDARY IMPORTANCE, BUT
THEY SHOULD BE SET LARGE ENOUGH TO CLEARLY DIF-
FERENTIATE FROM THE TEXT COPY, BUT SMALL ENOUGH
NOT TO INTERFERE WITH THE HEADLINE. BECAUSE THEY
ARE SECONDARY, THEY CAN BE SET IN A FONT THAT DIF-
FERS FROM THE TEXT COPY, THAT CONTRASTS WITH IT, OR
IS A BOLD VERSION OF THE TEXT TYPE AT A LARGER SIZE.
THE SUBHEADS THROUGHOUT A PIECE SHOULD ALL BE SET
CONSISTENTLY WITH EQUAL LEADING AND SPACING.

HEADS AND SUBHEADS ARE ELEMENTS FOR WHICH A
DESIGNER CAN USE TYPE CREATIVELY. FOR EXAMPLE, YOU
CAN INTEGRATE THE HEADLINE FONT WITH SOME IMAGES,
COLORS, OR TEXTURES TO INTERPRET THE MEANING OF
THE ARTICLE VISUALLY FOR THE READER. HEADLINES CAN
BE AN AREA TO EXPERIMENT AND TO TAKE CHANCES. IN
PUBLICATION DESIGN, THEY SHOULD BE THE MOST DYNAM-
IC ELEMENTS ON THE PAGE AND INTEGRATE WITH THE
LAYOUT OF THE TEXT AND IMAGES WELL.

SIDEBARS CONTAIN INFORMATION

THAT EITHER ELABORATES ON SOME-

THING MENTIONED IN THE TEXT, OR

THEY GIVE INSTRUCTIONS ON HOW TO

DO SOMETHING. THEY CAN ALSO

CONTAIN CHARTS OR GRAPHS THAT

RELATE TO OR EXPLAIN DATA FROM THE

TEXT. TYPOGRAPHICALLY, SIDEBARS

SHOULD BE RELATED TO THE TEXT

COPY, BUT DIFFERENT, PERHAPS SET IN

ITALICS, OR IN CAPS AND SMALL CAPS.

15-24. In the sidebar above, the text is set in Optima, in caps and small caps.

*Sidebars can also be
very small and have
tidbits of information in
them, depending on the
nature of the publication
and the layout.*

15-25. This short sidebar is set in Embassy Script.

This page is set in
Copperplate 29 8.5/12.

15 Typographic
Hierarchy

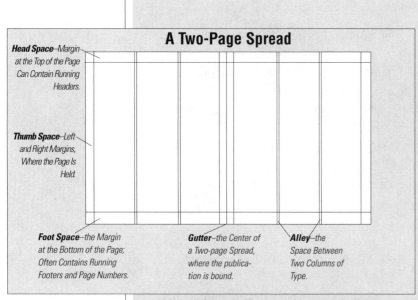

A Two-Page Spread

Head Space–Margin at the Top of the Page Can Contain Running Headers.

Thumb Space–Left and Right Margins, Where the Page Is Held.

Foot Space–the Margin at the Bottom of the Page; Often Contains Running Footers and Page Numbers.

Gutter–the Center of a Two-page Spread, where the publication is bound.

Alley–the Space Between Two Columns of Type.

15-26. In this diagram, the different areas of the page are identified.

howard pyle

Their wit and wisdom, pain and pageantry captured the imaginations of their audiences and continue to remain timely through to today.

15-27. This editorial spread, by KU student Doug Irwin, uses type creatively and with clear hierarchy on the page.

This page is set in Copperplate 29 8.5/12.

TYPOGRAPHIC HIERARCHY ON A TWO-PAGE SPREAD

A *SPREAD* IS THE TERM USED TO DESCRIBE TWO FACING PAGES IN A PIECE. THEY USUALLY SHARE COMMON MARGINS AND COLUMNS, OR HAVE SEPARATE FORMATS BASED ON WHETHER THEY ARE A LEFT OR A RIGHT PAGE. THE MARGIN AT THE CENTER OF A SPREAD IS REFERRED TO AS A *GUTTER*, AND THE SMALL MARGIN BETWEEN COLUMNS OF COPY IS CALLED AN *ALLEY*. THE SPACE AT THE OUTER EDGES OF THE SPREAD IS CALLED *THUMB SPACE*, FOR HOLDING THE BOOK. THESE TERMS CAN BE HELPFUL IN DESCRIBING A PAGE THAT HAS BEEN LAID OUT. THEY ARE COMMON IN BOOK PUBLISHING, AS WELL AS IN MAGAZINE PUBLICATION AND NEWSLETTER DESIGN.

TYPOGRAPHIC HIERARCHY IN SUMMARY

TYPOGRAPHIC HIERARCHY REFERS TO THE CLEAR STRUCTURE OF THE TYPE ON THE PAGE TO SHOW EMPHASIS THROUGH THE USE OF SIZE, COLOR AND PLACEMENT. THE HIERARCHY OF THE TYPE DETERMINES WHAT TYPE GETS READ FIRST–WHAT CALLS THE READER'S ATTENTION MOST PROMINENTLY. AS A DESIGNER, IT IS IMPORTANT TO UNDERSTAND AND UTILIZE TYPOGRAPHIC HIERARCHY TO ADD EMPHASIS TO THE INFORMATION ON THE PAGE. A DESIGNER CAN MAKE DECISIONS OF SCALE, PLACEMENT, WEIGHT AND COLOR THAT WILL AFFECT THE HIERARCHY. EXTREMELY LARGE TYPE, PRINTED IN YELLOW, WILL NOT BE PROMINENT IN THE OVERALL DESIGN. LIKEWISE, SMALL, BOLD TYPE, REVERSED OUT OF BLACK BARS, WILL STAND OUT NOTICEABLY ON THE PAGE. DESIGNERS CAN UTILIZE KNOWLEDGE OF TYPOGRAPHIC HIERARCHY IN AN EDITORIAL LAYOUT TO EMPHASIZE PARTS OF A MESSAGE OR HEADLINE. MASTERING THE USE OF HIERARCHY IS SIMILAR TO MASTERING THE USE OF COLOR WHEN "PAINTING" WITH TYPE.

PROJECT: OXYMORON POSTER

For this project, select an oxymoron that you will try to represent typographically. An *oxymoron* is a phrase that has an inherent contradiction in it. The following are some to choose from, but you should feel free to come up with your own:

OXYMORONS

- Military Intelligence
- Same Difference
- Jumbo Shrimp
- Black Light
- Together Alone
- Near Miss
- Peace Officer

Using an oxymoron, design a poster to interpret the concept in type. You can try to present the contradiction or the meaning that the phrase has come to suggest. Type should be the primary visual in the final piece. Consider your selection of fonts carefully. Write a few paragraphs of text type that relate to the oxymoron. Make this piece as creative as you can. The final size of the poster is up to you as the designer, and there is no limit to the number of colors to be used.

Begin by doing fifteen thumbnail sketches for your oxymoron. Then progress to two half-sized sketches, and lastly assemble the final piece on the computer.

OBJECTIVES

- To reinforce the use of type for readability in design.
- To reinforce the three stage process of design from thumbnails, to roughs, to finish.
- To apply the concept of creating a relationship between the message and the type solution.
- To appreciate the detailed nuances of different typefaces.
- To view letters as forms and experiment with combinations.
- To utilize type as a visual element, and an abstract and interpretive design element.

15-28. In this oxymoron poster, by KU student Kimberly L. Snyder, the text type is placed within the bulb to create the connection that makes the light.

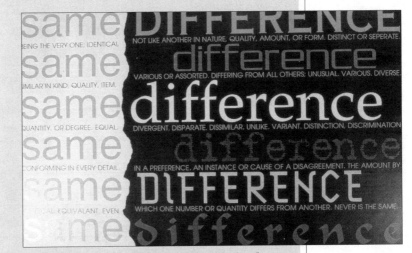

15-29. In this oxymoron poster, by KU student Rhonda Schmig, the phrase "same difference" is repeated with changes only to the word difference. The text runs in long lines placed in between the headlines.

Typographic Hierarchy-Review

1. What is a pull quote? _____

2. What is a sidebar? _____

3. What is an alley? _____

4. What is type hierarchy ? _____

5. What is a stand-up capital? _____

6. What is a drop cap? _____

7. What is a hanging capital? _____

8. What is thumb space? _____

9. What is a dateline? _____

10. What is the gutter in a spread? _____

11. What is a header? _____

12. What is a running footer? _____

13. What are captions? _____

14. What are author s bylines? _____

15. What are illustration/photo credits? _____

16. What are bullets? How are they used? _____

17. What are runovers? _____

18. What is the folio? _____

19. What is tabular material? _____

Using Type Creatively

16-1. This logo uses contrasting fonts. The serif Roman font in "Mix," and the serif italic font in "Soup & Salad Bar" differ in structure and weight from the word "MATCH" which is a bold sans serif font. Although very different, these fonts work together in harmony successfully.

INTRODUCTION

In this chapter we review how to use type innovatively while paying attention to nuances of typefaces for mixing them appropriately. Type can be a wonderfully communicative element in design. The single choice of a font can denote silliness, seriousness, a staid outlook, or conservative or contemporary attitudes. Aside from these obvious associations that designers become more attuned to, the treatment of a font's size, weight, color, texture, slant, edges, and background can also be used by a skilled designer to communicate.

There are innumerable ways to use type creatively, and no doubt all designers must find their own personal style of creating and interpreting with type. But it is imperative that designers begin with a concept before they embark on manipulating type creatively. The *concept*, or idea behind the design of a logo or headline, will determine which creative option a designer selects as appropriate for the given problem. Using type gimmicks to cover up a lack of ideas results in poor design. If you start with a concept either from the text or from your interpretation of the message, you will make sound choices in your type.

The written word still has tremendous power to move people and influence ideas, and sophisticated use of type makes this influence stronger and more powerful. Now, while you're planning which font you'll use for the next revolution, let's consider a few options of using type creatively.

CONTRASTING FACES, VARYING STRUCTURE

Contrasting various faces can be as simple as contrasting the *style* of an italic version of a serif face with the Roman version of the same face. Or, you can contrast the *weight* of the face as well as the *style*, so that you would contrast a serif, light, italic face with a serif bold Roman face. Then, you can contrast the *structure* of a face so that you would use a *sans serif*, bold, Roman font contrasted with a *serif*, light, italic font for maximum contrast.

16-2. The example above uses type placed on an angle to emphasize the angles in downhill skiing. The mixing of serif and sans serif fonts, some of which are condensed, creates variety and interest in the overall design. Spacing and scale variations also create a sense of rhythm in the lines of type in the logo.

CONTRASTING FONTS
A A
STYLE=ITALIC VS. ROMAN *Contrast of STYLE : Roman vs. Italic*
A A
WEIGHT=LIGHT VS. BOLD *Contrast of STYLE & WEIGHT: Bold Roman vs. Italic*
A A
STRUCTURE=SERIF VS. SANS SERIF *Contrast of STYLE & STRUCTURE: Roman Sans Serif vs. Italic Serif*
A A
WEIGHT=BOLD VS. LIGHT *Contrast of STYLE, WEIGHT & STRUCTURE: Bold Roman Sans Serif vs. Italic Serif*
A a
CASE=UPPER VS. LOWERCASE *Contrast of STYLE, WEIGHT, STRUCTURE & CASE: Bold Roman Sans Serif Cap vs. Italic Serif Lower Case*
A a
WIDTH=CONDENSED VS. REGULAR *Contrast of STYLE, WEIGHT, STRUCTURE, CASE & WIDTH: Bold Roman Sans Serif Condensed Cap vs. Italic Serif Lower Case*

16-3. This table shows a variety of ways to contrast type.

KEY CONCEPTS

Contrast in Style

Contrast in Weight

Contrast in Structure

Adjusting a Character

Reversing Characters

Replacing a Character with an Image

Using Leading Creatively

Using Rules, Dingbats & Directionals

Use of White Space

Shaped Text

Type as Texture

Active Type

Hand-Rendered Type

Abstracted Type

Varying Placement of Lines

Using Drop Shadows & Outlines

Relating Shape of Text to Layout Shape

This page is set in Stone Sans Regular 8.5/12.

16 *Using Type Creatively*

16-4. Sans serif is a good option for reversed type; serifs can close up when reversed.

16-5. In the example above, both fonts are serif fonts. The two fonts contrast in terms of their structure; one is bold, and the other is italic. Integrating fonts of different structures accentuates their differences. A pepper replaces the apostrophe in this logo.

16-6. The contrast of fonts from different eras can be effective to bridge different time periods. In the example above, the fonts that resonate with historic overtones are juxtaposed with a contemporary font to reflect the range of articles from different eras found in a secondhand store. The greatest contrast in fonts' structure is a script font opposed to a bold sans serif font.

16-7. The logo above, by KU student Rachael Waters, replaces the "I" in WHISPERS with a calligraphic figure in a gown; notice how well the thickness of strokes of the figure reflects the line weight of the strokes of the letter, creating aesthetic unity.

16-8. This story logo features all sans serif fonts; these differ in their structure, their weight, and their width. The tall, condensed, fine-weight font of "INTERRA-CIAL" contrasts with the bold sans serif "COUPLES" font. Spacing also differs; "RACIAL" is more tightly spaced than "COUPLES." Also notice the even space above and below "COUPLES." The distance to the rule below is the same as the distance to the box above.

Contrasting the style, structure and weight of fonts while maintaining harmony accentuates the characteristics of each font. The light, italic font *looks* lighter next to a bold, sans serif font, especially if it is printed in a lighter color.

You can also choose to contrast type that was created in different eras, so that you could contrast a detailed illuminated cap with a computer-generated, dot-matrix font. You can even contrast type that is of different languages if you have the right audience, such as Kanji calligraphic Japanese characters contrasted with a word in English. You can contrast the width of typefaces, so that you would use a tall, condensed serif font with an extended font. In addition, if you use different spacings for these fonts, you could tightly kern the extended font, and letter-space out the condensed font.

Why is contrasting type an effective way to use type creatively? Well, when you place two radically different fonts next to each other, you call attention to the inherent differences in the fonts, their appearances, and their impact on the viewer. You can often use contrasting type to show two different sides of an issue or two faces of a person, etc. The heavy, bold, sans serif font can supply a stable ground for an elegant, light, script face to be reversed out of.

The use of contrasting typefaces adds an unexpected element to the work, as well as sets up a very interesting typographic rhythm, or in this case syncopation. Without contrasts, the design might be pale, monotone, and predictable. Contrasting faces force a designer to look longer and harder for just the right face rather than settling for something ordinary. Remember that the fonts should only contrast if it's appropriate to the client's message.

VARY WEIGHTS

Varying the weights of type creates different tones of gray and black on the page. Using very light faces gives an open, light, airy feel to the page. If the next paragraph is set in a bold font, the contrast will be extreme, and the text will appear as though two different people are talking to one another. The weights can be used to call attention to some information, or to highlight certain issues. It is best to vary the weight of text type not simply for design reasons, but so that it makes sense with the meaning of the text. Although you will rarely vary the weight of fonts in text type, it can be used effectively in headlines to indicate weight loss, opposing points of view, conservative versus liberal attitudes, time of day, or tiredness, etc.

Complementary weights of fonts can be effective in the design of logos or in directional signage to clarify for the viewer which word or phrase is considered of primary importance. In logos, type weight should only be varied when it is appropriate, when there is a reason for the change in weight, and when it is used to enhance a harmonious design.

REVERSAL OF CHARACTERS

Reversed characters are letters that are printed white against a black or colored background. When reversed out of black, you should use at least a book-weight font because anything lighter may cause problems in printing by filling in with ink. It is usually preferable to reverse a mono-weight font, such as a sans serif, rather than a serif font, which has thicks and thins in its strokes; this is because when reversing, the thin areas can easily fill in with ink. It is also not advisable to reverse script or tiny type under 6 points due to the thinness of the strokes.

The black area that the type is reversed out of can cause an impression of depth or darkness on the page. The background can be a shape as well as a solid area of color, such as a star or cross, or a pattern, assuming that it doesn't have much white in the pattern. Letters can reverse out of a landscape, out of faces, or out of the shadow in any photo. Letters can be reversed from vibrant patterns that frolic across the page in endless variations. These reversed characters start to become one with the image they are reversed out of, and their placement on the image should be considered carefully. Sometimes a dropped shadow of white, gray or black helps the type to separate from the midtones in the background.

VARY LEADING—RHYTHM

Leading, along with the point size and the boldness of the font, creates typographic density on the page. A bold font heavily leaded will appear lighter than a light font set solid. Leading can create a very consistent rhythm on the page, as if to the beat of music. You can also turn type 90° on the page for effect, or interweave the lines of type from varying angles. You can screen large type in the background of text type, or you can reverse lines of type out of black bars–or combine some of the above ideas.

Varying the leading of a selection of text copy sets up a visual rhythm on the page as the lines define white areas between them. If you vary both the leading and the weights of the lines, you can create visual poetry with the type, calling for emphasis or delicacy as required in the text. Varied leading is not appropriate in all settings of text, but for clients willing to take

16-9. This logo, by KU student Joseph D. Roslin III, adapts an existing character, the "V," and simply adds horns to it to give the resonance of the Viking culture. You can add simple elements to letters to create a visual using the type.

16-10. This nameplate for a magazine on the topic of wine, by KU student Allison Jeffery, simply adjusts the tail of the lowercase "g," to make it reflect the spiraling of grapevines. Altering a single letter in a word can create a type and visual solution in one.

16-11. This packaging label uses a variety of fonts, with contrasting qualities. Notice that this label is predominantly typographic. Dingbats and decorative rules are used, as well as frames. Drop shadows highlight the type and give the label a more detailed sensibility.

16-12. Contrasting the structure of fonts means contrasting serif versus sans serif, italic versus Roman, and the weights of the fonts. The serif Roman font in the name VALENCIA'S of this restaurant logo contrasts with the structure of the italic serif font below to accentuate the differences in each font, yet they create a sense of harmony and balance.

When you reverse type, be sure to select a heavy weight stroke on the font, *because thin stroked letters tend to fill in and they're tough to read!*

16-13. Notice how difficult the script is to read when it's reversed due to the fine weight of the stroke.

This page is set in Tiffany 8.5/12.

16 *Using Type Creatively*

You can also use leading for creative effects, by placing type on a slant you can refer to noise, as if someone's screaming!

16-14. In this example, placing the type on angles gives the sense that it's radiating from a common point.

Some experts say that
        Yet, I find that when I
exercise makes you better
        exercise regularly
able to handle stress,
        I'm more tired and
gives you a positive
        more prone to illness,
attitude, makes you
        not to mention the
sleep better and
        time loss of an hour
ultimately makes you
        and a half a day to get
more efficient.
        to the gym, work out,

        and get back home.
        ■

16-15. Above is an example of interlaced columns of type. This is most readable when the fonts are distinctly different from each other, and there is plenty of leading to help the reader not get confused between lines.

16-16. Type is used above to accentuate the visual contrast and to reinforce the message of opposites. If the fonts were more similar in appearance, this would not have the visual impact. Also, notice how clearly the mono-stroked font reverses out of the gray background above. The script font requires a white drop shadow to improve readability against a mid-range gray and the white of "OPPOSITES."

16-17. The logo above uses the arm of the Liberty statue to replace the "I" in the word "LIBERTY" above. Replacing one letter of a word with a visual can be effective in typographic design for logos, headlines, and ads, and in editorial layouts.

This page is set in Tiffany 8.5/12.

a few risks to get noticed, it might be an interesting twist. Varied leading can be used to reflect the effect of an earthquake or a bomb, or to represent the passage of time, steps leading somewhere, the loud sound coming from speakers, or the type that is dropping to build the foundation of a house.

Along with varying the leading, you can occasionally vary the placement of the lines on the page. You can sometimes interlace two columns of text type that are set in different weights with very wide leading for an interesting effect. This is often used when representing contradictory points of view.

VARYING LEADING—WHITE SPACE

Whenever you place a line of type on the page, that line is seen in relation to the four edges of the page. Does the line of type hang across the top of the page, run down the side, sit contentedly in the middle of the page, or hug a corner? Does the line reverse out of a bar, sit on a diagonal, or fall to the bottom of the page?

Once the placement of the first line is determined, the other lines must be placed accordingly. White space in the layout can be used very dramatically to call attention to an extremely small headline, particularly when the environment that it is seen in is crowded. Sometimes, on a crowded page, white space screams for more attention than all of the flashy, bold headlines.

A small amount of type on an expansive white canvas can look lost, or floundering. It's important to place such phrases very carefully, paying attention to the edges of the page and the tension that is created between the type and the edge. This attention must also be given when type is placed in relation to the edges of photographs or illustrations.

REPLACING A LETTER WITH AN IMAGE

You can use an image to replace one letter of a headline or a logo. This can be effective because it combines type and image into one element, but you should not compromise readability in such a design. In order to be successful in transposing an image into the design, you first have to ascertain that the image and the letter have roughly the same shape— for example, using a coin to replace an "O" in a word. Then size the image so that it relates to the scale of rest of the type in the word.

Although this is a simple design solution, it can be extremely effective in the immediacy of its interpretation. You may want to try to match the stroke weight of the letters with the stroke weight in a line drawing that you create to replace a letter in a logo. Likewise, the curves and angles of the font can relate to the curves and angles in your drawing of an image to replace a letter. The replacement works best when the weights of the characters and the drawing are coordinated.

USE OF RULES, DINGBATS, AND DIRECTIONALS

Rules are lines that organize, separate and structure the type on the page. *Directionals* are pointing hands, lines, arrows or bullets that direct the viewer's eye in a certain way on the page.

Arrows and directionals can be used on forms, in headlines when appropriate, or as paragraph breaks for text that you want to set solid. They can direct the reader from one paragraph to another in a complex layout.

Dingbats are decorative images created by type designers to enhance the layout of the title page of a book, to separate type on the page, or to add a sense of flourish to a design. Dingbats have a long tradition in type design, and the refined use of them often requires great restraint. They include little symbols, leaves, vines, snowflakes, pencils, frames, borders, diamonds and all kinds of interesting little doodads.

There are entire fonts made up of dingbats, and they are created from the keyboard, with the dingbat font highlighted. Dingbats can be used to create fun borders in the margins of a page or at the top or bottom of a column of type, as a sort of formal ending or beginning device.

Dingbats can also be used in packaging and label design to accentuate or surround a word. They sometimes are used to create a visual filigree on a label, or to give historic resonance to a poster or book cover. Depending on the type designer, dingbats can look retro, contemporary, silly, rough, ancient, or Cubist. Because they are fonts, they are very easy to size, can be made into outlines, line up, and are simple to utilize.

Rules (or borders) can be made of any dingbat or a series of dingbats printed one after another. Rules are often used to call attention to headlines, but they can also be used in place of characters in a headline, or to separate areas of text where needed. Rules sometimes separate a subhead from prior text. *Vertical* or *alley rules* are used to separate columns of type. *Ruled boxes* are often used to set off a sidebar from the rest of the text. They can also be used to separate an image with a white background from the space on the rest of the page. It's a good idea to change the tone within a ruled box so that the rule separates one color or area of tone from another. Decorative rules are often used to give a historic or detailed sensibility to the layout.

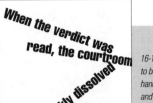

16-18. In this example, the type appears to be jumbled and falling into the right-hand corner. There is a sense of motion, and disruption from this unusual and awkward placement. In this case, the placement of the type attempts to reflect the chaos caused by a court proceeding. The type reiterates the mixed feelings and disorganization following the announcement of the jury's verdict.

16-21. Choose dingbats and directionals that are appropriate for the message and audience when directing the readers.

16-19. In the example above, two different fonts are used, but numerous dingbats and ornament or picture fonts are also used. These fonts offer the designer handsome rules for placement above or below headlines, elaborate dividers to replace bullets, and fancy ornaments to end or begin, or to sandwich around a selection of type. Mastering the use of ornaments takes some restraint and a broad familiarity with those available. Determining the appropriateness of ornaments is just as refined as selecting the font.

16-20. In the example above, the beginning of the sneeze sound gradually expands, and the "Os" appear to spray forth from the "H." Type that conforms to a shape can effectively imply the shape on the page, but shaping type should ideally not compromise the readability of the word or text.

16-22. Rules can organize elements on a page or subdivide unrelated areas of text. The dingbats are from the icon font Big Cheese.

This page is set in Athens 8.5/12.

16-25. The layout above, by KU student Lenore (lenn-e) Snell, uses reversed type and a separation of black and white in the layout to represent the male and female in Adam and Eve. When reversing type, it is best to keep the font simple and bold.

Contrast of size has to be exaggerated with type for the best effect.

16-23. When you use size contrast, it has to be extreme differences of size in text.

16-24. These fonts are still readable even though they've been manipulated on the computer.

When the conservative point of view wants to be heard, it attempts to scream in the media, but often there is little or no media coverage of the many issues that conservatives consider crucial.

16-26. The layout above uses overlapped type to try to get across the idea of competing messages in the media.

16-27. In the example above, the sans serif font in "MOONROCK" contrasts with the structure and forms of the serif italic font in "FASHIONS."

BREAK FROM PERPENDICULAR LAYOUT

Breaking from the perpendicular layout is one of the most enjoyable creative tools a designer can use. After you have created numerous traditional 90° pieces, it is refreshing to tilt a picture, or rotate or curve some copy. You can even take the entire perpendicular layout and twist it to an angle on the page, or just tilt the images. It can really be fun to turn type on its side and run it up a margin, or plaster a screened image on an angle across the background of text type. But you should use these devices only when it is appropriate to the message of the text itself, or to present a visual interpretation of the text.

Ads frequently set type on a slant merely to get their information to stand out against the rigid format of magazine grids. Some typographic applications really lend themselves more naturally to angled type than others. When you are trying to show a sport vehicle that can handle mountain travel, or a company that is growing, the typographic connection is obvious.

WHITE SPACE USED EFFECTIVELY

White space can also be a refreshing tool for a designer to use. By leaving a lot of space on the page and placing the type and image very small in one corner, you can force the curious reader to read the type even though it's so small. Or you can place very small type between someone whispering into someone else's ear to illustrate the quietness of the whispering communication. White space often makes an ad stand out tremendously against pages that are chock full of information all the time. White space in a newspaper ad enables it to really stand out from the gray text of the rest of the page.

White space can also be used effectively when you place a column of small type with wide leading on the opening page of a brochure. Rather than trying to scream the message, you get people's attention with understatement. White space can create visual tension between two unequal areas in an asymmetrical layout, or it can work as a frame around a very small quote placed perfectly in the center of the page.

VARY SIZE OF TYPE GREATLY

Varying the size of type greatly on the page is very striking. If you blow one character up so large that it bleeds off the page edges and then place the rest of the type in 11- or 12-point text, there is a dramatic contrast. This should only be employed where it makes sense, perhaps for a seed company to show how large their crops grow, or maybe to advertise a tall-men's-clothing store.

USE OF SCREENED TYPE OR ELEMENTS

Screened type can be very effective behind body copy, as long as the percentage of the screen does not overwhelm the body copy or render it illegible. Words, headlines, letters, or phrases can be screened and placed as a light texture behind body copy. Sometimes it is helpful to enlarge the test and place the screened type on an angle, or off to one side, so that it doesn't interfere with the text copy. Images and shapes can also be screened in a light tone and placed behind the text copy as design elements.

SHAPED TEXT TYPE

Shaped text is typeset to form a silhouetted image, such as a horse, a road, a fence, or a lamp. The shape that you choose should logically relate to the text copy. The connection should be evidently clear, so that the reader puts it all together. By using different weights of type, some computers can even represent a person's face, in pretty accurate detail. Type can be used as the bow and arrow head in an article on bow collecting. (It could even be used as the line of the arrow as well!) It can be shaped like a sail full of wind for an article on the America's Cup, or shaped like the milk in a glass for an article on the dairy industry, etc. There are no limits to the possibilities as long as designers are creative in their thinking and remember that the type, above all else, should be readable and easy for the reader to follow.

ACTIVE TYPE

Active type is the antithesis to stable or restrained type. I think of active type as letters that run and jump and play all over the page...with just one little problem: it still has to be readable as a headline or subhead. Active type can incorporate letterforms that you've made up yourself, or letters from many different sources . . . but it should not resemble ransom note lettering, unless that's what you're after. Active type can be used to describe an amusement park or a new kid's toy. Active text type curves and swirls and appears to move; it does *not* just sit there boring on the page.

EXPRESSIVE TYPE

Expressive type is a bit harder to define than the others. Expressive type conveys the emotive quality of the message in the text. In a story on death and dying, for example, expressive type could take many different turns, depending on the attitude of the article. It could be somber and depressing, upbeat and enlightening, or dark and oppressive; it could incorporate a tunnel with light at the end. Expressive type is very closely related

16-28. In the example above, the "A" in "GARDENERS" is replaced with pruning shears to give the sense of gardening. Notice that the gardening clippers are shaped like an "A," which helps the readability of the title.

16-29. The newsletter banner above uses hand-rendered typefaces to create a child-like scrawl to the type. Even the font for "CREATIONS" appears friendly and informal.

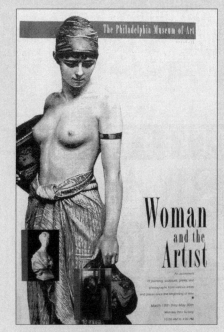

16-30. The poster design above, by KU student Ronald Pushkar, shows how effective the use of white space can be in a layout to call attention to the type. In this poster, the headline is prominent because of the vastness of the white space around it.

Elements that are screened behind the text will affect the reader's interpretation of the words, their truth, or their accuracy.

16-31. In this example, you are set up to question the text before you read it because of the screened question mark.

This page is set in Athens 8.5/12.

16-32. In the example above, the
message is redundant: we see
plaid, and we read plaid. This
would be more creative if the word
read "SUIT" or BLAZER."

16-33. Outlined type is difficult
to read; when shadowed, it is
even harder to read.

STRIKE–THROUGH
TYPE IS USED
WHEN COPY HAS
TO GO THROUGH
MULTIPLE ROUNDS
~~OF~~ OF EDITING
~~EDITING,~~ SO THAT
SUBSEQUENT
PEOPLE CAN SEE
WHAT EARLIER
PEOPLE DELETED.

16-34. Strike-through type is only
used in editing text, to show
what has been deleted.

16-35. Although the fonts in the logo above are the same point size,
just varying whether they are serif or sans serif creates a complementary relationship between the fonts in the two words

16-36. This brochure cover, by KU student Doug Irwin, uses hand-lettered type
to create an overall design of integrated
type, using a variety of tones. Type is
turned sideways, letters are read for two
different words, type from one line is
integrated into the next. This cover may
break some standard rules of design, but
often breaking the rules is fine—as long
as it works.

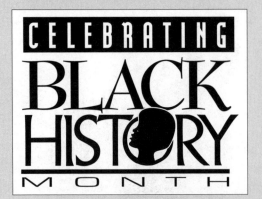

16-37. The logo above uses a variety of fonts, in fact one for each word, to
create an overall harmonious whole. The fonts do not call attention to themselves because they work together well.

to the intent of the copy, and is used to convert the views of
the author into a visually appropriate typographic solution.

INTEGRATE TYPE INTO IMAGE OR IMAGE INTO TYPE

Images can be integrated into type by placing an image into
a headline in place of a character of type. It is sometimes challenging to find the right image that reads as the letter as well
as the image, but the effort can bring the type and image
together so that they reinforce one another. The intent of the
words of the headline should reflect the sense of the image as
well. They should clarify the intent rather than fight one another or simply be redundant.

An image can be turned into type by cutting the letters out
of the image, so that the only areas of the image that you see
are those areas that fall where the characters are. Images can be
incorporated into the counter forms of letters, and they can be
placed into areas between letters or in place of the dot on an
"i," for example. If you can free yourself from predictable expectations of type, the options are enormous.

LARGE LETTERFORM OF IMAGE

One large letterform can be used on the page, with the image
printed directly onto the letter, so that you see a celebrity's face
in the counter of a big, bold Tiffany "D" that stands for her name.
Or a model could sit nestled into a huge, no-nonsense sans serif
Gill Sans "C." One large, decorative capital letter that parallels
the personality of a celebrity can be used as the backdrop of an
article, and have the text type knocked out of the large letter
or have the celebrity's face printed over the letter.

ABSTRACTED LETTERFORMS

Abstracted letterforms can be created from your own imagination, or manipulated from objects in the article, such as seafood,
or letterforms from a particular typeface that you distort. When
you create type out of physical or edible objects, make sure that
you can photograph or illustrate them easily. Letterforms that
you make up can be as abstract and unusual as is appropriate for
the subject matter. Type that you distort can be stretched,
curved, curled, twisted, flopped over or gradated for effect.
Always remember that these creative, innovative ideas should
be grounded in something that's in the text of the article or the
intended message of the piece, or they won't make sense to the
reader. Innovation in type for the sake of novelty alone is a poor
design choice and often smacks of a new designer. In type solutions, the designer must always have an idea that is visually represented with type.

TEXTURED TYPE

Textured type can take three forms: either type that is filled
in with a texture, type that you enlarge on a copier that has very
ragged edges, or type that you distort to give a rough-hewn edge.
For an article on Oriental rugs, you could do some interesting

textural treatments of the type. For an article on recognizing different woods by their grain, you could use wood-grain texture in the type. Enlarging small type so that the edges get ragged can be a very effective tool for an arts organization or a bookstore that specializes in alternative-lifestyle books, or for an article on branding cows because the brands are not very clear or accurate, etc.

UNTRADITIONAL LAYOUT SHAPE OR FORMAT SIZE

Untraditional layout shape or *format size* means to take the traditional vertical rectangular page and turn it on its side, make it into a square, or cut it so it's a circle or triangle. This can require more expensive press costs due to die cutting, or you can design a triangular poster that would print two up on a square sheet, and then be trimmed at an angle to a triangle. The uniqueness of these unusual shapes often forces the designer to try new type treatments and layouts once they're freed from the straightjacket of the rectangle. Perhaps you should design a long, thin poster next time.

VARY LINES, NOT ONLY PLACE HORIZONTALLY

Varying line placement on the page means to incorporate lines placed vertically or on random angles. Sometimes it is even appropriate to place type on a curve or on an irregularly drawn line. This can give a layout a tremendous amount of visual energy and might be appropriate for an article on gymnasts or the circus—something that seems to be going in all directions at once. Once you begin to free type from its standard placement, you are able to come up with all kinds of treatments that could work well for selected topics. Computers can hamper this creativity at times because the font-manipulation components of programs are not yet well integrated. It requires a high degree of user proficiency with a variety of programs.

HAND-RENDERED TYPE

Hand-rendered type, whether it is calligraphy, carefully measured capitals, graceful script or scrawled handwriting, can be effective in expressing the idea of the text. Hand-rendered type often stands out from typeset headlines just because it retains the mark of the individual. Beautiful hand-rendered type of the word Olympic with the word "winners" scrawled across it gives a feeling of careful study and spontaneity that could never be achieved in a typeset headline. It also reflects the years of practice that an Olympic athlete undergoes, only to be measured in one short-lived event.

Often it can be powerful to incorporate hand-rendered type with typeset copy. The immediacy of hand-rendered type creates a sense of the human element when contrasted with the clean crispness of mechanically typeset copy. When a spontaneous lettered element is placed next to rigid type, they accentuate their differences.

NEW HORIZONS
Real Estate

16-38. Both fonts in the above example are light in weight, but are very different in structure. The sans serif is square, while the script flows and is angled. These two fonts create a light and airy feel when used together.

16-39. In the poster above, by KU student Gelinde Buettner, different fonts and hand-rendered letters are used to spell out the composer's name, and a free-flowing calligraphic solution is used for the word "Festival."

TOM'S REPAIR
TYPEWRITER

16-40. The fonts in the example above are complements in terms of width and structure. The serif is very condensed and feels somewhat historic. The sans serif seems more contemporary and appears a little informal.

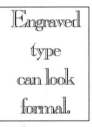

16-41 Curved type set on a path is exciting but should be clearly legible in terms of point size or font, or it's too much work for the reader.

Engraved type can look formal.

16-42. Engraved type attempts to approximate type carved in stone; usually it's a variation on outlined type.

It should be against the law to put a shadow on engraved type.

16-43. Shadowing engraved type only complicates the legibility for the reader.

This page is set in Weiss 8.5/12.

16 | *Using Type Creatively*

Outline type is difficult to work with.

16-44. Because outlined type is so light, it is hard to discern characters.

Outline type is easier to read when it is filled.

16-45. Using a screen to fill in outlined type helps the readability.

Shadowed type is often low on the legibility scale.

16-46. The best use of a drop shadow on type is when the type has to be distinguished from the background. This use is gratuitous.

16-47. This logo design, by KU student Tina M. Anthony, for a contemporary furniture manufacturer, uses type to transmit its style and modernity. Each letter is treated differently in the logo, but together they set the scene for eclectic, innovative, and contemporary furniture design.

The long, pointed bill aids in fishing.

16-48. Large type can be set sideways to call attention, even when it wouldn't fit horizontally in the layout.

16-50. This typographic identity, by KU student Eugene Yoder, tries to present the modern, high-tech sense of this project through the creative placement of type and partial reversals of characters. The use of geometric rules and shapes also reinforces a technical feel to the logo.

16-49. Unconventional shapes, such as a circle, can be appropriate when the topic warrants a break from tradition, such as in new energy sources.

16-51. Type can be used as a line to direct attention to an image or to guide the viewer's eye between two elements. Because the type is placed on a slant in the example above, it seems to balance precariously in space, demanding attention.

TYPE AS ILLUSTRATION

Illustrated type is type that illustrators create for the subject matter at hand. It may consist of characters made out of auto parts for an article on car design, or it may be type made up of pieces of sushi for an article on exotic eating. When the type and the illustration can come together like this, the editorial appearance of the page is usually very strong. Short headlines are a must for this, though, because the characters can be tough to read, and long headlines would be tedious. Another option is just to illustrate only one word of a typeset headline, for emphasis. Usually less is more in type design, and a single illustrated capital or word in a headline is plenty to get the idea across.

DROP SHADOW & OUTLINE FONTS

These special-effects fonts are used more rarely than new designers would assume. They are often difficult to read and don't really add that much either visually or emotively to a phrase. They should be used large when possible, and in limited applications. I would not advocate their use as body copy, but some daring young designer might experiment with them and succeed.

Shadowed type is most effective when used against photographs that have a variety of tones. It can prevent dark type from melding into the dark tones, and vice versa. The shadow makes the type appear to jump off the page and have a 3-D effect. It can also create a layered look in packaging that can be very effective and help readability.

Outlined type is tedious on the eyes because it takes longer to recognize the letters. Simply filling in the outline with a tone helps readability. Outlines can often be avoided by the judicious use of shadowed type, created by placing two layers of different tones of type on top of each other.

FITTING TYPE TO LAYOUT SHAPE

It is a good idea to place your text on the page so that it relates to the page shape. For example, if you only have four lines of copy on a page, you may want to set it in a thinner column and lead out the lines of type, so that it has an even border of white space around it, rather than setting the two lines on a long column width and creating four horizontal lines at the top of the page. Likewise, if you're working in a triangular or circular layout, shape the text to fit the respective shape, rather than having an awkward square block of text on the page. It's important to pay attention not only to the shape that you are creating with the text on the page, but to the white spaces that you are creating as well.

16-53. Large type, either a single letter or a few words, can provide a strong background and is usually legible behind simple images.

16-54. Unconventional shapes, such as a diagonal, and type on a slant can stand out in a 90° type environment.

16-52. In the example above, by KU student Susan M. Closi Reichert, the "i" explodes with activity and joyous spectacle to represent the concept of surprise. The "i" could be a cylinder of snakes bursting forth, or it could represent a surprise party.

Thousands have been killed. Don't support the massacre.

Don't buy ivory.

16-55. The large screened type above reinforces the message and gets to the point immediately. The large screened type is also very legible from a distance and encourages the reader to get further involved and read the smaller text.

If you want it

to be read

at a glance,

keep it simple

and direct.

The small, subordinate type

will only be read by those

who are very interested in the details.

16-56. Like the example above, you can use spacing, weight of font, and scale to establish type priority on the page and to call attention to it.

16-59. The example above uses a capital "L" as a grounding element. The large shape catches the viewer's attention because of its darkness, and because of the type reversed out of it. A large-scale single character can command a lot of attention in a layout because of its massive impact visually. Lighter fonts, however, such as a script, imply a lighter or more elegant message, as opposed to this serious, no-frills sans serif font.

Varying the leading

can create
rhythm on the page.

**The use of visual space
on the page insinuates
difference of opinion,
or direction, or
allows the reader time,
or represents separation of ideas.**

16-57. White space between sections of type can be used effectively by a designer to create a pause on the page as the reader tracks down the page to get to the next line of type.

We're hearing more

and **What are we teaching?**

more these days about cooperative

learning in the classroom, and

values-based education,

but **What are students learning?**

the truth is, test scores

of basic reading and math

skills continue to lower

each year, on average.

16-58. The layout above uses type reversed in bars to call attention to the main issues in the ad. Notice how the typeface in the bars contrasts with the type in the text, but does not overpower it.

This page is set in Souvenir Light 8.5/12.

RESTAURANTS

Marinda's Indian Cafe

Benny's Seafood Ship

The Granite Inn

Marino's Homemade Italian Food

Engine 49 Lunch Café

The Terraced Chef

Tiaria's Brain Foods & Juices

Bite Sized Delights Appetizer Bar

Thailand Emporium

Broadway Pizza & Wings

Torino's Fine Dining

The Elm Tree Inn

Chocolate Heaven Café

The Good Earth Vegetarian Restaurant

The Salsa Bar

Bob's Breakfast Buffet

The After Hours Club

The Wholistic Retreat

Ujugobani's Nigerian Cuisine

Over the Coals Grill Bar

Sweet Tooth's Desserts

Macrobiotic Service

Exclusively Crépes Café

The Home Cookin' Restaurant

Simply Sushi Dining

The Croaking Rooster Breakfast Diner

The Stew and Soup Shop

The Luscious Cheesecake Coffee Shop

The Zodiac New Age Cuisine Inn

Cappuccino to Go!

Essence of Bombay Indian Restaurant

Sweet Expectations Dessert Bar

This page is set in ITC Fenice Light 8.5/12.

PROJECT: CREATING A RESTAURANT IDENTITY

Utilize the examples for using type creatively in this chapter for inspiration to design a restaurant logo and menu for one of the following fictitious restaurants listed in the sidebar at left.

You may need to go to the library and determine the kinds of foods, spices, unique ingredients, recipes and flavors that are associated with the restaurant you are designing for. You will also need this information for putting together the menu entries, which often include a description of the food. It's a good idea to also research the particular country that the food is associated with, and get a sense of its textile design, fashion, crafts, typography, furniture design, lettering, painting and sculpture. Often this background research can be helpful in designing the logo.

Start with thumbnails of your design. Use each of the typographic techniques listed below to help you utilize type more creatively. Try to do a thumbnail sketch applying each technique to your restaurant logo. Later refine the half-sized sketches and then finally the full-scale logo. You should plan to design the signage for the restaurant in color, as well as the menu and a daily specials table tent; you may want to adapt the logo to a circular coaster. All of these designs should be consistent in terms of their use of typography and the application of the logo.

CREATIVE OPTIONS WITH TYPE

Contrast the styles (Roman vs. italic) of the fonts in the different words that make up the name of the restaurant.

- Contrast the weight (light vs. bold) of the fonts in the different words.
- Contrast the structure (script vs. serif vs. sans serif) of the fonts in the different words.
- Contrast the widths (extended vs. condensed) of the fonts in the different words.
- Contrast the spacing (letter-spaced out vs. kerned with ligatures) of the fonts in the different words.
- Contrast the point size of the type in different words.
- Try the reversal of characters or words.
- Vary the leading or spacing of letters to create rhythm.
- Incorporate rules, directionals, dingbats, decorative underlines, and flourishes.
- Replace a letter with an image.
- Contrast fonts from different time periods.
- Place type vertically or on a diagonal.
- Design a circular or triangular logo.
- Use screened-type elements.
- Use type to create a shape, or use characters in a word to create an image, without regard for readability.
- Use brush-stroke hand-lettering for a letter, word, a calligraphic image, or an abstract calligraphic element.
- Cut the letters of a word out of a texture.

- Put a small visual into the counters of letters, balance the visual on horizontals or hang a visual from crossbars.
- Abstract a single letter or all of the letters of a word.
- Hand-render the type in an elegant or a funky style.
- Base the design around one large letter in one of the words.
- Use the type to create a visual.
- Use engraved or inline type.
- Break from the traditional rectangular layout shape, and create a logo that is irregular in shape.
- Base the logo design on the lettering of the culture.
- Incorporate a textural element from the culture.
- Use colors from the flag of the country.
- Use art or craft images recognized from the country.

When you've done a number of thumbnails, it's a good idea to try to mix and match some of your ideas further to generate additional ideas. Also, it can be helpful to try entirely new directions based on your research as well.

OBJECTIVES

- To reinforce information on using type creatively from the text.
- To apply the innovative type in a hands-on process.
- To experience how you can be more inventive with type by going through the exercises in this chapter.
- To consider type as an art medium that can be experimented with.
- To appreciate the associations of fonts from different eras and how these fonts affect a logo design.
- To encourage you to understand type as an interpretive medium.
- To introduce you to the concept of organizing information using typeface distinction.
- To familiarize you with the hierarchy of typographic information.
- To reinforce your sense of kerning and ligatures.
- To develop a your ability to choose appropriate fonts for a project.
- To rekindle your ability to see type as an abstract design element.

16-61. Above is a logo, designed by KU student Erin Earley, for a Louisiana-based restaurant called Zydeco. Below are the fronts of the menus for different seasons of the year, and the interiors of the menus with type and images integrated.

16-62. This shows the exterior of the 3-fold menus for the Zydeco Café Bistro; the logo is shown above.

16-63. When opened, the Zydeco Café menus feature type interspersed with images.

16-64. In this restaurant logo, by KU student J. Daniel Kilgore, the letters were altered to create a delicate trumpet-flower shape.

16-65. This restaurant logo utilizes type to create a classic feel integrating a variety of different fonts.

16-66. This is the menu design for the Keswick Café logo above.

This page is set in ITC Fenice Light 8.5/12.

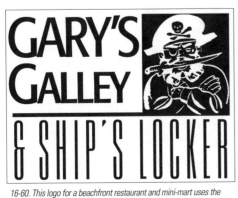

16-60. This logo for a beachfront restaurant and mini-mart uses the pirate motif to connect it to its environment.

Using Type Creatively-Review

16 *Using Type*
Creatively

1. What are three ways that you can vary the structure of fonts for contrast? _____

2. How can leading be used creatively on the page? _____

3. How does the leading of a selection of type affect readability? _____

_____

4. How should the nature of the font affect leading decisions? _____

_____

5. What do you have to be aware of when reversing type? _____

6. How can type be used to make a texture? _____

7. How can type be sensitive to the layout space that it is placed into? _____

8. How can you use rules creatively or effectively in design? _____

9. Name three uses of dingbats that are untraditional. _____

10. How can type be made to look spontaneous on the page? _____

11. Name two ways to use white space effectively in type design. _____

12. When you're contrasting the size of type, what should you be aware of? _____

13. Name three ways to use screened elements of type innovatively. _____

14. Below, draw three examples of active type.

15. Below, draw three examples of expressive type.

16. How can you integrate the type into the image and vice versa? Draw examples below.

17. How can texture be used in type? _____

18. What should you be aware of when shadowing type? _____

19. What is strike-through used for in type? _____

20. How should engraved fonts be handled? _____

Type in Black, White & Gray

INTRODUCTION

In this chapter we discuss the relationship between black, white, and gray in type, and considerations of readability when type is screened at less than 100% black. There are examples of black, white and screened type against a variety of background screens throughout this chapter for you to refer to. We will consider some of the fundamentals of working with type in tints of black in a piece. We will also review some basics of color theory and color associations and how these are affected by the viewer's cultural experience.

BLACK, WHITE AND GRAY

Black and white are complements of one another. When you mix pigments, white is added to black to create dark gray, and black is added to white to create light grays. When you work in printing, which is different from mixing paint on a palette, the black is screened as a series of dots to create grays. The size of the dots and their closeness determine the density or darkness of the screen. 70% black screened dots will be larger than 20% black screened dots. This process of screening to create gray is usually done in increments of 10% in printing. When you realize this, you realize that there are ten ranges of gray to print your type in, and ten possible background colors; for a total of one hundred different possible combinations.

These combinations are shown as examples in this chapter. You will notice that when the percentage screen of the background is the same as the percentage screen of the type, you cannot see any type in the box, because the type blends into the background. Using just one ink color and a range of screened type and screened backgrounds, you can create a piece that gives a feeling of color—even though you work with just one ink.

CONTRAST OF TONE

The *contrast of tone* refers to the dark intensity of an object in relation to its background and the other elements on the page. The greatest contrast when you're working in black and white is 100% black on 100% white, or the reverse, 100% white on a field of 100% black. When you're working on a layout where the photo or image is 30% black, it is a good idea to choose your backgrounds carefully. 30% black would show up well against 100% black. It is important to understand that any image that is 40% black and under in intensity is best offset against black, and that values or tones greater than 60% black are best when treated against a white background. The 50% range is the toughest to make decisions on, and often

100% Black type against a White background.

90% Black type against a White background.

80% Black type against a White background.

70% Black type against a White background.

60% Black type against a White background.

50% Black type against a White background.

40% Black type against a White background.

30% Black type against a White background.

20% Black type against a White background.

10% Black type against a White background.

17-1. On a 100 percent white background, screened type needs to be at least 30 percent black to be readable. 10 percent type on a 10 percent background cannot be seen.

KEY CONCEPTS

Contrast of Tone

Warm & Cool Colors

Type Color & Readability

Color & Value

Complements

Split Complements

Analogous Colors

Monochromatic Colors

Simultaneous Contrast

Hue

Value

Saturation

Tints

Shades

Luminosity

Color Symbolism

Color Associations

Color & Status

Color Projections

Utilizing Warm Colors

Harmony of Color

Type in Boxes & Bars

This page is set in Matrix Book 8.5/12.

17 *Type in Black,*
    White & Gray

100% Black type against a 10% Black background.

90% Black type against a 10% Black background.

80% Black type against a 10% Black background.

70% Black type against a 10% Black background.

60% Black type against a 10% Black background.

50% Black type against a 10% Black background.

40% Black type against a 10% Black background.

30% Black type against a 10% Black background.

20% Black type against a 10% Black background.

100% White type against a 10% Black background.

17-2. On a 10 percent black background, screened type needs to be at least 30 percent black to assure readability.

This page is set in Matrix Book 8.5/12.

requires the most careful analysis. It is a good idea to consider using no more than a 20% black background for type or a product that is about 50% black. These principles are only guidelines; they are not set in stone.

WARM AND COOL COLORS

When you work in color, it is important to remember a few things. First, the warm colors are in the ranges of the reds, yellows and oranges. The cool colors are the blues and greens. If it helps you to remember this by thinking of the colors associated with water (for the cool colors) and the colors associated with fire (for the warm colors) then use that short rule of thumb. Violets, lavenders, tans and grays are tough to give a blanket category to because they can be either cool or warm.

Warm colors always *project,* or come forward, and cool colors always recede from the viewer's eye. This information should prove valuable for you when deciding on background colors. It is also important to remember the psychological impact of colors: pink always seems passive and good, blue seems to conjure up images of calmness and cleanness, yellow can indicate references to the freshness of morning light, and yellow-green often has sickness associated with it. Sometimes you must not only consider the choice of the background color, but the mental impact that the color has on the viewer and the combination with other colors in the piece.

TYPE COLOR AND READABILITY

The darkness of type also plays a role in the readability of the copy. Black type is by far the easiest color copy to read, especially when it's on a light-colored stock. However, stark white paper, while it may be very good for halftones, can be harsh to the eye, depending on the lighting. A coated, bright white paper may produce a glare in the reader's eyes when read under normal office lighting due to the shiny surface and reflective quality of the coating on the paper. Type on a highly coated white paper can be difficult for people with bifocals to read because there is often a glare from the glossy coating when viewed under indoor lighting.

A good rule of thumb to consider is that the intensity of the type to the background should be at least 50% different in value from each other, so that type the equivalent screen of 20% black should be printed ideally on a tone equivalent to 100% black, but never on a screen lighter than 70% black when the point size is small and readability is an issue.

Likewise, type that has a tonal range equivalent to 50% black will work equally effectively against both a pure black or a pure white background. The choice of which is better is up to the designer's eye, the colors, the font selected and the overall message involved.

COLOR AND VALUE

Some colors defy this general rule, though. Red and black as a color combination can be very tricky. Red type does not read well against a black background, and black type does not read well against a red background although the tones of these colors appear different when looked at separately. Because their values are so close, they are hard to discern from each other when used together. The *value,* or *light-reflective qualities,* of both colors is very dark. The same complication and lack of readability applies to yellow and white. Both are light colors, but when they surround each other they tend to flow from one to the other. Yellow type on a white background is as illegible as white type on a yellow background. Because of their value closeness, these two colors have poor readability when used for type. These color combinations (white on yellow, and red on black) should be avoided, particularly in small type when the readability of the text is an issue. The type will be a texture; it will not be readable.

VIBRATING COMPLEMENTARY COLORS

Certain hot or fluorescent colors can be overwhelmingly bright to the eye, causing the viewer to look away and get an after-image when blinking, similar to the after-image of neon lights. Color combinations of contrasting colors can cause the type to vibrate on the surface, also reducing readability. This principle was used extensively in the '60's when Op or Optical Art was in vogue. All of the work was literally "hard" to look at, causing tiredness in the eye because the nerves were forced to fire so rapidly. Designers were trying to recreate on a limited scale the effects of psychedelic drugs through the vibrating complementary colors that they placed together. Needless to say, this vibration effect did not last too long in popularity and would not be considered the ideal treatment for a message that a client is trying to disseminate to the public (depending on who the client is). Complementary colors of type against background should be used only when the type is extremely large and simple, and when it enhances the concept of the words of the type. Of course, you could find just the right application for vibrating colors in a piece, and if so, have fun with them.

FUNDAMENTALS OF COLOR

Color is broken down into categories based on mixing colors. The *primary colors*—red, yellow and blue—are those that are combined with an additive color to make all of the other colors. *Secondary colors*—orange, green, and purple—are created by mixing two of the primaries. *Tertiary colors*—red-orange, yellow-orange, red violet, blue-violet, yellow green, and blue-green—are combined by mixing a primary and a secondary color. This process of mixing colors to broaden the color wheel can go on indefinitely. Although the human eye can distinguish between roughly 16 million colors, paint and ink companies can use computers to generate a wider range than those that humans are capable of differentiating. Some color theorists believe that as humans evolve, our eyes develop the ability to distinguish subtler nuances of color.

COLOR PROPERTIES

Color has three properties: hue, value and saturation. The *hue* is the name by which we identify color—the purest pigment of the color, the true chroma without black or white added. Examples of hues would be the pure pigment of red, green, magenta, or orange.

The *value* is the degree of lightness or darkness of a pure hue, the tendency of the hue to reflect or absorb light. Certain hues absorb more light and are darker in their pure state, such as purple. Other pure hues are very light in their pure state, such as yellow, which is very luminous and has a tendency to reflect light and, therefore, appears lighter than purple.

The *saturation* is the measure of color's purity, brightness of the pure pigment. This refers to the intensity of the pigment in the medium in a

---

100% Black type against a 20% Black background.

90% Black type against a 20% Black background.

80% Black type against a 20% Black background.

70% Black type against a 20% Black background.

60% Black type against a 20% Black background.

50% Black type against a 20% Black background.

40% Black type against a 20% Black background.

30% Black type against a 20% Black background.

10% Black type against a 20% Black background.

100% White type against a 20% Black background.

17-3. In these examples with a 20% black background, the reversed type is legible, and the 40% black type can be discerned. 20% type on a 20% black background cannot be seen.

This page is set in Matrix Book 8.5/12.

**100% Black type against a
30% Black background.**

**90% Black type against a
30% Black background.**

**80% Black type against a
30% Black background.**

**70% Black type against a
30% Black background.**

**60% Black type against a
30% Black background.**

**50% Black type against a
30% Black background.**

**40% Black type against a
30% Black background.**

**20% Black type against a
30% Black background.**

**10% Black type against a
30% Black background.**

**100% White type against a
30% Black background.**

17-4. In this series with a 30% black background, the screened type
is most legible at 60%, or reversed to white. 30 % type on a 30%
black background cannot be seen.

painting model. There are two ways of reducing intensity. You can either mix the pure pigment with gray of the same value, or mix the pure pigment with its complement, which creates a grayed-down tone of the color.

Tints and shades are when the pure pigment is mixed with either white or black. A *tint* is the pure hue of a color plus white, which makes it lighter than the pure hue. (In printing, tints are created as percentage screens from 10 to 100% of the original ink color). A *shade* is the pure hue of a color plus black, which makes it darker than the pure hue. (In printing, shades are created by the original ink color overprinted with a percentage screen from 10% to 90% of black).

COLOR-WHEEL COMBINATIONS

The *color wheel* is an organized diagram that places colors in relation to their properties of mixing. It is based on equal placement of primary, secondary and tertiary colors. Below are some principles of the relationships between colors on the color wheel.

Complements are colors that are directly opposite each other on the color wheel, such as green and red, blue and orange, and purple and yellow. Complements are often bold and jarring when juxtaposed; they appear to vibrate and often tire the eyes of the viewer.

Split complements are one or both of the hues on either side of its direct complement across the color wheel. Split complements create contrast without tiring the eyes as much as direct complements do. Examples of split complements are purple and yellow-orange or yellow-green; and blue and red-orange or yellow-orange.

Analogous colors are colors that are next to each other on the color wheel. Because these colors are close in their hue range, they often produce a soothing, restful quality. Examples would be yellow-orange, yellow, and yellow-green; or green, blue-green and blue. In printing, you can select two colors, such as green and blue, and use screen combinations to create a range of blue-greens.

Monochromatic colors are the pure hue of the color and its tints and shades. This would be similar in printing with two colors—for example, magenta and black—and utilizing all of the screen percentages of the pure magenta to create the tints, as well as all of the screen combinations of percentages of the magenta and black combined to create the shades.

Simultaneous contrast refers to the fact that the appearance of a color is affected by the colors that surround it; color is relative to the colors that butt up against it. Our eyes automatically adjust the intensity of a color depending upon its environment. For example, red looks brighter against yellow than against black; this is because the luminosity of the yellow brightens the red placed against it. Conversely, the red

Type in Black, White & Gray 17

appears darker against black, which causes both to absorb more light.

Neutral colors are highly affected by their environment and the principle of simultaneous contrast. A neutral gray placed beside a color will appear to have a tinge of that color's complement because our eyes automatically search for it. A neutral gray placed against a black ground will appear lighter than that same neutral gray placed against a white ground because of the effect of the surrounding color on the gray.

Printed ink colors are affected by the color of the paper they are printed on because inks are transparent. The light they are viewed under can affect how colors appear, and the environment they are viewed in can affect the appearance of colors.

COLOR PLANNING IN DESIGN

Color can be used by a designer as an effective tool to emphasize or understate information. It can determine the legibility of type, and it can alter perceptions of images. It has been found that yellows, reds and oranges work the most effectively in point-of-purchase and packaging applications. This may be because these warm colors grab people's attention, are more noticed, and, therefore, are more effective in their response rate. Some marketers assume that because women are the primary family consumers, their preference in colors determines packaging decisions. People seem to be born with preferences in colors; some studies indicate that men generally like dark blues, browns and blacks, and that women prefer reds and pinks. Ads or products that are determined for one audience or another may capitalize on this in their planning. For toddlers, primary colors are generally the rule, and for adolescent youths, harsh, bright neon colors may be the best choice because the intensity and visual excitement of these colors catch the adolescent attention.

Even with neutral colors, it is important to remember that grays and tans have warm and cool tendencies. When a color is too cool, it is depressing and recedes from the viewer; it may feel sterile or metallic. When a neutral tone is too warm, it is stimulating and may call more attention to itself than planned. When you work with neutrals, it is important to pay attention to the warmth or coolness of the color. Some studies have shown that certain warm colors seem to make prison inmates more complacent and less aggressive. Some psychologists believe that the colors we surround ourselves with in our homes, in our clothes, in our foods, and our offices affect our moods and outlook in general.

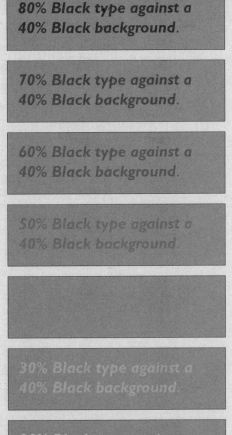

17-5. In these examples with a 40% black background, the black type is legible, and the reversed type is clear. Type on same percent background disappears.

This page is set in Walbaum Book 8.5/12.

17 *Type in Black, White & Gray*

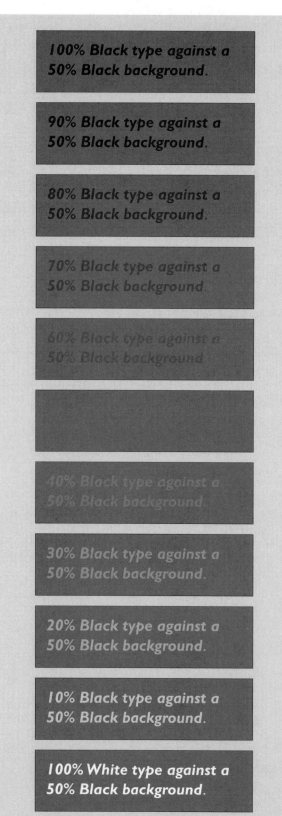

100% Black type against a 50% Black background.

90% Black type against a 50% Black background.

80% Black type against a 50% Black background.

70% Black type against a 50% Black background.

60% Black type against a 50% Black background.

40% Black type against a 50% Black background.

30% Black type against a 50% Black background.

20% Black type against a 50% Black background.

10% Black type against a 50% Black background.

100% White type against a 50% Black background.

17-6. With a 50% black background, the 100% white type should be equally legible. Type on same percent background disappears.

COLOR SYMBOLISM THROUGHOUT TIME

Colors not only carry moods, they also carry symbolism. This symbolism may vary in different cultures, so that a color may actually be "read" differently in various countries of the world. A single color may say opposite things. Yellow, for example, is a sacred color in Asia and yet in the Western tradition, when it is close to gold in tone, it can symbolize treachery and a lack of courage.

In contrast, in Victorian America, yellow was considered the color of elegance and sophistication, associations that it has since lost. Yellow does radiate a sense of light, brightness, and sunniness in interiors, but it is not considered the color of elegance in this century.

Trends in colors determine which colors will be popular, which will be used in interior decorating, and which will be commonly in vogue for a particular fashion season. If you doubt the truth of this, it takes only a moment to recall the avocado greens, the harvest golds, and the red-oranges that were common in all households painted in the 1960s and 70s. These colors in their heyday seemed very modern and fresh; their intensity represented a new era in interior design. Now they seem unlivable to those who look back at them or who are living with them. They seem so garish, dark and overstated when compared to the light tints currently in favor.

Blue was considered a very healing and soothing color by the ancient Egyptians who devised rooms of azure blue with pools of water where people went to be healed. Some color therapists today believe in the healing power of colors. They believe that even the colors of the food you eat can affect your physical health, mental disposition and energy level.

Red, according to color theorists, is considered a color that will give the wearer energy. Whether it is merely a matter of your eyes being stimulated by the red or the meridians of the body picking up on the energy of the color, no one knows for sure. Although color therapy seems somewhat farfetched today, it may be as fully accepted as acupuncture in the future. And, like acupuncture, it is a centuries-old tradition that has been handed down as a set of beliefs and practices, without any "hard" scientific data to support its effectiveness until thousands of years after its development and centuries of curative processes.

COLOR ASSOCIATIONS

Colors have the power to evoke specific emotional responses in the viewer. Some are personal, some are cultural, and some are universal. Warm colors seem to stimulate most people, and cool colors relax most people.

Type in Black,
White & Gray 17

**100% Black type against a
60% Black background.**

**90% Black type against a
60% Black background.**

80% Black type against a
60% Black background.

70% Black type against a
60% Black background.

50% Black type against a
60% Black background.

40% Black type against a
60% Black background.

30% Black type against a
60% Black background.

20% Black type against a
60% Black background.

10% Black type against a
60% Black background.

**100% White type against a
60% Black background.**

**100% Black type against a
70% Black background.**

**90% Black type against a
70% Black background.**

80% Black type against a
70% Black background.

60% Black type against a
70% Black background

50% Black type against a
70% Black background.

40% Black type against a
70% Black background.

30% Black type against a
70% Black background.

20% Black type against a
70% Black background.

10% Black type against a
70% Black background.

**100% White type against a
70% Black background.**

*17-7. On background percentages higher than 50%, as in this series of 60%
black backgrounds, the lighter type is more legible than the black type. Type
on same percent background disappears.*

*17-8. In these 70% black backgrounds, the screened type at 20%
seems very legible. Type on same percent background disappears.*

This page is set in
Gill Sans Bold Italic 8.5/12.

17 *Type in Black,*
White & Gray

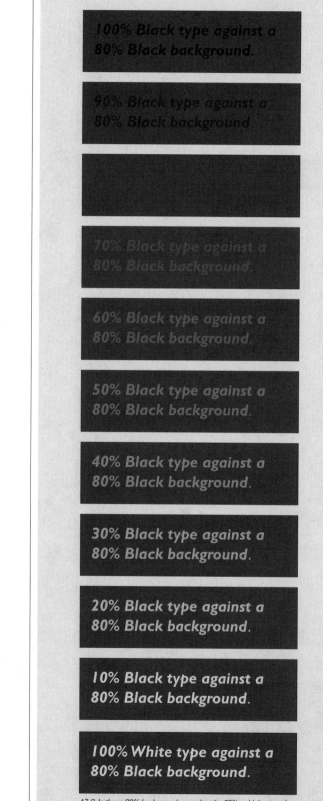

100% Black type against a
80% Black background.

90% Black type against a
80% Black background.

70% Black type against a
80% Black background.

60% Black type against a
80% Black background.

50% Black type against a
80% Black background.

40% Black type against a
80% Black background.

30% Black type against a
80% Black background.

20% Black type against a
80% Black background.

10% Black type against a
80% Black background.

100% White type against a
80% Black background.

*17-9. In these 80% background examples, the 60% or higher type is
very difficult to read. Type on same percent background disappears.*

Red is a color of multiple associations; it symbolizes love and extremely strong emotions. Red is considered the color of sexuality, aggression, passion, and violence. Interestingly enough, red is found in most national color combinations. Because it is also the color of blood, it represents war and suffering as well as military strength in some cultures. Throughout history, some believed that red raised the pulse of those around it and, therefore, aroused passion or violence in viewers.

Red is the color that has been shown to stimulate the brain waves of infants the most; it is thought that red can be good in the play environment of young children, but is undesirable in an environment where they are to rest. Also, when used in kitchens, some researchers think that red may stimulate people's eyes so much that they overeat, while others think that it can stimulate their digestion to work more rapidly. Red and purple have overtones of religious affiliation in some cultures because they have been the colors worn by religious clergy for for generations at ritual holidays.

Blue in darker values is associated with authority, conservative values and tradition. In middle values, such as royal blue, the color represents cleanliness, honesty, and has a cooling soothing effect, it has quiet positive associations. Even at full intensity blue retains calming quality.

Yellow is considered the color of warmth, good health, optimism and sunshine. In the U.S., bright yellow is the color of warning, and precaution because its luminous quality makes it stand out and call attention to itself even in dim light. With a bit of green added, yellow becomes distasteful and is associated with sickness.

Black and brown are considered staid, masculine colors of tradition. Gold and black, or silver and black are combinations that reflect a restrained elegance or style.

Green has been considered by many color theorists to be a very peaceful, restive color, one that puts the human spirit in a tranquil state. Dark green is supposed to help in re-centering one's spirit, which may be why retreats to nature are so cleansing to the soul. It is the primary color most prevalent in nature and, therefore, green pigment is extremely cheap. It is because of this economic factor that institutional green is green and not blue.

Due to its restive qualities, back in the early 1900s, a cool greenish blue was adopted for surgical garb in operating rooms instead of white. The coolness provided a contrast to the hot tones of the human flesh on which the doctors were working. This color offered relief to the staff's eyes against all the warm human tones and the stark white and metal operating-room furnishings.

It is important to consider your audience when selecting colors. It's also a good idea to get color reviews from local people at international offices to assure

100% Black type against a
90% Black background.

80% Black type against a
90% Black background.

70% Black type against a
90% Black background.

60% Black type against a
90% Black background.

50% Black type against a
90% Black background.

40% Black type against a
90% Black background.

30% Black type against a
90% Black background.

20% Black type against a
90% Black background.

10% Black type against a
90% Black background.

100% White type against a
90% Black background.

90% Black type against a
100% Black background.

80% Black type against a
100% Black background.

70% Black type against a
100% Black background.

60% Black type against a
100% Black background.

50% Black type against a
100% Black background.

40% Black type against a
100% Black background.

30% Black type against a
100% Black background.

20% Black type against a
100% Black background.

10% Black type against a
100% Black background.

100% White type against a
100% Black background.

17-10. In these 90% background examples, the 70% and
above type is very difficult to read. Type on same percent
background disappears.

17-11. In these 100% black backgrounds, the 80% and above type
seems to be quite easy to discern. Type on same percent background
disappears.

This page is set in Gill Sans
Bold Italic 8.5/12.

17 Type in Black, White & Gray

This type appears crammed left and right in the bar.

17-12. The type appears very tight in this skimpy little bar. There is not much space surrounding the type in this bar, the space is very tight around the type, and it appears to visually be cramped into the space.

This is too little type for a long bar.

17-13. The type appears to be swimming in this oversized bar. The space around the type visually swallows up the type within the bar. The black box becomes more visually prominent than the type itself, which may prevent the type from being read. To prevent this visual overwhelming of the type, you could use a taller font, a bolder font, a smaller box size, or a lighter box.

This type is too close to the top of this bar.

17-14. The type needs to be aligned and centered vertically in the box. It should also be centered left and right to appear comfortable in the space created by the box. Right now it appears to float in the box, or hug the upper edge of the box. The type seems oblivious of the space that it occupies and its relation to the edges of the box.

This type appears comfortable in the bar.

17-15. The type is aligned to center both vertically and side to side in the box. The type visually has even space above, below, and all around its perimeter; this includes the distance to the edge of ascenders and descenders.

This is type sized to fit in the bar.

17-16. The type appears to fit in the box more logically and comfortably.

SIMULTANEOUS   CONTRAST

17-17. The boxes above illustrate simultaneous contrast. Both gray boxes are the same screen percentage, 30%, but they appear different because of the background colors.

This page is set in Univers Condensed 47 8.5/12.

---

that the color in your packaging or corporate identity doesn't have negative overtones in another culture. In the global marketplace, colors need to be selected, researched and reviewed with care.

COLOR AND STATUS

Color could even symbolize one's financial status during certain historic periods. Color was used to signify financial status in earlier times; if a particular red, blue or purple pigment was rare in nature, it was more costly to procure for dying material, and the resulting material was likewise expensive to buy. Particularly dark saturated colors of material were expensive throughout history because the quantity of pigment required to attain the richness of the hue was very costly. The sumptuary laws throughout history limited the amount of expensive fabric that could be used for different articles of clothing, or could be worn by people of certain status. People were using the magnificently dyed cloth to show off their wealth, and these laws limited their excessive tendencies.

USING COLOR IN DESIGN

It can be helpful to think in terms of groups of colors when you design. You might consider the earth tones—the russets, tans, umbers, mustards, olive greens, gray-blues, and ambers—when designing a project. In contrast, *high-key colors* are those pure pigments saturated with a lot of intensity; they are the candy-coated yellows, greens, reds, oranges, and blues. These are pure, undiluted colors, perhaps reminiscent of jelly beans or some other candies. They are bright and attention-grabbing. In terms of pastels, they can be divided into two categories; the *spring pastels* (those that are very pure and pristine: lavender, light blue, pink, mint green, peach, and a soft yellow), and the *muted pastels* (those that appear to have a bit of gray added to the hue—mauves, tans, blue-grays, and light green-gray; these are very subtle, subdued, unscreaming colors). They can symbolize sophistication, taste and quality, or something that you don't want to overstate.

COLOR PROJECTIONS

Trend-watchers predict that during the twenty-first century, the jewel tones (saturated, deep, dark colors, such as emerald green, sapphire blue, and ruby red) that now predominate in fashion, interior design, and graphic design will be replaced by rich colors that are slightly off the perfect hue, such as eggplant, a deep olive green, rich mustard-ochre, and a maroonish red. Rich, thick colors will replace the mauves and teals of former years. Colors do have a life cycle, and the colors we are wearing today will date us all in another decade. It can sometimes be effective for a designer *to use* the date relationships of colors to their benefit when designing an historical piece. So that if you are doing a piece for the Victorian era when dark somber colors were fashionable, you might choose to design with deep maroons, golds, and pine greens in your palette. Or, by contrast, you may want to show a new look at the Victorian era by consciously deciding to design with neon colors.

UTILIZING WARM COLORS

As a rule of thumb, you may want to try to use a warm tone in every piece you design. It may be a russet color, a peach, a mustard, or a magenta. But it is important to realize how your placement of warm tones, even in a typographic layout, will affect the viewers' eye; they will notice the warmer tones first. Warm areas of an illustration may tend to be intense or prominent in the overall finished piece. This knowledge can be used to emphasize parts of a page or specific words in a headline skillfully.

Mostly, it is important to remember that warm colors project forward, and cool colors recede. Blacks, like grays, can have overtones of warmth or coolness based on the pigment and the ink base with which they are mixed. It is a good idea, because of the projection of warm colors, to consider using a warm color in your palette of colors. You may choose to use a warm black in a piece with a cool second color so that there is even more contrast between the two colors.

HARMONY OF COLOR

It is helpful at first to consider an overall color scheme for your piece, and then to make sure that the colors are harmonious with each other. With earth tones, it would be tans, russets, umbers, olive greens, mustards, browns, etc. One candy color amidst these earth tones will stand out like a sore thumb. You don't need to be overbearing with your use of color for attention. The attention-grabbing color should look out of place only when it is absolutely appropriate to the piece, and then it can be very effective. Don't be afraid to experiment with your work and take some chances with it; you can learn a great deal about color and its interactions.

TYPE IN BOXES AND BARS

When you place type in boxes and bars, there are a few rules of placement that you should be aware of. You want the type to be centered top and bottom in the bar. You want equal spacing above the type to the edge of the box, and below the type to the edge of the box. The type should appear comfortable within the bar. It should not look as though it is cramped in there, and it should not look as though it is floating within a huge bar. The type should be centered within the bar, rather than set flush left or flush right, which can have an awkward space of bar on one end or the other. The size of the type and the proportion of the width of the bar should be in relation to one another. You do not want the bar to appear skimpy around the type, nor too vast for a small line of type.

When you place type in a box (as is often done for callouts), you want to be sure that the text is inset from the edges of the box quite a bit. You also want to be sure that the type is paying attention to the box shape that it inhabits. The type should visually have an equal border of space on the top, on the bottom, and on both sides.

You should also pay attention to the text runaround, and how far the text is outset from the box. When you put a runaround feature on a box, and then place that box into text, depending on where you place it, you can wind up with an uneven white space above or below the box. This happens because of the interaction of the leading of the lines of text type and the text outset that you selected. Move the box small nudges to even out the white space, or change the runaround setting accordingly.

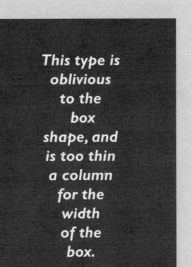

This type is
oblivious
to the
box
shape, and
is too thin
a column
for the
width
of the
box.

17-18. The type appears very uncomfortable in this box. It seems to be placed too tightly in the middle, with large amounts of space on the left and right that seem visually awkward.

This type hugs
the top of the box
too much.

17-19. The type appears very awkward in this box. It appears to hug the top of the box, with excessive space left at the bottom.

This type pays attention
to the box shape and
seems to fit comfortably
in the box without feel-
ing too crowded, or as if
it were simply floating.

17-20. The type appears comfortable in the box and reflects the space of the box. There's an even amount space around the type on all sides, which means that the placement of the type does not distract the reader from the message of the type.

This page is set in Univers Condensed 47 8.5/12.

17 *Type in Black,
White & Gray*

17-21. The serial relationship between this postcard and the next
one can be seen in the repeated
use of the fonts and color.

17-22. This postcard relies on a layered
pattern of type to create the visual.

17-23. Reversing the text type
on this postcard helps its
readability against the pattern
of type.

17-24. This postcard relies on a layered
pattern of type to create the visual. Type becomes a gray patterned background on this
postcard.

PROJECT: TYPOGRAPHIC POSTCARDS

This project requires that you design a series of four typographic postcards. You are limited to black, white and gray for
your design. You can plan the postcards so that they are related
in design, or so that when placed together, they form an overall design. The postcards will be sent out as reminders over a
series of four weeks.

These postcards will be used to promote an exhibit of poetry that is typographically designed. The sponsor of the show
is the NY Type Director's Club. You should think about placing
type on the page to create rhythm with the lines of type. You
can consider textures of type, screened type in the background,
etc. You can do a great deal with these by using the type creatively. Also, refer to the examples of black, white, and gray text
in this chapter to assist with creating postcards that take advantage of all of the screens possible.

The essential information that must be on the postcards is:
Poetry for the New Millennium

An Exhibit at the NY Type Director's Club
Opening December 1, 2015 from 6-8PM
50 Madison Avenue
For more information, call 212.278.2336

You can incorporate images into the postcards, but they
should be secondary to the type itself. You need to use type as
a design element in these cards. These postcards are meant
for designers, so they can be quite creative in layout. You can
use type experimentally. You can also come up with a type logo
for the name of the show that you design, and use it on each
card. The type should be carefully considered. Think about the
resonance of the fonts that you are planning to use. You can
create the letters by hand as well, if that's appropriate, or adjust them on the computer. Think about whether the font
should be elegant, simple, childlike, retro, new age, funky,
uptight, relaxed, etc.

OBJECTIVES

- To work in black, white and shades of gray.
- To refine your knowledge of computer-layout programs.
- To consider designs in a series, and those that work
  individually.
- To use type creatively as a visual element on the page.
- To encourage the exploration of unusual typographic so-
  lutions.
- To balance typographic readability with type inventiveness.
- To think of type as an interpretive, creative medium.
- To begin an awareness of foreground and background
  distinctions and readability considerations.

Type in Black, White & Gray-Review

1. What are some general principles regarding the tone of type, and readability? _____

_____

_____

_____

_____

_____

_____

_____

2. What should you be aware of when placing type in a box or a bar? _____

_____

_____

_____

_____

_____

_____

_____

_____

_____

This page is set in
Fenice Light 8.5/12.

17 *Type in Black,*
White & Gray

3. What is the hue of a color? _____

_____

4. What are split complements? _____

_____

5. What are analogous colors? _____

_____

6. What is simultaneous contrast as it applies to color? _____

_____

7. What is color harmony? _____

_____

8. When you use only black and shades of gray, what are some considerations of foreground and background tints to be aware of?

_____

_____

9. What are tints and shades? _____

_____

10. What are color associations, and how do they affect your decisions as a designer? _____

_____

11. What are some color combinations that are difficult to read? and why are they difficult? _____

_____

_____

Unique Considerations of Text Type

INTRODUCTION

In this chapter we consider the point size, spacing, leading, line length and alignment of type as it relates to text type. We also cover the details of typography, such as distinctions between prime marks and curly quotes, the single space after a period in text, as well as the placement of text copy in relation to bullets, parentheses and dashes.

Overall, the goal in text copy is to create an even tone of gray on the page, with the type set at a reasonable point size, with sufficient leading, well-planned tracking, a comfortable line length, and consistent spacing. The tone of gray created by type should not be interrupted by undesirable gaps of white, or characters placed too closely together creating an area of black. As a designer, you want the reader to feel that the text is readable and accessible. If you get the copy read by the reader, you have accomplished your goal.

You may want to begin to trace your own reading habits, whether in the newspaper, a magazine, instructions in a manual, or in this book. What do you tend to read first, and why? What grabs your attention on the page and gets you involved in the first place? Are you always drawn to color, or does texture attract you more? Is a large photo a lure for you? Do you read captions first? As you start to become conscious of your own reading/attention patterns, you may want to try to apply this knowledge to your own design.

LEADING CONSIDERATIONS FOR READING

Leading is connected to many other decisions you make about typesetting. The leading should be increased as you increase the line length. Studies of optimum readability show that our eyes can easily comprehend short line lengths because we can glimpse the entire line at one time. Short column widths, such as those of

18-1. This poster, one of a series by KU student Cheryl L. Long (Barends), uses lines of type as the web for the spiders. Text type can be active to enhance a layout.

18-2. In this poster, one of a series by KU student Cheryl L. Long (Barends), the type creates waves of water. Notice how the headline type and layout are consistent to make the series appear cohesive.

KEY CONCEPTS

Leading Considerations for Reading

Column Width & Reading

Line Length & Leading

Eye Tracking on Lines of Text

Using White Space Creatively

Leading as Rhythm on the Page

Hyphens

"Em" Dashes

"En" Dashes

Setting AM, PM

Italics in Text Copy

Subheads & Text

Paragraph Indents & Column Width

Hard & Soft Returns

Set Solid

Type Alignment

Rivers

Shaped Body Copy

Widows

Orphans

Bullets, Runovers & Dingbats

Parentheses & Key Commands

This page is set in Centennial Light 8.5/12.

18-3. This brochure, designed by KU student Erin Earley, separates the text copy into wide and thin columns depending on the content of the copy; quotes are set off in thinner columns.

Upper and lowercase words are easier TO READ THAN ALL UPPERCASE BECAUSE WITH ALL UPPERCASE, ALL OF THE WORDS ARE SHAPED THE SAME.

18-4. The ascenders and descenders in upper- and lowercase type make reading a lot faster due to the unique shapes of words.

Tightly leaded text is much harder to read than text that has sufficient leading.
The additional spaces of white between the lines of type prevent our eyes from tracking over the same line.

18-5. Frequently it's the amount of leading that helps readability, more so than the point size of the type.

newspaper columns, give the best results in reading ease because they require little horizontal eye tracking, and people rarely mistake which line they're on.

It is not only the column width that helps readability, but the number of characters that can fit on one line in a given font, at a given point size. Optimally, the ideal number of characters per line is at least thirty. This means that the smaller your line length, the smaller the point size of your type (or the more condensed your font) should be in order to get more characters on the line. And, conversely, a longer line length requires a slightly larger leading and slightly larger point size of type.

When reading, the eyes have to track horizontally across a line of text, then shift back to the left side of the column, skip down to the next line, and start tracking across again. If the designer insists on making the reader track across a line length of more than 18 picas, you should increase the leading to more than 3 points between lines. The reader's eyes tend to get confused between long lines of copy if the leading is not increased. The extra area of white *between* lines keeps the reader on the correct line. (This book is set in 8.5/12 with 3.5 points of leading between lines, which is, I hope, quite readable.)

INCREASED LEGIBILITY WITH UPPER- AND LOWERCASE

Studies have shown that upper- and lowercase characters are significantly easier to read than all caps or small caps in text copy. The lowercase letters with ascenders and descenders are more distinct in their forms than the uppercase characters. Because ascenders and descenders reach out from the x-height, we read faster by recognizing the shapes of entire words rather than being forced to read each individual character, which can slow down the reader. Because all capital letters line up along their baseline and cap line, the reader has to decode each individual character in order to read the word; there are no distinguishing parts. This process takes more time and is tedious on the eyes, hence the difficulty of all-caps copy.

CREATIVE USES OF LEADING/WHITE SPACE

In design, leading can be used for design effect, to make a selection of copy take up an entire page, or to separate different selections of type effectively from each other. By changing the leading and the font, the designer signals the reader that the two areas of type should be read separately.

Leading can be used to add dramatic impact to a piece, or to determine the "rhythm" of the type on the page. Depending on how you use the leading and line length, you can take the same selection and make a long, thin, narrow column of type with tremendous leading between the lines. Or you can set the text with very little leading in a shape that is a square. Or using small caps, you can set the text in a longer line length and really lead out the lines and stretch the letters across the entire page by opening up the tracking of the text type. Using a bold face, you can set the selection to a 2" wide column width, and have the selection leaded out to fill the page vertically. When leading is used creatively, it can enliven a page and spruce up its typographic rhythm.

Leading can insinuate the passage of time or a pause to the reader or it can make type feel as though it is crowded in the corner. The white space that is created by the use of open leading is very important in page design. It can give a sense of airy lightness, or a vast expanse between lines. White space on the page can balance a few asymmetrically placed lines of type.

REFINEMENTS IN TEXT COPY: SINGLE SPACES AFTER PERIODS

In text type, it is important to realize that there is only one space after a period. The two-space habit after a period can be tough for many typists to break. The reason for the double space is that in typewriter fonts (or mono-spaced fonts), all of the characters are allotted the same width of space, whether it's an "m," an "i," or a period. The two spaces after a period calls attention to the punctuation mark at the end of each sentence and creates a visual pause. In digital typesetting, the fonts are variably spaced, meaning each letter is encoded with its own set space that is different based on the width of the character. Especially when tracked negatively, the type can have a very tight fit. The punctuation is also designed to be slightly larger so that it is easily recognizable at small point sizes. Therefore, one space after a period has been the standard in typeset copy for some time; two spaces creates an awkward visual white space that interrupts the smooth, even gray of the text on the page.

You can utilize the "Find/Change" option in many layout programs to find all of the double spaces in manuscript copy and change them at once to single spaces. It's also a good idea to show the invisibles on the screen when working in a layout program. Spaces are represented by small dots between words; this way you can check that there are no double spaces in your text.

HYPHENS, SHORT DASHES AND LONG DASHES

A few other details in setting text copy involve using hyphens, short dashes and long dashes correctly. Hyphens are used when the syllables of a word break over two lines, or when two words, an adjective and a verb modify a noun, as an adjective, for example in "the long-awaited trial." Hyphens are the shortest and are obtainable from the hyphen or dash key on the keyboard.

Double spaces were used to create a visual pause after periods when all typewriter fonts were mono-spaced. In digital variable-spaced fonts, only one space is needed after a period in text.

18-6. One space after a period is the rule in computer copy.

Hyphens are used in copy when the syllables of a word break over two lines of text.

18-7. To get a hyphen in text, use the hyphen key on the keyboard.

Short dashes–"en" dashes–are used in copy to indicate a lapse of time or the word "to" in text.

18-8. To get a short dash, or an "en" dash, in text, use the option hyphen on the keyboard.

This page is set in
Futura Light 8.5/12.

18 **Unique Considerations of Text Type**

Long dashes—"em" dashes—are used in copy to indicate a sudden change of direction in text; "em" dashes—are also used to credit authors.

18-9. To get an "em" dash in text, hit option, shift, hyphen.

WHEN USING (PARENTHESES), – "EN" OR — "EM" DASHES, OR • BULLETS IN ALL CAPS or NUMERALS, YOU HAVE TO BASELINE-SHIFT THEM UP. These marks are designed so that they center on the lowercase x-height. The parentheses are designed so that they take into account lowercase descenders: (212) 622-6222.

18-10. Bullets, dashes and parentheses need to be shifted up in all-cap copy.

Prime marks, " and ', are used to indicate feet and inches. Curly quotes and apostrophes " such as " and ' ' are used to indicate speaking and contractions.

18-11. Curly quotes differ from prime marks in that they are angled and rounded. Avoid the use of prime marks for apostrophes, especially in headlines, where they stand out like a sore thumb!

AM and PM should always be set as small caps.

18-12. The example above shows the correct setting of AM and PM.

An ellipsis … (option + ;) is not the same as three periods with spaces. . .

18-13 The example above shows that an ellipsis takes up less space than three periods.

Short dashes, or *"en" dashes*, are used in copy or phrases to replace the word "to" in the copy, as in "from Feb. 1–Feb. 6." The en dash replaces the word "to" in this example.

Long dashes, or *"em" dashes*, are used in copy (not two hyphens!) to indicate a dramatic shift in the content of the text—as in a shift to a new topic. They are also used to attribute a quote to an author or speaker. All three use different key commands (see the table at end of this chapter for reference). When using hyphens or dashes in all-cap copy, it is necessary to baseline-shift them up because they are designed to center on the middle of the x-height of the font, and will look too low in all-caps copy.

Setting AM and PM in Small Caps in Text

It is considered correct to set AM and PM in small caps for most uses. This is the correct format for them in all typeset copy, and prevents them from being perceived as part of a word which might happen if they were set in lowercase; uppercase calls too much attention to them in text and in relation to the size of the numerals and is distracting.

Prime Marks vs. Curly Quotes

Another detail in typeset copy as opposed to typewriter manuscripts is the difference between ' , ", or prime marks used to indicate feet and inches, and true curly quotes, " ", and apostrophes '. In some programs, you must memorize the key commands to get smart quotes; other programs have application-wide default settings that can be set to activate smart quotes. When importing text, use the "Find/Change" option to change prime marks to curly quotes. As a designer, it is imperative to recognize the difference between these two marks and to use them accordingly. The prime marks are used for feet and inch marks; the single curly quotes are used for apostrophes, or quotes within a quote. Double curly quotes are correctly used to indicate words that someone is speaking. Be alert in copy not to switch these marks, or you will appear ignorant of typographic fundamentals.

The Ellipsis … vs. Three Periods with Spaces . . .

When it comes to punctuation, another difference between manuscripts and typeset copy is the presence of the ellipsis (…) that can be typed with a key command rather than using three periods with spaces between them (. . .). You'll notice that in the ellipsis, the periods are much closer together; this is the correct format for text. If you use the spaced-out periods, you'll create a gaping white hole in the text that will be noticeable and distracting, ultimately slowing down the reader. It is important to remember these details of typesetting so that your work won't be picked apart by design professionals.

Tips on Using Bullets Correctly

If you are using bullets in your text, it is important to make sure that the bullets are not oversized (if so, reduce the point size of the bullets and baseline-shift them up into place). Also pay attention to the *runovers*, or secondary lines of text under the bullet; the runovers should line up flush left with the first line of text—*not the bullet*. (Use command + \ at the beginning of the first line of the bullet copy to get the text to automatically align and wrap underneath.) The bullets should sort of hang to the left of the column of type. You may want to kern the space after the bullet to reduce the visual white space. It is a good shortcut to set up one bullet and kerned space as you want, and then copy and paste this into place for the other bullets. Also, it is a good idea to put extra leading between items in a bulleted list, so that each item is separated from the others. Lastly, bullets, parentheses, and dashes must all be shifted up in all-caps copy because they're designed to center on x-height, and look too low in all-caps copy.

SUBHEADS SPACING IN TEXT AND PARAGRAPH INDENTS

Take care to pay attention to spacing in subheads. Make sure that there is space before and not after the subhead (as throughout this book). This is so that the subhead is clearly linked to the paragraph it refers to. Space before *and* after a subhead creates a solo subhead wandering in space between text copy, and it appears ambiguous. Group subheads close to the text copy that they logically relate to; don't let them confuse the reader.

In text copy, correct paragraph indents require that you learn to use the tab settings in the layout program you're using. The width of the paragraph indent should be relative to the column width of the paragraph. Therefore, a wide paragraph indent should be reserved for wider column widths, and short indents are used with thinner column widths. If you don't follow this principle, you wind up with large gaps of white at the beginning of each paragraph, followed by a few words on the first line. This reads poorly and is awkward.

It's also common to use a line of space between paragraphs. When using this formatting style in text, it is not necessary to indent the first line as well. Both indenting and skipping a line are redundant; using one *or* the other is enough to indicate the paragraph break in text copy.

HARD AND SOFT RETURNS

It is wise to master the difference between *hard* and *soft returns* or *shift returns*. In the hard return, the computer assumes that you want to start a new paragraph; it snakes body copy back and forth across the column. But a hard return means to start a new paragraph; the first line after a hard return will automatically indent. The soft return is used when you want to move a word or syllable to the next line, but *do not* want the line to indent. The soft return can be used to eliminate hyphens at the end of lines; simply hit a shift return before the hyphenated word, and it will flow down to the right margin without an indent.

Unique
Considerations
of Text Type 18

• Bullets (option 8) are often designed to be too large for the point size of the type. (This text is not aligned correctly under the bullet.)

• Reduce the point size of the bullet, baseline-shift it up into place, then copy and paste it into other places. (You often have to kern the space after a bullet in most text faces.)

• Also, be sure to pay attention to the lines of text under the bullets. They should align left with the first line of text, *not* with the bullet. Use the command \ key command before your text to align text F/L easily.

• You may also want to add an extra line of space between bulleted items.

18-14. The example above shows the correct format for runovers: flush with the type, not the bullet.

▬ Paragraph indents should be a width that relates to the width of the column. Longer column widths should have wider paragraph indents to appear balanced.

18-15. Pay attention to paragraph indents when setting text type; they should be in proportion to the column width.

▬ Paragraph indents should be a width that relates to the width of the column. Shorter column widths should have shorter indents.

18-16. If you set a wide paragraph indent on a short line length, the first line will look uncomfortably short and awkward.

Hard returns give a paragraph indent. Shift returns (soft returns) do not indent; they just move copy to the next line.

18-17. Understanding hard and soft returns is essential when working with text copy.

This page is set in
Futura Light 8.5/12.

For titles in copy, *Set Them in Italics*, rather than bold or under-lined.

18-18. Underlines and boldface are not used for emphasis in body copy; use italics.

THE LONGER YOUR LINE OF TEXT COPY, THE MORE IMPORTANT IT IS TO OPEN UP THE LEADING, TO MAKE IT EASIER ON THE READER'S EYES. THIS PREVENTS THEM FROM TRACKING OVER THE SAME LINE REPEAT EDLY, CAUSING EYE FATIGUE. It's also wise to set the text in caps and lowercase, which is easier on the eyes.

18-19. Long line lengths of text should be set in caps and small caps for ease of reading, and with sufficient leading between the lines.

CHANGING THE LEADING

OF A HEADLINE CALLS

ATTENTION TO IT

ON THE PAGE

BECAUSE IT SETS UP

A NEW RHYTHM.

18-20. Leading in headlines can be used to create rhythm on the page.

STRATEGIES FOR IMPROVING THE RAG IN FLUSH-LEFT COPY (THE GOAL IS LINE ENDINGS THAT ARE ROUGHLY THE SAME)

• Tighten the tracking a bit.

• Hyphenate a word to improve rag.

• Make the column slightly wider.

• Reduce the size of copy by .5 points.

• Change to a condensed font.

• Add words of copy to short lines.

18-21. Use the tips above when the ragged edge of your copy is uneven.

EMPHASIS IN TEXT COPY

In text copy, you do not underline words for emphasis. Instead, use italics to call attention to a word or a title of an article or book. Bold is rarely used for emphasis within copy but is sometimes used to introduce a term or phrase, followed by a definition. With the advent of desktop layout, designers have had to learn typographic details that had previously been the domain of typesetters. Some designers resent this additional responsibility, others pay typesetters to review their files and proof-read, and still others feel empowered by the control they have over the typographic details of a piece and have incorporated the new knowledge into their design. It is best to be apprised of these details as early as possible in your design career when you can adopt and embrace this information.

TEXT-TYPE ALIGNMENT & COLUMN WIDTH

Decisions about the placement of type in the column can affect readability as much as the line length and leading. There are four standard options to choose from when having your text typeset: Flush Left (F/L), Flush Right (F/R), Justified (F/L and F/R), and Centered. These options can make a difference in the appearance of your final type. Some studies show that *justified type,* or type that is even on both the left and right edge of the column, like the text throughout this book, can be more tedious to read because the clean, even right margin doesn't give the eye any clues as to which is the next line to track down onto. These studies argue that the ragged right edge of type set F/L helps readers know which line they are on more clearly because each line ending is a slightly different length.

It is important to realize that justified copy is created by adjusting the *word spaces* within the text. This means that word spaces are crunched together or spread out so that the edges of the column are perfectly even. The break from consistent word spacing can slow down the eyes as they track across the copy. This variable word spacing can cause *rivers,* or uneven vertical white spaces running through the text block. Unfocus your eyes, and squint at the justified text to check for rivers. The text block should ideally have a uniform gray texture on the page. Rivers in your justified copy are a sure sign of poor typesetting. They can be alleviated by hyphenating some words, or in some cases rewriting a few words for a better fit. Rivers should be avoided at all costs, and you may consider changing the setting to rag right if you can't seem to get rid of them. Adjusting the line length just slightly can also help to overcome some rivers in your justified text.

Clearly, the typeset format we are most accustomed to seeing is the flush-left, ragged-right version. This means that the text is *flushed,* or *lined up,* along the left column edge and uneven along the right edge (as in this paragraph). One of the advantages of ragged-right copy is that the word spacing is consistent and should help readability, as well as create a fine, even gray in the text area. A "good" ragged right edge should be subtle down the right column edge. If you have some very short lines, you may want to hyphenate a word on the line above so that the short line lengths won't stand out from the text. But you also want to limit the number of hyphenated words that appear at the ends of succeeding lines. Generally, it is not acceptable to have more than one hyphen in a row at the end of lines of copy. (Two or three hyphens in a row at line endings should be avoided.) Sometimes you have to rewrite to improve line endings; either adding a word or changing a word to a shorter or a longer synonym works.

Flush-right copy has many of the advantages that flush-left copy has but some are reversed. In the flush-right column (like this paragraph), the ragged-left margin is sometimes a little harder for the reader to follow, and can cause some retracking on the same line, which slows down reading.

Centered copy is the most time-consuming of the four options because you must indicate the line breaks to create a harmonious visual on the page, making sure that the phrasing of the selection makes sense. When you center body copy, it is a good idea to create line lengths that are dramatically different. You do not want line lengths for centered copy that are all approximately the same length (like in this setting), or there is no sense in centering the copy. Similar line lengths will appear as poor planning. You should consider determining the line breaks so that you have long and short lines interspersed. This way, the uneven shape of both the left and right edges

Beware of rivers in copy that is justified. They are formed when extended word spaces line up on top of each other. The rivers break up the even tone of gray that you are striving for to assure the best readability.

18-22. Rivers are distracting when reading body copy; the erratic rhythm of the type on the page is difficult because it forces the eyes to continually readjust.

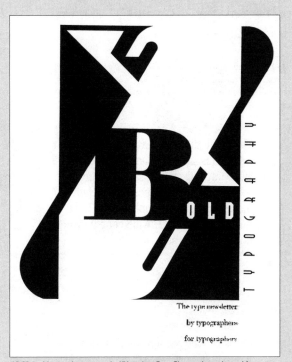

18-23. In this newsletter cover, by KU student Geno Simonetti, type is used for the visual element. Varying the leading of the text type at the bottom creates a contrasting texture to the other expanses of type elements.

In text copy, it's a good idea to omit hyphens at the end of lines of flush-left copy whenever possible. It's considered poor typography to have copy with more than one hyphen in a row at the end of subsequent lines.

18-24. More than one hyphen in a row at the end of lines is considered poor typography. Avoid hyphenations whenever possible.

This page is set in Avant Garde Book 8.5/12.

18 **Unique
Considerations
of Text Type**

These words are letterspaced
using positive tracking. Opening
the tracking in text can be difficult for readability. On the other
hand, sometimes the light type
calls attention to itself, which
can be desirable.

*18-25. In the letterspaced example above, notice that the spaces between words, as
well as the punctuation, are opened up. Sometimes, it's necessary to adjust the mechanical spacing to meet optical evenness of spacing; this usually holds true around the
thinner letters, such as "l" and "i," and the wider letters such as "w" and "m."*

This is the same copy as in the paragraph
below. It is set in the same font, with the
same tracking and the same leading. The
only difference is the point size relative to
the leading. This example is 11/12; the
one below is 9.5/12. Which one do you
find easier to read?

*18-26. This setting of text type in Garamond Condensed shows the
importance of leading in readability of body copy. This text is set in a large
point size with very little leading. The reader tracks across the lines easily.*

This is the same copy as in the paragraph above.
It is set in the same font, with the same tracking
and the same leading. The only difference is the
point size relative to the leading. This example is
9.5/12; the one above is 11/12. Which one do
you find easier to read?

*18-27. In this example, the point size of the text is considerably smaller
than the point size of the leading, creating channels of write space between the lines.*

This is the same copy as in the paragraph
above. One change is that it is set in the
font Berkeley Oldstyle Medium rather
than Garamond Condensed, with the
same tracking and the same leading. This
example is set in 9.5/12. Which font do
you find easier to read, and why?

*18-28. This copy, set in a different font, with a smaller x-height, should be
compared to the lower example above. Try to assess which sample is easier for
you to read, and why. How does the condensed face affect readability?*

becomes a design element
and has some character.
If you set similar length lines of copy centered, it
will look as though
you made a mistake,
or as though the equipment was flawed,
because the human eye cannot perceive
the subtle differences of lines
that are almost all the same length.

SETTING TEXT TYPE SOLID

Every font has a hairline of space built into the tops
and bottoms of characters so that even if you specify a setting of text type without any additional leading—which is called *set solid,* for example, 10/10 or
9/9, the ascenders and descenders will not touch
from one line to the next. (This paragraph is set solid,
and you can feel how difficult it is to read, and how
dense and cramped the type appears in the column.) The clearance is not great between lines, and
the lack of leading does make the text difficult to
read. But, sometimes set solid is the only option, especially when you have a great deal of type to fit
into a very limited space. Set solid is not advised for
long sequences of text, nor for setting detailed, technical information…it's so hard on the eyes, that people will not read the information—or will do so grudg-
ingly, like in this paragraph.

In order to get copy to fit into a predetermined
space, it is sometimes necessary to reduce the leading. A rule of thumb for leading is that it should be two
or three points higher than the point size of the type—
for instance, 9/11 or 9/12. (The text setting throughout this book has an additional 3.5 points of leading;
it's set in 8.5/12 copy.) Frequently it is the space *between* the lines of type, *not* the size of the letters
themselves, that improves the readability of the type.
For example, 9-point type on 12 points of leading may
actually appear *easier* to read on the page than 11-
point type set on 12 points of leading. The extra
white space gives the eye more room to move back
and forth on the page. Three points of leading in text
type is a good rule to strive for when specifying text
type, but you should experiment and find the setting
that feels comfortable to you depending on the
font, the line length, the tracking and the x-height of
the font.

SPACING TEXT TYPE/TRACKING

Just as spacing the lines of type on the page creatively can give unity and rhythm to the page layout, the letter-spacing out of words or letters can be
used creatively by a designer. In traditional typesetting, the spacing of characters in a font for text
setting is based on a unit system in most typesetting equipment. This system breaks each character
down into smaller equivalent units, and allots each

character a specific number of units or units plus fractions of units as the *set space* of the character.

The set space of a font can be adjusted overall for a more tightly fitted text type, or it can be opened up tremendously. In digital text typesetting, overall spacing is referred to as *tracking*. To review different trackings of text type, it's a good idea to print out one sample of text at a variety of tracking settings in the font and size you plan to use, and then to select the most comfortable tracking. When text is tracked at -5, it means that an even amount has been subtracted from the variable set space allotted for each character and each word space at the particular size requested. This means that the characters are brought together by fractions of an em space all throughout the text, evenly. This global tightening of letter spacing in body copy is referred to as tracking. Positive numbers in tracking open up the letter spacing of type and add consistent amounts of white space between letters and word spaces.

Tracking can be adjusted in layout programs, and body copy is usually tracked in negative numbers unless you are purposely letter spacing out the text. Increased tracking settings open up the spaces between letters and words.

Tracking can have serious effects on the design of a piece. First it can change the value of gray on the page that your text block appears: the closer together the characters are, the denser the appearance of the text on the page and the darker the tone of the text block. Tracking does, though, often improve the visual smoothness of the gray of the text on the page. It also helps to tighten up words, which can ultimately make them easier to read. Second, it is important to realize that tracking, when done throughout a long selection of text, will affect your character-per-pica count (CPP), which may affect how long the selection runs. Tightening the tracking gives the designer a very refined control over the letter and word spacing in text. This subtle adjustment can improve readability, reduce the number of typeset pages in long manuscripts like books, improve the regularity of the rag in flush-right body copy, and frequently improve the gray of the text on the page.

In some page-layout programs, the tracking options are simply no tracking, very tight, tight, normal, loose, and very loose. More and more computer-layout programs are enabling designers to refine the tracking of text through more accurate numeric typographic controls that are accessible

Shaped text boxes can be simple or complex; they can be created from angles or curves. Usually they will restrict the readability of the text a bit since all of the line lengths will keep changing and are irregular. In most cases, however, shaping text can be an effective design tool, and can create interest on a text heavy page or when photos are not possible.

18-29. When selecting the font for shaped text boxes, you should choose a simple, highly legible font.

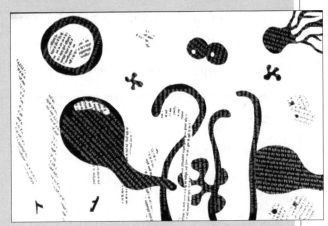

18-30. This whimsical use of shaped text type, by KU student Alison Burnside, uses type as a pattern rather than worrying about readability concerns.

As a designer, you can shape body copy so that it will fit into the shape that you have created for it. Sometimes this process is more successful than others. It's a good idea to keep the shape relatively simple, both for readability and for recognizability. You may want to justify type that's formed to a shape, so that the shape is more clear. Justifying helps to define both the left and right edges of the shaped copy. As always, with justified copy, beware of rivers, and change copy to get rid of them if possible.

18-31 When choosing text type for a shaped body copy, keep in mind that a condensed font can fit more characters on a very short line length.

18 *Unique
Considerations
of Text Type*

> ## A type widow is when the last line of a paragraph (usually a short line) is excessively short–that is, less than half the width of the column.

18-32. The example above shows a typographic widow; widows should be avoided in text.

STRATEGIES FOR REMOVING A WIDOW

- Tighten the tracking a bit.
- Make the column slightly wider.
- Make the column slightly narrower.
- Reduce the size of copy by .5 points.
- Change to a condensed font.
- Remove a few words of copy.

18-33. When faced with an undesirable widow in text, the principles above can be used to delete it.

> ## An orphan is when either the first or last lines of a paragraph are separated in a different column from the rest of the lines of the para- graph, all alone.

18-34. The example above shows a typographic orphan; orphans should be avoided in text.

to the user. It is still a good idea to set a paragraph in a variety of tracking settings and then to evaluate them on paper before deciding on the tracking setting for a long job.

AVOIDING WIDOWS AT THE END OF PARAGRAPHS

A *widow* is a typesetting term for a bad break at the end of a paragraph of type. A widow is the last line of a paragraph that is excessively short—that is, less than half the width of the column. This short line smacks of poor planning and creates an awkward rag on the right edge of the text type. It is much better to have new paragraphs at the top of columns, or a break that comes in a logical area of the text, such as after a comma or period. This is not always possible to do, but it is the *ideal*.

Widows are undesirable in text type, and they should be avoided. How do you avoid them? The first option would be to tighten up the tracking just a bit, which might make that short line bounce back into the prior line of type. Another is to reset the column width slightly wider, say one half pica more, which will change the line breaks and the number of lines. You could reduce the point size of your body copy by one half point or one tenth of a point to get the rid of the short line. Lastly, you could also change to a condensed version of the text type you are using, which would fit more characters on every line and allow the short line to bump back within the previous line. You could also rewrite the copy to fit better. When you apply these solutions, be prepared for new widows, orphans and hyphenations to crop up where you least expect them. Sometimes you have to choose between the lesser of two (or more) evils when setting body copy. "Kill the widow" means to get rid of the short last line by whatever means works the best!

AVOIDING ORPHANS IN COLUMNS AND OVER PAGE BREAKS

An orphan occurs when either the first or last line of a paragraph is separated in a different column from the rest of the lines of the paragraph. For example, the first line of a paragraph will be at the bottom of one column, and the rest of the paragraph will be at the top of the next column. This looks awkward in the column and reads poorly. If you must break a paragraph over columns, it is much better to do it so that at least three lines at the beginning of the paragraph or three lines at the end of the paragraph are together in the column. Anything less than three lines starts to call attention to itself and is considered an orphan.

The same tricks for removing a widow apply to removing an orphan, but sometimes you should apply them in reverse to get the first line of the paragraph to bounce into the following column. When trying to get the last line of a paragraph to stay at the bottom of a column, one option is to make the column just slightly longer in depth so that the line ends up at the bottom of the first column. If you want the line to bounce into the next column, make the column depth shorter, or increase the point size of the text by one half point to get the line to move into the next column. You could also decrease the column width by one half pica in order to reunite the orphan with the rest of the lines in the family paragraph.

The last, and most infrequently used, option when faced with widows and orphans is to...rewrite the copy, either shortening or extending a paragraph by a few words, or a phrase here or there to make the column of type end where you want it. Not many copy editors are fussy enough to consider doing this to make a designer's life easier, so don't count on it. Sometimes you will be blessed with a design-sensitized copy editor who will say, "How many characters do you need to lose?" and they'll call you back with their shorter version. With computers, you can type in the change and see that it works right before your eyes. Voila! And, if you're writing your own copy (as is often the case in school projects or nonprofit projects), you can add or subtract lines as you see fit to make the breaks in lines and columns work out. The beauty of the computer is that you can fool around with column width, adjusting it by little nudges to get the effect that you want for your line breaks and column breaks.

More and more computer-layout programs are enabling the user to set defaults for widow and orphan control. These can, however, be somewhat confusing when the program activates them. With these controls activated, you, the designer, keep opening a text block to allow a few more lines of copy to flow into the box at the end of a column, and the computer won't let you, because three lines won't fit at the bottom of that column, and it doesn't want to make an orphan for you to have to contend with; this can be frustrating!

ORNAMENTS: DINGBATS, FLOURISHES, FILLETS, AND FLEURONS

Ornaments are used in text copy in a variety of ways: they are used to separate areas of text; to replace paragraph breaks in copy; to signify the end of a story in a magazine or journal and to identify printers in colophons at the end of books. They have been created by type designers throughout all eras and are beautiful, quirky, and elegant depending on the taste and whim of the type designer.

Name	Symbol	Key Command
Hyphen	-	Dash on keyboard
"En" Dash	–	Option + Dash
"Em" Dash	—	Option + Shift + Dash
No Dot "i"	ı	Shift + Option + B
Bullet	•	Option + 8
Degree symbol	°	Option + Shift + 8
Prime Marks	",'	From Keyboard
Open Quotes	"	Option + [
Close Quotes	"	Option + Shift + [
Single Open Quote	'	Option +]
Single Close Quote	'	Option + Shift +]
Cents Symbol	¢	Option + 4
Trademark Symbol	™	Option + 2
Copyright Symbol	©	Option + g
Registered Symbol	®	Option + r
Pound Symbol	£	Option + 3
Yen Symbol	¥	Option + Y
Ellipsis	…	Option + ;
Black Box	■	n in Zapf Dingbats
Hanging Leaf	❦	Option + 7 in Zapf Ding.
Side Leaf	☙	Option + s in Zapf Ding.
Diamond	◆	u in Zapf Dingbats
Quartered Diamond	❖	v in Zapf Dingbats
Aligning type under bullet		Command + \ (located above the return key).

18-35. This chart features many of the common symbols and dingbats used in design and their corresponding key combinations, which are universal in most fonts; the examples above are shown in Times Roman or Zapf Dingbats.

This page is set in
Belwe Light8.5/12.

18 *Unique Considerations of Text Type*

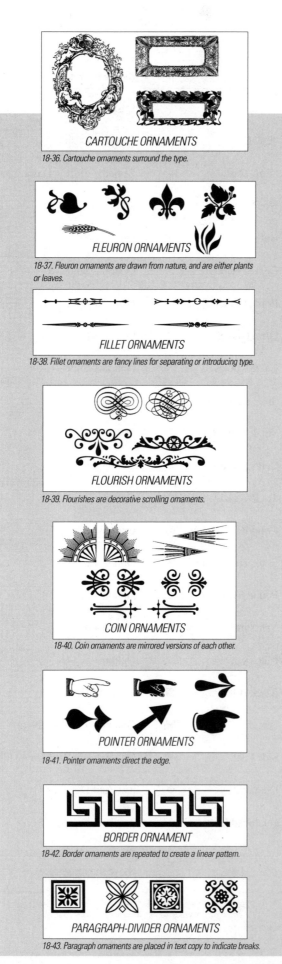

CARTOUCHE ORNAMENTS

18-36. Cartouche ornaments surround the type.

FLEURON ORNAMENTS

18-37. Fleuron ornaments are drawn from nature, and are either plants or leaves.

FILLET ORNAMENTS

18-38. Fillet ornaments are fancy lines for separating or introducing type.

FLOURISH ORNAMENTS

18-39. Flourishes are decorative scrolling ornaments.

COIN ORNAMENTS

18-40. Coin ornaments are mirrored versions of each other.

POINTER ORNAMENTS

18-41. Pointer ornaments direct the edge.

BORDER ORNAMENT

18-42. Border ornaments are repeated to create a linear pattern.

PARAGRAPH-DIVIDER ORNAMENTS

18-43. Paragraph ornaments are placed in text copy to indicate breaks.

They fall into a few different categories if you want to identify them correctly.

The cartouche ornament is a rectangular or oblong element; it's usually a frame with space inside for a word or a title. Sometimes these are simply created out of repeated border elements and are, thus, adjustable in length.

The fleuron ornament is based on a plant or leaf; it is designed from organic elements in nature. These ornaments may include a linear element in their design. They are often used in colophons, identifying the printer and fonts at the end of a book, and as end of story ornaments.

Fillets are decorative lines; they may include a scroll in the center or multiple lines, or angled lines. These decorative lines are often used in historic title pages of books.

A flourish is quite handsome; it is an elegant, curving scroll that usually is placed to divide two sections of copy. Sometimes a flourish is placed at the end of copy, as a space filler, or on the title page of a book.

The coin ornaments are usually triangular in shape, and are mirror images of each other; there is a left and a right component. Coin ornaments are used most frequently in posters and in packaging, especially in a symmetric design.

A pointer is somewhat self-explanatory; it is a hand or an arrow used to direct the attention of the reader. Pointers can be simple, architectural, whimsical or practical depending on the application, and they direct the eye to information.

A border is a pattern that can be repeated to create a line.

A paragraph dingbat indicates the end of a paragraph in place of a return. It is usually a box shape, so that it does not stand out from the text too much; it can also be used only at the end of a story. Most often end-of-story ornaments are characters of a dingbat typeface that can be sized up or down in points just like type, and kerned left or right.

PROJECT: PSA ONE-COLOR, TYPOGRAPHIC-AD SERIES

This is a series of three newspaper ads. Typographic ads rely on the creativity of the message. Good copy writing is a must. The message must be clear, with no ambiguities. The concept must be presented through the creative use of type.

The font must live up to the intent of the ad. Type can be used to its extremes; you can set up contrast between the sizes and weights of the type on the page. There are numerous options to visualize the concept with type:

- You can vary the tonal colors of the type.
- You can make the type interpret the message visually.
- You can exaggerate the type in the space.
- You can contrast the type with the intent of the verbal message.
- You can repeat the message numerous times.
- You can mix typefaces to emphasize the message.

TOPICS

- Multiple Sclerosis • Cancer • Alzheimer's
- Parkinson's • Glaucoma • AIDS
- Hodgkin's • Cystic Fibrosis • Diabetes

Two ads will be single-page ads; the other will be a double-page spread. The intent is to raise public awareness of the illness, and to try to get people to donate to its research foundation. Your audience comes from all ages and financial backgrounds.

The three headlines should be related; they comprise a series. Viewers should recognize the continuity of the message, and the type treatment. They should appear as a set so they will be connected when seen separately.

The most difficult part of a type ad is the brainstorming that's necessary beforehand. Read articles on the disease, its progress, its symptoms, and its complications in its advanced stages. Utilize your library and its holdings. The more you know about a topic, the more resources you have to be creative with in the design.

Come up with sixty ideas for headlines, twenty for each. The final sizes are: 8 1/2" x 11" for two single-page ads, and one 11" x 17" double-page spread. Choose the font carefully; think about its impact on the viewer. You're limited to type, but a small image can be incorporated into the ad.

OBJECTIVES

- To encourage the generation of creative verbal concepts.
- To "think," using type as a visual element.
- To review headlines, leading, kerning, and ligatures.
- To consider the appropriateness of fonts for a topic.
- To review a campaign, and how pieces relate visually.
- To challenge designers with an unusual topic.
- To consider the importance of research in design.
- To apply the details of spacing headlines and text.
- To gain hands-on experience setting headlines and text.
- To understand the creative potentials of type.

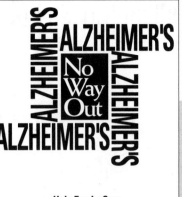

18-44. This ad, by KU student Carolyn Keer, uses types to transmit the lack of communication experienced by Alzheimer's patients.

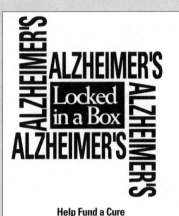

18-45. This ad, by KU student Carolyn Keer, uses the same layout and fonts, but simply changes the headline and box shape slightly.

18-46. This ad series, by KU student Carolyn Keer, uses the words Alzheimer's to reinforce the idea of being shut inside one's own mind, unable to communicate with the outside world. The type serves to both convey the message and create the visual. Notice the consistent use of type to carry the visual cohesiveness of this ad series.

This page is set in ITC Fenice Light 8.5/12.

Unique Considerations of Text Type–Review

18 Unique Considerations of Text Type

1. How does leading affect reading type? _____

2. What should you do for emphasis in body copy? _____

3. What is the difference between a hard and a soft return, and how are they used? _____

4. What are the standard versions of type alignment? _____

5. Why is upper- and lowercase easier to read than all uppercase? _____

_____

6. How should paragraph-indent width relate to the column width? _____

7. How does column length affect ease of reading? _____

8. What is considered optimum word spacing? _____

9. What does set solid mean when it comes to type? _____

10. When are long dashes used in copy? _____

11. In headlines, what type of leading is normally used? _____

12. What is tracking? _____

13. What is a widow? _____

14. What is an orphan? _____

15. What are rivers, and when do you have to be alert for them? _____

16. What is a bullet, and what do you have to be aware of when using them? _____

_____

17. What are two tricks a designer can use when the copy is running too long for the space allotted? ____

_____

18. What should a designer do to improve the rag in flush-left copy? _____

_____

19. When you use parentheses in all-cap copy, what do you have to do? _____

20. How should am and pm be used correctly in body copy? _____

21. Why is there only one space after a period in body copy? _____

22. What is the difference between and en dash and an em dash? _____

23. What is the difference between the prime sign and quotation marks? _____

24. What are runovers in bulleted copy, and how should they be set? _____

25. Draw two examples below of leading used creatively, to enhance the meaning of the written message.

26. Draw two examples of shaped text type used creatively in a layout for a dog-food ad.

27. What do you do to get text to align under a bullet? _____

28. Define a Fleuron ornament. _____

29. Define a Fillet ornament. _____

30. Define a Flourish ornament. _____

31. Define a Coin ornament. _____

32. Define a Cartouche ornament. _____

33-36. List four different ways in which printers' dingbats are used in body copy:

33. _____

34. _____

35. _____

36. _____

The Grid Structure

19 | *The Grid Structure*

This page is set in New Century Schoolbook 8.5/12.

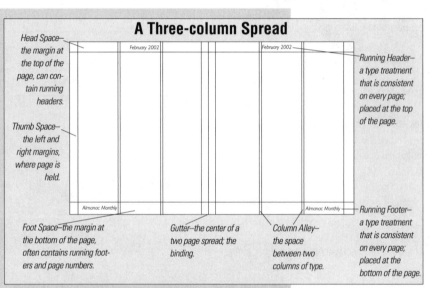

A Three-column Spread

Head Space—the margin at the top of the page, can contain running headers.

Thumb Space—the left and right margins, where page is held.

February 2002

February 2002

Almanac Monthly

Almanac Monthly

Running Header—a type treatment that is consistent on every page; placed at the top of the page.

Foot Space—the margin at the bottom of the page, often contains running footers and page numbers.

Gutter—the center of a two page spread; the binding.

Column Alley—the space between two columns of type.

Running Footer—a type treatment that is consistent on every page; placed at the bottom of the page.

19-1. The three-column grid is a standard structure for organizing information on a page. It is rather simple and practical, and for these reasons can be confining in design. Generally, the more complex the grid is, the more flexible the design is.

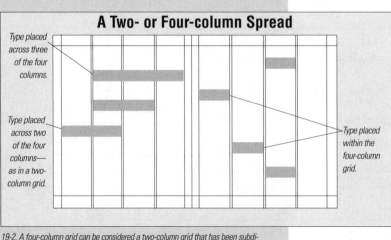

A Two- or Four-column Spread

Type placed across three of the four columns.

Type placed across two of the four columns— as in a two-column grid.

Type placed within the four-column grid.

19-2. A four-column grid can be considered a two-column grid that has been subdivided. Usually, additional columns allow a designer more flexibility in the placement and alignment of information and images.

INTRODUCTION

In this chapter, we'll explore how the grid is an underlying structure used to guide the design and placement of elements on the page. Grids can create the sense of family resemblance throughout a great number of different design pieces, or promote unity in a single piece of 100 pages. Grid systems today are designed for individual projects and are not based on any one standard proportion or format. Designers create grids based on their judgment of shapes and proportions, as they relate to the information and images that need to be organized in the space.

GRIDS IN EDITORIAL DESIGN

Grid systems are prevalent throughout the newspaper and magazine industries, and are used to speed up layout and create a constant, uniform appearance in monthly, weekly or daily publications. Grids are also useful for a single printed piece when numerous visual elements and copy have to be united into a cohesive layout. Ads, newsletters, brochures, annual reports, books, posters, and even television graphics utilize a grid to give order to information.

The grid usually begins with the division of the space for the margins on the left- and right-hand edge of the page (the thumb space), as well

as space at the top and bottom of the page. Next, the page is divided into a number of columns. Remember that the columns will mostly be used for body copy, so rational decisions regarding the width of these columns is essential. Traditionally, a three-column grid is practical for brochure and magazine work. This gives a wide enough column for text and also gives even more options when you further subdivide each column in half.

When further broken down into a six-column grid, the page can be set up alternately as either a two- or three- column format, as well as the six-column page. The six-column grid can be even more effective in the double spread or brochure interior, which gives the option of six to twelve columns over the entire area.

Two-column grids create a heavier textbook appearance, but can be converted to a lighter, four-column grid structure by subdividing the two columns into four. The three/six-and the two/four-column grid structures are the most commonly used formats because of their appropriate text-column-width measurement. Additionally, designs with five or seven columns can be flexible.

FACING- VS. NONFACING-PAGE GRIDS AND MARGINS

Facing-page-based grids are those where the margins are mirror images of each other. This means that the *inner margins,* near the gutter, are the same, and that the *outer margins*, or the *thumb space,* is the same. Nonfacing-page grids are those where the left margins are the same and the right margins are the same regardless of whether the page is a left or a right page.

In a nonfacing-page spread, the amount of thumb space on each page is different. The spread does not attempt to create a unified whole with a small gutter margin, as facing pages do. Every page is the same, and the gutter is visually wide on one side. The facing-page spread is the version that we are more accustomed to; it is symmetrical and harmonious.

However, in book design, it can be easier to design with nonfacing-page spreads, so that the pages are all the same, regardless of which side of the book they fall on. The type of spread you use or prefer is largely a matter of personal style and aesthetics, but is also determined by the type of information and visuals that you are working with. The book you are reading is based on facing pages that are mirror images of each other.

DETERMINING THE MARGINS

Having decided on the number of columns your grid will have, the next step is to determine the column height or depth. In a three-column grid, 11" x 8 1/2" *horizontal* page, your column can be a maximum height (if

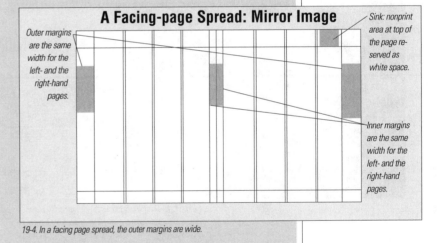

A Two-, Three- or Six-column Spread

Type placed across three of the six columns—as in a two-column grid.

Type placed within the six-column grid.

Type placed across two of the six columns—as in a three-column grid, but with more flexibility of placement.

Type placed across two of the six columns.

19-3. The grid above can be used for three columns or for six columns. It can even be used as a two-column grid. Generally, there are more design options with the six-column grid.

A Facing-page Spread: Mirror Image

Outer margins are the same width for the left- and the right-hand pages.

Sink: nonprint area at top of the page reserved as white space.

Inner margins are the same width for the left- and the right-hand pages.

19-4. In a facing page spread, the outer margins are wide.

A Non-facing-Page Spread: Same Margins on Left & Right Pages

Left margins are the same width for the left- and the right-hand pages.

Right margins are the same width for the left- and the right-hand pages.

19-5. In a nonfacing-page document, the larger margin is on the left regardless of whether it is a left or right page.

This page is set in New Century Schoolbook 8.5/12.

19   *The Grid*
Structure

A Two-, Three- or Six-Column Spread with Horizontal Alignment Rules

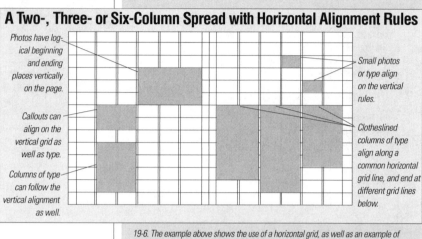

Photos have logical beginning and ending places vertically on the page.

Callouts can align on the vertical grid as well as type.

Columns of type can follow the vertical alignment as well.

Small photos or type align on the vertical rules.

Clotheslined columns of type align along a common horizontal grid line, and end at different grid lines below.

19-6. The example above shows the use of a horizontal grid, as well as an example of clotheslined columns of type.

19-7. The spread above, by KU student Keith Johnson, uses a curved grid to align type. The grid can be extremely unconventional and inventive; it does not have to be composed of evenly spaced vertical lines. The type becomes part of the photo manipulation and creates a shape; the type works around the elements in the spread and completes the photos.

A Diagonal Grid with Horizontal Alignment Rules

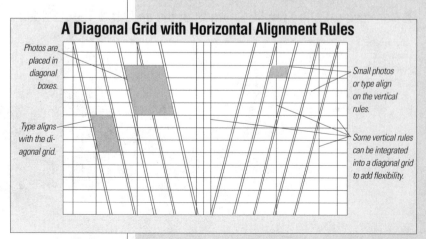

Photos are placed in diagonal boxes.

Type aligns with the diagonal grid.

Small photos or type align on the vertical rules.

Some vertical rules can be integrated into a diagonal grid to add flexibility.

This page is set in
New Century Schoolbook 8.5/12.

19-8. The example above shows the use of a diagonal grid, which incorporates some vertical and horizontal rules for alignment.

it were to bleed off the top and bottom) of 8 1/2" tall or preferably less, perhaps 7" tall, leaving room at the top and bottom. This space is known as a *margin,* and there are different terms for different areas of margins.

The place where type begins on each page should be consistent from one page to the next in a newsletter, magazine, or book. The white space above the type is referred to as the *sink.* There should be enough of a sink so that the type doesn't feel too crowded on the page, and the sink should be in proportion to the page; shorter pages have shorter sinks, and taller pages need taller sinks.

HEAD SPACE AND FOOT SPACE

The margin area at the top of the column is called the *header* or *head space,* and the margin area below the columns is referred to as the *footer* or *foot space.* The area between the columns is called the *inner-column margin,* or the *alley.* The space on the outside of the column group (to the left and right of the three columns) is termed the *border margins,* or the *thumb space.* On a single-page grid you refer to the border margins as "right" and "left." In a double-page-spread format, you label the margins near the center of the two pages the *gutter,* the *center,* or the *inner margins*; and the margins on the outer edges of the spread are the *outer margins.*

Normally the specific proportions for margins vary, but generally the largest measurements are reserved for the head and foot space, with the foot larger than the head. This allows for the page to feel *planted,* or *balanced,* and not appear to be too top heavy.

Next in size (and sometimes the same size as the header) would be the inner and outer page margins, which are usually equal on a single page. In facing-page spreads, the gutter width is reduced to half the width of the outer margins to cause the two areas of type on the facing pages to hold together visually as a unit. The gutter width is also narrowed because when viewing the overall spread, the gutter is read together as a single margin.

The smallest margins are the inter-column spaces or alleys. They can be anywhere between 1 pica up to 3.5 or 4 picas depending on whether there is some visual treatment in the inner column space such as a decorative rule, a dot series or another design device.

USING THE GRID FOR ORGANIZATION & CONSISTENCY

The grid is now assembled and ready for layout options. Begin by placing elements within the structure and experimenting with visual proportions, location and relationships. The grid helps to determine the placement of images and text in the design space. Initially you might make thumb-sized grid formats, and begin by experimentally placing the headline on each grid in a variety of positions, and in different fonts, sizes and weights.

Next, place variations of your largest image, alternating its scale, cropping and location. Photos and illustrations can break across columns and into margins, or work silhouetted with body text wrapped around them to create an unpredictable shape. Photos can be repeated and duplicated, reduced and placed into a grid, screened back, or can bleed off the page, depending on the message intended. Follow through the design process by placing your body copy on the format.

CLOTHESLINING BODY COPY

When working with body copy across columns, it's important to make sure that the baselines of text align in adjacent columns. Perhaps a natural treatment for your body text will be to run lengths of it down adjacent columns, lining up the tops of each column and allowing the bottoms to run different lengths. This is a common placement, known as *clotheslining*, and it gives the page a clean, horizontal head margin. Clotheslined columns have a straight, even top margin but an uneven, ragged bottom edge that creates energy and interesting placement options for the other visual elements on the page. Columns that are clotheslined look the most interesting when the lengths of the column endings are radically different; if the columns end within 1/4" or 1/2" of each other, it may not be dramatic enough and it may appear as though you had to cut a few lines out of one column at the last minute. Remember to be guided by the lines of the grid for placement of the elements. However that doesn't mean that text type couldn't go across two or more columns, or that photographs should never be one column wide.

HORIZONTAL GRID LINES FOR CONSISTENCY

You can also include a series of evenly spaced horizontal rules to assist you in laying out an editorial spread. These rules help you to place type and images so that there is continuity from one spread to the next. These rules are simply guidelines; they are not the *only* place you can align elements. But horizontal grid lines can simplify your work as a designer and further the harmony of the overall piece. A designer must still use discretion regarding when and where to break the grid, to bleed photos off the edge of the page, and to relax the sense of constraint that a tight grid can give a piece if it is overly confining.

Some designers are more comfortable with complex grid structure where the components are not merely column divisions, but each column is further divided into rectangular or square modular units through the addition of a series of horizontal grid lines on which they can align elements.

If you're utilizing horizontal rules in your layout, try to make boxed images or illustrations relate to the horizontal grid lines. Remember that you need white space in your design. The point is not to fill every available inch with text and image, but to

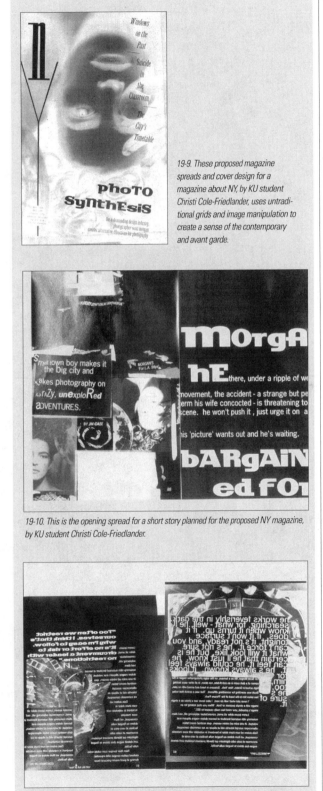

19-9. These proposed magazine spreads and cover design for a magazine about NY, by KU student Christi Cole-Friedlander, uses untraditional grids and image manipulation to create a sense of the contemporary and avant garde.

19-10. This is the opening spread for a short story planned for the proposed NY magazine, by KU student Christi Cole-Friedlander.

19-11. This is the jump spread for the feature story above in NY magazine, by KU student Christi Cole-Friedlander.

19   *The Grid*
Structure

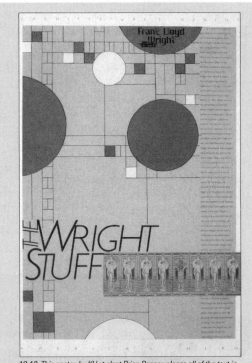

19-12. This poster, by KU student Brian Benner, places all of the text in a vertical column to create a tall, thin element down one side of the piece. This does conform to the grid, as do the other linear elements in this work. The overall effect is not, however, a highly grid-oriented piece because of the effective use of negative space.

create clear hierarchy and focus on the page through the placement of the elements. White space is often needed to balance a large expanse of an image or extensive body copy.

A grid is more than just a series of lines. It is a set of boundaries seen and used differently by as many personalities and visual styles as individuals who use it. A column is a column, but may be composed of any amount of leading. One designer may use interior column rules, while another will drop a tint over all text copy and leave the inner alleys untreated. Photographs and illustrations may line up with the type, bleed off the page, be silhouetted, or be placed on an angle. The grid is a useful tool, but the personal taste of the designer and the intent of the editorial content will still be evident on the printed page.

WHITE SPACE AND GRIDS

Special attention needs to be paid to the use of *white* or *negative*, space in the grid structure. The white space built into the grid is in the margins. A solid page filled with either type or image or a combination of the two, however, rarely looks well designed if every inch of the page is occupied. White space helps bring harmony and comfort to the page and should be considered a very important element in the design process. It provides a space of calmness to offset a very dynamic design. Extensive white space can create a sense of the vastness of space and cause the appearance of minimizing the text and visuals on the page. White space can create a harmony between densely designed and sparsely designed areas of the spread. Not only should you consider the placement of your heading, artwork, and body copy in a design, but you should think about the placement of some white space as well. You shouldn't feel compelled to fill in every available area of the grid. In fact, you can leave entire columns of white space for the eye to rest if it is appropriate and enhances your overall design and content.

VARYING THE GRID

Sometimes, for additional layout options, you may choose to overlap grids on a single page, to use different grids on two facing pages, to use a diagonal grid for an offbeat effect, or to integrate a variety of grids to create immediate visual contrast. Overlapping two different grid formats might be employed by using a three-column-grid for all text, while using a two-column design for the images

19-13. This typographic spread on the topic of different forms of love, for a philosophy journal, designed by KU student Lenore (lenn-e) Snell, breaks from the traditional placement of type horizontally on the page. Type runs vertically and interlaces with other lines of type to create a texture on the page. The headline creates the most prominent visual on the page.

This page is set in
News Gothic 8.5/12.

and captions. Careful planning is needed to prevent the page from appearing crowded or confused, and it is helpful to repeat specific, established, horizontal or vertical reference points, by either aligning text vertically or clotheslining the text.

Using a three-column grid on a right-hand page and a six-column grid on the left-hand page is best done after clear consideration of the design elements at hand. When you deal with a large diagram that has a lot of supplemental blurbs of copy, relevant to different areas of the diagram, a six-column grid could be very helpful to organize all of the captioned information. In contrast to this, the text could be on the facing page, placed neatly in two columns of a three-column grid, with some small supplemental art in the third mostly open column. Logic and practicality are the governing principles behind choosing the most appropriate grid format available for the specific problem.

FINAL GRID CONSIDERATIONS

The grid is used to create harmony and uniformity among a number of graphic elements. It is not designed to be the "end all" for visual solutions. How well individual designers stick to the grid is up to them. If a layout is created that goes outside of the grid boundaries, or "breaks the grid," but seems effective, then use it. The grid is only a tool created by the designer to help, not hinder, the flow of layout ideas. As a designer, you have to make the final decisions.

19-14 . This poster on palm reading, by KU student Amy Lapides, uses a very simple grid to organize the information. The characteristics of different-shaped fingers are listed under a silhouette of each finger shape.

19-15. For this companion poster, KU student Amy Lapides uses a horizontal listing of information with the related word screened in the background.

19-16. In this editorial layout, KU student Kelly Swisher uses a gridded layout and reversals of color to organize the type and images.

This page is set in News Gothic 8.5/12.

19 *The Grid Structure*

19-17. This spread on Isaac Asimov, by KU student Layne F. Lyons, introduces the copy with broad initial capitals. The headline creatively reverses letters out of the name.

19-18. This poster on soccer star Pélé, by KU student Kristopher J. Hammer, conforms to a grid, but also breaks up the space with reversed areas and patterns of soccer balls.

PROJECT: TWO-PAGE CELEBRITY SPREAD

Select a celebrity or historical figure that you can find sufficient data on. Write information about this person. Be sure to choose someone who is well known; it should not be an obscure, local rock star. Determine the age and disposition of your audience—whether this article would be designed for a children's audience, an elderly audience, or a youthful, mixed-gender audience.

The final size will be an 11" x 17" two-page spread. Try to integrate the headline, subhead, body copy, etc., creatively. Your focus should be on the use of the typography. Do not forget the lessons you've learned in kerning, tracking, ligatures, setting a headline, creating texture, rhythm, hierarchy, and shades of gray on the page with the density and leading of the body copy. You may want to choose a family of body-copy typefaces to work with on the spread, or mix and match from two families. It's a good idea to match a serif with a sans serif type. Look at the sample settings of different faces at the back of this book to determine which setting would be best for your use.

Incorporate only one image, photograph, illustration, collage, or caricature of the person into your layout. Try to use the type in the headline creatively in your layout. Once you have written your article (it can be straight, it can be a review of a movie or event, it can be satirical, it can be biographical, it can be political), brainstorm and write a creative headline and subhead.

Once your headline, subhead and article are refined, work on the layout of your two-page spread. Try three different grids for your thumbnails. Don't feel constrained to make all elements conform to the grid. You can be creative and flexible as well as organized.

Write at least twenty possible headlines for the article. They do not all have to be brilliant; some can be silly, irreverent, thought-provoking, or eye-catching. Next, match a subhead to it. Complete a series of 15 thumbnail sketches focused on the headline meaning. Type should work in concert with the message it conveys. A handsome type layout is meaningless if it does not relate to the idea behind the words. In editorial design, the words must come first; you must always read an article before you design a layout for it. Proceed to a half-sized rough draft to work from on the computer.

OBJECTIVES

- To understand how grids are used to structure information.
- To experiment with grids in the formative design process.
- To learn to work within a grid without feeling too constrained.
- To utilize a grid to enhance hierarchy and clarity.
- To experience the process of interpreting an article visually.
- To analyze different settings of copy typefaces closely.
- To organize information using typeface distinction.
- To reinforce a sense of kerning and ligatures in headlines.
- To encourage the refinement of the hierarchy of type on a page.
- To review the process of copy fitting of body copy.
- To develop a sense for choosing the appropriate copy type for a project.

The Grid Structure-Review

1. What is the difference between a two- and a four-column grid, and how are they similar ? _____

_____

2. What's the advantage of a six-column grid as opposed to a three-column grid? _____

_____

3. What's the gutter in a spread? _____

4. What's the space between columns of type called? _____

5. What's the space at the top edge of a spread called? _____

6. What's the space at the bottom of a spread called? _____

·7. What's the type in the space at the bottom of a spread called? _____

8. Why would you use a consistently spaced series of horizontal lines in your layout? _____

_____

9. What does clotheslining type mean? _____

10. What is the sink in editorial design? _____

11. Why does a designer use a grid, and then "break" it? Describe a few ways in which the grid is broken. _____

_____

_____

_____

_____

_____

This page is set in
Fenice Light 8.5/12.

Computers & Typography

*20 Computers &
Typography*

This page is set in
Equinox 8.5/12.

Operating System (harness): Software that channels the raw microprocessor into usable, controllable form.

Program Applications (reigns): Determine the kind of functions the computer will do.

User (driver): Coaxes and directs outcome.

Monitor/Screen (running lights): Illuminate the course pursued.

Ports & Disk Drive (horse eyes; ears): receives outside input into the system.

Hard Drive (wagon): Holds stable quantities of data for safe keeping.

RAM (horse brain): Where short-term, rapid-fire information from ports or the user are retained just when used.

Microprocessor Chip (horse heart): Provides speed and vitality for circulation and operating on all data.

Motherboard (horse body): Links and coordinates the other components.

ROM (legs; wheels): Runs automatic functions.

MegaHertz (horsepower): Speed at which system can function.

HORSE & BUGGY MODEL OF A COMPUTER

20-1. This illustration compares the parts of a horse and buggy with a computer.

ROM= Read-only Memory
Reads information only–does not change it.

RAM= Random-access Memory
Reads temporary information; is constantly changing–like screen redraw.

MHz= Megahertz
How fast electrons are speeding through your computer's microcircuits.

MB= Megabytes
How much stuff you can put in your hard disk; like an attic, larger=more space.

20-2. This list shows what some computer acronyms stand for.

INTRODUCTION

In this chapter we cover the difference between RAM, ROM and megahertz. We will also review the basics of the structure of a computer, how digital fonts work, and simple networking concepts. Before you plan to sit down and design your own digital font, there are a few basic concepts that you must know, and you must master the use of existing computer fonts.

There are some terms in computer jargon which take a while to master because they are so close to each other. *ROM* stands for *Read-only Memory*; it controls the routine functions of a computer, or compact disk, where data is *read* but *not changed*. (ROM is somewhat like the involuntary nervous system that controls heart rate, breathing, blood pressure, etc.) *RAM* stands for *Random-access Memory*; it performs computer-intensive functions like redrawing the screen and working in graphic programs. RAM is a *temporary access memory*; it functions only while the computer is on. (RAM is more like your attention span, or lack of attention—your immediate decisions that you make.) *MHz* is the *megahertz*, or speed, at which the small microprocessing chip in your computer is able to cram the electrons through its microcircuits. This is measured in *nanoseconds*, or thousandths of a second. There's also *MB*, which means *megabytes* and refers to the storage capacity of your hard drive. This is roughly similar to your memory.

THE HORSE-AND-WAGON MODEL OF A COMPUTER

The metaphor of the horse and wagon may shed some light on the differences between these terms. Assume that the horse and wagon are your computer. The size of the wagon determines the amount of stuff that can be held; this is like the hard drive of the computer, which determines how many megabytes of information can be stored. The horse's heart, pumping away, is like the computer chip. The faster the heart rate, the faster the processing happens. The brain of the horse is like the RAM of the computer; it determines how many commands the horse can do at once and how fast and how well the horse will perform those tasks. The RAM in computers can be updated by installing new chips (think of it as brain surgery on the horse). The ROM can be compared to the wheels and legs of the horse–the more there is in the wagon (applications and files), the slower the horse will move or process information (the slower the processing of the ROM). The motherboard of the computer is like the body of the horse that connects the speed-cranking device (heart or chip) to the brain (or RAM) to the hard drive or wagon. Larger hard drives (or wagons) can be installed when larger versions come out. But you have to make sure that your "stuff" is safely stowed, where it's retrievable while you hook up the new hard drive (wagon). Microprocessing chips are rarely changed in computers (the metaphoric equivalent of open heart surgery) without changing the entire motherboard, so you get a whole new horse, and the old one is retired. ROM, the involuntary repetitive functions, or the horse's legs and the wagon wheels, are intricately tied to the size of the wagon, or hard drive, and the amount of RAM (the brain) in the computer as well as the rate of the chip, or heart, so ROM changes only as a result of other upgrades. The running lights are like the monitor; they allow you to see where you're going with the computer. The operating system is like the harness of the computer and the training that the horse underwent when it was young. The harness is how the user directs the horse or computer. You can attach fancy bits and weights (extensions and units) to the harness, but it still is the directing device for the horse; you can even upgrade to a newer, faster, more sensitive harness, or operating system. Sometimes it is simpler to relate something new (the computer) to something that you already know, the horse and buggy, yet if the horse metaphor is too complex, forget it.

APPLICATIONS AND DOCUMENTS

The words "program" and "application" are interchangeable; they mean the same thing—a piece of software. Programs on the computer are complex, specific pieces of software code, written by a team of software engineers, designed to make the computer complete certain tasks in a predetermined fashion. There are applications used only for spreadsheets and accounting; there are programs for three-dimensional modeling, for page layout, for font design, and for photo editing. When you work in any program, you create a document using the program or application. You can usually determine which program a document was created in by looking at its icon on the screen; the document icon reflects the icon of the program used to create the document.

Documents are created using programs on the computer. (The terms *document* and *file* are interchangeable; they mean the same thing.) The document icons look similar to the icons of the programs used to create that file. If a document icon comes up as a simple sheet of paper (no recognizable icon), this often indicates that you don't have the program of creation loaded, or that you don't have the latest version loaded.

Users have to learn to load the software programs onto their machines. Computers often come with the operating system loaded, but that is it. Users have to learn to restart the computer and hold the "shift" key down during the startup, before loading any software onto the computer. Holding down the "shift" key turns off the Extensions, which can conflict with the installing of new software. After loading new software, hit the "restart" option, then launch the new program by double-clicking on its program icon.

LAUNCHING SOFTWARE

Launching software means opening it and bringing it to the front of your screen. There are a number of different ways to launch a piece of software once it is on your hard drive. One way is to find the icon of the software program and to double-click on it. Another way is to double-click on a document that was

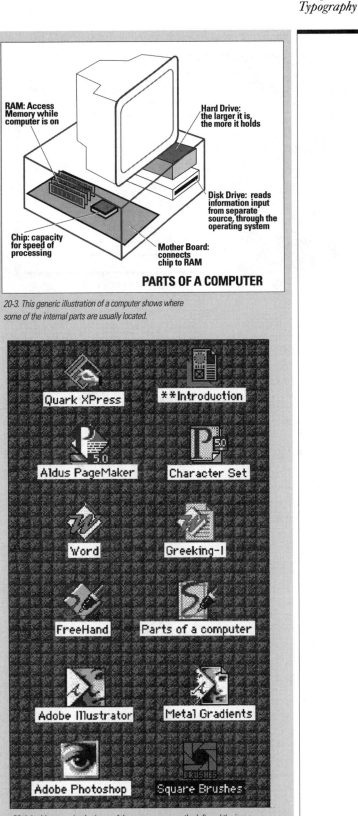

20-3. This generic illustration of a computer shows where some of the internal parts are usually located.

20-4. In this example, the icons of the programs are on the left, and the icons of the documents are on the right. Notice how the icons for the documents resemble the applications used.

This page is set in Equinox 8.5/12.

20 Computers & Typography

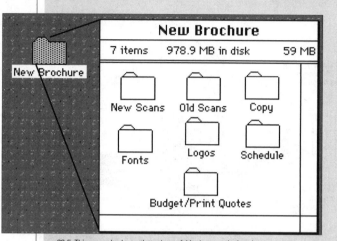

20-5. This example shows that when a folder is open, the icon is dimmed to indicate the open status.

> ### NOTE: Restart and hold down the shift key before loading any software onto a computer.

20-6. Holding down the shift key turns off any extensions that might conflict with the program-loading software.

> ### NOTE: All applications must be quit before fonts are loaded, then relaunch to make fonts accessible to the program.

20-7. Programs left running when fonts are installed will not be able to access the new fonts.

created using that piece of software. You cannot work on a document without having the program active. The only way to look at a document (or file) that you or someone else has created is to launch the software used to create it.

COMPUTER FOLDERS

The computer uses folders much the same as we use folders in our daily lives: to organize papers that are on a similar topic. However, with computers, you can have even *greater* organization by subdividing the information within the folder into subcategories in separate folders.

For instance, when you are working on a design project, you might have a folder named "New Brochure." Within that folder, you might have a folder named Old Scans, New Scans, Copy, Fonts, Logos, Schedule, or Budget/Print Quotes. Within each of the subcategories of folders, there will be numerous documents, but they'll be easier to find since the similar ones are grouped together. In the example on the left, notice that when a folder is open (or a program is launched) the icon gets grayed out, in a tone, yet it still retains the customized perimeter of the icon. This is to show you which applications or folders are open, at a glance.

FONTS ON THE COMPUTER

Fonts are often confounding to computer newcomers. One basic rule is to realize that Times Roman is recognized as a separate entity from Times Roman Bold or Times Roman Italic. These are each seen as separate, distinct computer documents, and they were created separately on the computer. Yet, they each must be present to print out a document correctly. The variations of Times Roman are linked as a family, and when all versions are present in the "Fonts" folder, they make it faster for the variations to print efficiently. Also, for every font to work correctly on the monitor *and* from the printer, two files are necessary. You must have the printer *and* the screen fonts loaded in your "System Folder."

In the Macintosh system, there are two parts to every font. Both files must be present for the font to print. There is a screen font (found in a suitcase) and a printer font, which downloads the PostScript code to the printer, so that the font appears correct on the printed page or the film.

SCREEN FONTS

The screen font (in a suitcase) creates a 72 pixel-per-inch rendition of the font, to assure accurate depiction on the screen. This is the only function of the suitcased files of fonts—to create the screen version of the font. Suitcases come from the manufacturer with numerous-sized versions of the screen fonts, but you need only one point size of *each* of the various weights and style of the font (Times Roman 10, Times Roman Bold 10, Times Roman Italic 10, Times Roman Bold Italic 10) if you have , Adobe Type Manager™(ATM) installed (ATM is discussed in detail below). When you double-click on a screen font inside the suitcase, you will see a sample of that font in the weight and point size named.

Screen fonts help to alleviate problems of inaccuracy between what you see on the screen and what you get out of the printer. The term "WYSIWYG" (pronounced whissywhig), which stands for "What You See Is What You Get," has not been perfectly refined yet on the computer. Screen fonts approximate on the screen what you will get from the printer. But if you're doing crucial spacing for a logo, you should go by the paper output, regardless of how the spacing looks on the screen. However, if you're doing a web page, which will be viewed on-screen, go by the monitor spacing.

PRINTER FONTS

Printer fonts are designed to interact with the printers and to make printing efficient; they describe the font in PostScript™, the language of the printers. The bulk of the printer fonts are designed with vector outlines of the shape of the font, producing a font outline that is always smooth and infinitely scalable using PostScript. PostScript is a computer language developed by Adobe™. In short, it is the language of PostScript printers. It uses mathematical calculations to plot the points of a font and the arcs between the points that make up the outline of a letter. Because it relies on this vector creation of characters, the edges of the fonts at all sizes are smooth and clean. Printer fonts are downloaded to the printer when you print a document. Unlike screen fonts, printer fonts are not point-sensitive. There is just one printer font for each weight or style.

PLACING FONTS WITHIN THE SYSTEM FOLDER

Both the screen fonts and the printer fonts are needed in the "Fonts" folder of the "System Folder" for a typeface to appear correctly on the screen and for it to print out correctly from the printer. If you do not have the printer font for a document, most programs will balk and alert you that it should be loaded when you try to launch the document. Some programs will allow you to open the document, and only balk or give a PostScript error when you try to print the page. If you don't have the correct screen font loaded, the font will show up on the screen with a terrible case of the jaggies; it won't be spaced or shaped correctly on the screen. The printer font will usually print jagged as well when the screen font is missing. This is because the printer font looks to the screen font for some of its encoding for the curves of the outline. Both the printer and screen fonts need to be placed in the "Fonts" folder of the "System Folder" in order for fonts to print correctly.

In addition, it is important to realize that you need the documents for every variation of weight and typestyle of a face in the "Fonts" folder of the "System Folder" in order to output them correctly from either a laser output or a service bureau. If you have only the screen and printer font of Goudy Oldstyle, for example, but you have some headings in the document that are in italics, the computer will not print the italics correctly until you load Goudy Oldstyle Italic, or Bold, or Bold Italic, as needed. It is necessary to quit any open applications when loading new fonts in order for them to be accessed in that program. Once the fonts are loaded, you can relaunch the program.

New computer users are often confounded when they place the folder with the screen and printer fonts into the "Fonts" folder in the "System Folder", relaunch the application, and the fonts are not present. Their mistake is that they must take the suitcase and printer fonts out of the "Storage" folder and place only these documents (not the "Storage" folder) into the "Fonts" folder of the "System Folder."

THE EFFICIENCY OF A FONT FAMILY

There is an efficiency of size that occurs when a family of fonts is all placed together in its family suitcase. This causes the size of each individual font document to be reduced. If all of the font

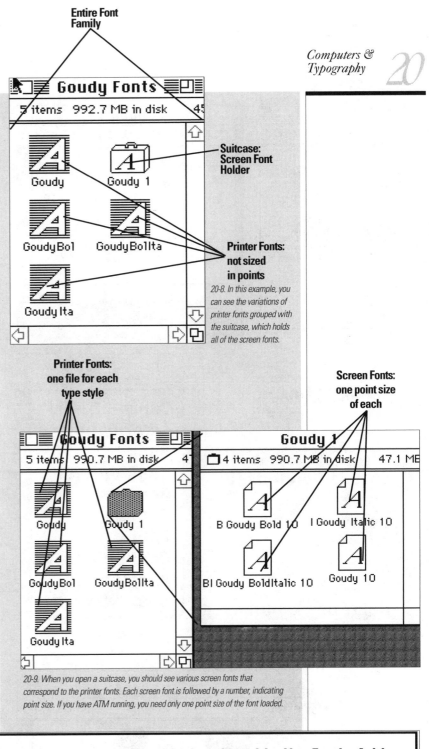

20-8. In this example, you can see the variations of printer fonts grouped with the suitcase, which holds all of the screen fonts.

20-9. When you open a suitcase, you should see various screen fonts that correspond to the printer fonts. Each screen font is followed by a number, indicating point size. If you have ATM running, you need only one point size of the font loaded.

20-10. This alert box comes up whenever you try to drop a font into the "System Folder." Selecting "OK" places the font correctly in the "Fonts" folder to be accessed by programs. You must be sure to take font files out of their folder before dropping them into the "System Folder."

This page is set in Elektrix Light 8.5/12.

20 Computers &
Typography

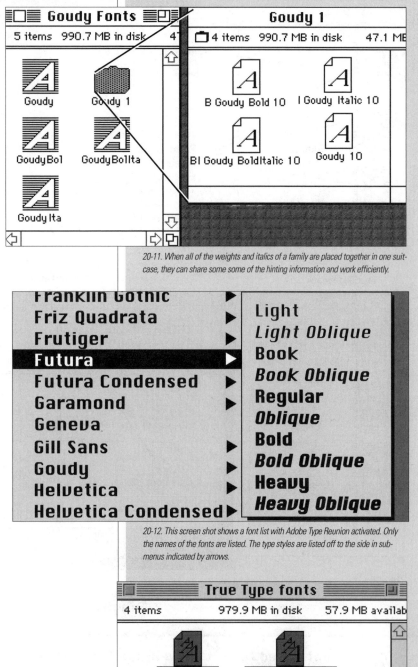

20-11. When all of the weights and italics of a family are placed together in one suit-case, they can share some some of the hinting information and work efficiently.

20-12. This screen shot shows a font list with Adobe Type Reunion activated. Only the names of the fonts are listed. The type styles are listed off to the side in sub-menus indicated by arrows.

20-13. This screen shot shows what True Type font icons look like. Notice that with True Type fonts, there is only one document; there is no printer-font/screen-font distinction. With True Type, the encoding is all built into one file.

This page is set in Clearface
Regular 8.5/12.

styles of one family are placed together, they will usually show up as a sub-menu off to the side on your font-selection list in programs (assuming that you have Adobe Type Reunion loaded). Adobe Type Reunion lists the name of the font, such as Garamond, then places the style and weight variations to the side as a sub-menu. This makes your overall font list shorter (even for font hogs) and faster to scroll through.

When you use the variations of bold or italic, it is most efficient for your output if you select variations of the font style, such as bold, etc., from this sub-menu list. If you make Palatino Bold by clicking on a bold style under "Type," rather than by highlighting Palatino Bold from the sub-menu, you're forcing the computer to extrapolate and either find the file for Palatino Bold or create it from the regular weight of Palatino. Two things happen: your page takes far longer to print because of this, and you may get an inaccurate font, which will not be consistent. To prepare your files correctly, it is important to select variations of a font from the font sub-menu, where you can highlight Palatino Bold, Palatino Italic, etc. This will ensure smoother and faster running files.

ENCAPSULATED POSTSCRIPT OR EPS

Encapsulated PostScript (EPS) is a format for saving files that makes them easily readable by any printer. When saved as an EPS, files are no longer able to be worked on; they are frozen. Many graphics, photo-editing and illustrating programs offer the option of saving your final document as an EPS version. This should be done only when you are quite sure that there will be no more rounds of changes, and you should always make sure to save the source file as well, in case you want to edit it.

EPS files import into layout programs very well, and are preferred at most output bureaus because they run smoothly. However, EPS versions of files are larger than the original document because the PostScript data adds to the size of your file; in the long run, the additional disk space is a small price to pay for fast-printing graphic files.

For importing into page-layout programs, the EPS versions of images are no longer adjustable, so if you want the image to be screened, etc., it's a good idea to do that *before* you save it as an EPS file. However, TIFF (Tagged Information File Format) versions of images are editable when taken into page-layout programs; they can be screened, colored, changed, etc., in the layout programs. They may take a bit longer to print out, but they are more fluid in the design process. Sometimes it's a good idea to use TIFF versions of your images for flexibility in the design-assembly process, then to go back into the photo-manipulation program, edit the photos accordingly, and then save them as EPS files so that they will print seamlessly.

NETWORKS

A *network* is when more than one computer share a printer(s). A network assumes that you have a couple of computers that are wired together, or daisy-chained to a printer. A simple AppleTalk network consists of cables that connect into small boxes, each of which has a cable that connects to the back of a computer. Cables from the printer port of one computer plug into the connector that plugs into the printer port of the next computer. This type of network is called a *daisy chain*. This cabling goes around from one computer to the next, and usually the printer is placed at the end or beginning of the chain. Printers are placed in the chain as one of the links. The daisy chain must be unbroken in order for all computers to access the printer. A break in the chain will render all computers after the break unable to print. Some networks are more complex, with a few printers on the network and a greater number of computers.

Ethernet™ is a different type of network cabling system. It requires specific computer cards and special cables. It's a faster, dedicated network that requires specific cards installed in each computer and cabling for each station on the network. It allows the transfer of large or complex files from one station to another very quickly.

Assuming that you've created your document efficiently using fonts correctly, you'll try to print it. There are two terms in the print process that you must become familiar with. There is the "Chooser" and the "Print Monitor." Both of these are software that interact with the Operating System to give flexibility when printing on a network.

TROUBLESHOOTING NETWORK PROBLEMS

On the right half of the "Chooser" window, you'll see a list of the available printers. Note that if a printer is off, your network cable is disconnected, or AppleTalk is inactive (check in the "Chooser"), you will not see any printers listed. You will not be able to print anything under these circumstances. Troubleshoot to make sure that the printer is on, that the printer's network cable is intact, that your network cable is intact, and that any other cables to computers between your station and the printer are intact. If there is any break in the daisy chain, you cannot access the printer. Lastly, if you are unable to print, check the AppleTalk option in the "Chooser" window at the bottom right. Make sure that AppleTalk is on; if it's off, your cabling may be fine, but the software to send out a signal to the network is off.

THE CHOOSER, PAGE-SETUP, & PRINTER DRIVERS

The "Chooser" itself is software designed to select from a variety of printers on a network. A larger network with many printers will require use of the software called the "Chooser" more often. The "Chooser" allows you to check which printer your computer is activated to print to; it also allows you to select to print out of a different printer if the one that's selected is busy printing a long job, or loaded with the wrong size paper.

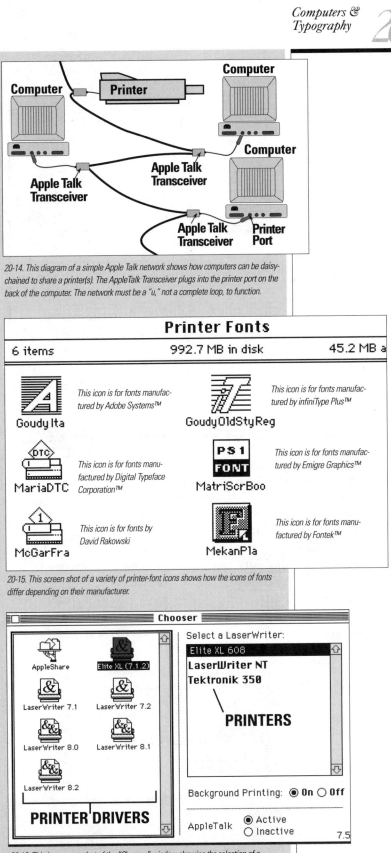

20-14. This diagram of a simple Apple Talk network shows how computers can be daisy-chained to share a printer(s). The AppleTalk Transceiver plugs into the printer port on the back of the computer. The network must be a "u," not a complete loop, to function.

20-15. This screen shot of a variety of printer-font icons shows how the icons of fonts differ depending on their manufacturer.

20-16. This is a screen shot of the "Chooser" window showing the selection of a printer driver. Also notice that "Background Printing" is on and AppleTalk is activated.

This page is set in Geneva 8.5/12.

20   *Computers &*
Typography

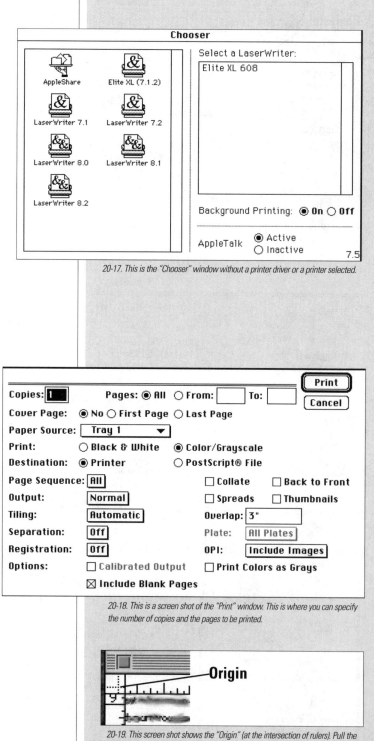

20-17. This is the "Chooser" window without a printer driver or a printer selected.

20-18. This is a screen shot of the "Print" window. This is where you can specify the number of copies and the pages to be printed.

20-19. This screen shot shows the "Origin" (at the intersection of rulers). Pull the "Origin" down to determine the left corner of the page you want tiled.

When the "Chooser" is launched, on the right half will be a list of the names of possible printers you have to choose between. The one that is highlighted is the one that is active. Simply click twice on the one that you want to change to and you have changed the printer.

This will usually activate the program to request that you review the "Page Setup Options" box since you've just changed the printer and the PostScript Printing Device (PPD) file. (Different printers have different specifications for the closeness to the edge that they are able to print, as well as the page sizes, dots per inch, etc.) It's wise to get into the habit of always checking "Page Setup Options" before printing. That should be your next step, after checking the "Chooser" for "Printer Drivers" and selection of printer.

The "Chooser" also enables you determine which version of the "Printer Driver" software you'll be using, and whether "Background Printing" is on. "Background Printing" allows the user to continue working once the document to be printed is spooled to the "Print Monitor."

The "Printer Driver" software determines how the PostScript code to the printer is prepared. "Printer Drivers" come with Apple Operating System software, and with any non-Apple printer that you buy. "Printer Driver" software is printer-sensitive, date-sensitive, and "Operating System" sensitive, depending on whether the programmer wrote it for PostScript Level 1 or 2, etc., or with RISC compatibility for Power PC computers. You must have the "Printer Driver" software loaded that is compatible with the specific printer that's attached to your computer. You will usually have a different "Printer Driver" software for each printer you have to select from.

APPLETALK AND THE PRINT MONITOR

AppleTalk is software that allows multiple users to send documents to the printer via phone-line networking; it creates a queue or line of documents determining the order of printing. Nanoseconds (thousandths of a second) make a difference in AppleTalk to determine who prints first. To clear a print that you've sent, you have to launch the "Print Monitor" from under the "Finder" icon (upper right of the menu bar); click on the document you want to cancel, and hit the "Remove from List" option twice, then close the window.

The "Print Monitor" is a piece of spooling software that saves your document in spooled format, enabling it to download to the printer efficiently. If you want to cancel a print you have to clear your document from the "Print Monitor," where it is spooled before printing. With AppleTalk on, the "Print Monitor" spools your document and then allows you to return to work in a few seconds…on the same document! (It will print out the version you had when you hit "Print.")

Computers &
Typography 20

STARTING THE PRINT CYCLE: "PRINT" DIALOGUE BOX

When you start a print cycle, it's important to realize whether or not you're Tiling (manually or automatically), the percentage size that the page is printing out at, and whether or not you've activated "Larger Print Area" as an option. Also it is important to check the "Chooser" to know where (physically) your work will be printed. You also want to make sure that you are printing "Separations" if needed, and to include the option for "Registration Marks" as needed. "Separations" mean that you are printing out each color as a separate page; this is usually done when you are preparing a job for service- bureau output. The color "Registration Marks" and "Crop Marks" show how to align the different color ink plates on the press, and where to crop the final piece.

PRINT MONITOR: A GREAT BACKGROUND SPOOLER

Once you hit "OK to Print," the information that is sent to the printer is spooled, or temporarily held in the Print Monitor on your machine. At this point, the only way to cancel a print cycle is to open the "Print Monitor," click on the document to be cancelled, and hit "Remove from List" twice, and then close the "Print Monitor" window. When your document is in the "Print Monitor," it is in limbo. Any changes made subsequent to the print activation will not be reflected in the printed document. It is better to cancel the print cycle and continue to make adjustments, then print.

As a spooling software, the "Print Monitor" is quite impressive. It holds the version you had when you decided to print, while not tying up the computer, and allowing you to work further on the same document. The "Print Monitor" waits until AppleTalk indicates that your document is next in line, and then it sends the signals of your document to the printer. This is all done seamlessly, in the background, while you work away. Sometimes, particularly if there is complex artwork or numerous scans in a document, spooling to the "Print Monitor" takes a few minutes, but the computer is cleared quite quickly while the "Print Monitor" holds the spooled document for printing in turn.

You generally cannot print a document without launching the application that created it, and without the correct fonts that are needed for the document. Some programs allow you to substitute in a different font, but this can cause havoc with your line endings, text blocks, tracking, etc. It's best to try to have the fonts as needed in the document loaded correctly into the "Fonts" folder of the "System Folder" before printing.

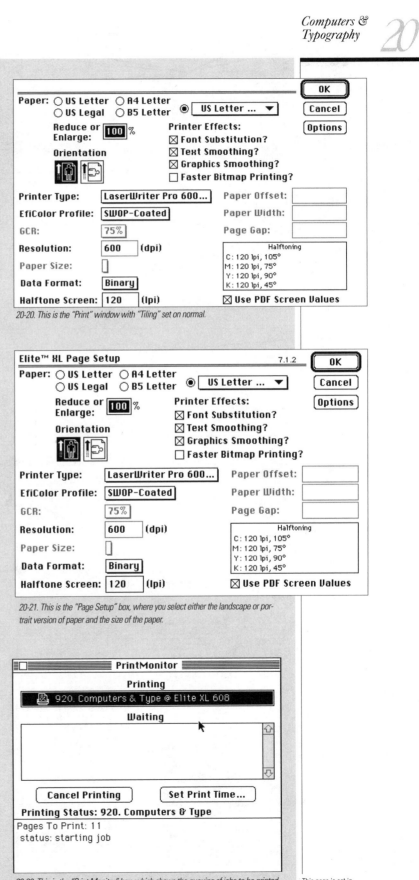

20-20. This is the "Print" window with "Tiling" set on normal.

20-21. This is the "Page Setup" box, where you select either the landscape or portrait version of paper and the size of the paper.

20-22. This is the "Print Monitor" box, which shows the queuing of jobs to be printed.

This page is set in Geneva 8.5/12.

20 Computers &
Typography

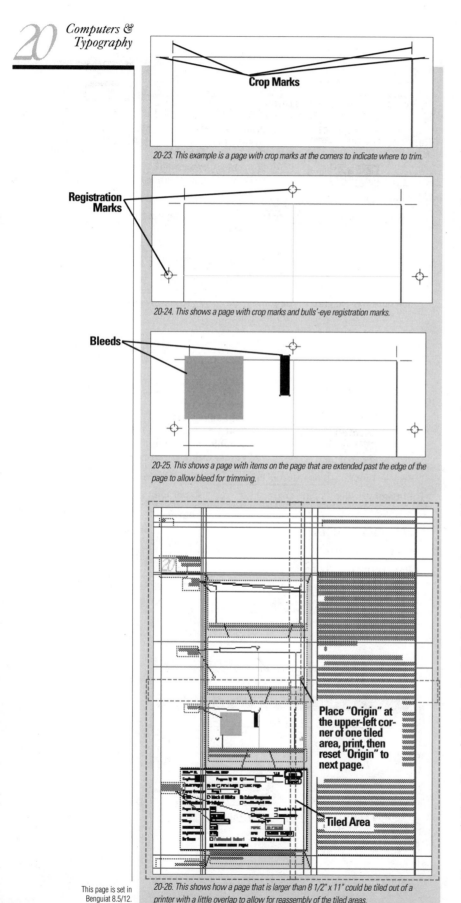

20-23. This example is a page with crop marks at the corners to indicate where to trim.

20-24. This shows a page with crop marks and bulls'-eye registration marks.

20-25. This shows a page with items on the page that are extended past the edge of the page to allow bleed for trimming.

Place "Origin" at the upper-left corner of one tiled area, print, then reset "Origin" to next page.

Tiled Area

This page is set in Benguiat 8.5/12.

20-26. This shows how a page that is larger than 8 1/2" x 11" could be tiled out of a printer with a little overlap to allow for reassembly of the tiled areas.

You also need to verify that your service bureau has the fonts for the output of your job. When preparing files for a service bureau, you need to have all of the linked artwork documents on the disk that you provide, along with your page-layout file. For any page-layout documents that have EPS files placed in (or linked to) them, you have to have the source file (usually an illustration program file) as well as the EPs version on your disk for output.

CROP MARKS, BLEEDS AND REGISTRATION MARKS

Crop marks are lines placed parallel to the edges of the paper, at the four corners of the sheet; they're usually placed 1/8" away from the edge. These marks tell the printer where to trim the piece. In order for an image or line to print to the edge of the sheet, you must give the printer *bleed*, or an extra 1/8" of the image or line past the intended edge of the page. This bleed provides for minor inaccuracies in trimming the final piece.

Bull's-eye *registration marks* are for aligning the different negatives or plates once the job goes to press. These registration marks print out on all four sides of a piece beyond the crop marks. They also print on all the negatives, outside the crop marks, and will print in precisely the same place on each color-printing plate if they are registered correctly. The registration marks allow the printers to check whether the cylinders with the different plates on them need to be moved miniscule amounts by computer to register the colors correctly.

AUTOMATIC AND MANUAL TILING

Tiling is a process that allows you to "tile" out an image area that is larger than the page size of the printer. The computer has an "Automatic Tile" option and a "Manual Tile" option. When using "Automatic Tile," set the measurement for the overlap of tiling, and the computer will tile your document; then you'll have to piece the pages together. (The default setting for the amount of overlap can be set in the "Print Dialogue" box.)

If you opt for "Manual Tile," you'll have to go into your program and set the "Origin." The "Origin" is the two intersecting dotted lines located at the intersection of the rulers. To select the "Origin" of the page, you have to drag the cross hairs found in the upper left-hand corner of the intersection of the rulers (they appear as dotted lines) to the upper left-hand corner of the page area that you want to print tiled onto a sheet of paper. Then you print each of the manually tiled pages one at a time.

To do this, select "Print," and print from page 1 to page 1, making sure that "Manual Tile" is activated in the Print Dialogue box. Then move the "Origin" to the upper left hand corner of the next page area that you want to tile out onto a sheet of paper and proceed, until the entire area has been tiled.

The advantage of "Manual Tile" over "Automatic Tile "is that although it's more tedious to tile manually, it does give you control over where the page breaks will fall for reassembly. This means that you can make sure that your text type will all tile onto one page, rather than having the computer automatically tile and having to piece the text type together from multiple copies.

FONT SUPPLIERS

There are numerous manufacturers of fonts today; the computer has enabled a proliferation of font design paralleled only in the heydays of Victorian type design. There are the large font suppliers Monotype™, Bitstream™, Adobe™, International Typeface Corporation (ITC)™; midsize specialty-font suppliers, such as Emigré™, FontHaus™, Letraset™; and small suppliers, such as House Industries™ (to name just a few). Those listed above have a wide array of quality digital fonts for sale, and provide designers with a sample list and price list of the fonts they have designed.

There are bargain-basement font suppliers, where you can buy a full CD of fonts for 30 dollars or so, rather than the standard price of around 25 dollars for a typeface. These "bargain" fonts are often not worth the price; they have often ripped-off the designs of legitimate type designers, making only minor modifications and changing the name only slightly, so that the bargain font is a close approximation of the name of the original font. Besides being questionable in terms of ethics, the "knockoff" fonts frequently give PostScript™ errors, do not have a comfortable fit on the page as body copy, or look badly balanced in text type. There are also lots of fonts available in the public domain, or for a nominal user charge on the internet. These have to be tested on a case-by-case basis to see whether they are well designed enough to use for body copy, and whether or not they will print smoothly from your printer and service bureau.

TRUE TYPE™ VS. POSTSCRIPT™ FONTS

In the world of fonts, there is a bit of a controversy underway. A variety of different font formats is vying for dominance in the world of fonts. PostScript fonts still seem to be winning the battle for ease of use. The others sound easy in theory but currently present frustrating implementation snags.

TrueType™ is a font format created by Apple Computer™. At first glance, it seems less cumbersome than the printer-friendly, two-part PostScript fonts. True

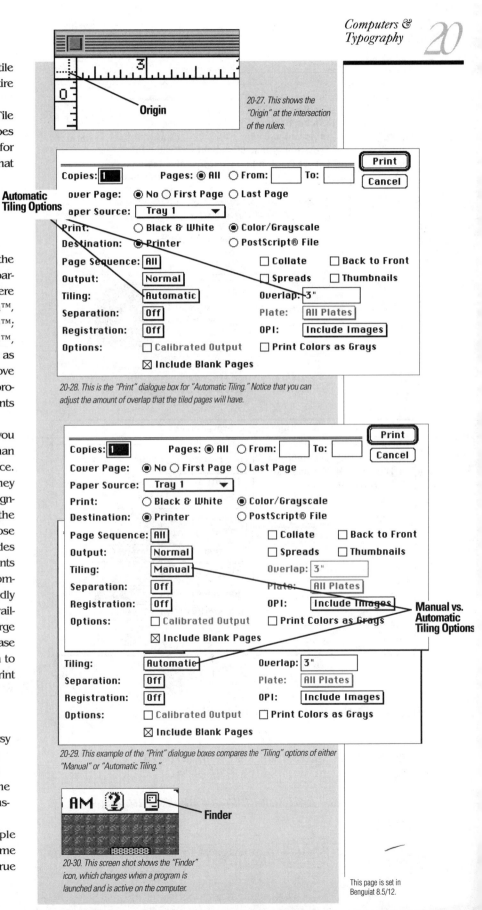

20-27. This shows the "Origin" at the intersection of the rulers.

20-28. This is the "Print" dialogue box for "Automatic Tiling." Notice that you can adjust the amount of overlap that the tiled pages will have.

20-29. This example of the "Print" dialogue boxes compares the "Tiling" options of either "Manual" or "Automatic Tiling."

20-30. This screen shot shows the "Finder" icon, which changes when a program is launched and is active on the computer.

This page is set in Benguiat 8.5/12.

20 **Computers &**
   Typography

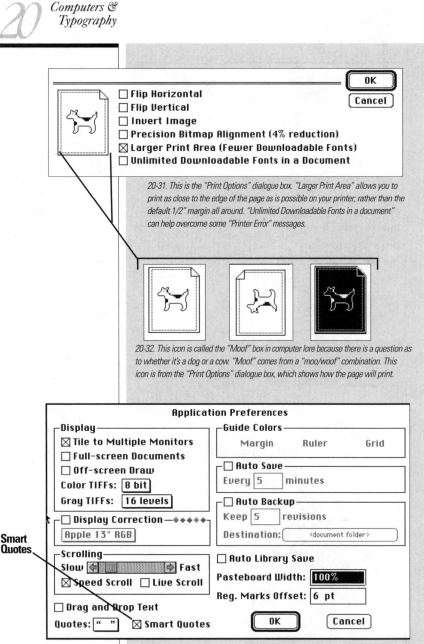

20-31. This is the "Print Options" dialogue box. "Larger Print Area" allows you to print as close to the edge of the page as is possible on your printer; rather than the default 1/2" margin all around. "Unlimited Downloadable Fonts in a document" can help overcome some "Printer Error" messages.

20-32. This icon is called the "Moof" box in computer lore because there is a question as to whether it's a dog or a cow. "Moof" comes from a "moo/woof" combination. This icon is from the "Print Options" dialogue box, which shows how the page will print.

20-33. This is an application-wide preferences box that allows you to turn "Smart Quotes" on.

"These are Curly Quotes, shaped like 69."

"These are Prime Marks; there's no shape to them."

Use Prime Marks;" and ' are italic for inches and feet, respectively.

20-34. These examples compare Curly Quotes, the correct format, with Prime Marks, the incorrect format.

This page is set in
Benguiat 8.5/12.

Type is an attempt to combine the printer and screen font into one document. There is only one file for True Type, and it allows for clean screen display and in theory is infinitely scalable for printing and allows printout at the maximum dpi of the printer. Yet, TrueType fonts are notorious for glitches in laser printers and at service bureaus; many service bureaus refuse to handle documents with TrueType unless the fonts have been brought into a vector program, changed to outlines, and saved as an Encapsulated Postscript File, or EPS File (which makes them similar to PostScript fonts, so they will print more efficiently). TrueType fonts print well from dot-matrix or some ink jet printers that rely on QuickDraw software rather than PostScript language. TrueType is also slow on screen redraw and printing from PostScript printers.

Quick Draw printers are printing from the bit-based screen language and are, therefore, more jagged than laser or PostScript printers; they are called StyleWriters, ImageWriters, and Ink Jet printers depending on their dpi. Even when a printer is called PostScript, it's important to determine whether it is PostScript native or interpolated. *Native* PostScript is better, and means that the printer understands the PostScript language. *Interpolation* means that the printer has to have the PostScript run through another program to decipher the PostScript language, which leads to slower printing and more printer error signals, especially with complex images.

CURLY QUOTES

Under the "Edit" menu of some layout programs, you can find "Preferences." By going to the "Application Preferences," you'll have the option to set curly quotes on or off. For most copy, you'll want the curly quotes activated; it is only when you're putting in measurements in feet and inches that it makes sense to turn off the curly quotes so that you get the correct prime marks in the text; these straight quotes should be set in italics for feet and inch symbols.

ADOBE TYPE MANAGER ATM™ & ADOBE TYPE REUNION™

Adobe Type Manager, or ATM, is a "Control Panel" utility that allows users to load only one point size of a typestyle (bold, italic) from the suitcase into their "Font" folder in the "System Folder." Loading only one point size of a font saves on hard-disk space. Without ATM loaded, the fonts on the screen would appear correct only if used at the one size that corresponded to the point size loaded in the suitcase in your "System Folder." With ATM, you can, for example, have only the 10 -point versions of the screen fonts loaded (plus the printer fonts), and all point sizes of the font will appear correct on the screen. Without ATM and only one point size loaded, you would get jaggies if you used any other point size. *ATM prevents the jaggies in your screen fonts, and allows you to streamline your "Fonts" folder by loading only one point size of screen fonts.*

ATM is bundled with some programs made by Adobe, or it can be purchased separately through Adobe. You have to make sure that you load the version that corresponds to the chip in your computer (all versions come on the CD) since some versions are different depending on the chip speed and whether or not the chip uses RISC processing. Like most software, minor upgrades are available online.

Virtually every computer user should have ATM installed to make screen fonts work more effectively and accurately. Computer manufacturers would be wise to build this code into their operating systems. You may find that occasionally, if you have a screen freeze, ATM will default to "Off." You can check it through the "Control Panel"; there is an "On/Off" button in its Control Panel box; make sure that it is on before panicking.

Adobe Type Reunion is another essential utility for designers. It groups families of fonts together, and displays the variations of a font style in a list to the side of the main font list; this sub-menu is indicated by an arrow. Adobe Type Reunion makes scrolling through the font list faster and more efficient, and lets you access the styles of a font very quickly. It also shows you which versions of the font style and weight are loaded into the "System Folder."

PRINTER ERRORS & UNLIMITED DOWNLOADABLE FONTS

Occasionally, when printing, you will get a message back that the printer was unable to print your document, and there will be an error message followed by a sequence of numbers. Sometimes, the problem is that there are too many fonts in the document to be held in the RAM of the printer. To overcome this, you can go to the "Print" box, to "Options," and highlight "Unlimited Downloadable Fonts." This allows more fonts to be downloaded by first flushing the RAM of the printer, and then loading only your fonts in fresh. It usually takes the document longer to print with this option activated, but it will print, and this often overcomes the error message. You may also want to deselect the options for "Text Smoothing" and "Graphics Smoothing" at the same time since these require some extra RAM to be devoted to them.

If this does not alleviate your PostScript error, you may have to go through the tedious task of figuring out what is causing the offending command; this will take a while. First, systematically print one page of the document at a time; print from page 1 to page 1, then page 2 to page 2, etc. This will enable you to narrow down which page has the problem. Once you know which page has the glitch, move one image or type box from the page systematically– trying to print after one item has its printout suppressed. This methodical process will point to

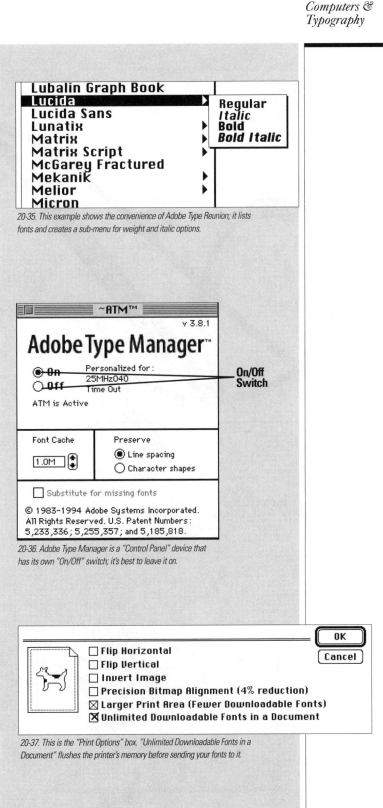

20-35. This example shows the convenience of Adobe Type Reunion; it lists fonts and creates a sub-menu for weight and italic options.

20-36. Adobe Type Manager is a "Control Panel" device that has its own "On/Off" switch; it's best to leave it on.

20-37. This is the "Print Options" box. "Unlimited Downloadable Fonts in a Document" flushes the printer's memory before sending your fonts to it.

20 **Computers &
    Typography**

20-38. When sending a document and its linked art to a service
bureau, it's a good idea to change any TrueType fonts into EPS
versions by bringing them into a drawing program and converting
them to paths. TrueType fonts may give you glitches in output and
are not yet practical for body copy.

*which image or text box is giving you the troubled sig-
nal in its Post Script code.*

*PostScript errors are dreaded by designers. They are
unpredictable; sometimes errors are caused by garbled
code in a scan; sometimes it's a font file that's gotten cor-
rupted. When you know what the problem is, delete
that type or image box, and recreate it, either by re-
scanning, or re-flowing in the text from the word-pro-
cessing document, or reloading the font from backups.
If the scan or type caused a problem once, it will continue to be a problem; there is little hope of rescuing
that damaged piece of information. It is, however, faster
to recreate only the offending scan or text than to have
to recreate the entire document.*

OUTLINE FONTS VS. MULTIPLE MASTER FONTS

*The outline format in which a font is created becomes
important; it can affect the appearance of the laser-out-
put font. The quality of the printed font at small sizes
can be dramatically different depending on whether
the font is encoded or directed with additional adjustments for better type at the small sizes. In Multiple
Master fonts, hinting, or the encoding that improves the
resolution of laser fonts at small sizes, makes the font
files larger because they take up more space to incorporate the hinting. But the resolution of the type at
small sizes is much better and truer to the font. Hinting
allows the font to be slightly adjusted depending on the
size it is printed. This is considered a preferable format to
straight outline encoding, which simply scales one outline of
a character to the required size, regardless of how large or small
the type is.*

*The hinted versions of fonts are more similar to the fonts
that punchcutters created by hand-cutting. The hinting reflects
the tendency in lead type to design the letters differently depending on their point size. Body text had one version of the letters, then there was the headline version and the display version. Hinted fonts are, in effect, recreating this multiple drawing
of a font by slightly adjusting the curves and counters of characters depending on the size at which they are used. This
practice of multiple fonts had gone out of use with digitized typesetting, where one font was scaled to all the necessary sizes. The
encoding of fonts as mathematical information has provided
the opportunity for type designers to return to an older standard of quality craftsmanship in type that was not possible
in the early digital technology. Rather than diminish the quality of type, laser and imagesetters will likely improve the overall quality and accuracy of the letterforms, restoring levels of
craftsmanship that had been considered obsolete.*

Computers & Typography-Review

1. What is RAM? _____

2. How does RAM differ from ROM? _____

3. What is the Disk Drive? _____

4. What is the Hard Drive? _____

5. What is the Motherboard? _____

6. What is the Microprocessor? _____

7. What is Megahertz? _____

8. What is a Program/Application? _____

9. What is a File/Document? _____

10. What is a Folder? _____

11. What is a screen font? _____

12. How does a screen font differ from a printer font? _____

13. What is a TrueType font, and how does it differ from a PostScript font? ____

14. What is the Chooser? _____

15. What is a Printer Description File? _____

16. What is the Print Monitor? _____

17. What is Tiling? _____

18. What is the difference between Manual and Automatic Tiling? _____

19. What is a Printer Driver? _____

20. What is a strategy for overcoming Print Cycle errors? _____

This page is set in
Fenice Light 8.5/12.

21 *Type Samples*

ITC American Typewriter Medium

ABCDEFGHIJ
KLMNOPQRST
UVWXYZabcd
efghijklmnop
qrstuvwxyz
1234567890
.,?*#$&'%!:;">

American Typewriter is based on the old mono-spaced font designed for typewriters; this version was designed by Joel Kadan with Tony Stan in 1974. The ITC version is not mono-spaced, yet it retains some of the details of the older version, such as the ball terminals; the overly wide, bulbous serifs; and the overall oval design to many of the bowls of the letters. Due to the large x-height, it is extremely legible at small sizes. Some of the numerals in this font, the "2" and the "7" are quite interesting in their curvaceousness. This is a nuts-and-bolts font: it appears practical and down-to-earth, and it has no pretensions of great elegance.

This is a sample of the text version of this font, to give you an idea of how easily the font reads at a variety of text settings. This allows you to compare fonts at a glance before using them in text type. Because of the differences in x-height, some fonts that measure the same point size appear to be different sizes for reading.

This example is set in 8.5 points, with -6 tracking, on 11 points of leading.

This is a sample of the text version of this font, to give you an idea of how easily the font reads at a variety of text settings. This allows you to compare fonts at a glance before using them in text type. Because of the differences in x-height, some fonts that measure the same point size appear to be different sizes for reading.

This example is set in 9 points, with -6 tracking, on 11 points of leading.

This is a sample of the text version of this font, to give you an idea of how easily the font reads at a variety of text settings. This allows you to compare fonts at a glance before using them in text type. Because of the differences in x-height, some fonts that measure the same point size appear to be different sizes for reading.

This example is set in 9.5 points, with -6 tracking, on 11 points of leading.

ITC Americana

ABCDEFGHIJ KLMNOPQRS TUVWXYZabc defghijklmno pqrstuvwxyz 1234567890., ?*#$&'%!:;">

Americana was designed by Isbell; it is particularly wide and has a very large x-height, giving it great legibility at small sizes. It has an informal flair and a graceful light-ness to the strokes; they taper beautifully into the spur serifs. These spur serifs are rather understated and subdued, giving Americana a light, contemporary feel. Because of the broad width of the characters, you won't fit many per line. This font should be used on a longer line length, at relatively small point sizes. It even looks rather large and clear at 7.5 points here and in the 8.5-point text sample, so you can use it in small point sizes for text.

This is a sample of the text version of this font, to give you an idea of how easily the font reads at a variety of text settings. This allows you to compare fonts at a glance before using them in text type. Because of the differences in x-height, some fonts that measure the same point size appear to be different sizes for reading.

This example is set in 8.5 points, with -6 tracking, on 11 points of leading.

This is a sample of the text version of this font, to give you an idea of how easily the font reads at a variety of text settings. This allows you to compare fonts at a glance before using them in text type. Because of the differences in x-height, some fonts that measure the same point size appear to be different sizes for reading.

This example is set in 9 points, with -6 tracking, on 11 points of leading.

This is a sample of the text version of this font, to give you an idea of how easily the font reads at a variety of text settings. This allows you to compare fonts at a glance before using them in text type. Because of the differences in x-height, some fonts that measure the same point size appear to be different sizes for reading.

This example is set in 9.5 points, with -6 tracking, on 11 points of leading.

This page is set in ITC Americana.

ITC Avant Garde Book

ABCDEFGHIJK
LMNOPQRSTU
VWXYZ abc
defghijklmn
opqrstuvwxyz
1234567890
.,?*#$&'%!:;">

Avant Garde is a very mechanical, rigid font built of perfect circles and right angles. It was originally designed as the nameplate for a magazine of the same name by Herb Lubalin, who later developed the entire alphabet with Tom Carnase in 1970, complete with alternate ligatured characters. The overall sense of this face is very round and very engineered–yet somehow it also looks very elementary in a typographic sense; it's reminiscent of geometry or letters in a tracing template. Rudimentary and basic describe the simplicity of this no-nonsense font. The lowercase is wide, and it should be used preferably on a long line length.

This is a sample of the text version of this font, to give you an idea of how easily the font reads at a variety of text settings. This allows you to compare fonts at a glance before using them in text type. Because of the differences in x-height, some fonts that measure the same point size appear to be different sizes for reading.

This example is set in 8.5 points, with -6 tracking, on 11 points of leading.

This is a sample of the text version of this font, to give you an idea of how easily the font reads at a variety of text settings. This allows you to compare fonts at a glance before using them in text type. Because of the differences in x-height, some fonts that measure the same point size appear to be different sizes for reading.

This example is set in 9 points, with -6 tracking, on 11 points of leading.

This is a sample of the text version of this font, to give you an idea of how easily the font reads at a variety of text settings. This allows you to compare fonts at a glance before using them in text type. Because of the differences in x-height, some fonts that measure the same point size appear to be different sizes for reading.

This example is set in 9.5 points, with -6 tracking, on 11 points of leading.

Balmoral Script Plain

*A B C D E F G H
I J K L M N O P
Q R S T U V W X
Y Z abcdefghijklmnopqrstuvwxyz
1234567890 .,?*$&'%!:;"*

Balmoral script has an overall circular sensibility to the uppercase letters, while the lowercase letters are quite condensed. The numerals are very handsome. The uppercase "I," "J," and "S" are difficult to discern from one another. This font would have to be set in 20 or more points for legibility (this is 20 pt.) because the lowercase is proportionally so much smaller than the caps. It is unreadable in the examples shown due to the excessively small x-height; notice that the lowercase is very condensed, so you fit a lot of letters on each line. This font could be set on a short line length successfully, without too many hyphens popping up.*

This is a sample of the text version of this font, to give you an idea of how easily the font reads at a variety of text settings. This allows you to compare fonts at a glance before using them in text type. Because of the differences in x-height, some fonts that measure the same point size appear to be different sizes for reading.

This example is set in 8.5 points, with -6 tracking, on 11 points of leading.

This is a sample of the text version of this font, to give you an idea of how easily the font reads at a variety of text settings. This allows you to compare fonts at a glance before using them in text type. Because of the differences in x-height, some fonts that measure the same point size appear to be different sizes for reading.

This example is set in 9 points, with -6 tracking, on 11 points of leading.

This is a sample of the text version of this font, to give you an idea of how easily the font reads at a variety of text settings. This allows you to compare fonts at a glance before using them in text type. Because of the differences in x-height, some fonts that measure the same point size appear to be different sizes for reading.

This example is set in 9.5 points, with -6 tracking, on 11 points of leading.

This is a sample of the text version of this font, to give you an idea of how easily the font reads at a variety of text settings. This allows you to compare fonts at a glance before using them in text type. Because of the differences in x-height, some fonts that measure the same point size appear to be different sizes for reading.

This example is set in 15 points, with -6 tracking, on 14 points of leading.

New Baskerville Roman

ABCDEFGHIJ KLMNOPQR STUVWXYZ abcdefghijklm nopqrstuvwxyz 1234567890 .,?*#$&'%!:;">

New Baskerville is a redesign of the original font of the same name. Many of the typographic nuances were maintained, but the width of the lower-case letters was reduced, and the serifs became a bit thicker; they no longer taper to points. The characters that seem to stick out in this font are the uppercase "E," whose bottom leg feels as though it juts out too far, almost as if it had a lower overbite. The "G" also seems as if its vertical stroke is too far extended from the bowl. Likewise, the lowercase "f" seems as if the arc is just a bit too wide. The numerals in this font are quite handsome. As a text font, this is extremely readable and clear. The italic is very vivacious; there are curly terminals on the "v" and "w," and the "f" and "y" are elegantly designed.

This is a sample of the text version of this font, to give you an idea of how easily the font reads at a variety of text settings. This allows you to compare fonts at a glance before using them in text type. Because of the differences in x-height, some fonts that measure the same point size appear to be different sizes for reading.

This example is set in 8.5 points, with -6 tracking, on 11 points of leading.

This is a sample of the text version of this font, to give you an idea of how easily the font reads at a variety of text settings. This allows you to compare fonts at a glance before using them in text type. Because of the differences in x-height, some fonts that measure the same point size appear to be different sizes for reading.

This example is set in 9 points, with -6 tracking, on 11 points of leading.

This is a sample of the text version of this font, to give you an idea of how easily the font reads at a variety of text settings. This allows you to compare fonts at a glance before using them in text type. Because of the differences in x-height, some fonts that measure the same point size appear to be different sizes for reading.

This example is set in 9.5 points, with -6 tracking, on 11 points of leading.

Bellevue

ABCDEFGHIJ
KLMNOPQR
STUVWXYZ
abcdefghijklmn
opqrstuvwxyz
1234567890
.,?* $&'%!:;"

Bellevue was designed by Jaeger; it is an interesting font that appears as a hybrid between a script and an italic typeface. It maintains the swashes and flourishes of a script, but also boasts the legibility of the lowercase, which is similar to an italic face. The exaggerated ball terminals call attention to themselves, even in text, so this might not be the best choice as a book font. These terminals add an air of whimsy to the typeface that is refreshing. The hooked finials on the lowercase are very tight and are almost vertical. Some of the characters, such as the uppercase "F," "L," and "M" are indeed unique and reveal the script influence in their design. The lowercase is slightly condensed and fits quite a quite a few characters per line; it reads well at small sizes.

This is a sample of the text version of this font, to give you an idea of how easily the font reads at a variety of text settings. This allows you to compare fonts at a glance before using them in text type. Because of the differences in x-height, some fonts that measure the same point size appear to be different sizes for reading.

This example is set in 8.5 points, with -6 tracking, on 11 points of leading.

This is a sample of the text version of this font, to give you an idea of how easily the font reads at a variety of text settings. This allows you to compare fonts at a glance before using them in text type. Because of the differences in x-height, some fonts that measure the same point size appear to be different sizes for reading.

This example is set in 9 points, with -6 tracking, on 11 points of leading.

This is a sample of the text version of this font, to give you an idea of how easily the font reads at a variety of text settings. This allows you to compare fonts at a glance before using them in text type. Because of the differences in x-height, some fonts that measure the same point size appear to be different sizes for reading.

This example is set in 9.5 points, with -6 tracking, on 11 points of leading.

This page is set in Bellevue.

Belwe Light

ABCDEFGHIJ KLMNOPQR STUVWXYZ abcdefghijklm nopqrstuvwxyz 1234567890 .,?*#$&'%!:;">

Belwe was designed by Georg Belwe in 1926. This font seems to take a legible face and push it to the limits of uniqueness, while still maintaining readability. This font calls attention to itself in text sizes, yet it is still very readable. It seems as though it would be perfect for a magazine geared toward adolescent girls; somehow the tails and angled serifs would appeal to their quirky sense of type. The flag-like extensions on the "v," "w," and "y" seem extraneous and unrelated to the other characters. The overly tight loop on the "2" and the "g" and the shoulder of the "f" seem wonderful design elements that harmonize well with the uppercase letters. The loop on the lowercase "k" is quite a unique feature in a Roman face.

This page is set in Belwe Light.

This is a sample of the text version of this font, to give you an idea of how easily the font reads at a variety of text settings. This allows you to compare fonts at a glance before using them in text type. Because of the differences in x-height, some fonts that measure the same point size appear to be different sizes for reading.

This example is set in 8.5 points, with -6 tracking, on 11 points of leading.

This is a sample of the text version of this font, to give you an idea of how easily the font reads at a variety of text settings. This allows you to compare fonts at a glance before using them in text type. Because of the differences in x-height, some fonts that measure the same point size appear to be different sizes for reading.

This example is set in 9 points, with -6 tracking, on 11 points of leading.

This is a sample of the text version of this font, to give you an idea of how easily the font reads at a variety of text settings. This allows you to compare fonts at a glance before using them in text type. Because of the differences in x-height, some fonts that measure the same point size appear to be different sizes for reading.

This example is set in 9.5 points, with -6 tracking, on 11 points of leading.

Bembo Regular

ABCDEFGHIJ KLMNOPQR STUVWXYZ abcdefghijklmn opqrstuvwxyz 1234567890 .,?★#$&'%!:;">

Bembo is a classic, standard face in book design and, therefore, may look very familiar to you in the text sizes. The clarity of its lowercase letters is admirable; they are clear yet they maintain their own identity, and work together as a team very well in text. Bembo was designed by Francesco Griffo for Cardinal Bembo in 1495 for Manutius's publication of De Aetna. The capital "R" has quite an extended, elegant tail, and the balance of the lowercase letters is poetic without being as predictable as Times Roman. Surprisingly, Bembo has quite a small x-height, which makes it most readable at the 9.5-point size in the examples of text type listed. This font marries functionality with artistry to create a unified whole. The italic version of Bembo, which you are reading, is very condensed, and it fits a lot of letters on this short line length, with relatively few hyphens. The flatness of the bowl on the lowercase "a" and the tail of the uppercase "R" help to distinguish this font.

This is a sample of the text version of this font, to give you an idea of how easily the font reads at a variety of text settings. This allows you to compare fonts at a glance before using them in text type. Because of the differences in x-height, some fonts that measure the same point size appear to be different sizes for reading.

This example is set in 8.5 points, with –6 tracking, on 11 points of leading.

This is a sample of the text version of this font, to give you an idea of how easily the font reads at a variety of text settings. This allows you to compare fonts at a glance before using them in text type. Because of the differences in x-height, some fonts that measure the same point size appear to be different sizes for reading.

This example is set in 9 points, with –6 tracking, on 11 points of leading.

This is a sample of the text version of this font, to give you an idea of how easily the font reads at a variety of text settings. This allows you to compare fonts at a glance before using them in text type. Because of the differences in x-height, some fonts that measure the same point size appear to be different sizes for reading.

This example is set in 9.5 points, with –6 tracking, on 11 points of leading.

Benguiat Book

ABCDEFGHIJ
KLMNOPQRST
UVWXYZabcd
efghijklmnop
qrstuvwxyz
1234567890
.,?*#$&'%!:;">

Benguiat is a font that you will never forget once you see it. It was designed by Edward Benguiat. The exaggerated points on the serifs are reminiscent of rose thorns or knife tips, and they seem to conjure up the danger of horror films. It is a very pointed font, one that could pierce you. It should be used sparingly in body copy–even though it is legible at small sizes—because of the harshness of the serifs. It also is very dark on the page in the book weight, which may make the text appear heavier and less inviting to the reader. The cross bars of many of the letters are arched and are higher than standard, giving this font a lighter, less serious flair.

This is a sample of the text version of this font, to give you an idea of how easily the font reads at a variety of text settings. This allows you to compare fonts at a glance before using them in text type. Because of the differences in x-height, some fonts that measure the same point size appear to be different sizes for reading.

This example is set in 8.5 points, with -6 tracking, on 11 points of leading.

This is a sample of the text version of this font, to give you an idea of how easily the font reads at a variety of text settings. This allows you to compare fonts at a glance before using them in text type. Because of the differences in x-height, some fonts that measure the same point size appear to be different sizes for reading.

This example is set in 9 points, with -6 tracking, on 11 points of leading.

This is a sample of the text version of this font, to give you an idea of how easily the font reads at a variety of text settings. This allows you to compare fonts at a glance before using them in text type. Because of the differences in x-height, some fonts that measure the same point size appear to be different sizes for reading.

This example is set in 9.5 points, with -6 tracking, on 11 points of leading.

ITC Berkeley Book

ABCDEFGHIJ
KLMNOPQR
STUVWXYZ
abcdefghijklmn
opqrstuvwxyz
1234567890
.,?*#$&'%!:;">

Berkeley is an interestingly designed font–its serifs are unevenly bracketed! This is most noticeable on the verticals of the "K," the "L," and the "N." You'll see, upon careful inspection, that the left serif has no bracketing to connect it to the stem, and the right serif has bracketing that eases it into the stem. Berkeley is an elegant font, originally drawn by Frederic Goudy, then redesigned by Tony Stan. It still appears to have its feet on the ground. It's well balanced and has subtle nuances in its design that make it handsome and readable, yet unique in body copy. It looks as though more care went into designing its letters than those of many other serif fonts. It appears very light and airy on the page even in book weight; and its italic, which you are reading, is very condensed, allowing for a lot of letters on this short line length. The italic is as readable as the Roman and clearly very beautiful in its own right.

This is a sample of the text version of this font, to give you an idea of how easily the font reads at a variety of text settings. This allows you to compare fonts at a glance before using them in text type. Because of the differences in x-height, some fonts that measure the same point size appear to be different sizes for reading.

This example is set in 8.5 points, with -6 tracking, on 11 points of leading.

This is a sample of the text version of this font, to give you an idea of how easily the font reads at a variety of text settings. This allows you to compare fonts at a glance before using them in text type. Because of the differences in x-height, some fonts that measure the same point size appear to be different sizes for reading.

This example is set in 9 points, with -6 tracking, on 11 points of leading.

This is a sample of the text version of this font, to give you an idea of how easily the font reads at a variety of text settings. This allows you to compare fonts at a glance before using them in text type. Because of the differences in x-height, some fonts that measure the same point size appear to be different sizes for reading.

This example is set in 9.5 points, with -6 tracking, on 11 points of leading.

This page is set in
ITC Berkeley Book.

21

Type Samples

Bernhard Modern Bold

ABCDEFGHI
JKLMNOPQR
STUVWXYZ
abcdefghijklmn
opqrstuvwxyz
1234567890
.,?*#$$&'%!.:;">

Bernhard Modern is a font that harkens back to the days of cuneiform and chisel-cut lettering. It was designed in 1929 by Lucien Bernhard. The horizontal strokes and some vertical strokes are shaped like triangles, and the serifs are curved lines with no bracketing. Because it is so simply structured, this font has an Ancient Greek feel to it. But it does work well in body copy, and it is legible at small sizes, regardless of the small x-height. The clarity and uniqueness of the design of the letters help the readability at small sizes. The font does not look heavy in body copy, even though the characters are bold; this must be due to the small x-height. Bernhard Modern is a good choice for body copy that you want to have distinction and show a sense of history.

This is a sample of the text version of this font, to give you an idea of how easily the font reads at a variety of text settings. This allows you to compare fonts at a glance before using them in text type. Because of the differences in x-height, some fonts that measure the same point size appear to be different sizes for reading.

This example is set in 8.5 points, with -6 tracking, on 11 points of leading.

This is a sample of the text version of this font, to give you an idea of how easily the font reads at a variety of text settings. This allows you to compare fonts at a glance before using them in text type. Because of the differences in x-height, some fonts that measure the same point size appear to be different sizes for reading.

This example is set in 9 points, with -6 tracking, on 11 points of leading.

This is a sample of the text version of this font, to give you an idea of how easily the font reads at a variety of text settings. This allows you to compare fonts at a glance before using them in text type. Because of the differences in x-height, some fonts that measure the same point size appear to be different sizes for reading.

This example is set in 9.5 points, with -6 tracking, on 11 points of leading.

This page is set in Bernhard Modern Bold.

Berthold Script Regular

ABCDEFGH
IJKLMNOP
QRSTUVWX
YZabcdefghijklmnop
qrstuvwxyz 1234567890
.,?*$&%!:;""

Berthold Script is a script whose stroke appears to be a monoweight line; there is not a lot of thick/thin contrast in this font. Overall there is a lightness to the script, especially in body copy. This is one of the more legible scripts, especially in the design of the uppercase letters. The lowercase owes a great deal to hand penmanship, as is evidenced in the design of the lowercase "f" with the loop at the top and the capital "Q," which is gracefully designed. The capital "S (s)" is difficult to understand, but the "M" and "N" are truly exquisitely designed. This text is set in 11.5 point, which is probably the smallest size to use this script due to the small x-height.

This is a sample of the text version of this font, to give you an idea of how easily the font reads at a variety of text settings. This allows you to compare fonts at a glance before using them in text type. Because of the differences in x-height, some fonts that measure the same point size appear to be different sizes for reading.

This example is set in 8.5 points, with -6 tracking, on 11 points of leading.

This is a sample of the text version of this font, to give you an idea of how easily the font reads at a variety of text settings. This allows you to compare fonts at a glance before using them in text type. Because of the differences in x-height, some fonts that measure the same point size appear to be different sizes for reading.

This example is set in 9 points, with -6 tracking, on 11 points of leading.

This is a sample of the text version of this font, to give you an idea of how easily the font reads at a variety of text settings. This allows you to compare fonts at a glance before using them in text type. Because of the differences in x-height, some fonts that measure the same point size appear to be different sizes for reading.

This example is set in 9.5 points, with -6 tracking, on 11 points of leading.

Bodoni Regular

ABCDEFGHIJ
KLMNOPQRS
TUVWXYZ
abcdefghijklm
nopqrstuvwxyz
1234567890.,
?*#$&'%!:;">

Bodoni is an engineer's font; it extols practicality before beauty. Designed in 1785 by Giambattista Bodoni, it looks as though it was drafted with rulers and triangles rather than drawn by hand and with an artistic sensibility. The double barbs on the "C" look too dark, and the tail on the "Q" appears as though it could slip off the "Q." Bodoni does evoke a technical sense and looks clean and crisp in body copy. The font has a practical appeal and has no extraneous curves or flourishes in body copy. Because of the vertical stress of the letters, it appears very vertical and rigid in body copy, which also emits a strength and durability. In body copy, it looks a bit dark. The italic reveals far more of the lettering ability of the designer than the Roman.

This page is set in Bodoni Regular.

This is a sample of the text version of this font, to give you an idea of how easily the font reads at a variety of text settings. This allows you to compare fonts at a glance before using them in text type. Because of the differences in x-height, some fonts that measure the same point size appear to be different sizes for reading.

This example is set in 8.5 points, with -6 tracking, on 11 points of leading.

This is a sample of the text version of this font, to give you an idea of how easily the font reads at a variety of text settings. This allows you to compare fonts at a glance before using them in text type. Because of the differences in x-height, some fonts that measure the same point size appear to be different sizes for reading.

This example is set in 9 points, with -6 tracking, on 11 points of leading.

This is a sample of the text version of this font, to give you an idea of how easily the font reads at a variety of text settings. This allows you to compare fonts at a glance before using them in text type. Because of the differences in x-height, some fonts that measure the same point size appear to be different sizes for reading.

This example is set in 9.5 points, with -6 tracking, on 11 points of leading.

ITC Bookman Light

ABCDEFGHIJ KLMNOPQRS TUVWXYZabc defghijklmno pqrstuvwxyz 1234567890.,? *#$&'%!:;">

Bookman is an extremely wide, bold font, even in its book weight; it is credited to Wadsworth A. Parker around 1900, and was redesigned by Edward Benguiat for ITC. The font has a large x-height, which makes it very easy to read at small sizes. Many children's books are set in Bookman because of its clarity. The barbs on the "C," "G" and "S" look exaggerated at large scale but feel comfortable at text sizes. The swirling tail of the "Q" is light-hearted. Bookman is a functional, clean face that can be used at small sizes because of its x-height, but should be set on a reasonably long line length because of the width of the characters to avoid numerous hyphens. The italic version is much softer and smoother than the Roman version.

This is a sample of the text version of this font, to give you an idea of how easily the font reads at a variety of text settings. This allows you to compare fonts at a glance before using them in text type. Because of the differences in x-height, some fonts that measure the same point size appear to be different sizes for reading.

This example is set in 8.5 points, with -6 tracking, on 11 points of leading.

This is a sample of the text version of this font, to give you an idea of how easily the font reads at a variety of text settings. This allows you to compare fonts at a glance before using them in text type. Because of the differences in x-height, some fonts that measure the same point size appear to be different sizes for reading.

This example is set in 9 points, with -6 tracking, on 11 points of leading.

This is a sample of the text version of this font, to give you an idea of how easily the font reads at a variety of text settings. This allows you to compare fonts at a glance before using them in text type. Because of the differences in x-height, some fonts that measure the same point size appear to be different sizes for reading.

This example is set in 9.5 points, with -6 tracking, on 11 points of leading.

This page is set in ITC Bookman Light.

21 Type Samples

Caslon 540 Roman

ABCDEFGHIJ KLMNOPQRS TUVWXYZ abcdefghijklm nopqrstuvwxyz 1234567890 .,?*#$&'%!:;">

Originally designed by William Caslon in 1725, Caslon 540 is a font that resonates with history. The lowercase is slightly extended and has a short x-height. There are some details of Caslon 540 that are quite notable: the tail on the "Q" is creatively designed, and the apex of the "A" is very comfortable yet unique. The "T" is very broad, and the teardrop terminals on the "f" and the "c" are quite full. Caslon works very well as body copy. Hopefully, you have also noticed how splendid Caslon's italic version is! The "w's," "y's" and "v's" almost look as though they were handwritten. The lowercase "f" is very graceful and delicate. The italic Caslon 540 is also very condensed, which allows more letters to the line, with less tendency for hyphens. This is an exceptional italic that successfully fuses style and creativity into one font, without sacrificing readability.

This page is set in Caslon 540 Roman.

This is a sample of the text version of this font, to give you an idea of how easily the font reads at a variety of text settings. This allows you to compare fonts at a glance before using them in text type. Because of the differences in x-height, some fonts that measure the same point size appear to be different sizes for reading.

This example is set in 8.5 points, with -6 tracking, on 11 points of leading.

This is a sample of the text version of this font, to give you an idea of how easily the font reads at a variety of text settings. This allows you to compare fonts at a glance before using them in text type. Because of the differences in x-height, some fonts that measure the same point size appear to be different sizes for reading.

This example is set in 9 points, with -6 tracking, on 11 points of leading.

This is a sample of the text version of this font, to give you an idea of how easily the font reads at a variety of text settings. This allows you to compare fonts at a glance before using them in text type. Because of the differences in x-height, some fonts that measure the same point size appear to be different sizes for reading.

This example is set in 9.5 points, with -6 tracking, on 11 points of leading.

Centennial Light

ABCDEFGHIJ
KLMNOPQRS
TUVWXYZab
cdefghijklmn
opqrstuvwxyz
1234567890
.,?*#$&'%!:;">

Centennial is a slightly condensed font, with a very large x-height which produces outstanding readability, particularly at small point sizes. Because it is slightly condensed, Centennial fits many characters to the line, which reduces the need for hyphenation. It has the potential to appear technical because of its vertical stress, but the bracketing on the serifs softens the engineered sense of the font a bit. It looks durable and as though it will withstand the changes of fashion. There are no gimmicks about this font. The italic version is creative and well designed; it has far more flair than the Roman version.

This is a sample of the text version of this font, to give you an idea of how easily the font reads at a variety of text settings. This allows you to compare fonts at a glance before using them in text type. Because of the differences in x-height, some fonts that measure the same point size appear to be different sizes for reading.

This example is set in 8.5 points, with -6 tracking, on 11 points of leading.

This is a sample of the text version of this font, to give you an idea of how easily the font reads at a variety of text settings. This allows you to compare fonts at a glance before using them in text type. Because of the differences in x-height, some fonts that measure the same point size appear to be different sizes for reading.

This example is set in 9 points, with -6 tracking, on 11 points of leading.

This is a sample of the text version of this font, to give you an idea of how easily the font reads at a variety of text settings. This allows you to compare fonts at a glance before using them in text type. Because of the differences in x-height, some fonts that measure the same point size appear to be different sizes for reading.

This example is set in 9.5 points, with -6 tracking, on 11 points of leading.

New Century Schoolbook

ABCDEFGHI JKLMNOPQR STUVWXYZ a bcdefghijklmn opqrstuvwxyz 1234567890.,? *#$&'%!:;">

New Century Schoolbook is a redesign of a classic face that was designed exclusively for the text of Century Magazine in 1896 by Lynn Boyd Benton and T. L. deVinne; it was redesigned by Morris Fuller Benton in 1920. Based on legibility research, it was widely used in children's reading primers. This is a bold, clear font, with easily distinguishable characters. Large ball terminals are modulated into gracefully. The serifs are tall and square on this serious font. This reads very well in text faces of all sizes, and is particularly legible at small point sizes due to the large x-height. Although there is a practical sense about this font, the letters harmonize well together in text. Also the italic is handsome, with a notable design to the "z," which is beautifully proportioned.

This page is set in New Century Schoolbook.

This is a sample of the text version of this font, to give you an idea of how easily the font reads at a variety of text settings. This allows you to compare fonts at a glance before using them in text type. Because of the differences in x-height, some fonts that measure the same point size appear to be different sizes for reading.

This example is set in 8.5 points, with -6 tracking, on 11 points of leading.

This is a sample of the text version of this font, to give you an idea of how easily the font reads at a variety of text settings. This allows you to compare fonts at a glance before using them in text type. Because of the differences in x-height, some fonts that measure the same point size appear to be different sizes for reading.

This example is set in 9 points, with -6 tracking, on 11 points of leading.

This is a sample of the text version of this font, to give you an idea of how easily the font reads at a variety of text settings. This allows you to compare fonts at a glance before using them in text type. Because of the differences in x-height, some fonts that measure the same point size appear to be different sizes for reading.

This example is set in 9.5 points, with -6 tracking, on 11 points of leading.

Cheltenham Light

ABCDEFGHIJ KLMNOPQRS TUVWXYZ abcdefghijklm nopqrstuvwxyz 1234567890 .,?*#$&'%!:;">

Cheltenham was designed in 1896 by Bertram Goodhue, an architect, and this font seems to have a sense of stability and structure to it. Cheltenham is a strong, readable text font. Its short, stocky serifs are clear at small sizes, and the ample x-height makes it extremely legible, even at 8.5 points. The font has a wide range of weights and condensed and extended versions. The strokes appear slender at large sizes, and the font is clean and light on the page. The characters of Cheltenham are slightly condensed, which means that quite a few characters fit on each line. This font lacks any distracting nuances, which make it a strong text font with great legibility. It is designed with a beauty of simplicity and a classic sense of restraint. It reads well for headlines and for text, the hallmark of a truly versatile font.

This is a sample of the text version of this font, to give you an idea of how easily the font reads at a variety of text settings. This allows you to compare fonts at a glance before using them in text type. Because of the differences in x-height, some fonts that measure the same point size appear to be different sizes for reading.

This example is set in 8.5 points, with -6 tracking, on 11 points of leading.

This is a sample of the text version of this font, to give you an idea of how easily the font reads at a variety of text settings. This allows you to compare fonts at a glance before using them in text type. Because of the differences in x-height, some fonts that measure the same point size appear to be different sizes for reading.

This example is set in 9 points, with -6 tracking, on 11 points of leading.

This is a sample of the text version of this font, to give you an idea of how easily the font reads at a variety of text settings. This allows you to compare fonts at a glance before using them in text type. Because of the differences in x-height, some fonts that measure the same point size appear to be different sizes for reading.

This example is set in 9.5 points, with -6 tracking, on 11 points of leading.

This page is set in Cheltenham Light.

Clarendon Regular

ABCDEFGHIJ
KLMNOPQR
STUVWXYZ
abcdefghijklm
nopqrstuvwx
yz123456789
0.,?*#$&'%!:;"

Designed as a bold text in 1845 by Robert Besley, Clarendon is an Egyptian font with heavy, thick serifs that provide a sense of stability and a darkness to the copy in text sizes. This dense, rich, broad font has handsome bracketing on the serifs, tightly curled ball terminals, and artistic transitions from stem to hairline weights. For all of its blockiness, Clarendon still has some curves and graceful transitions between stem and hairline strokes. When used in text type, Clarendon can set up a dark texture on the page, in contrast to lighter fonts. There is a classic style to the design of Clarendon, and for a headline font it is very well balanced.

This is a sample of the text version of this font, to give you an idea of how easily the font reads at a variety of text settings. This allows you to compare fonts at a glance before using them in text type. Because of the differences in x-height, some fonts that measure the same point size appear to be different sizes for reading.

This example is set in 8.5 points, with -6 tracking, on 11 points of leading.

This is a sample of the text version of this font, to give you an idea of how easily the font reads at a variety of text settings. This allows you to compare fonts at a glance before using them in text type. Because of the differences in x-height, some fonts that measure the same point size appear to be different sizes for reading.

This example is set in 9 points, with -6 tracking, on 11 points of leading.

This is a sample of the text version of this font, to give you an idea of how easily the font reads at a variety of text settings. This allows you to compare fonts at a glance before using them in text type. Because of the differences in x-height, some fonts that measure the same point size appear to be different sizes for reading.

This example is set in 9.5 points, with -6 tracking, on 11 points of leading.

ITC Clearface Regular

ABCDEFGHIJ
KLMNOPQR
STUVWXYZ
abcdefghijklm
nopqrstuvwxyz
1234567890
.,?*#$&'%!:;">

Clearface is a slightly condensed font with very little bracketing on the rectilinear serifs. It was originally designed by Morris Fuller Benton in 1907, and then redesigned by Caruso for ITC. The bottom of the eye of the "e" is slanted, and there are teardrop terminals in unexpected places–such as on the "k," the "v," the "w" and the "y." These delicate terminals soften the otherwise stringently designed face and give it more of a human quality. The beaks on the "F," "E" and "T" appear rather dark at large sizes, but seem appropriate in body copy. The gracefully sloping arc of the lowercase "a" is a distinguishing characteristic of this font. As its name states, it is extremely legible at small point sizes and has a good fit in text sizes.

This is a sample of the text version of this font, to give you an idea of how easily the font reads at a variety of text settings. This allows you to compare fonts at a glance before using them in text type. Because of the differences in x-height, some fonts that measure the same point size appear to be different sizes for reading.

This example is set in 8.5 points, with -6 tracking, on 11 points of leading.

This is a sample of the text version of this font, to give you an idea of how easily the font reads at a variety of text settings. This allows you to compare fonts at a glance before using them in text type. Because of the differences in x-height, some fonts that measure the same point size appear to be different sizes for reading.

This example is set in 9 points, with -6 tracking, on 11 points of leading.

This is a sample of the text version of this font, to give you an idea of how easily the font reads at a variety of text settings. This allows you to compare fonts at a glance before using them in text type. Because of the differences in x-height, some fonts that measure the same point size appear to be different sizes for reading.

This example is set in 9.5 points, with -6 tracking, on 11 points of leading.

COPPERPLATE 29

ABCDEFGHIJ
KLMNOPQRST
UVWXYZ ABC
DEFGHIJKLMNO
PQRSTUVWXYZ
1234567890
.,?*#$$&'%!:;">

COPPERPLATE WAS DESIGNED IN 1904 BY FREDERIC GOUDY. IT IS AN INTERESTING FONT; IT SPORTS MINUTE SPUR SERIFS THAT ARE BARELY VIEWABLE AT SMALL TEXT SIZES. ALTHOUGH THIS IS CONSIDERED A SERIF FONT, IT APPEARS MONO-WEIGHT IN THE DESIGN OF THE STROKE. THE ONLY LOWERCASE IN THIS FONT IS THE SMALL CAPITALS–THERE ARE NO CHARACTERS WITH ASCENDERS AND DESCENDERS. THIS FORMAT, CAPS, AND SMALL CAPS MEANS THAT COPPERPLATE SHOULD BE USED ONLY FOR LIMITED AMOUNTS OF TEXT TYPE, TO AVOID EXCESSIVE EYE STRAIN ON THE READER. IF YOU READ THE TEXT AT THE RIGHT, YOU WILL SEE THAT IT IS TEDIOUS TO DECODE EACH LETTER.

THIS IS A SAMPLE OF THE TEXT VERSION OF THIS FONT, TO GIVE YOU AN IDEA OF HOW EASILY THE FONT READS AT A VARIETY OF TEXT SETTINGS. THIS ALLOWS YOU TO COMPARE FONTS AT A GLANCE BEFORE USING THEM IN TEXT TYPE. BECAUSE OF THE DIFFERENCES IN X-HEIGHT, SOME FONTS THAT MEASURE THE SAME POINT SIZE APPEAR TO BE DIFFERENT SIZES FOR READING.

THIS EXAMPLE IS SET IN 8.5 POINTS, WITH -6 TRACKING, ON 11 POINTS OF LEADING.

THIS IS A SAMPLE OF THE TEXT VERSION OF THIS FONT, TO GIVE YOU AN IDEA OF HOW EASILY THE FONT READS AT A VARIETY OF TEXT SETTINGS. THIS ALLOWS YOU TO COMPARE FONTS AT A GLANCE BEFORE USING THEM IN TEXT TYPE. BECAUSE OF THE DIFFERENCES IN X-HEIGHT, SOME FONTS THAT MEASURE THE SAME POINT SIZE APPEAR TO BE DIFFERENT SIZES FOR READING.

THIS EXAMPLE IS SET IN 9 POINTS, WITH -6 TRACKING, ON 11 POINTS OF LEADING.

THIS IS A SAMPLE OF THE TEXT VERSION OF THIS FONT, TO GIVE YOU AN IDEA OF HOW EASILY THE FONT READS AT A VARIETY OF TEXT SETTINGS. THIS ALLOWS YOU TO COMPARE FONTS AT A GLANCE BEFORE USING THEM IN TEXT TYPE. BECAUSE OF THE DIFFERENCES IN X-HEIGHT, SOME FONTS THAT MEASURE THE SAME POINT SIZE APPEAR TO BE DIFFERENT SIZES FOR READING.

THIS EXAMPLE IS SET IN 9.5 POINTS, WITH -6 TRACKING, ON 11 POINTS OF LEADING.

Embassy

Embassy is more legible than most other scripts. The design of the uppercase letters shows great restraint in the limitation of curlicues and flourishes. The ball terminals are simple in their gracefulness. This understated font should be set at a minimum of 12-point type (the size you are reading is 14) for the best legibility. Due to its classic design, Embassy provides a sense of history and tradition.

This is a sample of the text version of this font, to give you an idea of how easily the font reads at a variety of text settings. This allows you to compare fonts at a glance before using them in text type. Because of the differences in x-height, some fonts that measure the same point size appear to be different sizes for reading.

This example is set in 8.5 points, with -6 tracking, on 11 points of leading.

This is a sample of the text version of this font, to give you an idea of how easily the font reads at a variety of text settings. This allows you to compare fonts at a glance before using them in text type. Because of the differences in x-height, some fonts that measure the same point size appear to be different sizes for reading.

This example is set in 9 points, with -6 tracking, on 11 points of leading.

This is a sample of the text version of this font, to give you an idea of how easily the font reads at a variety of text settings. This allows you to compare fonts at a glance before using them in text type. Because of the differences in x-height, some fonts that measure the same point size appear to be different sizes for reading.

This example is set in 9.5 points, with -6 tracking, on 11 points of leading.

This page is set in Embassy.

ITC Eras Book

ABCDEFGHIJ
KLMNOPQRST
UVWXYZ

abcdefghijklm
nopqrstuvwxyz

1234567890

.,?*#$&'%!:;">

Designed by Albert Hollenstein and Albert Boton for ITC in 1976, Eras is an unusual font; it has a bit of a slant to it, even in the Roman face. The lowercase "a" is unique because it has an open rather than a closed bowl. There is also a smoothness to the arc of the "a" meeting the bowl; they almost form an upside down "s" because they are so continuous. The lowercase "p" and "q" seem as if their bowls hang a bit low on the baseline; they look as though they are a bit too heavy for the stem. The "c," "r" and "f" have terminals that are slightly slanted. The "6," the "9," the "P" and the "R" also have open bowls in Eras. This is a very readable font at small sizes and has a clean, contemporary, informal feel to the characters.

This is a sample of the text version of this font, to give you an idea of how easily the font reads at a variety of text settings. This allows you to compare fonts at a glance before using them in text type. Because of the differences in x-height, some fonts that measure the same point size appear to be different sizes for reading.

This example is set in 8.5 points, with -6 tracking, on 11 points of leading.

This is a sample of the text version of this font, to give you an idea of how easily the font reads at a variety of text settings. This allows you to compare fonts at a glance before using them in text type. Because of the differences in x-height, some fonts that measure the same point size appear to be different sizes for reading.

This example is set in 9 points, with -6 tracking, on 11 points of leading.

This is a sample of the text version of this font, to give you an idea of how easily the font reads at a variety of text settings. This allows you to compare fonts at a glance before using them in text type. Because of the differences in x-height, some fonts that measure the same point size appear to be different sizes for reading.

This example is set in 9.5 points, with -6 tracking, on 11 points of leading.

Eurostile Extended

ABCDEFGHI JKLMNOPQ RSTUVWX YZabcdefghij klmnopqrstu vwxyz1234 567890.,? *#$$&'%!:;">

Designed by Aldo Novarese and Alessandro Butti in 1962, Eurostile Extended is a broad, square, architectural face that has a sense of the futuristic about it due to its angular design. This font seems to scream "less is more," and attempts to omit all curves and replace them with rounded corners on characters. In text sizes, Eurostile appears very large, even at 8.5 points, so it can be used in quite small sizes. However, because this font is so extended, it will fit only a few characters to the line, and text will tend to run longer than expected.

This is a sample of the text version of this font, to give you an idea of how easily the font reads at a variety of text settings. This allows you to compare fonts at a glance before using them in text type. Because of the differences in x-height, some fonts that measure the same point size appear to be different sizes for reading.
This example is set in 8.5 points, with -6 tracking, on 11 points of leading.

This is a sample of the text version of this font, to give you an idea of how easily the font reads at a variety of text settings. This allows you to compare fonts at a glance before using them in text type. Because of the differences in x-height, some fonts that measure the same point size appear to be different sizes for reading.
This example is set in 9 points, with -6 tracking, on 11 points of leading.

This is a sample of the text version of this font, to give you an idea of how easily the font reads at a variety of text settings. This allows you to compare fonts at a glance before using them in text type. Because of the differences in x-height, some fonts that measure the same point size appear to be different sizes for reading.
This example is set in 9.5 points, with -6 tracking, on 11 points of leading.

This page is set in Eurostile Extended.

ITC Fat Face Normal

ABCDEFGHIJ
KLMNOPQR
STUVWXYZ
abcdefghijklm
nopqrstuvwxyz
1234567890
.,?*#$S&'%!:;"" ›

Fat Face, designed by Alessandro Butti and Aldo Novarese in 1946, is a highly condensed font that has overly heavy stem strokes that contrast with very thin hairline strokes. This combination makes for limited readability for text sizes, but this font can be effective for display or headline purposes. Because it is so condensed, it allows a lot of words to be crammed into a small space, and have them still appear readable and bold. Like many bold fonts, Fat Face should be kerned very carefully and judiciously; if it's kerned too tightly, it will be almost impossible to read; if it's too loosely spaced, the words will be hard to connect. This text is set in 10 points.

This is a sample of the text version of this font, to give you an idea of how easily the font reads at a variety of text settings. This allows you to compare fonts at a glance before using them in text type. Because of the differences in x-height, some fonts that measure the same point size appear to be different sizes for reading.

This example is set in 8.5 points, with 6 tracking, on 11 points of leading.

This is a sample of the text version of this font, to give you an idea of how easily the font reads at a variety of text settings. This allows you to compare fonts at a glance before using them in text type. Because of the differences in x-height, some fonts that measure the same point size appear to be different sizes for reading.

This example is set in 9 points, with 6 tracking, on 11 points of leading.

This is a sample of the text version of this font, to give you an idea of how easily the font reads at a variety of text settings. This allows you to compare fonts at a glance before using them in text type. Because of the differences in x-height, some fonts that measure the same point size appear to be different sizes for reading.

This example is set in 9.5 points, with 6 tracking, on 11 points of leading.

ITC Fenice Regular

ABCDEFGHIJ
KLMNOPQR
STUVWXYZ
abcdefghijklm
nopqrstuvwxyz
1234567890
.,?*#$$&'%!:;">

Designed in 1980 by Aldo Novarese, Fenice is a condensed font that owes a lot of its design to the mechanical simplicity of Bodoni. One of the major differences between the two is that where Bodoni has ball terminals, Fenice has triangularly shaped terminals, beaks and barbs. The beaks on the "E," "F," "L" and "T" are shaped like triangles; they are bold without seeming too out of place. Fenice has great legibility at small sizes; even the 8.5-point sample is easy to read. This is due to the large x-height of the font. The lowercase "g" has a unique structure to it; it almost looks as if the link curves out too far before joining the loop below. The italic is very closely related to the Roman, with few character changes. It is more of an oblique rather than a new font.

This is a sample of the text version of this font, to give you an idea of how easily the font reads at a variety of text settings. This allows you to compare fonts at a glance before using them in text type. Because of the differences in x-height, some fonts that measure the same point size appear to be different sizes for reading.

This example is set in 8.5 points, with -6 tracking, on 11 points of leading.

This is a sample of the text version of this font, to give you an idea of how easily the font reads at a variety of text settings. This allows you to compare fonts at a glance before using them in text type. Because of the differences in x-height, some fonts that measure the same point size appear to be different sizes for reading.

This example is set in 9 points, with -6 tracking, on 11 points of leading.

This is a sample of the text version of this font, to give you an idea of how easily the font reads at a variety of text settings. This allows you to compare fonts at a glance before using them in text type. Because of the differences in x-height, some fonts that measure the same point size appear to be different sizes for reading.

This example is set in 9.5 points, with -6 tracking, on 11 points of leading.

Franklin Gothic Roman

21 *Type Samples*

ABCDEFGHIJ KLMNOPQRS TUVWXYZabc defghijklmnop qrstuvwxyz12 34567890.,? *#$&'%!:;">

Franklin Gothic is an outstanding sans serif font in terms of legibility; it was designed in 1904 by Morris Fuller Benton. Although it is sans serif, the structure of the characters is very close to some elements of serif design. This is seen in the thick-and-thin transitions, and the structure of the lowercase "a" and the lowercase "g." Franklin Gothic is a very handsome font. It is designed with a great sense of overall appropriateness to the characters; they seem as if they are the quintessential letters. There is an air of authority to this font because of the timelessness of its design. For body copy, this is a rather dark choice and should be used sparingly.

This is a sample of the text version of this font, to give you an idea of how easily the font reads at a variety of text settings. This allows you to compare fonts at a glance before using them in text type. Because of the differences in x-height, some fonts that measure the same point size appear to be different sizes for reading.

This example is set in 8.5 points, with -6 tracking, on 11 points of leading.

This is a sample of the text version of this font, to give you an idea of how easily the font reads at a variety of text settings. This allows you to compare fonts at a glance before using them in text type. Because of the differences in x-height, some fonts that measure the same point size appear to be different sizes for reading.

This example is set in 9 points, with -6 tracking, on 11 points of leading.

This is a sample of the text version of this font, to give you an idea of how easily the font reads at a variety of text settings. This allows you to compare fonts at a glance before using them in text type. Because of the differences in x-height, some fonts that measure the same point size appear to be different sizes for reading.

This example is set in 9.5 points, with -6 tracking, on 11 points of leading.

This page is set in Franklin Gothic Roman.

Friz Quadrata Roman

ABCDEFGHIJK LMNOPQRST UVWXYZ

abcdeghijklmn opqrstuvwxyz

1234567890

.,?*#$&'%!:;">

Friz Quadrata is a quirky font with spur serifs that are barely noticeable at text sizes. It was designed by Friz for ITC. Most of the bowls are open, particularly in the lowercase letters. The "v" and "w" appear as if their base has been cut off on a slant, and they look as though they could tip over. The lowercase "g" has some graceful sweep to the curves, and overall there is a clarity to the structure of the letters. Friz reads well as a text font, but it does appear a bit dark on the page. Also, it looks rather informal due to the uniqueness of design of the letters. The open bowls can be distracting at small sizes, and they can easily be mistaken for broken type at first glance.

This is a sample of the text version of this font, to give you an idea of how easily the font reads at a variety of text settings. This allows you to compare fonts at a glance before using them in text type. Because of the differences in x-height, some fonts that measure the same point size appear to be different sizes for reading.

This example is set in 8.5 points, with -6 tracking, on 11 points of leading.

This is a sample of the text version of this font, to give you an idea of how easily the font reads at a variety of text settings. This allows you to compare fonts at a glance before using them in text type. Because of the differences in x-height, some fonts that measure the same point size appear to be different sizes for reading.

This example is set in 9 points, with -6 tracking, on 11 points of leading.

This is a sample of the text version of this font, to give you an idea of how easily the font reads at a variety of text settings. This allows you to compare fonts at a glance before using them in text type. Because of the differences in x-height, some fonts that measure the same point size appear to be different sizes for reading.

This example is set in 9.5 points, with -6 tracking, on 11 points of leading.

This page is set in Friz Quadrata Roman.

Frutiger Roman

ABCDEFGHIJ KLMNOPQR STUVWXYZ abcdefghijklm nopqrstuvwxyz 1234567890., ?*#$&'%!:;">

Frutiger Roman was designed in 1976 by Adrian Frutiger, who also designed the Univers family. It is an exceptionally well-designed sans serif font. It is unusual because even though it is sans serif, it retains a sense of a business attitude and seriousness. This is a font that would be comfortable set next to any serif font. It is clear and elegantly designed with a sense of simplicity. Because the letters are so cleanly designed, Frutiger reads well at very small text sizes, and its large x-height makes it appear very large at 9.5 in the example at the right. There are no distracting nuances to call attention to this font. The artistry was put into creating letters so beautiful that they look perfectly balanced.

This is a sample of the text version of this font, to give you an idea of how easily the font reads at a variety of text settings. This allows you to compare fonts at a glance before using them in text type. Because of the differences in x-height, some fonts that measure the same point size appear to be different sizes for reading.

This example is set in 8.5 points, with -6 tracking, on 11 points of leading.

This is a sample of the text version of this font, to give you an idea of how easily the font reads at a variety of text settings. This allows you to compare fonts at a glance before using them in text type. Because of the differences in x-height, some fonts that measure the same point size appear to be different sizes for reading.

This example is set in 9 points, with -6 tracking, on 11 points of leading.

This is a sample of the text version of this font, to give you an idea of how easily the font reads at a variety of text settings. This allows you to compare fonts at a glance before using them in text type. Because of the differences in x-height, some fonts that measure the same point size appear to be different sizes for reading.

This example is set in 9.5 points, with -6 tracking, on 11 points of leading.

Futura Regular

ABCDEFGHIJ KLMNOPQR STUVWXYZ abcdefghijklm nopqrstuvwxyz 1234567890 .,?*#$$&'%!:;">

Futura was designed during the Art Deco era of the 1920s by Paul Renner in 1927. It is a font that appears as though it was drafted using a perfect square, a triangle and a circle template. The lowercase "i" is unusual in its lack of a curved terminal on the descender. All of the bowls of the characters are perfect circles. This makes the round characters very wide in comparison to the other characters, which can make Futura appear a bit spotty when used as a text font. Although the full circles are a welcome break in the lowercase, they can be distracting in text type. Futura reads well at small sizes because of the good legibility of the characters. There is a variety of weights and condensed versions of Futura, making it a versatile text choice.

This is a sample of the text version of this font, to give you an idea of how easily the font reads at a variety of text settings. This allows you to compare fonts at a glance before using them in text type. Because of the differences in x-height, some fonts that measure the same point size appear to be different sizes for reading.

This example is set in 8.5 points, with -6 tracking, on 11 points of leading.

This is a sample of the text version of this font, to give you an idea of how easily the font reads at a variety of text settings. This allows you to compare fonts at a glance before using them in text type. Because of the differences in x-height, some fonts that measure the same point size appear to be different sizes for reading.

This example is set in 9 points, with -6 tracking, on 11 points of leading.

This is a sample of the text version of this font, to give you an idea of how easily the font reads at a variety of text settings. This allows you to compare fonts at a glance before using them in text type. Because of the differences in x-height, some fonts that measure the same point size appear to be different sizes for reading.

This example is set in 9.5 points, with -6 tracking, on 11 points of leading.

This page is set in Futura Regular.

Galliard Roman

ABCDEFGHIJ
KLMNOPQR
STUVWXYZ
abcdefghijklm
nopqrstuvwxyz
1234567890
.,?*#$&'%!:;">

Designed in 1978 by Matthew Carter, the font Galliard is a Transitional font that owes much of its design to historic stone carvings. As with most Transitional fonts, the stem strokes almost appear too thick to be supported by the hair-line strokes. The serifs seem an odd mixture of heavy bracketing that quickly tapers down to pointed serifs. In general, the bracketing seems over-bearing for many of the uppercase characters. However, the structure of the lowercase "a" is worthy of note, with the top of the bowl angled, and with a corner at the transition into the curve of the bowl. The italic Galliard is very different from the Roman version; it is much more condensed, looks more like calligraphy than the Roman, and reads very well at small sizes.

This is a sample of the text version of this font, to give you an idea of how easily the font reads at a variety of text settings. This allows you to compare fonts at a glance before using them in text type. Because of the differences in x-height, some fonts that measure the same point size appear to be different sizes for reading.

This example is set in 8.5 points, with -6 tracking, on 11 points of leading.

This is a sample of the text version of this font, to give you an idea of how easily the font reads at a variety of text settings. This allows you to compare fonts at a glance before using them in text type. Because of the differences in x-height, some fonts that measure the same point size appear to be different sizes for reading.

This example is set in 9 points, with -6 tracking, on 11 points of leading.

This is a sample of the text version of this font, to give you an idea of how easily the font reads at a variety of text settings. This allows you to compare fonts at a glance before using them in text type. Because of the differences in x-height, some fonts that measure the same point size appear to be different sizes for reading.

This example is set in 9.5 points, with -6 tracking, on 11 points of leading.

This page is set in Galliard Roman.

ITC Garamond Light

ABCDEFGHIJ
KLMNOPQR
STUVWXYZ
abcdefghijklm
nopqrstuvwxyz
1234567890
.,?*#$&'%!:;">

*ITC Garamond is a
redrawing by Tony
Stan of the original
font designed in 1530
by Claude Garamond,
with a higher x-height
to improve readability.
As an Old Style font,
Garamond has organ-
ic, rounded ends to the
serifs and a cupped
bottom that makes the
letters appear very sta-
ble. The beaks on the
"T" and the "Z" in this
font are interesting: the
left one is slanted, and
the right one is vertical.
Also, the lowercase "a"
is distinguishable
because the bowl looks
very flat and angled in
text sizes. This is a very
curvaceous, comfort-
able font; it doesn't
appear too business-
like, or too casual. The
numerals are hand-
somely designed, and
the italic has some
wonderful finials.*

This is a sample of the text version of this font, to give you an idea of how easily the font reads at a variety of text settings. This allows you to compare fonts at a glance before using them in text type. Because of the differences in x-height, some fonts that measure the same point size appear to be different sizes for reading.

This example is set in 8.5 points, with -6 tracking, on 11 points of leading.

This is a sample of the text version of this font, to give you an idea of how easily the font reads at a variety of text settings. This allows you to compare fonts at a glance before using them in text type. Because of the differences in x-height, some fonts that measure the same point size appear to be different sizes for reading.

This example is set in 9 points, with -6 tracking, on 11 points of leading.

This is a sample of the text version of this font, to give you an idea of how easily the font reads at a variety of text settings. This allows you to compare fonts at a glance before using them in text type. Because of the differences in x-height, some fonts that measure the same point size appear to be different sizes for reading.

This example is set in 9.5 points, with -6 tracking, on 11 points of leading.

Gill Sans Regular

ABCDEFGHIJ
KLMNOPQR
STUVWXYZ
abcdefghijklm
nopqrstuvwxyz
1234567890
.,?*#$&'%!:;">

Gill Sans was designed in 1928 by the type designer Eric Gill, a British typophile who was trained as a stone engraver and studied lettering under Britain's Edward Johnston. Many say that this font owes a great tribute to Johnston's font designed for the London subways; the two are very similar. Gill Sans has some unique characteristics: the vertex of the uppercase "M" does not touch the baseline, the lowercase "a" has a tail on it , and the tail of the uppercase "R" is graceful and has a taper to it. The bowls of the lowercase "p" and "q" meet the stem stroke at a right angle. The structure of the italic is extremely different from the Roman, the "f" has a descender, and the "p's" bowl crosses the stem with a decorative tail. For all of its nuances, Gill is still an outstandingly flexible, unique font with a timelessness to the clarity of the letters.

This is a sample of the text version of this font, to give you an idea of how easily the font reads at a variety of text settings. This allows you to compare fonts at a glance before using them in text type. Because of the differences in x-height, some fonts that measure the same point size appear to be different sizes for reading.

This example is set in 8.5 points, with -6 tracking, on 11 points of leading.

This is a sample of the text version of this font, to give you an idea of how easily the font reads at a variety of text settings. This allows you to compare fonts at a glance before using them in text type. Because of the differences in x-height, some fonts that measure the same point size appear to be different sizes for reading.

This example is set in 9 points, with -6 tracking, on 11 points of leading.

This is a sample of the text version of this font, to give you an idea of how easily the font reads at a variety of text settings. This allows you to compare fonts at a glance before using them in text type. Because of the differences in x-height, some fonts that measure the same point size appear to be different sizes for reading.

This example is set in 9.5 points, with -6 tracking, on 11 points of leading.

Goudy Oldstyle Regular

ABCDEFGHIJ
KLMNOPQR
STUVWXYZ
abcdefghijklm
nopqrstuvwxyz
1234567890
.,?*#$&'%!:;">

Goudy Oldstyle, named after its designer, Frederic Goudy, was created in 1915, and is an outstanding combination of beauty and balance. Goudy researched the structure of his fonts from historic references, and he had an exquisite eye for type design. The serifs in this font are organic and gentle, without being overstated. The legs of the "L" and the "E" have a curvilinear structure to them; they appear almost spoon-shaped in their upward, sweep. The ear on the lowercase "g" tilts upward and the dots on the "i," the "j" and the periods and punctuation are actually diamond-shaped. Somehow, you can almost feel the human hand drawing this font, especially in the sweeping curves and arcs of the uppercase letters. This is a fine text font, but probably reads best over 9 points because the x-height is not too large. The italic is a refreshing break from the Roman, but often appears tiny by comparison to the Roman.

This is a sample of the text version of this font, to give you an idea of how easily the font reads at a variety of text settings. This allows you to compare fonts at a glance before using them in text type. Because of the differences in x-height, some fonts that measure the same point size appear to be different sizes for reading.

This example is set in 8.5 points with -6 tracking, on 11 points of leading.

This is a sample of the text version of this font, to give you an idea of how easily the font reads at a variety of text settings. This allows you to compare fonts at a glance before using them in text type. Because of the differences in x-height, some fonts that measure the same point size appear to be different sizes for reading.

This example is set in 9 points, with -6 tracking, on 11 points of leading.

This is a sample of the text version of this font, to give you an idea of how easily the font reads at a variety of text settings. This allows you to compare fonts at a glance before using them in text type. Because of the differences in x-height, some fonts that measure the same point size appear to be different sizes for reading.

This example is set in 9.5 points, with -6 tracking, on 11 points of leading.

This page is set in Goudy Oldstyle Regular.

Harting Regular

ABCDEFGHIJ
KLMNOPQRST
UVWXYZabcde
fghijklmno
pqrstuvwxyz
1234567890
.,?*#$£%!:;">

Harting is a specialty font that should be used only in limited text applications. It has an irregular baseline, and the texture of burlap to the letters. The spacing is very staccato, which makes it quite tedious to read. For headlines, Harting has to be kerned carefully. It has a rustic, rough-hewn feel to it, a sort of homemade quality. It screams that it's for a low-budget and non corporate environment.

This is a sample of the text version of this font, to give you an idea of how easily the font reads at a variety of text settings. This allows you to compare fonts at a glance before using them in text type. Because of the differences in x-height, some fonts that measure the same point size appear to be different sizes for reading.

This example is set in 8.5 points, with -6 tracking, on 11 points of leading.

This is a sample of the text version of this font, to give you an idea of how easily the font reads at a variety of text settings. This allows you to compare fonts at a glance before using them in text type. Because of the differences in x-height, some fonts that measure the same point size appear to be different sizes for reading.

This example is set in 9 points, with -6 tracking, on 11 points of leading.

This is a sample of the text version of this font, to give you an idea of how easily the font reads at a variety of text settings. This allows you to compare fonts at a glance before using them in text type. Because of the differences in x-height, some fonts that measure the same point size appear to be different sizes for reading.

This example is set in 9.5 points, -6 tracking, on 11 points of leading.

Helvetica Regular

ABCDEFGHIJ
KLMNOPQR
STUVWXYZ
abcdefghijklm
nopqrstuvwxyz
1234567890
.,?*#$$&'%!:;">

Probably the most overused of all fonts, Helvetica was designed in the 1950s by Max Meidinger and Eduoard Hoffman. Helvetica has, as a result, become synonymous with generic design. It no longer has a specific identity; it is used on generic packaging, and in numerous corporate logos. It no longer evokes any specific associations due to its broad overuse. However, if your message is about the generic in our visual environment, this is the perfect font. Helvetica is a very basic font. It is clear, it is readable, but alas, it is not beautiful. There is no soul to it, no grace, no personality, no luster. Perhaps, then, it has found its ideal niche in the nameless world of generic existence.

This is a sample of the text version of this font, to give you an idea of how easily the font reads at a variety of text settings. This allows you to compare fonts at a glance before using them in text type. Because of the differences in x-height, some fonts that measure the same point size appear to be different sizes for reading.

This example is set in 8.5 points, with -6 tracking, on 11 points of leading.

This is a sample of the text version of this font, to give you an idea of how easily the font reads at a variety of text settings. This allows you to compare fonts at a glance before using them in text type. Because of the differences in x-height, some fonts that measure the same point size appear to be different sizes for reading.

This example is set in 9 points, with -6 tracking, on 11 points of leading.

This is a sample of the text version of this font, to give you an idea of how easily the font reads at a variety of text settings. This allows you to compare fonts at a glance before using them in text type. Because of the differences in x-height, some fonts that measure the same point size appear to be different sizes for reading.

This example is set in 9.5 points, with -6 tracking, on 11 points of leading.

This page is set in Helvetica Regular.

Industrial 736

ABCDEFGHIJ
KLMNOPQR
STUVWXYZ
abcdefghijklmn
opqrstuvwxyz
1234567890
.,?*#$&'%!:;">

Industrial 736 is an outstanding font in terms of all qualifications: it is beautiful, it is readable, it has a great italic version, and it has a sense of artfulness and balance to the design of the letters. Even the punctuation is handsome—look at the question mark! The numerals are even exceptional in their own right–isn't that "2" fabulous? Interestingly, this font has no bracketing on the serifs, but it does have enough artistic design to the letters so that it doesn't feel mechanized or rigid. The letters are also condensed a bit, which means that you fit more characters to the line, resulting in fewer hyphens and bad line breaks. The italic is elegant, light and curvy, without feeling frilly. This is a versatile and an aesthetic font.

This is a sample of the text version of this font, to give you an idea of how easily the font reads at a variety of text settings. This allows you to compare fonts at a glance before using them in text type. Because of the differences in x-height, some fonts that measure the same point size appear to be different sizes for reading.

This example is set in 8.5 points, with -6 tracking, on 11 points of leading.

This is a sample of the text version of this font, to give you an idea of how easily the font reads at a variety of text settings. This allows you to compare fonts at a glance before using them in text type. Because of the differences in x-height, some fonts that measure the same point size appear to be different sizes for reading.

This example is set in 9 points, with -6 tracking, on 11 points of leading.

This is a sample of the text version of this font, to give you an idea of how easily the font reads at a variety of text settings. This allows you to compare fonts at a glance before using them in text type. Because of the differences in x-height, some fonts that measure the same point size appear to be different sizes for reading.

This example is set in 9.5 points, with -6 tracking, on 11 points of leading.

Ingrid

ABCDEFGHIJ
KLMNOPQR
STUVWXYZ
abcdefghijklm
nopqrstuvwxyz
1234567890
..?*#$&'%!:;"

Ingrid appears to have been drawn with a brush: it has a light-hearted, loose spontaneity that has been captured in the design of the letters. Usually it makes sense to use hand lettering, rather than use a font when seeking spontaneity because the font is sort of fake—all of the "a's" look the same, and all of the "s's" are the same. Ingrid seems to maintain a fresh-ness and a freedom that are not always captured in hand-rendered fonts. Each character seems to have its own life and per-sonality: the characters do not look like cookie-cutter letters. Ingrid is also sur-prisingly readable at text sizes, and could be used successfully as body copy in the right applications. Ingrid has grace and lightness, as well as a sense of personality and flair in limited text-type use.

This is a sample of the text version of this font, to give you an idea of how easily the font reads at a variety of text settings. This allows you to compare fonts at a glance before using them in text type. Because of the differences in x-height, some fonts that measure the same point size appear to be different sizes for reading.

This example is set in 8.5 points, with -6 tracking, on 11 points of leading.

This is a sample of the text version of this font, to give you an idea of how eas-ily the font reads at a variety of text set-tings. This allows you to compare fonts at a glance before using them in text type. Because of the differences in x-height, some fonts that measure the same point size appear to be different sizes for reading.

This example is set in 9 points, with -6 tracking, on 11 points of leading.

This is a sample of the text version of this font, to give you an idea of how easily the font reads at a variety of text settings. This allows you to compare fonts at a glance before using them in text type. Because of the differences in x-height, some fonts that measure the same point size appear to be different sizes for reading.

This example is set in 9.5 points, with -6 tracking, on 11 points of leading.

This page is set in Ingrid.

21 *Type Samples*

Insignia Alternate

ABCDEFGHIJ KLMNOPQRST UVWXYZ abc defghijklmnop qrstuvwxyz 1234567890 .,?*#$&'%!:;">

Insignia is a very bold, contemporary-looking font. The design of many of the characters is quite different from our expected norms of the letters. The "S" has a flat spine, and the "E" and the "F" have bars that cross the stems. The uniqueness of this font makes it call attention to itself. There is a sharpness and a sense of geometry to the design of the charac- ters. The uppercase seems very blocky and angular, yet strong, due to the heavy stroke weight. Although this is legible for body copy, it is rather dark on the page, and should be used with limited amounts of text, so that the reader is not over- whelmed. The boldness of the strokes would allow this font to reverse out of black well.

This is a sample of the text version of this font, to give you an idea of how easily the font reads at a variety of text settings. This allows you to com- pare fonts at a glance before using them in text type. Because of the dif- ferences in x-height, some fonts that measure the same point size appear to be different sizes for reading.

This example is set in 8.5 points, with -6 tracking, on 11 points of leading.

This is a sample of the text version of this font, to give you an idea of how easily the font reads at a vari- ety of text settings. This allows you to compare fonts at a glance before using them in text type. Because of the differences in x- height, some fonts that measure the same point size appear to be different sizes for reading.

This example is set in 9 points, with -6 tracking, on 11 points of leading.

This is a sample of the text ver- sion of this font, to give you an idea of how easily the font reads at a variety of text settings. This allows you to compare fonts at a glance before using them in text type. Because of the differences in x-height, some fonts that mea- sure the same point size appear to be different sizes for reading.

This example is set in 9.5 points, with -6 tracking, on 11 points of leading.

IRIS PLAIN

ABCDEFGHIJKLM
NOPQRSTUVWXYZ
1234567890
.,?* $&'0%!.;"›

Iris Plain is an extremely condensed font that is not used in text because it is illegible. As with most condensed fonts, it is necessary to set Iris with extra tracking so that the letters are readable. This font does have thick-and-thin contrasts to the letters, and is similar to a font called Empire from the 1920s. The transition in stroke weight gives Iris a unique and a historic association. Iris resonates with a sense of the Art Deco era because of its verticality and the weight variations, as well as its overall rounded-corner rectangular shape. The numerals in this font are quite interesting; the "5" is unique in the height of the bowl, and the cross bar on the "4" is very low by comparison.

THIS IS A SAMPLE OF THE TEXT VERSION OF THIS FONT, TO GIVE YOU AN IDEA OF HOW EASILY THE FONT READS AT A VARIETY OF TEXT SETTINGS. THIS ALLOWS YOU TO COMPARE FONTS AT A GLANCE BEFORE USING THEM IN TEXT TYPE. BECAUSE OF THE DIFFERENCES IN X-HEIGHT, SOME FONTS THAT MEASURE THE SAME POINT SIZE APPEAR TO BE DIFFERENT SIZES FOR READING.

THIS EXAMPLE IS SET IN 8.5 POINTS, WITH -6 TRACKING, ON 11 POINTS OF LEADING.

THIS IS A SAMPLE OF THE TEXT VERSION OF THIS FONT, TO GIVE YOU AN IDEA OF HOW EASILY THE FONT READS AT A VARIETY OF TEXT SETTINGS. THIS ALLOWS YOU TO COMPARE FONTS AT A GLANCE BEFORE USING THEM IN TEXT TYPE. BECAUSE OF THE DIFFERENCES IN X-HEIGHT, SOME FONTS THAT MEASURE THE SAME POINT SIZE APPEAR TO BE DIFFERENT SIZES FOR READING.

THIS EXAMPLE IS SET IN 9 POINTS, WITH -6 TRACKING, ON 11 POINTS OF LEADING.

THIS IS A SAMPLE OF THE TEXT VERSION OF THIS FONT, TO GIVE YOU AN IDEA OF HOW EASILY THE FONT READS AT A VARIETY OF TEXT SETTINGS. THIS ALLOWS YOU TO COMPARE FONTS AT A GLANCE BEFORE USING THEM IN TEXT TYPE. BECAUSE OF THE DIFFERENCES IN X-HEIGHT, SOME FONTS THAT MEASURE THE SAME POINT SIZE APPEAR TO BE DIFFERENT SIZES FOR READING.

THIS EXAMPLE IS SET IN 9.5 POINTS, WITH -6 TRACKING, ON 11 POINTS OF LEADING.

This page is set in Iris Plain.

21   *Type Samples*

Janson Text

ABCDEFGHI JKLMNOPQR STUVWXYZ abcdefghijklmn opqrstuvwxyz 1234567890 .,?*#$&'%!:;">

Janson Text was based on Jenson's font by Nicholas Kis, in 1690, the punch-cutter who designed the original font. It was redesigned by both Rogers and Janson. It is an extremely functional serif font. The uppercase is a bit full and wide, particularly the "T" and the "W." There is a slight angularity to the arc of the lowercase "a," but in general the lowercase is eloquently designed. Janson does have a beautiful italic. Janson works well as a text font; it is clear at a variety of sizes. It does have a historic sense to it, even in text sizes. The question mark is also unique, with the small spur on it. The "J" in the italic is wonderful, with the small cross bar and the sweep to the upper stroke. The italic is far more condensed than the Roman, and it fits more characters to the line with a beautiful sense of handwriting.

This page is set in Janson Text.

This is a sample of the text version of this font, to give you an idea of how easily the font reads at a variety of text settings. This allows you to compare fonts at a glance before using them in text type. Because of the differences in x-height, some fonts that measure the same point size appear to be different sizes for reading.

This example is set in 8.5 points, with -6 tracking, on 11 points of leading.

This is a sample of the text version of this font, to give you an idea of how easily the font reads at a variety of text settings. This allows you to compare fonts at a glance before using them in text type. Because of the differences in x-height, some fonts that measure the same point size appear to be different sizes for reading.

This example is set in 9 points, with -6 tracking, on 11 points of leading.

This is a sample of the text version of this font, to give you an idea of how easily the font reads at a variety of text settings. This allows you to compare fonts at a glance before using them in text type. Because of the differences in x-height, some fonts that measure the same point size appear to be different sizes for reading.

This example is set in 9.5 points, with -6 tracking, on 11 points of leading.

ITC Kabel Book

ABCDEFGHIJ
KLMNOPQR
STUVWXYZ
abcdefghijklm
nopqrstuvwxyz
1234567890
.,?*#$&'%!:;">

Kabel is a unique, carefree font designed by Rudolf Koch in 1927. It seems playful and energetic, with a lot of vitality. Because of the angled terminals on the baseline, it seems perched on the baseline, as if it is skipping along, rather than sitting on the baseline solidly. The structure of the lowercase letters is also somewhat informal and lighthearted. The lowercase "g" is creatively designed. Kabel is based on a very circular structure, and its details tend to be a bit distracting in body copy. It does have a large x-height, but the roundness of some characters, contrasted with the thin verticals, tends to give an overall spottiness to the font in text settings. Kabel has a variety of weights that work well in headlines. It seems particularly well suited for children's products.

This is a sample of the text version of this font, to give you an idea of how easily the font reads at a variety of text settings. This allows you to compare fonts at a glance before using them in text type. Because of the differences in x-height, some fonts that measure the same point size appear to be different sizes for reading.

This example is set in 8.5 points, with -6 tracking, on 11 points of leading.

This is a sample of the text version of this font, to give you an idea of how easily the font reads at a variety of text settings. This allows you to compare fonts at a glance before using them in text type. Because of the differences in x-height, some fonts that measure the same point size appear to be different sizes for reading.

This example is set in 9 points, with -6 tracking, on 11 points of leading.

This is a sample of the text version of this font, to give you an idea of how easily the font reads at a variety of text settings. This allows you to compare fonts at a glance before using them in text type. Because of the differences in x-height, some fonts that measure the same point size appear to be different sizes for reading.

This example is set in 9.5 points, with -6 tracking, on 11 points of leading.

This page is set in ITC Kabel Book.

Kauflinn Script

ABCDEFGHI
JKLMNOPQR
STUVWXYZ
abcdefghijklm
nopqrstuvwxyz
1234567890
.,?*#$&'%!:;">

Designed by Kauflinn, this is a mono-weight script, and like most scripts it must be set at a larger point size for text; this is 13-point type. Kauflinn is an un-stuffy script; it seems more appropriate for the name of a car from the 1950s or for the name of a retro diner than it does for a fancy invitation. This is a more casual, everyday type of script, not just one for special occasions. It sort of looks as though it is made out of neon. There are loops on some of the uppercase characters, and the "2" (q) is virtually unrecognizable. But the letters link together very well in this script.

This is a sample of the text version of this font, to give you an idea of how easily the font reads at a variety of text settings. This allows you to compare fonts at a glance before using them in text type. Because of the differences in x-height, some fonts that measure the same point size appear to be different sizes for reading.

This example is set in 8.5 points, with -6 tracking, on 11 points of leading.

This is a sample of the text version of this font, to give you an idea of how easily the font reads at a variety of text settings. This allows you to compare fonts at a glance before using them in text type. Because of the differences in x-height, some fonts that measure the same point size appear to be different sizes for reading.

This example is set in 9 points, with -6 tracking, on 11 points of leading.

This is a sample of the text version of this font, to give you an idea of how easily the font reads at a variety of text settings. This allows you to compare fonts at a glance before using them in text type. Because of the differences in x-height, some fonts that measure the same point size appear to be different sizes for reading.

This example is set in 9.5 points, with -6 tracking, on 11 points of leading.

This page is set in Kauflinn Script.

ITC Korinna Regular

ABCDEFGHI
JKLMNOPQ
RSTUVWXYZ
abcdefghijklm
nopqrstuvwxyz
1234567890
.,?*#$£&'%!:;">

Korinna has short, stocky serifs that are reminiscent of Cheltenham, but it also has other interesting design features. It was designed by Edward Benguiat and V. Caruso for ITC. The balance of the "G" and the "C" seems to be off; it feels as though they could tip over. There are unusual spurs on the "b" and the "g." The "N," with its truncated angled stroke, is unusual; it feels as though it intersects the stem too high. For all of its design, Korinna is a very readable text font, even at small sizes. Many of these nuances are not distracting when they are reduced. Also, the italic is called Korinna Kursive, and its form is very different from the Roman face.

This is a sample of the text version of this font, to give you an idea of how easily the font reads at a variety of text settings. This allows you to compare fonts at a glance before using them in text type. Because of the differences in x-height, some fonts that measure the same point size appear to be different sizes for reading.

This example is set in 8.5 points, with -6 tracking, on 11 points of leading.

This is a sample of the text version of this font, to give you an idea of how easily the font reads at a variety of text settings. This allows you to compare fonts at a glance before using them in text type. Because of the differences in x-height, some fonts that measure the same point size appear to be different sizes for reading.

This example is set in 9 points, with -6 tracking, on 11 points of leading.

This is a sample of the text version of this font, to give you an idea of how easily the font reads at a variety of text settings. This allows you to compare fonts at a glance before using them in text type. Because of the differences in x-height, some fonts that measure the same point size appear to be different sizes for reading.

This example is set in 9.5 points, with -6 tracking, on 11 points of leading.

Latin Classic Condensed Roman

21 *Type Samples*

ABCDEFGHIJKLM
NOPQRSTUVWXYZ
abcdefghijklm
nopqrstuvwxyz
1234567890
.,?*$&'!:;"

Latin Classic is a font that conjures up the Wild West and "Most Wanted" posters. The exaggerated, angular beaks on the letters and the unbracketed, angled serifs seem sinister and dangerous. The lowercase does not seem as threatening as the uppercase letters. There is even an awkwardness to the drawing of the letters that refers to old printing methods and uneven weights of the letters. The "4" seems very dark in comparison to the other numerals. This font is a poor choice for text; it's so condensed that it is almost impossible to read. This font should probably be limited to headline and subhead use.

This is a sample of the text version of this font, to give you an idea of how easily the font reads at a variety of text settings. This allows you to compare fonts at a glance before using them in text type. Because of the differences in x-height, some fonts that measure the same point size appear to be different sizes for reading.

This example is set in 8.5 points, with -6 tracking, on 11 points of leading.

This is a sample of the text version of this font, to give you an idea of how easily the font reads at a variety of text settings. This allows you to compare fonts at a glance before using them in text type. Because of the differences in x-height, some fonts that measure the same point size appear to be different sizes for reading.

This example is set in 9 points, with -6 tracking, on 11 points of leading.

This is a sample of the text version of this font, to give you an idea of how easily the font reads at a variety of text settings. This allows you to compare fonts at a glance before using them in text type. Because of the differences in x-height, some fonts that measure the same point size appear to be different sizes for reading.

This example is set in 9.5 points, with -6 tracking, on 11 points of leading.

This page is set in Latin Classic Condensed Roman.

LITHOS REGULAR

ABCDEFGHIJ KLMNOPQR STUVWXYZ 1234567890 .,?*$&'%!:;"

LITHOS, DESIGNED BY TWOMBLY, IS A DISPLAY FONT THAT DOES NOT EVEN HAVE A LOWER-CASE. IT HAS THE ESSENCE OF EARLY GREEK WRITING. THE LETTERS LOOK AS IF THEY COULD HAVE BEEN CARVED IN STONE. THE ROUND LETTERS ARE BASED ON AN ELLIPSE THAT IS FULL AND WIDE. THE "Y" HAS A GREAT SENSE OF CURVES TO A LETTER THAT IS USUALLY CONSIDERED ALL ANGLES. BECAUSE OF THE ASSOCIATION WITH ANCIENT GREEK WRITING, LITHOS HAS AN ANCIENT OR HISTORIC FEEL TO THE LETTERS. EVEN THE NUMBERS ARE QUITE UNIQUE. THIS FONT WORKS WELL IN HEADLINES AND IN SHORT AREAS OF TEXT WHEN TIGHTLY TRACKED AND WHEN BROADLY LEADED.

THIS IS A SAMPLE OF THE TEXT VERSION OF THIS FONT, TO GIVE YOU AN IDEA OF HOW EASILY THE FONT READS AT A VARIETY OF TEXT SETTINGS. THIS ALLOWS YOU TO COMPARE FONTS AT A GLANCE BEFORE USING THEM IN TEXT TYPE. BECAUSE OF THE DIFFERENCES IN X-HEIGHT, SOME FONTS THAT MEASURE THE SAME POINT SIZE APPEAR TO BE DIFFERENT SIZES FOR READING.

THIS EXAMPLE IS SET IN 8.5 POINTS, WITH -6 TRACKING, ON 11 POINTS OF LEADING.

THIS IS A SAMPLE OF THE TEXT VERSION OF THIS FONT, TO GIVE YOU AN IDEA OF HOW EASILY THE FONT READS AT A VARIETY OF TEXT SETTINGS. THIS ALLOWS YOU TO COMPARE FONTS AT A GLANCE BEFORE USING THEM IN TEXT TYPE. BECAUSE OF THE DIFFERENCES IN X-HEIGHT, SOME FONTS THAT MEASURE THE SAME POINT SIZE APPEAR TO BE DIFFERENT SIZES FOR READING.

THIS EXAMPLE IS SET IN 9 POINTS, WITH -6 TRACKING, ON 11 POINTS OF LEADING.

THIS IS A SAMPLE OF THE TEXT VERSION OF THIS FONT, TO GIVE YOU AN IDEA OF HOW EASILY THE FONT READS AT A VARIETY OF TEXT SETTINGS. THIS ALLOWS YOU TO COMPARE FONTS AT A GLANCE BEFORE USING THEM IN TEXT TYPE. BECAUSE OF THE DIFFERENCES IN X-HEIGHT, SOME FONTS THAT MEASURE THE SAME POINT SIZE APPEAR TO BE DIFFERENT SIZES FOR READING.

THIS EXAMPLE IS SET IN 9.5 POINTS, WITH -6 TRACKING, ON 11 POINTS OF LEADING.

This page is set in Lithos Regular.

ITC Lubalin Graph Book

21 Type Samples

ABCDEFGHIJ
KLMNOPQRS
TUVWXYZ
abcdefghijkl
mnopqrstuv
wxyz1234567
890.,?*#$$&'%!:;"

Lubalin Graph is a mono-weight, Egyptian serif font designed by Herb Lubalin, one of the founders of ITC. It has very few distinguishing character-istics, and it creates spotty text type due to the perfectly cir-cular bowls. Certainly this font is legible at small sizes, but the bowls are distracting to the eye at any size and disrupt the flow of reading. This is an engineer's font; it is designed more by mathematical prin-ciples than by an artistic eye and typographic sensitiv-ity. It is functional and practical, but because it is so wide, text runs very long.

This is a sample of the text version of this font, to give you an idea of how easily the font reads at a vari-ety of text settings. This allows you to compare fonts at a glance before using them in text type. Because of the differences in x-height, some fonts that measure the same point size appear to be different sizes for reading.

This example is set in 8.5 points, with -6 tracking, on 11 points of leading.

This is a sample of the text ver-sion of this font, to give you an idea of how easily the font reads at a variety of text settings. This allows you to compare fonts at a glance before using them in text type. Because of the differences in x-height, some fonts that mea-sure the same point size appear to be different sizes for reading.

This example is set in 9 points, with -6 tracking, on 11 points of leading.

This is a sample of the text ver-sion of this font, to give you an idea of how easily the font reads at a variety of text set-tings. This allows you to com-pare fonts at a glance before using them in text type. Because of the differences in x-height, some fonts that mea-sure the same point size appear to be different sizes for reading.

This example is set in 9.5 points, with -6 tracking, on 11 points of leading.

ITC Lucida Regular

ABCDEFGHIJ KLMNOPQRS TUVWXYZab cdefghijklmn opqrstuvwxyz 1234567890. ,?*#$&'%!:;">

Lucida is reminiscent of Cheltenham, with its compact serifs. But Lucida has a more business, practical, and contemporary sense to it than Cheltenham. It was designed by C. Bigelow and Holmes for ITC. The rigid verticals seem to conjure up early computer fonts, as do the rectangular spurs on the "a," the "j," the "r" and the "f." These are no-nonsense characters that will withstand the test of time. This is an exceptionally legible font, even at small point sizes, because the x-height is so large. The italic, which you are reading, bears little relation to the Roman; it appears more informal, and the serifs are reduced to wedges. The real test is how well the Roman and the italic look together on the same line.

This is a sample of the text version of this font, to give you an idea of how easily the font reads at a variety of text settings. This allows you to compare fonts at a glance before using them in text type. Because of the differences in x-height, some fonts that measure the same point size appear to be different sizes for reading.

This example is set in 8.5 points, with -6 tracking, on 11 points of leading.

This is a sample of the text version of this font, to give you an idea of how easily the font reads at a variety of text settings. This allows you to compare fonts at a glance before using them in text type. Because of the differences in x-height, some fonts that measure the same point size appear to be different sizes for reading.

This example is set in 9 points, with -6 tracking, on 11 points of leading.

This is a sample of the text version of this font, to give you an idea of how easily the font reads at a variety of text settings. This allows you to compare fonts at a glance before using them in text type. Because of the differences in x-height, some fonts that measure the same point size appear to be different sizes for reading.

This example is set in 9.5 points, with -6 tracking, on 11 points of leading.

Melior Regular

ABCDEFGHIJ
KLMNOPQRS
TUVWXYZ̃ab
cdefghijklmno
pqrstuvwxyz
1234567890
.,?*#$&'%!:;">

Melior, designed in 1925 by Hermann Zapf, is a very square face that is reminiscent of the old punch-card computer fonts. It has a technical feel to the design of the letters. Even the beaks and barbs are small rectangular boxes. Melior has very wide serifs that are squared off. The round characters appear to have been drawn within a box. As a text font, it is very readable, but it can run long due to the width of the characters. This is a practical font; it reads well, and is not distracting. It is not a particularly aesthetic font, but it is handsomely balanced in text. Considered more appropriate for corporate communication rather than for sensitive poetry, Melior has strength and candor due to its simple, no-nonsense aesthetic.

This page is set in Melior Regular.

This is a sample of the text version of this font, to give you an idea of how easily the font reads at a variety of text settings. This allows you to compare fonts at a glance before using them in text type. Because of the differences in x-height, some fonts that measure the same point size appear to be different sizes for reading.

This example is set in 8.5 points, with -6 tracking, on 11 points of leading.

This is a sample of the text version of this font, to give you an idea of how easily the font reads at a variety of text settings. This allows you to compare fonts at a glance before using them in text type. Because of the differences in x-height, some fonts that measure the same point size appear to be different sizes for reading.

This example is set in 9 points, with -6 tracking, on 11 points of leading.

This is a sample of the text version of this font, to give you an idea of how easily the font reads at a variety of text settings. This allows you to compare fonts at a glance before using them in text type. Because of the differences in x-height, some fonts that measure the same point size appear to be different sizes for reading.

This example is set in 9.5 points, with -6 tracking, on 11 points of leading.

Modula Regular

A B C D E F G H I J K L M N

O P Q R S T U V W X Y Z

a b c d e f g h i j k l m

n o p q r s t u v w x y z

1 2 3 4 5 6 7 8 9 0

. , ? * # $ & ´ % ! : ; ” ”

This is a sample of the text version of this font, to give you an idea of how easily the font reads at a variety of text settings. This allows you to compare fonts at a glance before using them in text type. Because of the differences in x-height, some fonts that measure the same point size appear to be different sizes for reading.

This example is set in 8.5 points, with -6 tracking, on 11 points of leading.

This is a sample of the text version of this font, to give you an idea of how easily the font reads at a variety of text settings. This allows you to compare fonts at a glance before using them in text type. Because of the differences in x-height, some fonts that measure the same point size appear to be different sizes for reading.

This example is set in 9 points, with -6 tracking, on 11 points of leading.

This is a sample of the text version of this font, to give you an idea of how easily the font reads at a variety of text settings. This allows you to compare fonts at a glance before using them in text type. Because of the differences in x-height, some fonts that measure the same point size appear to be different sizes for reading.

This example is set in 9.5 points, with -6 tracking, on 11 points of leading.

Modula is an extremely condensed font that is best used for headlines and display applications. It does have some interesting design features; the spurs on some of the lowercase letters are unusual for a sans serif font. The lowercase ``l″ has an interesting curve to it. The ``x″ is a fun mix of verticals and angles. There is a syncopation to the angles in the letters, making this an informal, unconventional font. As seen in the examples at left, it is illegible at text-font point sizes. This copy is set at 18 points on 21 point leading.

This page is set in Modula Regular.

NEULAND

ABCDEFGH IJKLMNOP QRSTUVW XYZ123456 7890.,?☆★#$ &'%!◆;";>

NEULAND IS A FONT THAT WAS DESIGNED BY RUDOLF KOCH, WITH A RUSTIC CRUDENESS; IT LOOKS AS THOUGH IT WERE CARVED FROM WOOD. THERE IS NO LOWERCASE TO THE FONT, AND IT IS THICK AND BLOCKY. THE CURVES ARE SIMPLIFIED AND SOMEWHAT ANGULAR. THERE IS A CHOPPINESS TO THIS FONT. IT IS USED PRIMARILY IN HEADLINES, AND SHOULD BE USED IN TEXT ONLY SPARINGLY.

THIS IS A SAMPLE OF THE TEXT VERSION OF THIS FONT, TO GIVE YOU AN IDEA OF HOW EASILY THE FONT READS AT A VARIETY OF TEXT SETTINGS. THIS ALLOWS YOU TO COMPARE FONTS AT A GLANCE BEFORE USING THEM IN TEXT TYPE. BECAUSE OF THE DIFFERENCES IN X-HEIGHT, SOME FONTS THAT MEASURE THE SAME POINT SIZE APPEAR TO BE DIFFERENT SIZES FOR READING.

THIS EXAMPLE IS SET IN 8.5 POINTS, WITH -6 TRACKING, ON 11 POINTS OF LEADING.

THIS IS A SAMPLE OF THE TEXT VERSION OF THIS FONT, TO GIVE YOU AN IDEA OF HOW EASILY THE FONT READS AT A VARIETY OF TEXT SETTINGS. THIS ALLOWS YOU TO COMPARE FONTS AT A GLANCE BEFORE USING THEM IN TEXT TYPE. BECAUSE OF THE DIFFERENCES IN X-HEIGHT, SOME FONTS THAT MEASURE THE SAME POINT SIZE APPEAR TO BE DIFFERENT SIZES FOR READING.

THIS EXAMPLE IS SET IN 9 POINTS, WITH -6 TRACKING, ON 11 POINTS OF LEADING.

THIS IS A SAMPLE OF THE TEXT VERSION OF THIS FONT, TO GIVE YOU AN IDEA OF HOW EASILY THE FONT READS AT A VARIETY OF TEXT SETTINGS. THIS ALLOWS YOU TO COMPARE FONTS AT A GLANCE BEFORE USING THEM IN TEXT TYPE. BECAUSE OF THE DIFFERENCES IN X-HEIGHT, SOME FONTS THAT MEASURE THE SAME POINT SIZE APPEAR TO BE DIFFERENT SIZES FOR READING.

THIS EXAMPLE IS SET IN 9.5 POINTS, WITH -6 TRACKING, ON 11 POINTS OF LEADING.

News Gothic Regular

ABCDEFGHIJ
KLMNOPQR
STUVWXYZ
abcdefghijklm
nopqrstuvwxyz
1234567890
.,?*#$&'%!:;">

News Gothic is a sans serif font that has a timelessness to the design of the letters. It is clean and essential, yet it still has a great sense of personality on the page. It is slightly condensed, so that it fits well in text type, and its overly large x-height makes it extremely easy to read, even at small point sizes. News Gothic does not call attention to itself in text; it is clear and comfortable on the eyes. It has a very good fit in text, and gives a well-balanced gray tone in text. It is a classic sans serif font.

This is a sample of the text version of this font, to give you an idea of how easily the font reads at a variety of text settings. This allows you to compare fonts at a glance before using them in text type. Because of the differences in x-height, some fonts that measure the same point size appear to be different sizes for reading.

This example is set in 8.5 points, with -6 tracking, on 11 points of leading.

This is a sample of the text version of this font, to give you an idea of how easily the font reads at a variety of text settings. This allows you to compare fonts at a glance before using them in text type. Because of the differences in x-height, some fonts that measure the same point size appear to be different sizes for reading.

This example is set in 9 points, with -6 tracking, on 11 points of leading.

This is a sample of the text version of this font, to give you an idea of how easily the font reads at a variety of text settings. This allows you to compare fonts at a glance before using them in text type. Because of the differences in x-height, some fonts that measure the same point size appear to be different sizes for reading.

This example is set in 9.5 points, with -6 tracking, on 11 points of leading.

This page is set in News Gothic Regular.

Onyx

ABCDEFGHIJKLM
NOPQRSTUVWXYZ
abcdefghijklm
nopqrstuvwxyz
1234567890
.,?*$&'%!:;"

Designed by Powell, Onyx is an extremely condensed vertical font with very heavy stem strokes contrasted with very light hairline strokes. The characters look as though they have all been squished in a vice. The font has a vertical sensibility to the letters and is used mainly in headline copy. It is illegible at text size, and is too dark to set text in. This font seems as if it is appropriate for models or high fashion due to the tall proportions; there is a feeling that conjures up tuxedos and traditional formality in this font.

This is a sample of the text version of this font, to give you an idea of how easily the font reads at a variety of text settings. This allows you to compare fonts at a glance before using them in text type. Because of the differences in x-height, some fonts that measure the same point size appear to be different sizes for reading.

This example is set in 8.5 points, with -6 tracking, on 11 points of leading.

This is a sample of the text version of this font, to give you an idea of how easily the font reads at a variety of text settings. This allows you to compare fonts at a glance before using them in text type. Because of the differences in x-height, some fonts that measure the same point size appear to be different sizes for reading.

This example is set in 9 points, with -6 tracking, on 11 points of leading.

This is a sample of the text version of this font, to give you an idea of how easily the font reads at a variety of text settings. This allows you to compare fonts at a glance before using them in text type. Because of the differences in x-height, some fonts that measure the same point size appear to be different sizes for reading.

This example is set in 9.5 points, with -6 tracking, on 11 points of leading.

Optima Regular

ABCDEFGHIJ KLMNOPQR STUVWXYZ abcdefghijklm nopqrstuvwxyz 1234567890 .,?*#$&'%!:;">

Hermann Zapf, a prolific type designer and the creator of Zapf dingbats, designed Optima in 1958. He based it on ancient stone engravings of letters in Rome and Greece. Optima is classified as a sans serif font, but careful inspection of the strokes reveals a splaying or swelling of the stroke at top and bottom; there is also a cupping to the terminals, almost implying a spur serif.

Optima is outstanding in legibility and clarity on the page, and it is light and airy with a contemporary balance. The rounded characters are full without feeling too geometric and rigid. There are graceful transitions between stem and hairline weights. It feels as if it has captured the essence of those clean, classic letters. The italic harmonizes well with the Roman to create a overall unified design.

This is a sample of the text version of this font, to give you an idea of how easily the font reads at a variety of text settings. This allows you to compare fonts at a glance before using them in text type. Because of the differences in x-height, some fonts that measure the same point size appear to be different sizes for reading.

This example is set in 8.5 points, with -6 tracking, on 11 points of leading.

This is a sample of the text version of this font, to give you an idea of how easily the font reads at a variety of text settings. This allows you to compare fonts at a glance before using them in text type. Because of the differences in x-height, some fonts that measure the same point size appear to be different sizes for reading.

This example is set in 9 points, with -6 tracking, on 11 points of leading.

This is a sample of the text version of this font, to give you an idea of how easily the font reads at a variety of text settings. This allows you to compare fonts at a glance before using them in text type. Because of the differences in x-height, some fonts that measure the same point size appear to be different sizes for reading.

This example is set in 9.5 points, with -6 tracking, on 11 points of leading.

This page is set in Optima Regular.

Palatino

ABCDEFGHIJ
KLMNOPQR
STUVWXYZa
bcdefghijklmn
opqrstuvwxyz
1234567890
.,?*#$&'%!:;">

Another Hermann Zapf design, from 1950, Palatino seems to capture the sense of proportions that was so sought after during the Italian Renaissance. Palatino feels as if you could sense the letters being drawn with an angled, ink-tipped pen, held at a consistent angle. It is a serif font with the presence of hand lettering. The serifs are square without being blocky, and there is a great sensitivity to the transitions between stem and hairline strokes. As a text face, Palatino is quite legible, even though the x-height is not overly large. The italic is very condensed, and it also maintains the presence of the calligraphic sense that Zapf was so well known for in his typefaces. This is a very well-balanced font.

This page is set in Palatino.

This is a sample of the text version of this font, to give you an idea of how easily the font reads at a variety of text settings. This allows you to compare fonts at a glance before using them in text type. Because of the differences in x-height, some fonts that measure the same point size appear to be different sizes for reading.

This example is set in 8.5 points, with -6 tracking, on 11 points of leading.

This is a sample of the text version of this font, to give you an idea of how easily the font reads at a variety of text settings. This allows you to compare fonts at a glance before using them in text type. Because of the differences in x-height, some fonts that measure the same point size appear to be different sizes for reading.

This example is set in 9 points, with -6 tracking, on 11 points of leading.

This is a sample of the text version of this font, to give you an idea of how easily the font reads at a variety of text settings. This allows you to compare fonts at a glance before using them in text type. Because of the differences in x-height, some fonts that measure the same point size appear to be different sizes for reading.

This example is set in 9.5 points, with -6 tracking, on 11 points of leading.

ITC Panache

ABCDEFGHI
JKLMNOPQ
RSTUVWXYZ
abcdefghijklm
nopqrstuvwxyz
1234567890
.,?*#$&'%!:;">

ITC Panache, designed by Edward Benguiat, is quite a striking font. It is very legible for text type, but it is designed with such a flair that it is a bit distracting in body copy. The curves in the lowercase "a" are very sensuous, and the "v," "w" and "y" also have sinuous curves in their design. Panache seems a bit flamboyant and striking. The uppercase "K," "R" and "Q" are almost whimsical in the design of their tails; it's as if the designer were trying to put nuances of serif fonts into this sans serif font. This is a font that doesn't take itself too seriously; it has an informal and casual air to it. Because of its clarity, it can be successful as a text font, assuming that the subject matter is light-spirited. The numerals are quite attractive.

This is a sample of the text version of this font, to give you an idea of how easily the font reads at a variety of text settings. This allows you to compare fonts at a glance before using them in text type. Because of the differences in x-height, some fonts that measure the same point size appear to be different sizes for reading.

This example is set in 8.5 points, with -6 tracking, on 11 points of leading.

This is a sample of the text version of this font, to give you an idea of how easily the font reads at a variety of text settings. This allows you to compare fonts at a glance before using them in text type. Because of the differences in x-height, some fonts that measure the same point size appear to be different sizes for reading.

This example is set in 9 points, with -6 tracking, on 11 points of leading.

This is a sample of the text version of this font, to give you an idea of how easily the font reads at a variety of text settings. This allows you to compare fonts at a glance before using them in text type. Because of the differences in x-height, some fonts that measure the same point size appear to be different sizes for reading.

This example is set in 9.5 points, with -6 tracking, on 11 points of leading.

This page is set in ITC Panache.

Park Avenue

21 *Type Samples*

ABCDEFGHIJ
KLMNOPQR
STUVWXYZ

abcdefghijklm

nopqrstuvwxyz

1234567890

.,?*#$&'%!:;"
>

As its name implies, Park Avenue is a font with an attitude. It is elegant and clear; it differs from traditional scripts in the design of the lowercase "e" and "l," which are uncharacteristic. The loops on the lowercase ascenders are hooked rather than being complete, like those in most script faces. There is a flatness to the bottom of this font that gives it a clean, technical feel in text.

This is a sample of the text version of this font, to give you an idea of how easily the font reads at a variety of text settings. This allows you to compare fonts at a glance before using them in text type. Because of the differences in x-height, some fonts that measure the same point size appear to be different sizes for reading.

This example is set in 8.5 points, with -6 tracking, on 11 points of leading.

This is a sample of the text version of this font, to give you an idea of how easily the font reads at a variety of text settings. This allows you to compare fonts at a glance before using them in text type. Because of the differences in x-height, some fonts that measure the same point size appear to be different sizes for reading.

This example is set in 9 points, with -6 tracking, on 11 points of leading.

This is a sample of the text version of this font, to give you an idea of how easily the font reads at a variety of text settings. This allows you to compare fonts at a glance before using them in text type. Because of the differences in x-height, some fonts that measure the same point size appear to be different sizes for reading.

This example is set in 9.5 points, with -6 tracking, on 11 points of leading.

This page is set in Park Avenue.

Pretoria

ABCDEFGHI JKLMNOPQ RSTUVWXY Zabcdefghij klmnopqrstu vwxyz1 2345 67890.,?*#$ &'%!:;"

Clearly designed for a display font rather than a text font, this dark face has a Gothic sensibility to the design of the characters. They seem Medieval in their structure and in their flourishes. This is a substantial font with unique qualities and detail to many of the letters. The horizontals are curved in many of the letters, giving Pretoria a funky or groovy appearance. This font embodies the design sense of the 1960s with its "cool" rustic quality.

This is a sample of the text version of this font, to give you an idea of how easily the font reads at a variety of text settings. This allows you to compare fonts at a glance before using them in text type. Because of the differences in x-height, some fonts that measure the same point size appear to be different sizes for reading.

This example is set in 8.5 points, with -6 tracking, on 11 points of leading.

This is a sample of the text version of this font, to give you an idea of how easily the font reads at a variety of text settings. This allows you to compare fonts at a glance before using them in text type. Because of the differences in x-height, some fonts that measure the same point size appear to be different sizes for reading.

This example is set in 9 points, with -6 tracking, on 11 points of leading.

This is a sample of the text version of this font, to give you an idea of how easily the font reads at a variety of text settings. This allows you to compare fonts at a glance before using them in text type. Because of the differences in x-height, some fonts that measure the same point size appear to be different sizes for reading.

This example is set in 9.5 points, with -6 tracking, on 11 points of leading.

21 *Type Samples*

Ribbon

ABCDEFGHI
JKLMNOPQ
RSTUVWXYZ

abcdefghijklm

nopqrstuvwxyz

1234567890

.,?* #$&'%!.:; ">

Ribbon is an informal script font. It has very simple uppercase characters that are clearly legible. The "M" and "N" are unusual in their loop structure. The x-height of Ribbon is extremely small, which means that it probably should be set at a minimum of 16 points for best readability. Ribbon conjures up the 1950s with drive-ins and hamburger stands; it has a nostalgic sense to it. As a script, the letters join very neatly and regularly, and the design of the characters is very clear and clean. Even the numerals are handsomely designed in this font.

This is a sample of the text version of this font, to give you an idea of how easily the font reads at a variety of text settings. This allows you to compare fonts at a glance before using them in text type. Because of the differences in x-height, some fonts that measure the same point size appear to be different sizes for reading.

This example is set in 8.5 points, with -6 tracking, on 11 points of leading.

This is a sample of the text version of this font, to give you an idea of how easily the font reads at a variety of text settings. This allows you to compare fonts at a glance before using them in text type. Because of the differences in x-height, some fonts that measure the same point size appear to be different sizes for reading.

This example is set in 9 points, with -6 tracking, on 11 points of leading.

This is a sample of the text version of this font, to give you an idea of how easily the font reads at a variety of text settings. This allows you to compare fonts at a glance before using them in text type. Because of the differences in x-height, some fonts that measure the same point size appear to be different sizes for reading.

This example is set in 9.5 points, with -6 tracking, on 11 points of leading.

This page is set in Ribbon.

Sabon Roman

ABCDEFGHIJ
KLMNOPQR
STUVWXYZ
abcdefghijklmn
opqrstuvwxyz
1234567890
.,?*#$&'%!:;">

Sabon is one of the most commonly used fonts in book design. It is a well-balanced serif font, with great legibility at small sizes, and few extraneous details to distract the reader. The counters in this font seem very open and reproduce well. There are few distinctive qualities to this font, although the "5," "6" and "9" are a bit unusual in their design, making them more unique. As a standard, reliable font, Sabon should be well noted. It is not a paragon of typographic creativity, but it is a formidable, consistent choice for text. The italic is more condensed than the Roman, but maintains the open counters and overall readability.

This is a sample of the text version of this font, to give you an idea of how easily the font reads at a variety of text settings. This allows you to compare fonts at a glance before using them in text type. Because of the differences in x-height, some fonts that measure the same point size appear to be different sizes for reading.

This example is set in 8.5 points, with -6 tracking, on 11 points of leading.

This is a sample of the text version of this font, to give you an idea of how easily the font reads at a variety of text settings. This allows you to compare fonts at a glance before using them in text type. Because of the differences in x-height, some fonts that measure the same point size appear to be different sizes for reading.

This example is set in 9 points, with -6 tracking, on 11 points of leading.

This is a sample of the text version of this font, to give you an idea of how easily the font reads at a variety of text settings. This allows you to compare fonts at a glance before using them in text type. Because of the differences in x-height, some fonts that measure the same point size appear to be different sizes for reading.

This example is set in 9.5 points, with -6 tracking, on 11 points of leading.

Senator Thin

ABCDEFGHIJKLM
NOPQRSTUVWXYZ
abcdefghijklm
nopqrstuvwxyz
1234567890
.,?*#$&'%!:;"

Senator is a font best suited for display purposes or limited body-copy applications. It is very rectangular, and is Egyptian in the design of its block serifs. There is no bracketing, and most of the curves have been squared off. Some have been converted to angles, as in the "h," the "n" and the "a." The numerals are very well designed and interesting in this font; they are an unusual combination of arcs and verticals with an artistic sensibility. Because of its squareness and slab serifs, Senator does have associations with fonts used for the names of long-established schools. Its structure seems like an update of those older, university fonts seen on jackets and sweatshirts. Still, this font maintains a contemporary sensibility through the use of sharp angles.

This is a sample of the text version of this font, to give you an idea of how easily the font reads at a variety of text settings. This allows you to compare fonts at a glance before using them in text type. Because of the differences in x-height, some fonts that measure the same point size appear to be different sizes for reading.

This example is set in 8.5 points, with -6 tracking, on 11 points of leading.

This is a sample of the text version of this font, to give you an idea of how easily the font reads at a variety of text settings. This allows you to compare fonts at a glance before using them in text type. Because of the differences in x-height, some fonts that measure the same point size appear to be different sizes for reading.

This example is set in 9 points, with -6 tracking, on 11 points of leading.

This is a sample of the text version of this font, to give you an idea of how easily the font reads at a variety of text settings. This allows you to compare fonts at a glance before using them in text type. Because of the differences in x-height, some fonts that measure the same point size appear to be different sizes for reading.

This example is set in 9.5 points, with -6 tracking, on 11 points of leading.

ITC Souvenir Light

ABCDEFGHIJ
KLMNOPQR
STUVWXYZ
abcdefghijklm
nopqrstuvwxyz
1234567890
.,?*#$&'%!:;">

Souvenir is a font that is soft and fuzzy in its appearance. It was first designed by Morris Fuller Benton in 1914, then redesigned for ITC by Edward Benguiat. The serifs grow out of the stem strokes in an organic, well-bracketed fashion. The design of the lowercase letters is smooth and very curved. This font is almost too soft, too flowing to have any sense of stability; it is appropriately used in infant ads or on pillows. Because the serifs are so short, it is almost as though the creators were undecided about them during the design phase. Since it is so soft in structure, Souvenir has a friendly, informal air to it. There is nothing too serious or business-like about this font. It does have a generous x-height and is readable at small text sizes. The italic works well with the Roman.

This page is set in ITC Souvenir Light.

This is a sample of the text version of this font, to give you an idea of how easily the font reads at a variety of text settings. This allows you to compare fonts at a glance before using them in text type. Because of the differences in x-height, some fonts that measure the same point size appear to be different sizes for reading.

This example is set in 8.5 points, with -6 tracking, on 11 points of leading.

This is a sample of the text version of this font, to give you an idea of how easily the font reads at a variety of text settings. This allows you to compare fonts at a glance before using them in text type. Because of the differences in x-height, some fonts that measure the same point size appear to be different sizes for reading.

This example is set in 9 points, with -6 tracking, on 11 points of leading.

This is a sample of the text version of this font, to give you an idea of how easily the font reads at a variety of text settings. This allows you to compare fonts at a glance before using them in text type. Because of the differences in x-height, some fonts that measure the same point size appear to be different sizes for reading.

This example is set in 9.5 points, with -6 tracking, on 11 points of leading.

21 *Type Samples*

ITC Stone Sans Regular

ABCDEFGHIJ
KLMNOPQR
STUVWXYZ
abcdefghijklmn
opqrstuvwxyz
1234567890
.,?*#$&'%!:;">

Stone Sans was designed by Sumner Stone, a contemporary type designer. It is an outstandingly well-designed sans serif face. It has exceptionally beautiful transitions from the hairline to stem weights, and the letters are exceedingly clear in terms of legibility at very small text sizes, even 6-point type! For a sans serif font, which we often think of as less crafted than a serif font, Stone Sans has an artistry and beauty to each of the letters; they look as though they've been redrawn with exceptional care and attention paid to the nuances of weight and subtle curves. The italic is also an exceptionally handsome font, and it complements the Roman magnificently.

This is a sample of the text version of this font, to give you an idea of how easily the font reads at a variety of text settings. This allows you to compare fonts at a glance before using them in text type. Because of the differences in x-height, some fonts that measure the same point size appear to be different sizes for reading.

This example is set in 8.5 points, with -6 tracking, on 11 points of leading.

This is a sample of the text version of this font, to give you an idea of how easily the font reads at a variety of text settings. This allows you to compare fonts at a glance before using them in text type. Because of the differences in x-height, some fonts that measure the same point size appear to be different sizes for reading.

This example is set in 9 points, with -6 tracking, on 11 points of leading.

This is a sample of the text version of this font, to give you an idea of how easily the font reads at a variety of text settings. This allows you to compare fonts at a glance before using them in text type. Because of the differences in x-height, some fonts that measure the same point size appear to be different sizes for reading.

This example is set in 9.5 points, with -6 tracking, on 11 points of leading.

ITC Stone Serif Regular

ABCDEFGHIJ KLMNOPQRS TUVWXYZab cdefghijklmn opqrstuvwxyz 1234567890 .,?*#$&'%!:;">

ITC Stone Serif, also by Sumner Stone, is a highly readable and legible font. It, too, maintains high readability at even small text sizes. Although unique in its design, Stone Serif seems to owe a lot of its details to some of the timeless fonts, such as Palatino, Baskerville, Times Roman and Clearface. The tail on the lowercase "a" is tipped up a bit, and the ear of the "r" seems a bit short. The italic reveals the calligraphic sensibility of the type designer; it has nuances, such as the lowercase "p" with a bit of a tail, and a very graceful lowercase "f" with a long descender. Because the x-height of this font is so large, it may read better with additional leading between the lines of text.

This page is set in ITC Stone Serif Regular.

This is a sample of the text version of this font, to give you an idea of how easily the font reads at a variety of text settings. This allows you to compare fonts at a glance before using them in text type. Because of the differences in x-height, some fonts that measure the same point size appear to be different sizes for reading.

This example is set in 8.5 points, with -6 tracking, on 11 points of leading.

This is a sample of the text version of this font, to give you an idea of how easily the font reads at a variety of text settings. This allows you to compare fonts at a glance before using them in text type. Because of the differences in x-height, some fonts that measure the same point size appear to be different sizes for reading.

This example is set in 9 points, with -6 tracking, on 11 points of leading.

This is a sample of the text version of this font, to give you an idea of how easily the font reads at a variety of text settings. This allows you to compare fonts at a glance before using them in text type. Because of the differences in x-height, some fonts that measure the same point size appear to be different sizes for reading.

This example is set in 9.5 points, with -6 tracking, on 11 points of leading.

ITC Tiffany

ABCDEFGHI
JKLMNOPQR
STUVWXYZab
cdefghijklmno
pqrstuvwxyz
1234567890
.,?*#$$&'%!:;">

Tiffany is a font that is very aptly named; it seems to be very delicate and decorative, just as the name sounds. It was designed by Edward Benguiat for ITC. There are very sharp barbs on the "T," "E" and "F," which can be distracting in body copy. The lowercase is rather extended, meaning that text will run longer than expected. The unusual flairs on the letters give this font a decorative rather than a serious appearance. Tiffany seems as though it would be appropriate for a florist or a dress shop, but not for a construction company–unless it specialized in one-of-a-kind artistic buildings. Even the italic is fancy in its appearance on the page. The "2," "3," "4" and "5" have a curvy, whimsical, feminine feel to them.

This is a sample of the text version of this font, to give you an idea of how easily the font reads at a variety of text settings. This allows you to compare fonts at a glance before using them in text type. Because of the differences in x-height, some fonts that measure the same point size appear to be different sizes for reading.

This example is set in 8.5 points, with -6 tracking, on 11 points of leading.

This is a sample of the text version of this font, to give you an idea of how easily the font reads at a variety of text settings. This allows you to compare fonts at a glance before using them in text type. Because of the differences in x-height, some fonts that measure the same point size appear to be different sizes for reading.

This example is set in 9 points, with -6 tracking, on 11 points of leading.

This is a sample of the text version of this font, to give you an idea of how easily the font reads at a variety of text settings. This allows you to compare fonts at a glance before using them in text type. Because of the differences in x-height, some fonts that measure the same point size appear to be different sizes for reading.

This example is set in 9.5 points, with -6 tracking, on 11 points of leading.

Times Roman

ABCDEFGHIJ KLMNOPQR STUVWXYZ

abcdefghijklm nopqrstuvwxyz

1234567890

.,?*#$&'%!:;">

Times Roman is the quintessential serif font. It appears to be perfectly designed; few characteristics can be noted which are distinctive about the characters. Even the numerals feel as though they are ideally designed. If ever there was a typographic paradigm, Times Roman is it for a serif font. As a text font, it is extremely clean and legible. It has a serious, no-nonsense attitude to it. The italic is equally easy to read, with a well-designed lowercase. It's almost as if Times Roman is too perfect and too devoid of any artistic sensitivity for us to comment on its structure and design. It's so timeless that it lacks any specific personality or associations. Perhaps we've seen too much of it in our visual environment?

This is a sample of the text version of this font, to give you an idea of how easily the font reads at a variety of text settings. This allows you to compare fonts at a glance before using them in text type. Because of the differences in x-height, some fonts that measure the same point size appear to be different sizes for reading.

This example is set in 8.5 points, with -6 tracking, on 11 points of leading.

This is a sample of the text version of this font, to give you an idea of how easily the font reads at a variety of text settings. This allows you to compare fonts at a glance before using them in text type. Because of the differences in x-height, some fonts that measure the same point size appear to be different sizes for reading.

This example is set in 9 points, with -6 tracking, on 11 points of leading.

This is a sample of the text version of this font, to give you an idea of how easily the font reads at a variety of text settings. This allows you to compare fonts at a glance before using them in text type. Because of the differences in x-height, some fonts that measure the same point size appear to be different sizes for reading.

This example is set in 9.5 points, with -6 tracking, on 11 points of leading.

This page is set in Times Roman.

TRIPLE CONDENSED GOTHIC

21 *Type Samples*

ABCDEFGHIJKLM
NOPQRSTUVWXYZ

ABCDEFGHIJKLM
NOPQRSTUVWXYZ
1234567890
.,?*$&'!:;"

Triple Condensed Gothic is an extremely condensed font designed for display purposes only. It is illegible in text sizes. There is no lowercase, just small caps. It has an exaggerated vertical structure, with most of the curves replaced by modified rectangles. There are times when Triple Condensed can work exceptionally well in design, but it always has to be spaced with care. If it gets too tight, the eye starts to see only a series of vertical lines, and the letters become too difficult to discern. At an adequate size and well spaced, Triple Condensed is very legible for headlines or display uses. It also can be used in logo design to create a very contrasting typographic texture when placed next to a script or a serif font.

THIS IS A SAMPLE OF THE TEXT VERSION OF THIS FONT, TO GIVE YOU AN IDEA OF HOW LEGIBLE THE FONT READS AT A VARIETY OF TEXT SETTINGS. THIS ALLOWS YOU TO COMPARE FONTS AT A GLANCE BEFORE USING THEM IN TEXT TYPE. BECAUSE OF THE DIFFERENCES IN X-HEIGHT, SOME FONTS THAT MEASURE THE SAME POINT SIZE APPEAR TO BE DIFFERENT SIZES FOR READING.

THIS EXAMPLE IS SET IN 9.5 POINTS, WITH 6 TRACKING, ON 11 POINTS OF LEADING.

THIS IS A SAMPLE OF THE TEXT VERSION OF THIS FONT, TO GIVE YOU AN IDEA OF HOW LEGIBLE THE FONT READS AT A VARIETY OF TEXT SETTINGS. THIS ALLOWS YOU TO COMPARE FONTS AT A GLANCE BEFORE USING THEM IN TEXT TYPE. BECAUSE OF THE DIFFERENCES IN X-HEIGHT, SOME FONTS THAT MEASURE THE SAME POINT SIZE APPEAR TO BE DIFFERENT SIZES FOR READING.

THIS EXAMPLE IS SET IN 9 POINTS, WITH 6 TRACKING, ON 11 POINTS OF LEADING.

THIS IS A SAMPLE OF THE TEXT VERSION OF THIS FONT, TO GIVE YOU AN IDEA OF HOW LEGIBLE THE FONT READS AT A VARIETY OF TEXT SETTINGS. THIS ALLOWS YOU TO COMPARE FONTS AT A GLANCE BEFORE USING THEM IN TEXT TYPE. BECAUSE OF THE DIFFERENCES IN X-HEIGHT, SOME FONTS THAT MEASURE THE SAME POINT SIZE APPEAR TO BE DIFFERENT SIZES FOR READING.

THIS EXAMPLE IS SET IN 8.5 POINTS, WITH 6 TRACKING, ON 11 POINTS OF LEADING.

Trump Medieval Roman

ABCDEFGHIJ
KLMNOPQR
STUVWXYZ

abcdefghijklm
nopqrstuvwxyz

1234567890

.,?*#$&'%!:;">

Designed by Georg Trump, Trump Medieval Roman has a historic feel to it, particularly caused by the angled structure of the serifs, and the lack of bracketing. Trump also has very wide capitals that can seem out of place with the slightly condensed lowercase. In text-type applications, the font is very legible due to the tall x-height. The characters also have a very fine fit when placed together in text. The angularity of the serifs gives a slightly Germanic, engineered feel to this font. The horizontal spur on the "G" is an unusual detail of this typeface. Trump appears very bold on the page in display sizes, and is a bit dark as a text font unless adequate leading is used.

This is a sample of the text version of this font, to give you an idea of how easily the font reads at a variety of text settings. This allows you to compare fonts at a glance before using them in text type. Because of the differences in x-height, some fonts that measure the same point size appear to be different sizes for reading.

This example is set in 8.5 points, with -6 tracking, on 11 points of leading.

This is a sample of the text version of this font, to give you an idea of how easily the font reads at a variety of text settings. This allows you to compare fonts at a glance before using them in text type. Because of the differences in x-height, some fonts that measure the same point size appear to be different sizes for reading.

This example is set in 9 points, with -6 tracking, on 11 points of leading.

This is a sample of the text version of this font, to give you an idea of how easily the font reads at a variety of text settings. This allows you to compare fonts at a glance before using them in text type. Because of the differences in x-height, some fonts that measure the same point size appear to be different sizes for reading.

This example is set in 9.5 points, with -6 tracking, on 11 points of leading.

21   *Type Samples*

Univers Condensed 47 Light

ABCDEFGHIJ KLMNOPQR STUVWXYZ abcdefghijklm nopqrstuvwxyz 1234567890 .,?*#$&'%!:;">

Univers was designed by Adrian Frutiger and was conceived as an entire family of fonts, with weights and widths desig-nated by numbers. Univers 47 is an extremely legible and easily readable font, especially at small sizes. All of the captions in this book were set in Univers 47. Univers 48 is the italic version that you are read-ing now. The lowercase letters are very carefully crafted in this font; they have an artistic sensibility in their drawing and a clean elegance. This is a font that seems both seri-ous and authoritative when set as text type. It seems official; you don't want to disagree with what it says. There is a squareness to the corners of the Univers bowls, but this subtlety adds an eloquence and refinement to the font.

This is a sample of the text version of this font, to give you an idea of how easily the font reads at a variety of text settings. This allows you to compare fonts at a glance before using them in text type. Because of the differences in x-height, some fonts that measure the same point size appear to be different sizes for eading.

This example is set in 8.5 points, with -6 track-ing, on 11 points of leading.

This is a sample of the text version of this font, to give you an idea of how easily the font reads at a variety of text settings. This allows you to compare fonts at a glance before using them in text type. Because of the differences in x-height, some fonts that measure the same point size appear to be different sizes for reading.

This example is set in 9 points, with -6 track-ing, on 11 points of leading.

This is a sample of the text version of this font, to give you an idea of how easily the font reads at a variety of text settings. This allows you to compare fonts at a glance before using them in text type. Because of the differences in x-height, some fonts that measure the same point size appear to be different sizes for read-ing.

This example is set in 9.5 points, with -6 tracking, on 11 points of leading.

Walbaum Book Regular

ABCDEFGHI
JKLMNOPQ
RSTUVWXYZ
abcdefghijklmn
opqrstuvwxyz
1234567890
.,?*#$&'%!:;">

Walbaum, at first glance, appears quite similar to Bodoni. It was designed by Lange, and has a very square design to many of the characters; the "B," the "D" and the "R" are all very square, especially the tail on the "R." Even the "U" and the "O" are squared off. The lowercase "a" has a very full, rectangular bowl on it. There is no bracketing on the thin, ruled serifs, and the stem weight is quite a bit heavier than the hairline stroke. The stress of the characters is very vertical, but the transitions are graceful, preventing this font from feeling too technical. The juncture of the lowercase "k" arms to the stem is unique: it looks like a supporting piece of welded metal. Walbaum has great readability at small point sizes, and a handsome, artistic italic.

This is a sample of the text version of this font, to give you an idea of how easily the font reads at a variety of text settings. This allows you to compare fonts at a glance before using them in text type. Because of the differences in x-height, some fonts that measure the same point size appear to be different sizes for reading.

This example is set in 8.5 points, with -6 tracking, on 11 points of leading.

This is a sample of the text version of this font, to give you an idea of how easily the font reads at a variety of text settings. This allows you to compare fonts at a glance before using them in text type. Because of the differences in x-height, some fonts that measure the same point size appear to be different sizes for reading.

This example is set in 9 points, with -6 tracking, on 11 points of leading.

This is a sample of the text version of this font, to give you an idea of how easily the font reads at a variety of text settings. This allows you to compare fonts at a glance before using them in text type. Because of the differences in x-height, some fonts that measure the same point size appear to be different sizes for reading.

This example is set in 9.5 points, with -6 tracking, on 11 points of leading.

Weiss Regular

ABCDEFGHIJ KLMNOPQR STUVWXYZ abcdefghijklm nopqrstuvwxyz 1234567890 .,?*#$&'%!:;">

Weiss is a quirky typeface with a great sense of history to the design. Designed by Weiss, the letters appear very carefully crafted with subtle nuances, such as the blending of the cross bar into the stem on the lowercase "f," and the short bottom curve on the "s." Many of Weiss's uppercase characters have peculiarities, such as the short vertical stroke on the "G," the "N," and the "S" that look as though they're upside down, and the very wide "W." In italic, Weiss is extremely condensed and very angular, but it harmonizes very well with the Roman version. As a text font, Weiss is very readable and legible even at small sizes, despite its relatively small x-height. This clarity is a tribute to the fine design of the characters, which makes them easy to discern at text sizes. The numerals and punctuation are even interesting in Weiss; the "2" is great, and the question mark is rather odd looking but fun. This is a very versatile font for either text or headlines.

This is a sample of the text version of this font, to give you an idea of how easily the font reads at a variety of text settings. This allows you to compare fonts at a glance before using them in text type. Because of the differences in x-height, some fonts that measure the same point size appear to be different sizes for reading.

This example is set in 8.5 points, with -6 tracking, on 11 points of leading.

This is a sample of the text version of this font, to give you an idea of how easily the font reads at a variety of text settings. This allows you to compare fonts at a glance before using them in text type. Because of the differences in x-height, some fonts that measure the same point size appear to be different sizes for reading.

This example is set in 9 points, with -6 tracking, on 11 points of leading.

This is a sample of the text version of this font, to give you an idea of how easily the font reads at a variety of text settings. This allows you to compare fonts at a glance before using them in text type. Because of the differences in x-height, some fonts that measure the same point size appear to be different sizes for reading.

This example is set in 9.5 points, with -6 tracking, on 11 points of leading.

Wilhelm Klingspor Gothic

ABCDEFGHI
JKLMNOPQ
RSTUVWXYZ

abcdefghijklm
nopqrstuvwxyz

1234567890

.,?áß_&'%!::;k>

Wilhelm Klingspor Gothic is a calligraphic-based Fraktur font that is very decorative and graceful. Some of the uppercase characters have decorative secondary strokes and flags that accentuate the flourishes. For a Gothic-style font, Wilhelm has a lot of personality to the design of the uppercase, and they incorporate many curves in their design. In contrast, the lowercase is very condensed and angular, with fewer flourishes. In text type, the condensed lowercase is tough to read, but in headlines its darkness is an asset.

This is a sample of the text version of this font, to give you an idea of how easily the font reads at a variety of text settings. This allows you to compare fonts at a glance before using them in text type. Because of the differences in x-height, some fonts that measure the same point size appear to be different sizes for reading.

This example is set in 8.5 points, with -6 tracking, on 11 points of leading.

This is a sample of the text version of this font, to give you an idea of how easily the font reads at a variety of text settings. This allows you to compare fonts at a glance before using them in text type. Because of the differences in x-height, some fonts that measure the same point size appear to be different sizes for reading.

This example is set in 9 points, with -6 tracking, on 11 points of leading.

This is a sample of the text version of this font, to give you an idea of how easily the font reads at a variety of text settings. This allows you to compare fonts at a glance before using them in text type. Because of the differences in x-height, some fonts that measure the same point size appear to be different sizes for reading.

This example is set in 9.5 points, with -6 tracking, on 11 points of leading.

This page is set in Wilhelm Klingspor Gothic.

Windsor

ABCDEFGHIJ
KLMNOPQR
STUVWXYZ
abcdefghijklm
nopqrstuvwxyz
1234567890
.,?*#$&'%!:;">

Windsor is a casual font that breaks many of the rules of typography. The cross bars for the uppercase shift up and down; there is no standard placement. The "J" and the "S" have a serpentine quality to their finials. The lowercase "f" also has a whimsical curlicue terminal. It is a cavalier font, with the bowls of some uppercase characters very full and those of others rather tight; compare the "R" to the "U." The numerals even have curls, the "2," "3," "5," "6" and "9" are rather elaborate and sinewy. There is a lot of energy in the design of this font, but it is not too distracting to read. It has good legibility at text sizes, and it is interesting on the page. Although Windsor is not appropriate for serious topics, it does have its niche for light-hearted text uses.

This page is set in Windsor.

This is a sample of the text version of this font, to give you an idea of how easily the font reads at a variety of text settings. This allows you to compare fonts at a glance before using them in text type. Because of the differences in x-height, some fonts that measure the same point size appear to be different sizes for reading.

This example is set in 8.5 points, with -6 tracking, on 11 points of leading.

This is a sample of the text version of this font, to give you an idea of how easily the font reads at a variety of text settings. This allows you to compare fonts at a glance before using them in text type. Because of the differences in x-height, some fonts that measure the same point size appear to be different sizes for reading.

This example is set in 9 points, with -6 tracking, on 11 points of leading.

This is a sample of the text version of this font, to give you an idea of how easily the font reads at a variety of text settings. This allows you to compare fonts at a glance before using them in text type. Because of the differences in x-height, some fonts that measure the same point size appear to be different sizes for reading.

This example is set in 9.5 points, with -6 tracking, on 11 points of leading.

Adobe Wood Ornaments 2

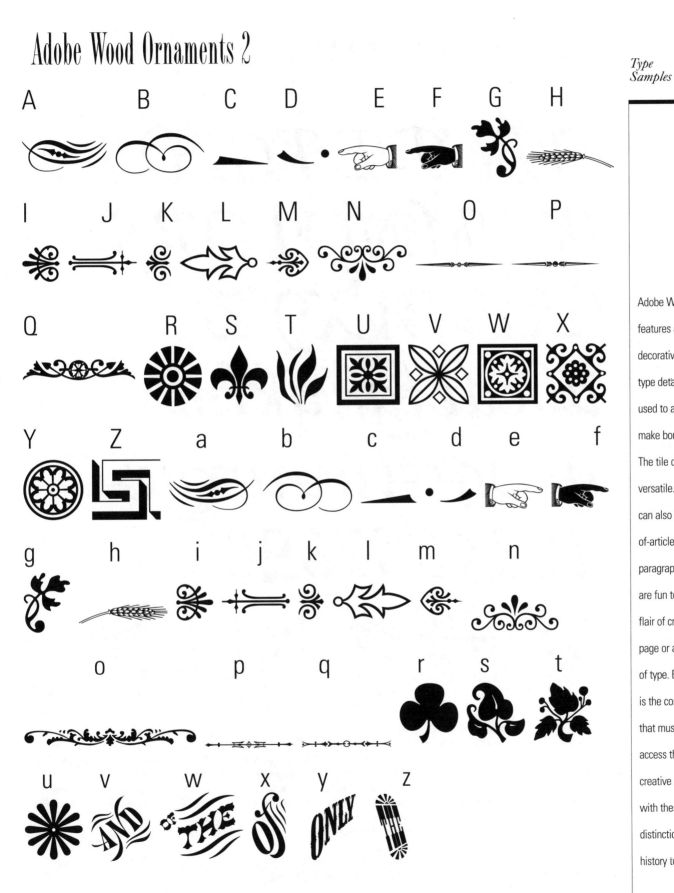

Adobe Wood Ornaments 2 features a series of historic decorative flourishes and type details that can be used to accentuate type, to make borders or patterns. The tile designs are very versatile. These images can also be used as end-of-article markers or as paragraph dividers. They are fun to use and add a flair of creativity to a title page or a subdividing line of type. Below each image is the corresponding letter that must be used to access the ornament. Be creative and experimental with these; they can add distinction or a sense of history to your work.

This page is set in Univers Condensed.

Zapf Chancery Medium Italic

ABCDEFGHIJ
KLMNOPQRS
TUVWXYZ
abcdefghijklm
nopqrstuvwxyz
1234567890
.,?*#$&'%!:;">

Zapf Chancery was designed by Hermann Zapf. Clearly based in the calligraphic hands, Zapf Chancery makes no pretense that it is hand drawn, yet it is more of a font than a spontaneous creation. The swashes on the uppercase characters are too repetitive, and there is little artistry or uniqueness to the letters. As a text font, Zapf is poorly suited because its x-height is so small that it prohibits clarity, even at sizes as large as 10 or 11 points. This font is best used for a few words in a headline, but even in that application, hand-drawn calligraphy will have more heart than this standardized font.

This is a sample of the text version of this font, to give you an idea of how easily the font reads at a variety of text settings. This allows you to compare fonts at a glance before using them in text type. Because of the differences in x-height, some fonts that measure the same point size appear to be different sizes for reading.

This example is set in 8.5 points, with -6 tracking, on 11 points of leading.

This is a sample of the text version of this font, to give you an idea of how easily the font reads at a variety of text settings. This allows you to compare fonts at a glance before using them in text type. Because of the differences in x-height, some fonts that measure the same point size appear to be different sizes for reading.

This example is set in 9 points, with -6 tracking, on 11 points of leading.

This is a sample of the text version of this font, to give you an idea of how easily the font reads at a variety of text settings. This allows you to compare fonts at a glance before using them in text type. Because of the differences in x-height, some fonts that measure the same point size appear to be different sizes for reading.

This example is set in 9.5 points, with -6 tracking, on 11 points of leading.

This page is set in Zapf Chancery.

Zapf Dingbats Regular

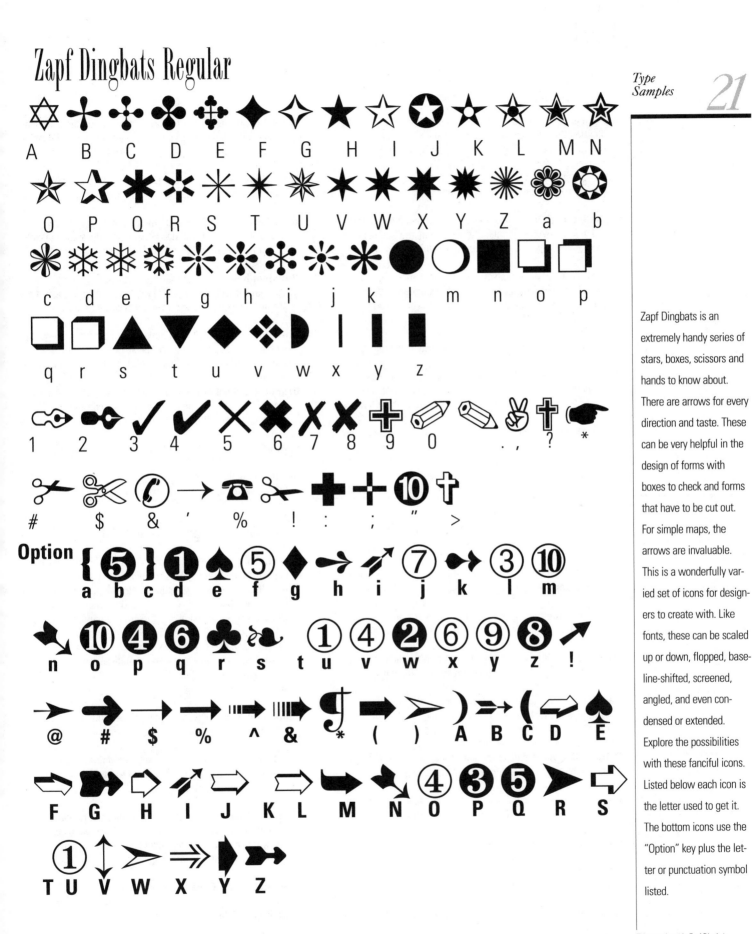

Zapf Dingbats is an extremely handy series of stars, boxes, scissors and hands to know about. There are arrows for every direction and taste. These can be very helpful in the design of forms with boxes to check and forms that have to be cut out. For simple maps, the arrows are invaluable. This is a wonderfully varied set of icons for designers to create with. Like fonts, these can be scaled up or down, flopped, baseline-shifted, screened, angled, and even condensed or extended. Explore the possibilities with these fanciful icons. Listed below each icon is the letter used to get it. The bottom icons use the "Option" key plus the letter or punctuation symbol listed.

This page is set in Zapf Dingbats.

Glossary

Glossary

AA–stands for Author's Alteration; used in proofing as an indication that changes are requested and will be paid for by the client; changes are not due to printer's error.

Alley–the space between two columns of set type; sometimes also called a column gutter or column margin.

Alphabet–a set of visual letters or characters arranged in an order fixed by custom, used to represent the sounds of a spoken language; 26 characters in English.

Alternate Character–a version of a letterform that is designed as a part of a font, but is not the standard letterform. It may incorporate a swash, or be a different structure of the letter.

Ampersand–the symbol for "and" (&) that is a monogrammatic.

Apex–the upper point of letters with an ascending pointed form–the point usually extends past the cap line; examples of different types: rounded, pointed, hallow, flat, and extended.

Arabic Number–a numeral from 0 through 9; can be set as Old Style or Lining Figures.

Arc of the Stem–a curved stroke that is continuous with a straight stem, not a bowl; examples: bottom of "j, t, f, a, and u." Also called a shoulder.

Arm–the horizontal or diagonal upward sloping stroke that attaches to the stem and is free on one end.

Ascender–the part of lowercase letters, "b, d, f, h, k, l, and t" extending above the x-height line.

Ascender Line–the horizontal rule that aligns along the top of the lowercase letters that extend above the waist line.

Back Matter–the book information placed after the text copy; includes index, glossary, bibliography, and appendix.

Bad Break–refers to widows or orphans in text copy, or a break that does not make sense of the phrasing of a line of copy, causing awkward reading.

Banner–the type design of the name of a repetitive publication, such as a newspaper, newsletter, or magazine.

Bar–the horizontal or oblique short stroke connected at both ends as in an "A" or "H;" also called a cross bar.

Barbs–the half serifs at ends of the arcs of "C, G, and S."

Baseline–the horizontal rule on which all the bottom serifs or terminals of letters align.

Beaks–the half serifs on the horizontal arms of "E, F, L, and T."

Black Letter–an angular fourteen-fifteenth century European Gothic lettering, having closely spaced and heavy miniscule stems; also called Old English or Textura faces.

Body Copy–the textual matter set in one face and point size, with a common leading and column width.

Bold Face–a heavy, stroked typeface, in which the negative space of counters is minimized; appears thick and massive; calls attention to itself in contrast to regular text for emphasis.

Boustrophedon–writing with alternating lines written in opposite directions; one line is written from left to right, then the next line's letters are reversed, written from right to left.

Bowl–the curved stroke that makes an enclosed space within a character. In an open bowl, the stroke does not meet with the stem completely; a closed-bowl stroke meets the stem.

Bracketed Serif–a serif in which the transition from the stem stroke to the serif stroke is one continuous curve. Serifs may have differing degrees of bracketing.

Brackets–the symbols used in algebraic formulas, {,}.

Break–the place where type is divided; may be the end of a line or paragraph, or as it *reads* best in display type.

Bullet–a small, solid circle that is used to introduce either a section that is important or items that are listed.

Calendaring–named for a stack of smooth calendar rollers made of metal that paper is run across to give a smooth finish to the sheet. Often the paper is flooded with a liquid clay-like coating before it's run through the calendaring stacks, which gives a hard, shiny surface to the paper.

California Job Case–the large drawers of shallow height used to sort hand-set lead type into small compartments that were arranged based on the frequency of use of the characters.

Callout–a selection of type (word or phrase) that is set in larger or bolder type from the body-copy font for emphasis.

Cap Height–the typesetting term referring to the size of a typeface–often a headline–measured from the baseline to the top of the capital letters.

Capital–the large letters of the alphabet; the original form of ancient Roman characters. The letters are based on a design within a square–no ascenders or descenders; also called uppercase, majuscule, and caps.

Caps and Small Caps–the typesetting option in which the lowercase letters are set as small capital letters; usually 75% the height of the size of the uppercase.

Caption–a small amount of copy, placed near an illustration or photo, describing the image or identifying people.

Character–a letter of the alphabet; also a punctuation mark, symbol, numeral, etc.

Character Count–an estimation of the number of characters in a selection of type.

Character Per Pica–(CPP) computerized estimate of the number of letters of a font at a given size that will fit in one pica.

Centered Line for Line–(CLL) typesetting term referring to text type whose center points are aligned vertically.

Codex–a book of paper or parchment leaves bound with boards; distinct from the ancient volume in scroll form.

Cold Type–the general term for type which is created by photocomposition, in which no heat is required.

Colophon–an inscription at the end of a manuscript or book that contains facts about its production; identifies artists, designers, or printers, and specifies the typefaces and papers used.

Column Rule–a line used between two columns of type.

Comp–short for comprehensive layout; used to show a client how the printed piece will look.

Condensed Type–type that has been compressed visually from left to right, giving a tall, thin appearance. Usually a condensed face is much taller than it is wide.

Copperplate–1. a printing process that is engraved into copper plates for intaglio printing; 2. the style of type derived from this engraving process.

Copy–the text for a project, supplied by the client; usually typewritten to be marked up for typesetting.

Copy-fitting–the process of speccing type to see if it will fit into a given space provided.

Counter–a negative space within a character of type; it can be either fully or partially enclosed.

Crop Marks–small lines placed outside the corners of a piece to indicate where the piece should be trimmed.

Cross Bar–the horizontal bar connecting two strokes of a letterform, as in "H" and "A", the ends are not free.

Cross Stroke–the horizontal stroke cutting across the stem of a letter, as in "t" and "f," where both ends of the stroke are free.

Crotch–the pointed space where an arm or arc meets a stem; an acute crotch less is than 90 degrees, and an obtuse crotch is more than 90 degrees.

Cuneiform–the Sumerian writing style of wedge-shaped characters that are pressed into damp clay with a stylus.

Cursive–handwriting or typefaces that are joined and slanted; when typeset, referred to as scripts.

Descender–the part of the lowercase letters "g, j, p, q, and y" and capital "J," extending below the baseline.

Descender Line–the horizontal rule that aligns along the bottom edge of the lowercase letters that extend below the baseline.

Dingbat–the decorative, visual printer's mark that is designed and sized as a font and used for typesetting accent.

Display–large type that is used for emphasis–usually for a title or headline; can be set in caps or caps/lowercase.

Drop Cap–an initial capital that is larger than the point size of the copy; insets into the column of type.

Ear–the small stroke (sometimes rounded) projecting from the top of lowercase Roman "g, r, f, and a."

Ellipsis–three periods (...) set in text type to indicate omitted material or a pause; (option + ;).

Em Dash or Mutt Dash–also known as a long dash; a dash that is the width of an em space; used for attributing a quote to an author; (option + shift + dash).

Em Space or Mutt Space–a typesetting measure equal to a square of the point size of the type; often used as a paragraph indent, and to indicate space in typesetting.

En Dash or Nut Dash–dash that is the length of an en space; used to replace "to" in text, as in 6–9PM; (option + dash).

En Space or Nut Space–a typesetting measure equal to half an em from left to right; used for spaces in typesetting.

Extended or Expanded–type that appears to have been stretched from left to right; is wide in appearance; usually an extended font is wider than the corresponding regular font.

Extenders–both ascenders and descenders together; called this because they extend beyond the body of the font.

Eye–the counter or enclosed area at the top of the lowercase "e."

Family of Type–variations of one primary font that have similar characteristics of serifs, strokes, proportion, and

Glossary

balance; examples of different variations: light, condensed, extended, italic, bold, etc.

Finial–the non-serif ending added to a stroke (e.g., ball, swash, spur, or hook finials). Finials often taper.

Flags–decorative, curved strokes connected to the stem of an uppercase Gothic letterform.

Fleuron–the decorative typesetting unit, often floral, for assembling into borders and fanciful dividers.

Flush Left–a typesetting term referring to text type that aligns along the left-hand margin; usually the text is rag right.

Flush Right–a typesetting term referring to text type that aligns along the right-hand margin; usually the text is rag left.

Folio–the page number; can also include any type, date or flourish that is placed with the page number on each page.

Font–the characters, numbers, punctuation marks, symbols, etc., composing one typeface; refers to a specific type design.

Foundry Set or Machine Set–a typesetting term that refers to type composition done mechanically on a machine without any specific spacing adjustments or kerning.

Fraktur–a sixteenth-century German style of letterforms that incorporated curved strokes to soften the angularity of earlier Gothic styles of calligraphy.

Galley–1. a typeset proof from the typesetter that is run out as one long column of type; 2. the frame that holds and locks up the metal type in letterpress printing.

Grain–the direction that the fibers run in paper. It is important to determine for folding and scoring paper successfully without cracking along the score.

Gravure–the printing process in which the plate is etched and the ink lies in the grooves; also called intaglio printing.

Greeking–nonsense type set in a particular font, size; and column width; used to indicate body copy for a client on a comp.

Grid–the underlying format of a piece in non-repro blue, or on a computer screen, determined by the designer to indicate column width, margins, gutters, and image placement.

Grotesk–the European designation for sans serif type or letters when they first appeared.

Gutter–the inner margin in a piece at the place where two pages or panels come together; where the piece is bound.

H & J–the hyphenation and Justification computer option for justified copy. Some programs allow users to refine the standard settings to their own preferences.

Hairline–1. the secondary stroke of a letter; usually thinner than the stem; 2. the weight of the finest rule a typesetter can set for rules or boxes.

Half-Uncial–a lettering style dating from the third century; so named because the letterforms are constructed on four horizontal guidelines, one-half uncial (Roman inch) apart. More cursive strokes, ascenders and descenders were introduced in uncials than were in Gothic.

Hanging Indention–a typesetting instruction used to indicate that the first line will be set flush left and the following lines will be indented (the format for bibliographies).

Hanging Initial–the initial letter of text set larger and in a different margin; placed partially or entirely in left margin next to text.

Hanging Punctuation–the punctuation set outside of the margins of the type, so that the type aligns vertically, either F/L or F/R.

Hanging Quote–quotation marks that hang in the left margin, so that flush left copy has all the letters aligned flush left.

Head Margin–the space above the type appearing on every page.

Head or Headline–the introductory title usually set in display type; set larger than text type, and sometimes in a different font to call attention to the text material below.

Hieratic–a cursive script that represented a simplified form of hieroglyphics; developed and used by ancient Egyptian priests.

Hieroglyphics–a writing system developed in ancient Egypt that used pictographs to represent words and sounds.

Hot Type–the general term for type which is cast from molten metal; heat is used to cast the letters in lead.

Hyphenation–a setting on some computer programs allowing the user to determine how many characters can precede a hyphen and the number of hyphenated line endings that will be set in a row in a column of type.

IBC– the abbreviation for the Inside Back Cover.

Ideograph–a sign or character that represents an idea or concept; often combines two or more pictographs.

IFC–the abbreviation for the Inside Back Cover.

Illuminating–lighting up the pages of a sacred book by decorating with gold or silver in illustrations, borders, or initial caps.

Indent–the space placed at the beginning of a line to indicate a paragraph break, or to offset a selection of text or tabular matter.

Index–an alphabetized reference list at the end of the text of the names, items, and subjects and the corresponding page on which they are found.

Inferior Character–also called subscript; a small number placed below the baseline; used in chemical formulas.

Initial Capital–the first letter of text is set as a larger or decorative letter used to introduce a section of text type. Used for design purposes and to draw readers into the text.

Inline–a typeface that incorporates a white line in the letters to simulate a raised surface or a chiseled, dimensional quality.

Intaglio or Gravure–the method of printing in which ink lies into incisions on the plate's surface.

Italic–denotes letters slanted to the right, distinct from Roman letters in their form, construction and terminals; used for emphasis or in titles, etc.

Jump Head–a headline placed over a story that is continued from a previous page; usually shorter and smaller than the original head.

Justified–a typesetting term referring to text type that is aligned vertically along both the left- and right-hand margins.

Kerning–adjusting (usually tightening) the space between individual characters in a headline so that they visually appear correct and evenly spaced. Leading can also be reduced to improve readability.

Keyline–the outline on a mechanical to indicate the placement of art.

Laid Paper–paper with parallel lines to simulate the texture of the surface of handmade paper that is imparted by the screens. Paper without the lines (smooth paper) is called wove finished.

Leaders–a series of dots, dashes or periods used to "lead" the eye across from one section of type to the next.

Leading–the space between lines of type, measured from baseline to baseline. The term comes from the thin lead spacers of different-point-sized widths used in letterpress printing that were sandwiched between slugs from a linotype machine.

Leaflet–a single printed sheet, folded but not bound.

Leg–a downward, angled stroke that is attached to the stem of a letter on one end and free on the other terminal end.

Letterpress–the printing method in which the raised surface of the type or blocks transfers the ink onto the paper with the application of pressure.

Letter-spacing–adding space between letters to allow headlines or running heads to extend to a specific pica measure.

Ligature–a combination of two or more letters that are joined to make one form; originally cast as one piece of lead designed to simulate the hand lettering in manuscripts.

Light Face–a thin-stroked typeface in which the negative space is far greater in mass than the weight of the strokes; appears open and airy.

Line Length or Measure–the length of a type line given in picas; usually is the width of a column of type.

Linespacing–another term for leading; the space from the center of one line to the center of the next line.

Lining Figures–numerals that align along the baseline of the font and are the same height as the uppercase characters, unlike Old Style figures, which have ascenders and descenders.

Link–the stroke connecting bowl and loop of a lowercase g.

Linotype–a hot metal typesetting system that utilizes a keyboard and sets one line of type at a time, as a solid piece of lead, when the text is typed in at a keyboard. (Invented by Mergenthaler.)

Lithography–printing from a flat surface in which the area to print is receptive to the ink and the rest of the plate is coated with a liquid mixture so that it resists the ink.

Logotype–the name, symbol or trademark that incorporates consistent type and is designed to identify a company; used on all company communication and products.

Loop–the lower portion of the Roman lowercase "g" added as a flourish rather than an essential part of the letter.

Lowercase–small letterforms, originating from the semi-uncial lettering style; includes ascenders and descenders. The name comes from the placement of the letterpress case of small letters in the lower of the two wooden type cases used by hand compositors; placed so that they were within hands' reach; also called lc or miniscule.

Ludlow–a hand composing bar usually used for setting or proofing headlines and display fonts in lead type.

Main Stem–the thickest stroke of a character.

Majuscule–the capital letterform, "A, B, and C," etc.; also uppercase.

Glossary

Margin–the white space from the edge of the text to the edge of the page, on all four sides of a printed or lettered piece.

Markup–the placing instructions for a typesetter on typed copy to insure correct typesetting; also called speccing.

Masthead–the editorial credit box of a regular publication.

Matte Finish–a coated paper having a dull finish without luster or glare, yet still a uniformly smooth surface.

Matrix–the piece of brass into which the punch is driven to create an impression of a letter. The matrix is then placed at the bottom of the precision mold to cast a letter.

Mean Line–the imaginary line defining the height of the lowercase letters, excluding ascenders; called the waist or x-height line.

Mechanical–the accurate assemblage and pasting down of all the type, images, rules, etc., on illustration board, so that they are ready for printing.

Miniscule–the letterform evolved from half uncials, incorporating ascenders and descenders and a smaller body height.

Minusing–decreasing the space between typeset characters in text settings; minusing affects the entire selection of text equally. Called tracking on computer programs. Text is set in minus one unit, minus 1.5 units, minus two units, etc.

Modern Typeface–a mechanical-looking typeface; has no bracketing; has thin, hairline strokes, serifs, and a vertical stress.

Monotone or Monoline typeface–a font in which all the lines appear to be of the same thickness.

Mutt or Mutton Quad–an alternate term for an em space; used to differentiate from an en space when spoken.

Mutt Dash or Em Dash–also known as a long dash; a dash that is the width of an em space; used for attributing a quote to an author; (option + shift + dash).

Nameplate– a type design of the name of a publication, such as a newspaper, newsletter, or magazine; also called banner.

Non-repro Blue–a light blue ink that is not picked up by the camera; used for designers to align type, images, and edges of the page on mechanical boards.

Nut Dash or En Dash–a dash that is the length of an en space; used to replace "to" in text, as in 6–9PM; (option + dash).

Nut Quad–another name for en space piece of lead; used to differentiate from em space when spoken.

OBC–the abbreviation for the Outside Back Cover.

Oblong Binding–a book that is bound on the shorter side.

OFC–the abbreviation for the Outside Front Cover.

Offset Lithography–a method of printing in which the image is transferred from the plate via a rubber roller to the paper.

Old English–a term for the Gothic style of lettering that was angular and condensed, or for fonts in this style.

Open Leaders–also called dot leaders; refer to a line of periods that are spaced widely apart.

Ornament–a small type decoration, such as a floret, a graceful curvilinear swash, or a dingbat; used to indicate paragraph breaks; set at the end of a selection for decoration, etc.

Orphan–the first line of a paragraph left at the bottom of a column of type, separated from the rest of the paragraph. This is undesirable because of reading interruption. Also, when the last line of a paragraph is at the top of a new column. The worst-case scenario is when one line of a paragraph is separated on a column on an entirely separate page.

Pagination–the numbering of pages in consecutive order.

Paragraph Mark–(¶) a type-speccing symbol used to indicate the beginning of a new paragraph; handwritten as a reversed cap "P" when marking up text; (option + 7).

Parchment–dried animal skins that are processed to write on.

Paste-up–the process of putting a mechanical together, often using heated wax as the adhesive, with which pieces are burnished in place, and checked for squareness and alignment.

PE–a mark used to indicate a printer's error when marking up typesetting, a proof, or a blueline; as opposed to designer's error.

Petroglyph–an elemental sign or pictograph carved or drawn on a rock.

Photocomposition–phototypesetting; the use of negatives of a font through which light is passed to expose the type onto photosensitive paper or film.

Phototypesetting–another term for photocomposition; photographically produced type; cold type.

Pica–a horizontal measure for line lengths equal to 1/6 of an inch, 12 points, or 0.013837 inches.

Pictograph–an elementary picture symbol that represents the object or word depicted.

Point–a typesetting measure used to determine the height of a typeface; equal to 1/72 of an inch, or 1/12 of a pica.

Point Size–a typesetting term that refers to the size of a character; measured from the ascender line to the descender line.

Press Type–alphabets on clear plastic film that can be rubbed down for a comp for a client's approval.

Proofreader–the person who checks the final typeset galleys for spelling, punctuation, consistency, and grammatical errors.

Proportional Spacing–fonts in which each letter has a space designated for that character; improves readability of the face.

Pull Quote–words repeated from the text and displayed larger and in a different typeface as a quotation by the author.

Punch-cutting–the cutting of a letter of the alphabet at the end of a steel bar so that it can be punched into a brass mould or matrix from which to cast lead type.

Quad–a space in typeset lead type; comes from the names of the word spacers used in hand-set composition.

Ragged Center–the type-speccing instruction for type that is set with each line centered; usually the designer indicates line breaks.

Ragged Left–type set with an aligned right margin and an uneven left margin.

Ragged Right–type set with an aligned left margin and an uneven right margin.

Raised Initial–an initial cap that projects above the first line of text type; it may or may not align with the baseline of the first line of text type. Also called a stick-up or stand-up initial capital.

Ranging Figures–another term for Old Style figures, or figures that are not aligned along the baseline of the font.

Readability–the relative ease with which type on a printed page can be read; based on the column width to point size ratio, the x-height of the font, the leading, the color of type, and the color of page.

Rebus–the use of pictures and/or pictographs to represent the syllables of the object.

Recto–the right-hand page in a book or spread.

Reference Mark–a mark used to indicate a footnote, an asterisk, a numeral, or a dagger symbol. Can also be used for the notes the author wants to inform the reader of as sidenotes to the text.

Relief–projecting from a flat surface; embossed. The opposite of incuse, engrave, or deboss.

Reversed Type–type that is white against a black background; will always appear slightly smaller and thinner than its corresponding face in black. Very fine-line type should not be reversed out of black: it will have tendency to close in during printing and will be difficult to read.

Revised Proof–a printing proof pulled after corrections are made.

River–a series of white spaces running through several consecutive lines of type, creating a vertical white "river" through the gray block of copy. Occurs most frequently in justified copy when word spacing is opened up; rivers should be changed.

Roman Face–denotes the upright vertical position of a letter, as opposed to a slanted, italic form.

Roman Numerals–the ancient Roman numbering system; uses letters to denote different quantities in the base-ten numbering system: I=1, V=5, X=10, L=50, C=100, D=500, and M=1000.

Rotolus–a scroll made from sheets of papyrus pasted together to make a writing scroll, approximately 9" x 35'. Used in ancient Greece and Rome.

Rough–a preliminary sketch or idea, frequently created in markers, to give a client a general idea of how the piece will look.

Roundhand–penmanship of rounded strokes and graceful curves; written with split pointed pens and controlled pressures.

Rule–a typeset line; can be used alone or as a box outline; comes in varying thicknesses specified by point sizes.

Run-around–text copy that is set to wrap around a silhouetted image or other element of the design. Also called contour set, skew, or wrap-around.

Run-in Head–a head set into the first line of text; usually set large, bold, or italic, or in a different font.

Running Foot or Feet–(running footer) a title, design element, rule, etc., repeated on every page; usually includes the folio.

Running Head–(running header) a headline or title that is repeated on every page, usually at the top; may include folio; can be chapter names or book title.

Saddle Stitch–appears like staple binding. Wire is inserted and bent back through the middle fold of the sheets to secure them together. Bent wire is on the inside of the finished document.

Glossary

Sans Serif–letterforms without serifs.

Scaling–determining the desired size for an image that will be reduced or enlarged to fit a given area in the layout.

Scanner–an electronic device that translates a visual image into digital information that can be saved on disk and printed.

Screen–a pattern of dots or lines that are extremely fine and appear as an area of gray when printed; can choose darkness of tone in 10% increments from 0 to 100%. Screens are measured in fineness as dots per inch (dpi)–the larger the dpi, the finer and smoother the tone. There are also specialty screens that give a spiral effect, or a mezzotint effect to a half-tone image.

Script–typefaces based on handwritten linked letters; usually incorporates a slant to the right and flourishes on the caps.

Serif–a line crossing the terminal of a character that extends beyond the main stroke; believed to be residuals of chisel-cut letters in ancient Rome;

Set-in Initial–a large first letter of the text that is inset into the body of the text; also called a cut-in initial.

Set Solid–a typesetting term that refers to typesetting with no additional leading between the lines, 12/12.

Shoulder–a curved stroke of the lowercase "h, m, and n."

Side Head–a heading set to the side of the page or column of text. A heading set partially into the outer margin of the text, and partially into the column of text is called a cut-in side heading.

Silhouette–an image whose background is removed.

Sinaitic Script–a writing system found in Sinaitic mines that may link Egyptian hieroglyphs to the Phoenician alphabet.

Sink–a term for the distance to the first line of type on a page, usually larger on chapter-opening pages to fit in the chapter head.

Slash Mark–a diagonal line (/) used to represent the per, as in miles/hour; or to represent alternatives as in and/or; also called a virgule.

Slug–1. a line of type cast as a single piece of metal, from a linotype machine; 2. strips of metal used for spacers to create vertical space on the page in letterpress printing.

Small Caps–smaller capital letters; designed with many fonts; usually about 75% the height of the uppercase characters; can be specified to be set instead of lowercase.

Speccing–a shortened version of type specifications; the term for marking up copy with accurate instructions for typesetting.

Spine–the main curved stroke of the letter "s."

Splayed–the stem of a character that is wider at the top and bottom than it is toward the center.

Spur–the nodule descending from the vertical stroke of an uppercase G connecting the straight stroke to the curved stroke.

Square or Hairline Serif–the stem stroke and serif are entirely separate; no bracketing; mechanical appearance to the font.

Squeeze–when text copy is set with less than the normal spacing between characters; also referred to as minusing or tracking.

Stand-up Initial–an initial cap that projects above the first line of text type; it aligns with the baseline of the first line of text type. Also called a stick-up or raised initial.

Stem–the main vertical, diagonal, or curved stroke of a character.

Stet–the term used when speccing copy that means to leave a selection the way it was typed; to disregard the typesetting marks; "Let the original stand."

Stress–the thickening in a curved stroke caused by a flat pen changing direction; the thickest point is "maximum stress." The direction of thick strokes in curves, either an oblique or a vertical stress.

Strike-on Composition–type that is made by direct impression, such as a typewriter.

Stroke–any line necessary to the basic form of a letter (not serif or swash, etc.).

Subhead–a subordinate heading; usually requires a different type treatment than the headlines or text.

Subscript–small numerals placed below the baseline for chemical formulas; also known as inferior characters.

Sunken Initial–a large initial cap whose top edge aligns with the ascenders of the top line of the text; also called "drop cap."

Superior Character–an undersized numeral placed so it hangs above the x-height; used for footnote reference and exponents; also called superscript.

Swash–a fancy flourish that replaces a terminal or serif in scripts.

Tabloid–1. a small-sized newspaper, about half the size of a full newspaper page; 2. in computer printers, this size indicates a vertical 11" x17" or 10" x 14".

Tail–a downward sloping stroke or arc of a character starting from the ending free–stroke on an uppercase "R, K, and the Q."

Terminal–the free end of a stroke. Different types: sheared, ball, straight, acute, horizontal, convex, concave, flared, hooked, and tapered and pointed terminals.

Text–the body copy set in a consistent size with uniform line length and leading; usually forms a block of copy with the appearance of a gray texture on the page, as opposed from heads, subheads, etc.

Thin Space–a space used between a bullet and text that is less than a 3 to the em space; usually about 1/4 or 1/5 em space.

Thumbnail–comprises small, quick sketches used to get down a variety of ideas when working on a project; usually very rough; done in a visual shorthand.

Tip-in–an illustration or image that is printed separately and trimmed out and pasted by hand into the space left for it in a book.

Title Page–the page in the front of the book listing the title, subtitle, author, publisher and date of publication.

TOC–abbreviation for the Table of Contents.

TR–means to transpose or switch the order of the letters.

Tracking–the function on computers that determines the character-to-character spacing, as well as the word spacing. Can be tightened for a closer fit; also called minusing or squeezing for text type and kerning in display type.

Typeface–the specific design of an alphabet's letters, numerals, monetary symbols, etc., in all sizes, to be used together.

Type Family–all of the various weights and versions of a particular typeface, including italics, outline faces, bold weights, light weights, condensed and extended varieties, etc.

Type-High–.918 in.; the precise height that a plate must be to be printed on a letterpress.

Type Size–the size of type, measured in points from the top of the ascenders to the bottom of the descenders. In the days of metal type, the term referred to the size of the piece of metal that the face was cut on. Also called the point size.

Typo–a shortened form of the phrase typographical error.

U&lc–1. abbreviation for upper- and lowercase; means set in capitals and lowercase letters as in the type manuscript; 2. also the name of the quarterly newsletter published by the International Typeface Corporation.

Uncials–a rounded manuscript style used as early as the third century in ancient Greece; frequently drawn on guidelines placed one inch (uncial) apart.

Uppercase–capital letters, historically placed in the upper of the two drawers used in hand composition.

Verso–the left-hand page in a book or spread.

Vertex–the outer, downward-pointing, free-ending juncture of two angled stems; the point touches just below the baseline; examples of different types: rounded, pointed, hallow flat, extended.

Virgule–the name of the slash mark (/) used to represent the per, as in miles/hour; or alternatives, as in and/or.

Waist Line–an imaginary horizontal rule that aligns on the body of the lowercase alphabet; also called the x-height line.

Watermark–a design or word placed in the screen when making paper; visible when paper is held up to the light; identifies the mill and the paper stock.

Weight–1. the boldness of the strokes of a character, both serif or sans serif; different examples include: light, medium, or book, semi-bold, bold, or extra bold; 2. the weight of a paper or card stock. The higher the weight of the paper, the thicker the sheet.

WF–typesetting mark that indicates the wrong font.

Widow–the line of type at the end of a paragraph that is less than half the column width. Undesirable in text copy.

Wood Type–type made from wood cut to type high; used for large type in place of lead because they were cheaper and lighter.

Word Spacing–the standard white space placed between words in body copy, usually 1/3 em space for l/c body copy, and one en space for capital text. (Also width of lowercase "l.")

Wove Paper–paper manufactured with a uniform, smooth surface.

Wrap-around Type–typeset lines that fit around a silhouetted or irregular image that projects into the column of type.

X-Height–the height of the body of the small or lowercase letters; does not include ascenders or descenders; measured from baseline to waist line.

Image Credits &
Acknowledgments

Image Credits & Acknowledgments

1-6. Gift of Mr. and Mrs. Donald P. Edgar, Courtesy, Museum of Fine Arts, Boston.

1-16 Friedrich. *Extinct Languages*. 1957. Philosophical Library, New York.

1-17. The Metropolitan Museum of Art, New York.

1-18. Lehner. *Symbols, Signs & Signets*. 1950. Dover Books.

1-22. Lehner. *Symbols, Signs & Signets*. 1950. Dover Books.

1-23. Lehner. *Symbols, Signs & Signets*. 1950. Dover Books.

1-24. Gift of Horace L. Meyer. Museum of Fine Arts, Boston.

1-30. The Metropolitan Museum of Art, New York, The Casnola Collection. Purchased by subscription, 1874-76.

1-37. © The British Museum.

2-3. Hutchinson. *Letters*. 1983. Van Nostrand Reinhold.

2-5. Hutchinson. *Letters*. 1983. Van Nostrand Reinhold.

2-9. The Metropolitan Museum of Art, New York.

2-14. Lieberman. *Types of Typefaces*. 1978. Oak Knoll Publishing. New Castle, DE. 19870.

2-20. Carter/Day/Meggs. *Typographic Design: Form & Communication, 2e*. 1993. John Wiley & Sons.

2-21. Lehner, *Symbols, Signs & Signets*. 1950. Dover Books.

2-24. Sibbett. *Celtic Design Coloring Book*. 1979. Dover Books.

2-49. Lehner. *Symbols, Signs & Signets*. 1950. Dover Books.

3-1. Hutchinson. *Letters*. 1983. Van Nostrand Reinhold.

3-2. Lieberman. *Types of Typefaces*. 1978. Oak Knoll Publishing. New Castle, DE. 19870.

3-5. Illustration by Ali Jeffery, based on Lieberman. *Types of Typefaces*. 1978. Oak Knoll Publishing. New Castle, DE. 19870.

3-10. Lehner. *Symbols, Signs & Signets*. 1950. Dover Books.

3-15. Lieberman. *Types of Typefaces*. 1978. Oak Knoll Publishing. New Castle, DE. 19870.

3-18. Rosenwald Collection, Library of Congress.

3-20. Lieberman. *Types of Typefaces*. 1978. Oak Knoll Publishing. New Castle, DE. 19870.

3-21. Grafton. *Trades & Occupations*. 1986. Dover Books.

3-22. Grafton. *Trades & Occupations*. 1986. Dover Books.

3-23. Hutchinson. *Letters*. 1983. Van Nostrand Reinhold.

3-24. Lieberman. *Types of Typefaces*. 1978. Oak Knoll Publishing. New Castle, DE. 19870.

3-25. Illustration by Ali Jeffery, based on Lieberman. *Types of Typefaces*. 1978. Oak Knoll Publishing. New Castle, DE. 19870.

3-26. Carter/Day/Meggs. *Typographic Design: Form & Communication, 2e*. 1993. John Wiley & Sons.

3-27. Illustration by Ali Jeffery, based on Lieberman. *Types of Typefaces*. 1978. Oak Knoll Publishing. New Castle, DE. 19870.

3-28. Lieberman. *Types of Typefaces*. 1978. Oak Knoll Publishing. New Castle, DE. 19870.

3-31. Carter/Day/Meggs. *Typographic Design: Form & Communication, 2e*. 1993. John Wiley & Sons.

3-32. Hutchinson. *Letters*. 1983. Van Nostrand Reinhold.

3-33. DŸrer. *Of the Just Shaping of Letters*. 1965. Dover Books.

3-34. Illustration by Ali Jeffery, based on Haley. *Typographic Milestones*. 1992. John Wiley & Sons.

3-35. Carter/Day/Meggs. *Typographic Design: Form & Communication, 2e*. 1993. John Wiley & Sons.

3-36. Lehner, *Symbols, Signs & Signets*. 1950. Dover Books.

3-37. Hutchinson. *Letters*. 1983. Van Nostrand Reinhold.

3-43. Illustration by Ali Jeffery, based on Lieberman. *Types of Typefaces*. 1978. Oak Knoll Publishing. New Castle, DE. 19870.

3-44. Lieberman. *Types of Typefaces*. 1978. Oak Knoll Publishing. New Castle, DE. 19870.

3-45. Hutchinson. *Letters*. 1983. Van Nostrand Reinhold.

3-49. Illustration by Ali Jeffery, based on Lieberman. *Types of Typefaces*. 1978. Oak Knoll Publishing. New Castle, DE. 19870.

3-50. Lieberman. *Types of Typefaces*. 1978. Oak Knoll Publishing. New Castle, DE. 19870.

3-52. Lambert. *Letterforms:110 Alphabets*. 1972. Dover Books.

Image Credits &
Acknowledgments

4-6. Lieberman. *Types of Typefaces.* 1978. Oak Knoll Publishing. New Castle, DE. 19870.

4-7. Carter/Day/Meggs. *Typographic Design: Form & Communication, 2e.* 1993. John Wiley & Sons.

4-12. Carter/Day/Meggs. *Typographic Design: Form & Communication, 2e.* 1993. John Wiley & Sons.

4-15. Lieberman. *Types of Typefaces.* 1978. Oak Knoll Publishing. New Castle, DE. 19870.

4-16. Haley. *Typographic Milestones.* 1992. John Wiley & Sons.

4-17. Illustration by Ali Jeffery, based on *Haley. Typographic Milestones.* 1992. John Wiley & Sons.

4-18. Lieberman. *Types of Typefaces.* 1978. Oak Knoll Publishing. New Castle, DE. 19870.

4-19. Haley. *Typographic Milestones.* 1992. John Wiley & Sons.

4-23. Illustration by Ali Jeffery, based on Lieberman. *Types of Typefaces.* 1978. Oak Knoll Publishing. New Castle, DE. 19870.

4-24, Museo Bodoniano. Parma, Italy.

4-25. Museo Bodoniano. Parma, Italy.

4-26. Illustration by Ali Jeffery, based on Lieberman. *Types of Typefaces.* 1978. Oak Knoll Publishing. New Castle, DE. 19870.

4-27. Meggs. *History of Graphic Design, 3e.* 1998. text © Philip B. Meggs. John Wiley & Sons.

4-28. Lieberman. *Types of Typefaces.* 1978. Oak Knoll Publishing. New Castle, DE. 19870.

4-29. Lieberman. *Types of Typefaces.* 1978. Oak Knoll Publishing. New Castle, DE. 19870.

4-30. Grafton. *Trades & Occupations.* 1986. Dover Books.

4-32. Solo. *Victorian Display Alphabets.* 1976. Dover Books.

4-33. Solo. *Victorian Display Alphabets.* 1976. Dover Books.

4-34. Solo. *Victorian Display Alphabets.* 1976. Dover Books.

4-35. Solo. *Victorian Display Alphabets.* 1976. Dover Books.

4-36. Meggs. *History of Graphic Design, 3e.* 1998. text © Philip B. Meggs. John Wiley & Sons.

4-40. Solo. *Victorian Display Alphabets.* 1976. Dover Books.

4-41. Solo. *Condensed Alphabets.* 1986. Dover Books.

4-45. Rowe. *Goods & Merchandise.* 1982. Dover Books.

4-46. Rowe. *Goods & Merchandise.* 1982. Dover Books.

4-47. Rowe. *Goods & Merchandise.* 1982. Dover Books.

4-48. Rowe. *Goods & Merchandise.* 1982. Dover Books.

4-49. Grafton. *Trades & Occupations.* 1986. Dover Books.

4-50. Solo. *Condensed Alphabets.* 1986. Dover Books.

4-51. Solo. *Extended Alphabets.* 1992. Dover Books.

4-54. Grafton. *Historic Alphabets & Initials.* 1977. Dover Books.

4-55. Grafton. *Trades & Occupations.* 1986. Dover Books.

4-56. Lambert. *Letterforms:110 Alphabets.* 1972. Dover Books.

4-60. Rohrbach Library Collection, Kutztown University.

4-61. Rohrbach Library Collection, Kutztown University.

4-62. Grafton. *Trades & Occupations.* 1986. Dover Books.

4-65. Rohrbach Library Collection, Kutztown University.

4-66. Rohrbach Library Collection, Kutztown University.

6-1. Illustration by Ali Jeffery based on Lieberman. *Types of Typefaces.* 1978. Oak Knoll Publishing. New Castle, DE. 19870.

6-2. Lieberman. *Types of Typefaces.* 1978. Oak Knoll Publishing. New Castle, DE. 19870.

6-3. Meggs. *History of Graphic Design, 3e.* 1998. text © Philip B. Meggs. John Wiley & Sons.

6-12. Grafton. *Art Nouveau Initials.* 1989. Dover Books.

6-13. Grafton. *Art Nouveau Initials.* 1989. Dover Books.

6-16. Gillon. *Art Nouveau.* 1969. Dover Books.

6-17. Gillon. *Art Nouveau.* 1969. Dover Books.

6-20. Illustration by Ali Jeffery based on Lieberman. *Types of Typefaces.* 1978. Oak Knoll Publishing. New Castle, DE. 19870.

This page is set in
Fenice Light 8.5/12.

Image Credits &
Acknowledgments

6-22. Carter/Day/Meggs. *Typographic Design: Form & Communication, 2e.* 1993. John Wiley & Sons.

6-23. Illustration by Kate Clair based on *U &lc* vol 21, fall 1994.

6-26. Illustration by Ali Jeffery based on Lieberman. *Types of Typefaces.* 1978. Oak Knoll Publishing. New Castle, DE. 19870.

6-29. Carter/Day/Meggs. *Typographic Design: Form & Communication, 2e.* 1993. John Wiley & Sons.

6-30. Raoul Hausmann, *Poeme Phonetique,* 1919.

6-31. Kennedy. *Modern Display Alphabets.* 1974. Dover Books.

6-34. Estate of Herbert Bayer.

6-35. Estate of Herbert Bayer.

6-36. From Meggs, *History of Graphic Design, 3e.* 1998. text © Philip B. Meggs. John Wiley & Sons.

6-37. From Meggs, *History of Graphic Design, 3e.* 1998. text © Philip B. Meggs. John Wiley & Sons.

6-38. From Meggs, *History of Graphic Design, 2e.* 1992. text © Philip B. Meggs, Van Nostrand Reinhold.

6-39. Athenaeum-Polak & Van Gennep.

6-40. The Estate of Jan Tschichold.

6-42. Illustration by Ali Jeffery based on *Lieberman. Types of Typefaces.* 1978. Oak Knoll Publishing. New Castle, DE. 19870.

6-43. Illustration by Kate Clair based on Haley. *Typographic Milestones.* 1992. John Wiley & Sons.

6-48. Illustration by Kate Clair based on *U &lc* vol 21, fall 1994.

6-49. Adrian Frutiger.

6-52. Illustration by Kate Clair based on *U &lc* vol 21, fall 1994.

6-58. Illustration by Kate Clair based on *U &lc* vol 21, fall 1994.

6-59. Kennedy. *Modern Display Alphabets.* 1974. Dover Books.

6-60. Kennedy. *Modern Display Alphabets.* 1974. Dover Books.

6-61. Illustration by Kate Clair based on *U &lc* vol 21, fall 1994.

6-67. © Bill Graham Presents. 1967. Artist Wes Wilson.

6-68. Kennedy. *Modern Display Alphabets.* 1974. Dover Books.

6-69. Seymour Chwast.

6-70. Illustration by Kate Clair based on Snyder/Peckolick. *Herb Lubalin.* 1985. American Showcase.

6-71. The Estate of Herb Lubalin.

6-72. From Avant Garde magazine.

6-80. With permission from M. Kisman.

6-86. With permission from M. Kisman.

6-87. With permission from J. Barnbrook.

6-88. With permission from M. Kisman.

6-91. With permission from B. Deck.

7-34. With permission from M. Kisman.

20- 4. Freehand¨ icon with permission of Macromedia Inc.¨.; PageMaker¨, Illustrator¨, and Photoshop¨ icons with permission of Adobe Systems Inc.¨; Quark¨ icon with permission of Quark, Inc.¨. Microsoft Word¨ icon, trade-mark Microsoft¨, Redmond, WA.

20-5. , 20-6., 20-7., 20-10. , 20-13., 20-16.Ñ20-32., 20-37., 20-38. With permission from Apple Computers, Inc. ¨.

20-8., 20-9., 20-11., 20-12. with permission from Adobe Systems Inc.¨.

20-15. With permission from Adobe Systems Inc.¨., Digital Typeface Corp.¨, David Rakowski, infiniType Plus¨, Emigre Graphics¨, Letraset Esselte¨.

20-35., 20-36. With permission from Adobe Systems Inc.¨.

with permission from Adobe Systems Inc.¨.

Bibliography

World Sign Design, No. 2-1994: Marks & Logos. Roman Nippan Books.

Adler, E. 1993. *Everyone's Guide to Successful Publications.* Peach Pit Press.

Aldrich-Ruenzel, N., ed. 1991. *Designer's Guide to Typography.* Watson-Guptill.

Annual of the Type Directors' Club Staff. 1990-present. *Typography 11-18.* Watson-Guptill.

Arnold, E. 1969. *Modern Newspaper Design.* Harper & Row.

Berger, A. A. 1998. *Seeing Is Believing.* Mayfield Publishing Co.

Bigelow, C. 1977-1988. *Fine Print on Type.* Pro Arte Libri.

Bradbury, T. 1988. *Bradbury Thompson: The Art of Graphic Design.* Yale U. P.

Brier, D. 1994. *International Typographic Design 2.* Madison Square.

————. 1992. *Great Type and Lettering Designs.* F & W Publications.

Brier, D., ed. 1992. *Typographic Design.* Madison Square.

Buchannan, C. 1994. *Quick Solutions for Great Type Combinations.* F & W Publications.

Carter, R. 1993. *American Typography Today.* Van Nostrand Reinhold.

Carter, R., and P. Meggs. 1993. *Typographic Specimens.* John Wiley & Sons.

Chijiiwa, H. 1987. *Color Harmony.* Rockport Publishers.

Chwast, S., and S. Heller, ed. 1985. *The Left-Handed Designer.* Abrams Publishing.

Cliff, S. 1994. *The Best in Cutting Edge Typography.* Quarto Publishing.

Craig, J. 1990. *Production for the Graphic Designer.* Watson-Guptill.

————. 1992. *Designing with Type: A Basic Course in Typography.* Watson-Guptill.

Cropper, M., and L. Haller. 1994. *Fresh Ideas in Corporate Identity.* F & W Publications.

Davis, G. 1993. *Quick Solutions to Great Layouts.* North Light Books.

de la Croix, H., and R. G. Tansey. 1986. *Gardner's Art Through the Ages.* Harcourt, Brace, Jovanovich Publishers, Inc.

————. 1986. *Gardner's Art Through the Ages.* Harcourt, Brace, Jovanovich Publishers, Inc.

Denton, Gillian, and G. Allen. 1984. *The Doring Kindersley History of the World.* Doring Kindersley Publishing.

Drogin, M. 1980. *Medieval Calligraphy.* Dover Publications.

Elam, K. 1990. *Expressive Typography.* Van Nostrand Reinhold, Inc.

Evans, P. 1996. *The Graphic Designer's Sourcebook.* F & W Publications.

Fenton, E. 1989. *The Macintosh Font Book.* Peachpit Press.

Friedman, M. et al. 1989. *Graphic Design America.* Harry N. Abrams, Inc.

Friedrich, J. 1957. *Extinct Languages.* Rowman & Littlefield Publishers.

Glorya Hale Staff. 1996. *Classic Clip Art.* Random House Value Publishing.

Gottschall, E. 1989. *Typographic Communications Today.* MIT Press.

Goudy, F. 1922. *Alphabet & Elements of Lettering.* Dover Books.

————. 1978. *Goudy's Type Designs: His Story & Specimens.* Oak Knoll.

Grafton, C. 1984. *Treasury of Victorian Printers' Frames, Ornaments & Initials.* Dover Books.

————. 1986. *Treasury of Book Ornament & Decoration.* Dover Books.

Graphis. 1992-present. Graphis Press.

Gray, N. 1986. *A History of Lettering.* David R. Godine Publisher, Inc.

Haley, A. 1992. *Typographic Milestones.* Van Nostrand Reinhold.

Harrower, T. 1989. *The Newspaper Designer's Handbook.* Wm. C. Brown Communications, Inc.

Harter, J. 1978. *Harter's Picture Archive for Collage & Illustration.* Dover Books.

Hartt, F. 1976. *ART: A History of Painting, Sculpture, and Architecture.* Harry N. Abrams, Inc.

Heller, S., and G. Anderson, 1994. *American Typeplay.* Hearst Books International.

Heller, S., and S. Chwast. 1994. *Graphic Style: From Victorian to Post-Modern.* Abrams Publishing.

Henrikson, A. 1983. *Through the Ages.* Crown Publishers, Inc.

Hinrichs, K., and D. Hirasuna. 1990. *Type Wise.* F & W Publications.

Hurlburt, A. 1977. *Layout: The Design of the Printed Page.* Watson-Guptill Publications.

Hutt, A. 1967. *Newspaper Design.* Oxford University Press

Jeavons, T., and M. Beaumont. 1990. *An Introduction to Typography.* Chartwell Books.

Kennedy, P. E. 1974. *Modern Display Alphabets.* Dover Books.

King, J. C. 1993. *Designer's Guide to PostScript Text Type.* Van Nostrand Reinhold.

Koren, L., and R. W. Meckler. 1989. *Graphic Design Cookbook.* Chronicle Books.

Labuz, R. 1988. *Typography & Typesetting.* Van Nostrand Reinhold, Inc.

Bibliography

Lambert, F. 1972. *Letterforms: 110 Complete Alphabets.* Dover Books.

Landa, R. 1996. *Graphic Design Solutions.* Delmar Publishers.

Lieberman, J. B. 1978. *Type & Typefaces.* Oak Knoll.

———. 1978. *Type & Typefaces & How to Recognize Them.* Sterling Publishing.

Livingston, A. and I. Livingston. 1992. *The Thames & Hudson Encyclopaedia of Graphic Design & Designers.* Thames Hudson.

Margolin, V. 1975. *American Poster Renaissance.* Watson-Guptill Publishing, Inc.

Martin, D., and M. Cropper. 1993. *Fresh Ideas in Letterhead & Business Card Design.* F & W Publications.

Martin, D., and L. Haller. 1996. *Street Smart Design.* North Light Books.

Meggs, P. 1992. *A History of Graphic Design.* Van Nostrand Reinhold.

———. 1992. *Type & Image: The Language of Graphic Design.* Van Nostrand Reinhold.

Mendenhall, J. 1992. *Scan This Book.* Art Direction Books

———. 1994. *Typographic Specimens.* Van Nostrand Reinhold.

Nesbitt, A. 1959. *Decorative Alphabets and Initials.* Dover Publications, Inc.

Parker, R. C. 1990. *Looking Good in Print.* Ventana Press.

Parsons, B. 1994. *Electronic Pre-Press: A Hands-on Introduction.* Delmar Publishing.

Perfect, C. and J. Austen. 1992. *The Complete Typographer.* Prentice Hall.

Phornirunlit, S., & Supon Design Group Staff. 1992. *Great Design Using One, Two & Three Colors.* Madison Square.

Phornirunlit, S., ed. 1996. *Innovative Low-Budget Design.* Madison Square.

Pipes, A.1992. *Production for Graphic Designers.* Prentice-Hall

Place, J. 1995. *Creating Logos & Letterheads.* North Light Books.

Poynor, R., and E. Booth-Clibborn, ed. 1991. *Typography Now.* L & W Publications, Inc.

Quimn G. 1994. *The Clip Art Book.* Crescent Books, Crown Publishers.

Rabb, M. Y., ed. 1990. *The Presentation Design Book.* Ventana Press, Inc.

Rand, P. 1993. *Design, Form & Chaos.* Yale University Press.

Robinson, W. 1991. *How'd They Design & Print That?* Quarto Publishing.

Scarre, C. 1993. *Smithsonian Timelines of the Ancient World.* Dorling Kindersley, Inc.

Seibert, L., and L. Ballard. 1992. *Making a Good Layout.* North Light Books.

Siebert, L. and M. Cropper. 1993. *Working with Words & Pictures.* North Light Books.

Snyder, G. and A. Peckolick. 1985. *Herb Lubalin.* American Showcase, Inc.

Solo, D. X. 1986. *Condensed Alphabets: One Hundred Complete Fonts.* Dover Books.

———. 1989. *Circus Alphabets.* Dover Books.

———. 1992. *Extended Alphabets: One Hundred Complete Fonts.* Dover Books.

———. 1995. *One Hundred Ornamental Fonts.* Dover Books.

———. 1979. *Sans Serif Display Alphabets: 100 Complete Fonts.* Dover Books.

Soloman, M. 1994. *Art of Typography.* Art Direction Books.

Supon Design Group, Inc. 1993. *International Women in Design.* Van Nostrand Reinhold.

Supon Phornirunlit Staff. 1993. *Iconopolis: A Collection of City Iconographics.* North Light Books.

Swann, A. 1991. *How to Understand & Use Design & Layout.* North Light Books.

———. 1989. *How to Use Grids.* North Light Books.

Tschichold, J. 1992. *Treasury of Alphabets and Lettering.* Design Press.

———. 1995. *The New Typography.* University of California Press.

Van Nostrand Reinhold Staff. 1974. *The Type Specimen Book.* Van Nostrand Reinhold.

von Wodtke, M. 1993. *Mind Over Media.* McGraw-Hill, Inc.

Watson-Guptill Staff. 1997. *Graphic Design USA.* Watson-Guptill.

Wells, H. G. 1961. *The Outline of History.* Garden City Books.

Whalley, J. I. 1980. *The Art of Calligraphy.* Bloomsbury Books.

White, A. 1987. *How to Spec Type.* Watson-Guptill.

White, J. V. 1988. *Design for the Electronic Age.* Watson-Guptill.

———. 1990. *Graphic Idea Notebook.* Rockport Publishing.

Will-Harris, D. 1990. *Type Style.* Peachpit Press.

Wolfe, G. 1991. *Type Recipes.* F & W Publications.

Wotzkow, H. 1952. *The Art of Hand Lettering.* Dover Publications.

Index

Index

This page is set in
ITC Fenice Light 8.5/10.5

Index

Index

Index

This page is set in
ITC Fenice Light 8.5/10.5

Index

This page is set in
ITC Fenice Light 8.5/10.5

Index

Index

This page is set in
ITC Fenice Light 8.5/10.5

Index

Index

This page is set in
ITC Fenice Light 8.5/10.5

Index

Index

This page is set in
ITC Fenice Light 8.5/10.5